DATA STRUCTURES

Theory and Practice

Second Edition

This is a volume in
COMPUTER SCIENCE AND APPLIED MATHEMATICS
A Series of Monographs and Textbooks

Editor: WERNER RHEINBOLDT

A complete list of titles in this series appears at the end of the volume.

DATA STRUCTURES
Theory and Practice

Second Edition

A. T. Berztiss

University of Pittsburgh

ACADEMIC PRESS   New York San Francisco London

A Subsidiary of Harcourt Brace Jovanovich, Publishers

ACADEMIC PRESS, INC.
111 Fifth Avenue, New York, New York 10003

United Kingdom Edition published by
ACADEMIC PRESS, INC. (LONDON) LTD.
24/28 Oval Road, London NW1

Library of Congress Cataloging in Publication Data

Berztiss, A T
    Data structures. Second edition

    (Computer science and applied mathematics)
    Bibliography: p.
    Includes index.
    1.   Data structures (computer science)
2.   Electronic digital computers—Programming.
I.   Title.
QA76.6.B475 1975   001.6'42   74-17977
ISBN 0–12–093552–X

AMS (MOS) 1970 Subject Classifications: 00-01; 04-01, 04-04,
04A05, 05-01; 05-04, 05A10, 05C20; 68-01, 68A15; 90-01,
90-04, 90B10, 90B35

Contents

Chapter 3.   Graph Theory

Chapter 4.   Algebras and Strings

Part II
APPLICATIONS OF STRUCTURES

Chapter 5.   Trees

Chapter 6.   **Paths and Cycles in Digraphs**

Chapter 7.   **Digraphs of Programs**

Chapter 8.   **Other Applications of Graphs**

Part III
COMPUTER REPRESENTATION OF STRUCTURES

Chapter 9.   **Arrays**

Chapter 10.   **Lists and List Structures**

Chapter 11. Organization of Files

Chapter 12. Application Studies

Preface

A man looking at a road map wishes to go from place X to place Y. His problem: Which of the numerous possible routes should he follow? Let us interpret the road map as the picture of a mathematical object, namely of a graph. Then the choosing of the shortest route translates into the well-known shortest path problem of graph theory, and an algorithm for solving this problem exists. The remaining task is the computer implementation of the algorithm, and this requires a suitable computer representation of the graph. Here we can identify three distinct phases in the complete solution process. First, a mathematical model has to be found. Second, an algorithm has to be developed within the mathematical model (we hope, however, that somebody has already done this for us). Third, a computer representation has to be selected for the data on which the algorithm is to operate.

The three parts of this book correspond more or less to the three phases. The selection of a mathematical model requires knowledge of the basic properties of some mathematical systems. These fundamentals form the subject matter of Part I, Discrete Structures in Mathematics. Part II, Applications of Structures, deals mainly with algorithms, but, in addition, the examples should help one gain experience in the selection of mathematical models for real life problems. Part III is precisely described by its title, Computer Representation of Structures.

In broad terms, this book aims at developing a productive *attitude* to the solution of problems. Of course, the main purpose is sometimes obscured by the details.

Part I, taken as a whole, is a selection of mathematical topics that are essential background knowledge for anyone who wishes to study data structures in depth. Despite appearances, the selection is highly pragmatic. Some of the topics may be irrelevant to an understanding of later parts of *this book,* but they have direct relevance to the proper understanding of journal articles dealing with mathematical models of computer data structures. The order of courses in a computer science curriculum varies so much from place to place that I could not take any specific item of background knowledge for granted. This practical consideration has prevented inclusion of more examples from computer science, which would have made the general relevance of discrete mathematics more apparent. The instructor, being familiar with the background of the students, can, and should, enliven the presentation with appropriate examples.

The first two chapters deal with topics in set theory, and most readers will find them familiar. I feel, however, that a student having just a knowledge of set theory is inadequately prepared. One must be able to think in abstract terms. That is why these chapters belabor set theory in great detail. They aim at dispelling false conceptions that a student may have and at improving his or her intuitive understanding of the nature of a mathematical proof. By the end of Chapter 2 the student should be able to digest an abstract argument fairly rapidly. Fluency in the language of basic discrete mathematics is essential for a serious study of computer science.

However, the very detailed development in Chapters 1 and 2 is not necessarily a suggestion that much class time should be spent on these chapters. On the contrary, the detail is there to enable the instructor to adopt a much more rapid pace than he or she could if the detail had to be supplied in class.

Chapter 3, which introduces graph theory, is the core of the book in that nearly all of Part II is based on this chapter and the various list structures of Chapter 10 are merely computer representations of directed graphs. Chapter 4 is needed for background to the applications discussed in Part II.

Part II establishes links with a number of disciplines in which mathematical structures can be put to good use. This way the mathematical structures are transformed into data structures, but the actual computer representation is understated. The object here is to unify various disciplines by the use of similar data structures.

In Part III efficiency is considered. There, for example, it is shown that the designer of a representation of a data structure must consider the peculiarities of his computer and of the operations that are to be performed on the data structure. Because of the rapid changes in computer science, one of the hardest tasks in writing a text is to decide which parts of the subject are basic. I hope to have avoided the ephemeral.

The material in this book covers much of what the ACM Curriculum Committee on Computer Science recommends for course B3 (Introduction to Discrete Structures) and Il (Data Structures) [see *CACM* **11,**151–197 (1968)].

* * *

In preparing this new edition I have been fortunate in being able to draw on the experience of many instructors who have used the text in their courses. The basic structure of the first edition has been retained, but there are major changes, motivated by extensive classroom experience. Here follows a summary of the more important of these changes:

(a) A discussion of minimization of Boolean functions has been added to Section 2b. The general tone of this section is rather formal. My main aim for Section 2b is a justification of the highly practical technique of binary valuation and the formalism is unavoidable for achieving this objective. The discussion of minimization has deliberately been made comparatively informal to provide the reader with some relief.

(b) A section on group codes has been added in Chapter 4.

(c) The discussion of pushdown stores has been brought forward from Chapter 10 to Chapter 5, and it has been considerably expanded. Algorithms for the traversal of trees have been added in Chapter 5.

(d) The sections on shortest paths and on cycles in Chapter 6 have been completely revised to bring them up to date.

(e) Chapter 10, "Lists and List Structures," has been greatly expanded. Since very few computer scientists write chess playing programs and suchlike for a living, linked lists do not in their own right have as great a practical importance as arrays, say. Consequently list structuring was not given much prominence in the first edition. However, list structuring methodology is gaining in importance because it is the basis for some important organizational techniques in the structuring of large files. Chapter 10 was expanded in response to this trend.

(f) The sections on scatter storage techniques and sorting in Chapter 11 have been extensively revised and expanded. New sections on tape sorting and on disk files have been added.

(g) Chapter 12, "Application Studies," is all new. It replaces a chapter on programming languages for information structures.

(h) The number of exercises has been increased by 200, bringing the total to 484. Since many instructors have indicated that the first edition contained too few exercises without solutions, very few of the new exercises have been provided with solutions.

(i) The bibliography contains 195 new entries. To prevent the bibliography from becoming too awesome by its size, just 164 of the 305 references of the first edition have been retained. Only by means of these cuts, which in many instances were done with much regret, was it possible to keep the bibliography within reasonable bounds. The proportion of books and survey articles compared to research papers has increased. This should help the instructor, who can on occasion present in class material not covered in the text, and illustrate the subject matter of the text with additional examples. The primary purpose of the bibliography is to assist the instructor in this task.

The first edition of this book has seen classroom use in so many different contexts, at levels ranging from sophomore to graduate, that there is no point in making detailed recommendations as to how it should be used. At my own university it serves three courses. In the first, Introduction to Information Structures, the subject matter of the entire book is covered in a necessarily superficial manner. This initial exposure is followed up with two more advanced courses in which we aim at reinforcement, solidification, and in-depth coverage of this same material. Part I of the book is the basis for our course Discrete Mathematical Structures, and Part III for a course that we have named Data Structures and Files. Part II of the book consists mainly of algorithms. With some of the algorithms we emphasize their mathematical formulation, with others their computer implementation. The particular emphasis given to an algorithm determines the course in which it is discussed.

The important topic of disk files is given much briefer treatment in this book than it would seem to warrant. Let me explain. There are two parts to the study of this topic: one is an investigation of how records are structured into files, the other is an examination of the practicalities relating to large files, and the two are quite distinct. Our Chapters 10 and 11 give an adequate introduction to structuring concepts, but the practicalities are a different matter. Indeed, they are sufficiently important to be covered in a separate course on file processing. Our concern here is more with principles than with the equally important practicalities.

Although the relation between mathematical structures and computing is not stressed in the earlier chapters, nearly all chapters contain some algorithms put in the form of computer programs and some programming exercises. The programming language was selected after much deliberation. It is Fortran. The primary reason for this choice is that Fortran is the only general purpose language for which a national standard has been established (in the United States). Fortran is also the most widely used general purpose language. Since a computer provided with a Fortran compiler, a magnetic tape drive, and a continuing supply of tape reels is equivalent in computing power to a Turing machine, there are no algorithms that cannot be implemented in Fortran, but some of the algorithms discussed in the text would be very awkward to implement in this language. Such algorithms could be presented as assembler language programs, but, since there is no standard assembler language, one would then have to play at being a computer manufacturer and design one's own computer with its assembler language. Alternatively, the algorithms could be left in the form of flowcharts or English sentences. Since translation of an algorithm from one assembler language into another is at least as difficult as translation of a flowchart, the latter course is followed here. Some instructors may decide to combine the study of material from this book with the study of a programming language for nonnumerical computation, and express some of the algorithms in this language. Alternatively, students can be asked to extend a general purpose language to enable it to deal with some class of nonnumerical problems.

Acknowledgments

I have received much assistance from my students and colleagues over the years in which a rough set of lecture notes has changed into the present version of the book. In particular, I am grateful to Walter Burkhardt, William Conner, Gerald Fisher, Koichi Furukawa, Norman Gibbs, Rex Harris, Dale Isner, Donald Knuth, William Kraynek, Gary Lindstrom, Michael McManus, Michael Matzek, Werner Rheinboldt, Francis Sullivan, Antons Susts, Stanley Walljasper, and Richard Watkins for their comments, suggestions, and corrections.

PART I

DISCRETE STRUCTURES IN MATHEMATICS

Set Theory

1a. Basic Definitions

Mathematics investigates relations between abstract objects. The objects might be natural numbers, or real numbers, or points in the plane, or letters in some alphabet. Some objects, such as points on the real line, cannot be counted. These objects form the basis of continuum mathematics. Other objects are countable; they are the basis of discrete mathematics. We use natural numbers in counting, and it is well known that there is no largest natural number. In other words, there is no limit at which counting has to stop. Thus we have a further subdivision of sets of countable objects into infinite sets and finite sets. Since our ultimate interest is in the application of finite discrete devices, digital computers, we shall be primarily concerned with finite sets of objects.

As the concept of a set is basic to mathematics and the theory of sets close to its foundations, we had to refer to sets rather freely in the paragraph above. We should therefore define a set, but this we cannot do. The closest we can come to a definition is to say that a set is a collection of *distinguishable* objects sharing some common feature that qualifies them for membership in the set. The objects comprising a set are called *members* of the set or *elements* of the set. Just as in geometry the terms *point* and *line* cannot be defined, so in set theory the terms *set* and *member* are undefined terms. *Membership* is an undefined relation. A way of specifying a particular set is to enclose its elements in braces: $\{\cdots\}$.

Examples of finite sets

Decimal digits: $\{0, 1, 2, \ldots, 9\}$.
Binary digits: $\{0, 1\}$.
Letters of an alphabet: $\{a, b, c, \ldots, z\}$.
Solutions of $x^2 - x = 0$: $\{0, 1\}$.

Examples of infinite sets

Natural numbers: $\{1, 2, 3, \ldots\}$.
Even natural numbers: $\{2, 4, 6, \ldots\}$.
Integers: $\{0, -1, 1, -2, 2, \ldots\}$.

DEFINITION 1.1   Two sets are equal if and only if they have the same members.

Example

$\{1, 2, 3\} = \{3, 1, 2\} = \{1, 2, 3, 3\} \neq \{1, 3, 4\}$. The first equality holds because elements of a set may be written down in any order. The second equality holds because the two 3s in $\{1, 2, 3, 3\}$ are indistinguishable. Since set $\{1, 2, 3, 3\}$ *is* the set $\{1, 2, 3\}$, one would not normally list an element more than once. Sets $\{1, 2, 3\}$ and $\{1, 3, 4\}$ have the same number of elements, but the elements are not the same.

An alternative notation for specifying the elements of a set uses a formula $P(x)$. If the formular notation is used, a set is defined by $\{x \mid P(x)\}$, read as " the set of *all* objects x such that $P(x)$ is true." Either notation can be used to represent the same set, e.g.,

$$\{0, 1, 2, \ldots, 9\} = \{i \mid i \text{ is a decimal digit}\},$$
$$\{1, 2, 3, \ldots\} = \{n \mid n \text{ is a natural number}\},$$
$$\{0, 1\} = \{x \mid x^2 - x = 0\}.$$

Formular notation specifies the feature common to elements of a set. Therefore, there is more information in $\{x \mid x^2 - x = 0\}$, say, than in $\{0, 1\}$. The increase in the information content is due to the fact that a set of elements can be specified by more than one formula. Thus $\{0, 1\}$ is also equal to $\{b \mid b \text{ is a binary digit}\}$ and to $\{c \mid c = 0 \text{ or } c = 1\}$. Note, however, that sets $\{x \mid x^2 - x = 0\}$, $\{b \mid b \text{ is a binary digit}\}$, and $\{c \mid c = 0 \text{ or } c = 1\}$ are exactly equal (by D.1.1). The increase of information relates entirely to the context in which the sets are being studied.

We shall use lower case Latin letters for elements of sets and Latin capitals for sets, e.g., $I = \{i \mid i \text{ is a decimal digit}\}$, $E = \{x \mid x < 1 \text{ and } x > 2\}$, $L = \{a, b, \ldots, z\}$. Note that E contains no elements. Membership will be indicated by the symbol $\in$, e.g., $k \in L$, $9 \in I$. If an object does not belong to a set, we shall use the symbol $\notin$, e.g., $coffee \notin L$, $5 \notin L$, $5 \notin E$, $15 \notin I$, $-5 \notin I$.

Let A be a finite set. We shall use the symbol $|A|$ to denote the number of elements in A. For example, if $A = \{1, 2, 2, 5\}$, then $|A| = 3$. The number of elements in a finite set is sometimes called the *cardinality* or the *cardinal number* of the set. (There also exist infinite cardinal numbers, which arise in discussions regarding the size of infinite sets, but the topic of infinite cardinal numbers is beyond the scope of this book.)

DEFINITION 1.2   A *null* (*empty, zero*) set has no elements. It is denoted by $\{\ \}$, or by $\varnothing$.

Examples

1. $\{x \mid x < 1 \text{ and } x > 2\} = \varnothing$.
2. $\{x \mid x \neq x\} = \varnothing$.
3. $\{0\} \neq \varnothing$, since the set $\{0\}$ contains an element, namely the digit 0.
4. $\varnothing \neq 0$, since $\varnothing$ is a set and 0 is not a set.
5. $\{\varnothing\} \neq \varnothing$, since set $\{\varnothing\}$ contains an element, the null set $\varnothing$.

DEFINITION 1.3   A *family* (*class, collection*) of sets is a set whose elements are themselves sets. Families of sets will be denoted by script letters.

Examples

1. $\mathscr{A} = \{\{0\}, \{1, 2\}, \{3, 4, 5\}, \{6, 7, 8, 9\}\}$.
2. $\mathscr{B} = \{\{0, 9\}, \{1, 8\}, \{2, 7\}, \{3, 6\}, \{4, 5\}\}$.
3. $\mathscr{C} = \{\{1, 2, 3\}, \{1, 2\}, \{2, 3\}, \{3, 1\}, \{1\}, \{2\}, \{3\}, \varnothing\}$.
4. $\mathscr{D} = \{A \mid A = \{x \mid x \text{ is a letter in a particular word}\}\} = \{\{g, u, m\}, \{a, c, t\}, \{a, c, t, i, o, n\}, \ldots\}$. Note that $\{x, y, w\} \notin \mathscr{D}$, that the words *mug* and *gum* both give rise to the same set $\{g, u, m\}$, and that *act, cat, tact* give rise to the set $\{a, c, t\}$.

DEFINITION 1.4   If A and B are sets, then A is *included* in B, written $A \subseteq B$, if and only if each member of A is a member of B. Note that B *includes* A, written $B \supseteq A$, is synonymous with $A \subseteq B$. If $A \subseteq B$, then A is a *subset* of B, and B is a *superset* of A. If $A \subseteq B$, and there exists an object x such that $x \in B$, $x \notin A$, then A is a *proper* subset of B, written $A \subset B$. If $A \subseteq B$ does not hold, we write $A \nsubseteq B$.

Examples

1. Let $I_1 = \{d \mid d \text{ is a digit}\}$, $I_2 = \{i \mid i \text{ is an integer}\}$. Then $I_1 \subseteq I_2$ and $I_1 \subset I_2$.
2. The family of sets $\mathscr{C}$ in Example 3 of D.1.3 is the family of all subsets of set $\{1, 2, 3\}$. In particular, $\varnothing \subseteq \{1, 2, 3\}$. The subset relation may not be obvious here because we have difficulty associating the phrase *each member*

of D.1.4 with something that has no members; see, therefore, Th.1.1 below.

3. $\{1, 2, 3\} \subseteq \{1, 2, 3, 3\}$, and also $\{1, 2, 3\} \supseteq \{1, 2, 3, 3\}$,

THEOREM 1.1   For any set A, $\varnothing \subseteq A$.

Proof. Assume $\varnothing \nsubseteq A$. Then there exists at least one object x such that $x \in \varnothing$, $x \notin A$. But $\varnothing$ has no members (D.1.2). Hence $x \notin \varnothing$. Since the assumption leads to a contradiction, the assumption must be wrong.

THEOREM 1.2   Sets A and B are equal if and only if $A \subseteq B$ and $B \subseteq A$.

Proof. We note first that the *if* part of the theorem tells that conditions $A \subseteq B$ and $B \subseteq A$ are sufficient for $A = B$. The *only if* part tells that the conditions are also necessary. We shall prove sufficiency and necessity separately.

Sufficiency. Let $A \subseteq B$ and $B \subseteq A$. Assume $A \neq B$. Then by D.1.1 there is at least one member in one of the sets but not in the other. Let this member be x, and assume $x \in A$. Then $x \notin B$. But, if $x \in A$ and $A \subseteq B$, then $x \in B$ by D.1.4. This is a contradiction. Similarly, assuming $x \in B$ leads to the contradiction $x \notin A$ and $x \in A$. Hence $A = B$ if $A \subseteq B$ and $B \subseteq A$.

Necessity. Assume that one or other of conditions $A \subseteq B$, $B \subseteq A$ does not hold. Then there is an element in one of the sets and not in the other. But then $A \neq B$ (by D.1.1). Hence $A = B$ only if $A \subseteq B$ and $B \subseteq A$.

DEFINITION 1.5   The family of all subsets of a set A is the *power set* of A, symbolized $\mathscr{P}(A)$ or 2^A.

Example

Let $C = \{1, 2, 3\}$. Then $2^C = \{C, \{1, 2\}, \{1, 3\}, \{2, 3\}, \{1\}, \{2\}, \{3\}, \varnothing\}$.

THEOREM 1.3   If a finite set A has n members, then $\mathscr{P}(A)$ has 2^n members.

Proof. (i) $n = 0$. Then, by Th.1.1, $\varnothing \subseteq A$. Since A has no members, this is the only subset of A, i.e., $\mathscr{P}(A)$ has 1 member. But $1 = 2^0$, as required.

(ii) $n > 0$. Write the n elements of A as the sequence $a_1 a_2 \cdots a_n$. Then describe a subset B of A by a sequence of binary digits $d_1 d_2 \cdots d_n$ in which $d_i = 1$ if $a_i \in B$ and $d_i = 0$ if $a_i \notin B$. To each subset there corresponds just one sequence of digits, and each such sequence uniquely identifies a particular subset. The sequences range from $00 \cdots 0$ (for the null set) to $11 \cdots 1$ (for A itself). We interpret the sequences as binary numbers. The decimal equivalent of a binary number composed of n 1s is $2^n - 1$, and the total number of sequences is 2^n. Consequently A has 2^n distinct subsets.

Example

Let $A = \{1, 2\}$. Then $\mathscr{P}(A)$ has four members. The binary notation associates four binary sequences with these four subsets of A:

$$\begin{array}{cccc} \{\ \} & \{2\} & \{1\} & \{1, 2\} \\ 00 & 01 & 10 & 11 \end{array}$$

If the sequences are interpreted as binary numbers, the leading zeros may be removed.

DEFINITION 1.6   The *union* (*set sum*) of sets A and B is defined by

$$A \cup B = \{x \mid x \in A \quad \text{or} \quad x \in B\},$$

where *or* has the inclusive meaning, i.e., $x \in A$ or $x \in B$ means that one of the following three statements holds: $x \in A$ and $x \notin B$; $x \notin A$ and $x \in B$; $x \in A$ and $x \in B$. The *intersection* (*set product*) of sets A and B is defined by

$$A \cap B = \{x \mid x \in A \quad \text{and} \quad x \in B\}.$$

If $A \cap B = \varnothing$, sets A and B are said to be *disjoint*.

Examples

1. $A = \{1, 3, 5, \ldots\}, B = \{2, 4, 6, \ldots\}. A \cup B = \{1, 2, 3, 4, \ldots\}, A \cap B = \varnothing.$
2. $X = \{1, 2, 3\}, Y = \{2, 3, 4, 5\}. X \cup Y = \{1, 2, 3, 4, 5\}, X \cap Y = \{2, 3\}.$

1b. Indexed Sets

Here we shall study families of sets. Consider the power set of some set A. In formular notation the family can be defined $\mathscr{P}(A) = \{B \mid B \subseteq A\}$. Alternatively, if the elements of A are known, the power set can be written out in full, e.g., $\mathscr{P}(A) = \{A, \{1\}, \{2\}, \varnothing\}$ when $A = \{1, 2\}$. Assume now that we are primarily interested in the number of sets in a family. Formular notation, as we have it, does not give this number. Explicit listing, while enabling us to count the number of sets in the family, is too detailed for our purposes here. The superfluous detail makes the notation cumbersome; imagine listing the 256 elements of the power set of a set having eight elements. (Counting commas, opening braces, and closing braces, there are at least 2,545 symbols in the list.)

A notation that gives the number of elements without requiring the elements to be written out in full is suggested by the binary sequences of Th.1.3. Write the four subsets of $A = \{1, 2\}$ as $B_{00}, B_{01}, B_{10}, B_{11}$, and collect the subscripts into a set I; we have $I = \{00, 01, 10, 11\}$. We can then write

$$\mathscr{P}(A) = \{B_i \mid i \in I\}, \tag{1.1}$$

where

$$I = \{i \mid i \text{ is a binary integer} \quad \text{and} \quad 00 \leqq i \leqq 11\}. \tag{1.2}$$

If next we want to describe the power set of a set consisting of eight elements, (1.1) does not have to be changed. We simply redefine I:

$$I = \{i \mid i \text{ is a binary integer} \quad \text{and} \quad 00000000 \leqq i \leqq 11111111\}. \tag{1.3}$$

In (1.2) and (1.3) the binary sequences are interpreted as binary numbers.

We can even change to decimal numbers and express (1.3), say, as

$$I = \{n \,|\, n \text{ is a decimal integer} \quad \text{and} \quad 0 \leqq n \leqq 255\}.$$

Sometimes it is more convenient *not* to interpret the binary sequences as numbers. Let A be a set of eight elements. Suppose that we have to define a family $\mathscr{A}$, comprised of subsets of A having less than three elements. For an arbitrary binary sequence s we let $\lambda(s)$ be the length of the sequence, and $\kappa(s)$ be the number of 1s in it. Then

$$\mathscr{A} = \{B_i \,|\, B_i \in \mathscr{P}(A) \quad \text{and} \quad \kappa(i) < 3\},$$

where $\mathscr{P}(A)$ is defined by (1.1) and (1.3). Alternatively, without direct reference to the power set:

$$\mathscr{A} = \{B_i \,|\, i \in I\},$$

$$I = \{i \,|\, i \text{ is a binary sequence with } \lambda(i) = 8 \quad \text{and} \quad \kappa(i) < 3\}.$$

DEFINITION 1.7   Let $\mathscr{A}$ be the family of sets $\{A_{s_1}, A_{s_2}, A_{s_3}, \ldots\}$, where $A_{s_i} = A_{s_j}$ if $s_i = s_j$. Then the elements of $\mathscr{A}$ are identified by elements of the set

$$I = \{s_1, s_2, s_3, \ldots\}.$$

We can therefore write

$$\mathscr{A} = \{A_i \,|\, i \in I\}.$$

An element of I is called an *index*, set I itself is the *index set*, and $\mathscr{A}$ is an *indexed set*.

Examples

1. The power set of a set of n elements A is the family $\mathscr{P}(A) = \{A_i \,|\, i \in I\}$, where the index set I is defined by $I = \{i \,|\, i \text{ is a binary sequence and } \lambda(i) = n\}$.
2. $I = \{a, b, c\}$. $\mathscr{B} = \{A_i \,|\, i \in I\} = \{A_a, A_b, A_c\}$.
3. $I = \{2, 4, 4, 6, 6\}$. $\mathscr{X} = \{X_i \,|\, i \in I\} = \{X_2, X_4, X_6\}$.
4. Consider set $A = \{1, 2, 3, 4\}$ and the family of sets $\mathscr{A} = \{A_i \,|\, i \in I\}$, where each A_i is a set of two elements, selected from A at random. Let ten selections be made, i.e., let $I = \{1, 2, 3, \ldots, 10\}$. But only six *distinct* selections are possible: $\{1, 2\}, \{1, 3\}, \{1, 4\}, \{2, 3\}, \{2, 4\}, \{3, 4\}$. This means that some sets in $\mathscr{A}$ will have the same elements. By D.1.1 such sets are indistinguishable. Yet we may need to distinguish among them. Indexing gets around the difficulty in a rather subtle way. Let m and n be members of I. Normally $m \neq n$ means that A_m and A_n do not have the same elements, but note that there is no such *requirement* in D.1.7. This means that A_m and A_n may have the same elements when $m \neq n$. The symbols A_m and A_n are certainly not

equal, and this suggests two interpretations of A_i. When appropriate, A_i is interpreted as standing for a set of elements. An alternative interpretation takes A_i as a symbol, and the indexed set as a set of symbols. Under the first interpretation $\mathscr{A}$ can have at most six elements; if the second interpretation is taken, having ten elements is in order.

DEFINITION 1.8 Let I be an index set. We generalize the operations of union and intersection:

$$\bigcup_{i \in I} A_i = \{a \,|\, a \in A_i \quad \text{for at least one } i \in I\},$$
$$\bigcap_{i \in I} A_i = \{a \,|\, a \in A_i \quad \text{for all } i \in I\}.$$

Examples

1. Let $I = \{1, 2, 3, 4\}$, and $A_1 = \{1, 2\}$, $A_2 = \{1, 3\}$, $A_3 = \{1, 4\}$, $A_4 = \{1, 2, 4, 5\}$. Then $\bigcup_{i \in I} A_i = \{1, 2, 3, 4, 5\}$, and $\bigcap_{i \in I} A_i = \{1\}$. Note that $\bigcup_{i \in I} A_i$ can be written also as $\bigcup \{A_i \,|\, i \in I\}$, or as $\bigcup_i A_i$ (if the index set need not be emphasized). In this example we can also have $\bigcup_{i=1}^{i=4} A_i$ for the union. Similar notational variants can be used for intersection, e.g., $\bigcap_i A_i$.

2. $\bigcup_{i \in \varnothing} A_i = \varnothing$. Since there is no A_i, the set of objects belonging to at least one A_i is empty.

3. $\bigcap_{i \in \varnothing} A_i$ is more difficult to interpret. Let us consider objects that do *not* satisfy the formula of D.1.8. If, for some object a, it is not true that $a \in A_i$ *for all* $i \in I$, then there must exist at least one A_i, with $i \in I$, such that $a \notin A_i$. But if $I = \varnothing$, no A_i exists. This is a contradiction. Hence there are no objects that do not satisfy the formula, i.e., all objects satisfy the formula. We shall discuss the meaning of *all objects* in Section 1c.

4. $\bigcup_{i \in \{1\}} A_i = \bigcap_{i \in \{1\}} A_i = A_1$.

DEFINITION 1.9 A *partition* $\mathscr{A}$ of a set A, $\mathscr{A} = \{A_i \,|\, i \in I\}$, is a family of nonempty and distinct subsets of A such that $\bigcup_{i \in I} A_i = A$, and $A_i \cap A_j = \varnothing$ for all $i, j \in I$ $(i \neq j)$. Sets A_i are *blocks* of the partition.

Examples

1. Some partitions of $A = \{1, 2, 3, 4\}$: $\mathscr{A}_1 = \{\{1, 2\}, \{3, 4\}\}$, $\mathscr{A}_2 = \{\{1\}, \{2, 4\}, \{3\}\}$, $\mathscr{A}_3 = \{\{1, 2, 3, 4\}\}$.

2. Families $\mathscr{A}$ and $\mathscr{B}$ in Examples 1 and 2 of D.1.3 are partitions of $\{d \,|\, d$ is a decimal digit$\}$.

3. There is nothing sacred about definitions. What we make our terms mean is purely a matter of convenience. Here, for example, we could permit some A_i to be empty sets, but we do not because such a definition of a partition would cause inconvenience in the later development of the theory. In

the interests of communication we should not, of course, radically alter well-established definitions.

1c. Complement of a Set

DEFINITION 1.10   If all sets under consideration in a certain discussion are subsets of a set U, then U is the *universal set* or the *universe of discourse* for that discussion.

Examples

1. In elementary number theory U is the set of integers.
2. In plane analytic geometry U is the set of coordinate pairs.
3. If we consider sets of students taking particular courses at a university, U is the set of all students of that university.
4. $\bigcap_{i \in \varnothing} A_i = U$ identifies the *set of all objects*, which arose in Example 3 of D.1.8, with the universal set (or, more precisely, *a* universal set).

The definition of the universal set is rather vague. If I is the set of integers, and S is the set of all students of Example 3, we could use the set $\{x \mid x \in I$ or $x \in S\}$ as the universal set for both Examples 1 and 3. Indeed, we might consider the set of *all* objects in the universe (everything we can conceive) as the universal set for any discussion. Let us see what consequences this has. Define the set $R = \{x \mid x \notin x\}$. The defining formula seems reasonable. Consider, for example, the integer 5. We know that 5 is not a set. Hence 5 cannot have any members, $5 \notin 5$ is true, and $5 \in R$. For a further example, we know that $\mathscr{P}(\{1, 2\})$ is not a member of itself (Example of Th.1.3), and hence $\mathscr{P}(\{1, 2\}) \in R$. But if the universal set is the set of all objects, then R itself belongs to it, and the defining formula has to be applied to R. If $R \notin R$ is true, then R qualifies for membership of R, i.e., $R \in R$. On the other hand, if $R \notin R$ is false, which is equivalent to $R \in R$ being true (a possibility that cannot be dismissed, however unlikely it may appear), then R does not qualify for membership of R, i.e., $R \notin R$. Thus we have the contradiction $R \in R$ *if and only if* $R \notin R$. Unrestricted application of the defining formula $x \notin x$ is the basis of this contradiction, which is one of several possible formulations of what is known as the Russell paradox.

The Russell paradox is just one of a number of contradictions that arose in early formulations of set theory. These formulations permitted one to talk about the set of all sets, which means that one could consider a set as a member of itself. The contradictions can be traced back to this particular membership. They disappear if the manner of introducing the objects that set theory can talk about is such that a set can no longer be considered as a member of itself. This is done by making sure that the axioms of set theory can produce the theorem

For any set a, a ∉ a.

One axiomatic theory in which this is a theorem is known as Zermelo–Fraenkel set theory.

We still have to find out how one should select the universal set for a particular discussion. D.1.10 is very permissive in this respect. We have found, however, that the permissiveness lets us make a selection that leads to contradictions. The proper way is to take an axiomatic set theory that is free of contradictions and to select from the objects this theory can talk about the smallest set that contains as subsets all sets used in the discussion. In practice we let the context in which the sets are used determine the universal set, and we will find that a universal set so selected is an acceptable set in terms of the axiomatic theory. Unless stated otherwise, the universal sets that we shall select will not have sets as members.

DEFINITION 1.11   The *relative complement* of a set A with respect to a set X, written $X - A$ (and sometimes called *set difference*), is the set

$$X - A = \{x \,|\, x \in X \quad \text{and} \quad x \notin A\}.$$

The *absolute complement* of a set A, written $\bar{A}$, is the set $U - A$. In terms of the absolute complement we have $X - A = X \cap \bar{A}$.

Example

Let $A = \{1, 2, 3, 4\}$ and $B = \{3, 4, 5\}$. Then $A - B = \{1, 2\}$, $B - A = \{5\}$. In this discussion we can take the set of natural numbers for U. This choice gives $\bar{A} = \{5, 6, 7, \ldots\}$, and $B \cap \bar{A} = \{3, 4, 5\} \cap \{5, 6, 7, \ldots\} = \{5\}$. Note that $\bar{A}$ depends on the choice for the universal set, but that $B \cap \bar{A}$ is independent of the choice. In the context here we can equally well select the set of decimal digits for the universal set. Then $\bar{A} = \{0, 5, 6, 7, 8, 9\}$, but $B \cap \bar{A} = \{5\}$ again.

THEOREM 1.4   Let A be a set and let U be the universal set. Then $A \cup \bar{A} = U$ and $A \cap \bar{A} = \varnothing$.

Proof. By D.1.6 $A \cup \bar{A} = \{x \,|\, x \in A \text{ or } x \in \bar{A}\}$ and $A \cap \bar{A} = \{x \,|\, x \in A \text{ and } x \in \bar{A}\}$. But (by D.1.11) $\bar{A} = U - A = \{x \,|\, x \in U \text{ and } x \notin A\} = \{x \,|\, x \notin A\}$, since it is understood that all elements belong to the universal set. Then we can put $A \cup \bar{A} = \{x \,|\, x \in A \text{ or } x \notin A\}$ and $A \cap \bar{A} = \{x \,|\, x \in A \text{ and } x \notin A\}$. The defining formulas are satisfied by all elements and by no elements, respectively. Hence $A \cup \bar{A} = U$, $A \cap \bar{A} = \varnothing$.

COROLLARY   If $A \neq \varnothing$ and $A \neq U$, i.e., if $\varnothing \subset A \subset U$, then the family $\{A, \bar{A}\}$ is a partition of U.

Examples

1. Prove that $\bar{A} \subseteq \bar{B}$ if and only if $A \supseteq B$. Assume $A \not\supseteq B$. Then there exists an element $x \in B$ such that $x \notin A$, and (by Th. 1.4) $x \in \bar{A}$. But if $x \in B$, then $x \notin \bar{B}$ (Th.1.4). Thus there exists an element x such that $x \in \bar{A}$ and $x \notin \bar{B}$, i.e., $\bar{A} \not\subseteq \bar{B}$. Hence $\bar{A} \subseteq \bar{B}$ only if $A \supseteq B$. The sufficiency proof is similar.

2. Prove $\overline{A \cap B} = \bar{A} \cup \bar{B}$. We have to show (i) $\overline{A \cap B} \subseteq \bar{A} \cup \bar{B}$, and (ii) $\bar{A} \cup \bar{B} \subseteq \overline{A \cap B}$ (Th.1.2). To show that (i) holds, let $x \in \overline{A \cap B}$. Then $x \notin A \cap B$, i.e., $x \in A$ and $x \in B$ cannot both be true. Consequently $x \in \bar{A}$ or $x \in \bar{B}$, and, by the defining formula of D.1.6, $x \in \bar{A} \cup \bar{B}$. But x is *any* element of $\overline{A \cap B}$. This means that every element of $\overline{A \cap B}$ is an element of $\bar{A} \cup \bar{B}$, or $\overline{A \cap B} \subseteq \bar{A} \cup \bar{B}$. To prove inclusion (ii) *assert* that $\bar{A} \subseteq \overline{A \cap B}$ and $\bar{B} \subseteq \overline{A \cap B}$, and let $x \in \bar{A} \cup \bar{B}$. Then $x \in \bar{A}$ or $x \in \bar{B}$. If $x \in \bar{A}$, then $x \in \overline{A \cap B}$; and also if $x \in \bar{B}$, then $x \in \overline{A \cap B}$ (on the basis of the assertion). Hence $\bar{A} \cup \bar{B} \subseteq \overline{A \cap B}$. It remains to prove the assertion. We show that $\bar{A} \subseteq \overline{A \cap B}$. Let $y \in A \cap B$. Then $y \in A$ and $y \in B$, in particular $y \in A$. Hence $A \supseteq A \cap B$, and consequently, by Example 1, $\bar{A} \subseteq \overline{A \cap B}$. The proof of $\bar{B} \subseteq \overline{A \cap B}$ is similar.

DEFINITION 1.12   The *symmetric difference* of sets A and B, written $A + B$, is the set defined by

$$A + B = (A - B) \cup (B - A).$$

Example

In terms of defining formulas $A - B = \{x \mid x \in A \text{ and } x \notin B\}$, and $B - A = \{x \mid x \in B \text{ and } x \notin A\}$. Then $A + B = \{x \mid x \in A \text{ or } x \in B\}$, where *or* has the exclusive meaning, i.e., $x \in A$ *or* $x \in B$ here means $x \in A$ or $x \in B$ *but not* $x \in A$ and $x \in B$ (cf. definition of $A \cup B$ in D.1.6). Let $A = \{1, 2, 3, 4\}$ and $B = \{2, 3, 4, 5, 6\}$. Then $A \cup B = \{1, 2, 3, 4, 5, 6\}$, but $A + B = \{1, 5, 6\}$. Defining formulas of $A + B$ and $A \cup B$ are identical except for the interpretation of the word *or*, and there is nothing in the word itself to indicate the intended meaning. All *natural* languages (e.g., English, French) contain ambiguities. But ambiguities have no place in mathematics. This has led to the use of unambiguous symbolic languages in formal developments. In such languages there are different symbols for *or* (inclusive) and *or* (exclusive).

1d. Algebra of Sets

The properties of the complement of a set discussed in Th.1.4 and in the examples following the theorem are results in an algebra of sets. The results were obtained without a plan: The complement has been discussed, but we still have no knowledge of the basic properties of union and intersection. A consequence of the unplanned approach was the need for separate proofs of $\bar{A} \subseteq \overline{A \cap B}$ and $\bar{B} \subseteq \overline{A \cap B}$ in Example 2 of Th.1.4. We know, of course, that $\bar{B} \subseteq \overline{B \cap A}$ follows from $\bar{A} \subseteq \overline{A \cap B}$ (simply change every A to B, and every B to A), but we have as yet no theorem that would enable us to deduce $\bar{B} \subseteq \overline{A \cap B}$ from $\bar{B} \subseteq \overline{B \cap A}$; our intuitive belief that $A \cap B$ should equal $B \cap A$ is, of course, no proof. There is a need then for a systematic development of an algebra of sets.

Operators $\cup, \cap, {}^-, -, +$ have been defined. Expressions in $-$ or $+$ can be changed to equivalent expressions in which the only operators to appear are $\cup$, $\cap$, and ${}^-$, i.e., any expression in $-$ or $+$ can be interpreted as a shorthand version of the equivalent expression in $\cup$, $\cap$, and ${}^-$, e.g., $A + B$ as an abbreviation for $(A \cap \bar{B}) \cup (B \cap \bar{A})$. Properties of the relative complement and symmetric difference are, therefore, only of secondary interest. Operators $\cup$ and $\cap$ take two operands—union and intersection are binary operations; ${}^-$ takes a single operand—complementation is a unary operation.

We need commutative laws for the binary operations. Interpretation of generalizations $\bigcup_i A_i$ and $\bigcap_i A_i$ of D.1.8 as repeated applications of binary operators $\cup$ and $\cap$, respectively, points out the need for associative laws. Since $\cup$ and $\cap$ can both occur in the one expression, e.g., $(A \cap \bar{B}) \cup (B \cap \bar{A})$, we also need distributive laws. Finally, a set needs to be related to the two special sets U and $\varnothing$, and to the complemented set. The laws are listed in the form of equalities in Th.1.5.

THEOREM 1.5 Let A, B, C be any subsets of the universal set U. Then the following equalities hold.

1A. $A \cup B = B \cup A$.
1B. $A \cap B = B \cap A$.
2A. $A \cup (B \cup C) = (A \cup B) \cup C$.
2B. $A \cap (B \cap C) = (A \cap B) \cap C$.
3A. $A \cup (B \cap C) = (A \cup B) \cap (A \cup C)$.
3B. $A \cap (B \cup C) = (A \cap B) \cup (A \cap C)$.
4A. $A \cup \varnothing = A$.
4B. $A \cap U = A$.
5A. $A \cup \bar{A} = U$.
5B. $A \cap \bar{A} = \varnothing$.

Proof. Parts 5A and 5B are Th.1.4. Proofs of the other equalities can be based on interpretation of defining formulas or on the two-sided inclusion procedure suggested by Th.1.2 and followed in the proof of Example 2 of Th. 1.4.

Union, intersection, and complementation are operations, and they define new sets. Set inclusion is not an operation. It describes a condition. While $A \cap B$ is the set whose elements belong to both A and B, $A \subseteq B$ is not a set—it states that every member of set A belongs also to set B. We know that conditions $A \subseteq B$ and $B \subseteq A$ are equivalent to the equality $A = B$ (Th.1.2). We shall now show that $A \subseteq B$ on its own is equivalent to certain equalities.

THEOREM 1.6   Let A and B be any subsets of the universal set U. The following statements about A and B are equivalent to each other:

(a) $A \subseteq B$.
(b) $A \cup B = B$.
(c) $A \cap B = A$.

Proof. We have to show that statement (b) is true if (a) is true, and that (c) is true if (b) is true. Then it has to be shown that (a) is true if (c) is true. The last part enables us to say for any two of the statements that one is true if and only if the other is true, and this is what is meant by equivalence of the statements.

(a) implies (b). Assume $A \subseteq B$. The defining formula for set union gives $A \cup B = \{x \mid x \in A \text{ or } x \in B\}$. But every member of A is a member of B by assumption. Hence the $x \in A$ part in the defining formula is superfluous, and the definition reduces to $A \cup B = \{x \mid x \in B\}$ here. Also $B = \{x \mid x \in B\}$. Hence $A \cup B = B$.

(b) implies (c). Assume $A \cup B = B$. We shall use parts of Th.1.5 in the proof.

$$
\begin{aligned}
A \cap B &= A \cap (A \cup B) & \text{(Assumption)} \\
&= (A \cup B) \cap A & \text{(1B)} \\
&= (A \cup B) \cap (A \cup \varnothing) & \text{(4A)} \\
&= A \cup (B \cap \varnothing) & \text{(3A)} \\
&= A \cup (B \cap \varnothing) \cup \varnothing & \text{(4A)} \\
&= A \cup (B \cap \varnothing) \cup (B \cap \bar{B}) & \text{(5B)} \\
&= A \cup (B \cap (\varnothing \cup \bar{B})) & \text{(3B)} \\
&= A \cup (B \cap (\bar{B} \cup \varnothing)) & \text{(1A)} \\
&= A \cup (B \cap \bar{B}) & \text{(4A)} \\
&= A \cup \varnothing & \text{(5B)} \\
&= A. & \text{(4A)}
\end{aligned}
$$

(c) implies (a). Assume $A \cap B = A$. Let $y \in A \cap B$. Then $y \in A$ and $y \in B$, in particular $y \in B$. Hence $A \cap B \subseteq B$, and, by the assumption, $A \subseteq B$.

It must be understood that the equalities of Th.1.6 are essentially different from those of Th.1.5, although we have used the same symbol ($=$) in both theorems. The statements of Th.1.5 hold for all subsets of a universal set. They are therefore identities. In Th.1.6 particular sets have been singled out from the family of all subsets of a universal set, and the equalities hold only for those sets. Thus in $A \cap B = B \cap A$ the symbols A and B stand for any subsets of the universal set, but in $A \cap B = A$ the equality holds only if A is a subset of B. Some writers emphasize the difference by using a special symbol ($\equiv$) for identity.

We have been talking about algebra of sets without making clear what is meant by it. Consider a nonempty set U with power set $\mathscr{P}(U)$. For any sets $A, B \in \mathscr{P}(U)$ we have $A \cup B \in \mathscr{P}(U)$, $A \cap B \in \mathscr{P}(U)$, $\bar{A} \in \mathscr{P}(U)$. If an operation on any members of a set produces an object that is also a member of the set, then the set is said to be *closed* under this operation. The power set $\mathscr{P}(U)$ is closed under union, intersection, and complementation. For some U one can find proper nonempty subsets of $\mathscr{P}(U)$ that are also closed under the three operations. Since $A \cup \bar{A} = U$ and $A \cap \bar{A} = \varnothing$ for any set A, these subsets of $\mathscr{P}(U)$, in order to be closed, necessarily contain $\varnothing$ and U. A nonempty subset of $\mathscr{P}(U)$, closed under union, intersection, and complementation, in which elements $\varnothing$ and U are distinguished, is a closed system known as an algebra of sets. We summarize: The power set $\mathscr{P}(U)$ of a nonempty set U is an algebra of sets based on U (but the $\mathscr{P}(U)$ are not the only algebras of sets).

The use of the plural, algebras of sets, may be somewhat confusing. Set U can be any nonempty set (within the limits discussed in Section 1c) and we have a different algebra for each U. But the form of the theorems is the same in all algebras of sets. Therefore, it is customary to call the theorems, rather loosely, the algebra of sets.

The concept of membership of an element in a set is essential for proof of Th.1.5. This concept belongs to the general theory of sets, and the proof of Th.1.5 places the algebra of sets within the framework of that theory. We assert now that every theorem in the algebra of sets can be deduced from Th.1.5. Note that the statement of Th.1.5 makes no mention of membership and, if we consider the algebra of sets by itself, the question of membership does not arise in it. But then we cannot prove Th.1.5 and have to consider the algebra of sets as an axiomatic theory based on the statement of Th.1.5 as a set of axioms.

1e. Algebra of Sets as an Axiomatic Theory

Most students approach *abstract theories* with trepidation. The adjective *abstract* has come to acquire a forbidding sound; commonly it denotes something that the mind finds hard to grasp. Contrary to popular belief *abstract* does not have this meaning in mathematics. Abstraction in mathematics is the process of eliminating anything that is inessential to a particular discussion; the aim is clarity and generality. Abstraction is so important that one might even say that mathematics *is* abstraction: A child first experiences mathematics in realizing that putting two blue blocks and three blue blocks together is an operation that in its essence has nothing to do with the color of the blocks or the fact that the toys are blocks rather than beads. Despite appearances, the process that will take us from the algebra of sets to an abstract theory does not differ in kind from that through which a child goes in arriving at an understanding of the nature of addition.

The essentials of an algebra of sets are in the first place symbols representing sets and operations. The interpretation given to the symbols is necessary for proof of Th.1.5. New theorems, however, can be derived from Th.1.5 with no knowledge of the meaning of the symbols. Thus, in proving that $A \cup B = B$ implies $A \cap B = A$ (Th.1.6), symbols are manipulated according to rules supplied by Th.1.5 in a purely mechanical manner. The set of relations given in Th.1.5 is, therefore, another essential feature of the theory, but the meaning the symbols have in Th.1.5 is not. Here then the abstraction process consists of stripping symbols of their meaning. The result is a base for a generalized theory, comprising a system of undefined symbols and Th.1.5 as a set of axioms, expressing relations between symbols in this abstract system.

The idea that a mathematician builds an abstract theory out of nothing by taking a system of symbols, declaring axioms arbitrarily, and hoping for the best is a misconception. Axiomatic theories are abstractions of something already existing. For the purpose of introducing the terminology of axiomatic theories we shall, however, assume that there is nothing to start with. Then the first task is to create a base consisting of certain symbols and properties of the symbols. The symbols in the base cannot be defined; a definition gives meaning to a symbol in terms of other symbols, and there are no other symbols at the time the basic symbols are introduced. The basic symbols are called *primitives*. All other symbols, called *defined symbols*, must be defined in terms of primitives or other defined symbols. If nonprimitives are used in the definition of a new symbol, one must make sure that circular definitions are avoided, i.e., that all nonprimitives in the definition have in fact been defined.

Statements expressing relations between symbols are admitted to a theory only if they are *provable*. A *proof* is a sequence of statements in which each statement follows from one or more preceding statements by rules of logic. All statements in the sequence that are so derived by the system of logic employed are called *theorems*. A small set of statements expressing basic relations between primitives (and thus establishing their basic properties) is accorded special status. These statements, called *axioms*, are admitted to the theory without proof. (Alternatively, to be consistent with the principle that only provable statements are admitted to a theory, axioms can be considered as theorems that prove themselves.) It must be emphasized that *every* statement provable in a theory is a theorem in that theory. Since most provable statements in a theory are uninteresting, we tend to reserve the term *theorem* for those provable statements that we find particularly significant. For example, in Th.1.6 (assuming for the time being that we are dealing with an axiomatic theory), the fact that $A \cap B = A$ follows from $A \cup B = B$ is significant, and we would call "*if* $A \cup B = B$, *then* $A \cap B = A$" a theorem under any interpretation of the term. Looking at the proof of this theorem we see that the statement "*if* $A \cup B = B$, *then* $A \cap B = A \cup (B \cap (\varnothing \cup \bar{B}))$" is also a theorem in the technical sense. But we are not impressed by this theorem.

Most axiomatic theories are *informal*, by which is meant that the formulation presupposes and draws on rules of inference and general set theory. If rules of inference are assumed, one can, for example, infer equality of two things from the observation that the two things are equal to a third. A *formal* theory makes no presuppositions; consequently this rule of inference must be established as a theorem of the formal theory before it may be used in a proof. A formal theory will also contain a general set theory (e.g., the Zermelo–Fraenkel axiomatic set theory). Two clarifying remarks should be made. First, axiomatic set theory is not to be confused with axiomatized algebra of sets. While set theory investigates the relation of a member to a set, the algebra is concerned with relations between sets. Second, an informal theory is informal only in comparison with a formal theory. Even in an informal theory great attention is paid to the form of presentation.

In selecting a set of primitives and constructing the axioms of our theory we shall be guided by Th.1.5. An abstract algebra that results from an axiomatization based on Th.1.5 is known as a *Boolean algebra*. Subsequently the primitives of the general theory can be interpreted in set-theoretical terms, in which case the theory gives an algebra of sets, or they can be given some other interpretation.

Boolean algebra B

Primitives
> Set B.
> Binary operations $\oplus$ and $*$ under which B is closed.
> Unary operation $'$ under which B is closed.
> Distinct elements 0 and 1 of B. (By *distinct* we mean here that while symbols a, b, c, and the like stand for any elements of B, symbols 0 and 1 represent themselves.)

Axioms

For all a, b, $c \in B$:

1A. $a \oplus b = b \oplus a$.

1B. $a * b = b * a$.

2A. $a \oplus (b \oplus c) = (a \oplus b) \oplus c$.

2B. $a * (b * c) = (a * b) * c$.

3A. $a \oplus (b * c) = (a \oplus b) * (a \oplus c)$.

3B. $a * (b \oplus c) = (a * b) \oplus (a * c)$.

4A. $a \oplus 0 = a$.

4B. $a * 1 = a$.

5A. $a \oplus a' = 1$.

5B. $a * a' = 0$.

Some symbols appear in the set of axioms that are not listed as primitives. Certain symbols, such as (,), $\in$, *for each*, *there exists*, are symbols in the theories presupposed by the informal Boolean algebra (general set theory and the theory of inference), and as such can be admitted to the theory. General set theory also gives meaning to the terms *binary operation* and *unary operation*. The symbol $=$ is somewhat special in that different meanings are assigned to it in different interpretations of the abstract theory. We shall discuss this symbol in Section 2h.

A set of axioms is *independent* if no axioms can be removed without loss of a theorem in the theory; otherwise the set contains at least one *redundant* axiom. In our set of axioms 2A and 2B are redundant. They can be deduced from the other axioms (Exercise 1.29). As long as the set of axioms remains reasonably small, there is no harm in having redundant axioms. They may in fact help one get a better understanding of the structure of a theory.

Axioms of our algebra come in pairs and axioms in the one pair are similar. This similarity can be precisely defined, and a powerful result can then be deduced from it.

DEFINITION 1.13   Let S be a statement in Boolean algebra B, and replace in S symbols $\oplus$, $*$, 1, 0 according to the following scheme:

$\oplus$ becomes $*$, $*$ becomes $\oplus$;

1 becomes 0,   0 becomes 1.

The resulting statement is the *dual* of S.

Example

The dual of $a \oplus b = b \oplus a$ is $a * b = b * a$, and the dual of $a * b = b * a$ is $a \oplus b = b \oplus a$. Each axiom in each of the five pairs of axioms of the Boolean algebra is in fact the dual of the other.

THEOREM 1.7   (*Principle of duality*)   If S is a theorem in Boolean algebra B, then its dual is also a theorem in B.

Statements of Boolean algebra express relations between objects *in* the algebra. They certainly do not belong to the algebra as objects that the algebra relates. Therefore, statements *about* theorems are in a different system from that of the theorems. Theorems about theorems are known as *metatheorems*; Th.1.7 is an example of a metatheorem. It functions in the Boolean algebra as a rule of inference. A proper proof of Th.1.7 is difficult, but one might be convinced of its truth by the following argument. A statement S is established as a theorem by means of a proof. Since the dual of every axiom is also an axiom, the sequence of duals of statements in the proof of S should be a proof of the dual of S.

THEOREM 1.8   In Boolean algebra B:

1. If, for all a, $a \oplus b = a$, then $b = 0$.
2. If, for all a, $a * b = a$, then $b = 1$.

Proof. 1. Assuming $a \oplus b = a$, take in particular

$$\text{(i)} \quad a \oplus b_1 = a,$$
$$\text{(ii)} \quad a \oplus b_2 = a.$$

Then, putting b_2 for a in (i) and b_1 for a in (ii) (which we can do, since, by assumption, the relations hold for all a),

$$\text{(iii)} \quad b_2 \oplus b_1 = b_2,$$
$$\text{(iv)} \quad b_1 \oplus b_2 = b_1.$$

From (iv),

$$\text{(v)} \quad b_2 \oplus b_1 = b_1 \quad \text{(by Axiom 1A).}$$

From (iii) and (v), $b_2 = b_1$ (two things equal to third). Thus the element b in $a \oplus b = a$ is unique. But $a \oplus 0 = a$ (Axiom 4A). Hence the unique element is 0.

2. This follows from Part 1 by principle of duality.

Axioms 4A and 4B give properties of 0 and 1, but they do not say that 0 and 1 are the only elements having these properties. Thus 4A states that $a \oplus 0 = a$ holds, but the question of whether $a \oplus b = a$ can hold for *some* b other than 0 is left open. Part 1 of Th.1.8 excludes this possibility. Th.1.8 in fact states that 0 and 1 are unique elements of B in the sense that in forms $a \oplus b = a$ and $a * c = a$ element b can be only 0 and c can be only 1. A much shorter proof of Th.1.8 can be found (Exercise 1.27), but it does not point out the uniqueness of the distinct elements 0 and 1 as clearly. The next theorem is similar to Th.1.8 in that it establishes the uniqueness of a' for a given element a (an a' exists for every a since B is closed under $'$).

THEOREM 1.9   In Boolean algebra B: For every a, if $a \oplus b = 1$ and $a * b = 0$, then $b = a'$.

Proof. Exercise 1.28.

In defining Boolean algebra B we defined $\oplus$ and $*$ as binary operations and $'$ as a unary operation in this algebra. Use of the term *operation* implies that the application of $\oplus$, $*$, or $'$ gives unique elements (see D.2.1), e.g., if $a \oplus b = c_1$ and $a \oplus b = c_2$, then $c_1 = c_2$ by definition. Our ability to *prove* the uniqueness of a' for a given a shows that $'$ may be defined as something more general than operation (namely, as a relation—see Chapter 2).

THEOREM 1.10   In Boolean algebra B:

1. For all a, $a \oplus a = a$.
2. For all a, $a \oplus 1 = 1$.
3. For all a and b, $a \oplus (a * b) = a$.

Proof. 1. $\begin{aligned} a \oplus a &= (a \oplus a) * 1 & \text{(4B)} \\ &= (a \oplus a) * (a \oplus a') & \text{(5A)} \\ &= a \oplus (a * a') & \text{(3A)} \\ &= a \oplus 0 & \text{(5B)} \\ &= a. & \text{(4A)} \end{aligned}$

2. $\begin{aligned} a \oplus 1 &= a \oplus (a \oplus a') & \text{(5A)} \\ &= (a \oplus a) \oplus a' & \text{(2A)} \\ &= a \oplus a' & \text{(Part 1)} \\ &= 1. & \text{(5A)} \end{aligned}$

3. Exercise 1.28.

THEOREM 1.11   In Boolean algebra B:

1. For all a, $a * a = a$.
2. For all a, $a * 0 = 0$.
3. For all a and b, $a * (a \oplus b) = a$.

Proof. From Th.1.10 by principle of duality.

THEOREM 1.12   In Boolean algebra B:

1. For all a, $(a')' = a$.
2. $0' = 1$ and $1' = 0$.
3. For all a and b, $(a \oplus b)' = a' * b'$ and $(a * b)' = a' \oplus b'$.

Proof. 1. Axioms 5A and 5B give the following pairs of theorems:

(i) $a' \oplus (a')' = 1$, $a' * (a')' = 0$;
(ii) $a \oplus a' = 1$, $a * a' = 0$.

From (ii), by Axioms 1A and 1B,

(iii) $a' \oplus a = 1,$ $a' * a = 0.$

Then, by Theorem 1.9, from (i) and (iii), $(a')' = a$.

2. Exercise 1.28.

3. If it can be shown that $(a \oplus b) \oplus (a' * b') = 1$ and $(a \oplus b) * (a' * b') = 0$, then, by Th.1.9, $(a \oplus b)' = a' * b'$.

$$\begin{aligned}
(a \oplus b) \oplus (a' * b') &= ((a \oplus b) \oplus a') * ((a \oplus b) \oplus b') &\text{(3A)} \\
&= ((b \oplus a) \oplus a') * ((a \oplus b) \oplus b') &\text{(1A)} \\
&= (b \oplus (a \oplus a')) * (a \oplus (b \oplus b')) &\text{(2A)} \\
&= (b \oplus 1) * (a \oplus 1) &\text{(5A)} \\
&= 1 * 1 &\text{(Th.1.10, Part 2)} \\
&= 1. &\text{(Th.1.11, Part 1)}
\end{aligned}$$

Similarly one shows that $(a \oplus b) * (a' * b') = 0$, and $(a \oplus b)' = a' * b'$ then follows. Then $(a * b)' = a' \oplus b'$ by principle of duality. These two theorems are known as *de Morgan's laws*.

The theory has as yet no equivalent of the subset relation for sets. We introduce such a relation by definition, taking Th.1.6 for a guide.

DEFINITION 1.14   In Boolean algebra B, for two elements a and b, the relation $a \leq b$ holds if and only if $a \oplus b = b$. Relation $a \geq b$ is synonymous with $b \leq a$.

Examples

1. Show that $a * b = a$ if and only if $a \oplus b = b$. Then the statements $a \leq b$, $a \oplus b = b$, and $a * b = a$ are all equivalent to each other. First assume $a \oplus b = b$, and show that $a * b = a$ follows:

$$\begin{aligned}
a &= a * (a \oplus b) &\text{(Th.1.11, Part 3)} \\
&= a * b. &\text{(Assumption)}
\end{aligned}$$

Next assume $a * b = a$. Then

$$\begin{aligned}
b &= b \oplus (b * a) &\text{(Th.1.10, Part 3)} \\
&= b \oplus (a * b) &\text{(B1)} \\
&= b \oplus a &\text{(Assumption)} \\
&= a \oplus b. &\text{(A1)}
\end{aligned}$$

2. Statement $a \leq b$ is equivalent to $a \oplus b = b$ and to $a * b = a$, but they are not duals of each other. Hence, if the dual of a statement containing $\leq$ or $\geq$ has to be found, one must replace relations in these symbols by their

equivalents prior to making the replacements. Alternatively, since $a \geqq b$ is equivalent to $a * b = b$, which is the dual of $a \oplus b = b$, one can extend the replacement scheme of D.1.13 by adding to it

$$\leqq \text{ becomes } \geqq, \qquad \geqq \text{ becomes } \leqq.$$

3. For all a in B, $1 \geqq a \geqq 0$.

Nothing has been said about the truth of axioms. In order to tell whether a statement is true one must know what it means. The meaning of a statement is determined by the meaning of the symbols in it. In an abstract system the only meaning that a symbol has is its relation to other symbols in the system, expressed in the first place by axioms. Theorems other than axioms are of course true within the abstract theory, in the sense that they are logical consequences of the axioms, with the axioms having assigned meaning to the symbols in them. But the axioms themselves do not follow from anything. Hence axioms have no meaning, and one cannot talk about their truth. The lack of preconceived notions about the symbols is in fact the strength of an abstract theory. On the other hand, proving theorems in a theory that exists in complete isolation is a sterile game. We emphasize again that in setting up an abstract theory, interpretation of the theory in terms of objects from a world external to the theory is anticipated.

The process of *interpretation* consists in taking objects that have definite meaning in some theory external to the abstract theory and of interpreting the abstract system as these concrete objects. Meaning is thus assigned to the primitives, and the axioms become meaningful statements. One can then ask whether they are true for the concrete objects. If they are, the system of the concrete objects is a *model* of the abstract theory. All theorems of an abstract theory are true statements about objects in a model of the theory,

In using Th.1.5 as a guide for setting up the abstract Boolean algebra B we provided ourselves with a ready-made model—the algebraic system $\mathscr{P}(U)$, $\cup$, $\cap$, $^-$, $\varnothing$, U. All objects in this system have been defined earlier. Hence they have a meaning. Th.1.5 establishes the system as a model of algebra B, and all theorems in B are automatically theorems in the Boolean algebra of subsets of U [members of $\mathscr{P}(U)$]. The symbol $=$ is interpreted as set equality. To exemplify this process, we reformulate Th.1.11 and Th.1.12 as theorems about sets.

THEOREM 1.13   For all members of $\mathscr{P}(U)$:

1. $A \cap A = A$.
2. $A \cap \varnothing = \varnothing$.
3. $A \cap (A \cup B) = A$.

THEOREM 1.14   For all members of $\mathscr{P}(U)$:

  1. $\bar{\bar{A}} = A$.
  2. $\overline{\varnothing} = U$ and $\overline{U} = \varnothing$.
  3. $\overline{A \cup B} = \bar{A} \cap \bar{B}$ and $\overline{A \cap B} = \bar{A} \cup \bar{B}$.

Our approach still has the appearance of a game. Obviously Th.1.13 and Th.1.14 could have been deduced directly from Th.1.5. Instead, we axiomatized the algebra of sets, found theorems in the axiomatic theory, switched back to the original system, and restated the theorems in this system. The algebra of subsets of U is not, however, the only model of the abstract theory. This has considerable practical significance. The theorems of an abstract theory are true for all systems that can be shown to be models of the theory, and to establish a system as a model one merely has to show that the axioms of the abstract theory are true for the system. Without an abstract theory every theorem has to be proven separately in each of the systems.

1f. Venn Diagrams

It is much easier to prove something when we know precisely what we have to prove. Thus it is not as easy to "simplify" $A \cup (A \cap B)$ as it is to prove $A \cup (A \cap B) = A$. A graphical device known as a *Venn diagram* (or Venn–Euler diagram) can help one find a precise formulation of a theorem in the algebra of sets before one sets out to prove it. A Venn diagram represents sets by sets of points in plane regions. First, one draws a fairly large rectangle: Points within the rectangle represent the universal set. A subset of the universal set is represented by points in some region, usually the interior of a circle, within the rectangle.

In Figure 1.1 the interiors of the two circles represent sets A and B, the entire shaded region represents $A \cup B$, and the crosshatched region $A \cap B$. Since the entire rectangle and the shaded region represent U and $A \cup B$, respectively, the unshaded region within the rectangle represents $\overline{A \cup B}$. In

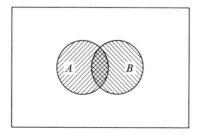

Figure 1.1

Figure 1.2 horizontal shading indicates the region representing $\bar{A}$ and vertical shading the region representing $\bar{B}$. The crosshatched region represents $\bar{A} \cap \bar{B}$, and the unshaded region $\overline{\bar{A} \cup \bar{B}}$. The crosshatched region in Figure 1.2 corresponds to the unshaded region in Figure 1.1, and the unshaded region in Figure 1.2 to the crosshatched region in Figure 1.1. These correspondences suggest $\bar{A} \cap \bar{B} = \overline{A \cup B}$ and $\overline{\bar{A} \cup \bar{B}} = A \cap B$ as possible identities.

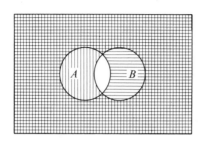

Figure 1.2

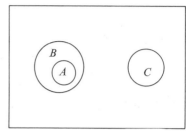

Figure 1.3

Figure 1.3 depicts set inclusion and disjoint sets. The region representing an included set lies entirely within the region representing the including set (circles A and B, for $A \subseteq B$). Disjoint sets, such as B and C, are represented by nonoverlapping regions. Looking again at Figure 1.2, regions shaded by vertical or horizontal lines alone represent the relative complements $A - B$ and $B - A$, respectively. They are two of the four nonoverlapping regions into which the rectangle has been partitioned by circles A and B. Provided each of the four regions contains at least one point, i.e., does not represent a null set, the sets represented by these regions constitute a partition of the universal set, $\{\bar{A} \cap \bar{B}, A - B, B - A, \overline{\bar{A} \cup \bar{B}}\}$.

Although we have shown that arguments based on Venn diagrams are useful for the appreciation of relations between sets, such arguments do not function well as *proofs*. Assume that we have to prove $\bar{A} \cup \bar{B} = \overline{A \cap B}$. In an algebraic proof A and B are variables throughout the proof, including the last line. It is clear that the result is an identity. In a Venn diagram A and B have to be represented by particular regions, and generality is lost at once. We can show that $\bar{A} \cup \bar{B} = \overline{A \cap B}$ is consistent with Figure 1.3, but so too is $\bar{A} \cup \bar{B} = \bar{A}$. There is no way of telling from Figure 1.3 alone that one of the equations is an identity while the other is a consequence of the relation $A \subseteq B$ in which A and B happen to stand as represented by Figure 1.3. To prove that $\bar{A} \cup \bar{B} = \overline{A \cap B}$ is an identity we have to demonstrate consistency with diagrams depicting all the different ways in which A may be related to B. An algebraic proof is much more direct.

Venn diagrams can be of great help in the solution of certain counting problems. Let us see whether we can determine the total number of computer science majors at a given college from the following data: 50 of the students taking course CS125 and 74 of those taking course CS133 are computer science majors, 38 computer science majors are in both CS125 and CS133, but 156 computer science majors are in neither of these two courses. Let A be the set of computer science majors in CS125, and B the set of computer science majors in CS133. Turn now to Figure 1.1. Let the set of all computer science majors be the universal set. Then $|U|$ is the number we want, and this is the sum of the members of the four disjoint sets represented by the four nonoverlapping regions of Figure 1.1. The crosshatched area represents the set of CS majors taking both courses, and we know that there are 38 such students. The unshaded region represents the set of CS majors in neither course, and there are 156 such students. It remains to determine the numbers in the sets represented by the remaining two regions, i.e., the set of CS majors in CS125 but not in CS133, and of those in CS133 but not in CS125. Clearly the students in these two sets number $50 - 38 = 12$ and $74 - 38 = 36$, respectively. Hence $|U| = 38 + 156 + 12 + 36 = 242$.

1g. The Ordered Pair and Related Concepts

It should be clearly understood that the order in which elements of a set are written down is unimportant. But often we have to deal with composite objects in which the order of components is important. One such object is the coordinate pair of analytic geometry: Points represented by coordinate pairs $\langle 2, 3 \rangle$ and $\langle 3, 2 \rangle$ are different; sets $\{2, 3\}$ and $\{3, 2\}$ are equal. Another example is a sequence of statements S_1, S_2, S_3, S_4 of a proof. Extending the notation for coordinate pairs, we can write the sequence as $\langle S_1, S_2, S_3, S_4 \rangle$. The sequence $\langle S_3, S_2, S_4, S_1 \rangle$ is probably not a proof, but, as sets, $\{S_1, S_2, S_3, S_4\} = \{S_3, S_2, S_4, S_1\}$.

We must find a definition of order in terms of sets. For generality we will no longer refer to $\langle a, b \rangle$ as a coordinate pair; we shall call the object an *ordered pair*. The main property of an ordered pair, which must be deducible from its definition, is uniqueness: If $\langle a, b \rangle$ and $\langle x, y \rangle$ are ordered pairs, and $\langle a, b \rangle = \langle x, y \rangle$, then $a = x$ and $b = y$. We shall see that this property is deducible from D.1.15.

DEFINITION 1.15   The *ordered pair* of a and b, written $\langle a, b \rangle$, is the set $\{\{a\}, \{a, b\}\}$. We call a the *first coordinate* and b the *second coordinate* of $\langle a, b \rangle$.

Examples

1. $\{\{a\}, \{a, b\}\} = \{\{b, a\}, \{a\}\}$, but, unless $a = b$, $\{\{a\}, \{a, b\}\} \neq \{\{b\}, \{a, b\}\}$. Indeed $\{\{b\}, \{a, b\}\} = \langle b, a \rangle$.

2. $\langle a, a \rangle = \{\{a\}, \{a, a\}\} = \{\{a\}, \{a\}\} = \{\{a\}\}$. Note that the unordered pair $\{a, b\}$ reduces to $\{a\}$ when $a = b$, and that $\{\{a\}\} \neq \{a\}$.

THEOREM 1.15   If $\langle a, b \rangle = \langle x, y \rangle$, then $a = x$ and $b = y$.

Proof. Write out the ordered pairs in full:

$$\text{(i)} \quad \{\{a\}, \{a, b\}\},$$
$$\text{(ii)} \quad \{\{x\}, \{x, y\}\}.$$

For convenience we shall call sets with two distinct elements pairs and sets with single elements singletons. We shall consider two cases.

(a) $x = y$. Then (ii) reduces to $\{\{x\}\}$. Since $\langle x, y \rangle = \langle a, b \rangle$ by hypothesis, and $\langle x, y \rangle$ is a singleton, $\langle a, b \rangle$ must also be a singleton. This means that $\{a, b\}$ must equal $\{a\}$, giving $a = b$. Hence (i) reduces to $\{\{a\}\}$, and, since (i) and (ii) are equal by hypothesis, $\{\{a\}\} = \{\{x\}\}$, giving $a = x$. It follows that all a, b, x, and y are equal, in particular $a = x$ and $b = y$.

(b) $x \neq y$. Then (ii) contains exactly one singleton and exactly one pair. Since $\langle a, b \rangle = \langle x, y \rangle$, (i) must contain one singleton and one pair. Hence we can equate: $\{a\} = \{x\}$, $\{a, b\} = \{x, y\}$. $\{a\} = \{x\}$ gives $a = x$, and this in turn gives $\{x, b\} = \{x, y\}$. Since $\{x, b\}$ is a pair, $b \neq x$. Hence $b = y$.

DEFINITION 1.16   The *product set* (*Cartesian product*), $A \times B$, of sets A and B is the set of ordered pairs such that the first coordinate of each pair is a member of A, and the second coordinate belongs to B:

$$A \times B = \{\langle a, b \rangle \mid a \in A \quad \text{and} \quad b \in B\}.$$

Examples

1. $A = \{1, 2\}$, $B = \{a, b, c\}$.

$$A \times B = \{\langle 1, a \rangle, \langle 1, b \rangle, \langle 1, c \rangle, \langle 2, a \rangle, \langle 2, b \rangle, \langle 2, c \rangle\},$$
$$B \times A = \{\langle a, 1 \rangle, \langle b, 1 \rangle, \langle c, 1 \rangle, \langle a, 2 \rangle, \langle b, 2 \rangle, \langle c, 2 \rangle\},$$
$$A \times A = \{\langle 1, 1 \rangle, \langle 1, 2 \rangle, \langle 2, 1 \rangle, \langle 2, 2 \rangle\}.$$

If set A has m (distinct) elements and set B has n elements, then the product sets $A \times B$ and $B \times A$ both have mn elements.

2. $X = \{1\}$, $Y = \{1, 2, 3\}$.

$$X \times Y = \{\langle 1, 1 \rangle, \langle 1, 2 \rangle, \langle 1, 3 \rangle\}.$$
$$(X \times Y) \cap (Y \times X) = \{\langle 1, 1 \rangle\}.$$

3. $X = \varnothing$, $Y = \{1, 2, 3\}$. $X \times Y = Y \times X = \varnothing$.

4. If A, B, C are sets, then $A \times B$ and $B \times C$ are also sets, and extended product sets such as $A \times (B \times C)$ and $(A \times B) \times C$ have meaning:

$$A \times (B \times C) = \{\langle a, \langle b, c \rangle \rangle \mid a \in A \quad \text{and} \quad \langle b, c \rangle \in B \times C\},$$
$$(A \times B) \times C = \{\langle \langle a, b \rangle, c \rangle \mid \langle a, b \rangle \in A \times B \quad \text{and} \quad c \in C\}.$$

5. Note that sets A and B of D.1.16 can be considered as the two members of the family $\{A_i \mid i \in I\}$, with $I = \{1, 2\}$. We can then write the product set $A_1 \times A_2$ as $\mathsf{X}_{i \in I} A_i$.

According to D.1.16 the product set $A \times B$ is constructed by going through all elements of the sets, taking element a from A, element b from B, and writing the elements in the order a, b. We are not at all dependent on the set-theoretical definition of $\langle a, b \rangle$. Similarly we want to look upon the generalized product set $A_1 \times A_2 \times \cdots \times A_n$ as a set of ordered objects $\langle a_1, a_2, \ldots, a_n \rangle$, with $a_1 \in A_1$, $a_2 \in A_2$, $\ldots$, $a_n \in A_n$. Intuitively we feel that there should be no essential difference between, say,

$$\langle a_1, \langle a_2, \ldots, a_n \rangle \rangle \quad \text{and} \quad \langle \langle a_1, \ldots, a_{n-1} \rangle, a_n \rangle,$$

i.e., $A_1 \times (A_2 \times \cdots \times A_n)$ should equal $(A_1 \times \cdots \times A_{n-1}) \times A_n$. All that really matters is that a_i comes from A_i and is written down between a_{i-1} and a_{i+1}. Quite clearly, however, product sets $A \times (B \times C)$ and $(A \times B) \times C$ of Example 4 are not equal; i.e., the operation $\times$ is not associative. This is a consequence of D.1.15, indicating a certain amount of artificiality in the set-theoretical definition of the ordered pair. The reason for persisting with this definition is conceptual economy, which outweighs the possible inconvenience of not being able to consider

$$\langle a_1, \langle a_2, \ldots, a_n \rangle \rangle \quad \text{and} \quad \langle \langle a_1, \ldots, a_{n-1} \rangle, a_n \rangle$$

as identical objects. We have to develop a completely new theory of ordered objects if D.1.15 is rejected. The way out of our difficulty is to define a product set in which the order of parentheses is unambiguously prescribed, to adhere to the definition consistently, and to interpret $A_1 \times A_2 \times \cdots \times A_n$ as the product set so defined. The mechanism for this approach is suggested by Example 5.

DEFINITION 1.17 Let I_n be the index set $\{1, 2, \ldots, n\}$. Define:

(i) $\mathsf{X}_{i \in I_1} A_i = A_1$,

(ii) $\mathsf{X}_{i \in I_k} A_i = (\mathsf{X}_{i \in I_{k-1}} A_i) \times A_k$ $(k > 1)$.

Examples

1. D.1.17 is a *recursive* definition. Another example of a recursive definition is the well known definition of *n factorial*:

$$0! = 1,$$
$$n! = (n-1)!\, n \qquad (n > 0).$$

2. $A_1 \times A_2 \times \cdots \times A_n$ is interpreted as $\mathsf{X}_{i \in I_n} A_i$. Under this interpretation $A_1 \times A_2 \times A_3 = ((A_1) \times A_2) \times A_3 = (A_1 \times A_2) \times A_3$, but $A_1 \times A_2 \times A_3$ cannot equal $A_1 \times (A_2 \times A_3)$ since D.1.17 does not assign a meaning to $A_2 \times A_3$.

3. Generalization of the ordered pair derives from D.1.17 and D.1.16. The general product set $\mathsf{X}_{i \in I_n} A_i$ is defined as the product set of two sets $\mathsf{X}_{i \in I_{n-1}} A_i$ and A_n, and D.1.16 defines the product set of two sets as a set of ordered pairs. Hence, provided $n > 1$, an element of $\mathsf{X}_{i \in I_n} A_i$ is an ordered pair. The first coordinate of this ordered pair is in turn an ordered pair (provided $n > 2$), and so on. An element of $\mathsf{X}_{i \in I_n} A_i$ then has the form $\langle \cdots \langle \langle a_1, a_2 \rangle, a_3 \rangle, \ldots, a_n \rangle$, which we shall write simply as $\langle a_1, a_2, \ldots, a_n \rangle$. The element $\langle a_1, a_2, \ldots, a_n \rangle$ is called an *ordered n-tuple*, Some *n*-tuples have special names: A 3-tuple is called a *triple*, a 4-tuple a *quadruple*, and so forth.

4. $\langle \langle a_1, a_2 \rangle, a_3 \rangle = \{\{\langle a_1, a_2 \rangle\}, \{\langle a_1, a_2 \rangle, a_3\}\} = \{\{\{\{a_1\}, \{a_1, a_2\}\}\}, \{\{\{a_1\}, \{a_1, a_2\}\}, a_3\}\}$. By interpretation $\langle \langle a_1, a_2 \rangle, a_3 \rangle \in A_1 \times A_2 \times A_3$, but $\langle a_1, \langle a_2, a_3 \rangle \rangle \notin A_1 \times A_2 \times A_3$.

5. The Boolean algebra of Section 1e is the 6-tuple $\langle B, \oplus, *, ', 0, 1 \rangle$. The 6-tuple $\langle \mathscr{P}(U), \cup, \cap, \bar{\ }, \varnothing, U \rangle$ is a model of the abstract algebra. Writing the systems as 6-tuples makes the interpretation unambiguous; here it is quite clear what the correspondence between the objects is.

6. We write A^n for the product set $A \times A \times \cdots \times A$ taken to n terms, e.g., $A \times A \times A = A^3$.

1h. Permutations and Combinations

DEFINITION 1.18   Let A be a set with $|A| = n$. If $\langle a_1, a_2, \ldots, a_m \rangle \in A^m$, then this ordered *m*-tuple is an *m-sample* of A. If all a_i in an *m*-sample are distinct, the *m*-sample is an *m-permutation* of A. In particular, an *n*-permutation is called simply a *permutation* of A. We shall denote the set of all *m*-samples of a set A by $S_m(A)$, the set of all *m*-permutations by $P_m(A)$, and the set of all permutations by $P(A)$.

Examples

1. $A = \{a, b, c\}$. Then $S_2(A) = \{\langle a, a\rangle,\ \langle a, b\rangle, \langle a, c\rangle, \langle b, a\rangle,\ \langle b, b\rangle,$ $\langle b, c\rangle, \langle c, a\rangle, \langle c, b\rangle, \langle c, c\rangle\}$, $P_2(A) = \{\langle a, b\rangle, \langle a, c\rangle, \langle b, a\rangle, \langle b, c\rangle, \langle c, a\rangle,$ $\langle c, b\rangle\}$, and $P(A) = \{\langle a, b, c\rangle,\ \langle a, c, b\rangle,\ \langle b, a, c\rangle,\ \langle b, c, a\rangle,\ \langle c, a, b\rangle,$ $\langle c, b, a\rangle\}$. Note that $S_k(A) = A^k$. In keeping with normal practice we shall abbreviate our notation, writing $\{ab,\ ac,\ ba,\ bc,\ ca,\ cb\}$ for $P_2(A)$, $\{abc, acb,$ $bac, bca, cab, cba\}$ for $P(A)$, etc.

2. For all k, $P_k(A) \subseteq S_k(A)$. Specifically, $P_1(A) = S_1(A)$, and $P_k(A) \subset S_k(A)$ for $k > 1$. If k exceeds the size of A, then $P_k(A) = \varnothing$. Samples whose size exceeds $|A|$ do not contradict the definition. Thus, for $A = \{a, b, c\}$, $baabba \in S_6(A)$. An m-sample is sometimes called an m-permutation with repetition, the terminology being suggested by the subset relation in which permutations stand to samples.

Set A of D.1.18 can be given various interpretations. Consider, for example, the set $\{1, 2, \ldots, 6\}$, interpreted as the set of possible outcomes for the throw of a die. If one throws the die repeatedly and scores the outcomes, the score might be 5 after the first throw, 56 after the second, 561 after the third, and so on to 5612263123 after the tenth throw. The abbreviated notation of Example 1 is very suggestive: In this notation $S_{10}(A)$ is in fact the list of all possible scores for ten throws. Alternatively, set A might represent a deck of 52 cards from which one draws five cards, one after the other. Repetition is not possible; all cards in the hand are distinct. Here $P_5(A)$ lists all possible hands of five cards that may be drawn from the deck. But a straight flush is a straight flush, irrespective of the order in which the cards have been drawn. Therefore we might not want to distinguish between hands that differ only in the order of draw. Similarly we might not be interested in the order of throws of the die, and consider scores 5612263123 and 1122233566 equivalent. There is thus a need to define unordered counterparts of samples and permutations.

Since elements of a permutation are all distinct, the natural unordered counterpart of the ordered m-tuple defining an m-permutation would seem to be the set of its elements. Unfortunately we cannot define the unordered object corresponding to a sample quite this way: the set of elements in $abab$, ab, $aaab$ is the same, namely $\{a, b\}$. The unordered samples should, however, be all different. One possibility is to take a set in which elements are paired with counts of their occurrences. Then $abab$ and $aabb$ both correspond to $\{\langle a, 2\rangle, \langle b, 2\rangle\}$, while ab corresponds to $\{\langle a, 1\rangle, \langle b, 1\rangle\}$, $aaab$ to $\{\langle a, 3\rangle,$ $\langle b, 1\rangle\}$, and $aabbbc$ to $\{\langle a, 2\rangle, \langle b, 3\rangle, \langle c, 1\rangle\}$. We do in fact use this scheme in our definition.

DEFINITION 1.19   Let A be a set. Then an m-selection of A is the set $\{\langle a_1, k_1 \rangle, \langle a_2, k_2 \rangle, \ldots, \langle a_r, k_r \rangle\}$ such that all $a_i \in A$, all k_i are integers $(k_i > 0)$, and $\sum_{i=1}^{r} k_i = m$. In particular, if all $k_i = 1$, the m-selection is called an m-combination of A. The k_i in $\langle a_i, k_i \rangle$ is the *multiplicity* of a_i. We denote the set of all m-selections of a set A by $Q_m(A)$, and the set of all m-combinations by $C_m(A)$.

Examples

1. $A = \{a, b, c\}$. Then $Q_2(A) = \{\{\langle a, 2 \rangle\}, \{\langle a, 1 \rangle, \langle b, 1 \rangle\}, \{\langle a, 1 \rangle, \langle c, 1 \rangle\}, \{\langle b, 2 \rangle\}, \{\langle b, 1 \rangle, \langle c, 1 \rangle\}, \{\langle c, 2 \rangle\}\}$, and $C_2(A) = \{\{\langle a, 1 \rangle, \langle b, 1 \rangle\}, \{\langle a, 1 \rangle, \langle c, 1 \rangle\}, \{\langle b, 1 \rangle, \langle c, 1 \rangle\}\}$. Again we shall abbreviate our notation, writing $\{(ab), (ac), (bc)\}$ for $C_2(A)$, $\{(aaa), (aab), (aac), (abb), (abc), (acc), (bbb), (bbc), (bcc), (ccc)\}$ for $Q_3(A)$, and so forth.

2. In a combination all multiplicities are equal to 1. Explicit specification of the multiplicities is, therefore, superfluous, and a definition of combinations of A as subsets of A would seem more natural than the definition we have given. Then, however, combinations would differ in *type* from selections. Since $P_k(A) \subseteq S_k(A)$ we also want $C_k(A) \subseteq Q_k(A)$. With our definition $C_k(A) \subseteq Q_k(A)$ for all k. For example, with $A = \{a, b, c\}$, $C_2(A) \cap Q_2(A) = \{\{\langle a, 1 \rangle, \langle b, 1 \rangle\}, \{\langle a, 1 \rangle, \langle c, 1 \rangle\}, \{\langle b, 1 \rangle, \langle c, 1 \rangle\}\} \cap Q_2(A) = C_2(A)$. Hence, by Th.1.6, $C_2(A) \subseteq Q_2(A)$. By contrast, because of the difference in type, $\{\{a, b\}, \{a, c\}, \{b, c\}\} \cap Q_2(A) = \varnothing$. An m-selection is sometimes called an m-combination with repetition.

It may be essential, e.g., for determination of probabilities, to know the total *number* of different m-combinations of a given set (with or without repetition). As preliminaries we define binomial coefficients and find the number of elements in a subset of a product set.

DEFINITION 1.20   Let n and r be nonnegative integers. Define

$$P(n, r) = n(n - 1) \cdots (n - r + 1),$$
$$C(n, r) = P(n, r)/r!.$$

Numbers $C(n, r)$ are called *binomial coefficients*. (The symbol $\binom{n}{r}$ is often used to denote a binomial coefficient. The reflex-like action, which may automatically "complete" $\binom{n}{r}$ to $\binom{n}{\frac{}{r}}$ makes it a dangerous symbol for the occasional user.)

Examples

1. Note that $0! = 1$, $P(n, n) = n!$, and $P(n, r) = 0$ if $n < r$. Hence $C(n, 0) = 1$ and $C(n, n) = 1$ ($n \geq 0$), and $C(n, r) = 0$ if $n < r$. If $n \geq r$ we can write

$$C(n, r) = \frac{n!}{r! \, (n - r)!}$$

but not if $n < r$, since then $(n - r)!$ is undefined.

2. $C(n, r) = C(n, n - r)$.
   $C(n, r) = C(n - 1, r) + C(n - 1, r - 1)$, $(n, r \geq 1)$.

3. Computation of $n!$ is difficult for large n, on account of the size of the numbers involved. Thus $10!$ is already $3,628,800$, and $50! \approx 3 \cdot 04 \times 10^{64}$. An approximation (*Stirling's formula*), $n! \approx \sqrt{2\pi n} \, (n/e)^n$, where e is the base of the natural logarithms, is widely used in computations involving factorials. The relative error introduced by the approximation is about $1/(12n)$.

ALGORITHM 1.1   Recurrence relation

$$C(n, r) = C(n - 1, r) + C(n - 1, r - 1)$$

is the basis of the following algorithm for the calculation of binomial coefficients for all n up to some maximum value n'.

1. Set $C(0, 0) = 1$. Set $n = 0$.
2. Set $n = n + 1$. If $n > n'$, stop.
3. Set $C(n, 0) = 1$. Set $r = 0$.
4. Set $r = r + 1$. If $r = n$, set $C(n, r) = 1$ and go to Step 2.
5. Set $C(n, r) = C(n - 1, r) + C(n - 1, r - 1)$. Go to Step 4.

Table 1.1 illustrates Algorithm 1.1. The algorithm generates a triangular array of numbers, known as *Pascal's triangle*. All entries in the array, except the 1s that border the array, are generated by the recurrence relation. With row $n - 1$ generated, an element in row n is found by adding two successive elements of row $n - 1$. The sum is inserted in row n immediately below the second (rightmost) of the two successive elements.

Consider a sequence of r elements. If the first element can be picked in n_1 different ways, the second in n_2 different ways, $\ldots$, the rth in n_r different ways, then the number of different sequences is $n_1 n_2 \cdots n_r$. Our next theorem is difficult to understand, but it is no more than a formalization of the above observation. The meaning of the theorem should become clearer when one has seen it put to use in the proof of Th.1.17.

TABLE 1.1

BINOMIAL COEFFICIENTS $C(n, r)$

n \ r	0	1	2	3	4	5	$\cdots$
0	1						
1	1	1					
2	1	2	1				
3	1	3	3	1			
4	1	4	6	4	1		
5	1	5	10	10	5	1	
$\vdots$	$\vdots$	$\vdots$	$\vdots$	$\vdots$	$\vdots$	$\vdots$	$\vdots$

THEOREM 1.16 (*Rule of product*)   Consider finite families of sets $\{A_i \mid i \in I\}$ and $\{M_i \mid i \in I\}$. With each M_i associate the number n_i ($n_i \leqq |A_i|$). Sets M_i are defined as follows:

   (i) $i = 1$: $M_1 \subseteq A_1$, with $|M_1| = n_1$;
   (ii) $i > 1$: $M_i \subseteq M_{i-1} \times A_i$, where M_i is constructed by pairing each element of M_{i-1} with exactly n_i elements of A_i (not necessarily the same n_i elements of A_i).
Then $|M_r| = \prod_{i=1}^{r} n_i$.
Proof. The proof is by induction on r.
   (i)   By definition, $|M_1| = n_1 = \prod_{i=1}^{1} n_i$.
   (ii) Assume that the rule of product holds for $r - 1$ and prove it for r on basis of the assumption. The elements of $M_r (r > 1)$ are formed by pairing each element of M_{r-1} with exactly n_r elements of A_r, i.e., $|M_r| = |M_{r-1}| \times n_r$. By assumption, $|M_{r-1}| = \prod_{i=1}^{r-1} n_i$. Hence $|M_r| = \prod_{i=1}^{r} n_i$.

Example

   If $n_i = |A_i|$ for all $i \leqq r$, then $M_r = \mathsf{X}_{i \in I_r} A_i$ and $|M_r| = \prod_{i=1}^{r} |A_i|$.

THEOREM 1.17   Let A be a set with $|A| = n$. Then

   (i) $|S_r(A)| = n^r$;
   (ii) $|P_r(A)| = P(n, r)$;
   (iii) $|C_r(A)| = C(n, r)$;
   (iv) $|Q_r(A)| = C(n + r - 1, r)$.
Proof. (i) In Th. 1.16 make

$$A_1 = A_2 = \cdots = A_r = A \quad \text{and} \quad n_1 = n_2 = \cdots = n_r = n.$$

Then $|M_r| = n^r$. But $M_r = A^r = S_r(A)$.

(ii) In Th.1.16 make $A_1 = A_2 = \cdots = A_r = A$ and $n_1 = n$. Since all elements of a permutation must be distinct, only $n - 1$ elements of A can be paired with an element of M_1 in the construction of M_2, only $n - 2$ elements of A remain to be paired with an element of M_2, and so on. Hence $n_2 = n - 1$, $n_3 = n - 2, \ldots, n_r = n - r + 1$. Thus $|P_r(A)| = |M_r| = P(n, r)$.

(iii) The number of r-combinations of A is equal to the number of subsets of A with r elements (see Example 2 of D.1.19). We shall find the number of subsets by investigating their r-permutations. Each subset gives rise to a different set of r-permutations, these sets are disjoint, and each member of $P_r(A)$ belongs to some set. Therefore the family of these sets is a partition of $P_r(A)$. By Part (ii), $P_r(A)$ has $P(n, r)$ elements, and the number of r-permutations of a subset of r elements, i.e., the number of elements in each set belonging to the partition, is $P(r, r)$. Hence the number of sets in the partition is $P(n, r)/P(r, r) = P(n, r)/r! = C(n, r)$. This is also the number of subsets of A with r elements, and hence the number of r-combinations of A.

(iv) Consider sets $S = \{1, 2, \ldots, n\}$ and $T = \{1, 2, \ldots, n + r - 1\}$. Clearly $|Q_r(S)| = |Q_r(A)|$. Also, by Part (iii), $|C_r(T)| = C(n + r - 1, r)$. Therefore, if $Q_r(S)$ and $C_r(T)$ can be shown to have the same number of elements, the theorem is proven. Every member of $Q_r(S)$ can be written in the form $(s_1 s_2 \cdots s_r)$, with $s_1 \leqq s_2 \leqq \cdots \leqq s_r$. Construct the r-combination $\{\langle s_1 + 0, 1\rangle, \langle s_2 + 1, 1\rangle, \ldots, \langle s_r + r - 1, 1\rangle\}$, which is a member of $C_r(T)$. It is now easy to see that $Q_r(S)$ and $C_r(T)$ have the same number of elements: Elements of $Q_r(S)$ run through the sequence $(1\cdots11)$, $(1\cdots12)$, $(1\cdots22)$, $\ldots, (n\cdots nn)$, with a different element of $C_r(T)$ corresponding to each element in the sequence, and every element of $C_r(T)$ corresponds to some element in the sequence.

Examples

1. The English alphabet has 26 letters. The number of 5-letter "words" that can be constructed from letters of this alphabet is $26^5 = 11,881,376$. If repetition of symbols is not permitted, the total reduces to $P(26, 5) = 7,893,600$. Of course, most of the "words," such as *caabb* or *abxzy*, will not be found in any dictionary.

2. A poker hand is a 5-combination of a deck of 52 cards. The number of different hands is $C(52, 5) = 2,598,960$. The number of different bridge hands is $C(52, 13) = 635,013,559,600$. In the language of probability theory, each hand is an *event*, and there is a probability associated with the event. By convention the sum of the probabilities for all possible events is 1. Here each event can be assumed to have equal probability of occurrence. Hence the probability of receiving a particular poker hand is $1/2,598,960$, and that of receiving a particular bridge hand $1\cdot57 \times 10^{-12}$.

3. The score for 10 throws of a die, with order disregarded, is a 10-selection of a set of six elements. Hence the total number of unordered scores is

$C(15, 10) = 3003$. Here we cannot assume that all selections have an equal probability of occurrence; the events with equal probability are the ordered samples. There is only one sample that results in score 6666666666, but 10 samples result in score 5666666666.

The statement of the next theorem is known as the *principle of inclusion and exclusion*. It is very useful in the counting of objects that possess certain attributes. Consider again the counting problem discussed in the final paragraph of Section 1f. Suppose that the total number of computer science majors is known, and that the number of such students in neither CS125 nor CS133 is the unknown to be determined. To arrive at this number we start with our total of 242. From this total we *exclude* the 50 students in CS125 and the 74 students in CS133. However, some students have now been excluded twice, namely those taking both courses, and, to compensate for this error, we next have to *include* these 38 students. The number of students in neither CS125 nor CS133 is thus $242 - 50 - 74 + 38 = 156$. Theorem 1.18 is merely a generalization of this approach to the case where the number of attributes is a general parameter.

THEOREM 1.18   Let A be a finite set, and consider n attributes or properties $p_1, p_2, \ldots, p_n$ that elements of A may or may not possess. Consider subsets of A defined as follows:

$$A_{i_1 i_2 \cdots i_k} = \{x \mid x \text{ possesses attributes } p_{i_1}, p_{i_2}, \ldots, p_{i_k}\}$$

(A_3 is the subset whose members possess attribute p_3; A_{235} is the subset whose members possess attributes p_2, and p_3, and p_5). Let B be the subset of A whose members possess *none* of the attributes $p_1, p_2 \ldots, p_n$. Then

$$|B| = |A| - \sum_i |A_i| + \sum_{ij} |A_{ij}| - \sum_{ijk} |A_{ijk}| + \cdots + (-1)^n |A_{i2 \cdots n}|,$$

where, for example, $\sum_{ijk} |A_{ijk}|$ indicates that the summation is to be over all 3-combinations of $\{1, 2, \ldots, n\}$.

Proof. Exercise 1.46.

Examples

1. For the problem of the computer science students discussed above the general expression becomes

$$|B| = |A| - |A_1| - |A_2| + |A_{12}|,$$

where B is the subset of students taking neither of the two courses, A is the set of all students, A_1 is the subset characterized by the attribute "takes CS125," A_2 the subset characterized by "takes CS133," and A_{12} the subset of students characterized by both attributes. Clearly, given any four of the five counts in the equation, we can determine the fifth. Thus, in the original formulation of the problem (at the end of Section 1f), we have

$$156 = |A| - 50 - 74 + 38,$$

and this is to be solved for $|A|$. What if we were told that the total number of CS students is 265, that 50 of these take CS125 and 74 take CS133, that 140 take neither course, and that the number of students taking both courses is to be determined? The equation now becomes

$$140 = 265 - 50 - 70 + |A_{12}|,$$

with the solution $|A_{12}| = -1$. Since this solution is impossible, the given data must be wrong.

2. The number of elements in $N = \{1, 2, \ldots, 10{,}000\}$ that are *not* divisible by 2, 3, 5, or 7 may be determined by evaluation of the inclusion–exclusion formula

$$|N| - |N_2| - |N_3| - |N_5| - |N_7| + |N_{23}| + |N_{25}| + |N_{27}| + |N_{35}|$$
$$+ |N_{37}| + |N_{57}| - |N_{235}| - |N_{237}| - |N_{257}| - |N_{357}| + |N_{2357}|,$$

where N_{237}, for example, is the subset of N consisting of numbers divisible by 2, by 3, and by 7, i.e., the subset of numbers divisible by $2 \times 3 \times 7 = 42$. We obtain

$$10{,}000 - 5000 - 3333 - 2000 - 1428 + 1666 + 1000 + 714 + 666 + 476$$
$$+ 285 - 333 - 238 - 142 - 95 + 47 = 2285.$$

($|N_{237}|$ is the integer part of the quotient $10{,}000/42$, namely, 238.)

We shall now consider some computational algorithms for generation of combinations and permutations. In some applications it is necessary to generate successive members of a sequence of combinations or permutations in some well-defined order. Normally this order is *lexicographic* order. It is therefore necessary to have at least an intuitive understanding of what is meant by lexicographic order. With m-combinations $(a_1 a_2 \cdots a_m)$ and m-permutations $a_1 a_2 \cdots a_m$ of the alphabet $\{a, b, \ldots, z\}$ lexicographic order is the normal alphabetic order. If the combinations (or permutations) are of a set of digits, a sequence of them is in lexicographic order if and only if, for any two members of the sequence, $(a_1 a_2 \ldots a_m)$ and $(b_1 b_2 \cdots b_m)$, or $a_1 a_2 \cdots a_m$ and $b_1 b_2 \cdots b_m$, $(a_1 a_2 \cdots a_m)$ precedes $(b_1 b_2 \cdots b_m)$ in the sequence, or $a_1 a_2 \cdots a_m$ precedes $b_1 b_2 \cdots b_m$, if and only if the number $a_1 a_2 \cdots a_m$ is smaller than the number $b_1 b_2 \cdots b_m$. A rigorous definition of lexicographic order is given in Section 2f.

ALGORITHM 1.2   Two algorithms for finding all *m*-samples of the set {0, 1}.

(a) The procedure represented by the flowchart of Figure 1.4 generates the next sample from a given sample $\langle d_1, d_2, \ldots, d_m \rangle$. The sequence of samples is in no special order. Therefore, the first entry to the procedure can be with any *m*-sample of {0, 1}. The first 2^m entries generate all 2^m samples. The sequence of samples then starts repeating itself.

(b) The procedure of Figure 1.4 is modified in subroutine NEXTS, which generates *m*-samples in lexicographic order. First entry must be with $\langle 1, 1, \ldots, 1 \rangle$ in array SAMPLE.

```
      SUBROUTINE NEXTS (SAMPLE, M)
      INTEGER SAMPLE(M)
      K = M
   1  IF (SAMPLE(K).EQ.0) GO TO 2
      SAMPLE(K) = 0
      K = K-1
      IF (K) 1,3,1
   2  SAMPLE(K) = 1
   3  RETURN
      END
```

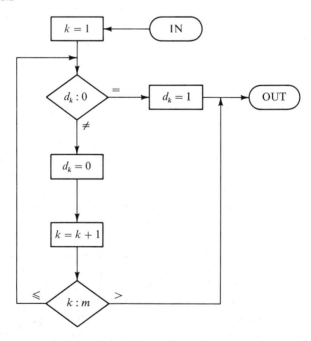

Figure 1.4

ALGORITHM 1.3   Subroutine NEWSAM finds all m-samples corresponding to a particular m-selection of $\{0, 1\}$, i.e., it finds all orderings of this selection. If an m-selection of $\{0, 1\}$ contains n_0 zeros, there are $C(m, n_0)$ such samples. Prior to the first call to NEWSAM array SAM must be set to $\langle 0, 0, \ldots, 0 \rangle$. The m-selection is specified by NZ, the value of which determines the number of zeros in the selection. With M and NZ having the values 5 and 3, respectively, successive calls to NEWSAM generate samples 00011, 00101, 00110, 01001, 01010, 01100, 10001, 10010, 10100, 11000. The samples are in lexicographic order. The next call generates 00011 again, i.e., the sequence starts to repeat itself. A given sample can be represented as the pattern: $m - n - z - 1$ digits, zero, n ones, z zeros. The next sample is obtained by rearranging this pattern to $m - n - z - 1$ digits, one, $z + 1$ zeros, $n - 1$ ones. In the case of a 7-sample 1011100 the rearrangement gives 1100011. Exceptions arise in the first call (the given sample is $00\cdots0$) and after the generation of the final sample (when $11\cdots10\cdots0$ has to be changed to $0\cdots011\cdots1$).

```
      SUBROUTINE NEWSAM (SAM, M, NZ)
      INTEGER SAM(M)
      J = M
C COUNT ZEROS (JNIL = NUMBER OF ZEROS + 1)
    1 IF (SAM(J).EQ.1) GO TO 2
      J = J-1
C TEST FOR SAM = 0,0,...,0
      IF (J) 1,102,1
    2 JNIL = M-J+1
C COUNT ONES (JONE = NUMBER OF ONES - 1)
      JONE = 0
    3 J = J-1
C TEST FOR FINAL SAMPLE (1,1,...,1,0,...,0)
      IF (J.EQ.0) GO TO 100
      IF (SAM(J).EQ.0) GO TO 4
      JONE = JONE+1
      GO TO 3
C INSERT A ONE
    4 SAM(J) = 1
C INSERT ZEROS (AT LEAST ONE ZERO)
      DO 5 K = 1,JNIL
      J = J+1
    5 SAM(J) = 0
```

```
C INSERT ONES (PERHAPS NONE)
      IF (JONE.EQ.0) RETURN
      DO 6 K = 1,JONE
      J = J+1
   6  SAM(J) = 1
      RETURN
C INITIATE OR REINITIATE
 100  DO 101 K = 1,NZ
 101  SAM(K) = 0
 102  KA = NZ+1
      DO 103 K = KA,M
 103  SAM(K) = 1
      RETURN
      END
```

ALGORITHM 1.4 Subroutine NEWCOM generates m-combinations of n integers $\{1, 2, \ldots, n\}$ in array COM. Initially COM must be set to $\langle n, n, \ldots, n \rangle$. $C(n, m)$ successive calls generate the sequence of combinations in lexicographic order. Further calls cause the sequence to be repeated.

```
      SUBROUTINE NEWCOM (COM,M,N)
      INTEGER COM(M)
C LOCATE REGION TO BE CHANGED
      DO 1 K = 1,M
      KA = M-K+1
      KB = N-K+1
      IF (COM(KA).LT.KB) GO TO 3
   1  CONTINUE
C INITIATE -- GENERATE FIRST COMBINATION
      DO 2 K = 1,M
   2  COM(K) = K
      RETURN
C MAKE CHANGES
   3  KB = COM(KA)
      DO 4 K = KA,M
      KB = KB+1
   4  COM(K) = KB
      RETURN
      END
```

There are many algorithms for the generation of permutations. If $|A| = m$, then $|P(A)| = m!$. Hence $m!$ is the minimum number of interchanges of elements necessary for the generation of all permutations of the elements of A. Algorithm 1.5 generates all permutations in just this number of interchanges. It is based on the following principle. Given the set

$$A = \{a_1, a_2, \ldots, a_m\}.$$

For $n = 1, 2, \ldots, m - 1$, if P_n is the set of permutations of elements of $A_n = \{a_1, a_2, \ldots, a_n\}$, then P_{n+1} can be generated from P_n by inserting element a_{n+1} in every position of every permutation belonging to P_n. Finally $P_m = P(A)$. For example, with $A = \{a, b, c\}$, we let $A_1 = \{c\}$, $A_2 = \{b, c\}$, $A_3 = \{a, b, c\}$. Then $P_1 = \{c\}$ and $P_2 = \{bc, cb\}$. Elements of P_3 are generated from those of P_2: From bc of P_2, by sending a forward, we obtain permutations abc, bac, bca; from cb, by sending a backward, we obtain cba, cab, acb. Given the initial permutation abc, $3! - 1$ successive calls to subroutine PERMER would in fact generate bac, bca, cba, cab, and acb, with the $(3!)$th call generating abc. The conceptual simplicity of the principle is obscured by programming detail. A program based on the flowchart of A.1.6 would be much simpler, but it would be rather inefficient if written in a higher-level language such as Fortran. An assembler language program for a computer that has an instruction for moving blocks of storage could, however, compare favorably with A.1.5. The storage movements would take more time than the interchanges of A.1.5, but the extreme simplicity of organization of A.1.6 might make total execution times comparable.

ALGORITHM 1.5 Subroutine PERMER generates the $m!$ permutations of m objects in sequence. The initial call is made with FIRST having the value .FALSE. and array PERM containing some permutation of M objects. FIRST is made .TRUE. and remains .TRUE. until the (M!)th call. Then PERM returns the original permutation and FIRST returns the value .FALSE.. Subsequent calls would cause the sequence to repeat itself. The value of M may not exceed 10.

```
      SUBROUTINE PERMER (PERM,M,FIRST)
      DIMENSION PERM(M), NP(10), ND(10)
      LOGICAL FIRST
      IF (FIRST) GO TO 2
C INITIATE REFERENCE ARRAYS FOR SUBSCRIPTING
      DO 1 K = 2,M
      NP(K) = 0
```

```
1   ND(K) = 1
    FIRST = .TRUE.
2   N = M
    K = 0
3   NP(N) = NP(N) + ND(N)
    NQ = NP(N)
    IF (NQ.NE.N) GO TO 4
    ND(N) = -1
    GO TO 5
4   IF (NQ.NE.0) GO TO 7
    ND(N) = 1
    K = K+1
5   IF (N.LE.2) GO TO 6
    N = N-1
    GO TO 3
C ALL PERMUTATIONS HAVE BEEN FOUND
6   NQ = 1
    FIRST = .FALSE.
C INTERCHANGE ELEMENTS
7   NQ = NQ+K
    TEMP = PERM(NQ)
    PERM(NQ) = PERM(NQ+1)
    PERM(NQ+1) = TEMP
    RETURN
    END
```

(Note that locations NP(1) and ND(1) are never in use.)

ALGORITHM 1.6   Figure 1.5 represents a procedure for generating all permutations of the set of numbers $\{1, 2, \ldots, m\}$. A new permutation results when all or part of a given permutation is rotated. The meaning of, *rotate the n lowest numbers*, is best explained by means of an example. Suppose we have the permutation 12345. Rotation of the three lowest numbers produces 23145. Schematically, one first transforms

| 1 | 2 | 3 | 4 | 5 | to | 1 | 2 | 3 | | 4 | 5 |

and then to

| 2 | 3 | 1 | 4 | 5 |.

Note that the initial configuration $d_1 d_2 \cdots d_m = 12 \cdots m$ is not printed by the procedure as shown in Figure 1.5 (see Exercise 1.54).

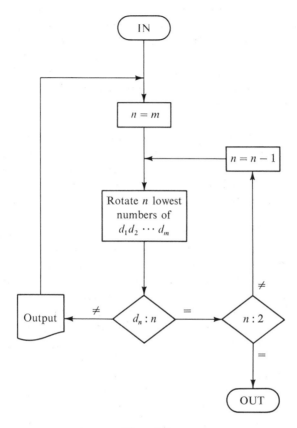

Figure 1.5

Notes

The best way of finding a text to one's liking is to go into a library and browse. Books are like acquaintances: some become friends, others don't. Since the author's style, a subjective manifestation judged according to one's own subjective likes and dislikes, determines to a great extent the regard one has for a book, it is somewhat presumptuous to make recommendations. Nevertheless, I cannot let this opportunity pass without acknowledging my high regard for [St61], which I found a most enjoyable intermediate text covering approximately the same ground as our Chapters 1 and 2. The larger

[St63] does not expand on the material covered by [St61]; the increase in size is due to the greater number of topics dealt with. In particular, it derives the basic properties of arithmetic in the sets of natural numbers and real numbers. [Ha60] is another good intermediate text; however, it may be too concise for collateral reading. A huge collection of worked examples and exercises can be found in [Li64]. This is a beginner's book, but Chapters 9 and 11–13 deal with material, which, while of little relevance to practical computing, is an important part of set theory when it is studied for its own sake. For really solid axiomatic developments of set theory one can consult [Fr66] or [Ha68b]. Boolean algebras are studied in a highly theoretical manner in [Si64].

Set theory is a well-established discipline, and nearly all the current research is of a very advanced nature. The study of fuzzy sets is an exception. Normally an object either is a member of a set or is not a member. There are, however, sets in which the question of membership cannot be precisely established, i.e., the range of the characteristic function associated with such a set (see Example 4 of D.2.2) is the interval [0, 1] rather than {0, 1}, and such sets are called fuzzy. Fuzzy sets were first studied by Zadeh [Za65]; a reasonably complete set of references (to 1971) to work on fuzzy sets and various extensions of the concept of fuzziness is provided in [Ch71a].

For general information on combinatorial mathematics one can consult [Ha67a, Li68, Be72]. An algorithmic approach to combinatorics is taken in [We71] and [Ev73]. For properties of binomial coefficients see [Ab64] or [Kn68]. An interesting technique for the exact computation of binomial coefficients is outlined in [Ko74, pp. 337–338]. The bounds on the value of a factorial given in Exercise 1.43 are due to Robbins [Ro55].

The Algorithms section of *CACM* contains many algorithms for generating permutations and combinations, and most of our algorithms derive from this source: A.1.3 from [Ho63a], A.1.4 from [Ku62], A.1.5 from [Tr62]. (If one intends to use an ACM algorithm, it is advisable to consult a recent subject index to the Algorithms section—generally published in the December issue of *CACM*—for references to remarks on the algorithm contributed after its publication.) The rotation algorithm A.1.6 derives from [La67]. A review of permutation generators can be found in [Or71]. Rosary permutations (see Exercises 1.45 and 1.57) are studied in [Ro73]. One way of generating combinatorial configurations (permutations, combinations) is to generate a set of integers such that each integer in the set uniquely defines one configuration, and to compute the complete set of configurations from this set of integers. Such sets of integers are defined in [Pa70, Mo70, Kn74]. Another recent development is the generation of combinatorial configurations by "loopless" algorithms [Eh73], where an algorithm is considered loopless if in all cases the generation of the next configuration of n objects from a given configuration can be carried out in less than k operations, where k is a constant independent of n.

Exercises

The letter in parentheses identifies the section to which the exercise has greatest relevance.

1.1 (a) In which instances are the sets A and B equal?
    (i) $A = \{1, 2, 3\}$, $B = \{i \mid i$ is an integer$\}$.
    (ii) $A = \{1, 2, 3, 4, 5\}$, $B = \{1, 10, 11, 100, 101\}$.
    (iii) $A = \{\alpha, \beta, \gamma\}$, $B = \{a, b, c\}$.
    (iv) $A = \{\alpha\}$, $B = \{x \mid x$ is the first letter of the Greek alphabet$\}$.
    (v) $A = \{a, b, ab, ba, b, a\}$, $B = \{a, b, ab\}$.

1.2 (a) Prove Th.1.3 by induction. (Consider a statement $P(n)$ about some nonnegative integer n. The *principle of induction* states: If $P(k)$ is true and $P(m)$ implies $P(m + 1)$, then $P(n)$ is true for all n such that $k \leq n \leq m + 1$. Proving $P(k)$ provides a basis for the proof; normally one takes $k = 0$ or $k = 1$. Showing that $P(m)$ implies $P(m + 1)$ is the induction step.)

1.3 (a) Find $A \cup B$ and $A \cap B$ in the following cases:

    (i) $A = \{1, 2, 3\}$, $B = \{i \mid i$ is an integer$\}$;
    (ii) $A = \{1, 2, 3\}$, $B = \{4, 5, 6, 7, \ldots\}$;
    (iii) $A = \{a, b, ab, ba, b, a\}$, $B = \{a, b, ab\}$;
    (iv) $A = \{\varnothing\}$, $B = \varnothing$;
    (v) Any A, $B = \{x \mid x \notin A\}$.

1.4 (a) Consider the sets of all rectangles, all squares, all trapezoids, all quadrilaterals, and all parallelograms. Use the set inclusion symbol to show how these sets are related.

1.5 (a) Show that if $A \subseteq B$ and $C \subseteq D$, then $A \cap C \subseteq B \cap D$.

1.6 (a) Find $\mathscr{P}(A)$ and $\mathscr{P}(B)$, where $A = \{\varnothing\}$ and $B = \{a, b, c, d\}$. How many members does the power set of $C = \{a, b, c, \ldots, z\}$ have?

1.7 (a) How many members does the power set of the power set of $B = \{a, b, c, d\}$ have?

1.8 (a) List the elements of $\mathscr{P}(\mathscr{P}(A))$ and $\mathscr{P}(\mathscr{P}(B))$, where $A = \varnothing$ and $B = \{\varnothing\}$.

1.9 (a) Let M be a set of J integers and N a set of K integers ($J, K \leq 1,000$). Assume that elements of M and N are stored in ascending order in locations $M(1), M(2), \ldots, M(J)$, and $N(1), N(2), \ldots, N(K)$, respectively. Write a subroutine for finding $M \cup N$ and $M \cap N$.

1.10   (b)   For $\{A_i | i \in I\}$, where $I = \{1, 2, \ldots, n\}$, show $B \cap (\bigcup_i A_i) = \bigcup_i (B \cap A_i)$ and $B \cup (\bigcap_i A_i) = \bigcap_i (B \cup A_i)$.

1.11   (b)   Let $\mathscr{X} = \{X_1, X_2, \ldots, X_m\}$ and $\mathscr{Y} = \{Y_1, Y_2, \ldots, Y_n\}$ be partitions of a set A. Show that $\mathscr{Z} = \{X_i \cap Y_j \mid X_i \in \mathscr{X}, \ Y_j \in \mathscr{Y}, \ X_i \cap Y_j \neq \varnothing\}$ is a partition of A (known as the *cross-partition* of $\mathscr{X}$ and $\mathscr{Y}$).

1.12   (b)   Let U be the set of students at a university and define the following subsets of U: A—males, B—females, C—undergraduates, D—graduates. $\mathscr{A} = \{A, B\}$ and $\mathscr{B} = \{C, D\}$ are partitions of U. Use formular notation to specify the elements of the sets comprising the cross-partition of $\mathscr{A}$ and $\mathscr{B}$.

1.13   (c)   For $\{A_i | i \in I\}$, where $I = \{1, 2, \ldots, n\}$, show $\overline{\bigcap_i A_i} = \bigcup_i \bar{A}_i$ and $\overline{\bigcup_i A_i} = \bigcap_i \bar{A}_i$.

1.14   (c)   For $\{X_i | i \in I\}$, where $I = \{1, 2, \ldots, n\}$, show $U - (\bigcup_i X_i) = \bigcap_i (U - X_i)$.

1.15   (c)   Is every family $\{A, \bar{A}\}$ a partition of the universal set?

1.16   (c)   Show that $(A - B) - C \subseteq A - (B - C)$. Is $(A - B) - C = A - (B - C)$?

1.17   (c)   Prove: (i) $(A \cup B) - C = (A - C) \cup (B - C)$,
　　　　　　　(ii) $A - (B \cup C) = (A - B) \cap (A - C)$,
　　　　　　　(iii) $A \cap (B - C) = (A \cap B) - (A \cap C)$.

1.18   (c)   Find a necessary and sufficient condition for $A + B = A \cup B$ to hold.

1.19   (c)   Prove: (i) $A + B = (A \cup B) \cap (\bar{A} \cup \bar{B})$,
　　　　　　　(ii) $A + B = (A \cup B) - (A \cap B)$.

1.20   (c)   Prove: (i) $A + A = \varnothing$,　　　　　(ii) $A + \varnothing = A$,
　　　　　　　(iii) $A + B = \bar{A} + \bar{B}$,　　　　(iv) $(A + B) + B = A$.

1.21   (c)   Show that (i) $|A \cup B| = |A| + |B| - |A \cap B|$,
　　　　　　　　(ii) $|A + B| = |A \cup B| - |A \cap B|$.

1.22   (d)   Show that $X \cap A = Y \cap A$ and $X \cap \bar{A} = Y \cap \bar{A}$ imply $X = Y$.

1.23   (d)   Prove again that $A \subseteq B$ and $C \subseteq D$ imply $A \cap C \subseteq B \cap D$.

1.24   (d)   Prove: (i) $A \cap (B + C) = (A \cap B) + (A \cap C)$,
　　　　　　　(ii) $A = B$ if and only if $A + B = \varnothing$.

1.25   (d)   Prove that $A - B = \bar{B} - \bar{A}$.

1.26   (d)   Modify your subroutine of Exercise 1.9 so that it finds $M - N$ as well. If, in addition, $M + N$ is required, is there a need to design a special routine or to modify the present subroutine for this purpose?

1.27   (e)   Give a shorter proof of Th.1.8.

1.28   (e)   Prove: (i) Th.1.9, (ii) Part 3 of Th.1.10, (iii) Part 2 of Th.1.12.

1.29   (e)   In Boolean algebra B show that $a \oplus (b \oplus c) = (a \oplus b) \oplus c$ and

$a * (b * c) = (a * b) * c$ can be deduced from the other axioms. (Hint: Prove first that $x * z = y * z$ and $x * z' = y * z'$ imply $x = y$.)

1.30   (f)   The eight nonoverlapping regions of Figure 1.6 represent a partition of the universal set just as the four regions of Figure 1.2 do. Write down expressions for the eight sets represented by these eight regions.

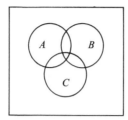

Figure 1.6

1.31   (f)   Is it true that $A \cup (B + C) = (A \cup B) + (A \cup C)$?

1.32   (f)   Simplify $[A \cap (B \cap C)] \cup [A \cap (B + C)]$.

1.33   (f)   Use Venn diagrams to find the relation between
$$(W \cup X) + (Y \cup Z) \quad \text{and} \quad (W + Y) \cup (X + Z).$$
Then prove the relation (the proof is tedious and lengthy).

1.34   (f)   Of a graduating class of 153 computer science majors 63 have taken English Composition (EC), 54 have taken Technical Writing (TW), 62 have taken Report Writing (RW), 43 have taken EC and TW, 46 have taken EC and RW, 45 have taken TW and RW, and 37 have taken all three of these courses. How many of the students have not taken any one of these three writing courses? Use a Venn diagram such as Figure 1.6.

1.35   (f)   A certain university has published the following data regarding its student population:

in-state students	7923
male students	6811
sophomores	3370
in-state males	5430
in-state sophomores	2877
male sophomores	1784
in-state male sophomores	1063

Show that these figures must be wrong.

1.36   (g)   Find the sets equal to $\langle a, \langle a, a \rangle \rangle$ and $\langle \langle a, a \rangle, a \rangle$.

1.37   (g)   It may appear that the definition $\langle a_1, a_2 \rangle = \{\{a_1\}, \{a_1, a_2\}\}$ could be generalized to $\langle a_1, a_2, a_3 \rangle = \{\{a_1\}, \{a_1, a_2\}, \{a_1, a_2, a_3\}\}$. Why is this definition of an ordered triple inadequate?

1.38   (g)   Show that $A \subseteq C$ and $B \subseteq D$ imply $A \times B \subseteq C \times D$. Under what conditions is it *not* true that $A \times B \subseteq C \times D$ implies $A \subseteq C$ and $B \subseteq D$?

1.39   (g)   Referring to Example 5 of D.1.17, show that $\langle \{\emptyset, U\}, \cup, \cap, ^-, \emptyset, U \rangle$ is a Boolean algebra.

1.40   (g)   If $\langle \mathscr{P}(U), \cup, \cap, ^-, \emptyset, U \rangle$ is a Boolean algebra, is $\langle \mathscr{P}(U), \cap, \cup, ^-, U, \emptyset \rangle$ also a Boolean algebra?

1.41   (h)   In Fortran the name of a variable may be 1–6 characters long, where the first character must be a letter from the set $\{A, B, \ldots, Z\}$, and the other characters (if any) may be taken from the set of letters or from the set of digits $\{0, 1, \ldots, 9\}$. How many different names are possible?

1.42   (h)   Show that $\sum_{k=0}^{n} C(n, k) = 2^n$. (Hint: Use Th.1.3.)

1.43   (h)   An accurate Stirling-like formula for the factorial is

$$n! = \sqrt{2\pi} \, n^{n+\frac{1}{2}} \exp(r_n - n),$$

where

$$\frac{1}{12n + 1} < r_n < \frac{1}{12n}.$$

This formula can be used to obtain two values between which the true value of the factorial lies. (i) Eight children attend a party to which each takes ten cookies. The cookies are mixed up, and each child is then given ten cookies. What is the probability that a particular child receives back precisely his or her own ten cookies? Use the formula given above to obtain two values between which the true probability lies. (ii) In the situation described above the probability that none of the cookies received by a child were taken to the party by this child is the ratio of the number of 10-combinations of the 70 cookies that were brought by the other children to the number of 10-combinations of all 80 cookies, i.e., $C(70, 10)/C(80, 10)$. Evaluate this expression. (iii) What would be the latter probability if there had been 20 children? Evaluate.

1.44   (h)   The recurrence relation of A.1.1,

$$C(n, r) = C(n-1, r) + C(n-1, r-1),$$

is derived by considering a specific element a in the set of n elements from which the $C(n, r)$ r-combinations are taken. An r-combination either contains this element, or it does not. The two terms on the right-hand side correspond to these two possibilities. If an r-combination does not contain the element a, then $C(n-1, r)$ is the number of ways r elements can be picked from the remaining $n-1$ elements. If an r-combination contains the element, then this element is fixed, and we count the number of ways of choosing the other

$r - 1$ elements from the $n - 1$ available elements. This count is $C(n - 1, r - 1)$. Use this technique to derive a similar recurrence relation for $P(n, r)$. Denoting the number of r-selections by $Q(n, r)$, derive a recurrence relation for $Q(n, r)$.

1.45 (h) Consider five balls that are colored blue, yellow, white, green, and red. Denote the balls by b, y, w, g, r, respectively. Permutations *wbrgy* and *rgywb* are distinct. However, if we drill holes through the balls, thread the balls onto a piece of string, and tie the two ends of the string together, we have the same arrangement when we thread the balls in the order w, b, r, g, y, in the order r, g, y, w, b, or even in the reverse order y, g, r, b, w. Each distinct arrangement of the balls on the string is called a *rosary* permutation (after rosary beads). How many rosary permutations of n elements are there?

1.46 (h) Prove Theorem 1.18 (by induction).

1.47 (h) Denote a permutation of the integers $\{1, 2, \ldots, n\}$ by $\langle a_1, a_2, \ldots, a_n \rangle$. The permutation is a *derangement* if $a_i \neq i$, $i = 1, 2, \ldots, n$. For example, $\langle 3, 1, 4, 2 \rangle$ is a derangement, but $\langle 3, 1, 2, 4 \rangle$ is not because here $a_4 = 4$. Use the principle of inclusion–exclusion to show that the number of derangements of $\{1, 2, \ldots, n\}$ is

$$D(n) = n! \left[1 - \frac{1}{1!} + \frac{1}{2!} - \cdots + (-1)^n \frac{1}{n!} \right].$$

Note that the expression in square brackets is an approximation of e^{-1}. Hence $D(n) \simeq n!/e$.

1.48 (h) How many 6-samples of $\{a, b, c\}$ are there such that no two adjacent letters in a sample are identical?

1.49 (h) A dinner party consists of k ($k \geq 3$) married couples. In how many ways can the couples be seated around a circular table so that no husband sits next to his wife? This problem is known as the problem of *menages*. (Hint: First prove that the problem is equivalent to the counting of permutations $a_1 a_2 \cdots a_n$ of $\{1, 2, \ldots, n\}$, where $n = 2k$, such that the three numbers in every column of the table

1	2	$\cdots$	$n - 1$	n
2	3	$\cdots$	n	1
a_1	a_2	$\cdots$	a_{n-1}	a_n

are different.)

1.50 (h) Given a set of integers $\{a_1, a_2, \ldots, a_n\}$. Write a subroutine that generates m-samples of this set of integers (cf. A.1.2).

1.51 (h)   Modify A.1.4 so that it finds an m-combination of n arbitrary distinct integers $\{a_1, a_2, \ldots, a_n\}$.

1.52 (h)   Subroutine NEWSAM (A.1.3) is not completely "safe." What happens when NZ = 0 and when M = NZ? Make appropriate improvements in the subroutine.

1.53 (h)   In the paragraph preceding A.1.5 we state that the algorithm is based on an insertion principle. Convince yourself of the essential correctness of this observation by a study of the pattern of interchanges giving the next permutation in the printout of all permutations of $\{1, 2, 3, 4, 5\}$.

1.54 (h)   The flowchart of Figure 1.5 requires only a slight modification to make the procedure print the initial configuration $d_1 d_2 \cdots d_m = 12 \cdots m$ as well. Make the modification. Next modify the flowchart of Figure 1.5 so that there is no output from the procedure, but $m!$ successive calls to the procedure return all $m!$ permutations of $\{1, 2, \ldots, m\}$.

1.55 (h)   Prove that the number of ways in which a set A of n elements can be partitioned into k blocks $A_1, A_2, \ldots, A_k$, such that $|A_1| = r_1, |A_2| = r_2, \ldots, |A_k| = r_k$, is given by the *multinomial coefficient*

$$\frac{n!}{r_1! \, r_2! \cdots r_k!}.$$

Write a program to generate a table of multinomial coefficients for $n = 1, 2, \ldots, 8$, and for $k = 1, 2, \ldots, n$.

1.56 (h)   Devise an algorithm for the generation of all derangements of the integers $\{1, 2, \ldots, n\}$.

1.57 (h)   Devise an algorithm for the generation of all rosary permutations of the integers $\{1, 2, \ldots, n\}$.

CHAPTER 2

Functions and Relations

2a. Functions

Throughout Chapter 1 we were relating objects: The proof of Th.1.3 depends on a correspondence between sequences of elements of a set and sequences of binary digits; D.1.19 pairs elements of a general set with elements of the set of natural numbers. Intuitive understanding of the correspondences was adequate, but only barely so when the correspondences became complicated, as in the proof of Part (iv) of Th.1.17. We shall now make our intuitive notions precise.

DEFINITION 2.1   The set f is a *function* from set A into set B if and only if it is a subset of a set of ordered pairs $A \times B$, and $\langle a, b \rangle \in f$ and $\langle a, c \rangle \in f$ imply $b = c$. (There are many synonyms for *function*, such as *transformation*, or *operation*, or *mapping* from set A into set B.) If $\langle a, b \rangle \in f$, then b is an *image* of the *argument* a under f, denoted $f(a)$. We also call $f(a)$ the *value* of f for a. When the function is from a set of n-tuples we shall abbreviate $f(\langle a_1, a_2, \ldots, a_n \rangle)$ to $f(a_1, a_2, \ldots, a_n)$.

Examples

1. The set $f = \{\langle beer, 4 \rangle, \langle is, 2 \rangle, \langle food, 4 \rangle, \langle for, 3 \rangle, \langle some, 4 \rangle\}$ is a function; the set $\{\langle 4, five \rangle, \langle 4, aces \rangle, \langle 5, spell \rangle, \langle 7, tragedy \rangle\}$ is not. The first coordinates must be distinct. Second coordinates need not be distinct.

We have the images $f(is) = 2, f(for) = 3, f(beer) = f(food) = f(some) = 4$. The reason why first coordinates must be distinct is that normally we identify a function with a computation process: Given an argument, we compute its image. The process has to be deterministic, which it would not be if an argument could have more than one image.

2. Consider sets $f = \{\langle x, x^2 \rangle \mid x \in R\}$ and $g = \{\langle x^2, x \rangle \mid x \in R\}$, with R the set of real numbers. Although f is a function, g is not a function (since, for example, both $\langle 1, -1 \rangle \in g$ and $\langle 1, 1 \rangle \in g$). Here $f(1) = 1, f(1.1) = 1.21$, and, in general, $f(x) = x^2$.

3. Selections and combinations are functions. An m-selection of A is a mapping from A into the set of natural numbers, and an m-combination is a mapping from A into the set $\{1\}$.

4. The binary set operations of union and intersection are mappings from $\mathscr{P}(U) \times \mathscr{P}(U)$ into $\mathscr{P}(U)$, and the unary operation of complementation is a mapping from $\mathscr{P}(U)$ into itself. Consider sets A, B, C. If $A \cup B = C$, the ordered triple $\langle \langle A, B \rangle, C \rangle$ (or $\langle A, B, C \rangle$) is a member of the operation of set union. Unary operations are sets of ordered pairs; binary operations are sets of ordered triples.

5. 2-combinations $\{\langle a, 1 \rangle, \langle b, 1 \rangle\}$ and $\{\langle b, 1 \rangle, \langle a, 1 \rangle\}$ are, of course, equal. Since functions are sets, equality of functions is defined by D.1.1.

DEFINITION 2.2   Let $f \subseteq A \times B$ be a function. The *domain D_f* and *range R_f* of the function are defined as follows:

$$D_f = \{a \mid \text{for some } b, \quad \langle a, b \rangle \in f\},$$
$$R_f = \{b \mid \text{for some } a, \quad \langle a, b \rangle \in f\}.$$

If $D_f = A$, function f is said to be *on* the set A or a *total* function with respect to this set. If $R_f = B$, the function is *onto* the set B. A total function from A into B is denoted by the symbol $f: A \to B$, or by the symbol $A \overset{f}{\to} B$.

Examples

1. The domain of $\{\langle beer, 4 \rangle, \langle is, 2 \rangle, \langle food, 4 \rangle, \langle for, 3 \rangle, \langle some, 4 \rangle\}$ is the set $A = \{beer, is, food, for, some\}$. The range is $\{2, 3, 4\}$. The function is on A, but not on the set of all words in the English language, i.e., it is total with respect to A, but not with respect to the set of all words. The function is both *into* and *onto* set $\{2, 3, 4\}$, but only *into* the set of natural numbers.

2. Let function f be an m-selection of set A, with $m < |A|$. Then $D_f \subset A$ and $R_f \subset \{1, 2, \ldots, m\}$. In general, with $f \subseteq A \times B$, $D_f \subseteq A$ and $R_f \subseteq B$. The notation $f: A \to B$ is used only if $D_f = A$, i.e., if f is a total function with respect to A.

3. Consider $f: A \to B$, with $|A| = m$ and $|B| = n$. Since f is on A, the function has m elements, and no other function from any subset of A can

have a greater number of elements. Hence at most $1/n$ of the mn elements of $A \times B$ can belong to a function from A.

4. The function $f: U \rightarrow \{0, 1\}$, where U is a universal set, is known as the *characteristic function* of a set A if $f(a) = 0$ when $a \in A$ and $f(a) = 1$ when $a \notin A$.

DEFINITION 2.3 If $f: A \rightarrow B$ and $C \subseteq A$, then the function $f \cap (C \times B)$ is the *restriction* of f to C, written $f \mid C$. A function f is an *extension* of a function g if and only if $g \subseteq f$. The *composite* of functions g and h, symbolized $h \circ g$, is the set $\{\langle x, z \rangle \mid$ there exists a y such that $\langle x, y \rangle \in g$ and $\langle y, z \rangle \in h\}$.

Examples

1. Consider the English alphabet $A = \{a, b, \ldots, z\}$. Let W be the set of all five-letter "words" constructed out of the letters of A (in the sense of Example 1 of Th.1.17), W' the set of five-letter English words, and $S_5(A)$ the set of five-samples of A. Then $f: W \rightarrow S_5(A)$ with $f(a_1a_2a_3a_4a_5) = \langle a_1, a_2, a_3, a_4, a_5 \rangle$ and $g: W' \rightarrow S_5(A)$ with $g(a_1a_2a_3a_4a_5) = \langle a_1, a_2, a_3, a_4, a_5 \rangle$ are functions, and $g = f \mid W'$ is the restriction of f to W'.

2. Let N be the set of nonnegative integers $\{0, 1, 2, \ldots\}$. Subtraction as a function into N is defined on the set $\{\langle a, b \rangle \mid a, b \in N$ and $a \geq b\}$. The function is $S = \{\langle a, b, a - b \rangle \mid a, b \in N$ and $a \geq b\}$. We define proper subtraction $P: N \times N \rightarrow N$ as $\{\langle a, b, a \dotminus b \rangle \mid a, b \in N\}$. Then

$$
\begin{aligned}
S(a, b) &= a - b && (a \geq b); \\
P(a, b) &= a - b && (a \geq b), \\
&= 0 && (a < b).
\end{aligned}
$$

Since $P \supseteq S$, proper subtraction is an extension of subtraction. Whereas P is a total function, S is not total (with respect to $N \times N$). A function that is not total is called a *partial* function.

3. Let R be the set of real numbers, I the set of integers, and N the set of natural numbers $\{1, 2, 3, \ldots\}$. Consider the function $f: N \rightarrow N$ with $f(n) = (n - 1)!$. A well-known extension of this factorial function is the gamma function $\Gamma: R - (I - N) \rightarrow R$ with $\Gamma(n) = (n - 1)!$ for $n \in N$ (in fact Γ can be defined on $C - (I - N)$, where C is the set of complex numbers). The set $R - (I - N)$ is the set of all real numbers with the set $\{0, -1, -2, \ldots\}$ excluded.

4. The composite $h \circ g$ of functions g and h is also a function. If $g: X \rightarrow Y$ and $h: Y \rightarrow Z$, then $h \circ g: X \rightarrow Z$, and $(h \circ g)(x)$ can be written as $g(h(x))$.

DEFINITION 2.4   A total function $f: A \to B$ is *one to one* if it maps distinct elements of A onto distinct elements of B; i.e., the function is one to one if and only if $f(a_1) = f(a_2)$ implies $a_1 = a_2$ [alternatively, the function is one to one if and only if $a_1 \neq a_2$ implies $f(a_1) \neq f(a_2)$]. A total function that is not one to one is a *many-to-one* function.

Examples

1. Function f of Example 1 of D.2.3 is one to one. Consider $Q_5(A)$, the set of 5-selections of $A = \{a, b, \ldots, z\}$. The function $h: W' \to Q_5(A)$, with W' the set of five-letter English words and $h(a_1a_2a_3a_4a_5) = (a_1a_2a_3a_4a_5)$, is many to one, since $h(heaps) = h(phase) = h(shape) = (aehps)$.

2. Let I be the set of integers and N the set of natural numbers. Define $f(n) = n^2$. Then $f: I \to N$ is many to one, but the restriction $f \mid N$ is one to one.

3. Consider the alphabet $A = \{a, b, c, \ldots, z\}$ and the set of odd numbers $B = \{3, 5, 7, \ldots, 53\}$. Let $f: A \to B$ be a one-to-one function that assigns the number $2n + 1$ to the nth letter of the alphabet, e.g., $\langle a, 3 \rangle \in f$, $\langle g, 15 \rangle \in f$. Let W be the set of all "words" constructed out of the letters of A and let $p_1, p_2, p_3, \ldots$ be the primes in ascending order. Products of powers of the primes belong to N, the set of natural numbers. A number-theoretical argument shows that the function $g: W \to N$ with $g(a_1a_2 \cdots a_k) = p_1^{n_1} p_2^{n_2} \cdots p_k^{n_k}$, where $n_i = f(a_i)$ is one to one. Some examples: $g(aabca) = 2^3 \cdot 3^3 \cdot 5^5 \cdot 7^7 \cdot 11^3 = 739,891,619,775,000$, $g(sapphire) = 2^{39} \cdot 3^3 \cdot 5^{33} \cdot 7^{33} \cdot 11^{17} \cdot 13^{19} \cdot 17^{37} \cdot 19^{11}$. This technique of mapping sequences of symbols into the set of natural numbers is known as Gödel numbering. It is very important in the study of the foundations of mathematics, but the size of the numbers makes the technique useless for representation of symbols in a computer.

4. A one-to-one function is sometimes called an *injection*, an onto function a *surjection*, and a function that is both one-to-one and onto is called a *bijection*.

THEOREM 2.1   Let $f: A \to B$ be a function and consider the *onto* function $g: f \to f'$ with $g(a, b) = \langle b, a \rangle$. The set f' is a function if and only if f is one to one. Moreover, f' is on B if and only if f is onto B.

Proof. Exercise 2.9.

DEFINITION 2.5   If $f: A \to B$ is a one-to-one function, then the *inverse function* of f, symbolized f^{-1}, is the range of the function $g: f \to f'$ with $g(a, b) = \langle b, a \rangle$. (If f is not one to one, f^{-1} does not exist.)

Examples

1. Consider functions $f: W \to S_5(A)$ and $g: W' \to S_5(A)$ of Example 1 of D.2.3. Both functions are one to one. Hence f^{-1} and g^{-1} exist, and f^{-1} is the

function $f^{-1}: S_5(A) \to W$ with $f^{-1}(a_1, a_2, a_3, a_4, a_5) = a_1 a_2 a_3 a_4 a_5$. The function g^{-1} from $S_5(A)$ onto W' is not total. The abbreviation for a sample, which we introduced in Example 1 of D.1.18, is actually the image of the sample under f^{-1}.

2. Consider function $f: I \to N$ of Example 2 of D.2.4. Here f^{-1} does not exist. The restriction $f \mid N$ has an inverse, but the inverse is not total with respect to N (the range of $f \mid N$ consists of squared numbers alone).

THEOREM 2.2　Consider sets A and B with $|A| = a$ and $|B| = b$. The number of functions on A into B is b^a.

Proof. Exercise 2.10.

2b. Boolean Functions and Forms

In this section we shall deal in general terms with functions of a special kind, the Boolean functions. The importance of some models of Boolean algebras is more a consequence of the part played in them by Boolean functions than of anything else. These interesting models will be discussed in Section 2c.

Although our definitions will be quite general, examples will be based on the simple system $\langle \{0, 1\}, \oplus, *, ', 0, 1 \rangle$. As a preliminary we will have to show that this system is a Boolean algebra.

THEOREM 2.3　The system $\langle \{0, 1\}, \oplus, *, ', 0, 1 \rangle$ is a Boolean algebra.

Proof. The given system is precisely the Boolean algebra $\langle B, \oplus, *, ', 0, 1 \rangle$ of Section 1e, with set B having just two elements, the distinct elements 0 and 1. To prove that the system is a Boolean algebra it suffices to show that $\{0, 1\}$ is closed under $\oplus$, $*$, and $'$. By Axioms 4A and 4B, Parts 1 and 2 of Th.1.10, Parts 1 and 2 of Th.1.11, and Part 2 of Th.1.12 (all of Section 1e) we have the following definitions of operations $\oplus$, $*$, $'$ for members of $\{0, 1\}$:

$$0 \oplus 0 = 0, \quad 0 \oplus 1 = 1 \oplus 0 = 1 \oplus 1 = 1;$$
$$0 * 0 = 0 * 1 = 1 * 0 = 0, \quad 1 * 1 = 1;$$
$$0' = 1, \quad 1' = 0.$$

Operations are functions ($\oplus: \{0, 1\}^2 \to \{0, 1\}$ is the function $\{\langle 0, 0, 0 \rangle,$ $\langle 0, 1, 1 \rangle, \langle 1, 0, 1 \rangle, \langle 1, 1, 1 \rangle \}$), and the three functions are all into (and onto) the set $\{0, 1\}$. The set is therefore closed under the operations.

DEFINITION 2.6　Consider the Boolean algebra $\langle B, \oplus, *, ', 0, 1 \rangle$. A function $f(x_1, x_2, \ldots, x_n)$ on B^n into B, $f: B^n \to B$, is a *Boolean function* of n variables.

Example

Let $B = \{0, 1\}$. There are 2 elements in B and 2^n elements in B^n (Th.1.16). By Th.2.2, the number of functions on B^n into B is, therefore, 2^{2^n}. In the case of $n = 1$ the four functions are $\{\langle 0, 0\rangle, \langle 1, 0\rangle\}$, $\{\langle 0, 0\rangle, \langle 1, 1\rangle\}$, $\{\langle 0, 1\rangle, \langle 1, 0\rangle\}$, $\{\langle 0, 1\rangle, \langle 1, 1\rangle\}$.

DEFINITION 2.7   Let $\langle B, \oplus, *, ', 0, 1\rangle$ be a Boolean algebra and let f, g, h denote functions on B^n into B, i.e., Boolean functions of n variables. We define the following *functional* equalities:

(i) $f \oplus g = h$ if and only if, for *every* element of the set of samples $S_n(B)$, the result of combining the images under f and g in accordance with the interpretation of $\oplus$ in B is equal to the image of the element under h;

(ii) $f * g = h$ is defined analogously;

(iii) $f' = h$ if and only if, for every element of $S_n(B)$, the complement (image under $'$) of the image of this element under f is equal to the image of the element under h.

Example

Let $B = \{0, 1\}$ and consider functions from B^2 into B. For this system operations $\oplus$, $*$, and $'$ are defined in the proof of Th.2.3. Take functions f and g such that $f(0,0) = 1, f(0, 1) = f(1, 0) = f(1, 1) = 0; g(0, 0) = g(0, 1) = g(1, 0) = 1$, $g(1, 1) = 0$. Take also functions $s(x_1, x_2) = x_1 \oplus x_2$ and $p(x_1, x_2) = x_1 * x_2$. Table 2.1 represents f, g, s, p, $f \oplus g$, $f * g$, f', and g' in tabular form, one row for each member of $S_2(B)$. Since $|S_2(B)| = 4$, we have four rows. Consider the first row. The entries for f and g are given by the definitions above. The other entries are generated using definitions of $\oplus$, $*$, and $'$ for the set $\{0, 1\}$ given in the proof of Th.2.3. From the table it is seen that $f \oplus g = g, f * g = f, f' = s, g' = p$.

TABLE 2.1

FUNCTIONAL EQUALITIES

$\langle x_1, x_2\rangle$	f	g	s	p	$f \oplus g$	$f * g$	f'	g'
$\langle 0, 0\rangle$	1	1	0	0	1	1	0	0
$\langle 0, 1\rangle$	0	1	1	0	1	0	1	0
$\langle 1, 0\rangle$	0	1	1	0	1	0	1	0
$\langle 1, 1\rangle$	0	0	1	1	0	0	1	1

In D.2.7 we have defined functional equality. We now have to show that $f \oplus g, f * g$, and f' as defined in D.2.7 are in fact functions. For example, we have to show that if $f \oplus g = h_1$ and $f \oplus g = h_2$, then $h_1 = h_2$.

THEOREM 2.4   Let $\langle B, \oplus, *, ', 0, 1 \rangle$ be a Boolean algebra. Let f and g denote Boolean functions on B^n into B. Then

(i) $f \oplus g$,
(ii) $f * g$,
(iii) f'

are also functions.

Proof. (i) Consider an n-tuple $a \in S_n(B)$, and assume that $(f \oplus g)(a) = c_1$ and $(f \oplus g)(a) = c_2$. By D.2.7, $(f \oplus g)(a) = f(a) \oplus g(a)$. Hence $f(a) \oplus g(a) = c_1$ and $f(a) \oplus g(a) = c_2$. But, by definition of a function, $f(a)$ and $g(a)$ are unique elements of B. Also, by definition of the Boolean algebra, $\oplus$ is an operation in B (i.e., a function from B^2). Hence $c_1 = c_2$, implying that $f \oplus g$ is a function.

(ii) The proof is similar.
(iii) By Th.1.9 (uniqueness of the complement).

Our next theorem asserts that the set of all functions on B^n into B is a Boolean algebra as well.

THEOREM 2.5   Let $\langle B, \oplus, *, ', 0, 1 \rangle$ be a Boolean algebra. Then $\langle F_n, \oplus, *, ' f_0, f_1 \rangle$, where F_n is the set of all functions on B^n into B and the operations are defined by D.2.7, is a Boolean algebra.

Proof. We shall not prove the theorem because the proof is rather lengthy. It consists of showing that F_n is closed under the operations and that its elements satisfy the axioms of Section 1e.

Example

Let $B = \{0, 1\}$ and consider F_2. We have $|F_2| = 16$, with each member of F_2 consisting of four triples. We take f_0 and f_1 as the functions with ranges $\{0\}$ and $\{1\}$, respectively, e.g., $f_0 = \{\langle 0, 0, 0 \rangle, \langle 0, 1, 0 \rangle, \langle 1, 0, 0 \rangle, \langle 1, 1, 0 \rangle\}$. Here it is easy to convince oneself that F_2 is closed under the operations and that its elements satisfy the axioms.

Consider the expression $(x_1 \oplus x_2)' \oplus (x_1' * x_2)$, where x_1 and x_2 are variables denoting elements of B. Although we tend to call such an expression a function, it is certainly not a set of ordered pairs and hence not a function. The expression is a *formula* or *form*. The reason why we sometimes loosely describe forms as functions is that a form of n variables has a function on B^n into B *associated* with it. We shall investigate this association further on.

DEFINITION 2.8   Let $\langle B, \oplus, *, ', 0, 1 \rangle$ be a Boolean algebra, and let variables $x_1, x_2, \ldots, x_n$ denote elements of B. A *Boolean form* (*Boolean formula*) is defined recursively as follows:

1. 0 and 1 are Boolean forms.
2. A variable x_i $(i = 1, 2, \ldots, n)$ is a Boolean form.
3. If α is a Boolean form, then so is (α).
4. If α is a Boolean form, then so is α'.
5. If α and β are Boolean forms, then so is $\alpha \oplus \beta$.
6. If α and β are Boolean forms, then so is $\alpha * \beta$.
7. Only expressions given by Statements 1–6 are Boolean forms.

Example

Consider the expression $(x_1 \oplus x_2)' \oplus (x_1' * x_2)$. Let us determine whether or not it is a Boolean form. This is a recognition problem. We find successively that $x_1, x_2, x_1 \oplus x_2, (x_1 \oplus x_2), (x_1 \oplus x_2)', x_1', x_1' * x_2, (x_1' * x_2)$ are Boolean forms. Finally, by Statement 5, we recognize the entire expression as a Boolean form. It is easy to see that $(x_1 \oplus x_2)' \oplus * (x_1' * x_2)$, say, is not a Boolean form. In the model $\langle \mathscr{P}(U), \cup, \cap, \bar{\ }, \varnothing, U \rangle$, with variables A and B, expression $\overline{A \cup B} \cup (\bar{A} \cap B)$ is a Boolean form, but not $\overline{A \cup B} \cup \cap (\bar{A} \cap B)$.

D.2.8 is not a workable algorithm for recognizing Boolean forms. Although every reader should be able to recognize a Boolean form, most readers will be hard put to give a precise formal description of the recognition procedure they used. A detailed algorithm is, however, necessary if recognition is to be by computer. The algorithm will be an exercise in Section 5e. For the time being we shall assume a recognition algorithm and investigate equivalence of Boolean forms.

Let $\langle B, \oplus, *, ', 0, 1 \rangle$ be a Boolean algebra, and consider a Boolean form in which n variables $x_1, x_2, \ldots, x_n$ denote elements of B. In this context we shall give a special name to elements of the set of n-samples of B; we shall call the elements of $S_n(B)$ *value assignments*. For example, with $B = \{0, 1\}$ and three variables $x_1, x_2,$ and x_3, we have $S_n(B) = \{\langle 0, 0, 0 \rangle, \langle 0, 0, 1 \rangle, \langle 0, 1, 0 \rangle, \langle 0, 1, 1 \rangle, \langle 1, 0, 0 \rangle, \langle 1, 0, 1 \rangle, \langle 1, 1, 0 \rangle, \langle 1, 1, 1 \rangle\}$, a set of eight assignments. We shall associate the ith coordinate of an assignment with the variable x_i. Take, for example, the Boolean form $x_1 * (x_1 \oplus (x_2 * x_3))$ and the assignment $\langle 1, 0, 1 \rangle$. With this assignment the form becomes $1 * (1 \oplus (0 * 1))$, which can be evaluated using the definitions of the operations for members of $\{0, 1\}$ as given in the proof of Th.2.3: $1 * (1 \oplus (0 * 1)) = 1$. The association between coordinates of an assignment and the variables thus enables us to reduce the form to a value. The reduction, which we call a *valuation*, gives a link between forms and functions. Here one member of the function on B^3 into B associated with the form $x_1 * (x_1 \oplus (x_2 * x_3))$ is seen to be $\langle\langle 1, 0, 1\rangle, 1\rangle$ or $\langle 1, 0, 1, 1\rangle$. Valuations for all assignments give all elements of the functions. Table 2.2 displays valuations of $x_1 * (x_1 \oplus (x_2 * x_3))$. The principles of construction are as for Table 2.1.

We call two Boolean forms *equivalent* if their valuations are equal for every value assignment. Table 2.2 shows that forms x_1 and $x_1 * (x_1 \oplus (x_2 * x_3))$ are equivalent in Boolean algebra $\langle \{0, 1\}, \oplus, *, ', 0, 1\rangle$. The equivalence lets us write $x_1 * (x_1 \oplus (x_2 * x_3)) = x_1$. Note, however, that this is no new result; the equivalence is only a special case of Part 3 of Th.1.11. Since the forms are equivalent, the functions associated with them are equal. Although x_1 is a form in a single variable, the function associated with it must be taken as being on $\{0, 1\}^3$ if we are to talk of equality of this function and that associated with $x_1 * (x_1 \oplus (x_2 * x_3))$.

It is feasible to determine equality of Boolean functions by means of valuations only if there are few elements in set B. Consider, for example, the model $\langle \mathscr{P}(U), \cup, \cap, \bar{\ }, \varnothing, U\rangle$, with $|U| = 3$. As algebras of sets go, the number of elements in U is very small. But, since $|\mathscr{P}(U)| = 8$, the number of 2-samples of $\mathscr{P}(U)$ is 64 and the number of 3-samples 512. Clearly valuations are impracticable here. Thus it would seem that valuations are in general a poor substitute for the more formal techniques of Section 1e. The study of canonical forms, to which we now turn, does, however, provide us with a powerful decision procedure for establishing equality of functions despite its dependence on a particular type of valuations.

This study makes difficult reading; indeed, at first sight, the treatment may seem unduly ponderous. The reader is advised not to worry about the details in the definitions and the theorems at first reading, but to concentrate on the examples, referring to the definitions only to the extent necessary to arrive at an intuitive understanding of the examples.

TABLE 2.2

VALUATION OF BOOLEAN FORM $x_1 * (x_1 \oplus (x_2 * x_3))$

$\langle x_1, x_2, x_3\rangle$	$\alpha = x_2 * x_3$	$\beta = x_1 \oplus \alpha$	$x_1 * \beta$
$\langle 0, 0, 0\rangle$	0	0	0
$\langle 0, 0, 1\rangle$	0	0	0
$\langle 0, 1, 0\rangle$	0	0	0
$\langle 0, 1, 1\rangle$	1	1	0
$\langle 1, 0, 0\rangle$	0	1	1
$\langle 1, 0, 1\rangle$	0	1	1
$\langle 1, 1, 0\rangle$	0	1	1
$\langle 1, 1, 1\rangle$	1	1	1

DEFINITION 2.9   Let $\langle B, \oplus, *, ', 0, 1 \rangle$ be a Boolean algebra and $\alpha(x_1, \ldots, x_n)$ a Boolean form in the variables $x_1, \ldots, x_n$, which stand for elements of B. Denote elements of the set of n-samples $S_n(\{0, 1\})$, which we call *binary value assignments*, by t_m^n $(m = 0, 1, \ldots, 2^n - 1)$. The sample $\langle m_1, \ldots, m_n \rangle$ is denoted by t_m^n when the binary number $m_1 \cdots m_n$ is equal to the (decimal) number m. Let F be the set of forms $\alpha(m_1, \ldots, m_n)$, and define a function $q: S_n \to F$ such that $q(t_m^n) = \alpha(m_1, \ldots, m_n)$ if and only if $t_m^n = \langle m_1, \ldots, m_n \rangle$. Next define the *binary valuation function* $v: F \to \{0, 1\}$ such that $v(\alpha(m_1, \ldots, m_n)) = 0$ if and only if $\alpha(m_1, \ldots, m_n)$ has the value 0 when evaluated according to the definitions of operations for members of $\{0, 1\}$ derived in the proof of Th.2.3.

Examples

1. Consider $\alpha(x_1, x_2, x_3) = x_1 * (x_1 \oplus (x_2 * x_3))$. Members of S_3 are given by the first column of Table 2.2, e.g., $t_5^3 = \langle 1, 0, 1 \rangle$. Then $q(t_5^3) = \alpha(1, 0, 1) = 1 * (1 \oplus (0 * 1))$, and $v(q(t_5^3)) = 1$. Images of $q(t_m^3)$ under v are given by the last column of the table. If $B = \{0, 1\}$, then the set $\{\langle t_m^3, v(q(t_m^3)) \rangle \mid m = 0, \ldots, 7\}$ is the function associated with the form $x_1 * (x_1 \oplus (x_2 * x_3))$.

2. The form $(x_1 \oplus x_2) * (x_1 \oplus x_3')$ is processed in Table 2.3.

TABLE 2.3

BINARY VALUATION OF $(x_1 \oplus x_2) * (x_1 \oplus x_3')$

m	t_m^3	$q(t_m^3)$	$v(q(t_m^3))$
0	$\langle 0, 0, 0 \rangle$	$(0 \oplus 0) * (0 \oplus 0')$	0
1	$\langle 0, 0, 1 \rangle$	$(0 \oplus 0) * (0 \oplus 1')$	0
2	$\langle 0, 1, 0 \rangle$	$(0 \oplus 1) * (0 \oplus 0')$	1
3	$\langle 0, 1, 1 \rangle$	$(0 \oplus 1) * (0 \oplus 1')$	0
4	$\langle 1, 0, 0 \rangle$	$(1 \oplus 0) * (1 \oplus 0')$	1
5	$\langle 1, 0, 1 \rangle$	$(1 \oplus 0) * (1 \oplus 1')$	1
6	$\langle 1, 1, 0 \rangle$	$(1 \oplus 1) * (1 \oplus 0')$	1
7	$\langle 1, 1, 1 \rangle$	$(1 \oplus 1) * (1 \oplus 1')$	1

DEFINITION 2.10   Let $\langle B, \oplus, *, ', 0, 1 \rangle$ be a Boolean algebra, let variables $x_1, x_2, \ldots, x_n$ stand for elements of B, and let a_i denote either x_i or x_i'. The form $a_1 * a_2 * \cdots * a_n$ is called a *minterm (minimal polynomial, complete product, fundamental product)*, and the form $a_1 \oplus a_2 \oplus \cdots \oplus a_n$ is called a *maxterm (maximal polynomial, complete sum, fundamental sum)* of the n variables. We shall write x_i^1 for x_i and x_i^0 for x_i' in these forms. Under this convention we shall denote the minterm $x_1^{m_1} * x_2^{m_2} * \cdots * x_n^{m_n}$ by min_m^n and the maxterm $x_1^{m_1'} \oplus x_2^{m_2'} \oplus \cdots \oplus x_n^{m_n'}$ by max_m^n when the binary number $m_1 m_2 \cdots m_n$ is equal to m. The a_i are called *literals*.

Examples

1. With n variables there are 2^n minterms and 2^n maxterms. Thus, if $n = 3$, there are 8 minterms and 8 maxterms. The minterms are $x_1^0 * x_2^0 * x_3^0$, $x_1^0 * x_2^0 * x_3^1$, $x_1^0 * x_2^1 * x_3^0$, $x_1^0 * x_2^1 * x_3^1$, $x_1^1 * x_2^0 * x_3^0$, $x_1^1 * x_2^0 * x_3^1$, $x_1^1 * x_2^1 * x_3^0$, $x_1^1 * x_2^1 * x_3^1$, denoted by min_0^3, min_1^3, ..., min_7^3, respectively; $max_7^3 = x_1^0 \oplus x_2^0 \oplus x_3^0$.

2. A form in which the literals are combined by the $*$ operator alone is a *simple product* or just *product*; a form is a *simple sum* or just *sum* if the literals are combined by the $\oplus$ operator alone. For example, $x_1 * x_3' * x_4'$ is a simple product, $x_1' \oplus x_2 \oplus x_3'$ is a simple sum, and the form x_2' is both. A form consisting of products combined by the $\oplus$ operator is a *sum of products*; a form in which sums are combined by the $*$ operator is a *product of sums*. For example, $(x_1' * x_3) \oplus x_1 \oplus (x_2 * x_3 * x_4)$ and $(x_1' \oplus x_2) * (x_1' \oplus x_3) * x_3'$ are, respectively, a sum of products and a product of sums. The form $x_1 * x_2' * x_3 * x_5$ is a sum of products consisting of a single product, and it is also the product of the sums x_1, x_2', x_3, and x_5. The form $(x_1' \oplus x_2) * ((x_1' * x_3) \oplus (x_2 * x_4))$ is neither a sum of products nor a product of sums.

THEOREM 2.6   Let $\langle B, \oplus, *, ', 0, 1 \rangle$ be a Boolean algebra, and let variables $x_1, x_2, \ldots, x_n$ denote elements of B. Every Boolean form $\alpha(x_1, x_2, \ldots, x_n)$ of n variables is equivalent to an expansion in minterms:

$$\alpha(x_1, x_2, \ldots, x_n) = \bigoplus_{m=0}^{m=2^n-1} v(q(t_m^n)) * min_m^n$$

(where we have used an obvious abbreviation for representing a repeated $\oplus$ operation).

Proof. We shall prove the theorem by induction on n.
(i) $n = 1$. Since

$$x_1 \oplus 1 = x_1' \oplus 1 = x_1' \oplus x_1 = 1,$$
$$x_1 * 0 = x_1' * 0 = x_1' * x_1 = 0,$$
$$x_1 * 1 = x_1 \oplus 0 = x_1 * x_1 = x_1 \oplus x_1 = x_1,$$
$$x_1' * 1 = x_1' \oplus 0 = x_1' * x_1' = x_1' \oplus x_1' = x_1',$$

every $\alpha(x_1)$ ultimately reduces to 1, 0, x_1, or x_1'. The images of the two binary value assignments $t_0^1 = 0$ and $t_1^1 = 1$ under q are $q(t_0^1) = \alpha(0)$ and $q(t_1^1) = \alpha(1)$. We have to consider the images $v(\alpha(0))$ and $v(\alpha(1))$. Clearly $v(\alpha(0)) = v(\alpha(1)) = 1$ when $\alpha(x_1) = 1$, and $v(\alpha(0)) = v(\alpha(1)) = 0$ when $\alpha(x_1) = 0$. When $\alpha(x_1) = x_1$ we have $\alpha(0) = 0$ and $\alpha(1) = 1$. Consequently $v(\alpha(0)) = 0$ and $v(\alpha(1)) = 1$. The images are reversed when $\alpha(x_1) = x_1'$: $\alpha(0) = 1$ and $\alpha(1) = 0$, giving

$v(\alpha(0)) = 1$ and $v(\alpha(1)) = 0$. Evaluation of $(v(\alpha(0)) * x_1') \oplus (v(\alpha(1)) * x_1)$ completes the proof for $n = 1$:

$$
\begin{aligned}
\alpha(x_1) &= 1, & (1 * x_1') \oplus (1 * x_1) &= 1, \\
\alpha(x_1) &= 0, & (0 * x_1') \oplus (0 * x_1) &= 0, \\
\alpha(x_1) &= x_1, & (0 * x_1') \oplus (1 . * x_1) &= x_1, \\
\alpha(x_1) &= x_1', & (1 * x_1') \oplus (0 * x_1) &= x_1'.
\end{aligned}
$$

(ii) Assume the theorem true for n. This enables us to write

$$
\alpha(x_1, \ldots, x_{n+1}) = \bigoplus_{m=0}^{m=2^n-1} \alpha(m_1, \ldots, m_n, x_{n+1}) * min_m^n. \tag{A}
$$

Also

$$
\alpha(m_1, \ldots, m_n, x_{n+1}) = (v(\alpha(m_1, \ldots, m_n, 0)) * x_{n+1}') \\
\oplus (v(\alpha(m_1, \ldots, m_n, 1)) * x_{n+1}),
$$

and it should be reasonably easy to see that use of this expression in (A) gives the theorem for $n + 1$:

$$
\alpha(x_1, \ldots, x_{n+1}) = \bigoplus_{m=0}^{m=2^{n+1}-1} v(\alpha(m_1, \ldots, m_{n+1})) * min_m^{n+1}.
$$

Theorem 2.7 For a given Boolean form $\alpha(x_1, \ldots, x_n)$ the equivalent expansion in minterms defined by Th. 2.6 is unique.

Proof. Assume that two different expanded forms are equivalent to $\alpha(x_1, \ldots, x_n)$. Since the forms are different, there exists at least one $t_m^n = \langle m_1, \ldots, m_n \rangle$ such that $v(q(t_m^n))$ is 0 in one of the forms and 1 in the other, but then, by D.2.9, we have the contradiction $\alpha(m_1, \ldots, m_n) = 0$ and $\alpha(m_1, \ldots, m_n) = 1$.

Theorem 2.8 Let $\langle B, \oplus, *, ', 0, 1 \rangle$ be a Boolean algebra, and let variables $x_1, x_2, \ldots, x_n$ denote elements of B. Every Boolean form $\alpha(x_1, x_2, \ldots, x_n)$ of n variables has a unique equivalent expansion in maxterms:

$$
\alpha(x_1, x_2, \ldots, x_n) = \mathop{\textstyle *}_{m=0}^{m=2^n-1} v(q(t_m^n)) \oplus max_m^n
$$

(where an obvious abbreviation is used for a repeated $*$ operation).

Proof. By principle of duality from Th.2.6 and Th.2.7.

Since the expanded forms are unique, we call them *canonical forms* or *normal forms*. The canonical expansion of Th.2.6 is known as the *disjunctive normal form*, and that of Th.2.8 as the *conjunctive normal form*. An obvious consequence of the uniqueness of normal forms is that two forms are equivalent if they have the same normal form. Then the associated functions are, of course, equal. Inspection of the canonical expansions shows that two Boolean forms $\alpha(x_1, \ldots, x_n)$ and $\beta(x_1, \ldots, x_n)$ have the same normal form, i.e., have equal associated functions, if $v(\alpha(m_1, \ldots, m_n)) = v(\beta(m_1, \ldots, m_n))$ for all n-samples $\langle m_1, \ldots, m_n \rangle$ of set $\{0, 1\}$.

Examples

1. Clearly a term min_m^n for which the corresponding $v(q(t_m^n))$ is 0 does not have to be included in a disjunctive normal form. Similarly, one does not have to include a term max_m^n for which $v(q(t_m^n))$ is 1 in a conjunctive normal form. From Table 2.3, the disjunctive and conjunctive normal forms equivalent to $(x_1 \oplus x_2) * (x_1 \oplus x_3')$ are, respectively, $(x_1' * x_2 * x_3') \oplus (x_1 * x_2' * x_3') \oplus (x_1 * x_2' * x_3) \oplus (x_1 * x_2 * x_3') \oplus (x_1 * x_2 * x_3)$ and $(x_1 \oplus x_2 \oplus x_3) * (x_1 \oplus x_2 \oplus x_3') * (x_1 \oplus x_2' \oplus x_3')$.

2. Sometimes we may be given a function and asked to find a formula describing it. Let function $f: \{0, 1\}^2 \to \{0, 1\}$ be the set $\{\langle 0, 0, 0 \rangle, \langle 0, 1, 1 \rangle, \langle 1, 0, 1 \rangle, \langle 1, 1, 0 \rangle\}$. The disjunctive normal form of the function is $(x_1' * x_2) \oplus (x_1 * x_2')$. The conjunctive normal form is $(x_1 \oplus x_2) * (x_1' \oplus x_2')$. Since the normal forms represent the same function, they are equivalent. Hence, in model $\langle \mathscr{P}(U), \cup, \cap, ^-, \varnothing, U \rangle$,

$$(\bar{A} \cap B) \cup (A \cap \bar{B}) = (A \cup B) \cap (\bar{A} \cup \bar{B}).$$

Since the left-hand side of the equation defines the symmetric difference, we can write $A + B = (A \cup B) \cap (\bar{A} \cup \bar{B})$.

3. Tables 2.4 and 2.5 show that the two forms $\alpha = ((x_1 * x_3) \oplus (x_2 * x_3'))'$ and $\beta = (x_1' * x_3) \oplus (x_2' * x_3')$ are equivalent. The disjunctive normal form of α and β is $(x_1' * x_2' * x_3') \oplus (x_1' * x_2' * x_3) \oplus (x_1' * x_2 * x_3) \oplus (x_1 * x_2' * x_3')$. The conjunctive form is $(x_1 \oplus x_2' \oplus x_3) * (x_1' \oplus x_2 \oplus x_3') * (x_1' \oplus x_2' \oplus x_3) * (x_1' \oplus x_2' \oplus x_3')$.

4. There is a fundamental difference between the valuations of Table 2.2 and the binary valuations here. In Table 2.2 variables x_1, x_2, x_3 stand for elements of the very special algebra $\langle \{0, 1\}, \oplus, *, ', 0, 1 \rangle$, and the valuations define the elements of a function. In Tables 2.4 and 2.5 the x_1, x_2, x_3 represent elements of the general Boolean algebra $\langle B, \oplus, *, ', 0, 1 \rangle$. The binary valuations of these tables let us make decisions about the equivalence of forms (and thus about equality of functions), but they do not define the elements of functions. Consider the model $\langle \mathscr{P}(U), \cup, \cap, ^-, \varnothing, U \rangle$ and functions $g: (\mathscr{P}(U))^3 \to \mathscr{P}(U), h: (\mathscr{P}(U))^3 \to \mathscr{P}(U)$, defined by the forms

$$g(A, B, C) = (A \cup B) \cap (B \cup C) \cap (C \cup A),$$
$$h(A, B, C) = (A \cap B) \cup (B \cap C) \cup (C \cap A),$$

TABLE 2.4

$$\alpha = ((x_1 * x_3) \oplus (x_2 * x_3'))' = (\alpha_1 \oplus \alpha_2)'$$

m	t_m^3	$v(\alpha_1)$	$v(\alpha_2)$	$v(\alpha_1 \oplus \alpha_2)$	$v(\alpha)$
0	$\langle 0, 0, 0 \rangle$	0	0	0	1
1	$\langle 0, 0, 1 \rangle$	0	0	0	1
2	$\langle 0, 1, 0 \rangle$	0	1	1	0
3	$\langle 0, 1, 1 \rangle$	0	0	0	1
4	$\langle 1, 0, 0 \rangle$	0	0	0	1
5	$\langle 1, 0, 1 \rangle$	1	0	1	0
6	$\langle 1, 1, 0 \rangle$	0	1	1	0
7	$\langle 1, 1, 1 \rangle$	1	0	1	0

TABLE 2.5

$$\beta = (x_1' * x_3) \oplus (x_2' * x_3')$$

m	t_m^3	$v(x_1' * x_3)$	$v(x_2' * x_3')$	$v(\beta)$
0	$\langle 0, 0, 0 \rangle$	0	1	1
1	$\langle 0, 0, 1 \rangle$	1	0	1
2	$\langle 0, 1, 0 \rangle$	0	0	0
3	$\langle 0, 1, 1 \rangle$	1	0	1
4	$\langle 1, 0, 0 \rangle$	0	1	1
5	$\langle 1, 0, 1 \rangle$	0	0	0
6	$\langle 1, 1, 0 \rangle$	0	0	0
7	$\langle 1, 1, 1 \rangle$	0	0	0

where A, B, C represent elements of $\mathscr{P}(U)$. The equality of g and h can be demonstrated by standard procedures of the algebra of sets applied to the formulas $(A \cup B) \cap (B \cup C) \cap (C \cup A)$ and $(A \cap B) \cup (B \cap C) \cup (C \cap A)$. Alternatively, the forms can be shown to be equivalent by showing that they have the same normal forms. This we do in Table 2.6. The disjunctive normal form of $(A \cup B) \cap (B \cup C) \cap (C \cup A)$ is $(\bar{A} \cap B \cap C) \cup (A \cap \bar{B} \cap C) \cup (A \cap B \cap \bar{C}) \cup (A \cap B \cap C)$. (Clearly, we have not been defining elements of the function here. Let $U = \{1, 2, 3, 4, 5\}$, say. Then $|\mathscr{P}(U)| = 32$, and the number of 3-samples of $\mathscr{P}(U)$ is 32,768. Since this is the number of elements in the function g—and in any other function on $(\mathscr{P}(U))^3$ when U has five elements—listing the elements would be a rather meaningless exercise.)

5. Consider $\alpha = (x_1 * x_2 * x_3) \oplus (x_1' * x_2 * x_3) \oplus x_2' \oplus x_3'$. Here $v(\alpha) = 1$ for all $\langle m_1, m_2, m_3 \rangle$. Hence the disjunctive normal form has eight terms. In the conjunctive normal form each term appears as $1 \oplus max_m^n$. Since, by convention, such terms are not included in the normal form, the conjunctive normal form would be written as 1 here.

TABLE 2.6

EQUALITY OF FUNCTIONS g AND h

m	t_m^3	$v(g(A, B, C))$	$v(h(A, B, C))$
0	$\langle \varnothing, \varnothing, \varnothing \rangle$	$\varnothing$	$\varnothing$
1	$\langle \varnothing, \varnothing, U \rangle$	$\varnothing$	$\varnothing$
2	$\langle \varnothing, U, \varnothing \rangle$	$\varnothing$	$\varnothing$
3	$\langle \varnothing, U, U \rangle$	U	U
4	$\langle U, \varnothing, \varnothing \rangle$	$\varnothing$	$\varnothing$
5	$\langle U, \varnothing, U \rangle$	U	U
6	$\langle U, U, \varnothing \rangle$	U	U
7	$\langle U, U, U \rangle$	U	U

2c. Applications of Boolean Functions

The system $\langle \{0, 1\}, \oplus, *, ', 0, 1 \rangle$, which by Th.2.3 is a Boolean algebra, is sometimes called *switching algebra*. Functions $s: \{0, 1\}^n \to \{0, 1\}$ are known as *switching functions*. The terminology reflects an important application of the functions s. Wherever information passes along wires, as in a computer, telephone switching system, or some other such system, the simplest information processing is performed by switches. A *switch* is a two-state device. It is either *closed* and passes information through, or it is *open* and stops the information flow. Switching functions have been found useful for describing circuits that contain switches and in the design of such circuits.

A circuit that links two terminal points t_1 and t_2, and consists of interconnected switches is known as a *combinatorial two-terminal switching circuit*. Depending on the states of the switches, information passes or does not pass from one terminal to the other. If information does pass, the circuit is *closed*. Otherwise it is *open*. Figure 2.1 shows two very simple circuits containing two switches x_1 and x_2. In the *series* connection the circuit is closed only if both switches are closed. In the *parallel* connection it is sufficient to have just one switch closed for the circuit to be closed.

We associate the element 0 of $\{0, 1\}$ with an open switch and the element 1 with a closed switch. The n switches in a circuit are associated with *circuit variables* $x_1, x_2, \ldots, x_n$, and the circuit itself with a function of these variables, $s(x_1, x_2, \ldots, x_n)$. We associate elements of $\{0, 1\}$ with the circuit as well: 0 with an open circuit and 1 with a closed circuit. States of the circuits of Figure 2.1 are investigated in Table 2.7. The four rows of the table correspond to the four possible states of the two switches (both open, x_1 alone open, x_2 alone open, both closed). The table shows the states of the circuits corresponding to the states of the switches, and $x_1 * x_2$ and $x_1 \oplus x_2$ (functions p

$$t_1 \circ\!\!-\!\!-\!\!-\, x_1 \,-\!\!-\!\!-\, x_2 \,-\!\!-\!\!-\!\!\circ\, t_2$$

(a) Series connection of two switches.

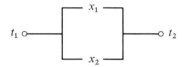

(b) Parallel connection of two switches.

Figure 2.1

and s of Table 2.1). We see that a series connection of x_1 and x_2 can be represented by $x_1 * x_2$, and a parallel connection by $x_1 \oplus x_2$.

Consider now the circuit of Figure 2.2. It can be represented by the switching function $s(x_1, x_2, x_3, x_4, x_5) = x_1 * (x_2 \oplus (x_3 * (x_4 \oplus x_5)))$. This form is equivalent to the form $(x_1 * x_2) \oplus (x_1 * x_3 * x_4) \oplus (x_1 * x_3 * x_5)$. The question arises: Can one represent a form containing more than one occurrence of a variable by a switching circuit? The answer is affirmative, with an understanding that in the physical realization of the circuit there is a mechanism to ensure that switches bearing the same label are simultaneously all open or all closed. In practice, however, one is not interested in designing an equivalent circuit more complicated than the original one. Rather, the practical problem is one of simplification.

The important application of switching functions is in the design of circuits. Assume that we are given some switching function and are required to design a switching circuit corresponding to this function. The circuit is to

TABLE 2.7

STATES OF SERIES AND PARALLEL CONNECTIONS OF TWO SWITCHES

$\langle x_1, x_2 \rangle$	Series connection	Parallel connection	$x_1 * x_2$	$x_1 \oplus x_2$
$\langle 0, 0 \rangle$	0	0	0	0
$\langle 0, 1 \rangle$	0	1	0	1
$\langle 1, 0 \rangle$	0	1	0	1
$\langle 1, 1 \rangle$	1	1	1	1

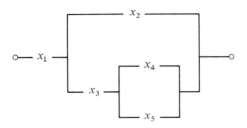

Figure 2.2

be open for those combinations of switches $x_1, x_2, \ldots, x_n$ for which $s(x_1, x_2, \ldots, x_n) = 0$ and closed for combinations giving $s(x_1, x_2, \ldots, x_n) = 1$. The theory of normal forms of Section 2b permits us to write down formulas of the function. If combinations with $s(x_1, x_2, \ldots, x_n) = 0$ predominate in the specification of the function, we choose the disjunctive normal form. Otherwise we select the conjunctive normal form. Probably there will be terms in x_i' as well as in x_i in the normal form. The state of switch x_i' is completely determined by that of x_i: If x_i is closed, x_i' is open; if x_i is open, x_i' is closed. In what follows we shall abbreviate $x_1 * x_2 * \cdots * x_n$ to $x_1 x_2 \cdots x_n$.

Example

Suppose we require a combinatorial two-terminal switching circuit of four switches to be closed whenever exactly two of the switches are closed and to be open otherwise. First, in Table 2.8, we specify the switching function.

TABLE 2.8
A Switching Function

$\langle x_1, x_2, x_3, x_4 \rangle$	$s(x_1, x_2, x_3, x_4)$
$\langle 0, 0, 0, 0 \rangle$	0
$\langle 0, 0, 0, 1 \rangle$	0
$\langle 0, 0, 1, 0 \rangle$	0
$\langle 0, 0, 1, 1 \rangle$	1
$\langle 0, 1, 0, 0 \rangle$	0
$\langle 0, 1, 0, 1 \rangle$	1
$\langle 0, 1, 1, 0 \rangle$	1
$\langle 0, 1, 1, 1 \rangle$	0
$\langle 1, 0, 0, 0 \rangle$	0
$\langle 1, 0, 0, 1 \rangle$	1
$\langle 1, 0, 1, 0 \rangle$	1
$\langle 1, 0, 1, 1 \rangle$	0
$\langle 1, 1, 0, 0 \rangle$	1
$\langle 1, 1, 0, 1 \rangle$	0
$\langle 1, 1, 1, 0 \rangle$	0
$\langle 1, 1, 1, 1 \rangle$	0

There are 6 nonzero images against 10 zero images. Therefore, the disjunctive normal form of the function is the simpler form:

$$s(x_1, x_2, x_3, x_4) = x_1'x_2'x_3x_4 \oplus x_1'x_2x_3'x_4 \oplus x_1'x_2x_3x_4'$$
$$\oplus x_1x_2'x_3'x_4 \oplus x_1x_2'x_3x_4' \oplus x_1x_2x_3'x_4'.$$

Figure 2.3 shows the circuit corresponding to this function.

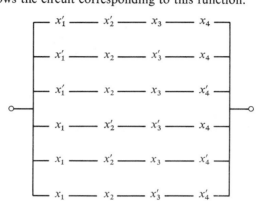

Figure 2.3

The circuit of Figure 2.3 contains 24 switches. This number seems excessive. Let us therefore try to simplify the formula. Using the theorems of Section 1e, we find

$$s(x_1, x_2, x_3, x_4) = x_1'x_2'x_3x_4 \oplus x_1x_2x_3'x_4' \oplus (x_1'x_2 \oplus x_1x_2')(x_3'x_4 \oplus x_3x_4').$$

The simpler circuit (16 switches) corresponding to this form is shown in Figure 2.4.

At the present stage of development of computer science the simplification of normal forms by algebraic manipulation cannot be expressed in the form of an algorithm, but there are algorithmic methods that utilize other

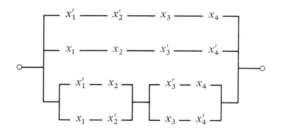

Figure 2.4

approaches. Since the dual of any algorithm for disjunctive normal forms is an algorithm for conjunctive normal forms, it will suffice to discuss disjunctive normal forms alone in what follows. Known as *minimization* methods, the simplification algorithms minimize normal forms in a rather special sense. Given a disjunctive normal form, a minimization method finds an equivalent sum of products that contains the least number of products, and, moreover, of all sums of products containing this number of products, the least number of literals. In this sense, the form corresponding to the circuit of Figure 2.3 is minimal. Even though the equivalent circuit of Figure 2.4 requires fewer switches, the form that defines this circuit does not count because it is not a sum of products.

The best-known minimization methods are the Karnaugh map technique and the Quine–McCluskey tabulation method. A Karnaugh map is constructed from the normal form that is to be minimized, and the minimal form is found by visual examination of the map. This technique is rather difficult to program for a computer, and as a pencil and paper method it becomes very complicated when the number of variables exceeds five. For these reasons the Quine–McCluskey method alone will be discussed here.

Minimization methods are based on the concept of prime implicants. A Boolean form α *covers* another Boolean form β if $v(\alpha) = 1$ for all value assignments that make $v(\beta) = 1$. If α covers β, and β is a simple product, then β is an *implicant* of α. If β is an implicant of α, and no other form obtainable from β by removal of literals is an implicant of α, then β is a *prime implicant* of α. For example, $s_1 = x_1 x_2 \oplus x_3 x_4$ covers $s_2 = x_1 x_2 x_3'$, and, since s_2 is a product, it is an implicant of s_1. Since also $x_1 x_2$ is an implicant of s_1, the product $x_1 x_2 x_3'$ is not a prime implicant. The products $x_1 x_2$ and $x_3 x_4$ are the two prime implicants of s_1.

The products in a minimal sum of products equivalent to a disjunctive normal form must all be prime implicants. Since a sum of products has the value 1 whenever a product in this sum has the value 1, every product in the minimal sum of products must be an implicant of the normal form. Further, if some product were not a prime implicant, then it could be replaced by an implicant containing fewer literals, i.e., the sum of products would not be minimal. The Quine–McCluskey procedure first generates the set of all prime implicants of the normal form, and then selects a subset of the prime implicants that defines a minimal sum of products. The second stage is, in general, the more difficult.

It is a trivial exercise to prove that $\alpha x \oplus \alpha x' = \alpha$, where α is any Boolean form. This theorem is used in the generation of the set of prime implicants. Consider a disjunctive normal form $s(x_1, x_2, \ldots, x_n)$. First apply the theorem to all pairs of minterms to which it is applicable. This produces a set of reduced products containing $n - 1$ literals. Next apply the theorem to all pairs

of these products to which it is applicable to produce products that contain
$n - 2$ literals, and so forth. When the theorem can be applied no further,
cross off all the products to which it has been applied. The set of products
that remain is the set of all prime implicants.

Consider the normal form defined by the set of minterms

$$P_1 = \{x_1'x_2'x_3'x_4, \, x_1'x_2x_3x_4', \, x_1x_2'x_3x_4', \, x_1x_2'x_3x_4, \, x_1x_2x_3x_4', \, x_1x_2x_3x_4\}.$$

The theorem is applicable to the following pairs of minterms:

$$x_1'x_2x_3x_4', \quad x_1x_2x_3x_4' \, ;$$
$$x_1x_2'x_3x_4', \quad x_1x_2'x_3x_4 \, ;$$
$$x_1x_2'x_3x_4', \quad x_1x_2x_3x_4' \, ;$$
$$x_1x_2'x_3x_4, \quad x_1x_2x_3x_4 \, ;$$
$$x_1x_2x_3x_4', \quad x_1x_2x_3x_4 \, .$$

The reductions result in the set of products

$$P_2 = \{x_2x_3x_4', \, x_1x_2'x_3, \, x_1x_3x_4', \, x_1x_3x_4, \, x_1x_2x_3\},$$

and the theorem is now applicable to the pairs

$$x_1x_2'x_3, \, x_1x_2x_3;$$
$$x_1x_3x_4', \, x_1x_3x_4 \, .$$

In both cases the reduced product is $x_1 x_3$, i.e.,

$$P_3 = \{x_1x_3\}.$$

In P_1 and P_2 all products except $x_1'x_2'x_3'x_4$ and $x_2x_3x_4'$, respectively, are
crossed off. Hence the set of prime implicants is

$$\{x_1'x_2'x_3'x_4, \, x_2x_3x_4', \, x_1x_3\}.$$

Note that the reduction theorem is applicable to a pair of products only if
one product contains an x_i, the other an x_i', and the other literals agree.
This observation is utilized in A.2.1, which is a systematization of the procedure outlined above.

ALGORITHM 2.1   An algorithm for finding the prime implicants of a disjunctive normal form.

1.   Represent every minterm $x_1^{m_1}x_2^{m_2}\cdots x_n^{m_n}$ in the disjunctive normal
form by the binary number $m_1 \, m_2 \cdots m_n$.
2.   Set $i = n$. Place the binary numbers into groups $G_0^i, G_1^i, \ldots, G_n^i$,

assigning a number containing k ones to group G_k^i.

3. Compare every number in group G_k^i with every number in group G_{k+1}^i for $k = 0, 1, \ldots, n - 1$. Use the theorem $\alpha x \oplus \alpha x' = \alpha$ where applicable, i.e., where the numbers being compared are identical except for one digit position. Where the theorem is applicable,

  (a)   flag both numbers being compared;
  (b)   generate a new number by taking the number in G_k^i and replacing the zero in the differing digit position by a dash;
  (c)   assign the new number to group G_k^{i-1} if this group does not already contain this number.

4. Set $i = i - 1$. If more than one group G_k^i is not empty, go to Step 3.

5. Stop. The unflagged numbers in *all* the groups represent the set of prime implicants.

Examples

1. Apply the algorithm to the normal form defined by the set of minterms $\{min_1^4, min_6^4, min_{10}^4, min_{11}^4, min_{14}^4, min_{15}^4\}$. The binary representations are 0001, 0110, 1010, 1011, 1110, 1111. Table 2.9 shows how the algorithm works. The groups in the first column are $G_1^4, G_2^4, G_3^4, G_4^4$. Compare 0001 of G_1^4 against 0110 of G_2^4. The numbers differ in three digit positions. Hence the theorem is not applicable. Next compare 0001 against 1010. The theorem is again not applicable. This completes the $G_1^4 : G_2^4$ comparisons, and the $G_2^4 : G_3^4$ comparisons are made next. The theorem is not applicable to 0110 and 1011, but it is applicable to 0110 and 1110, which differ only in the first digit. The flag is set to 1 against both 0110 and 1110, and the 0110 is changed

TABLE 2.9

FINDING OF PRIME IMPLICANTS

	Flag		Flag		Flag
0001		−110		1−1−	
		101−	1		
0110	1	1−10	1		
1010	1				
		1−11	1		
1011	1	111−	1		
1110	1				
1111	1				

to -110 and entered in the second column of the table. Next 1010 is compared against 1011 and 1110 in turn. The theorem is applicable in both cases, flags are set, and the numbers $101-$ and $1-10$ are entered in the second column of the table. All $G_2^4 : G_3^4$ comparisons have now been made, and the numbers -110, $101-$, $1-10$, which have resulted from the comparisons, define G_2^3. The other two numbers in the second column, which define G_3^3, arise from the comparisons of 1011 against 1111, and 1110 against 1111, respectively. Step 4 is now entered. Since there are two groups of numbers in the second column of the table, go to Step 3. Of the six pairings of the three numbers in G_2^3 with the two numbers in G_3^3 the theorem is applicable only to $101-$ and $111-$, which results in these numbers being flagged and $1-1-$ being entered in the third column of the table, and to $1-10$ and $1-11$. In the latter case the numbers are flagged, but $1-1-$ is not entered in the table because a $1-1-$ is already there. Since the third column contains only one group (G_2^2), the algorithm stops. The unflagged numbers are 0001 in G_1^4, -110 in G_2^3, and $1-1-$ in G_2^2. The prime implicants represented by these numbers are $x_1' x_2' x_3' x_4$, $x_2 x_3 x_4'$, and $x_1 x_3$, respectively. This was to be expected because the example here is precisely the example that was used in the informal discussion of the algorithm.

2. Table 2.10 shows the application of the algorithm to the normal form defined by the set of minterms $\{min_i^5 \mid i \in I\}$, where $I = \{0, 1, 2, 8, 9, 16, 17, 18, 20, 21, 24, 25, 26, 27, 28, 29\}$. The set of prime implicants is $\{x_2' x_3' x_5', x_1 x_3' x_5', x_1 x_2 x_3', x_3' x_4', x_1 x_4'\}$.

After the prime implicants have been found, the minimal sum of products is generated. First a table is set up in which rows correspond to the minterms of the normal form, and columns to the prime implicants. Rows and columns are labeled using binary representations. Consider a particular minterm and a particular prime implicant. Disregarding the dashes in the representation of the latter, compare the remaining digits with the corresponding digits in the representation of the minterm. If they agree, then the prime implicant covers the minterm, and then a 1 is entered in the table in the location defined by the intersection of the row of the minterm and the column of the prime implicant. This determination is made for all pairs of minterms and prime implicants. The result for Example 2 of A.2.1 is Table 2.11, which we call a table of covers.

Note now that if α covers β, and β covers α, then α and β are equivalent. The normal form covers every prime implicant and hence every sum of prime implicants. Consequently, a minimal sum of prime implicants that together cover all minterms defines a minimal sum of products equivalent to the normal form. This minimal set is determined from the table of total covers by selecting the smallest number of columns such that there is still at least one 1 in every row, and the number of literals in the prime implicants of the selected columns is the smallest possible for this number of columns.

TABLE 2.10

FINDING OF PRIME IMPLICANTS

	Flag		Flag		Flag		Flag
00000	1	0000-	1	0-00-	1	--00-	
		000-0	1	-000-	1		
00001	1	0-000	1	-00-0	1	1--0-	
00010	1	-0000	1	--000	1		
01000	1						
10000	1	0-001	1	--001	1		
		-0001	1	-100-	1		
01001	1	-0010	1	10-0-	1		
10001	1	0100-	1	1-00-	1		
10010	1	-1000	1	1-0-0			
10100	1	1000-	1	1--00	1		
11000	1	100-0	1				
		10-00	1	1--01	1		
10101	1	1-000	1	1-10-	1		
11001	1			110--			
11010	1	-1001	1	11-0-	1		
11100	1	10-01	1				
		1-001	1				
11011	1	1-010	1				
11101	1	1010-	1				
		1-100	1				
		1100-	1				
		110-0	1				
		11-00	1				
		1-101	1				
		110-1	1				
		11-01	1				
		1101-	1				
		1110-	1				

If a row contains just a single 1, then the prime implicant to which this 1 corresponds is called *essential*. Every essential prime implicant must go into the minimal set. In Table 2.11 four prime implicants are essential: $-00-0$ (single 1 in row 3), $110--$ (single 1 in row 15), $--00-$ (single 1 in row 2, and also in rows 4 and 6), and $1--0-$ (single 1 in rows 9, 11, 14, 16). The corresponding columns are 1, 3, 4; and 5, respectively. Now the rows are checked: if a row contains a 1 in one of the columns 1, 3, 4, or 5, then the row is flagged with a check mark. In our example every row is so flagged. This means that the four essential prime implicants cover the entire normal form, i.e., that $x_2' x_3' x_5' \oplus x_1 x_2 x_3' \oplus x_3' x_4' \oplus x_1 x_4'$ is a minimal sum of products equivalent to the normal form.

TABLE 2.11

TABLE OF COVERS

		-00-0	1-0-0	110--	--00-	1--0-	Check mark
1	00000	1			1		✓
2	00001				1		✓
3	00010	1					✓
4	01000				1		✓
5	10000	1	1		1	1	✓
6	01001				1		✓
7	10001				1	1	✓
8	10010	1	1				✓
9	10100					1	✓
10	11000		1	1	1	1	✓
11	10101					1	✓
12	11001			1	1	1	✓
13	11010		1	1			✓
14	11100					1	✓
15	11011			1			✓
16	11101					1	✓

In general the determination of the minimal sum of products is not as simple. Some minterms may not be covered by any of the essential prime implicants, and these rows remain unflagged. The minimal form then contains at least one prime implicant additional to the essential prime implicants. It may even happen that no prime implicant is essential (see Table 2.12). In such cases the minimization problem has in general more than one solution. In simpler cases the solution may be found by inspection (e.g., it is easy to see that $x_1' x_2' x_3' \oplus x_1 x_2' x_4' \oplus x_1' x_2 x_4 \oplus x_1 x_2 x_3$ is one solution of the problem of Table 2.12). Systematic techniques exist for the more complicated situations, but they are outside the scope of this book. References to texts describing these techniques can be found at the end of the chapter.

TABLE 2.12

TABLE OF COVERS WITH NO ESSENTIAL PRIME IMPLICANTS

	000-	-000	0-01	10-0	01-1	1-10	-111	111-
0000	1	1						
0001	1		1					
1000		1		1				
0101			1		1			
1010				1		1		
0111					1		1	
1110						1		1
1111							1	1

Next we consider *gating circuits*. In a gating circuit there are *n inputs* $x_1, x_2, \ldots, x_n$, and each input is either 0 (signal absent) or 1 (signal present). There is a single *output*, also 0 or 1. The simplest gating circuits consist of just two inputs, x_1 and x_2, and of a *gate*, either an OR-*gate* or an AND-*gate*. If the gate is an OR-gate, the output signal is 0 when $x_1 = x_2 = 0$ and 1 otherwise. If the gate is an AND-gate, the signal is 1 when $x_1 = x_2 = 1$ and 0 otherwise. In addition to gates we may have an *inverter*, which has a single input x. The output of the inverter is 1 when $x = 0$ and 0 when $x = 1$.

A gating circuit with *n* inputs corresponds to a *gating function* $g: \{0, 1\}^n \to \{0, 1\}$. The OR-gate corresponds to the $\oplus$-operation in $\{0, 1\}$, the AND-gate to the $*$-operation, and the inverter to complementation. There is a great similarity between gating circuits and switching circuits. In fact, there is a one-to-one correspondence between gating circuits with *n* inputs and switching circuits with *n* switches. Switches x_i and x_j in parallel correspond to an OR-gate with inputs x_i and x_j, and switches in series correspond to an AND-gate. Wherever there is an x_i' in the switching circuit, signal x_i is passed through an inverter in the gating circuit. To avoid confusion between switching and gating problems, and to adhere to generally accepted notation we shall use the symbol $\vee$ for the $\oplus$-operation and the symbol $\wedge$ for the $*$-operation; i.e., here our Boolean algebra, sometimes called *gating algebra*, is $\langle \{0, 1\}, \vee, \wedge, ', 0, 1 \rangle$. Again we shall abbreviate $x_i \wedge x_j$ to $x_i x_j$. In more complicated gating circuits there may be more than one output (see Exercise 2.29). When there are *m* outputs the gating function becomes $g: \{0, 1\}^n \to \{0, 1\}^m$.

Figure 2.5 shows the three fundamental gating circuits. In Figure 2.6 we show the gating circuit corresponding to the switching circuit of Figure 2.2,

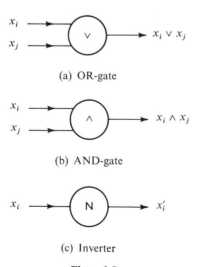

(a) OR-gate

(b) AND-gate

(c) Inverter

Figure 2.5

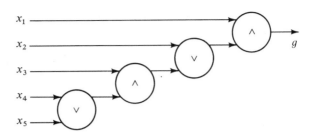

Figure 2.6

and in Figure 2.7 the gating circuit corresponding to the switching circuit of Figure 2.4.

Let us look at an everyday example. A circuit is to be designed that permits a stair light to be controlled by switches at the bottom and the top of the stairs. From each of the two switches there is an input to the system, and the state of the switch determines the value of the input: 0 if the switch is open, 1 if it is closed. Denote the inputs by x_1 and x_2. An appropriate gating function $g(x_1, x_2)$ is to be found. We stipulate $g(0, 0) = 0$. Then, if either of the switches is closed, we want the light to go on. This requires $g(0, 1) = g(1, 0) = 1$. The light is to go off when the remaining open switch is closed. Hence we require $g(1, 1) = 0$. From this specification we get the gating function $x_1 x_2' \vee x_1' x_2$. Alternatively, the problem can be considered as one of designing an appropriate switching circuit. The circuit would be defined by $x_1 x_2' \oplus x_1' x_2$, where x_1 and x_2 now denote the switches at the bottom and the top of the stairs.

The complexity of Figure 2.7 is best evidence that it would be difficult to construct a gating circuit corresponding to the function of Table 2.8 if we did not have the techniques based on canonical forms. These techniques enable us to find a formula involving functions $\oplus$, $*$, and $'$ for any Boolean function $f: B^n \to B$. The question arises whether it is still possible to find formulas for all functions if the basic set of operations is other than $\{\oplus, *, '\}$. This is the problem of functional completeness.

DEFINITION 2.11 A set of operations $\{p_1, \ldots, p_k\}$ in set B is *functionally complete* if and only if *every* Boolean function $f: B^n \to B$ can be represented by a form $\alpha(x_1, \ldots, x_n)$ in variables $x_1, x_2, \ldots, x_n$ and operations $p_1, \ldots, p_k$.

Examples

1. The set of functions $\{\oplus, *\}$ on $\{0, 1\}^2$ is not functionally complete. Since $0 \oplus 0 = 0 * 0 = 0$, there is no way of constructing a formula corresponding to a function that contains $\langle 0, 0, 1 \rangle$. Also, since $1 \oplus 1 = 1 * 1 = 1$,

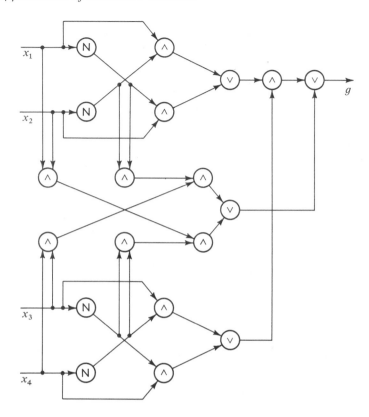

$$g = x_1 x_2 x_3' x_4' \lor x_1' x_2' x_3 x_4 \lor (x_1 x_2' \lor x_1' x_2)(x_3 x_4' \lor x_3' x_4)$$

Figure 2.7

there is no way of constructing a formula of a function with $\langle 1, 1, 0 \rangle$ as a member. Hence only 4 of the 16 functions on $\{0, 1\}^2$ into $\{0, 1\}$ can be represented by forms in $\oplus$ and $*$ alone. These forms are x_1, x_2, $x_1 \oplus x_2$, $x_1 * x_2$ (or forms equivalent to them). In the context of gating circuits this means that very few functions can be represented by gating circuits containing no inverters.

2. In Boolean algebra $\langle B, \oplus, *, ', 0, 1 \rangle$ we have, for any elements a, $b \in B$,

$$a \oplus b = (a' * b')'; \qquad a * b = (a' \oplus b')'.$$

Hence sets of functions $\{*, '\}$ and $\{\oplus, '\}$ are functionally complete in B.

3. In Table 2.1 we define function g on set $\{0, 1\}$. Since $g' = p$, where p is

defined by the form $x_1 * x_2$, we have $g(x_1, x_2) = (x_1 * x_2)'$. Function $g(x_1, x_2)$ is written $x_1 \,|\, x_2$ and called *stroke function*. We have

$$x_1' = x_1 \,|\, x_1,$$
$$x_1 \oplus x_2 = x_1' \,|\, x_2' = (x_1 \,|\, x_1) \,|\, (x_2 \,|\, x_2),$$
$$x_1 * x_2 = (x_1 \,|\, x_2)' = (x_1 \,|\, x_2) \,|\, (x_1 \,|\, x_2).$$

Hence $\{\,|\,\}$ is functionally complete. The gating circuit corresponding to the stroke function is known as a NAND-*gate* (NAND for Not AND). Any Boolean function can be represented by a circuit consisting of nothing but NAND-gates.

Our final application deals with statements. By a *statement* or *proposition* we mean a sentence that is either true or false. It is possible to determine the truth or falsity of the sentences

There are 23 lines of print on this page   (p)

$10 + 10 = 100$ (q)

Jack and Jill went up the hill   (r)

They are therefore statements. The sentence

What time is it?

is not a statement.

One can modify a statement by the word *not* or connect statements with words *and, or, if–then, if and only if*. The five words or combinations of words (or their synonyms, e.g., *implies* for *if–then*) are called *connectives*. Statements built up from simpler statements by means of the connectives are called *composite statements*. The different types of composite statements have been given special names. A statement modified by the connective *not* is the *negation* of the original statement. The statement that results when two statements are joined by *and* is the *conjunction* of the two statements. When two statements are joined by *or* the resulting statement is the *disjunction* of the two statements. The statement *if p then q* is a *conditional* statement having statement p as its *antecedent* and statement q as its *consequent*. The connective *if and only if* generates a *biconditional* statement.

Statements p and q are not composite. Such statements are called *prime statements* or *atomic statements*. Statement r, on the other hand, is composite if it is regarded as the conjunction of statements

Jack went up the hill   (s)

Jill went up the hill   (t)

(The presence of *and* in a statement does not necessarily make the statement composite. If Jill's actions always match Jack's actions, then r can be regarded as an atomic statement.) The following statements are composite:

$$10 + 10 \neq 100 \qquad\qquad\qquad (u)$$

$$10 + 10 = 100 \quad \text{or} \quad 10 + 10 \neq 100 \qquad (v)$$

$$10 + 10 = 100 \quad \text{if and only if} \quad 10 + 10 \neq 100 \qquad (w)$$

$$\text{If} \quad 3 < 5 \quad \text{and} \quad 4 < 5 \quad \text{then} \quad 4 < 3 \quad \text{or} \quad 3 < 5 \quad (x)$$

Statement u is the negation of q. It is true if q is false, and false if q is true. Hence v is true irrespective of the truth or falsity of q. Indeed, the disjunction of any statement and its negation is necessarily true. The biconditional of a statement and its negation, of which w is an example, is always false. The fact that the truth or falsity of certain statements is a consequence of their form alone suggests that statements can be studied in the framework of an abstract theory.

We shall denote statements by letters p, q, r, ..., and use the following symbols for the connectives:

$$\vee \qquad \text{for} \quad \textit{or,}$$
$$\wedge \qquad \text{for} \quad \textit{and,}$$
$$\neg \qquad \text{for} \quad \textit{not,}$$
$$\rightarrow \qquad \text{for} \quad \textit{if–then,}$$
$$\leftrightarrow \qquad \text{for} \quad \textit{if and only if.}$$

With this symbolism we can write statement r as $s \wedge t$, statement u as $\neg q$, statement v as $q \vee \neg q$ and statement w as $q \leftrightarrow \neg q$. We shall indicate the truth or falsity of a statement by assigning a *truth value* to it: T if the statement is true, F if it is false.

Ordinary (natural) language is ambiguous. Consider the phrase *visitors or guests*. Here the *or* may indicate *guest* as a synonym of *visitor*; i.e., *visitors or guests* may refer to just the one class of people. Under a different interpretation visitors and guests may be considered to belong to disjoint classes. Then *or* has the *exclusive* meaning. Under yet another interpretation a visitor may, but need not, be a guest, and *or* has the *inclusive* meaning. Usually the context enables one to decide which meaning is intended. But a process of abstraction isolates statements from context. Hence there is no way of determining the intended meaning of *or* in the statement $p \vee q$ of the abstract theory unless the connective is precisely defined. In Table 2.13 we define connectives by giving the truth value of the composite statement resulting from prime statements p and q for all assignments of truth values to p and q.

If every F in Table 2.13 is replaced by 0 and every T by 1, the table becomes familiar. Then the columns for $\neg p$, $p \vee q$, $p \wedge q$ represent binary valuations of

TABLE 2.13

DEFINITIONS OF CONNECTIVES

$\langle p,q \rangle$	$\neg p$	$p \vee q$	$p \wedge q$	$p \rightarrow q$	$p \leftrightarrow q$
$\langle F, F \rangle$	T	F	F	T	T
$\langle F, T \rangle$	T	T	F	T	F
$\langle T, F \rangle$	F	T	F	F	F
$\langle T, T \rangle$	F	T	T	T	T

Boolean forms p', $p \oplus q$, $p * q$, respectively. Hence the system $\langle \{F, T\}, \vee,$ $\wedge, \neg, F, T \rangle$ is a Boolean algebra. It is called the *algebra of truth values*. Just as a switch may be open or closed, a statement may be false or true, and just as a switching circuit may be open or closed depending on the states of the switches, a composite statement may be false or true depending on the assignment of truth values to its prime statements. In analogy with switching theory we denote the prime statements of a composite statement by variables $p_1, p_2, \ldots, p_n$, and associate the composite statement with a function $f(p_1, p_2, \ldots, p_n)$ of these variables, $f: \{F, T\}^n \rightarrow \{F, T\}$.

Clearly, the set of operations $\{\vee, \wedge, \neg\}$ is functionally complete on $\{F, T\}^n$. Although $\{\vee, \neg\}$ and $\{\wedge, \neg\}$ are also functionally complete (see Example 2 of D.2.11), by tradition the set of connectives $\{\vee, \wedge, \neg\}$ is considered basic to the theory, and its members are called *primary connectives*. Connectives $\rightarrow$ and $\leftrightarrow$ are called *secondary connectives*. Functional equality (in the sense of D.2.7) of $p \rightarrow q$ and $\neg p \vee q$ is demonstrated in Table 2.14. The table shows also that $p \leftrightarrow q$ is equivalent to $(p \rightarrow q) \wedge (q \rightarrow p)$, i.e., to $(\neg p \vee q) \wedge (\neg q \vee p)$. (A valuation table, such as Table 2.14, has a special name in the statement calculus; it is called *truth table*.)

We can show also that $p \rightarrow q$ is functionally equal to $p \vee q \leftrightarrow q$ (Exercise 2.32). Comparing this result with D.1.14 we see that the $p \rightarrow q$ of our model represents $p \leqq q$ of the abstract Boolean algebra $\langle B, \oplus, *, ', 0, 1 \rangle$. Note further that the statement $(p \rightarrow q) \leftrightarrow (p \vee q \leftrightarrow q)$ is true for every value

TABLE 2.14

FUNCTIONAL EQUALITIES

$\langle p,q \rangle$	$\neg p$	$\neg p \vee q$	$(p \rightarrow q) \wedge (q \rightarrow p)$		
$\langle F, F \rangle$	T	T	T	T	T
$\langle F, T \rangle$	T	T	T	F	F
$\langle T, F \rangle$	F	F	F	F	T
$\langle T, T \rangle$	F	T	T	T	T

assignment $\langle p, q \rangle$. Statements that are true for all value assignments are called *tautologies*. The symbol $\leftrightarrow$ has special significance in the context of a biconditional tautology. In the *tautology* $p \leftrightarrow q$ it symbolizes equivalence of formulas p and q. In the model $\langle \{F, T\}, \vee, \wedge, \neg, F, T \rangle$ it replaces the symbol $=$ of the general Boolean algebra of Section 1e.

Examples

1. Statement *If* $3 < 5$ *and* $4 < 5$ *then* $4 < 3$ *or* $3 < 5$ has the form *if p and q then r or p*, i.e., $(p \wedge q) \rightarrow (r \vee p)$. This form represents a function on $\{F, T\}^3$ into $\{F, T\}$. Table 2.15 is the truth table of this function. It shows that the statement $(p \wedge q) \rightarrow (r \vee p)$ is a tautology. Some readers may find the definition of the conditional of Table 2.13 hard to accept. Somehow it seems wrong that a conditional having a false antecedent and a true consequent should be true. The definition may be easier to accept if we rephrase *if p then q* to *p is a sufficient condition for q*. Then we see that a false antecedent is immaterial to the truth of $p \rightarrow q$ and that $p \rightarrow q$ can only be false if a false consequent results when a sufficient condition is satisfied, i.e., when the antecedent is true.

TABLE 2.15

A Tautology

$\langle p, q, r \rangle$	$(p \wedge q) \rightarrow (r \vee p)$		
$\langle F, F, F \rangle$	F	T	F
$\langle F, F, T \rangle$	F	T	T
$\langle F, T, F \rangle$	F	T	F
$\langle F, T, T \rangle$	F	T	T
$\langle T, F, F \rangle$	F	T	T
$\langle T, F, T \rangle$	F	T	T
$\langle T, T, F \rangle$	T	T	T
$\langle T, T, T \rangle$	T	T	T

2. Table 2.16 shows that the statement $((p \rightarrow q) \wedge (q \rightarrow r)) \rightarrow (p \rightarrow r)$ is a tautology. This tautology, known as the *law of syllogism*, is very important in logic. (The statement calculus is part of *symbolic logic*.)

Most higher level programming languages, such as Fortran and Algol, provide facilities for representation and evaluation of logical expressions. In Fortran operations .OR., .AND., .NOT. represent, respectively, $\vee$, $\wedge$, and $\neg$. Truth values, or logical constants, T and F are written .TRUE. and .FALSE.. Secondary connectives are not provided (Algol does provide them). For example, $p \rightarrow p \vee q$ has to be reformulated to $\neg p \vee (p \vee q)$ before it can be written as a Fortran expression, namely .NOT.P.OR.(P.OR.Q).

TABLE 2.16

The Law of Syllogism

$\langle p, q, r \rangle$	$((p \to q) \land (q \to r)) \to (p \to r)$				
$\langle F, F, F \rangle$	T	T	T	T	T
$\langle F, F, T \rangle$	T	T	T	T	T
$\langle F, T, F \rangle$	T	F	F	T·	T
$\langle F, T, T \rangle$	T	T	T	T	T
$\langle T, F, F \rangle$	F	F	T	T	F
$\langle T, F, T \rangle$	F	F	T	T	T
$\langle T, T, F \rangle$	T	F	F	T	F
$\langle T, T, T \rangle$	T	T	T	T	T

ALGORITHM 2.2 This is an algorithm, expressed as a Fortran function, for testing whether a given statement is a tautology. Logical function TAUT returns the value .TRUE. if the statement specified by the function FORM is a tautology and .FALSE. if it is not. Subroutine NEXT must be provided. Given an *n*-sample of {.FALSE., .TRUE.} in array SAMPLE, NEXT generates in SAMPLE the next *n*-sample (in lexicographic order, say). This subroutine would be very similar to that of A.1.2.

```
      LOGICAL FUNCTION TAUT (FORM, SAMPLE, N)
      LOGICAL SAMPLE(N), FORM
      DO 1 K = 1,N
   1  SAMPLE(K) = .FALSE.
      NN = 2**N
      TAUT = .FALSE.
      DO 2 K = 1,NN
      IF (.NOT.FORM(SAMPLE,N)) RETURN
   2  CALL NEXT (SAMPLE,N)
      TAUT = .TRUE.
      RETURN
      END
```

Example

Let us test whether $(p \to q) \to ((q \to r) \to (p \to r))$ is a tautology. We rewrite the statement as $\neg(\neg p \lor q) \lor (\neg(\neg q \lor r) \lor (\neg p \lor r))$, which can be simplified to $(p \land \neg q) \lor (q \land \neg r) \lor (\neg p \lor r)$ by means of the theorems of Section 1e. (The advisability of making the simplification is debatable. It may be argued that it defeats the purpose of mechanization.) Function FORM is now written as follows:

```
LOGICAL FUNCTION FORM (S, N)
LOGICAL S(N)
FORM = (S(1).AND..NOT.S(2)).OR.(S(2).AND..NOT.
X        S(3)).OR.(.NOT.S(1).OR.S(3))
RETURN
END
```

Symbolic logic reduces the determination of the validity of an argument to a mechanical procedure, which may employ the following laws.

Law of detachment: If p does imply q, and if p is true, then q is true.

Law of substitution: If $p \leftrightarrow q$, then the substitution of p for q, or of q for p, in an argument does not affect the validity of the argument.

Law of excluded middle: $p \wedge \neg p$ is always false, i.e., a statement may not be simultaneously true and false.

Law of syllogism: $((p \rightarrow q) \wedge (q \rightarrow r)) \rightarrow (p \rightarrow r)$ is a tautology.

From the conditional $p \rightarrow q$ we can construct *derived conditionals* by negating or interchanging statements p and q in various combinations. The more important of the derived conditionals are the *converse* $(q \rightarrow p)$, the *inverse* $(\neg p \rightarrow \neg q)$, and the *contrapositive* $(\neg q \rightarrow \neg p)$. It can be shown that $(\neg q \rightarrow \neg p) \leftrightarrow (p \rightarrow q)$ (Exercise 2.33).

An argument is expressed as follows: Given that statements $p_1, p_2, \ldots, p_n$ are true, statement p_{n+1} is also true. Statements $p_1, \ldots, p_n$ are called *premises* and statement p_{n+1} *conclusion* of the argument. The proof of the validity of an argument consists in showing that the truth of the conclusion does in fact derive from the premises by the laws of logic. In what follows we shall abbreviate the phrase *p is true* to *p*; i.e., we shall assume that the act of writing down p is in itself an assertion of the truth of p.

Examples

1. Given that p, $p \rightarrow q$, and $\neg r \rightarrow \neg q$, prove r. The forms $\neg r \rightarrow \neg q$, $\neg(\neg q) \rightarrow \neg(\neg r)$ (its contrapositive), and $q \rightarrow r$ (the contrapositive simplified) are equivalent. Hence the argument may be rewritten as p, $p \rightarrow q$, $q \rightarrow r$, r (by the law of substitution). Since $p \rightarrow q$ and $q \rightarrow r$, then also $p \rightarrow r$ (by the laws of detachment and syllogism). But if p and $p \rightarrow r$, then r (by the law of detachment). The following statements provide a specific example of the general argument.

Premises: Prices are high.
               If prices are high, one should sell stocks.
               If productivity is not low, one should not sell stocks.
Conclusion: Productivity is low.

2. In Example 1 a *direct proof* is employed. In a direct proof one derives the conclusion from the premises. Now we shall set up an *indirect proof* (also called *proof by contradiction*, or *reductio ad absurdum proof*) in which the premises and the *negation* of the conclusion are assumed, and an attempt is made to derive a contradiction $p \wedge \neg p$ in which p is any statement. If a contradiction can be derived, one of the assumed statements must be false. Since the premises are true, the false statement is the negated conclusion. Hence the conclusion is true. Consider the following argument.

Premises: There is unemployment, or productivity is high.
                    Prices are high if and only if there is an inflation.
                    If there is an inflation, there is no unemployment.
                    If prices are low, productivity is high.
Conclusion: Productivity is high.

We write the proof as a column of statements. The first five statements are the four premises and the negation of the conclusion. We interpret *low* as *not high*.

(1)	$u \vee p$	
(2)	$h \leftrightarrow i$	
(3)	$i \to \neg u$	
(4)	$\neg h \to p$	
(5)	$\neg p$	
(6)	$\neg p \to h$	(contrapositive of 4)
(7)	h	(from 5 and 6, law of detachment)
(8)	i	(from 7 and 2, substitution)
(9)	$\neg u$	(from 8 and 3, detachment)
(10)	p	(from 1 and 9, see Exercise 2.33)
(11)	$\neg p \wedge p$	(from 5 and 10)

Let $p_1, \ldots, p_n, p_{n+1}$ be an argument in which $p_1, \ldots, p_n$ are premises and p_{n+1} is the conclusion. The argument is valid if $(p_1 \wedge \cdots \wedge p_n) \to p_{n+1}$ is a tautology. This observation provides an alternative method for proving the validity of an argument. The proof is an examination of the Boolean function $f: B^{n+1} \to B$, where $B = \{F, T\}$, corresponding to the form $(p_1 \wedge \cdots \wedge p_n) \to p_{n+1}$. The argument is valid if the range of f is $\{T\}$.

Example

The forms corresponding to the arguments in Examples 1 and 2 above are

$$(p \wedge (p \to q) \wedge (\neg r \to \neg q)) \to r,$$
$$((u \vee p) \wedge (h \leftrightarrow i) \wedge (i \to \neg u) \wedge (\neg h \to p)) \to p.$$

2d. Relations

Correspondences between elements of sets A and B are defined by subsets of the set of ordered pairs $A \times B$. Correspondences may be one–one, many–one, one–many, and many–many. Only one–one and many–one correspondences have distinct first coordinates; they alone are functions from A into B. By a subterfuge we may also represent one–many correspondences by functions. While the subsets of $A \times B$ that define such correspondences are not functions, interchange of coordinates produces sets of ordered pairs in which first coordinates are all distinct. These sets are therefore functions from B into A. In Example 1 of D.2.1 we had the nonfunction $\{\langle 4, \mathit{five} \rangle, \langle 4, \mathit{aces} \rangle \langle 5, \mathit{spell} \rangle, \langle 7, \mathit{tragedy} \rangle\}$. The set $\{\langle \mathit{five}, 4 \rangle, \langle \mathit{aces}, 4 \rangle, \langle \mathit{spell}, 5 \rangle, \langle \mathit{tragedy}, 7 \rangle\}$, however, is a function. This expedient clearly does not work for many–many correspondences. Therefore, we need a theory more general than that of functions.

Let us assume that the four children of some family are called Thomas, Mary, Richard, and Henry. Abbreviating their names to initials, we have the set $C = \{T, M, R, H\}$. Consider now a subset of $C \times C$, the set of ordered pairs $\{\langle T, M \rangle, \langle T, R \rangle, \langle T, H \rangle, \langle R, T \rangle, \langle R, M \rangle, \langle R, H \rangle, \langle H, T \rangle, \langle H, M \rangle, \langle H, R \rangle\}$. The correspondence defined by this set is expressed by the formula *x is the brother of y*. Here x and y are variables, and *is the brother of* is a relation. If, on substituting constants for the variables, the formula becomes a true statement, the ordered pair of the constants belongs to the relation. Order is important: *T is the brother of M* is true, but *M is the brother of T* is not. Consequently $\langle T, M \rangle$ is a member of the relation, but not $\langle M, T \rangle$. All members of the set of ordered pairs given above belong to the relation *is the brother of*, and no other member of $C \times C$ belongs to this relation. The relation with formula *x and y are brothers* is the set $\{\langle T, R \rangle, \langle T, H \rangle, \langle R, T \rangle, \langle R, H \rangle, \langle H, T \rangle, \langle H, R \rangle\}$.

DEFINITION 2.12   A *binary relation* from set A to set B is a subset of $A \times B$. If R is a relation, we write $\langle x, y \rangle \in R$ and xRy interchangeably. If $\langle x, y \rangle \in R$, we say that x is *R-related* to y. (If $\langle x, y \rangle \notin R$, we may write $x\cancel{R}y$.)

Examples

1. Let $A = \{a, b, c\}$, and let $C_n(A)$ be the set of n-combinations and $P_n(A)$ the set of n-permutations of A. Let R_n be a relation from C_n to P_n such that $qR_n s$ if and only if the n elements of A in s are the same as in q. Here $C_2 = \{(ab), (ac), (bc)\}$ and $C_3 = \{(abc)\}$. Relation R_2 is $\{\langle (ab), ab \rangle, \langle (ab), ba \rangle, \langle (ac), ac \rangle, \langle (ac), ca \rangle, \langle (bc), bc \rangle, \langle (bc), cb \rangle\}$. All six members of R_3 have the same first coordinate. Some of them are $\langle (abc), abc \rangle, \langle (abc), bac \rangle, \langle (abc), cab \rangle$. Note that $R_3 = C_3 \times P_3$, but that $R_2 \subset C_2 \times P_2$ $(\langle (ab), ca \rangle \notin R_2)$.

2. Every function is, of course, a relation. Recall our note following Th.1.9 to the effect that $'$ does not have to be introduced in Boolean algebra B as a function. It is sufficient to introduce it more generally as a relation; the fact that it is also a function is derived in the theory as Th.1.9.

3. Let I be the set of integers. The formula $a < b$, where variables a and b stand for members of I and $<$ has the conventional meaning, defines a binary relation from I to I. Thus $2 < 5$ or $\langle 2, 5 \rangle \in <$, but $\langle 5, 2 \rangle \notin <$. We can, however, have a relation $\nless$ as well: then $\langle 5, 2 \rangle \in \nless$, and $\langle 2, 5 \rangle \notin \nless$.

DEFINITION 2.13   A subset of $A \times A$ is a binary relation *in* the set A. In particular, the set $A \times A$ is the *universal* relation in A.

Examples

1. Any relation in a set is a subset of the universal relation in this set. The relations $<$ and $\nless$ of Example 3 of D.2.12 are relations *in* I. Their union, $< \cup \nless$, is the universal relation in I, and $< \cap \nless = \varnothing$.

2. The set of 2-samples $S_2(A)$ is a universal relation in A.

3. Let R be the set of real numbers. The square root relation can be defined by $\{\langle x^{1/2}, x \rangle \mid x \in R\}$ or by $\{\langle x, x^{1/2} \rangle \mid x \in R\}$. Both sets are relations in R. Only one of the sets is a function (cf. Example 2 of D.2.1).

4. We shall see that the theory of relations is almost exclusively concerned with relations in a set. This has led some writers to define relations in a set as the only relations. Since $A \times B$ is a subset of $(A \cup B) \times (A \cup B)$, a relation from A to B is also a relation in $A \cup B$; i.e., every relation is in fact a relation in some set. The alternative definition is, therefore, not unduly restrictive.

DEFINITION 2.14   Let R be a relation and let A be a set. Then

$$R[A] = \{ y \mid \text{for some } x \text{ in } A, \, xRy \}$$

is called the set of *R-relatives* of the elements of A.

Examples

1. For relation R_2 of Example 1 of D.2.12, $R_2[\{(ab)\}] = \{ab, ba\}$ and $R_2[C_2(A)] = \{ab, ba, ac, ca, bc, cb\}$. $R_2[C_3(A)] = \varnothing$.

2. Let U be a universal relation in a set A. Then $U[A] = A$.

3. Let $I_n = \{1, 2, \ldots, n\}$. For relation $>$ in I_{100}, $>[I_1] = \varnothing$ and $>[I_n] = I_{n-1}$ $(n = 2, \ldots, 100)$.

DEFINITION 2.15   The *domain* D_ρ and *range* R_ρ of a relation ρ are defined as follows:

$$D_\rho = \{x \mid \text{for some } y, \, \langle x, y \rangle \in \rho\},$$
$$R_\rho = \{y \mid \text{for some } x, \, \langle x, y \rangle \in \rho\}.$$

Examples

1. The domain of a relation is the set of all first coordinates and the range is the set of all second coordinates of the relation. Let ρ be a relation. Then $\rho[D_\rho] = R_\rho$ and, for any set A, $\rho[A] \subseteq R_\rho$.

2. $D_{A \times B} = A$ provided $B \neq \emptyset$, and $R_{A \times B} = B$ provided $A \neq \emptyset$. If $B = \emptyset$ or $A = \emptyset$, then $A \times B = \emptyset$. Clearly a null relation cannot have a nonnull domain or range.

3. Consider the set $C = \{T, M, R, H\}$ defined at the beginning of this section. The domain of the relation x *is the brother of* y in C is $\{T, R, H\}$. The range is $\{T, M, R, H\}$. The relation x *and* y *are brothers* has the same domain, but the range contracts to $\{T, R, H\}$, i.e., the relation has the same set for its domain and range.

DEFINITION 2.16   If R is a relation, the *converse* (*reversed*) *relation* of R, written R^{-1}, is a relation such that $yR^{-1}x$ if and only if xRy.

Examples

1. Let R be the relation $\{\langle n^{1/2}, n \rangle \mid n \in I\}$ in the set of integers. The converse R^{-1} is the relation $\{\langle n, n^{1/2} \rangle \mid n \in I\}$.

2. The converse of relation R_2 of Example 1 of D.2.12 is $\{\langle ab, (ab) \rangle, \langle ba, (ab) \rangle, \langle ac, (ac) \rangle, \langle ca, (ac) \rangle, \langle bc, (bc) \rangle, \langle cb, (bc) \rangle\}$.

3. The set $\{x \mid$ for some y in set B, $x\rho y\}$ is the set of ρ^{-1}-relatives of B. Thus, $\rho^{-1}[R_\rho] = D_\rho$, and $\rho^{-1}[\{b\}]$ is the set of first coordinates of all ordered pairs belonging to ρ that have b as the second coordinate; e.g., for R_2 of Example 1 of D.2.12, $R_2^{-1}[\{(ac)\}] = \{ac, ca\}$.

4. The relation x *and* y *are brothers* is its own converse.

DEFINITION 2.17   A relation R in a set A is

   (i)   *reflexive* if xRx for all $x \in A$;
  (ii)   *irreflexive* if xRx for no $x \in A$;
 (iii)   *symmetric* if xRy implies yRx for all $x, y \in A$;
  (iv)   *antisymmetric* if xRy and yRx imply $x = y$ for all $x, y \in A$;
   (v)   *transitive* if xRy and yRz imply xRz for all $x, y, z \in A$.

Examples

1. The relation x *is the brother of* y in a set of males is irreflexive (no one is his own brother) and symmetric. At first sight the relation appears to be transitive: *Henry is the brother of Thomas* and *Thomas is the brother of Richard* do imply *Henry is the brother of Richard*. But *Henry is the brother of Thomas* implies *Thomas is the brother of Henry*, and, if the relation were transitive, the unacceptable *Henry is the brother of Henry* would be implied.

2. Let R be the relation *course a is a prerequisite for course b* in the set of courses offered by a university. Relation R is irreflexive and transitive. It is not symmetric.

3. The relation $\leq$ in a set of numbers is reflexive, antisymmetric, and transitive. The relation $<$ is irreflexive, antisymmetric, and transitive.

If a proper substitution is made in the ordered pair $\langle\langle$ *father, mother* $\rangle$, *their child* $\rangle$ for the variables, the resulting ordered pair is a member of the parenthood relation. Since here the ordered pair can be considered also an ordered triple, the parenthood relation may be called a *ternary relation*. Generalizing, a binary relation from a set of $(n - 1)$-tuples to a set of simple elements can be considered a set of n-tuples. It may be called, therefore, an *n-ary relation*. This is simply a matter of terminology: An n-ary relation is not a new concept; it is still essentially a set of ordered pairs of ordered $(n - 1)$-tuples and simple elements.

2e. The Equivalence Relation

DEFINITION 2.18   A relation in a set is an *equivalence relation* if it is reflexive, symmetric, and transitive.

Examples

1. Equality in a set of numbers is an equivalence relation. In the set of integers the relation $=$ is an identity relation, and this relation is a rather trivial equivalence relation (it makes little sense to speak of symmetry and transitivity when $x = y$ if and only if x and y are identical; in fact the relation $=$ is both symmetric and antisymmetric in a trivial sense here). In the set of rational numbers we can have, for example, $2/3 = 4/6$ and $4/6 = 200/300$. Therefore, equality in the set of rational numbers is a nontrivial equivalence relation. Equality of moduli in a set of complex numbers is another non-trivial equivalence relation: $\langle 2 + 5i, 5 + 2i \rangle$ belongs to the relation.

2. Let $\langle B, \oplus, *, ', 0, 1 \rangle$ be a Boolean algebra. The relation $=$ in the set of forms in variables standing for elements of B, the distinct elements 0 and 1, and the operations $\oplus$, $*$, and $'$ is an equivalence relation.

3. The relation $\leftrightarrow$ in a set of statements (prime or composite) is an equivalence relation. Note that the symbol $\leftrightarrow$ has two interpretations in the statement calculus: $p \leftrightarrow q$ can denote a statement, which may be false for certain truth values of p and q, or it can represent a biconditional tautology. We have the second interpretation in mind when we speak of the *relation* $\leftrightarrow$. (The tautology $p \leftrightarrow q$ is sometimes denoted $\vdash p \leftrightarrow q$.) ·

4. The relation *x has the same image as y* in the domain of a many–one function is an equivalence relation. The domain of the function is both domain and range of the relation. It is clear that the domain of any equivalence relation is the set in which the relation is defined. One can therefore speak of an equivalence relation *on* a set. The equivalence relation *x has the same image as y* is on the domain of a function.

DEFINITION 2.19   Let *R* be an equivalence relation on a set *A*. Consider an element *a* of *A*. The set of *R*-relatives of *a* in *A*, $R[\{a\}]$, is called the *R-equivalence class generated* by *a*. Where there is no danger of confusion, the symbol $R[\{a\}]$ can be abbreviated to $[a]$.

THEOREM 2.9   Let *R* be an equivalence relation on *A* and let $a, b \in A$. Then

    (i) $a \in [a]$,
    (ii) if aRb, then $[a] = [b]$.

Proof. The first part is a direct consequence of reflexivity of an equivalence relation. To prove the second part, assume aRb and let *x* be any element such that $x \in [b]$. Then bRx, and, by transitivity, aRx. Hence $x \in [b]$ implies $x \in [a]$, i.e., $[b] \subseteq [a]$. By symmetry, bRa. A similar argument gives $[a] \subseteq [b]$.

Part (i) of Th.2.9 implies that every element of a set on which an equivalence relation *R* is defined belongs to some *R*-equivalence class, i.e., that the union of all *R*-equivalence classes generated by elements of this set is the set itself. Part (ii) means that any element of an equivalence class can be used to represent the equivalence class. Looking at the examples of D.2.18 in the light of these results one begins to suspect that the *R*-equivalence classes constitute a partition of the set on which *R* is defined. In our next theorem we turn suspicion into fact.

THEOREM 2.10   Let *X* be the set of equivalence relations on a set *A* and *Y* the set of partitions of *A*. Let ρ be any member of *X*. There exists a one-to-one onto function $f: X \to Y$ such that $f(\rho)$ is the set of ρ-equivalence classes generated by elements of *A*.

Proof. The proof can be broken down into four parts.

(i) The set of ρ-equivalence classes is a partition of *A*. Part (i) of Th.2.9 implies that the union of the ρ-equivalence classes is *A*. Let $a, b \in A$. These elements generate $[a]$ and $[b]$. Now let $x \in [a]$ and $x \in [b]$. By part (ii) of Th.2.9 we have $[x] = [a]$ and $[x] = [b]$. Hence $[a] = [b]$, i.e., equivalence classes generated by members of *A* are either disjoint or equal.

(ii) The set of ρ-equivalence classes is unique, i.e., *f* exists. Assume that ρ defines two different partitions. Then there exists some $a \in A$ such that the equivalence classes generated by *a* are different in the two partitions. This, in turn, means that there exists some element *b* that belongs to one of the classes but not to the other, i.e., $\langle a, b \rangle \in \rho$ and $\langle a, b \rangle \notin \rho$. This is a contradiction.

(iii) Function *f* is one to one. Let ρ_1 and ρ_2 be equivalence relations on *A*. By D.2.4, function *f* is one to one if and only if $\rho_1 \neq \rho_2$ implies $f(\rho_1) \neq f(\rho_2)$. Assume $\rho_1 \neq \rho_2$. Then we may assume that there exist elements *a* and *b* such that $\langle a, b \rangle$ belongs to one of the relations but not to the other. Let the equivalence classes generated by *a* be denoted by $[a]_1$ in $f(\rho_1)$ and by $[a]_2$ in $f(\rho_2)$. Then $b \in [a]_1$ and $b \notin [a]_2$, or $b \notin [a]_1$ and $b \in [a]_2$. In either case $[a_1] \neq [a]_2$. But $[a]_1$ and $[a]_2$ are the only sets in the respective partitions containing element *a*. Hence $f(\rho_1) \neq f(\rho_2)$.

(iv) Function *f* is onto. Consider any partition $\mathscr{A} = \{A_1, A_2, \ldots, A_n\}$ of *A* and a relation α such that $\langle a, b \rangle \in \alpha$ if and only if both *a* and *b* belong to one and the same A_i for some $i \in \{1, 2, \ldots, n\}$. If α is an equivalence relation, then members of $\mathscr{A}$ are the α-equivalence classes, and—since $\mathscr{A}$ is any partition—*f* is onto. We show that α is an equivalence relation. Let $a \in A$. Since $\mathscr{A}$ is a partition, $a \in A_i$ for some $i \in \{1, 2, \ldots, n\}$ and $a \notin A_j$ when $j \neq i$. Hence $\langle a, a \rangle \in \alpha$; i.e., α is reflexive. Relation α is symmetric: If $\langle a, b \rangle \in \alpha$, then $a, b \in A_i$ for some *i*; hence $\langle b, a \rangle \in \alpha$. If $\langle a, b \rangle \in \alpha$ and $\langle b, c \rangle \in \alpha$, then $a, b \in A_i$ and $b, c \in A_j$ for some *i* and *j*. But if $b \in A_i$, then $b \in A_j$ only if $i = j$. Hence $a, c \in A_i$, giving $\langle a, c \rangle \in \alpha$; i.e., the relation is transitive.

Examples

1. It is easy to make errors in defining the equivalence relation that corresponds to a given partition. A population of males can be partitioned into sets of brothers. The relation of brotherhood, however, is not reflexive. Hence it is not an equivalence relation. The relation that corresponds to this partition might be formulated as *x is y or the brother of y* or as *x has the same parents as y*. The set $\{1, 2, \ldots, 100\}$ can be partitioned as $\{\{1, 100\}, \{2, 99\}, \ldots, \{50, 51\}\}$. The relation $101 - a = b$ has nothing to do with the partition.

2. Let *a*, *b*, *m* be integers $(m \neq 0)$. The relation *congruence modulo m* in the set of integers is defined as follows: *a* is congruent to *b*, modulo *m*, if and only if $a - b$ is divisible by *m*. We write $a = b(\bmod m)$, e.g., $15 = 5(\bmod 5)$, but $15 \neq 5(\bmod 4)$. Congruence modulo *m* is an equivalence relation with the number of equivalence classes in the partition defined by this relation being equal to *m*. Thus, when $m = 4$, the set of all integers is partitioned into the four equivalence classes $[0] = \{\ldots, -4, 0, 4, 8, \ldots\}, [1] = \{\ldots, -3, 1, 5, \ldots\}, [2] = \{\ldots, -2, 2, 6, \ldots\}, [3] = \{\ldots, -1, 3, 7, \ldots\}$.

2f. Ordering Relations

DEFINITION 2.20   A reflexive, antisymmetric, and transitive relation in a set is a *partial order relation* or a *partial ordering* in that set. If R is a partial ordering in A, the ordered pair $\langle A, R \rangle$ is a *partially ordered set.*

Examples

1. The relation *less than or equal*, symbolized $\leq$, in any subset of the set of real numbers is a partial ordering. The relation *less than* is irreflexive, and, hence, not a partial ordering.
2. The subset relation in a collection of sets is a partial ordering, but the proper subset relation is not.
3. The relations *is an integral multiple of* and *divides* in the natural numbers are partial orderings. Note that the relations are converses of each other. Generalizing, if a relation is a partial ordering, then so is its converse (Exercise 2.60).
4. Let R and R^* denote the relation *divides* in the set of natural numbers and in the set $\{3, 5, 15\}$, respectively. Then $R^* = \{\langle 3, 3 \rangle, \langle 3, 15 \rangle, \langle 5, 5 \rangle, \langle 5, 15 \rangle, \langle 15,15 \rangle\}$. This is a partial ordering. Now let $A = \{5, 15\}$ and $B = \{3, 30\}$. Then $R^* \cap (A \times A) = \{\langle 5, 5 \rangle, \langle 5, 15 \rangle, \langle 15, 15 \rangle\}$, a partial ordering in A. But $R^* \cap (B \times B)$ is not a partial ordering in B; since $\langle 30, 30 \rangle \notin R^* \cap (B \times B)$, the relation is not reflexive. Relation $R \cap (B \times B)$, however, is a partial ordering. If A and B are any sets, and R is a partial ordering in A, we say that R *partially orders* B if and only if $R \cap (B \times B)$ is a partial ordering in B. In particular, R partially orders B if $B \subseteq A$.

It is customary to use the symbols $\leq$ and $\geq$ for the designation of partial order relations. Although the symbols derive from the natural ordering of numbers, here they need not have anything to do with the comparison of numerical values. Thus, one may denote the partial ordering *is an integral multiple of* by $\leq$. We have then, for example, $\langle 30, 5 \rangle \in \leq$ or $30 \leq 5$. (It would be more suggestive, however, to use the symbol $\geq$ here.)

DEFINITION 2.21   Define relation $<$ in a set A as follows: For $a, b \in A$, $a < b$ if and only if $a \leq b$ and $a \neq b$. If $a < b$ we say that a *precedes* (is *less than*) b, or that b *follows* (is *greater than*) a.

Example

Consider the set R^* of Example 4 of D.2.20. It is a partial ordering, which we denote by $\leq$. Here relation $<$ is $\{\langle 3, 15 \rangle, \langle 5, 15 \rangle\}$. The set $R^* - <$ is the identity relation $\{\langle 3, 3 \rangle, \langle 5, 5 \rangle, \langle 15, 15 \rangle\}$.

DEFINITION 2.22   A partial order relation $\leq$ in a set A is a *simple* (or *linear*) *ordering* if and only if $a \leq b$ or $b \leq a$ for all $a, b \in A$. If $\leq$ is a simple ordering in A, the ordered pair $\langle A, \leq \rangle$ is a *simply ordered set* or *chain*. (If, for some $a, b \in A$, neither $a \leq b$ nor $b \leq a$, then a and b are said to be *incomparable*.)

Examples

1. The partial ordering *less than or equal* in the set of natural numbers $\{1, 2, 3, \ldots\}$ is a simple ordering. For any two numbers in the set, one is less than or equal to the other.

2. Consider $A = \{1, 2, 3, 5, 6, 10, 15, 30\}$, the set of numbers that divide 30. Set A is partially ordered by relation *less than or equal*, which we denote by $\leq$, or by the relation *divides*, denoted by $\leq'$. Then $\langle A, \leq \rangle$ and $(A, \leq')$ are different partially ordered sets. Only $\langle A, \leq \rangle$ is a chain.

3. The subset relation in any family of sets is a partial ordering. Only rarely is it a simple ordering. Let $A = \{1, 2, 3\}$. Then $\mathscr{P}(A) = \{\varnothing, \{1\}, \{2\}, \{3\}, \{1, 2\}, \{1, 3\}, \{2, 3\}, A\}$. The pair $\langle \mathscr{P}(A), \subseteq \rangle$ is not a simply ordered set: Since, for example, $\{1, 2\} \nsubseteq \{2, 3\}$ and $\{2, 3\} \nsubseteq \{1, 2\}$, sets $\{1, 2\}$ and $\{2, 3\}$ are incomparable. The pair $\langle \mathscr{A}, \subseteq \rangle$, where $\mathscr{A} = \{\varnothing, \{1\}, \{1, 3\}, A\}$, is a simply ordered set.

DEFINITION 2.23   Let ρ be a simple ordering in a set A.

We define a *lexicographic ordering* ρ' in set B, where B is A^n or $\bigcup_n A^n (n = 1, 2, 3, \ldots)$. Let $\langle a_1, \ldots, a_p \rangle$, $\langle b_1, \ldots, b_q \rangle \in B$ and assume $p \leq q$. Then $\langle a_1, \ldots, a_p \rangle \rho' \langle b_1, \ldots, b_q \rangle$ if one of the following holds:

(i) $\langle a_1, \ldots, a_p \rangle = \langle b_1, \ldots, b_p \rangle$;

(ii) $a_1 \neq b_1$ and $a_1 \rho b_1$ in A;

(iii) $a_i = b_i$, $i = 1, \ 2, \ldots, \ k$ $(k < p)$;   and $a_{k+1} \neq b_{k+1}$ and $a_{k+1} \rho b_{k+1}$ in A.

Otherwise $\langle b_1, \ldots, b_q \rangle \rho' \langle a_1, \ldots, a_p \rangle$.

Examples

1. Let $A = \{0, 1, \ldots, 9\}$ and $B = A^5$. Then, for example, using our abbreviated notation for samples, $12304, 00012, 12302 \in B$. Let ρ be the relation $\leq$ (less than or equal) in A. By Condition (i), $12304 \rho' 12304$. Consider 12304 and 00012. Since the first digits differ, and $0 \leq 1$, we have $00012 \rho' 12304$. Similarly, also by Condition (ii), $00012 \rho' 12302$. With 12304 and 12302, since the first four digits agree, and the fifth digits are different, we consider Condition (iii). Since $2 \leq 4$, $12302 \rho' 12304$. A natural interpretation of the samples is to consider them as numbers. The relation ρ' is then the numerical relation *less than or equal*.

2. Let $A = \{a, b, c, \ldots, z\}$ and $B = \bigcup_{i=1}^{i=6} A^i$; B is the set of all "words" of six letters or less on the alphabet A. We let ρ be a relation $\leq$ in A such that

$a \leq b \leq c \leq \cdots \leq z$. By Condition (i), *tableρ'tablet*. By Condition (ii) *sableρ'table* and *sableρ'tablet*. By Condition (iii), *tabletρ'taboo*. Relation ρ' defines the normal alphabetic order of words.

DEFINITION 2.24   A *least* member of a set A relative to a partial ordering $\leq$ in A is an element $b \in A$ such that, for all $a \in A$, $b \leq a$. Similarly, a *greatest* member of A relative to $\leq$ is a $b \in A$ such that, for all $a \in A$, $a \leq b$.

Examples

1. The least and greatest members of the set B of Example 1 of D.2.23 are 00000 and 99999, respectively. For set B of Example 2 of D.2.23 they are, respectively, a and $zzzzzz$.
   2. Consider the family of sets $\mathscr{A} = \{\{1\}, \{2\}, \{3\}, \{1, 2\}, \{1, 3\}, \{2, 3\}\}$. Relative to partial ordering $\subseteq$ in $\mathscr{A}$ there is neither a least nor a greatest member of $\mathscr{A}$. Now consider $\mathscr{A} \cup \{\varnothing\}$. There is still no greatest member, but $\varnothing$ is the least member. With $\mathscr{A} \cup \{\varnothing\} \cup \{\{1, 2, 3\}\}$ we have both a greatest and a least member relative to $\subseteq$. The greatest member is $\{1, 2, 3\}$. Relative to some partial ordering, a set can have at most one least member and one greatest member (Exercise 2.63).

DEFINITION 2.25   A *minimal* member of set A relative to a partial ordering $\leq$ in A is an element $b \in A$ such that, for no $a \in A$, $a < b$ (where $<$ is defined by D.2.21). Similarly, a *maximal* member is an element b such that $b < a$ for no $a \in A$.

Examples

1. If a set has a least (greatest) element, then the least (greatest) element is also a minimal (maximal) element (Exercise 2.63). If A is finite and $\langle A, \leq \rangle$ is a chain, then A has a least and a greatest element. $\langle B, \rho' \rangle$, where ρ' is a lexicographic ordering in B, is a chain, and the least (greatest) elements of sets B in the examples of D.2.24 are unique minimal (maximal) elements of the respective sets. The infinite set of integers $I = \{\ldots, -2, -1, 0, 1, 2, \ldots\}$, together with the *less than or equal* relation $\leq$, constitutes the chain $\langle I, \leq \rangle$. Set I has neither a least nor a greatest element, and there are no minimal or maximal elements.
   2. The fact that a set has a least (greatest) element implies that the set has exactly one minimal (maximal) element. The converse need not be true: The union of the infinite set of odd integers and the set $\{2, 4\}$ has exactly one maximal element, namely 4, with respect to the partial ordering *divides*. There is no greatest element.
   3. Consider family $\mathscr{A}$ of Example 2 of D.2.24. Relative to partial ordering $\subseteq$ the family has three minimal elements $\{1\}$, $\{2\}$, $\{3\}$, and three maximal

elements $\{1, 2\}, \{1, 3\}, \{2, 3\}$. The family $\mathscr{A} \cup \{\varnothing\} \cup \{\{1, 2, 3\}\}$ has unique minimal and maximal elements.

DEFINITION 2.26   Let $\leq$ be a partial ordering in set A, and let $<$ be the relation defined by D.2.21. Then $b \in A$ is a *cover* of $a \in A$ if and only if $a < b$ and there exists no $u \in A$ such that $a < u < b$.

Examples

1. The family $\{\{1\}, \{2\}, \{1, 2\}, \{1, 2, 3\}\}$ is partially ordered by $\subseteq$. Here $\{1, 2, 3\}$ is the cover of $\{1, 2\}$, and $\{1, 2\}$ covers both $\{1\}$ and $\{2\}$. But $\{1, 2, 3\}$ covers neither $\{1\}$ nor $\{2\}$ ($\{1\} \subset \{1, 2\} \subset \{1, 2, 3\}$ and $\{2\} \subset \{1, 2\} \subset \{1, 2, 3\}$). Members $\{1\}$ and $\{2\}$ are incomparable. Hence neither can cover the other.

2. Consider the partially ordered sets $\langle A, \leq \rangle$ and $\langle A, \leq' \rangle$ of Example 2 of D.2.22. We have 6 covering 5 with respect to $\leq$ but not with respect to $\leq'$ (6 covers 2 and 3 with respect to $\leq'$).

DEFINITION 2.27   Let set A be partially ordered by $\leq$ and let $\varnothing \subset B \subseteq A$. Then an element $a \in A$ is an *upper bound* (*lower bound*) of B if and only if, for all $b \in B$, $b \leq a$ ($a \leq b$). The least (greatest) element of the set of all upper (lower) bounds of B is the *least upper bound* (*greatest lower bound*) or *supremum* (*infimum*) of B, symbolized lub B (glb B) or sup B (inf B).

Examples

1. Let the power set $\mathscr{P}(\{1, 2, 3\})$ be partially ordered by $\subseteq$. Let $B_1 = \{\{1\}, \{2\}\}$ and $B_2 = \{\{1\}, \{1, 2\}\}$. The set of upper bounds of B_1 is $\{\{1, 2\}, \{1, 2, 3\}\}$. There is only one lower bound, the null set $\varnothing$. Then sup $B_1 = \{1, 2\}$ and inf $B_1 = \varnothing$. Neither belongs to B_1. The set of upper bounds of B_2 is also $\{\{1, 2\}, \{1, 2, 3\}\}$, but the set of lower bounds is $\{\varnothing, \{1\}\}$. Then sup $B_2 = \{1, 2\}$ and inf $B_2 = \{1\}$. Both supremum and infimum belong to B_2.

2. Let set $A = \{a, b, c\}$ be partially ordered by the identity relation $=$. The only subsets of A with upper or lower bounds are $\{a\}, \{b\}, \{c\}$. In each case the upper and lower bound is the single element belonging to the set. Each upper bound is a supremum and each lower bound an infimum, e.g., sup $\{a\} = \inf \{a\} = a$.

Algorithm 2.3 is a procedure for the construction of diagrams that represent partially ordered sets. The diagrams help identify least and greatest elements, minimal and maximal elements, and the various bounds of subsets. The basis of the algorithm is the observation that if $\langle A, \leq \rangle$ is a finite partially ordered set, then $a_1 < a_n$ in A if and only if there exists a chain $a_1 < a_2 < \cdots < a_n$ in which a_{i+1} covers a_i for $i = 1, 2, \ldots, n - 1$.

ALGORITHM 2.3   Consider the partially ordered set $\langle A, \leqq \rangle$. Represent each element $a_i \in A$ by a node α_i in the plane, and consider all ordered pairs $\langle a_i, a_j \rangle$ belonging to $A \times A$. Draw node α_i above node α_j if and only if $a_j < a_i$, and join nodes α_i and α_j by a line if a_i covers a_j. The result is a diagram for $\langle A, \leqq \rangle$ in which there is a sequence of joined lines ascending from node α_n to node α_m if $a_n < a_m$.

Example

Diagrams (a) and (b) of Figure 2.8 represent, respectively, the partially ordered sets $\langle A, \leqq \rangle$ and $\langle A, \leqq' \rangle$ of Example 2 of D.2.22. Diagram (c) represents the partially ordered set $\langle \mathscr{P}(\{1, 2, 3\}), \subseteq \rangle$. Diagram (d) represents $\langle \mathscr{A}, \subseteq \rangle$ of Example 2 of D.2.24, and Diagram (e) the partially ordered set $\langle A, = \rangle$ of Example 2 of D.2.27. Diagrams (b) and (c) are equal.

Any node from which there is no ascending line represents a maximal element, and, if there is only one such node, it also represents the greatest element. Nodes from which there are no descending lines represent minimal elements. If there is only one node with no descending lines, this node represents also the least element. We can have $A = B$ in the context of D.2.27. Therefore, the node representing the greatest (least) element of a partially ordered set also represents the supremum (infimum) of this set.

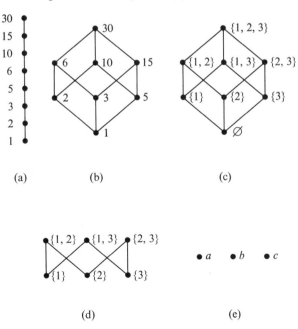

(a)   (b)   (c)

(d)   (e)

Figure 2.8

THEOREM 2.11 Every nonempty finite partially ordered set can be represented by a diagram.

Proof (by induction on n, the number of elements in the set).

(i) Basis. The only ordering of a set $\{a_1\}$ can be $a_1 \leq a_1$. This is represented by a single node.

(ii) Induction step. Assume the theorem for a partially ordered set on $n - 1$ elements. Let A be a set of n elements, partially ordered by $\leq$. Since A is finite, it has at least one maximal element, say a_m (see Exercise 2.64). If a_m is omitted, the set $A - \{a_m\}$ is still partially ordered by $\leq$, and it has $n - 1$ elements. But this set has a diagram (induction hypothesis). Therefore, take this diagram and place a node α_m above it. Then, for all a_i that are covered by a_m, join α_i and α_m in the diagram. The result is a diagram for A.

DEFINITION 2.28 A function $f: A \to A'$ is *order preserving* relative to an ordering $\leq$ for A and an ordering $\leq'$ for A' if and only if $a \leq b$ in A implies $f(a) \leq' f(b)$ in A'. If there exist order preserving functions $f: A \to A'$ and $f^{-1}: A' \to A$, then the partially ordered sets $\langle A, \leq \rangle$ and $\langle A', \leq' \rangle$ are said to be *order-isomorphic*.

Examples

1. Consider the sets $\{1, 2, 3, 5, 6, 10, 15, 30\}$, partially ordered by *divides*, and $\mathscr{P}(\{1, 2, 3\})$, partially ordered by the subset relation. Let f be the function $\{\langle 1, \varnothing \rangle, \langle 2, \{1\} \rangle, \langle 3, \{2\} \rangle, \langle 5, \{3\} \rangle, \langle 6, \{1, 2\} \rangle, \langle 10, \{1, 3\} \rangle, \langle 15, \{2, 3\} \rangle, \langle 30, \{1, 2, 3\} \rangle\}$. It is easy to see that both f and f^{-1} are order preserving. This is particularly easy to see by reference to the diagrams of the partially ordered sets, Diagrams (b) and (c) of Figure 2.8.

2. Let $A = \{a_1, a_2, a_3, a_4\}$ and $B = \{b_1, b_2, b_3, b_4\}$. Define a partial ordering in A: $a_1 \leq a_2$, $a_1 \leq a_3$, $a_1 \leq a_4$, $a_3 \leq a_4$. Define also a partial ordering in B: $b_1 \leq' b_2 \leq' b_3 \leq' b_4$. Then $f: A \to B$, defined by $\{\langle a_i, b_i \rangle \mid 1 \leq i \leq 4\}$, is order preserving. Clearly f is one to one. Hence $f^{-1}: B \to A$ exists. But f^{-1} is not order preserving; we have $b_2 \leq' b_3$, but $f^{-1}(b_2) = a_2$ and $f^{-1}(b_3) = a_3$ are incomparable. Figure 2.9 represents $\langle A, \leq \rangle$ and $\langle B, \leq' \rangle$.

THEOREM 2.12 Two partially ordered sets can be represented by the same diagram if and only if they are order-isomorphic.

Proof. Denote two partially ordered sets by $\langle A, \leq \rangle$ and $\langle A', \leq' \rangle$, and assume that both sets are represented by the one diagram. In the coincident diagram each node α_i represents an $a_i \in A$ and an $a_i' \in A'$. Therefore, there exist functions $f: A \to A'$ and $f^{-1}: A' \to A$ such that $\langle a_i, a_i' \rangle \in f$ and $\langle a_i', a_i \rangle \in f^{-1}$. Since we have the same diagram, clearly $a_i \leq a_j$ if and only if $a_i' \leq a_j'$. Hence having the same diagram implies order-isomorphism. Con-

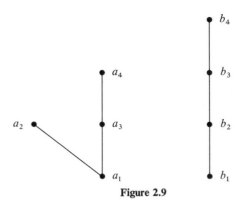

Figure 2.9

versely, assume that $\langle A, \leqq \rangle$ and $\langle A', \leqq' \rangle$ are order-isomorphic, and construct a diagram of A. There exists an order preserving function $f: A \to A'$, and, since f^{-1} also exists, f is one to one. Hence we can let node α_i, which represents $a_i \in A$, also represent the image of a_i under f. Clearly, since order-isomorphism means that $f(a_i) \leqq' f(a_j)$ if and only if $a_i \leqq a_j$, the diagram represents A' as well.

2g. Lattices

DEFINITION 2.29   Let $\langle A, \leqq \rangle$ be a partially ordered set. The system $\langle A, \leqq \rangle$ is a *lattice* if and only if each pair of elements a_i and a_j of A has a supremum and an infimum in A. We denote sup $\{a_i, a_j\}$ by $a_i \oplus a_j$ and inf $\{a_i, a_j\}$ by $a_i * a_j$.

Examples

1. Let $X = \{1, 2, 3, 5, 6, 10, 15, 30\}$ be partially ordered by relation *divides*, which we denote by D here. Every pair of elements of X has a supremum and an infimum. $\langle X, D \rangle$ is therefore a lattice. Since no subset of a set has more than one supremum and one infimum (relative to a given partial ordering $\leqq$), $\oplus$ and $*$ are well-defined operations (see Exercise 2.65). For a finite lattice $\langle A, \leqq \rangle$ we can therefore draw up a table of images for all elements of $A \times A$ under $\oplus$ and $*$. Table 2.17 is such an "addition" and "multiplication" table for $\langle X, D \rangle$. Since $x_i \oplus x_j = x_j \oplus x_i$, $x_i * x_j = x_j * x_i$, and $x_i \oplus x_i = x_i * x_i$, both operations can be defined by a single array in which the diagonal is shared. Entries above the diagonal constitute the rest of the "multiplication" table, and entries below the diagonal complete the "addition" table. We can denote a lattice $\langle A, \leqq \rangle$ by $\langle A, \oplus, * \rangle$. This notation emphasizes the operations in the lattice rather than its structure as a partially ordered set.

TABLE 2.17

OPERATIONS $\oplus$ AND $*$ IN $\langle X, D \rangle$

x_j \ x_i	1	2	3	5	6	10	15	30	
1	1	1	1	1	1	1	1	1	
2	2	2	1	1	2	2	1	2	
3	3	6	3	1	3	1	3	3	
5	5	10	15	5	1	5	5	5	
6	6	6	6	30	6	2	3	6	$x_i * x_j$
10	10	10	30	10	30	10	5	10	
15	15	30	15	15	30	30	15	15	
30	30	30	30	30	30	30	30	30	
					$x_i \oplus x_j$				

2. Any partially ordered set $\langle A', \leqq' \rangle$ that is order-isomorphic to a lattice $\langle A, \leqq \rangle$ is also a lattice. Let $f: A \to A'$ be the order preserving function associated with the isomorphism. Then, if a_k is the supremum (infimum) of $\{a_i, a_j\}$ relative to $\leqq$, $f(a_k)$ is the supremum (infimum) of $\{f(a_i), f(a_j)\}$ relative to $\leqq'$. The partially ordered set $\langle \mathscr{P}(\{1, 2, 3\}), \subseteq \rangle$ is order-isomorphic to the lattice $\langle X, D \rangle$ of Example 1; it is therefore also a lattice; i.e., the lattice may be denoted by $\langle \mathscr{P}(\{1, 2, 3\}), \cup, \cap \rangle$. The two lattices are represented by Diagrams (b) and (c) in Figure 2.8.

3. A partially ordered set need not be a lattice. Let $A = \{a, b, c\}$ be partially ordered by the identity relation $=$. Then $\langle A, = \rangle$ is a partially ordered set, but subsets $\{a, b\}$, $\{a, c\}$, $\{b, c\}$ of A have neither suprema nor infima (see Diagram (e) of Figure 2.8).

4. Consider lattice $\langle A, \oplus_A, *_A \rangle$. A lattice $\langle B, \oplus_B, *_B \rangle$, where $B \subseteq A$, is a *sublattice* of $\langle A, \oplus_A, *_A \rangle$ if $\oplus_B$ and $*_B$ are restrictions of $\oplus_A$ and $*_A$ to $B \times B$. Let $\langle X, D \rangle$ be the lattice of Example 1. Define the following subsets of X: $X_1 = \{2\}$, $X_2 = \{1, 2, 3\}$, $X_3 = \{2, 3, 6\}$, $X_4 = \{1, 2, 3, 6\}$, $X_5 = \{1, 2, 5, 6, 15, 30\}$. Now consider partially ordered sets $\langle X_i, D \cap (X_i \times X_i) \rangle$. They are lattices when $i = 1, 4, 5$, but not when $i = 2, 3$. The lattices are sublattices of $\langle X, D \rangle$ when $i = 1, 4$. But $2 \oplus 5 = 10$ in $\langle X, D \rangle$ and $2 \oplus 5 = 30$ in $\langle X_5, D \cap (X_5 \times X_5) \rangle$. Hence $\oplus$ is not a restriction in this instance (neither is $*$), and the lattice of X_5 is not a sublattice of $\langle X, D \rangle$.

5. Define a relation R in the family $\mathscr{P} = \{\mathscr{A}_i \mid \mathscr{A}_i \text{ is a partition of set } A\}$ as follows: $\mathscr{A}_m R \mathscr{A}_n$ if and only if every block of $\mathscr{A}_m$ is the subset of some block of $\mathscr{A}_n$. Relation R is expressed in words as *is a refinement of* (since $\mathscr{A}_m R \mathscr{A}_n$ implies that $\mathscr{A}_m$ has more blocks than $\mathscr{A}_n$ when $m \neq n$). Relation R is a partial ordering in $\mathscr{P}$ and the system $\langle \mathscr{P}, R \rangle$ is a lattice.

DEFINITION 2.30   A lattice $\langle A, \oplus, * \rangle$ is *distributive* if, for all $a, b, c \in A$,

$$a \oplus (b * c) = (a \oplus b) * (a \oplus c),$$
$$a * (b \oplus c) = (a * b) \oplus (a * c).$$

Examples

1. Diagrams (a), (b), and (c) of Figure 2.8 represent distributive lattices.

2. The lattice represented by Diagram (a) of Figure 2.10 is not distributive. We have $x_2 \oplus (x_3 * x_4) = x_2 \oplus x_5 = x_2$, but $(x_2 \oplus x_3) * (x_2 \oplus x_4) = x_1 * x_1 = x_1$. Diagram (b) of Figure 2.10 represents the lattice

$$\langle \{\varnothing, \{1\}, \{2\}, \{3\}, \{1, 2, 3\}\}, \subseteq \rangle.$$

Lattices represented by these diagrams are clearly order-isomorphic. Note here that lattice operations $\oplus$ and $*$ cannot be interpreted as set operations $\cup$ and $\cap$ in the lattice of the sets. We have, for example, $\{1\} \oplus \{2\} = \{1, 2, 3\} \neq \{1\} \cup \{2\}$.

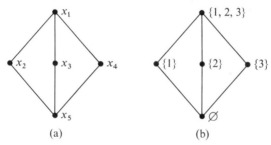

(a)   (b)

Figure 2.10

THEOREM 2.13   Let $\langle A, \leq \rangle$ be a lattice. Then A has exactly one minimal (maximal) element relative to $\leq$ if and only if it has a least (greatest) element relative to $\leq$.

Proof. For any partially ordered set $\langle A, \leq \rangle$, if A has a least element, then A has a unique minimal element (Exercise 2.63). The converse is true only for some partially ordered sets. To prove it for a lattice, let a and b be arbitrary elements of A. Since $a * b = \inf \{a, b\}$, it follows from D.2.27 that $a * b \leq a$. Now, in particular, if a is a minimal element of A, then $a * b < a$ does not hold, and we have $a * b = a$. Since $a * b = a$ implies $a \leq b$ (Exercise 2.74), and b is completely arbitrary, a is a least element. Analogously we can prove identity of maximal and greatest elements.

Example

Since finiteness of A guarantees existence of minimal and maximal elements (Exercise 2.64), we have a corollary: If $\langle A, \leq \rangle$ is a finite lattice, A has unique minimal and maximal elements. In the lattices of Figure 2.10 elements x_5 and $\varnothing$ are minimal, and elements x_1 and $\{1, 2, 3\}$ maximal.

DEFINITION 2.31   If $\langle A, \leqq \rangle$ is a lattice, and A has maximal and minimal elements relative to $\leqq$, the (unique) maximal and minimal elements are called *bounds* of the lattice and the lattice is called a *bounded* lattice. The bounds are distinguished by special names: The maximal and minimal elements are given names 1 and 0, respectively. (Note that every finite lattice is bounded.)

DEFINITION 2.32   Let $\langle A, \leqq \rangle$ be a bounded lattice. Then $\langle A, \leqq \rangle$ (or $\langle A, \oplus, * \rangle$) is a *complemented* lattice if, for every $a \in A$, there exists an element $a' \in A$ such that $a \oplus a' = 1$ and $a * a' = 0$. An element a' satisfying these conditions is a *complement* of a.

Examples

1. If a lattice is not bounded, then it cannot be complemented. Even a bounded lattice need not be complemented. Lattice $\langle \mathscr{A}, \subseteq \rangle$ of Figure 2.11 has bounds $\varnothing$ and $\{1, 2, 3\}$. The only elements b that satisfy the equation $\{1, 3\} \oplus b = \{1, 2, 3\}$ are $\{1, 2\}$, $\{2, 3\}$, and $\{1, 2, 3\}$. But for these elements $\{1, 3\} * b \neq \varnothing$. On the other hand, in the lattice of Diagram (c) of Figure 2.8, $\{1, 3\} \oplus \{2\} = \{1, 2, 3\}$ and $\{1, 3\} * \{2\} = \varnothing$.

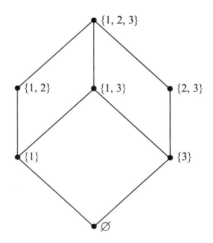

Figure 2.11

2. The lattices of Figure 2.10 are complemented, but only elements 1 and 0 have unique complements: $1' = 0$ and $0' = 1$. In the lattice of Diagram (a) we have that x_3 is a complement of x_2 ($x_2 \oplus x_3 = 1$ and $x_2 * x_3 = 0$), and

also that x_4 is a complement of x_2 ($x_2 \oplus x_4 = 1$ and $x_2 * x_4 = 0$). Similarly, x_3 has complements x_2 and x_4, and x_4 has complements x_2 and x_3. Since $x_3' = x_2$ and $x_2' = x_4$, we have $(x_3')' = x_4$.

DEFINITION 2.33   Let $\langle A, \leqq \rangle$ be a complemented lattice. If each $a \in A$ has a unique complement in A, then $\langle A, \leqq \rangle$ is *uniquely complemented.*

Example

Lattice $\langle \mathscr{P}(\{1, 2, 3\}), \subseteq \rangle$ is uniquely complemented. We have already seen that the complemented lattices of Example 2 of D.2.32 are not uniquely complemented.

Let us now summarize our knowledge about lattices. Let $\langle A, \leqq \rangle$ be a lattice and let a, b, c be any elements of A. The following results hold for all lattices (see Exercise 2.75):

$$a \oplus b = b \oplus a, \qquad a * b = b * a;$$
$$a \oplus (b \oplus c) = (a \oplus b) \oplus c, \qquad a * (b * c) = (a * b) * c.$$

If $\langle A, \leqq \rangle$ is distributive, we have, in addition,

$$a \oplus (b * c) = (a \oplus b) * (a \oplus c),$$
$$a * (b \oplus c) = (a * b) \oplus (a * c).$$

If $\langle A, \leqq \rangle$ is bounded, then $0 \leqq a$ and $a \leqq 1$ for all $a \in A$. But this implies (see Exercise 2.74)

$$a \oplus 0 = a, \qquad a * 1 = a.$$

Finally, if $\langle A, \leqq \rangle$ is complemented, then, for each $a \in A$, there exists some a' such that

$$a \oplus a' = 1, \qquad a * a' = 0.$$

The properties of distributive complemented lattices are precisely the axioms of Boolean algebra. Boolean algebras are therefore lattices of a special type. Since lattices are more general algebraic systems than Boolean algebras, all theorems that hold for lattices hold for Boolean algebras. Since Boolean algebras are in fact distributive complemented lattices, every theorem that has been proven for Boolean algebras holds for such lattices, but not necessarily for lattices in general.

THEOREM 2.14   A complemented distributive lattice is uniquely complemented.

Proof.   Th. 2.14 is Th. 1.9.

2h. Abstract Algebras

We have seen (in Section 2c) that some algebraic systems deriving from different application areas, such as switching algebra and the algebra of truth values, are so similar in most respects that they can be taken to be essentially the same system. The notion of similarity and sameness were, however, left vague. A formal discussion of these concepts has been deliberately postponed because their proper understanding requires reasonable familiarity with the abstract approach. This, we hope, has now been gained.

In quite general terms an algebra consists of a set A with some distinguished elements and functions from A^n into A. Since the partial ordering $\leq$ is not a function, a lattice written as $\langle L, \leq \rangle$ is not an algebra; written in the form $\langle L, \oplus, * \rangle$ is it an algebra.

DEFINITION 2.34   Let A be a nonempty set. Every function $f\colon A^n \to A$ ($n = 0, 1, 2, \ldots$) is an *n-argument operation* in A. By a 0-argument operation x in A we understand a *constant* (*distinguished*) *element* $x \in A$.

Example

In the complemented distributive lattice or Boolean algebra $\langle L, \oplus, *, ', 0, 1 \rangle$ we have the set of operations $\{\oplus, *, ', 0, 1\}$. Operations $\oplus$ and $*$ are functions from L^2 into L, operation $'$ is a function from L into L, and 0 and 1 are zero-argument operations.

DEFINITION 2.35   Let f be an *n*-argument operation in A. Then a set B, such that $B \subseteq A$, is said to be *closed* under f if $f(x_1, x_2, \ldots, x_n) \in B$ for all $\langle x_1, x_2, \ldots, x_n \rangle \in B^n$.

Example

Consider algebra $\langle X, \oplus, * \rangle$ of Example 1 of D.2.29 and subsets X_i of X as defined in Example 4 of D.2.29. Inspection of Table 2.17 shows that sets X_1 and X_4 are closed under both operations, set X_2 under $*$, set X_3 under $\oplus$, but that set X_5 is not closed under either operation.

DEFINITION 2.36   Let A be a nonempty set. The system $\langle A, f_1, f_2, \ldots, f_m \rangle$, where each f_i is an n_i-argument operation in A, is an *abstract algebra*. (The set of operations of an abstract algebra does not have to be finite. We have made it finite purely for convenience.)

Example

$\langle L, \oplus, * \rangle$, where $\oplus$ and $*$ are two-argument operations in L, and $\langle B, \oplus, *, ', 0, 1 \rangle$, where $\oplus$ and $*$ are two-argument operations in B, $'$ is a one-argument operation, and 0 and 1 are zero-argument operations, are abstract algebras. It is customary to denote an algebra by its set; here we may speak of the abstract algebras L and B. We cannot call L a lattice or B a a Boolean algebra unless we also specify the appropriate sets of axioms that the systems have to satisfy. But if we do so, then L and B cease to be *abstract* algebras.

DEFINITION 2.37   Let A be the abstract algebra $\langle A, f_1, f_2, \ldots, f_m \rangle$ and consider a subset B of A. An abstract algebra $\langle B, h_1, h_2, \ldots, h_m \rangle$, where each h_i is a restriction $f_i \mid B^{n_i}$ and B is closed under f_i, is a *subalgebra* of A.

Examples

1. It is customary to denote an operation and its restriction by the same symbol. The algebra $\langle \{0, 1\}, \oplus, *, ', 0, 1 \rangle$ is a subalgebra of $\langle B, \oplus, *, ', 0, 1 \rangle$. If $B \supset \{0, 1\}$, the $\oplus$ in algebra $\{0, 1\}$ is not the same as the $\oplus$ in algebra B. We use the same symbol because $\oplus$ in $\{0, 1\}$ is a restriction of the $\oplus$ in B to $\{0, 1\}^2$.

2. Consider algebra $\langle X, \oplus, * \rangle$ of Example 1 of D.2.29 and subsets X_i defined in Example 4 of D.2.29. The systems $\langle X_1, \oplus, * \rangle$ and $\langle X_4, \oplus, * \rangle$ are subalgebras of $\langle X, \oplus, * \rangle$. Although $\langle X_5, \oplus, * \rangle$ is an abstract algebra, it is not a subalgebra of $\langle X, \oplus, * \rangle$. Systems $\langle X_2, \oplus, * \rangle$ and $\langle X_3, \oplus, * \rangle$ are not even algebras ($2 \oplus 3$ is not defined in X_2 and $2 * 3$ is not defined in X_3). Note that $\langle X, \oplus, *, ', 1, 30 \rangle$ is also an abstract algebra. Then $\langle X_i, \oplus, *, ', 1, 30 \rangle$ can be an algebra only if 1 and 30 are members of X_i. Element 30 is not a member of X_1, X_2, X_3, or X_4. Both 1 and 30 are members of X_5, but $'$ is not an operation in X_5 (for example, 6 has both 5 and 15 for complements). The system $\langle X_4, \oplus, *, ', 1, 6 \rangle$ is an algebra, but, since an algebra and its subalgebras must have the same constant elements, this algebra cannot be a subalgebra of X.

DEFINITION 2.38   Abstract algebras $\langle A, f_1, f_2, \ldots, f_m \rangle$ and $\langle B, h_1, h_2, \ldots, h_n \rangle$ are *similar* if $m = n$ and each h_i has as many arguments as the corresponding f_i. Consider similar algebras A and B. A function $\phi \colon A \to B$ is a *homomorphism* of A into B (or onto B if ϕ is an onto function) if and only if $\phi(f_i(x_1, x_2, \ldots, x_{n_i})) = h_i(\phi(x_1), \phi(x_2), \ldots, \phi(x_{n_i}))$ for all $i = 1, 2, \ldots, m$ and for every n_i-sample of A. A homomorphism that is one to one and onto is an *isomorphism*. In particular, if sets A and B are equal, a homomorphism is called an *endomorphism* and an isomorphism is called an *automorphism*.

Examples

1. An algebra of sets $\langle A, \cup, \cap, ^-, \varnothing, U \rangle$ and the algebra of truth values $\langle \{F, T\}, \vee, \wedge, \neg, F, T \rangle$ are similar. Let $A = \mathscr{P}(\{a, b\})$ and define functions

α: $\{F, T\} \rightarrow A$, β: $\{F, T\} \rightarrow A$, γ: $A \rightarrow \{F, T\}$ such that $\alpha(F) = \{a, b\}$ and $\alpha(T) = \varnothing$, $\beta(F) = \varnothing$ and $\beta(T) = \{a, b\}$, and $\gamma(\{a, b\}) = \gamma(\{a\}) = T$ and $\gamma(\{b\}) = \gamma(\varnothing) = F$. Since, for example, $\alpha(F \wedge T) = \{a, b\}$ and $\alpha(F) \cap \alpha(T) = \varnothing$, α is not a homomorphism. Function β is a homomorphism into A (but not onto A). Function γ is a homomorphism onto $\{F, T\}$. Since, however, it is many to one, the function is not an isomorphism.

2. Let $A = \{\varnothing, U\}$ and $B = \{F, T\}$, and consider the algebras $\langle A, \cup, \cap, ^-, \varnothing, U \rangle$ and $\langle B, \vee, \wedge, \neg, F, T \rangle$. The function $\phi: A \rightarrow B$ such that $\phi(\varnothing) = F$, $\phi(U) = T$ is an isomorphism. If $\phi: A \rightarrow B$ is an isomorphism, then $\phi^{-1}: B \rightarrow A$ is also an isomorphism. We say then that algebras A and B are *isomorphic* to each other and that each algebra is an *isomorphic image* of the other.

3. Consider algebras of sets

$$\langle \mathscr{P}(A_1), \cup, \cap, ^-, \varnothing, U \rangle$$

and

$$\langle \mathscr{P}(A_2), \cap, \cup, ^-, U, \varnothing \rangle,$$

and let $A_1 = A_2$. Then the function $\phi: \mathscr{P}(A_1) \rightarrow \mathscr{P}(A_2)$ such that $\phi(X) = \overline{X}$ for all $X \in \mathscr{P}(A_1)$ is an automorphism.

THEOREM 2.15   Two lattices, considered as algebras, are isomorphic if and only if they are order-isomorphic when considered as partially ordered sets.

Proof. The proof is not particularly difficult. It does, however, depend on several theorems in the theory of lattices that we consider irrelevant to the purposes of this book.

Example

The partially ordered sets represented by Diagrams (b) and (c) of Figure 2.8 are order-isomorphic. They are lattices. The lattice of Diagram (b) can be considered as the algebra $\langle L_1, \mu, \delta \rangle$, where the two-argument operations μ and δ have as their respective images the least common multiple and the greatest common divisor of the arguments. The lattice of Diagram (c) can be considered as the algebra $\langle L_2, \cup, \cap \rangle$, where $\cup$ and $\cap$ have their usual set-algebraic meaning. The function $\{\langle 1, \varnothing \rangle, \langle 2, \{1\} \rangle, \langle 3, \{2\} \rangle, \langle 5, \{3\} \rangle, \langle 6, \{1, 2\} \rangle, \langle 10, \{1, 3\} \rangle, \langle 15, \{2, 3\} \rangle, \langle 30, \{1, 2, 3\} \rangle\}$ is an isomorphism. Hence L_1 and L_2 are isomorphic.

With the introduction of the concept of isomorphism we hope to have clarified the notion of essential sameness. If two abstract algebras are isomorphic, then, with respect to their structure, they can be regarded as one and the same algebra. We shall now link the concepts of isomorphism and equivalence classes and find that a number of results of great practical importance arise. Isomorphism is of particular importance in the study of Boolean algebras. Since a distributive complemented lattice is a Boolean algebra, we know already that finite Boolean algebras are isomorphic if and only if they have the same diagram when considered as partially ordered sets (Th.2.12 and Th.2.15). But we are interested in infinite (not necessarily Boolean) algebras as well. For example, turning to statement calculi, we find that no bound can be put on a sequence of statements in just p and $\lor$ alone: p, $p \lor p$, $p \lor p \lor p$, ... We shall, therefore, discuss isomorphism in rather general terms.

DEFINITION 2.39   If R is an equivalence relation on a set A, the partition of A induced by R is the *quotient set* of A by R, denoted A/R (and read *A modulo R*).

DEFINITION 2.40   An equivalence relation R on A is a *congruence* with respect to an operation $f\colon A^m \to A$ if, for all m-samples $\langle x_1, x_2, \ldots, x_m \rangle$ and $\langle y_1, y_2, \ldots, y_m \rangle$ of A, the conditions $x_1 R y_1$, $x_2 R y_2$, $\ldots$, $x_m R y_m$ imply $\langle f(x_1, x_2, \ldots, x_m), f(y_1, y_2, \ldots, y_m) \rangle \in R$. If relation R is a congruence with respect to every operation in an abstract algebra A, we call it a *congruence in A*.

Examples

1. The universal relation is a congruence. Then A/R has exactly one member. This member is the set A itself. If a congruence R is not a universal relation on A (i.e., if the quotient set has more than one member), relation R is called a *proper* congruence.

2. Consider a set of statements S and operations $\lor$, $\land$, $\lnot$ in S. The biconditional $\leftrightarrow$, interpreted as a relation, is clearly an equivalence. We can show that $p \leftrightarrow s$ and $q \leftrightarrow t$ for $p, s, q, t \in S$ imply $(p \lor q) \leftrightarrow (s \lor t)$, $(p \land q) \leftrightarrow (s \land t)$, and $\lnot p \leftrightarrow \lnot s$ by means of truth tables (we do so for the operation $\lor$ in Table 2.18, where we need only consider truth value assignments to p, s, q, t for which the conditions $p \leftrightarrow s$ and $q \leftrightarrow t$ hold). Hence $\leftrightarrow$ is

TABLE 2.18

CONGRUENCE OF $\leftrightarrow$ WITH RESPECT TO $\lor$

p	q	s	t	$p \leftrightarrow s$	$q \leftrightarrow t$	$(p \lor q) \leftrightarrow (s \lor t)$		
T	T	T	T	T	T	T	T	T
T	F	T	F	T	T	T	T	T
F	T	F	T	T	T	T	T	T
F	F	F	F	T	T	F	T	F

a congruence with respect to $\vee$, $\wedge$, and $\neg$. Since, for any $p \in S$, p and $\neg p$ belong to different equivalence classes, it is a proper congruence. Relation $\leftrightarrow$ is a congruence in the algebra $\langle S, \vee, \wedge, \neg \rangle$.

Theorem 2.16   Let R be a congruence in an algebra $\langle A, f_1, f_2, \ldots, f_m \rangle$. Then, corresponding to every f_i on A^{n_i}, there exists an operation f_i' on $(A/R)^{n_i}$ such that $f_i'([x_1], [x_2], \ldots, [x_{n_i}]) = [f_i(x_1, x_2, \ldots, x_{n_i})]$, i.e.,

$$\langle A/R, f_1', f_2', \ldots, f_m' \rangle$$

is an algebra similar to algebra A. (A/R is called the *quotient algebra* of A by R.)

Proof. Since $x_1 R y_1$, $x_2 R y_2$, $\ldots$, $x_{n_i} R y_{n_i}$ imply $\langle f_i(x_1, x_2, \ldots, x_{n_i}),$ $f_i(y_1, y_2, \ldots, y_{n_i}) \rangle \in R$, we have that $[f_i(x_1, x_2, \ldots, x_{n_i})]$ is independent of the choice of elements x_1, x_2, $\ldots$, x_{n_i} from the equivalence classes $[x_1]$, $[x_2]$, $\ldots$, $[x_{n_i}]$. Therefore, the definition of f_i' does in fact define an operation, $\langle A/R, f_1', f_2', \ldots, f_m' \rangle$ is an algebra, and clearly this algebra is similar to algebra $\langle A, f_1, f_2, \ldots, f_m \rangle$.

Theorem 2.17   If R is a congruence in an abstract algebra A, then $f: A \rightarrow A/R$ such that $f(x) = [x]$ is an onto homomorphism (called the *natural* homomorphism from A onto A/R). Conversely, if $g: A \rightarrow B$ is a homomorphism, there exists a congruence Q in A, and the algebra A/Q is isomorphic to B.

Proof. That f is a homomorphism follows at once from the definition of homomorphism and the definition of the operations in A/R. The homomorphism must be onto: If $[x] \in A/R$, then clearly $x \in A$ and $f(x) = [x]$. Next consider an n-argument operation k in algebra A and the corresponding operation k' in the similar algebra B. Define a relation Q in A such that xQy if and only if $g(x) = g(y)$, and assume that conditions $x_1 Q y_1$, $\ldots$, $x_n Q y_n$ hold for some $x_1, \ldots, x_n, y_1, \ldots, y_n \in A$. By definition of homomorphism and the equalities $g(x_1) = g(y_1), \ldots, g(x_n) = g(y_n)$,

$$\begin{aligned} g(k(x_1, \ldots, x_n)) &= k'(g(x_1), \ldots, g(x_n)) \\ &= k'(g(y_1), \ldots, g(y_n)) \\ &= g(k(y_1, \ldots, y_n)). \end{aligned}$$

But this means that $\langle k(x_1, \ldots, x_n), k(y_1, \ldots, y_n) \rangle \in Q$. Hence Q is a congruence in A. Now define relation h as follows: $h = \{ \langle [x], g(x) \rangle \mid [x] \in A/Q \}$. Clearly, by the definition of Q, h is a one-to-one function. Therefore, if h is a homomorphism, it is also an isomorphism. By Th.2.16, algebras A and A/Q are similar. Since g is a homomorphism, A and B are also similar, and, since similarity of algebras is clearly a transitive relation, algebras A, B, and A/Q are all similar. We introduce an n-argument operation ϕ in A/Q corresponding to operations k in A and k' in B. Then

$$h(\phi([x_1], \ldots, [x_n])) = h([k(x_1, \ldots, x_n)])$$
$$= g(k(x_1, \ldots, x_n))$$
$$= k'(g(x_1), \ldots, g(x_n))$$
$$= k'(h([x_1]), \ldots, h([x_n])),$$

and we have shown h to be a homomorphism and hence an isomorphism. (Since ϕ is an operation in a quotient algebra, Line 1 follows from Th.2.16. Lines 2 and 4 are given by the definition of h, and Line 3 is a consequence of the assumption that g is a homomorphism.)

By Th.2.17, the existence of a homomorphism $g \colon A \to B$ implies existence of a congruence R in A, and of an isomorphism from A/R onto B. Further, if homomorphism $g' \colon A \to C$ also determines congruence R, then A/R, B, and C are all isomorphic, i.e., they are essentially the same algebra, namely A/R. Since the algebras are isomorphic, homomorphisms g and g' are not essentially different from the natural homomorphism $f \colon A \to A/R$. Discussion of onto homomorphisms of an algebra and the images under the homomorphisms can therefore be reduced to a consideration of natural homomorphisms and quotient algebras. It should be clear that natural homomorphisms on an algebra are in one-to-one correspondence with congruences in the algebra.

In the discussion of Boolean algebra B in Section 1e we could not explain the significance of the relation $=$. We are now in a position to assign a precise meaning to it. From an examination of the axioms and theorems we note that this relation must be an equivalence relation, and that if $\alpha(x_1, \ldots, x_n)$ and $\alpha(y_1, \ldots, y_n)$ are Boolean forms in variables $x_1, \ldots, x_n, y_1, \ldots, y_n$, which stand for elements of B, then $x_1 = y_1, \ldots, x_n = y_n$ should imply $\alpha(x_1, \ldots, x_n) = \alpha(y_1, \ldots, y_n)$. We assert that these conditions constitute an adequate definition of the relation. Comparison of the definition with D.2.40 shows that $=$ is a congruence in B. In a model of an algebra the congruence $=$ should be precisely defined. The congruence is then called the *natural* congruence for the model. In an algebra of sets the natural congruence is equality of sets, and the symbol $=$ denotes it nicely. Sometimes, however, it is more suggestive to use a symbol other than $=$ for a natural congruence. Thus, the symbol for the natural congruence in the algebra of truth values is $\leftrightarrow$.

In Example 2 of D.2.40 we found that relation $\leftrightarrow$ is a congruence in an algebra of statements $\langle S, \vee, \wedge, \neg \rangle$. Perhaps we could find zero-argument operations that would make S a Boolean algebra. The algebra of truth values suggests that we should look for some statement that is always true and some statement that is always false. But $(p \vee \neg p)$ is always true and $(p \wedge \neg p)$

always false for *every* $p \in S$. Consequently there is nothing unique about the constants. Indeed we can find no unique pair of constants that would make S a Boolean algebra. But $S/\leftrightarrow$ is a Boolean algebra. Clearly $(p \vee \neg p) \leftrightarrow (q \vee \neg q)$ and $(p \wedge \neg p) \leftrightarrow (q \wedge \neg q)$ for any $p, q \in S$. We can therefore define equivalence classes $T = [p \vee \neg p]$ and $F = [p \wedge \neg p]$. Then the quotient algebra $\langle S/\leftrightarrow, \vee, \wedge, \neg, F, T \rangle$ is a Boolean algebra. Operations $\vee$, $\wedge$, and $\neg$ are analogs of the operations in S; they are defined by Th.2.16.

Notes

The general references of Chapter 1 cover much of the material of this chapter as well. To those we add [Ho66], which deals with applications of Boolean algebras; [Ru65], which is a clear introduction to lattice theory; and [Ab69], an intermediate text on sets, lattices, and Boolean algebras.

Chapter 4 of [Ko70] provides an exceptionally readable account of minimization of Boolean functions. The reader may also consult the more advanced [Pr67], which appears to be the most often cited text on minimization, and [Ha65a] or [Ed73]. The physical realization of switching and gating circuits is emphasized in [Sh72]. Work still goes on in this area: see, for example, [Zi73]. Exact minimization may be found impracticable in some cases because of excessive amounts of computer time required; minimization that is not exact, but leads to appreciable reductions in computer time, is studied in [Bo70, Sl70]. Exercise 2.25 has been suggested by [Qu59]. Besides parallel and series arrangements, there are bridge switching circuits (for an example see Exercise 2.21), which may need fewer switches than their equivalents in series and parallel form. They are studied in [Ha65a].

The CODASYL (Conference on Data System Languages) Development Committee has published a report on an Algebra of Information based on functions, [Zz62]—[C162] is a shortened version of the report; [Mc63a] contains an example of the use of the algebra of information in the formulation of data processing problems. [Me67] is a more recent paper taking the same approach. The Notes to Chapter 11 contain references to a later CODASYL paper, and to papers by Codd and by Childs in which discrete mathematics is used to provide theoretical bases for the design of file structures.

For a proof of Th.2.15 see [Sz63, p. 41]. A program for drawing lattices is described in [Fe70]. Stirling numbers of the second kind (see Exercise 2.55) are tabulated in [Ab64].

Exercises

2.1 (a) Which of the following sets are functions?

(i) $\{\langle 1, 1 \rangle, \langle 2, 4 \rangle, \langle 3, 9 \rangle, \langle 4, 16 \rangle, \ldots\}$.

(ii) $\{\langle a, b, c \rangle, \langle a, c, b \rangle, \langle b, a, d \rangle\}$.

(iii) $\{\langle a, \langle b, c \rangle\rangle, \langle a, \langle c, b \rangle\rangle, \langle b, \langle a, d \rangle\rangle\}$.

(iv) $\{\langle \{a, b\}, c \rangle, \langle \{a, c\}, b \rangle, \langle \{b, a\}, d \rangle\}$.

2.2 (a) Consider $f: A \to B$ and $g: A \to B$. Under what conditions is $f \cap g$ a function? Under what conditions is $f \cup g$ a function?

2.3 (a) A frequently used device in programming is an indexing vector. Suppose we have a vector $A = \langle a_3, a_2, a_5, a_1, a_4 \rangle$. Here the indexing vector I is $\langle 4, 2, 1, 5, 3 \rangle$. The ith element of the indexing vector tells one where element a_i is currently located in vector A. The indexing vector is updated by interchanging its ith and jth elements whenever a_i and a_j are interchanged in A. For example, if a_3 and a_4 were interchanged in A, elements $i_3 = 1$ and $i_4 = 5$ would be interchanged in I. Do we have a function here? If so, specify it.

2.4 (a) Consider the Cartesian product $A \times B$, with $|A| = m$ and $|B| = n$.

(i) What is the greatest number of elements that a set $C \subseteq A \times B$ may have if it is to be a function?

(ii) If $f: A \to B$ and $m < n$, can f be onto B?

2.5 (a) Let $A = \{1, 2, 3, 4, 5\}$, and define functions $f: A \to A$ and $g: A \to A$ as follows:

$$f(1) = 2, \quad f(2) = 3, \quad f(3) = 4, \quad f(4) = 5, \quad f(5) = 1;$$
$$g(1) = 5, \quad g(2) = 3, \quad g(3) = 1, \quad g(4) = 4, \quad g(5) = 2.$$

Define $f \circ g$ and $g \circ f$.

2.6 (a) Prove that if $f: A \to B$ and $g: B \to C$ are both onto functions, then $g \circ f: A \to C$ is also onto.

2.7 (a) Let $f: A \to B$, $g: B \to C$, $h: C \to D$. Prove that $h \circ (g \circ f) = (h \circ g) \circ f$.

2.8 (a) Show that $f: N \times N \to N$, where N is the set of natural numbers, and f is defined by $f(x, y) = \frac{1}{2}(x + y - 1)(x + y - 2) + y$, is a one-to-one function. (Note: this device shows that the set of ordered pairs of natural numbers is countable.)

2.9 (a) Prove Th.2.1.

2.10 (a) Prove Th.2.2.

2.11 (a) A function on a set S into the same set is said to be *in* S. How many one-to-one functions are there in a set of n elements? How many onto functions are there in this set? How many into functions?

2.12 (a) Show that the elements of the Cartesian product $A \times B$ are in one-to-one correspondence with the elements of $B \times A$.

2.13 (b) Let $B = \{0, 1\}$ and consider functions from B^2 into B. Let

$f(0, 0) = f(0, 1) = 0$, $f(1, 0) = f(1, 1) = 1$; $g(0, 0) = g(0, 1) = 1$, $g(1, 0) = g(1, 1) = 0$. Define $f \oplus g, f * g, f * f', g * f'$ by a table similar to Table 2.1.

2.14 (b) With reference to D.2.8, which of the following are Boolean forms?

   (i) $x_1 \oplus x_2 * x_3 \oplus x_4 * x_5 \oplus x_6$;
   (ii) $((((x_1))) * ((x_2))$;
   (iii) $((((x_1) * (x_2 \oplus x_3))) * x_4)$;
   (iv) $((((x_1)')')')$.

2.15 (b) What is the Boolean function corresponding to Boolean form $(x_1 \oplus x_2) * (x_1 \oplus x_3')$ of Table 2.3 when $B = \{0, 1\}$?

2.16 (b) Simplify the conjunctive normal form of Tables 2.4 and 2.5.

2.17 (b) Use the technique of binary valuations to prove the following set equalities:

   (i) $[(A \cap B) \cup (\bar{A} \cap \bar{B}) \cup A] \cap B = A \cap B$,
   (ii) $(A \cap B) - C = (A - C) \cap (B - C)$.

2.18 (b) Repeat the proof of Exercise 1.33.

2.19 (c) Write down the switching function corresponding to the circuit of Figure 2.12. Simplify the circuit.

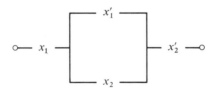

Figure 2.12

2.20 (c) Draw a circuit corresponding to the switching function $((x_1 * x_3) \oplus (x_2 * x_3'))'$.

2.21 (c) In all switching circuits considered in the text connections have been in series or in parallel. It is possible to reduce the number of switches necessary for the implementation of a switching function by means of bridge circuits. Figure 2.13 shows the bridge circuit corresponding to the series–parallel circuit of Figure 2.3. Show that the circuits are in fact equivalent.

2.22 (c) Minimize the normal form defined by the set of minterms $\{min_i^4 \mid i \in I\}$, where $I = \{0, 1, 5, 6, 10, 12, 14\}$, and then the normal form which results when min_7^4 is added to it.

2.23 (c) Use theorem $\alpha = \alpha x \oplus \alpha x'$ to convert $x_1 x_2 \oplus x_1 x_3 \oplus x_2' x_3$ to the equivalent disjunctive normal form. Minimize the normal form.

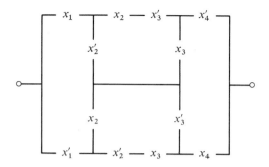

Figure 2.13

2.24 (c) Minimize the normal form defined by the set of minterms $\{min_i^5 \mid i \in I\}$, where

(i) $I = \{3, 4, 6, 9, 10, 11, 16, 17, 20, 21, 22, 23, 25, 30, 31\}$,
(ii) $I = \{0, 1, 3, 4, 7, 16, 22, 23, 24, 25, 30\}$.

2.25 (c) Devise an example to show that the number of prime implicants of a normal form can be greater than the number of minterms. (This exercise is more difficult than it looks. The given condition arises only when the number of variables exceeds 5.)

2.26 (c) Function f of Table 2.1 defines a NOR-gate. Using NOR-gates alone, design circuits that function as (i) inverter, (ii) OR-gate, (iii) AND-gate, (iv) NAND-gate.

2.27 (c) Design gating circuits with three inputs and a single output that give an output signal when

(i) exactly one of the inputs carries a signal,
(ii) at least two inputs carry signals,
(iii) exactly two inputs carry signals,
(iv) at least one and at most two inputs carry signals.

2.28 (c) A room has three doors with a light switch at each door. Design a circuit that allows lights in the room to be switched on or off by means of any one of the switches.

2.29 (c) A committee of five reaches its decisions by simple majority in secret ballot. Since the voting has been taking up too much time, a new scheme is being proposed. There would be a button under the table at each member's seat, and the member would vote *for* a measure by depressing the button with his or her foot. A green lamp would light up if the measure is passed by the committee; otherwise a red light would go on. Design the appropriate circuit.

2.30   (c)   A binary half-adder is a circuit having two inputs and two outputs, where the outputs are defined by Table 2.19. A full adder has three inputs (p, q, k) and two outputs (s, c), defined by Table 2.20. Design a half-adder, and, hence, using two half-adders and an OR-gate, the full adder.

TABLE 2.19

Input		Output	
p	q	s	c
0	0	0	0
0	1	1	0
1	0	1	0
1	1	0	1

TABLE 2.20

Input			Output	
p	q	k	s	c
0	0	0	0	0
0	0	1	1	0
0	1	0	1	0
0	1	1	0	1
1	0	0	1	0
1	0	1	0	1
1	1	0	0	1
1	1	1	1	1

2.31   (c)   Define a (Boolean) statement form in the algebra of truth values.

2.32   (c)   Show that $p \rightarrow q$ is functionally equal to $p \vee q \leftrightarrow q$.

2.33   (c)   Show that the following composite statements are tautologies.

(i) $\neg q \wedge (q \vee p) \rightarrow p$;
(ii) $(\neg q \rightarrow \neg p) \leftrightarrow (p \rightarrow q)$;
(iii) $((p \rightarrow q) \wedge (q \rightarrow p)) \leftrightarrow (p \leftrightarrow q)$;
(iv) $((p \rightarrow q) \wedge (\neg p \rightarrow \neg q)) \leftrightarrow (p \leftrightarrow q)$.

2.34   (c)   By means of a computer program show that the following are tautologies:

(i) $(p \wedge (p \rightarrow q) \wedge (\neg r \rightarrow \neg q)) \rightarrow r$;
(ii) $((p \leftrightarrow q) \wedge (q \rightarrow r) \wedge (\neg r \vee s) \wedge (\neg p \rightarrow s)) \rightarrow s$.

2.35 (c) Show that $(p \rightarrow q) \wedge (q \rightarrow r) \wedge (r \rightarrow p)$ implies (i) $p \leftrightarrow r$, (ii) $p \leftrightarrow q$, (iii) $q \leftrightarrow r$. (Note that these implications justify the form of the proof of Th.1.6.)

2.36 (c) Are the operations $\rightarrow$ and $\leftrightarrow$ associative?

2.37 (c) Given that $a < b$ if and only if both $a \leq b$ and $a \neq b$, show that the statement, "if $a \leq b$ then $a < b$ or $a = b$" is true.

2.38 (c) Examine the validity of the following argument, in which the last sentence is the conclusion.

If the balance of payments situation deteriorates, imports are high and exports are low. A surtax has been imposed. A surtax causes money to become scarce. If money is scarce, both imports and exports are low. The balance of payments situation does not deteriorate.

2.39 (c) Thomas, Richard, Harry, and Johndoe were the program advisors who were supposed to be on duty the morning of New Year's Day. Only one turned up. One of the absentees was later questioned as to who the conscientious program advisor was. Somewhat evasively, the absentee made the following revelations: "If Thomas turned up, then so did Harry. If Johndoe was absent, then Richard was there. Either Harry was there, or Johndoe was there, but clearly not both. If either Thomas or Johndoe was absent, then so was Richard." Who was on duty?

2.40 (c) At a penal reform symposium a speaker observed: "If the crime rate is not reduced, then there will be full prisons. It is impossible both to reduce the crime rate and not increase welfare payments, but, if welfare payments are increased, then taxpayers are unhappy." The audience was rather startled by his next statement: "In order to keep taxpayers happy, it is necessary to have full prisons." Does the conclusion follow from the premises? Is "If taxpayers are happy, then prisons are full" a valid conclusion?

2.41 (c) Instead of using truth tables to arrive at the truth value of a composite statement, one may use an arithmetic procedure with the following representations:

$$\neg p \quad - \quad 1 + p,$$
$$p \wedge q \quad - \quad p + q + pq,$$
$$p \vee q \quad - \quad pq.$$

When the value T (F) is assigned to a prime statement, the value 0 (1) is assigned to the corresponding variable in the arithmetic expression. Addition is performed modulo 2, i.e., we have

$$0 + 0 = 0, \quad 0 + 1 = 1 + 0 = 1, \quad 1 + 1 = 0.$$

A tautology is identically equal to 0. The representation of $\neg s \wedge (s \vee t)$, for example, is $(1 + s) + st + (1 + s)st = 1 + s + st + st + sst = 1 + s + st$ (since $p + p \equiv 0$ and $pp \equiv p$). We have then, corresponding to assignments F to s and T to t, $1 + 1 + 1 \cdot 0 = 0$. Find arithmetic representations of $p \rightarrow q$, $p \leftrightarrow q$ and $p \wedge q \wedge r$. Demonstrate the validity of the argument of Exercise 2.38 by arithmetic means.

2.42   (d)   If $|A| = m$ and $|B| = n$, how many binary relations are there from set A to set B? How many binary relations are there from A to B if $A \subseteq B$?

2.43   (d)   Let $I = \{1, 2, 3, 4, 5\}$. List members of the following relations in I:

    (i) $I \times I$;
    (ii) $\{\langle x, y \rangle \mid x, y \in I$ and $x < y\}$;
    (iii) $\{\langle x, y \rangle \mid x, y \in I$ and $x = y\}$.

Which of the relations is a function?

2.44   (d)   Can $\{\langle a, b \rangle, \langle a, b, c \rangle, \langle b, c \rangle, \langle b, c, d \rangle\}$ be a relation in a set?

2.45   (d)   Let R be a relation in set A, and let $X \subseteq A$, $Y \subseteq A$.

Prove: (i) $R[X \cup Y] = R[X] \cup R[Y]$,
        (ii) $R[X \cap Y] \subseteq R[X] \cap R[Y]$.

2.46   (d)   Let R and Q be relations in set A.

Prove: (i) $(R \cup Q)^{-1} = R^{-1} \cup Q^{-1}$,
        (ii) $(R \cap Q)^{-1} = R^{-1} \cap Q^{-1}$.

2.47   (d)   Give examples of relations ρ in $I = \{1, 2, 3, 4, 5\}$ such that $R_\rho = D_\rho$ and (i) $\rho = \rho^{-1}$, (ii) $\rho \neq \rho^{-1}$.

2.48   (d)   Characterize the following relations according to D.2.17:

    (i) $A \times A$ considered as a relation in A;
    (ii) $x > y$ in a set of integers;
    (iii) x and y are brothers;
    (iv)   identity relation;
    (v)   square root relation in the set of integers.

2.49   (d)   Let R and Q be relations in set A. Which of the following are true? Justify your answers with proofs.

    (i)   If R and Q are reflexive, then $R \cup Q$ is reflexive.
    (ii)   If R and Q are reflexive, then $R \cap Q$ is reflexive.
    (iii)   If R and Q are irreflexive, then $R \cup Q$ is irreflexive.
    (iv)   If R and Q are irreflexive, then $R \cap Q$ is irreflexive.
    (v)   If R and Q are symmetric, then $R \cup Q$ is symmetric.
    (vi)   If R and Q are symmetric, then $R \cap Q$ is symmetric.

(vii) If R and Q are antisymmetric, then $R \cup Q$ is antisymmetric.

(viii) If R and Q are antisymmetric, then $R \cap Q$ is antisymmetric.

(ix) If R and Q are transitive, then $R \cup Q$ is transitive.

(x) If R and Q are transitive, then $R \cap Q$ is transitive.

2.50 (d) Characterize the following:

(i) A relation that is both symmetric and antisymmetric.

(ii) A reflexive relation that is a function.

(iii) A relation R that satisfies $R \cap R^{-1} = \emptyset$.

(iv) A relation R that satisfies $R = R^{-1}$.

2.51 (d) Show that a nonempty transitive and symmetric relation cannot be irreflexive but need not be reflexive.

2.52 (e) Which of the following are equivalence relations?

(i) *x and y take the same course* in the set of students of a university.

(ii) $\{\langle\langle x_1, x_2\rangle, \langle x_3, x_4\rangle\rangle \,|\, x_1 + x_4 = x_2 + x_3\}$.

(iii) $\{\langle\langle x_1, x_2\rangle, \langle x_3, x_4\rangle\rangle \,|\, x_1 + x_3 = x_2 + x_4\}$.

2.53 (e) Let R be a relation in set A. Prove that if R is reflexive and transitive, then $R \cap R^{-1}$ is an equivalence relation.

2.54 (e) Find the equivalence classes corresponding to the following equivalence relations:

(i) $A \times A$;

(ii) identity relation in a set $\{x_1, x_2, \ldots, x_n\}$;

(iii) the relation of Part (ii) of Exercise 2.52 in the set $N = \{\langle 1, 2\rangle, \langle 3, 4\rangle, \langle 5, 6\rangle, \ldots\}$.

(iv) the relation of Part (ii) of Exercise 2.52 in the set $\{\langle 0, 2\rangle, \langle 1, 2\rangle, \langle 2, 4\rangle, \langle 3, 4\rangle, \langle 4, 6\rangle, \langle 5, 6\rangle, \ldots\}$.

2.55 (e) Define the numbers $S(n, m)$:

$$S(0, n) = S(n, 0) = 0 \qquad (n > 0),$$
$$S(n, n) = 1 \qquad (n \geq 0),$$
$$S(n, m) = mS(n - 1, m) + S(n - 1, m - 1) \qquad (n > 0).$$

These numbers are called Stirling numbers of the second kind. Show that $\sum_{m=1}^{m=n} S(n, m)$ is the number of equivalence relations in a set of n elements.

2.56 (f) Let X be the set $\{1, 4, 9, 16, \ldots\}$. Suggest one or more partial ordering relations on X.

2.57 (f) Show that the identity relation in a set is the only relation in this set that is both an equivalence relation and a partial ordering.

2.58 (f) Let $\langle A, R\rangle$ be a partially ordered set, and let $B \subseteq A$. Show that $\langle B, R \cap (B \times B)\rangle$ is a partially ordered set.

2.59   (f)   Let $\langle B, \oplus, *, ', 0, 1 \rangle$ be a Boolean algebra. Show that $\langle B, \leqq \rangle$, where relation $\leqq$ is defined by D.1.14, is a partially ordered set.

2.60   (f)   Show that if relation R is a partial ordering, then R^{-1} is also a partial ordering.

2.61   (f)   A reflexive and transitive relation is a preordering. Every partial ordering is, of course, a preordering. Give an example of a preordering that is not a partial ordering.

2.62   (f)   Consider set $A = \{2, 6, 10\}$, partially ordered by the relation *divides*. Find all subsets of A that are simply ordered by *divides*.

2.63   (f)   Show that, relative to a partial ordering, a set can have at most one least member and one greatest member, and that existence of a least (greatest) member implies existence of a unique minimal (maximal) member, which coincides with the least (greatest) member.

2.64   (f)   Show that, relative to a partial ordering, a finite set has at least one minimal (maximal) element.

2.65   (f)   Let $\langle A, \leqq \rangle$ be a partially ordered set. Show that each subset of A has at most one supremum (infimum).

2.66   (f) = Represent the following sets, partially ordered by the relation *divides*, by diagrams:

(i) $\{2, 3, 5, 7, 210\}$,   (ii) $\{2, 3, 4, 5, 9, 1080\}$,   (iii) $\{2, 3, 5, 10, 15, 300\}$.

2.67   (f)   Find least and greatest elements, and minimal and maximal elements of the partially ordered sets of Exercise 2.66.

2.68   (f)   Find subsets of the partially ordered sets of Exercise 2.66 that have three elements and are linearly ordered by the relation *divides*.

2.69   (f)   Find all upper bounds and the supremum for subset $\{2,5\}$ of each of the partially ordered sets of Exercise 2.66.

2.70   (f)   Represent the partially ordered set $\langle \mathscr{P}(\{a, b, c, d\}), \subseteq \rangle$ by a diagram and find a subset of the natural numbers, which, when partially ordered by the relation *divides*, is order-isomorphic to this partially ordered set. What does the diagram turned through 180° represent? What does the diagram turned through 90° represent?

2.71   (f)   Define sets $X = \{2, 4, 8, 16, 32\}$, $Y = \{2, 4, 8, 16, 96\}$, and $Z = \{2, 4, 8, 12, 96\}$, and denote relation *divides* by D, relation *less than or equal* by $\leqq$ and relation *greater than or equal* by $\geqq$. Which of the partially ordered sets of $\{X, Y, Z\} \times \{D, \leqq, \geqq\}$ are order-isomorphic to each other?

2.72   (g)   Are any of the partially ordered sets of Exercise 2.66 lattices? Is any of the partially ordered sets of Exercise 2.71 not a lattice?

2.73   (g)   Draw the operation table for lattice $\langle Z, D \rangle$ of Exercise 2.71.

2.74   (g)   Let $\langle A, \leqq \rangle$ be a lattice. Show that statements $a * b = a$, $a \leqq b$, $a \oplus b = b$ are equivalent for any $a, b \in A$.

2.75 (g) Let $\langle A, \leqq \rangle$ be a lattice. Show that, for any $a, b, c \in A$,

$$a \oplus b = b \oplus a, \qquad a * b = b * a;$$
$$a \oplus (b \oplus c) = (a \oplus b) \oplus c, \qquad a * (b * c) = (a * b) * c.$$

2.76 (g) Let $\langle A, \leqq \rangle$ be a lattice. Show that, for any $a, b \in A$, $a \oplus (a * b) = a = a * (a \oplus b)$.

2.77 (g) Is the set of all sublattices of a lattice again a lattice?

2.78 (g) Show that either of the distributive laws of D.2.30 implies the other.

2.79 (g) (i) Let $\langle A, \leqq \rangle$ be a lattice and let $x, y, z \in A$. Show that $x \leqq y$ implies $x \oplus z \leqq y \oplus z$ and $x * z \leqq y * z$, but that $x \oplus z \leqq y \oplus z$ or $x * z \leqq y * z$ need not imply $x \leqq y$.

(ii) Let $\langle A, \leqq \rangle$ be a distributive lattice with $x, y, z \in A$. Show that $x \oplus z = y \oplus z$ and $x * z = y * z$ imply $x = y$.

2.80 (g) Show that lattice $\langle A, \leqq \rangle$ is distributive if and only if, for any $a, b, c \in A$, $(a \oplus b) * c \leqq a \oplus (b * c)$. Hint: Results obtained in Exercises 2.74, 2.76, and 2.79 are required for the solution of this rather difficult exercise.

2.81 (g) Let $\leqq$ be a partial ordering and let $\geqq$ be the converse of $\leqq$. Show that if $\langle A, \leqq \rangle$ is a lattice, then there exists a lattice $\langle A, \geqq \rangle$, and that if $\langle A, \leqq \rangle$ is distributive, then so is $\langle A, \geqq \rangle$.

2.82 (g) Develop the theory of lattices as an axiomatic theory.

2.83 (g) Given a lattice $\langle X, \leqq \rangle$, where $X = \{x_1, x_2, \ldots, x_n\}$ is a set of integers. A convenient representation of the lattice in a computer is by means of its addition–multiplication table. A program for computing this table might consist of a logical function TEST, which returns .TRUE. if $x_i \leqq x_j$ and .FALSE. otherwise, subroutine SETUP, which generates an N-by-N array LESS in which LESS(I,J) = 1 if $x_i \leqq x_j$ and LESS(I,J) = 0 otherwise, and subroutine TABLE, which computes the addition–multiplication table (SETUP and TABLE are independent of the particular partial ordering).

(i) Write the program and test it on the lattice of Example 1 of D.2.29. For ease of programming assume that for elements $x_1, x_2, \ldots, x_n$, which are stored as LAT(1), LAT(2), ..., LAT(N), $x_i \leqq x_j$ does not hold if i is greater than j (this means that all LESS(I,J) with I greater than J are zero).

(ii) Indicate how the program could be used to determine whether or not the lattice is a chain and to compute an element such as $(x_1 \oplus x_2) * (x_2 \oplus (x_4 * x_6))$, say.

2.84 (g) Rewrite the program of Exercise 2.83 for the general case in which $x_i \leqq x_j$ may hold if i is greater than j. Test the modified program on the lattice of Example 1 of D.2.29 with LAT containing the elements of X in the order 2, 5, 15, 30, 10, 6, 1, 3.

2.85   (h)   (i)   Consider algebra $\langle B, \oplus, *, ', 0, 1 \rangle$ and define operation $+$ by $x + y = (x * y') \oplus (x' * y)$. Is B closed under $+$?
(ii)   Let $N = \{0, 1, 2, 3, \ldots\}$. Give examples of operations under which N is closed.

2.86   (h)   Let $\oplus$ and $*$ be two-argument operations, let $'$ be a one-argument operation, and let 0 and 1 be zero-argument operations in $B = \{0, 1, 2\}$. Which of the following algebras are similar?

   (i) $\langle B, \oplus, *, ', 0, 1 \rangle$.
   (ii) $\langle B, \oplus, *, 0, 1 \rangle$.
   (iii) $\langle B, *, \oplus, ', 0, 1 \rangle$.
   (iv) $\langle B, ', *, \oplus, 0, 1 \rangle$.
   (v) $\langle \{0, 1\}, \oplus, *, ', 0, 1 \rangle$.

2.87   (h)   Show that every sublattice and every homomorphic image of a distributive lattice is a distributive lattice. (Sublattices are subalgebras of lattices.)

2.88   (h)   Consider an algebra $\langle X, * \rangle$, where $X = \{x_1, x_2, x_3, x_4\}$ and the operation is defined by Table 2.21. How many automorphisms $f_k : X \to X$ are there such that the image algebra is also $\langle X, * \rangle$?

TABLE 2.21

$x_i * x_j$

x_i＼x_j	x_1	x_2	x_3	x_4
x_1	x_1	x_2	x_3	x_4
x_2	x_2	x_1	x_4	x_3
x_3	x_3	x_4	x_1	x_2
x_4	x_4	x_3	x_2	x_1

2.89   (h)   Show that, for Boolean algebras B and C, if $f : B \to C$ is an isomorphism, then $f^{-1} : C \to B$ is also an isomorphism.

2.90   (h)   Show that a sublattice of a Boolean algebra need not be a Boolean algebra.

2.91   (h)   Develop an algorithm for the construction of the diagram of a lattice from its addition table. Use the algorithm to show that lattices $\langle A, R_1 \rangle$ and $\langle A, R_2 \rangle$, where $A = \{a, b, c, d, e\}$ and Table 2.22 defines addition in the two lattices, are isomorphic.

TABLE 2.22

	a	b	c	d	e
a	a				
b	a	b			
c	a	a	c		
d	a	b	c	d	
e	a	b	c	d	e

$\langle A, R_1 \rangle$

	a	b	c	d	e
a	a				
b	b	b			
c	a	b	c		
d	a	b	c	d	
e	b	b	e	e	e

$\langle A, R_2 \rangle$

CHAPTER 3

Graph Theory

3a. Diagrams and Graphs

Consider again the diagrams of Figure 2.8. Assume that we have to store enough information in a computer for reconstruction of a diagram at some later date. First, we should store a list of the nodes. Secondly, we will need to know which pairs of nodes are joined by lines, and, for each line, which node covers the other. For example, we should store Diagram (b) as

Nodes $\{1, 2, 3, 5, 6, 10, 15, 30\}$;
Lines $\{\langle 1, 2\rangle, \langle 1, 3\rangle, \langle 1, 5\rangle, \langle 2, 6\rangle, \langle 2, 10\rangle, \langle 3, 6\rangle, \langle 3, 15\rangle,$
         $\langle 5, 10\rangle, \langle 5, 15\rangle, \langle 6, 30\rangle, \langle 10, 30\rangle, \langle 15, 30\rangle\}$,

where it is understood that the node represented by the second coordinate of an ordered pair covers the node represented by the first coordinate. This pair, a set of nodes and a set of lines, is precisely a directed graph.

DEFINITION 3.1   A *directed graph* (*digraph, oriented graph*) is the ordered pair $D = \langle A, R\rangle$, where A is a nonempty set of *nodes* (*points, vertices*) and R is a relation in A, i.e., R is a set of ordered pairs, which are called *arcs* (*lines, pointers*).

Set A may be infinite. We, however, shall deal only with finite digraphs, and the unqualified term *digraph* will always mean a *finite* digraph. Elements of A can then be represented by drawing points in the plane. An arc $\langle a, b\rangle$

is represented by joining a and b with a line, and providing the line with an arrowhead pointing from a to b. Note that if $a \in A$, and there exists no $b \in A$ such that $\langle a, b \rangle \in R$, then a point is still drawn for a in the plane. The notational device of arrowheads is much more explicit than the positional convention we adopted for diagrams of partially ordered sets. If our familiar diagram for $\{1, 2, 3, 5, 6, 10, 15, 30\}$, partially ordered by *divides*, is turned upside down, then the diagram represents partial ordering by the relation, *is a multiple of*. No such misunderstanding can arise with the arrowhead notation; every arrowhead has to be reversed before a picture of digraph $\langle A, R \rangle$ becomes a picture of digraph $\langle A, R^{-1} \rangle$.

A picture of a digraph can give very useful insight into the structure of the relation associated with the digraph, and we sometimes refer to pictures of digraphs as digraphs or even as graphs. We must clearly understand, however, that a digraph is the object defined by D.3.1; it is not a picture. Drawings of the same digraph can, in fact, be greatly different. The three drawings of Figure 3.1 represent the same digraph; it is Diagram (b) of Figure 2.8 inter-

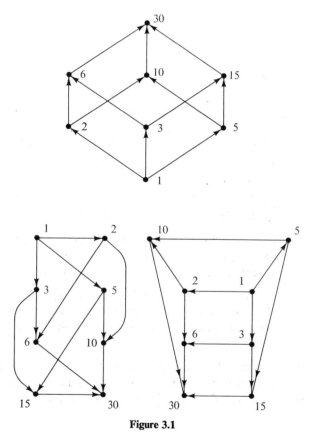

Figure 3.1

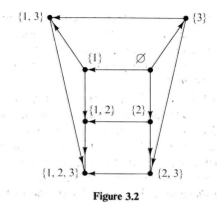

Figure 3.2

preted as the digraph $\langle A, R \rangle$, where $A = \{1, 2, 3, 5, 6, 10, 15, 30\}$ and R is the relation *is covered by*. The picture of Figure 3.2, on the other hand, represents a different digraph, despite its agreement in appearance with one of the drawings of Figure 3.1. Figure 3.2 represents the digraph $\langle \mathscr{P}(\{1, 2, 3\}), R \rangle$, where R is again the relation *is covered by*.

What has come to be known as the theory of graphs really comprises two distinct theories: the theory of digraphs and the theory of (nonoriented) graphs. D.3.1 makes *digraph* a synonym for a relation and the set in which the relation is defined. The theory of digraphs can, therefore, be considered an extension of the theory of relations. One should not, however, put too great an emphasis on the relations as relations. An empirical structure, which may not easily submit itself to characterization by a single meaningful relation, can still be profitably studied as a digraph. One such structure is a system of routes along which something or other moves, be it information, or control, or automobiles, or some commodity such as water or electricity. We might be interested in the accessibility of certain points in the system, or in the elimination of circular routes. The theory of digraphs provides algorithms for the solution of such problems for a general digraph $\langle A, R \rangle$, which are independent of any external interpretation given to relation R.

The theory of graphs proper has more of a combinatorial flavor. For example, the theory of graphs might address itself to the following problem: Given a crystal lattice, how many figures of some type can be formed from points of the lattice and lines between the points? Direction of lines has no importance here.

DEFINITION 3.2   A *graph* is the ordered pair $G = \langle A, P \rangle$, where A is a nonempty set of *nodes* (*points, vertices*) and P is a set of (unordered) pairs of elements of A. Elements of P are called *edges*.

One can convert any graph to a digraph by replacing every $\{a, b\} \in P$ by two ordered pairs $\langle a, b \rangle$ and $\langle b, a \rangle$. It would seem, then, that the theory of digraphs is more general and includes the theory of graphs. This is not so. The two theories deal with different classes of problems and employ different techniques. One is as important as the other. We shall be considering the theory of diagraphs more extensively here for no other reason but that it has more links with computer science.

It should be noted that there is no standard terminology in graph theory. Not only do synonyms abound, but the same word is sometimes used for different concepts. We shall try not to be too original in our choice of terminology. Nevertheless, one somewhat unorthodox term will be used. Normally an arc $\langle a, a \rangle$ is called a *loop*. To avoid confusion with the meaning of *loop* in programming, we shall call arcs of the form $\langle a, a \rangle$ *slings*. Moreover, we have included the term *pointer* in D.3.1 to emphasize the fact that certain data structures in which this term has become standard are in fact digraphs.

3b. Basic Definitions in the Theory of Digraphs

DEFINITION 3.3   If $G = \langle A, R \rangle$ is a digraph and Y is a subset of A, then digraph $G' = \langle Y, (Y \times Y) \cap R \rangle$ is a *subdigraph* of G; it is a *proper subdigraph* if $G \neq G'$. If Q is a subset of R, a digraph $G'' = \langle A, Q \rangle$ is a *partial digraph* of G. The concept of a *partial subdigraph* is an obvious extension.

Example

Consider a digraph $\langle A, R \rangle$ representing a chart of the system of streets in a city. Intersections and ends of streets are represented by nodes. If a street is two way, the segment between two adjacent intersections a and b is represented by arcs $\langle a, b \rangle$ and $\langle b, a \rangle$. If a street is one way in the direction from intersection c to an adjacent intersection d, we represent this segment by $\langle c, d \rangle$. The charts of all two-way streets and of all one-way streets are partial digraphs of $\langle A, R \rangle$. A chart showing only intersections provided with traffic lights and the arcs between such intersections when they adjoin is a subdigraph of $\langle A, R \rangle$. Other subdigraphs are the charts for sections of the city. A chart showing only the one-way streets in some section of the city is a partial subdigraph. Figure 3.3 shows digraph $\langle A, R \rangle$ and a subdigraph representing the system of streets in the eastern end of the city. Figure 3.4 shows the digraph of all one-way streets for the entire city (a partial digraph of $\langle A, R \rangle$) and for the eastern end (a partial subdigraph). Figure 3.5 shows the subdigraph of intersections with traffic lights.

DEFINITION 3.4   A digraph in which some or all nodes have labels associated with them (in addition to the identifying names of the nodes) is called a *labeled digraph*. A digraph in which arcs have weights associated with them is called a *weighted digraph* or *network*. A digraph that is both labeled and weighted is a *labeled network*.

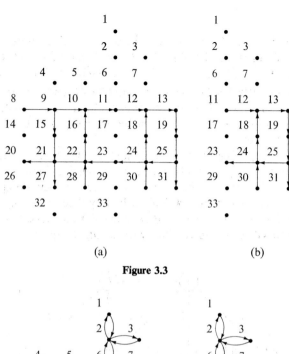

(a)   (b)

Figure 3.3

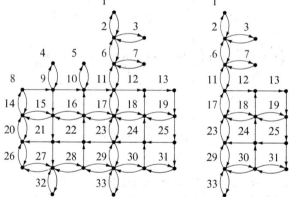

(a)   (b)

Figure 3.4

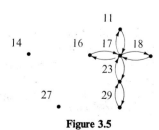

Figure 3.5

Examples

1. In the digraph of Figure 3.3 let nodes representing intersections provided with traffic lights receive the label *T*. The resulting object is a labeled digraph (with nodes 11, 14, 16, 17, 18, 23, 27, 29 labeled). Further, let the arcs have street names attached to them: the name *South Lane* to arcs $\langle 25, 24 \rangle$, $\langle 24, 23 \rangle$, etc.; the name *Main Street* to arcs $\langle 14, 15 \rangle$, $\langle 15, 14 \rangle$, $\langle 15, 16 \rangle$, $\langle 16, 15 \rangle$, etc.; and so on. These street names are weights and the digraph is now a labeled network.

2. The term *weight* is given a more general meaning here than is generally the case. Originally only numbers were used as weights, perhaps expressing the capacity of the arcs for the flow of some commodity along them. As Example 1 shows, we permit a weight to be any piece of information one wishes to associate with an arc. In Figure 3.6 we show a network in which the weights are capacities for flow. The network might represent a system of pipelines.

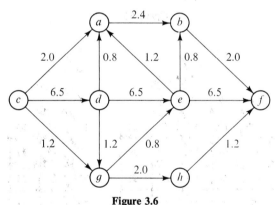

Figure 3.6

3. An $n \times n$ matrix X can be represented by a weighted digraph $\langle A, R \rangle$ in which $\langle i, j \rangle \in R$ if and only if element x_{ij} of matrix X is nonzero. The weight of arc $\langle i, j \rangle$ is the value of x_{ij}. Figure 3.7 shows a matrix and the network that represents it. The weighted digraph can be represented by an ordered pair $\langle A, Q \rangle$, where Q is a set of ordered triples $\langle i, j, x_{ij} \rangle$. $Q = \{ \langle 1, 1, 4 \rangle, \langle 1, 2, 3 \rangle, \langle 2, 1, 2 \rangle, \langle 2, 3, 4 \rangle, \langle 3, 5, -1 \rangle, \langle 4, 1, 8 \rangle, \langle 4, 4, -2 \rangle, \langle 5, 3, 1 \rangle, \langle 5, 5, 2 \rangle \}$.

DEFINITION 3.5 Let $\langle A, R \rangle$ be a digraph with arc $\langle a, b \rangle \in R$. Then a is the *initial node* and b the *terminal node* of $\langle a, b \rangle$. Arc $\langle a, b \rangle$ is said to *originate from* node a and to *terminate at* node b. Extending these concepts, consider $X \subseteq A$. Then $\langle a, b \rangle$ originates from set X if $a \in X$ and $b \notin X$, and the arc terminates in X if $a \notin X$ and $b \in X$. Arcs that originate from or terminate in a set are said to be *incident* with the set.

DEFINITION 3.6 Let $\langle A, R \rangle$ be a digraph and let $X \subseteq A$. We define the following subsets of R:

$$R_X^+ = \{\langle a, b \rangle \mid a \in X, \quad b \notin X\},$$
$$R_X^- = \{\langle a, b \rangle \mid a \notin X, \quad b \in X\}.$$

Then $|R_X^+|$ is the *outdegree* of X, written $od(X)$, and $|R_X^-|$ is the *indegree* of X, written $id(X)$. The *total degree* of X, written $td(X)$, is defined by $td(X) = od(X) + id(X)$. When X consists of a single node, say a, we write $od(a)$, $id(a)$, $td(a)$, and speak of the outdegree, indegree, and total degree of node a.

Example

In the digraph of Figure 3.7 let $X = \{1, 3, 5\}$. Then $R_X^+ = \{\langle 1, 2 \rangle\}$, $R_X^- = \{\langle 2, 1 \rangle, \langle 4, 1 \rangle, \langle 2, 3 \rangle\}$, and $od(X) = 1$, $id(X) = 3$, $td(X) = 4$. For node 1 we have $od(1) = 1$, $id(1) = 2$. Sling $\langle 1, 1 \rangle$ cannot contribute to the indegree or outdegree of node 1. The sum of the indegrees over all nodes of a digraph (or the sum of the outdegrees over all nodes) is the number of those arcs in the digraph that are not slings. The result would be aesthetically more satisfactory if we did not have the qualifier concerning slings. There are many

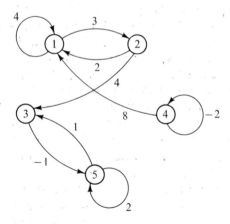

$$\begin{bmatrix} 4 & 3 & 0 & 0 & 0 \\ 2 & 0 & 4 & 0 & 0 \\ 0 & 0 & 0 & 0 & -1 \\ 8 & 0 & 0 & -2 & 0 \\ 0 & 0 & 1 & 0 & 2 \end{bmatrix}$$

Figure 3.7

other results in the theory of digraphs that would be simpler to express were it not for slings. This has led some authors to go as far as to completely exclude digraphs containing slings from their developments of the theory of digraphs.

DEFINITION 3.7   Let $D = \langle A, R \rangle$ be a digraph. If certain members of R can be placed in a sequence of the form $\langle a_1, a_2 \rangle$, $\langle a_2, a_3 \rangle$, ..., $\langle a_{n-1}, a_n \rangle$, then the set $P = \{\langle a_1, a_2 \rangle, \langle a_2, a_3 \rangle, ..., \langle a_{n-1}, a_n \rangle\}$ is a *path* from a_1 to a_n in D. The path is a *cycle* if $a_n = a_1$. A sequence of $n - 1$ arcs can be replaced by an equivalent sequence of n nodes $(a_1, a_2, a_3, ..., a_n)$. If all nodes in this sequence are distinct, the corresponding path is *simple* (*elementary*). If the node sequence corresponds to a cycle, and nodes $a_1, a_2, ..., a_{n-1}$ are distinct, then the cycle is *simple* (*elementary*). If the node sequence corresponds to a simple path (cycle), and it contains every node of A, then the path (cycle) is *Hamiltonian*. The *length* of a simple path (cycle) is $|P|$.

Example

In the digraph of Figure 3.7 we have an arc sequence $\langle 4, 1 \rangle$, $\langle 1, 2 \rangle$, $\langle 2, 3 \rangle$, $\langle 3, 5 \rangle$, and the equivalent node sequence $(4, 1, 2, 3, 5)$. Hence there exists a path $\{\langle 4, 1 \rangle, \langle 1, 2 \rangle, \langle 2, 3 \rangle, \langle 3, 5 \rangle\}$. The path is simple and Hamiltonian. Its length is 4. We also have a sequence $\langle 4, 1 \rangle$, $\langle 1, 2 \rangle$, $\langle 2, 1 \rangle$, $\langle 1, 2 \rangle$, $\langle 2, 1 \rangle$, $\langle 1, 2 \rangle$, $\langle 2, 3 \rangle$, $\langle 3, 5 \rangle$, and the path corresponding to this sequence is $\{\langle 4, 1 \rangle, \langle 1, 2 \rangle, \langle 2, 1 \rangle, \langle 2, 3 \rangle, \langle 3, 5 \rangle\}$. This path is not simple. Let us add the arc $\langle 5, 4 \rangle$ to the digraph, and to the two arc sequences. The equivalent node sequences are then $(4, 1, 2, 3, 5, 4)$ and $(4, 1, 2, 1, 2, 1, 2, 3, 5, 4)$. The former corresponds to a cycle that is simple and Hamiltonian; the cycle corresponding to the latter is not simple and, therefore, cannot be Hamiltonian. The digraph of Figure 3.7 contains simple cycles corresponding to node sequences $(1, 1)$, $(1, 2, 1)$, $(3, 5, 3)$, $(4, 4)$, and $(5, 5)$. None of these is Hamiltonian.

D.3.7 warrants several remarks. First, cycles are also paths, but a simple cycle cannot be a simple path. Second, the length of a path or cycle that is not simple is not defined. Sequences of different lengths can correspond to a single path. This prevents us from using the length of a sequence as a measure of the length of the corresponding path. Consider the path $\{\langle 4, 1 \rangle, \langle 1, 2 \rangle$, $\langle 2, 1 \rangle, \langle 2, 3 \rangle\}$ in the digraph of Figure 3.7. The path has only four members, but tracing of this path in the drawing involves traversal of at least five lines. Hence the number of arcs in a nonsimple path is not a satisfactory measure of its length either. Third, there is no fundamental reason why sequences should not define paths and cycles. Thus, in the digraph of Figure 3.7, sequences $(3, 5, 3)$ and $(5, 3, 5)$ could define two distinct cycles. But our intuitive feeling is that there should be only one cycle here. This intuitive feeling is recognized in our definition of paths and cycles in terms of sets rather than sequences. For reasons of economy we shall at times speak of a "cycle"

(3, 5, 3), or of a "cycle" (5, 3, 5), say, but it will be understood that the two sequences are equivalent, both standing for the set $\{\langle 3, 5\rangle, \langle 5, 3\rangle\}$.

DEFINITION 3.8   A digraph is *cyclic* if it contains at least one cycle; otherwise it is *acyclic*.

THEOREM 3.1   A path in a digraph D is not simple if and only if some subset of the path defines a cycle.

Proof. Assume that P is a nonsimple path in D. Then any node sequence corresponding to P contains a subsequence of the form $(a_i, \ldots, a_i)$, and this subsequence corresponds to a cycle. Next assume that subset Q of a path P in D defines a cycle. Any node sequence corresponding to Q has the form $(a_i, \ldots, a_i)$, and the sequence corresponding to any superset of Q will, therefore, contain a subsequence of this form. Consequently neither Q nor any superset of Q can define a simple path.

DEFINITION 3.9   In a digraph node b is *reachable* from node a if there exists a path from a to b. We assume that every node is reachable from itself along a path of zero length.

DEFINITION 3.10   If node a in digraph D is reachable from no other node in D, and no other node is reachable from a, then a is an *isolated* node. (Alternatively, a is isolated if $id(a) = od(a) = 0$.)

Example

In the digraph of Figure 3.8 every node in the set $N = \{a_1, a_2, a_3, a_5, a_6\}$ is reachable from any other node in N. Node a_7 is reachable from any node in N, but no node in N is reachable from it. Node a_7 is reachable also from a_8, but a_8 is reachable only from itself. Node a_4 is isolated, and so is node a_9.

DEFINITION 3.11   Let $D = \langle A, R\rangle$ be a digraph and let Y be a subset of A. If every node in A is reachable from some node in Y, and no proper subset of Y has this property, then Y is a *node base* of D.

Example

The node base of the digraph of Figure 3.8 comprises the nodes a_4, a_8, a_9, and any one member of $\{a_1, a_2, a_3, a_5, a_6\}$. This digraph, therefore, has five distinct node bases, one of which is $\{a_3, a_4, a_8, a_9\}$.

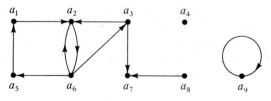

Figure 3.8

THEOREM 3.2 A node belonging to a node base is not reachable from any other node in the base.

Proof. Let nodes a and b belong to a node base, and assume that there exists a path $(a, \ldots, b)$. Then every node reachable from b is reachable from a as well, i.e., removal of b from the node base produces a proper subset of the node base such that all nodes of the digraph are still reachable from its members. Therefore, a path $(a, \ldots, b)$ cannot exist.

THEOREM 3.3 A node that does not have zero indegree and does not lie on a cycle cannot belong to a node base.

Proof. Let N be a node base of a digraph. Consider a node a that has non-zero indegree and does not lie on a cycle. Then there exists an arc that terminates at a, say $\langle b, a \rangle$. Node b belongs to N or is reachable from some node c that belongs to N. Neither b nor c is identical with a (a does not lie on a cycle). Hence a is reachable from some node other than itself in N, and, by Th.3.2, cannot belong to N.

THEOREM 3.4 The node base of an acyclic digraph (or a digraph in which all cycles are slings) $D = \langle A, R \rangle$ is defined by $N = \{a_i \mid a_i \in A, id(a_i) = 0\}$.

Proof. We note first that the presence of a sling affects the reachability of a node from itself alone. Since a node is reachable from itself in any case, the proof can be confined to acyclic digraphs. In the case of an acyclic digraph Th.3.3 states that a node that does not have zero indegree cannot belong to a node base. Hence all nodes belonging to the node base must have zero indegree. Moreover, every such node must belong to the node base. Otherwise, since a node having zero indegree can only be reached from itself, some node would not be reachable from any node belonging to the node base.

THEOREM 3.5 All node bases of a digraph have the same number of elements.

Proof. Consider node bases N_1 and N_2. We shall prove $|N_1| = |N_2|$ by showing that reachability, considered as a relation from N_1 to N_2, is a total one-to-one onto function. Clearly any member of N_2 must be reachable from some member of N_1, and vice versa. Assume that nodes a and b in N_2 are both reachable from node t in N_1. But t is in turn reachable from some node c in N_2, and both a and b are then reachable from c. By Th.3.2 this can be only if $a = b = c$. Similarly we can show that a node in N_2 is reachable from at most one node in N_1. Next assume that there exists a member of N_1 from which no member of N_2 is reachable. Then there exists a proper subset of N_1 from which all nodes of N_2, and hence of the diagram, are reachable; i.e., N_1 is then not a node base.

3c. Digraphs, Matrices, and Relations

A digraph having n nodes $a_1, a_2, \ldots, a_n$ can be completely specified by a square matrix of order n.

DEFINITION 3.12 Let $D = \langle A, R \rangle$ be a digraph, with $A = \{a_1, a_2, \ldots, a_n\}$. The *adjacency matrix* X of D is defined as follows:

$$x_{ij} = 1 \quad \text{if} \quad \langle a_i, a_j \rangle \in R,$$
$$x_{ij} = 0 \quad \text{if} \quad \langle a_i, a_j \rangle \notin R.$$

If D is weighted and w_{ij} is the weight associated with arc $\langle a_i, a_j \rangle$, then, assuming that w_{ij} is zero if and only if $\langle a_i, a_j \rangle$ is not an arc, the w_{ij} define a matrix W. This is the *variable adjacency matrix* of the weighted digraph.

Examples

1. The adjacency matrix of the digraph of Figure 3.8 is

$$X = \begin{bmatrix} 0 & 1 & 0 & 0 & 0 & 0 & 0 & 0 & 0 \\ 0 & 0 & 0 & 0 & 0 & 1 & 0 & 0 & 0 \\ 0 & 1 & 0 & 0 & 0 & 0 & 1 & 0 & 0 \\ 0 & 0 & 0 & 0 & 0 & 0 & 0 & 0 & 0 \\ 1 & 0 & 0 & 0 & 0 & 0 & 0 & 0 & 0 \\ 0 & 1 & 1 & 0 & 1 & 0 & 0 & 0 & 0 \\ 0 & 0 & 0 & 0 & 0 & 0 & 0 & 0 & 0 \\ 0 & 0 & 0 & 0 & 0 & 0 & 1 & 0 & 0 \\ 0 & 0 & 0 & 0 & 0 & 0 & 0 & 0 & 1 \end{bmatrix}.$$

2. The matrix shown in Figure 3.7 is the variable adjacency matrix associated with the weighted digraph of that figure. Our definition of the variable adjacency matrix is very general, but the main need for the matrix arises in the rather special situation in which arcs are given distinct identifying labels and one wants to derive new results from the pattern of the arcs (see A.6.2).

Another matrix of importance, which does not, however, completely specify a digraph, is the path matrix of the digraph.

DEFINITION 3.13   Let $D = \langle A, R \rangle$ be a digraph, with $A = \{a_1, a_2, \ldots, a_n\}$
The *path matrix* P of D is defined as follows:

$p_{ij} = 1$ if there exists a path (or cycle) of nonzero length from
a_i to a_j,

$p_{ij} = 0$ otherwise.

Examples

1. The path matrix of the digraph of Figure 3.8 is

$$
P = \begin{bmatrix}
1 & 1 & 1 & 0 & 1 & 1 & 1 & 0 & 0 \\
1 & 1 & 1 & 0 & 1 & 1 & 1 & 0 & 0 \\
1 & 1 & 1 & 0 & 1 & 1 & 1 & 0 & 0 \\
0 & 0 & 0 & 0 & 0 & 0 & 0 & 0 & 0 \\
1 & 1 & 1 & 0 & 1 & 1 & 1 & 0 & 0 \\
1 & 1 & 1 & 0 & 1 & 1 & 1 & 0 & 0 \\
0 & 0 & 0 & 0 & 0 & 0 & 0 & 0 & 0 \\
0 & 0 & 0 & 0 & 0 & 0 & 1 & 0 & 0 \\
0 & 0 & 0 & 0 & 0 & 0 & 0 & 0 & 1
\end{bmatrix}.
$$

The path matrix remains unchanged when arc $\langle a_6, a_2 \rangle$ is removed from the
digraph.

2. We want $p_{ii} = 1$ if there exists a cycle through a_i. However, since a
cycle is also a path, why do we have the explicit "(or cycle)" in the definition?
The reason is rather pedantic. Although a cycle is a path, a cycle cannot be
a simple path. But the length of a path that is not simple is not defined.
Hence a cycle cannot be a path of nonzero length.

THEOREM 3.6   Let X be the adjacency matrix of digraph D, and let $Y = X^h$.
Then y_{ij} is the total number of distinct sequences $\langle a_i, \ldots \rangle, \ldots, \langle \ldots, a_j \rangle$
that (i) have length h, and (ii) correspond to paths in D.

Proof. We prove the theorem by induction. The base is provided by
D.3.12: With $h = 1$ the theorem is in fact D.3.12. For the induction step
assume that the theorem is true for $h = h'$. Let $P = X^{h'}$. Then, by assumption,
p_{ik} is the number of sequences of length h' having the form $\langle a_i, \ldots \rangle, \ldots,$
$\langle \ldots, a_k \rangle$, and this is also the number of sequences of length $h' + 1$ having the
form $\langle a_i, \ldots \rangle, \ldots, \langle \ldots, a_k \rangle, \langle a_k, a_j \rangle$, i.e., $p_{ik} x_{kj} = p_{ik}$ if $\langle a_k, a_j \rangle$ is an arc,
and $p_{ik} x_{kj} = 0$ if $\langle a_k, a_j \rangle$ is not an arc. The total number of sequences of

length $h' + 1$ having the form $\langle a_i, \ldots \rangle, \ldots, \langle \ldots, a_j \rangle$ is therefore equal to the sum $\sum_{k=1}^{k=n} p_{ik}x_{kj}$, where n is the order of X. But this is the (i, j)th element of $X^{h'+1}$.

COROLLARY 1   If $X^h = 0$ for some $h \leq n$, then D is acyclic.

COROLLARY 2   If P is the path matrix of D and $Q = X + X^2 + \cdots + X^n$, then $p_{ij} = 1$ if and only if q_{ij} is nonzero.

Example

For the digraph of Figure 3.8 we have

$$X^3 = \begin{bmatrix} 0 & 1 & 1 & 0 & 1 & 0 & 0 & 0 & 0 \\ 1 & 1 & 0 & 0 & 0 & 1 & 1 & 0 & 0 \\ 0 & 1 & 1 & 0 & 1 & 0 & 0 & 0 & 0 \\ 0 & 0 & 0 & 0 & 0 & 0 & 0 & 0 & 0 \\ 0 & 0 & 0 & 0 & 0 & 1 & 0 & 0 & 0 \\ 0 & 2 & 1 & 0 & 1 & 1 & 0 & 0 & 0 \\ 0 & 0 & 0 & 0 & 0 & 0 & 0 & 0 & 0 \\ 0 & 0 & 0 & 0 & 0 & 0 & 0 & 0 & 0 \\ 0 & 0 & 0 & 0 & 0 & 0 & 0 & 0 & 1 \end{bmatrix}.$$

There are two sequences of length 3 corresponding to paths from a_6 to a_2: $\langle a_6, a_5 \rangle, \langle a_5, a_1 \rangle, \langle a_1, a_2 \rangle$ and $\langle a_6, a_2 \rangle, \langle a_2, a_6 \rangle, \langle a_6, a_2 \rangle$. The elements of X^9 are quite large:

$$X^9 = \begin{bmatrix} 2 & 8 & 4 & 0 & 4 & 5 & 2 & 0 & 0 \\ 4 & 11 & 5 & 0 & 5 & 8 & 4 & 0 & 0 \\ 2 & 8 & 4 & 0 & 4 & 5 & 2 & 0 & 0 \\ 0 & 0 & 0 & 0 & 0 & 0 & 0 & 0 & 0 \\ 2 & 5 & 2 & 0 & 2 & 4 & 2 & 0 & 0 \\ 5 & 17 & 8 & 0 & 8 & 11 & 5 & 0 & 0 \\ 0 & 0 & 0 & 0 & 0 & 0 & 0 & 0 & 0 \\ 0 & 0 & 0 & 0 & 0 & 0 & 0 & 0 & 0 \\ 0 & 0 & 0 & 0 & 0 & 0 & 0 & 0 & 1 \end{bmatrix}.$$

By Corollary 2 of Th.3.6, the path matrix can be found by generating powers of the adjacency matrix, but this brute-force approach produces a very slow procedure. Use of Boolean operations $\wedge$ and $\vee$ gives P more directly ($1 \wedge 1 = 1$, $1 \wedge 0 = 0 \wedge 1 = 0 \wedge 0 = 0$; $0 \vee 0 = 0$, $0 \vee 1 = 1 \vee 0 = 1 \vee 1 = 1$). We define Boolean matrix operations $C = A \wedge B$ and $D = A \vee B$ in a set of square matrices of order n by

$$c_{ij} = \bigvee_{k=1}^{n} (a_{ik} \wedge b_{kj}),$$

$$d_{ij} = a_{ij} \vee b_{ij}.$$

Then $P = X \vee X^2 \vee \cdots \vee X^n$, where $X^k = X^{k-1} \wedge X$. A very efficient algorithm for computing P follows. It is the well-known Roy–Warshall algorithm.

ALGORITHM 3.1 Given a square matrix X of order n with elements in $\{0, 1\}$.

1. Set $X^* = X$.
2. Set $j = 1$.
3. Set $i = 1$.
4. If $x_{ij}^* = 1$, then set $x_{ik}^* = x_{ik}^* \vee x_{jk}^*$ for all k from 1 to n.
5. Set $i = i + 1$. If $i \leqq n$, go to 4.
6. Set $j = j + 1$. If $j \leqq n$, go to 3; else stop.

THEOREM 3.7 If X is the adjacency matrix of a digraph, then the X^* generated by A.3.1 is the path matrix.

Proof. We show first that $x_{ik}^* = 1$ implies $p_{ik} = 1$. If $x_{ik} = 1$, then certainly $x_{ik}^* = 1$, and $p_{ik} = 1$. If $x_{ik} \neq 1$, then x_{ik}^* is set to 1 in Step 4. This means that at some stage of the process $x_{ij}^* = x_{jk}^* = 1$. Each of these, similarly, comes from X itself or from a previous application of Step 4; i.e., x_{ij}^* was set to 1 because $x_{ij} = 1$ or by virtue of $x_{ij'}^* = x_{j'j}^* = 1$ having held, and similarly for x_{jk}^*. Since the process is finite, the sequence of applications of Step 4 that finally leads to $x_{ik}^* = 1$ must have started out with X containing a finite set of elements $x_{ii_1} = x_{i_1i_2} = x_{i_2i_3} = \cdots = x_{i_mk} = 1$, but this means that $p_{ik} = 1$. Next prove that $p_{ik} = 1$ implies $x_{ik}^* = 1$. If $p_{ik} = 1$, then an expression of the form $x_{ii_1} = x_{i_1i_2} = \cdots = x_{i_mk} = 1$ must hold; i.e., $x_{ii_1}^* = x_{i_1i_2}^* = \cdots = x_{i_mk}^* = 1$ holds initially. Our purpose is to justify a series of replacements of subexpressions $x_{aj}^* = x_{jb}^*$ in this expression by x_{ab}^* that finally leaves the expression $x_{ik}^* = 1$. The iteration with $j = 1$ in A.3.1 produces in Step 4 $x_{i'k'}^* = 1$ for all i' and k' such that $x_{i'1}^* = x_{1k'}^* = 1$, and this justifies substitution of subexpression $x_{i'k'}^*$ for every subexpression $x_{i'1}^* = x_{1k'}^*$. The iteration with $j = 2$ similarly justifies substitution of $x_{i'k'}^*$ for every subexpression $x_{i'2}^* = x_{2k'}^*$. The substitutions are continued with increased j until $j = t$, where t is the largest of the subscripts $i_1, i_2, \ldots, i_m$. Clearly, at the end of the iteration, the expression has been reduced to $x_{ik}^* = 1$. Consequently $p_{ik}^* = 1$ implies $x_{ik}^* = 1$.

As an aid to the understanding of A.3.1 observe that after the iteration with $j = 1$ we have $x_{ik}^* = 1$ if and only if there exist paths (i, k) or $(i, 1, k)$, and that after the iteration with $j = 2$ have $x_{ik}^* = 1$ if and only if there exist paths (i, k), or $(i, 1, k)$, or $(i, 2, k)$, or $(i, 1, 2, k)$, or $(i, 2, 1, k)$, i.e., if and only if there exists a path from i to k that contains nodes belonging to $\{i, k, 1, 2\}$ alone. In general, after the iteration with $j = t$, $x_{ik}^* = 1$ if and only if there exists a path from i to k that contains nodes belonging to $\{i, k, 1, 2, \ldots, t\}$ alone. A proof of Th.3.7 based on this observation should provide greater insight into the structure of A.3.1 than the proof given above (Exercise 3.14).

A digraph is a set and a relation in the set, but the theory of digraphs is not the theory of relations. Although there is no distinct demarcation between the two theories, they do pursue different ends and use different techniques to achieve their ends. The theory of digraphs emphasizes explicit listing of the members of a relation; the theory of relations is more concerned with relations as defined by formulas. Selecting the proper approach to a problem involving a relation is a matter of utility. The pattern of flow of some commodity, say, is best represented by a digraph, and, if we were interested in accessibility of one point from another, or in some related problem, we would not try to express the relation in words or attempt to determine its type. Conversely, given a relation defined by some simple formula (e.g., the *less than* relation in a set of numbers), considering the relation as a digraph, i.e., listing all its elements, will rarely serve a useful purpose. Nevertheless, there are times when it may be profitable to apply the techniques of one theory to the problems of the other. We shall see that operations on the adjacency matrix, which belong to the theory of digraphs rather than the theory of relations, can give useful information about relations.

DEFINITION 3.14 Let $D = \langle A, R \rangle$. Digraph D is *reflexive* (*irreflexive, symmetric, antisymmetric, transitive*) if and only if R is a reflexive (irreflexive, symmetric, antisymmetric, transitive) relation.

In a reflexive digraph there is a sling on every node; in an irreflexive digraph there are no slings. In a symmetric digraph $\langle a, b \rangle \in R$ implies $\langle b, a \rangle \in R$, and in an antisymmetric digraph $\langle a, b \rangle \in R$ implies $\langle b, a \rangle \notin R$ when $a \neq b$. By definition, the existence of a simple path of length 2, $\{\langle i, k \rangle, \langle k, j \rangle\}$, in a transitive digraph implies existence of an arc $\langle i, j \rangle$. Equivalently, if $\langle i, j \rangle$ is not an arc, then there cannot exist a path $\{\langle i, k \rangle, \langle k, j \rangle\}$ for any $k \in A$. The following algorithm makes use of this property of a transitive digraph in determining whether or not a relation is a partial ordering.

ALGORITHM 3.2   Function ISPORD returns .TRUE. if the relation defined by the adjacency matrix MX is a partial ordering.

```
        LOGICAL FUNCTION ISPORD (MX,N)
        DIMENSION MX(N,N)
        ISPORD = .FALSE.
C1   TEST FOR REFLEXIVITY
        DO 10   K = 1,N
        IF (MX(K,K).EQ.0) RETURN
    10  CONTINUE
C2   TEST FOR ANTISYMMETRY AND TRANSITIVITY
        DO 20   I = 2,N
        JTOP = I - 1
        DO 20   J = 1,JTOP
C3   ANTISYMMETRY TEST
        IF (MX(I,J) * MX(J,I).EQ.1) RETURN
C4   TRANSITIVITY TEST - TEST FOR PATHS (I,K,J) IF
C4   MX(I,J) = 0   AND FOR PATHS (J,K,I) IF   MX(J,I) = 0
        IF (MX(I,J).EQ.1) GO TO 14
        DO 12   K = 1,N
        IF (MX(I,K) * MX(K,J).EQ.1) RETURN
    12  CONTINUE
        IF (MX(J,I).EQ.1) GO TO 20
    14  DO 16   K = 1,N
        IF (MX(J,K) * MX(K,I).EQ.1) RETURN
    16  CONTINUE
    20  CONTINUE
C5   EXIT FROM LOOP IMPLIES THAT THE RELATION IS A
C5   PARTIAL ORDERING
        ISPORD = .TRUE.
        RETURN
        END
```

A relation can be shown to be an equivalence by a procedure similar to A.3.2 (Exercise 3.20), but a faster procedure is one based on the fact that an equivalence relation is uniquely determined by a partition of the nodes in which each element belonging to a block is related to every element in that block, but to no element outside the block. Therefore, a relation is an equivalence if there exists a permutation of rows and corresponding columns of the adjacency matrix that transforms it to a block diagonal form exemplified by Figure 3.9 in which the shaded blocks consist of elements that are

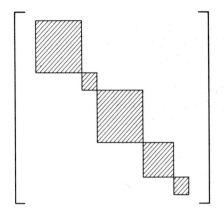

Figure 3.9

all 1, and all elements in the unshaded regions are 0. In our algorithm we shall not interchange the actual rows and columns. Instead, a reference vector will be used to keep track of the interchanges.

ALGORITHM 3.3   Function `ISEQUI` returns `.TRUE.` if the relation defined by the adjacency matrix `MX` is an equivalence. Vector `IREF` returns a permutation that would take `MX` to block diagonal form.

```
      LOGICAL FUNCTION ISEQUI (MX,IREF,N)
      DIMENSION MX(N,N), IREF(N)
C1    INITIALIZE THE REFERENCE VECTOR
      DO 5  I = 1,N
    5 IREF(I) = I
C2    IN (N-M) INTERCHANGES, WHERE M IS THE NUMBER OF
C2    BLOCKS, GENERATE A FORM THAT IS BLOCK DIAGONAL IF
C2    AND ONLY IF THE RELATION IS AN EQUIVALENCE
      IR = 1
   10 II = IREF(IR)
      IR = IR + 1
      IF (IR.GE.N) GO TO 25
      J = IR
   15 JJ = IREF(J)
      IF (MX(II,JJ).EQ.0) GO TO 20
      IREF(J) = IREF(IR)
      IREF(IR) = JJ
      IR = IR + 1
```

```
   20   J = J + 1
        IF (N-J) 10,15,15
C3   TEST THAT FORM IS BLOCK DIAGONAL
   25   ISEQUI = .FALSE.
        ILOW = 1
C4   FIND UPPER LIMIT OF BLOCK
   30   II = IREF(ILOW)
        DO 35  J = ILOW,N
        JJ = IREF(J)
        IF (MX(II,JJ).EQ.0) GO TO 40
   35   CONTINUE
C5   THIS IS THE LAST BLOCK - SKIP ZERO TESTS
        JM = N
        GO TO 50
C6   TEST DIAGONAL ELEMENT
   40   IF (J.EQ.ILOW) RETURN
C7   TEST THAT ALL ELEMENTS TO THE RIGHT AND BENEATH
C7   THE BLOCK ARE ZERO
        JM = J - 1
        DO 45  IROW = ILOW,JM
        II = IREF(IROW)
        DO 45  ICOL = J,N
        JJ = IREF(ICOL)
        IF (MX(II,JJ) + MX(JJ,II).GT.0) RETURN
   45   CONTINUE
C8   TEST THAT ALL ELEMENTS IN BLOCK ARE ONE (FIRST ROW
C8   OF BLOCK HAS ALREADY BEEN DONE)
   50   IF (ILOW.EQ.JM) GO TO 60
        ILOWP = ILOW + 1
        DO 55  IROW = ILOWP,JM
        II = IREF(IROW)
        DO 55  ICOL = ILOW,JM
        JJ = IREF(ICOL)
        IF (MX(II,JJ).EQ.0) RETURN
   55   CONTINUE
C9   TEST NEXT BLOCK
   60   ILOW = JM + 1
        IF (ILOW.LE.N) GO TO 30
        ISEQUI = .TRUE.
        RETURN
        END
```

Example

Given

$$
MX = \begin{bmatrix}
1 & 0 & 0 & 0 & 1 & 1 \\
0 & 1 & 0 & 1 & 0 & 0 \\
0 & 0 & 1 & 0 & 0 & 0 \\
0 & 1 & 0 & 1 & 0 & 0 \\
1 & 0 & 0 & 0 & 1 & 1 \\
1 & 0 & 0 & 0 & 1 & 1
\end{bmatrix},
$$

`ISEQUI` returns `.TRUE.`, and `IREF` returns (1, 5, 6, 4, 2, 3). To see how `IREF` is used, assume that we have to generate the block diagonal matrix explicitly, and that we are generating row 2 of this matrix. Since `IREF(2)` = 5, we go to the fifth row in `MX`: (1, 0, 0, 0, 1, 1). `IREF` now tells us to take elements of this row in the sequence 1, 5, 6, 4, 2, 3. By doing so we obtain (1, 1, 1, 0, 0, 0). The complete block diagonal matrix is

$$
\begin{bmatrix}
1 & 1 & 1 & 0 & 0 & 0 \\
1 & 1 & 1 & 0 & 0 & 0 \\
1 & 1 & 1 & 0 & 0 & 0 \\
0 & 0 & 0 & 1 & 1 & 0 \\
0 & 0 & 0 & 1 & 1 & 0 \\
0 & 0 & 0 & 0 & 0 & 1
\end{bmatrix}.
$$

DEFINITION 3.15   A digraph $\langle A, R \rangle$ is *complete* if, for every pair of nodes a and b in A, $\langle a, b \rangle \notin R$ implies $\langle b, a \rangle \in R$.

Examples

1. The definition is of the form $p \to q$, where p is "$\langle a, b \rangle \notin R$" and q is "$\langle b, a \rangle \in R$", and statement $p \to q$ is false if and only if p is true and q is false. With respect to $\langle a, a \rangle$ this means that $\langle a, a \rangle \notin R$ makes $p \to q$ false, i.e., that a complete digraph must have a sling on every node. By D.2.22, if R is a partial ordering in A, and digraph $\langle A, R \rangle$ is complete, then the relation is a simple ordering.

2. We shall refer to a complete digraph with all slings removed as a *complete slingless* digraph. A digraph in which one and only one of $\langle a, b \rangle \in R$ and $\langle b, a \rangle \in R$ holds for every distinct pair of nodes $a, b \in A$, and

$\langle a, a \rangle \notin R$ for all $a \in A$, is called a *tournament*. The number of arcs in a tournament on n nodes is the number of 2-combinations of a set of n elements. This is $C(n, 2) = \frac{1}{2}n(n - 1)$. Since every arc may be in one of two directions, the number of tournaments is $2^{n(n-1)/2}$. Consider a set of tennis players in round-robin competition. Every player plays every other player exactly once. The players are represented by nodes, and for each pair of players an arc is drawn from the winner to the loser. The resulting digraph is a tournament.

3. A symmetric complete digraph will be called a *total* digraph. A total digraph with slings removed will be called *total slingless*. A total digraph on a set represents the universal relation in the set.

3d. Connectedness in a Digraph

DEFINITION 3.16   Let $D = \langle A, R \rangle$ be a digraph. If, for every nonempty proper subset X of A one or both of $od(X) \neq 0$ and $id(X) \neq 0$ holds, then D is *connected*. Otherwise D is *disconnected*.

DEFINITION 3.17   A connected subdigraph $D' = \langle X, (X \times X) \cap R \rangle$ of D, such that $id(X) = od(X) = 0$, is a *(connected) component* of D.

Examples

1. Let $D = \langle A, R \rangle$ be a connected digraph, and let $X \subseteq A$. Condition $id(X) = od(X) = 0$ holds if and only if $X = A$. Therefore, a connected digraph has a single connected component, which is the digraph itself.

2. Every block of the partition induced by an equivalence relation defines a component. The only equivalence whose digraph is connected is the universal relation. In the digraph of the identity relation every node is isolated; consequently there are as many components as there are nodes.

In D.3.7 the node sequence $(a_1, a_2, \ldots, a_n)$ stands for the arc sequence $\langle a_1, a_2 \rangle, \langle a_2, a_3 \rangle, \ldots, \langle a_{n-1}, a_n \rangle$. We require the first coordinate of an arc to be the same as the second coordinate of its predecessor. Let us drop this requirement; i.e., let $(a_1, a_2, \ldots, a_n)$ stand for an arc sequence of which no more is required than that a_1 and a_2, a_2 and $a_3, \ldots, a_{n-1}$ and a_n be coordinates of successive arcs. For example, our node sequence could stand for $\langle a_1, a_2 \rangle$, $\langle a_3, a_2 \rangle, \ldots, \langle a_n, a_{n-1} \rangle$. Although we can no longer say that a_n is reachable from a_1, the relation between a_1 and a_n is similar to reachability, and we speak of a *semipath* between a_1 and a_n, or say that a_1 and a_n are *connected*, where we assume that a node is always connected with itself. An alternative definition of a connected digraph can now be given: A digraph is connected

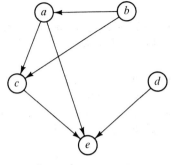

Figure 3.10

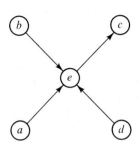

Figure 3.11

if all of its nodes lie on one semipath. In Figure 3.10 all five nodes lie on the semipath (a, b, c, e, d). The corresponding sequence of arcs is $\langle b, a \rangle$, $\langle b, c \rangle$, $\langle c, e \rangle$, $\langle d, e \rangle$. In Figure 3.11 the semipath is (a, e, b, e, c, e, d), and the arc sequence is $\langle a, e \rangle$, $\langle b, e \rangle$, $\langle b, e \rangle$, $\langle e, c \rangle$, $\langle e, c \rangle$, $\langle d, e \rangle$.

THEOREM 3.8   Let $\langle C_i, (C_i \times C_i) \cap R \rangle$ be the connected components of $\langle A, R \rangle$. Sets C_i form a partition of A.

Proof. We use the terminology of the paragraph above. By definition, connectedness in a set of nodes is reflexive. It is also symmetric and transitive. Therefore it is an equivalence relation. It is easy to see that the partition induced by this equivalence relation consists of the C_i.

It is important to realize that the equivalences discussed in Example 2 of D.3.17 differ from that of the proof of Th.3.8. The latter is not the relation R. Therefore, although the adjacency matrix of $\langle A, R \rangle$ can be transformed to block diagonal form, elements of a block need no longer be all ones. But, if Q denotes the relation *a and b are connected*, elements of blocks of the block diagonalized adjacency matrix of $\langle A, Q \rangle$ are all ones, and these blocks define the C_i of Th.3.8. Exercise 3.29 asks for the adjacency matrix of $\langle A, Q \rangle$ to be generated from the adjacency matrix of $\langle A, R \rangle$. Application of A.3.3 to $\langle A, Q \rangle$ produces the block diagonal form. It is then an easy matter to find the connected components of $\langle A, R \rangle$.

DEFINITION 3.18   A digraph is *strongly connected* if every node in the digraph is reachable from every other node.

DEFINITION 3.19   Subdigraph $D' = \langle X, (X \times X) \cap R \rangle$ of D is a *strongly connected component* (*strong component*) of D if it is strongly connected and there exists no pair of nodes $a \in X$, $b \notin X$ such that a and b lie on the same cycle in D.

Example

The strong components of the digraph of Figure 3.8 are $\{a_1, a_2, a_3, a_5, a_6\}$, $\{a_4\}$, $\{a_7\}$, $\{a_8\}$, $\{a_9\}$. Those of the digraph of Figure 3.10 are $\{a\}$, $\{b\}$, $\{c\}$, $\{d\}$, $\{e\}$.

DEFINITION 3.20   A partial digraph D'' of D is the *cycle digraph* of D if it contains all arcs belonging to cycles in D and only such arcs.

THEOREM 3.9   Digraph $D = \langle A, R \rangle$ is strongly connected if and only if there is a cycle (not necessarily simple) through every node in A.

Proof. Exercise 3.30.

COROLLARY   The strong components of a digraph are precisely the connected components of its cycle digraph.

ALGORITHM 3.4   Given the adjacency matrix X of digraph D.

1. Find path matrix P of D.
2. Compute matrix C, defined by $c_{ij} = x_{ij} \times p_{ji}$.

Matrix C is the adjacency matrix of the cycle digraph of D.

Example

The adjacency and path matrices of the digraph of Figure 3.8 are given by Example 1 of D.3.12 and the example of D.3.13, respectively. Then

$$
C = \begin{bmatrix}
0 & 1 & 0 & 0 & 0 & 0 & 0 & 0 & 0 \\
0 & 0 & 0 & 0 & 0 & 1 & 0 & 0 & 0 \\
0 & 1 & 0 & 0 & 0 & 0 & 0 & 0 & 0 \\
0 & 0 & 0 & 0 & 0 & 0 & 0 & 0 & 0 \\
1 & 0 & 0 & 0 & 0 & 0 & 0 & 0 & 0 \\
0 & 1 & 1 & 0 & 1 & 0 & 0 & 0 & 0 \\
0 & 0 & 0 & 0 & 0 & 0 & 0 & 0 & 0 \\
0 & 0 & 0 & 0 & 0 & 0 & 0 & 0 & 0 \\
0 & 0 & 0 & 0 & 0 & 0 & 0 & 0 & 1
\end{bmatrix}.
$$

DEFINITION 3.21   Let $D = \langle A, R \rangle$ be a digraph and define the following sets:

$\mathscr{S} = \{S_i \mid S_i \text{ is a strong component of } D\}$,
$Q = \{\langle S_i, S_j \rangle \mid s_i \in S_i, s_j \in S_j, \langle s_i, s_j \rangle \in R, S_i \neq S_j\}$.

Digraph $\langle \mathscr{S}, Q \rangle$ is the *condensation* of D.

Example

Figure 3.12 shows a digraph D and its condensation D^*. A condensed digraph is acyclic. This implies that, if $\langle h, i \rangle$ in D were replaced by $\langle i, h \rangle$, the condensation of the new digraph would consist of a single node.

THEOREM 3.10   Let $D = \langle A, R \rangle$ and $D^* = \langle \mathscr{S}, Q \rangle$ be a digraph and its condensation, respectively. Define a subset of $\mathscr{S}: \mathscr{S}' = \{ S_i \mid id(S_i) = 0 \}$. A node base of D is generated by taking exactly one element from each S_i in $\mathscr{S}'$.

Proof. Exercise 3.33.

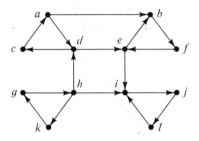

Digraph D

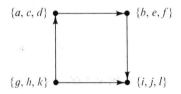

Condensation D^*

Figure 3.12

3e. Trees

DEFINITION 3.22   An acyclic digraph in which exactly one node has indegree 0 and every other node has indegree 1 is a *directed tree*. The node with indegree 0 is the *root* of the tree. Nodes with zero outdegree are *terminal nodes*. The length of the path from the root to a node is the *level* of the node. If $\langle a, b \rangle$ is an arc in a directed tree, then node b is a *successor* of node a, and a is the *predecessor* of b. Nodes that have the same predecessor are *neighbors* of each other.

Examples

1. Usually a directed tree is depicted with the root placed at the top of the drawing, nodes reachable from the root along a path of length 1 immediately below the root, nodes on level 2 immediately below these, etc. Figure 3.13 shows a directed tree with root *a* and terminal nodes *d, e, f, h, i*. Node *a* is on 0 level; nodes *b* and *c* are on level 1; nodes *d, e, f*, and *g* on level 2; nodes *h* and *i* on level 3. Node *a* has two successors, nodes *b* and *c*. Node *g* is the successor of node *c*. Nodes *d, e*, and *f*, which have the same predecessor, namely *b*, are neighbors. Similarly *b* and *c* are neighbors, as are *h* and *i*, but *f* and *g* are not. Every node in a directed tree, except the root, has exactly one predecessor. The root has no predecessor, and terminal nodes have no successors.

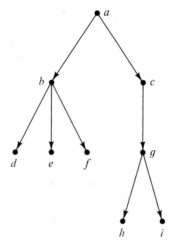

Figure 3.13

2. A single node is a directed tree.

3. If the arrows are removed from the drawing of a directed tree, then the result is the drawing of an undirected graph. *Provided the root is clearly identified*, no loss of information results from the removal of arrows because the original directed tree can always be derived from this undirected structure, which is called a *rooted tree* (see D.3.36 for a formal definition). Directed trees and rooted trees are exactly equivalent as regards their power to represent a given concrete situation in an application.

DEFINITION 3.23   A directed tree in which every node has outdegree 0 or 2 is a *binary tree*.

Example

The directed trees of Figure 3.14 are binary.

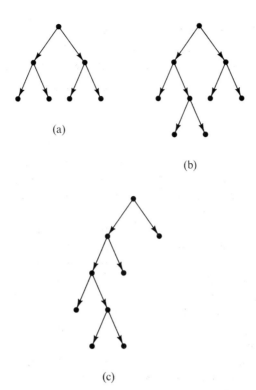

(a)

(b)

(c)

Figure 3.14

THEOREM 3.11   Let n be any positive nonzero integer. A binary tree T_n with n terminal nodes exists.

Proof. Assume that $T_n = \langle A_n, R_n \rangle$ exists. Let $a \in A_n$ be any terminal node in T_n. Introduce nodes $b, c \notin A_n$ and draw arcs $\langle a, b \rangle$, $\langle a, c \rangle$. Now $id(b) = id(c) = 1$, $od(b) = od(c) = 0$, $od(a) = 2$, and indegrees and outdegrees of all other members of A_n remain unchanged. Clearly the new structure is again a binary tree. Node a is no longer terminal, but two new terminal nodes have been created; i.e., the number of terminal nodes has increased to $n + 1$. Hence T_{n+1} exists if T_n exists. But T_1 exists; it is a single isolated node. (If you are not happy with basing the proof on the degenerate tree T_1, construct T_2 as well.)

THEOREM 3.12   Let $T = \langle A, R \rangle$ be a binary tree. Then $r = |R| = 2(n_t - 1)$, where n_t is the number of terminal nodes in T.

Proof. Exercise 3.37.

DEFINITION 3.24   Let n be the number of terminal nodes in a binary tree, and let m be a nonnegative integer; let d be the length of a path from the root to a terminal node. A binary tree is *balanced* if

(a) $n = 2^m$ implies $d = m$,

(b) $2^m < n < 2^{m+1}$ implies $d = m$ or $d = m + 1$.

A balanced binary tree with $n = 2^m$ is a *full binary tree* of order *m*.

Example

Binary trees (a) and (b) of Figure 3.14 are balanced. Tree (a) has four terminal nodes, and the length of every path from the root to a terminal node is 2. Tree (b) has five terminal nodes. Three of the paths have length 2, the other two have length 3. Binary tree (c) is not balanced. Only (a) is a full binary tree. It is of order 2.

The left-to-right order in which one draws arcs originating from a node of a directed tree is significant in most applications, so that usually the picture of a directed tree does not really correspond to a digraph. For reasons of conceptual economy we do, however, wish to consider directed trees as a species of digraphs. This can be done if the arcs are labeled according to some scheme that expresses the order they would have in a drawing. A canonical labeling scheme results if arcs originating from the one node are simply labeled 0, 1, 2, ..., reading from left to right.

There are many important applications of binary trees in which order is important, and we shall now apply the labeling scheme that has just been described to binary trees. Actually the structures we shall consider are somewhat more general than the binary trees of D.3.23 in that the outdegree of a nonterminal node is permitted to be 1 as well as 2, but the single arc originating from a nonterminal node with outdegree 1 still has direction: it may be directed to the left or to the right. We shall call these trees B-trees.

DEFINITION 3.25   A *B-tree* is the triple $\langle A, R, f \rangle$, where $\langle A, R \rangle$ is a directed tree in which every node has outdegree 0, 1, or 2, and function $f: R \to \{0, 1\}$ associates with each arc a label 0 or 1. An arc $\langle a, b \rangle \in R$ has *left orientation* if $f(a, b) = 0$; it has *right orientation* if $f(a, b) = 1$. Two arcs originating from one node cannot have the same orientation. If arc $\langle a, b \rangle$ has left (right) orientation, then node *b* is the *left (right) successor* of node *a*. The subtree rooted at the left (right) successor of node *a* is the *left (right) subtree* of the tree or subtree rooted at *a*.

Examples

1. The three structures of Figure 3.15 are distinct when considered as B-trees. On removal of the labels they revert to being ordinary digraphs, and then all three drawings represent the same digraph. (In practice, how-

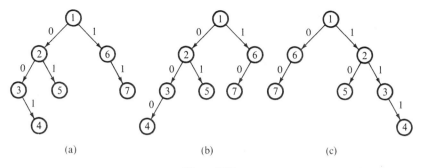

Figure 3.15

ever, one normally neglects to label the arcs in a drawing of a B-tree. The peculiar way the B-trees are drawn should be sufficient indication that order is considered important.)

2. We introduce three functions: the predecessor function p, the left successor function l, and the right successor function r. If node a is the predecessor of node b, then $p(b) = a$; if b is the left successor of a, then $l(a) = b$; if b is the right successor of a, then $r(a) = b$. The functions are undefined for certain nodes of a B-tree: p is undefined for the root, l for nodes having no left successor, and r for nodes having no right successor. Table 3.1 lists the images of the nodes of B-tree (a) of Figure 3.15 under the three functions. In this B-tree $r(r(1)) = r(6) = 7$, but $r(r(r(1)))$ is undefined; $p(l(2)) = p(3) = 2$; $p(p(p(4))) = 1$.

TABLE 3.1

B-Tree Functions

n	$p(n)$	$l(n)$	$r(n)$
1	—	2	6
2	1	3	5
3	2	—	4
4	3	—	—
5	2	—	—
6	1	—	7
7	6	—	—

3. The definition of balanced B-trees is analogous to D.3.24. However, a slightly more restrictive definition may be given: A B-tree is balanced if, for every subtree of the tree, the number of nodes in its right and left subtrees differ by at most 1. For the purposes of this definition, if the root of a subtree does not have one or other of the successors, then the corresponding number of nodes is taken to be zero. If trees (a) and (b) of Figure 3.14 are

interpreted as B-trees, then they are both balanced in terms of D.3.24, but
(b) is not balanced in the more restrictive sense. Adelson-Velskii and Landis
advance a more permissive definition: A B-tree is balanced if, for every node
in the tree, the number of arcs constituting a longest path from this node to a
terminal node through the left successor of the node differs by at most one
from the number of arcs constituting such longest path through the right
successor. B-trees that satisfy this last definition are called AVL trees.

3f. Linear Formulas of Digraphs

Instead of representing a digraph by its adjacency matrix, we can represent
it by a set of linear formulas. Let us first discuss the notation informally. It is
based on the representation of an arc by an operator * applied to the node
symbols: Arc $\langle a, b \rangle$ is represented by *ab*. We shall call operator * the
K-operator. If more than one arc originates from a node, a formula representing all these arcs consists of as many K-operators as there are arcs,
followed by the symbol of the node from which the arcs originate, followed
in turn by symbols of the nodes in which the arcs terminate. Referring to
Figure 3.16, we have, for arcs originating from nodes *a*, *b*, and *c*, formulas
***abce*, ***bbcd*, ***cbde*, respectively. The three formulas represent the
three digraphs shown in Figure 3.17. Note that the symbols of the terminal
nodes can be written in any order. Thus we can rewrite formula ***abce* as
***aebc*, or as ***aecb*, and so forth.

The formulas may be combined. We replace the *b* in the formula for *A* by
the formula for *B* to get ***a***bbcdce*, a formula representing the digraph
of Figure 3.18. If next we substitute ***cbde* for one of the occurrences of *c*
in this formula, we obtain ***a***bb***cbdedce* or ***a***bbcd***cbdee*,
depending on which occurrence of *c* we substitute for. Either of these final
formulas represents the digraph of Figure 3.16. We call the formulas K-
formulas.

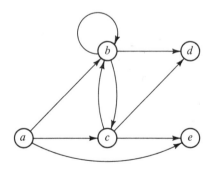

Figure 3.16

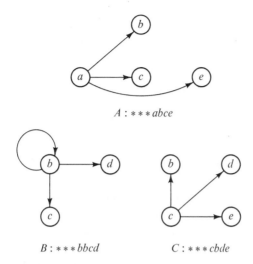

$A : * * * abce$

$B : * * * bbcd$ $\qquad$ $C : * * * cbde$

Figure 3.17

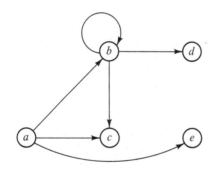

Figure 3.18

DEFINITION 3.26   We define a K-formula recursively:

(a) A node symbol is a K-formula.

(b) If α and β are K-formulas, then $*\alpha\beta$ is a K-formula.

[To be quite explicit, we should add (c): K-formulas are only those entities that are constructed under (a) and (b).]

DEFINITION 3.27   A K-formula is a K-formula *of the node* whose symbol is the leftmost node symbol in the K-formula, and this node is the *leading node* of the K-formula.

Example

cbbcdde* is a K-formula of leading node *c*.

Since D.3.26 is a recursive definition, we can consider subformulas of K-formulas as K-formulas in their own right, provided they are consistent with the definition. The definition enables us to tell whether or not a given formula is "well formed," but it does not relate a K-formula to a particular digraph. Hence we require an algorithm for generating K-formulas of given digraphs. In what follows we shall always assume that K-formulas are considered in the context of particular digraphs rather than as abstract objects.

ALGORITHM 3.5   Let $D = \langle A, R \rangle$ be a digraph.

1.   For every isolated node $a \in A$ that has no sling on it write the K-formula a.

2.   For every arc $\langle a, b \rangle \in R$ write the K-formula $*ab$.

3.   Apply the following *substitution rule* to combine the K-formulas until it can no longer be applied:

> If there exists a K-formula of a node and there exists another K-formula in which a symbol of the node appears, substitute the K-formula of the node for this symbol.

4.   (Check step) Denote the K-formulas produced in Step 3 by $k_1, k_2, \ldots, k_n$, and the leading node of a k_i by a_i. If some k_i contains as a subformula a K-formula of node b in which a_i appears, and the b occurs in one of $k_1, \ldots, k_{i-1}, k_{i+1}, \ldots, k_n$, extract the K-formula of b from k_i, inserting b in its place, substitute what now remains of k_i into this K-formula, and return to Step 3.

Examples

1. Consider the digraph of Figure 3.19. There are no isolated nodes, so, in applying A.3.5, we start in Step 2, and obtain the set

$$\{*ad, *bc, *cd, *db, *de, *ea\}.$$

Successive applications of the substitution rule produce

$$\{*a*de, *bc, *cd, *db, *ea\},$$
$$\{*a*d*ea, *bc, *cd, *db\},$$
$$\{*a**db*ea, *bc, *cd\},$$
$$\{*a**d*bc*ea, *cd\},$$
$$\{*a**d*b*cd*ea\}.$$

2.   With the digraph of Figure 3.20 we proceed from $\{*ab, *bc, *cb\}$ to $\{*ab, *c*bc\}$, but find then that the substitution rule cannot be applied any further. Therefore we go to Step 4 of the algorithm and find that subformula $*bc$ of $*c*bc$ contains c, and that $*ab$ contains b. We extract the $*bc$, and substitute into it what is left after the extraction, namely $*cb$. The resulting K-formula $*b*cb$ is substituted into $*ab$ to produce $*a*b*cb$.

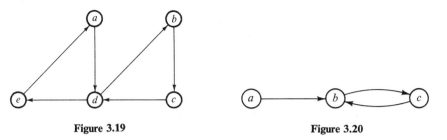

Figure 3.19   Figure 3.20

3. Step 2 of A.3.5 has been put in the form it has for the purposes of D.3.29. If we are interested in producing a set of K-formulas of a given digraph for a practical application, this step should be replaced by the following: " For every node $b \in A$ that has not been processed in Step 1 write a K-formula consisting of as many K-operators as there are arcs originating from b, followed by the symbol b, followed in turn by symbols of all the nodes at which these arcs terminate." The K-formulas produced by Step 1 and the modified Step 2 will be called *atomic* K-formulas.

DEFINITION 3.28   For a digraph D, a set of K-formulas produced by A.3.5 is a *minimal* set of K-formulas of D.

Although in practice one is mostly interested in minimal sets of K-formulas, for theoretical reasons we must be able to associate more general sets of K-formulas with a particular digraph. D.3.29 enables us to do so.

DEFINITION 3.29   A set of K-formulas *represents* a digraph D if and only if it can be obtained by applying the substitution rule of A.3.5 to the K-formulas generated from D in Steps 1 and 2 of A.3.5, where the number of applications of the rule may vary from zero to as many as are required to take A.3.5 to completion.

The following remarks apply to any set of K-formulas representing a digraph D. Since the substitution rule neither creates nor destroys any K-operators, all representative sets of D contain the same number of K-operators, and this number is equal to the number of arcs in D. Furthermore, the number of K-operators preceding occurrences of a particular node symbol a is equal to the number of arcs originating from a. For example, in a representation $\{**a***a*bc**dcbef, **bf**e**bad*ac\}$, symbol a occurs four times, preceded by 2, 3, 0, and 1 K-operators, respectively. Therefore, the total number of arcs originating from a is 6. Let us see where these arcs terminate. If a is preceded by n K-operators, then it is the leading node of a K-formula $** \cdots *a\alpha_1\alpha_2 \cdots \alpha_n$, where the $\alpha_1, \alpha_2, \ldots, \alpha_n$ are again K-formulas. The leading nodes of these K-formulas are terminal nodes of arcs originating from a. Continuing with our example, we have the following relevant K-formulas of

a: $**a(***a*bc**dcbe)(f)$, $***a(*bc)(**dcb)(e)$, $*a(c)$, where the α_i have been enclosed in parentheses for clarity. The set of arcs originating from a is, therefore, $\{\langle a, a\rangle, \langle a, f\rangle, \langle a, b\rangle, \langle a, d\rangle, \langle a, e\rangle, \langle a, c\rangle\}$. Applying the procedure to occurrences of b we get the set $\{\langle b, c\rangle, \langle b, f\rangle, \langle b, e\rangle, \langle b, a\rangle, \langle b, d\rangle\}$. There are no arcs originating from nodes c and f, and arcs originating from d and e constitute the sets $\{\langle d, c\rangle, \langle d, b\rangle\}$ and $\{\langle e, b\rangle, \langle e, a\rangle\}$, respectively. The union of these four sets is precisely the set of arcs of the digraph.

The recursive definition of a K-formula is not particularly well suited to identification of the α_i. Therefore, we give an equivalent iterative definition.

DEFINITION 3.26a   Consider a formula $s_1 s_2 \cdots s_i \cdots s_m$. Let k_i and n_i denote numbers of K-operators and node symbols, respectively, in the subformula $s_1 \cdots s_i$. The formula is a K-formula if and only if the following conditions are satisfied:

$$n_i \leqq k_i, \qquad i = 1, 2, \ldots, m - 1;$$
$$n_m = k_m + 1.$$

Example

Consider the formula $**a***a*bc**dcbef$. Set $n = 0$ and $k = 0$. Scan the formula from the left, setting $n = n + 1$ when a scanned symbol represents a node, or $k = k + 1$ when it is a K-operator. Throughout the scan we have $n \leqq k$, except when the symbol f is reached, and then $n = k + 1$. Therefore the formula is a K-formula. Writing the formula as $**a\alpha_1\alpha_2$, we can determine α_1 by repeating the procedure on the subformula $***a*bc**dcbef$. Again $n \leqq k$ while we are scanning $***a*bc**dcb$, and $n = k + 1$ when the e is reached. Therefore α_1 is $***a*bc**dcbe$. The rest of the subformula, namely f, must be α_2. In a similar fashion, expressing $***a*bc**dcbe$ as $***a\alpha_1\alpha_2\alpha_3$, we find that $\alpha_1 = *bc$, $\alpha_2 = **dcb$, $\alpha_3 = e$.

DEFINITION 3.30   Let F be a set of K-formulas.

(a) If a member of F or a subformula of a member has the form $** \cdots *a\alpha_1\alpha_2 \cdots \alpha_n$, where node symbol a is preceded by n K-operators ($n \geqq 2$), and $\alpha_1, \ldots, \alpha_n$ are K-formulas, a reordering of the $\alpha_1, \ldots, \alpha_n$ is an application of the *switch rule*.

(b) The interchange of two K-formulas of a node a, occurring as members or subformulas of members of F, provided the interchange does not produce a new member of F consisting of a single node symbol, is an application of the *interchange rule*.

D.3.29 does not specify the order in which the substitution rule is to be applied. Application of switch and interchange rules merely converts a given representative set to the set that would have resulted had a different sequence of substitutions been followed. Consider K-formula ****ac*b***c*db*edae*, which represents the digraph of Figure 3.21. Here $\alpha_1 = c$, $\alpha_2 = $ **b***c*db*eda*, $\alpha_3 = e$. One application of the switch rule produces ****a*b***c*db*edaec*. Interchange of ****c*db*eda* and c in this formula produces ****a*bce***c*db*-eda*. For another example consider the set {****a***bbcdce, ***cbde*}. Interchange of ****bbcd* and b to produce {****abce, ***c***bbcdde*} is valid, and so is the interchange of c and ***cbd*, but we may not interchange the c with ****cbde*. In the last instance {****a***bbcd***cbdee, c*} would be produced, which is not a representative set according to D.3.29.

In effect, the use of K-formulas for the representation of a directed graph converts the digraph to a labeled directed tree or set of trees. We introduce the notion of levels of K-formulas. A minimal set of K-formulas consists of K-formulas on level 0. If a K-formula k_i in this set can be written as **** $\cdots$ **a_i*$\alpha_1\alpha_2 \cdots \alpha_n$, where the α_j are again K-formulas, then the α_j are K-formulas on level 1. They are said to *derive* from k_i. If an α_j can in turn be expressed in terms of K-formulas, then these K-formulas are on level 2, and so forth. Consider again the K-formula

$$\text{\textit{***ac*b***c*db*edae,}}$$

which represents the digraph of Figure 3.21. Here the K-formulas on level 1 are $\alpha_1 = c$, $\alpha_2 = $ **b***c*db*eda*, $\alpha_3 = e$. The second level K-formula that derives from α_2 is ****c*db*eda*, and from this K-formula we can derive third level K-formulas, **db, *ed, a*. The first two of these give rise to fourth level

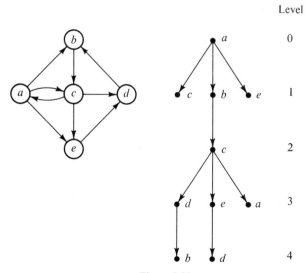

Figure 3.21

K-formulas b and d, respectively. The level structure is illustrated by the level tree of Figure 3.21.

The level tree of a K-formula will be called a *K-tree*. In particular, the level trees of atomic K-formulas will be called *atomic K-trees*. An application of the switch rule to a K-formula corresponds in its K-tree merely to a rearrangement of the order of the arcs originating from a node. An application of the interchange rule corresponds in the K-tree to the interchange of subtrees whose roots carry identical labels, i.e., the tree is transformed to a truly different tree. For example, in the K-tree of Figure 3.21, we can detach the subtree rooted at c, and reattach it to the terminal node labeled c. The K-tree of a digraph has the same number of arcs as the digraph it represents. The K-tree can in fact be regarded as the digraph "unraveled" into a more tractable form.

THEOREM 3.13   The leading nodes of K-formulas in a minimal set of a digraph constitute a base of the digraph.

Proof. It is easy to show that every node whose symbol appears in a K-formula of a node is reachable from this node. Also, K-formulas of a minimal set (indeed, of any representative set) contain symbols of all nodes. Hence all nodes of the digraph are reachable from the leading nodes of the K-formulas of a minimal set. We shall show that no proper subset of the leading nodes has this property. Let k_i and k_j be any two K-formulas in the minimal set, with leading nodes a and b, respectively, and assume that a is reachable from b. Then there exists a finite path $(b, n_1, n_2, \ldots, n_t, a)$. The original $*n_t a$ could not have been substituted into any formula other than k_i (otherwise k_i could now be substituted into this formula). Therefore n_t appears in k_i. Moreover, n_t is the leading node of a K-formula that contains a. Therefore, if $*n_{t-1}n_t$ had been substituted into a formula other than k_i, the check step of A.3.5 would be applicable. In a like manner we show that $*n_{t-2}n_{t-1}, \ldots, *n_1 n_2, *b n_1$ have been substituted into k_i. But $*b n_1$ could not have been so substituted (otherwise k_j could now be substituted into k_i). This contradiction establishes that the leading nodes are not reachable one from another, i.e., that there exists no proper subset of the leading nodes from which every node of the digraph could be reached.

The set of leading nodes of a minimal set of K-formulas is invariant under applications of switch and interchange rules. If a digraph has more than one node base, the leading nodes of the minimal set produced by A.3.5 can be made to constitute any one of the bases. Therefore, if a digraph has more than one node base, it is impossible to generate every minimal set of K-formulas of the digraph, starting from a given set, by means of switch and interchange rules alone. In order to generate all minimal sets we have to apply the procedure of Step 4 of A.3.5 as well. For example, we can split up ****a*b***c*db*edaec* into ****abec* and **b***c*db*eda*, and then substitute ****abec* for the *a* in the second formula to obtain **b***c*db*ed***abec*.

We now have three representations of a digraph that cover a wide scale. At one end of the scale is the drawing of the digraph, which gives immediate indication of the structure of the digraph, but is very awkward to operate on in a computer. At the other end of the scale is the adjacency matrix. Its computational properties are excellent, but the structure of the digraph is concealed. Representation in terms of K-formulas or K-trees is a compromise. The structure of the digraph is still reasonably explicit, and the manipulation of K-formulas and K-trees is not too difficult. In the next section we shall see how these properties of the K-formular representation can be put to good use.

3g. Isomorphism of Digraphs

DEFINITION 3.31   Two digraphs are *isomorphic* if some permutation of the rows and corresponding columns in the adjacency matrix of one of the digraphs produces the adjacency matrix of the other; i.e., isomorphic digraphs are identical except for the identifying names carried by their nodes.

Example

The digraphs of Figure 3.22 are isomorphic. Their adjacency matrices are equal when we make elements of $\{1, 2, 3, 4, 5\}$ and $\{a, b, c, d, e\}$ correspond to the $a_1, \ldots, a_5$ of D.3.12 as follows:

a_1	a_2	a_3	a_4	a_5
1	2	3	4	5
c	d	a	e	b

The isomorphism problem is very difficult. An algorithm for testing pairs of digraphs for isomorphism certainly exists: Permute the rows and corresponding columns of one of the adjacency matrices until it matches the other, or—in case the digraphs are not isomorphic—stop after $n!$ permutations. The algorithm fails on practical grounds: even with a digraph of only 16 nodes, a hypothetical computer that generates a new permutation and checks the two matrices for equality once every microsecond could take close to 40 years for the job. It is for this reason that heuristic procedures that examine the fine structure of the digraphs have been developed. Let us illustrate two such procedures with reference to the digraphs of Figure 3.22.

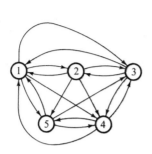 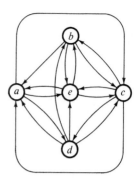

Figure 3.22

First, let us list the indegrees and outdegrees of the nodes.

n	$id(n)$	$od(n)$	n	$id(n)$	$od(n)$
1	4	4	a	4	3
2	2	4	b	3	3
3	4	3	c	4	4
4	4	3	d	2	4
5	3	3	e	4	3

The list shows at once that nodes 1, 2, and 5 can correspond only to nodes c, d, and b, respectively, and that nodes in the set $\{3, 4\}$ can correspond only to nodes in $\{a, e\}$. This is how far the first procedure takes us here.

Next let us list the arcs originating from 3 and 4, and from a and e.

$$\langle 3, 1 \rangle, \langle 3, 2 \rangle, \langle 3, 4 \rangle \qquad \langle a, c \rangle, \langle a, d \rangle, \langle a, e \rangle$$
$$\langle 4, 1 \rangle, \langle 4, 3 \rangle, \langle 4, 5 \rangle \qquad \langle e, a \rangle, \langle e, b \rangle, \langle e, c \rangle$$

Assume the correspondences 1–c, 2–d, 5–b, and assume that node 3 corresponds to node e. Existence of $\langle 3, 1 \rangle$ implies existence of $\langle e, c \rangle$, and existence of $\langle 3, 2 \rangle$ implies existence of $\langle e, d \rangle$. But $\langle e, d \rangle$ does not exist. Therefore 3 cannot correspond to e, and can correspond only to a. The only node to which 4 can then correspond is e. All that remains is to set up the two adjacency matrices according to the scheme

a_1	a_2	a_3	a_4	a_5
1	2	3	4	5
c	d	a	e	b

The digraphs are isomorphic if and only if the two matrices are equal. Here they are.

In the heuristic approach to the isomorphism problem sets of arcs are the data. One develops a number of procedures, each designed to extract from a set of arcs information relating to a particular aspect of the structure of a digraph. The procedures are finally combined and a very complicated program results. Although a set of arcs contains all the information required, the information is not directly accessible; it must be computed. Moreover, the computation takes a different form in each of the procedures. Hence the complexity. For example, in setting up a table of outdegrees, a list of first coordinates of the arcs has to be examined. The indegrees, on the other hand, are computed from a list of second coordinates. The procedure for extracting the arcs that originate from the same node is again different in form, and so on.

The linear formulas introduced in the preceding section contain structural information in a more readily accessible form. As a consequence, instead of having to test digraphs for isomorphism by a sequence of dissimilar tests, one can perform the task by letting a relatively simple unified procedure operate on minimal sets of K-formulas. We shall give only a very sketchy outline of the procedure by means of an example.

Consider the digraphs of Figure 3.22. We shall set up a reference K-formula of one of the digraphs, and then find all K-formulas representing the other that have the same pattern. Each correspondence defines an isomorphism. This will be done in stages, by comparing K-formulas of substructures. Here we generate the reference K-formula

$$****1****2***3***4***51341312145345.$$

The atomic K-formulas of the other digraph form the set {$***acde$, $***bace$, $****cabde$, $****dabce$, $***eabc$}. First we look for K-formulas belonging to this set that match subformula $***5134$, and we find that $***acde$, $***bace$, $***eabc$ do so. Next we substitute, *and apply the switch rule*, to produce K-formulas that have the same pattern as subformula $***4***513413$. Consider, for example, $***a***eabccd$. In the reference subformula 5 is followed by two occurrences each of 1 and 3. In the trial subformula only c occurs more than once among the corresponding final five symbols. By such examination we find that the only subformulas having the same structure as $***4***513413$ are

$$***b***eacbac, \qquad ***e***baceac.$$

Let us examine how the first was produced. By substitution we obtain $***bac$-$***eacb$, and then switch the first ac to the end of the formula. In the next stage try to extend these K-formulas in an attempt to produce K-formulas that match

$$***3***4***51341312.$$

Only the K-formula of e can be extended, to give

$$***acd***e***baceac,$$

which, after switching, becomes

$$***a***e***bcaecacd.$$

At this point we have a unique tentative node correspondence:

$$\begin{array}{ccccc} 1 & 2 & 3 & 4 & 5 \\ c & d & a & e & b \end{array}$$

All that now remains is to confirm that this node correspondence holds for the entire digraph. We can, and do, produce

$$****c****d***a***e***bcaecacdcebaeb,$$

which is the required confirmation.

Since all permutations of the node names are considered in the matching process, the procedure finds all isomorphisms, in case there is more than one. In terms of our example, we took a particular permutation of $\{1, 2, 3, 4, 5\}$, namely 12345, and tested permutations of $\{a, b, c, d, e\}$ against it. In the first stage of the process we found that any member of $\{a, b, e\}$ could correspond to 5. In the third stage we had found that only one of the 60 possible groups of symbols taken from $\{a, b, c, d, e\}$ could correspond to the 345 in 12345. Our stepwise procedure eliminated entire large classes of permutations from further consideration, and this is its strength, but the effect was the same as if every permutation of $\{a, b, c, d, e\}$ had been tested individually against 12345.

DEFINITION 3.32   Let $D = \langle A, R \rangle$ be a digraph. Then $D' = \langle A, R' \rangle$ is the *complement* of D if the following condition is satisfied: For all $a, b \in A$, $\langle a, b \rangle \in R'$ if and only if $\langle a, b \rangle \notin R$.

Example

Figure 3.23 shows the complements of the two digraphs of Figure 3.22.

THEOREM 3.14   Let A and B be two digraphs, and let A' and B' be their complements. A and B are isomorphic if and only if A' and B' are.

Proof. Consider adjacency matrices of A and A'. An element in the adjacency matrix of A is 1 just when the corresponding element in the adjacency matrix of A' is 0, and vice versa. The two matrices are therefore identical in

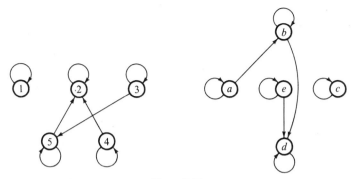

Figure 3.23

form, and the permutation of rows and corresponding columns of the adjacency matrix of B that makes it equal to the adjacency matrix of A is precisely the permutation that has to be applied to the adjacency matrix of B' to make it equal to the adjacency matrix of A'.

Quite often it is easier to establish isomorphism of complements than of the digraphs themselves. The digraphs of Figures 3.22 and 3.23 provide a good example. Let $D' = \langle A, R' \rangle$ be the complement of $D = \langle A, R \rangle$. Then $|R \cup R'| = |A|^2$. Complement D' has fewer arcs than D when $|R| > \frac{1}{2}|A|^2$, and there may then be an advantage in using complements in tests for isomorphism.

Isomorphism of digraphs can be defined also in terms of functions. Consider digraphs $\langle A, R \rangle$ and $\langle B, S \rangle$. They are isomorphic if and only if there exists a one-to-one onto function $f \colon A \to B$ such that $\langle a, b \rangle \in R$ implies $\langle f(a), f(b) \rangle \in S$ and $\langle c, d \rangle \in S$ implies $\langle f^{-1}(c), f^{-1}(d) \rangle \in R$ for all members of R and S. There may be more than one function on A onto B that satisfies the conditions. Functions $f \colon A \to A$ satisfying these conditions also exist, e.g., the identity function. In the extreme case, letting A be a set of n nodes, there are $n!$ such functions associated with, for example, the digraph $\langle A, A \times A \rangle$.

The formalism of D.2.38 is not applicable here. Taking a digraph $\langle A, R \rangle$, with $A = \{a_1, \ldots, a_n\}$, we can denote the set of arcs terminating at a_i by f_i. The $(n + 1)$-tuple $\langle A, f_1, \ldots, f_n \rangle$ defines the digraph just as well as $\langle A, R \rangle$, but, although the f_i are functions, they need not be operations.

3h. Planar Graphs

Planarity is a property studied in the theory of undirected graphs. Our problem: Given a graph, can it be drawn on a sheet of paper in such a way that no two edges cut each other? As usual with problems of some complexity, the solution is found in stages. In advancing to the solution we shall be developing a terminology, and a number of interesting results will be obtained, not always properly relevant to the problem at hand. This section, then, while motivated by the specific problem of planarity, serves as a more general introduction to the theory of graphs.

DEFINITION 3.33   Let $G = \langle A, P \rangle$ be a graph. Then $G' = \langle B, Q \rangle$, where $B \subseteq A$, is a *subgraph* of G if Q contains every edge of P whose elements are both in B. It is a *proper subgraph* if $G' \neq G$. The graph $G'' = \langle A, R \rangle$, with $R \subseteq P$, is a *partial graph* of G.

DEFINITION 3.34   If certain edges of a graph can be placed in a sequence of the form $\{a_1, a_2\}, \{a_2, a_3\}, \ldots, \{a_{n-1}, a_n\}$, where all edges are distinct, the set of these edges is a *chain*. It is a *circuit* if, moreover, $a_1 = a_n$. If all nodes in the corresponding sequence of nodes $(a_1, a_2, a_3, \ldots, a_n)$ are distinct, the chain is *simple*. If $a_1, \ldots, a_{n-1}$ are distinct, but $a_1 = a_n$, then the set of edges is a *simple* circuit.

THEOREM 3.15   A chain is simple if and only if it has no circuit for a subset.
Proof. Exercise 3.51.

DEFINITION 3.35   A graph G is *connected* if every two distinct nodes of the graph are joined by a chain. Let G' be a connected subgraph of G. G' is a *connected component* of G if there exists no further connected subgraph of which G' is a proper subgraph. A *disconnected* graph is not connected.

In studying a disconnected graph one can treat each of its connected components as a graph in its own right. Therefore, we can limit the discussion that follows to connected graphs with no loss of generality.

DEFINITION 3.36   A *tree* is a connected graph that contains no circuits. Considering the tree $T = \langle B, Q \rangle$ as a partial subgraph of a connected graph $G = \langle A, P \rangle$, members of $P - Q$ are *chords* of T. If $B = A$, then T is a *spanning tree* of G. If $T = \langle C, S \rangle$ is a tree, and a particular node $r \in C$ is designated as the root of T, then the structure $\langle C, S, r \rangle$ is a *rooted tree*.

Example

In Figure 3.24 trees T_1 and T_2 span G, and they are not the only spanning trees of G. With respect to T_1 we have the set of chords $\{\{a, b\}, \{a, c\}, \{a, d\}, \{b, c\}, \{b, d\}, \{c, d\}\}$. With respect to T_2 the set of chords is $\{\{a, b\}, \{a, c\}, \{b, c\}, \{b, e\}, \{c, e\}, \{d, e\}\}$. One aspect of the theory of graphs is its concern with enumeration. Finding all trees on a given number of nodes would be a typical problem.

THEOREM 3.16   Let $\langle A, P \rangle$ be a tree with n nodes. Then $|P| = n - 1$.

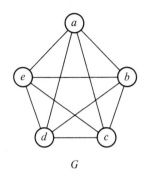

G

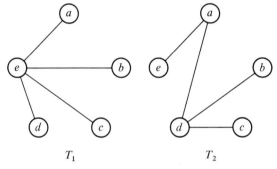

T_1 T_2

Figure 3.24

Proof. Consider some $a_1 \in A$. Since a tree is connected and has no circuits, there is one and only one chain between a_1 and a member of $\{a_2, a_3, \ldots, a_n\}$. The final edges in the $n - 1$ sequences defining the chains are, of course, distinct. To show that the set of final edges is in fact P assume that there exists a final edge $\{a_i, a_k\}$ and some other edge $\{a_j, a_k\}$. But then there exists a chain $(a_1, \ldots, a_i, a_k, a_j)$; i.e., $\{a_k, a_j\}$ is a final edge.

THEOREM 3.17 Let $T = \langle A, Q \rangle$ be a spanning tree of $G = \langle A, P \rangle$, and let edge e be a chord of T. The graph $\langle A, Q \cup \{e\} \rangle$ contains exactly one circuit.

Proof. Exercise 3.54.

DEFINITION 3.37 Let $T = \langle A, Q \rangle$ be a spanning tree of $G = \langle A, P \rangle$, and write $P - Q = \{e_1, e_2, \ldots, e_k\}$. The k circuits contained in the k graphs $\langle A, Q \cup \{e_i\} \rangle$ form a *fundamental set of circuits* (not necessarily unique) of G. The quantity $|P - Q|$ is the *cyclomatic number* of G.

Let $T = \langle A, Q \rangle$ be a spanning tree of $G = \langle A, P \rangle$, and let $|A| = n$ and $|P| = m$. Then, by Th.3.16, $|P - Q| = m - n + 1$. This is the number of fundamental circuits of G. It is obvious that a graph contains no circuits when its cyclomatic number is zero. It contains a single circuit when $m - n + 1 = 1$, i.e., when $m = n$. When $m > n$, a graph may contain simple circuits additional to those in a fundamental set. Algorithms have been found for deriving the fundamental set and, from it, the set of all simple circuits of a graph.

DEFINITION 3.38   Represent a connected graph in the geometric plane by drawing nodes as distinct points, and edges as simple curves. The graph is *planar* if it possesses a geometric representation in which edges intersect only at points representing nodes. In this representation a region of the plane that is bounded by a circuit, and that encloses no other circuit sharing a common edge with it, is a *face*. The unbounded infinite region exterior to the finite faces is also considered a face. (A finite face may enclose another face, provided that the circuits defining the two faces are disjoint.)

Example

Graph G_1 of Figure 3.25 is planar, as shown by the construction. Its faces are z_0, z_1, z_2, z_3 (z_0 is infinite, the others are finite). Graph G_2 is nonplanar.

THEOREM 3.18   The circuits defining the finite faces of a planar connected graph form a fundamental set of circuits.

Proof. Consider a planar graph G_{f+1} with $f + 1$ finite faces. It is possible to construct this graph from some planar graph G_f with f finite faces by drawing a simple chain between two nodes a and b in G_f, $(a, n_1, \ldots, n_k, b)$, where $n_1, \ldots, n_k$ do not belong to G_f. (If some n_i belonged to G_f, the resulting structure would have at least $f + 2$ finite faces.) The construction increases the number of nodes by k and the number of edges by $k + 1$; i.e., the cyclomatic number, in going from G_f to G_{f+1}, is increased by $(k + 1) - k = 1$. Therefore, by D.3.37, the theorem is true for G_{f+1} if it is true for G_f. But the theorem is true for G_1, a graph with one finite face—G_1 contains a single circuit, and this circuit must be the fundamental set.

We have shown that the cyclomatic number of a planar connected graph is equal to the number of finite faces in the graph. Therefore, putting n for the number of nodes, m for the number of edges, and f for the *total* number of faces (including the infinite face), we can express Th.3.18 as a formula: $n - m + f = 2$. This expression is known as *Euler's formula*. A connected graph is planar if and only if it satisfies Euler's formula.

DEFINITION 3.39   A graph $G = \langle A, P \rangle$ is *complete* if P contains every 2-element subset of A. A complete graph on n nodes is denoted by K_n. A complete subgraph of a graph such that this subgraph is not a proper

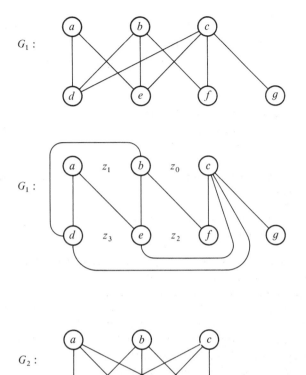

Figure 3.25

subgraph of another complete subgraph of this graph is a *clique*, i.e., a clique is a maximal complete subgraph of a graph.

Example

Graph G of Figure 3.24 is a complete graph on 5 nodes. A complete graph $\langle A, P \rangle$ having n nodes contains the greatest possible number of edges on n nodes. This number is equal to the number of 2-combinations of A, and, by Th.1.17, $C_2(A) = C(n, 2) = \frac{1}{2}n(n - 1)$. Note that a set $\{a, a\}$ has only one element and cannot be an edge; i.e., we have no counterpart of slings in the theory of graphs. Graph G_1 of Figure 3.26 contains two cliques. They are the complete subgraphs on nodes $\{a, b, c, d\}$ and on $\{a, b, c, e\}$. Graph G_2 of Figure 3.26 has only one clique. It is G_2 itself.

DEFINITION 3.40   A graph $\langle B \cup C, P \rangle$ is *bipartite* if $B \cap C = \varnothing$ and every member of P has one element in B and the other in C. A bipartite graph in which every member of B is joined by an edge to every member of C is known as a *utility graph*. The utility graph in which the disjoint sets of nodes have s and t members, respectively, is denoted by $K_{s,\,t}$.

Example

Graphs G_1 and G_2 of Figure 3.25 are bipartite. In the case of G_1 we have $B = \{a, b, c\}$ and $C = \{d, e, f, g\}$. In the case of G_2 the sets are $B = \{a, b, c\}$ and $C = \{d, e, f\}$. G_2 is a utility graph. The term has arisen from the use of this species of graphs to represent situations in which each of s consumers is to be supplied with each of t public utilities (e.g. water, gas, electricity) from their supply stations.

THEOREM 3.19   Graphs K_5 (graph G of Figure 3.24) and $K_{3,3}$ (graph G_2 of Figure 3.25) are nonplanar.

Proof. Assume that K_5 is planar. Then Euler's formula gives $f = 2 - n + m = 2 - 5 + 10 = 7$. A circuit defining a face must contain at least three edges, and each edge lies on a boundary of two faces. Hence $m/3 \geq f/2$ or $2m \geq 3f$, leading to the contradiction $20 \geq 21$. Next assume that $K_{3,3}$ is planar. Circuits in a bipartite graph must contain at least four edges. (If a circuit had only three edges, one edge would have to have both members in one of the disjoint sets.) Hence we must have $m/4 \geq f/2$ or $m \geq 2f$. But here $f = 2 - 6 + 9 = 5$, again implying an absurdity, namely $9 \geq 10$.

DEFINITION 3.41   An *elementary contraction* in a graph is the removal of an edge $\{a, b\}$, and the coalescing of the two nodes a and b into a single node (either a or b).

Example

In graph G_1 of Figure 3.26 removal of edge $\{z, b\}$ and coalescing of nodes z and b into b results in the disappearance of edge $\{a, z\}$ as well. Two further elementary contractions lead to the absorption of nodes x and y into nodes e and d, respectively. These two contractions give rise to a new edge $\{e, d\}$. By means of three elementary contractions G_1 has been contracted to graph G_2 of Figure 3.26.

THEOREM 3.20 (Kuratowski's theorem).   A graph is planar if and only if it does *not* contain as a subgraph the graph K_5, or the graph $K_{3,3}$, or a graph that can be contracted to K_5 or $K_{3,3}$ by a sequence of elementary contractions.

Proof. Necessity follows from Th.3.19. The sufficiency proof is very difficult. We shall not give it here.

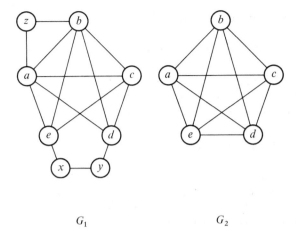

$$G_1 \qquad\qquad G_2$$

Figure 3.26

Notes

The most useful general text for this chapter appears to be [De74b]; this book gives the basic theory of directed and undirected graphs, contains numerous examples of applications, takes an algorithmic approach throughout, and is provided with excellent sets of references. In short, an outstanding book. [Ha65b] is a specific text on digraphs. It is primarily addressed to social scientists, and is rather easy to read. The theory of undirected graphs is covered in [Ha69], and [Ha73] deals specifically with enumeration problems Further examples of applications of graphs and digraphs can be found in [Bu65] and [Ma71a]; [Ch71b] deals primarily with applications found in engineering. The present interest in applications of graph theory has been to a large extent due to Berge's *Theory of Graphs and its Applications*, [Be58], which put a strong stress on the use of graphs in operations research.

A.3.1 was discovered independently by Roy [Ro59], and by Warshall [Wa62]. More than one digraph may have the same path matrix: The inverse problem of finding the digraph of fewest arcs corresponding to a given path matrix is solved in [Si65, Ba69, Mo69]. For additional references to work relating to the determination of the path matrix see the Notes to Chapter 6.

The K-trees and K-formulas of Section 3f were introduced by Krider [Kr64] as an aid to automatic flowcharting of computer programs. Th.3.13 has been stated without proof in [Be69a]. The heuristic procedures for testing pairs of digraphs (or graphs) for isomorphism were independently developed by

Suthenguth [Sa64], and Unger [Un64]. Other papers dealing with the isomorphism problem are [Co70b, Le74b]. A detailed account of the algorithm for detecting isomorphism of digraphs based on K-formulas can be found in [Be73]. This algorithm is a backtrack procedure. Backtrack programming is described in [Go65, F167] (see also [Pe66] for a specific example). A very brief introduction to backtracking can be found in [Ni74, pp. 44–50]. Some attempts have been made to find a function from the set of graphs under which two graphs would have the same image if and only if they were isomorphic. To date all conjectures in this area have come to nothing—see [Tu68].

A canonical scheme for labeling the nodes of a tree is described in [Go63]. Solutions to the problem of finding circuits in graphs are to be found in [We66a, Pa69]. The algorithm for generating all circuits from the fundamental set in [We66a] has been found faulty and is corrected in [Gi69]. [Mc69a] is an algorithm for finding all spanning trees of a graph. The Notes to Chapter 8 contain references to papers dealing with the detection of cliques. For a discussion of AVL trees (introduced in Example 3 of D.3.25) see [Kn73a].

A proof of Th.3.20 can be found in [Be58, Bu65]. Kuratowski's theorem is the basis of an algorithm that tests a graph for planarity, see [Me70]. An algorithm for deriving a planar geometric representation of a planar graph can be found in [De64]; this paper contains also a discussion of the reduction of the number of intersections of edges in a nonplanar graph.

Special purpose programming languages have been devised for the implementation of graph and digraph algorithms; references to such languages are given in the Notes to Chapter 10.

Exercises

3.1 (a) Draw pictures of the following digraphs:

(i) $\langle A, A \times A \rangle$, where $A = \{a, b, c, d\}$;

(ii) $\langle \{1, 2, 3, 4, 5\},$ greater than$\rangle$;

(iii) $\langle A, R \rangle$, where $A = \{a, b, c, d\}$ and R is the identity relation;

(iv) $\langle \mathcal{P}(\{1, 2, 3\}), R \rangle$, where R is the subset relation;

(v) $\langle \mathcal{P}(\{1, 2, 3\}), Q \rangle$, where Q is the relation *covers* with respect to the subset relation in $\mathcal{P}(\{1, 2, 3\})$;

(vi) $\langle S \cup C, R \rangle$, where S is a set of five students of your acquaintance, C is the set of courses attended by these students, and $R = \{\langle a, b \rangle \mid$ student a takes course $b\}$;

(vii) $\langle S \cup L, R \rangle$, where S is the set of students of Part (vi) and L is the set of localities where they live, and $R = \{\langle a, b \rangle \mid$ student a lives in $b\}$;

(viii) the *structure* of Figure 2.7.

3.2 (a) The digraphs of Parts (vi) and (vii) of Exercise 3.1 are *bipartite* digraphs. Try to abstract their distinguishing feature and hence devise a definition of bipartite digraphs.

3.3 (a) Using the information you collected for Part (vi) of Exercise 3.1, draw an undirected graph $\langle S, P \rangle$, where $P = \{\{a, b\} \mid a, b \in S,\ a \text{ and } b \text{ have at least one course in common}\}$.

3.4 (b) Find indegrees and outdegrees of all nodes in the digraphs of Figures 3.7 and 3.8.

3.5 (b) Show that the sum of total degrees of all nodes of a digraph is even, and hence that in every digraph there is an even number of nodes with odd total degrees. (Note that zero is an even number.)

3.6 (b) Find all cycles in the digraph of Figure 3.8.

3.7 (b) Show that if a digraph contains paths $(a, \ldots, b)$ and $(b, \ldots, a)$, then the digraph contains a cycle, but that there need not exist a *simple* cycle $(a, \ldots, b, \ldots, a)$.

3.8 (b) Show that an acyclic digraph has at least one node with zero indegree and at least one node with zero outdegree.

3.9 (b) Show that if A and B are cycles, and the node sequences that define them have at least one node in common, then $A \cup B$ is also a cycle.

3.10 (b) Show that the greatest number of arcs in an acyclic digraph on n nodes is $\frac{1}{2}n(n - 1)$.

3.11 (b) Consider a digraph that has a node base of n elements. Show that at least $n - 1$ arcs have to be added to the digraph to convert it to a digraph whose node base consists of a single node.

3.12 (b) The proof of Th.3.5 consists of four parts: it is proven that reachability is a function, that it is total, that it is one-to-one, and that it is onto. Identify the four parts.

3.13 (b) Implement A.3.1 as a Fortran subroutine, and use the subroutine to find path matrices of the digraphs of Figures 3.6, 3.7, and 3.8. Write the subroutine in such a way that the input to it may be a variable adjacency matrix.

3.14 (c) Prove Th.3.7 by induction, using an approach based on the observation given as the example of Th.3.7.

3.15 (c) Let $D = \langle A_n, R \rangle$, where $A_n = \{a_1, a_2, \ldots, a_n\}$, be a digraph with adjacency matrix X, and let $A_k = \{a_1, a_2, \ldots, a_k\}$ ($A_k \subset A_n$). Given X, and the path matrix of the subdigraph $\langle A_k, R \cap (A_k \times A_k) \rangle$, find the path matrix of $\langle A_{k+1}, R \cap (A_{k+1} \times A_{k+1}) \rangle$.

3.16 (c) In A.3.1 interchange iteration indices j and k so that Steps 2, 4, and 6 become

    2. Set $k = 1$.

  4. If $x_{ij}^* = 1$, then set $x_{ik}^* = x_{ik}^* \lor x_{jk}^*$ for all j from 1 to n.
  6. Set $k = k + 1$. If $k \leqq n$, go to 3; else stop.

What effect does the interchange have on the algorithm? What effect would interchange of j and i have?

3.17   (c)   Write a Fortran subroutine that computes from the adjacency matrix of a digraph $\langle A, R \rangle$ a matrix S such that s_{ij} is the length of the *shortest* path from a_i to a_j and $s_{ij} = 10^{10}$ (or some other very large number) if there is no path from a_i to a_j. Can S be computed from the path matrix of the digraph?

3.18   (c)   Characterize the digraphs of Exercise 3.1 according to D.3.14.

3.19   (c)   In A.3.2 make MX a logical array in which an element is .TRUE. if the corresponding element of the adjacency matrix is 1, and .FALSE. if it is 0. Modify ISPORD accordingly.

3.20   (c)   What is to be changed in ISPORD to make it into a function subprogram that determines whether or not a relation is an equivalence?

3.21   (c)   Write a Fortran logical function that, given the *path* matrix of a digraph, returns .TRUE. if the digraph is cyclic, and .FALSE. if it is not.

3.22   (c)   Attempt to get an understanding of ISEQUI of A.3.3 by following through the actions of the procedure on the matrix of the example of A.3.3. Then modify ISEQUI so that it also prints the equivalence classes generated by the equivalence relation defined by the adjacency matrix MX (as sets of row numbers).

3.23   (c)   Write a Fortran function subprogram that determines whether or not a digraph is complete.

3.24   (c)   Draw all tournaments for $n = 3$, 4, 5. These digraphs represent all possible outcomes of round-robin tournaments with 3, 4, and 5 players. Identify the instances in which there is a definite winner of the tournament.

3.25   (c)   Show that every tournament contains a Hamiltonian path.

3.26   (c)   Let $\langle A, R \rangle$ be a total slingless digraph. Show that there exists a partition of R into sets R_1 and R_2 such that $\langle A, R_1 \rangle$ and $\langle A, R_2 \rangle$ are acyclic.

3.27   (d)   Let $D = \langle A, R \rangle$ be a connected digraph. A node $v \in A$ is an *articulation point* of D if the subdigraph obtained by deleting v is disconnected. Show that v is an articulation point if and only if there exist two nodes $a, b \in A$ such that every semipath joining a and b passes through v.

3.28   (d)   What is the form of the path matrix of a strongly connected digraph?

3.29   (d)   Write a Fortran subroutine that computes from the adjacency matrix of a digraph $\langle A, R \rangle$ a matrix C such that $c_{ij} = 1$ if a_i and a_j are connected and $c_{ij} = 0$ if they are not connected.

3.30 (d) Prove Th.3.9.

3.31 (d) Devise an algorithm for finding the strong components of a digraph.

3.32 (d) Let $D = \langle A, R \rangle$ be a digraph. Show that D must be connected if for every pair of nodes $a, b \in A$, $td(a) + td(b) \geq n - 1$.

3.33 (d) Prove Th.3.10 and devise an algorithm for finding all node bases of a digraph.

3.34 (e) Produce an example of a digraph in which exactly one node has indegree 0 and every other node has indegree 1 that is not a directed tree.

3.35 (e) Show that D.3.22 defines the same objects when the condition that the digraph must be acyclic is replaced by the condition that the digraph must be connected and without slings.

3.36 (e) If the arrows in Figure 3.13 are removed, and each of the nine nodes is in turn identified as the root, then nine different rooted trees result. Draw the nine directed trees corresponding to these rooted trees.

3.37 (e) Prove Th.3.12.

3.38 (e) Define the predecessor function, the left successor function, and the right successor function for B-trees (b) and (c) of Figure 3.15.

3.39 (f) Find minimal sets of K-formulas for the digraphs of Figures 3.7 and 3.8 (disregard weights in Figure 3.7).

3.40 (f) Implement A.3.5 as a Fortran program.

3.41 (f) Which of the following are K-formulas?

> (i) $**{*}aba*dc.$ (ii) $**{*}aba*dcd.$
> (iii) $**aba**dc.$ (iv) $*a*b*a*dc.$

Draw the digraphs corresponding to the K-formulas.

3.42 (f) Implement a recognition algorithm for K-formulas based on D.3.26a as a Fortran program.

3.43 (f) Draw K-trees corresponding to the following K-formulas:

> (i) $***{*}aca*dbb,$
> (ii) $***a***bbcd***cbdee,$
> (iii) $***{*}1***{*}2***3***4***51341312145345.$

Draw the digraphs represented by the K-formulas.

3.44 (f) Draw K-trees of the following K-formulas:

> (i) $***a*b*c*d***eabdcd,$
> (ii) $*1**2*64*3**425,$
> (iii) $***a***bb***ebdedce.$

Is there a simple way of determining the number of levels in a K-tree from the form of its K-formula?

3.45 (f) Show that the interchange rule of D.3.30 does not lose any of its power if it is defined in the following, more restricted, fashion: The interchange of a K-formula of node a, occurring as a (proper) subformula of a member of F, and a node symbol a, occurring in any member of F, is an application of the interchange rule.

3.46 (g) Let $D_1 = \langle X_1, R_1 \rangle$, $D_2 = \langle X_2, R_2 \rangle$, where $X_1 = \{a, b, c, d, e, f\}$ and $X_2 = \{1, 2, 3, 4, 5, 6\}$, $R_1 = \{\langle c, a \rangle, \langle b, c \rangle, \langle e, b \rangle, \langle e, f \rangle, \langle f, a \rangle, \langle b, f \rangle, \langle c, f \rangle, \langle b, e \rangle, \langle a, c \rangle, \langle d, a \rangle, \langle d, f \rangle, \langle e, d \rangle, \langle d, b \rangle, \langle f, b \rangle, \langle f, e \rangle, \langle c, e \rangle, \langle b, d \rangle, \langle a, f \rangle, \langle a, d \rangle, \langle d, e \rangle, \langle a, e \rangle, \langle f, c \rangle, \langle f, d \rangle, \langle d, c \rangle\}$, $R_2 = \{\langle 1, 2 \rangle, \langle 5, 4 \rangle, \langle 6, 4 \rangle, \langle 4, 1 \rangle, \langle 2, 4 \rangle, \langle 1, 3 \rangle, \langle 6, 1 \rangle, \langle 5, 6 \rangle, \langle 3, 2 \rangle, \langle 2, 5 \rangle, \langle 1, 6 \rangle, \langle 3, 4 \rangle, \langle 2, 3 \rangle, \langle 3, 1 \rangle, \langle 4, 2 \rangle, \langle 3, 5 \rangle, \langle 6, 5 \rangle, \langle 2, 6 \rangle, \langle 1, 4 \rangle, \langle 2, 1 \rangle, \langle 4, 3 \rangle, \langle 5, 1 \rangle, \langle 1, 5 \rangle, \langle 6, 2 \rangle\}$. Are the digraphs D_1 and D_2 isomorphic?

3.47 (g) Given digraphs represented by the K-formula

$$**1**2**3**5**4352114$$

and the set of K-formulas $\{**abd, **bce, **cab, **dce, **ead\}$, respectively. Find all isomorphisms between the two digraphs.

3.48 (g) Given that there are k isomorphisms between digraphs A and B, and that digraph A is isomorphic to digraph C. What can you say regarding the number of isomorphisms between digraphs B and C?

3.49 (g) Let $D = \langle X, R \rangle$ be a complete symmetric digraph on n nodes $x_1, x_2, \ldots, x_n$. Let $D' = \langle X, R' \rangle$ be a digraph that results when the subscripts of the nodes are permuted. Discuss the isomorphism of D and D'.

3.50 (g) Prove that a digraph is disconnected if and only if its complement is connected.

3.51 (h) Prove Th.3.15.

3.52 (h) Find all spanning trees for graph G of Figure 3.24.

3.53 (h) Show that the definition of a tree in D.3.36 is consistent with the following definition: A tree is a connected graph that becomes disconnected when *any* one of its edges is removed.

3.54 (h) Prove Th.3.17.

CHAPTER 4

Algebras and Strings

4a. Algebraic Structures

As we have pointed out before, abstraction is the process of eliminating everything that is inessential to a particular investigation. Thus, when we had to *define* concepts such as similarity, homomorphism, and the like, we found the truly abstract algebras of Section 2h most effective, precisely because they are devoid of structure. On the other hand, when we look for a useful mathematical model of a real system, we want a model with as much structure as possible. The more structure an algebra possesses, the richer its stock of theorems. Consequently, the more features of the system are reflected in the model, the more information about the system is the model capable of providing.

Structure is imposed on an abstract algebra by means of rules that must be satisfied by operations in the algebra. We might require an operation to be associative, or commutative. For a pair of operations, we might have an axiom defining the way one operation distributes over the other. The simplest nontrivial abstract algebra is the system $\langle A, * \rangle$, where $*$ denotes a binary operation in A. D.4.1 is a set of statements, subsets of which define specific algebras A. These statements are then the axioms of A.

DEFINITION 4.1   Let $\langle A, * \rangle$ be an algebra. We say that algebra A satisfies the associative law if statement A_1 is true. Similarly for statements A_2, A_3, and A_4.

A_1. *Associative law*: $a * (b * c) = (a * b) * c$ for all $a, b, c \in A$.

A_2. *Commutative law*: $a * b = b * a$ for all $a, b \in A$.

A_3. *Identity law*: There exists an element $e \in A$ such that $e * a = a * e = a$ for every $a \in A$.

A_4. *Inverse law*: For every $a \in A$ there exists an element $a' \in A$ such that $a' * a = a * a' = e$.

Statement A_3 actually comprises two identity laws: a left identity law, expressed by $e * a = a$, and a right identity law, expressed by $a * e = a$. Similarly A_4 comprises left inverse and right inverse laws.

DEFINITION 4.2   An algebra $\langle A, * \rangle$ that satisfies A_1 of D.4.1 is a *semigroup*. If, in addition, the algebra satisfies A_3, it is a *semigroup with identity* or a *monoid*. (It is easy to show that the identity element of a monoid is unique.)

Examples

1. If A is a nonempty set, then algebras $\langle \mathscr{P}(A), \cup \rangle$ and $\langle \mathscr{P}(A), \cap \rangle$ are semigroups with identity, the identity elements being the null set and the set A, respectively.

2. If N is the set of nonnegative integers, then $\langle N, + \rangle$ and $\langle N, \cdot \rangle$ are semigroups with identity elements 0 and 1, respectively.

In keeping with D.2.34 we should consider the identity element a 0-argument operation, and write the algebras of the examples above as $\langle \mathscr{P}(A), \cup, \varnothing \rangle$, $\langle \mathscr{P}(A), \cap, A \rangle$, $\langle N, +, 0 \rangle$, and $\langle N, \cdot, 1 \rangle$.

Semigroups without identity elements are not particularly interesting. Therefore, it is quite normal to find the term *semigroup with identity* abbreviated to *semigroup*. This usage is based on the assumption that no confusion would arise because semigroups without identity elements are not worth talking about. When one goes as far as to speak of a *semigroup* $\langle A, *, e \rangle$, of course no confusion can arise.

DEFINITION 4.3   A semigroup with identity that satisfies A_4 is a *group*. If, in addition, it satisfies A_2, it is an *Abelian group*.

Examples

1. The set of all integers under addition is a group. Addition is clearly associative. There exists an identity element, namely $e = 0$, and the inverse law is satisfied if we take $a' = -a$. The group is Abelian.

2. The set of all integers is not a group under multiplication (A_4 does not hold), but the set of all rational numbers is an Abelian group. The inverse of an element of this group is defined by $x' = 1/x$.

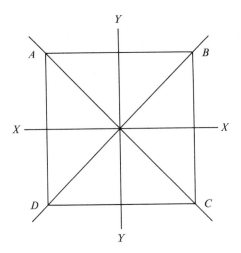

Figure 4.1

3. Consider the square *ABCD* shown in Figure 4.1. The square can be rotated (clockwise) through 90°, 180°, 270°, and 360° with no change to its appearance. It can be rotated also about axes *XX*, *YY*, *AC*, and *BD*. We denote these eight rotations by *a*, *b*, *c*, *d*, *e*, *f*, *g*, and *h*, respectively, and let *x* ∗ *y* stand for rotation *x* followed by rotation *y*. It is easy to see that ∗ is an operation in {*a*, ..., *h*}. For example, *a* ∗ *e* = *h* and *e* ∗ *a* = *g*. Table 4.1 is a "multiplication" table for this operation. The operation is associative, but not commutative. Rotation *d* is a (unique) identity element, and each element possesses an inverse. Algebra ⟨{*a*, ..., *h*}, ∗, *d*⟩ is, therefore, a group (known as the dihedral group D_4).

TABLE 4.1

OPERATION *x* ∗ *y* IN {*a*, ..., *h*}

x \ *y*	*a*	*b*	*c*	*d*	*e*	*f*	*g*	*h*
a	*b*	*c*	*d*	*a*	*h*	*g*	*e*	*f*
b	*c*	*d*	*a*	*b*	*f*	*e*	*h*	*g*
c	*d*	*a*	*b*	*c*	*g*	*h*	*f*	*e*
d	*a*	*b*	*c*	*d*	*e*	*f*	*g*	*h*
e	*g*	*f*	*h*	*e*	*d*	*b*	*a*	*c*
f	*h*	*e*	*g*	*f*	*b*	*d*	*c*	*a*
g	*f*	*h*	*e*	*g*	*c*	*a*	*d*	*b*
h	*e*	*g*	*f*	*h*	*a*	*c*	*b*	*d*

DEFINITION 4.4 If a group G has n elements, it is called a group of *order n*. If G is infinite, it is called a group of *infinite order* or an *infinite group*.

Example

The dihedral group D_4 is a finite group of order 8. The groups of the other examples of D.4.3 are infinite.

DEFINITION 4.5 Let $\langle G, *, e \rangle$ be a group. Consider $G_1 \subseteq G$ such that $e \in G_1$. If $\langle G_1, *, e \rangle$ is a group, then G_1 is a *subgroup* of G. A subgroup that is neither G nor $\{e\}$ is a *proper* subgroup of G.

Examples

1. Strictly speaking the $*$ in $\langle G_1, *, e \rangle$ is not the same as in $\langle G, *, e \rangle$. The operation in G_1 is the restriction of the operation in G to this subset, and it would be more precise to write $\langle G_1, *|G_1, e \rangle$ in place of $\langle G_1, *, e \rangle$.

2. With reference to D_4 of Example 3 of D.4.3, both $\{d\}$ and the entire group itself are subgroups of D_4, but they are not proper subgroups. Examples of proper subgroups: $\{a, b, c, d\}$ and $\{b, d\}$.

DEFINITION 4.6 Let G_1 be a subgroup of G, and let $a \in G$. Then $aG_1 = \{a * b | b \in G_1\}$ is a *left coset* of G_1 in G, and $G_1 a = \{b * a | b \in G_1\}$ is a *right coset* of G_1 in G.

Examples

1. Since $a = a * e$, and the identity element e belongs to G_1, consequently $a \in aG_1$ for all $a \in G$.

2. Consider subgroup $S = \{a, b, c, d\}$ of D_4 (see Example 2 of D.4.5). Then, for example, $cS = \{c * a, c * b, c * c, c * d\} = \{d, a, b, c\}$ (using Table 4.1). Evaluation of all left cosets of S gives $aS = bS = cS = dS = \{a, b, c, d\}$ and $eS = fS = gS = hS = \{e, f, g, h\}$.

THEOREM 4.1 Let G_1 be a subgroup of $\langle G, *, e \rangle$. Then the family of left cosets of G_1 constitutes a partition of G. (This partition is called a *left decomposition* of G with respect to G_1.)

Proof. It is sufficient to prove that every element of G is in some left coset of G_1, and that two left cosets of G_1 are equal when they are not disjoint. We have $a = a * e$ for every $a \in G$, but the identity is in every subgroup of G, in particular $e \in G_1$. Consequently, $a * e$ satisfies the definition $aG_1 = \{a * b | b \in G_1\}$, i.e., every element of G is in some coset. For the second part suppose that cosets aG_1 and bG_1 have element c in common. Then $c = a * x = b * y$, where $x, y \in G_1$. This permits us to write $a * x * x' = b * y * x'$, and hence $a = b * y * x'$. Then $a * z = b * y * x' * z$ for all $z \in G_1$, but $y * x' * z \in G_1$. Consequently, $aG_1 \subseteq bG_1$. Reversing the roles of a and b gives $bG_1 \subseteq aG_1$ and hence $aG_1 = bG_1$.

THEOREM 4.2 Let G be a finite group, G_1 a subgroup of G, and aG_1 any left coset of G_1 in G. Then $|aG_1| = |G_1|$.

Proof. The function from G_1 defined by $f(x) = a * x$ is total and onto aG_1. It has to be shown that it is one to one. Let $f(x) = f(y)$, i.e., let $a * x = a * y$. Then $a' * a * x = a' * a * y$, which implies $x = y$. But if $f(x) = f(y)$ implies $x = y$, then f is one to one (see D.2.4).

Example

From the two theorems it follows at once that the order of a subgroup of a finite group is a divisor of the order of the group. This result is known as *Lagrange's theorem*.

We shall now study permutations in the context of the theory of groups. In Section 1h a permutation of n objects was defined as something static, an n-tuple with distinct elements. Here we take a dynamic approach; we identify a permutation with the *action* taken to transform one n-tuple into another by defining a permutation of a set A having n elements as a one-to-one transformation (function) $p: A \to A$. There are $n!$ such transformations. Since an algorithm generates permutations by a sequence of transformations, and algorithms are of greater relevance in computer science than static definitions, the definition given here should hold a greater appeal for us.

We write a permutation as

$$p = \begin{pmatrix} a_1 & a_2 & a_3 & \cdots & a_n \\ b_1 & b_2 & b_3 & \cdots & b_n \end{pmatrix},$$

where $\langle a_i, b_i \rangle \in p$. The order in which the a_i are written is immaterial, but if $\langle a_i, b_i \rangle \in p$, the b_i must be written below the a_i:

$$p = \begin{pmatrix} a_1 & a_2 & \cdots & a_n \\ b_1 & b_2 & \cdots & b_n \end{pmatrix} = \begin{pmatrix} a_2 & a_n & \cdots & a_1 \\ b_2 & b_n & \cdots & b_1 \end{pmatrix}.$$

The product of permutations p and q, written pq, is obtained by carrying out transformations p and q in sequence. For example, if

$$p = \begin{pmatrix} 1 & 2 & 3 \\ 2 & 1 & 3 \end{pmatrix} \quad \text{and} \quad q = \begin{pmatrix} 1 & 2 & 3 \\ 3 & 1 & 2 \end{pmatrix},$$

then

$$pq = \begin{pmatrix} 1 & 2 & 3 \\ 2 & 1 & 3 \end{pmatrix}\begin{pmatrix} 1 & 2 & 3 \\ 3 & 1 & 2 \end{pmatrix} = \begin{pmatrix} 1 & 2 & 3 \\ 2 & 1 & 3 \end{pmatrix}\begin{pmatrix} 2 & 1 & 3 \\ 1 & 3 & 2 \end{pmatrix} = \begin{pmatrix} 1 & 2 & 3 \\ 1 & 3 & 2 \end{pmatrix}.$$

Note that $pq \neq qp$ here:

$$qp = \begin{pmatrix} 1 & 2 & 3 \\ 3 & 1 & 2 \end{pmatrix}\begin{pmatrix} 1 & 2 & 3 \\ 2 & 1 & 3 \end{pmatrix} = \begin{pmatrix} 1 & 2 & 3 \\ 3 & 1 & 2 \end{pmatrix}\begin{pmatrix} 3 & 1 & 2 \\ 3 & 2 & 1 \end{pmatrix} = \begin{pmatrix} 1 & 2 & 3 \\ 3 & 2 & 1 \end{pmatrix}.$$

Let us consider $P(A)$, the set of all permutations of a set A. Obviously the product function is an operation in $P(A)$. It is easy to prove that this operation obeys the associative law. The identity function provides an identity element; we write

$$i_n = \begin{pmatrix} a_1 & a_2 & \cdots & a_n \\ a_1 & a_2 & \cdots & a_n \end{pmatrix},$$

and each $p \in P(A)$ has a unique inverse $p^{-1} \in P(A)$ such that if

$$p = \begin{pmatrix} a_1 & a_2 & \cdots & a_n \\ b_1 & b_2 & \cdots & b_n \end{pmatrix}, \quad \text{then} \quad p^{-1} = \begin{pmatrix} b_1 & b_2 & \cdots & b_n \\ a_1 & a_2 & \cdots & a_n \end{pmatrix}.$$

Clearly $pp^{-1} = p^{-1}p = i_n$. $P(A)$ is therefore a group under the product operation. It is called the *symmetric permutation group* or *symmetric group* of order $n!$ (when A has n elements).

Let $C = \{c_1, c_2, \ldots, c_m\}$ be a subset of $A = \{a_1, a_2, \ldots, a_n\}$. A *cycle* of length m is a permutation p such that

$$p(c_i) = c_{i+1} \quad (i = 1, 2, \ldots, m - 1),$$
$$p(c_m) = c_1,$$
$$p(a_i) = a_i \quad (a_i \in A - C).$$

For example,

$$\begin{pmatrix} 1 & 2 & 3 & 4 & 5 & 6 & 7 \\ 1 & 4 & 3 & 6 & 2 & 5 & 7 \end{pmatrix}$$

is a cycle of length 4 ($c_1 = 2$, $c_2 = 4$, $c_3 = 6$, $c_4 = 5$). It is customary to abbreviate a cycle to just those elements changed in the transformation, e.g., to (2 4 6 5) here. Two or more cycles that have no elements in common in the abbreviated notation are called *disjoint*, and every permutation can be expressed as a product of disjoint cycles. The disjoint cycles are very easily detected when a permutation is represented by a digraph. Figure 4.2 is the digraph representing the permutation

$$p = \begin{pmatrix} 1 & 2 & 3 & 4 & 5 & 6 \\ 5 & 6 & 3 & 1 & 4 & 2 \end{pmatrix}.$$

We see at once that $p = (154)(26)(3)$. A cycle of length 1 represents an unchanged element and may be omitted from the specification of a permutation, e.g., we could write $p = (154)(26)$ here. A permutation that consists

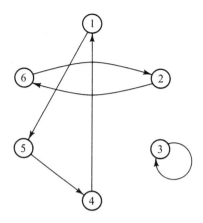

Figure 4.2

entirely of cycles of length 1 is an *identity permutation*. In this case, of course, at least one of the cycles must be retained to denote the permutation. Indeed, a notation that includes every element in the domain of the permutation is preferable in any case.

A cycle of length 2 is called a *transposition*, and every permutation can be expressed as the product of transpositions. If it is the product of an even number of transpositions, the permutation is called *even*; otherwise it is called *odd*. A permutation cannot be both even and odd. Half the permutations in $P(A)$ are even, half are odd. The permutation (1 5 4)(2 6) becomes, in terms of transpositions, (1 5)(1 4)(2 6); it is odd. Note that (15)(14)(26) $\neq$ (14)(15)(26).

We shall now consider algebras with two binary operations: $\langle R, +, \cdot \rangle$. It is common practice to call operations $+$ and $\cdot$ "addition" and "multiplication," respectively, and to abbreviate expressions of the form $a \cdot b$ to ab.

DEFINITION 4.7   The algebra $\langle R, +, \cdot, 0, 1 \rangle$ is a *ring* if $\langle R, +, 0 \rangle$ is an Abelian group, $\langle R, \cdot, 1 \rangle$ is a semigroup, and the following additive distribution laws hold for all $a, b, c \in R$:

$$a(b + c) = ab + ac, \qquad (b + c)a = ba + ca.$$

Examples

1. The algebra $\langle I, +, \cdot, 0, 1 \rangle$, where I is the set of integers, and the operations are the conventional arithmetic operations, is a ring.

2. The Boolean algebra $\langle B, \oplus, *, ', 0, 1 \rangle$ is not a ring ($a' \oplus a \neq 0$ in B), but if we define a new operation in B, $a + b = (a * b') \oplus (b * a')$, then $\langle B, +, *, 0, 1 \rangle$ is a ring.

3. The ring $\langle R, +, \cdot, 0, 1 \rangle$ is a *field* if $\langle R - \{0\}, \cdot, 1 \rangle$ is an Abelian group. Element 0 is excluded from R here because this element cannot satisfy A_4 of

D.4.1. Examples of fields: the set of real numbers under conventional addition and multiplication, the set of complex numbers under complex addition and complex multiplication.

Strictly speaking the structures defined in D.4.7 are *rings with multiplicative identity*. The more precise definition of a "bare" ring would not be as restrictive as D.4.7 because it would not require the semigroup to have an identity element, but, as we have pointed out before, semigroups without identity elements excite little interest.

DEFINITION 4.8   The algebra $\langle Q, +, \cdot, 0, 1 \rangle$ is a *Q-semiring* if $\langle Q, +, 0 \rangle$ and $\langle Q, \cdot, 1 \rangle$ are semigroups, and the following laws hold for all $a, b, c \in Q$:

$$a + b = b + a;$$
$$a(b + c) = ab + ac, \qquad (b + c)a = ba + ca;$$
$$a + 1 = 1;$$
$$a \cdot 0 = 0 \cdot a = 0.$$

Examples

1. The Boolean algebra $\langle B, \oplus, *, 0, 1 \rangle$ is a Q-semiring.
2. $\langle R_+^\infty, min, +, \infty, 0 \rangle$, where R_+^∞ is the set of nonnegative real numbers, together with positive infinity, *min* is an operation that takes the smaller of two numbers, and $+$ is conventional addition, is a Q-semiring, and $\langle R_+^\infty, max, min, 0, \infty \rangle$, where *max* is the operation of taking the larger of two numbers, is also a Q-semiring.

Our interest in Q-semirings will be justified in Section 6a.

4b. Group Codes

An interesting application of group theory arises in coding. People in general regard codes as devices for preserving the secrecy of messages in transmission. A programmer may refer to a segment of a program as a "piece of code," but the programmer may also speak of a character code, meaning a function that associates with each character in a permissible character set a unique bit pattern of fixed size, which then serves as the representation of the character inside a computer. To a communications scientist a code means something else again. Although communications scientists are at times concerned with preserving secrecy of messages, their more important interest is in preserving the messages themselves. Communications channels are affected by "noise." Just as surrounding noise at a party may distort spoken words beyond recognition by a listener, so the environment introduces "noise" into a communications channel that may distort the messages being sent through it. Codes have been devised that make it possible to detect and correct the errors introduced by this distortion. They are called, respectively, *error detecting codes* and *error correcting codes*, where an error correcting code is obviously also an error detecting code. It is these codes that will be looked at here.

We regard a message to be transmitted as a sequence of *words* or *blocks* where each word belongs to $\{0, 1\}^m$. The message is encoded prior to transmission by means of a one-to-one encoding function $f : \{0, 1\}^m \to \{0, 1\}^n$, where $n > m$. Note that encoding introduces redundancy. Either function f or the range of f is called a *code*. The code words are transmitted, but the noise in the channel may change some zeros to ones and some ones to zeros, and the coded message may arrive at its destination contaminated. Here a decoding function from $\{0, 1\}^n$ onto $\{0, 1\}^m$ attempts to change each word in the coded message back to its original form. Use is made of the redundancy to detect, and possibly correct, words that have been corrupted in the transmission process.

A very simple error detecting code is used in many computers. Consider a machine in which the word length is m bits. An $(m + 1)$th *parity check bit* is added to the word. The value of this bit is made such that the number of 1 bits in the $(m + 1)$-bit extended word is always odd (*odd parity check*), or always even (*even parity check*). In the odd parity check situation, if the number of 1 bits in the $(m + 1)$-bit extended word is detected to be even, then an error has arisen. Clearly there is insufficient information to determine which bit is in error, and, moreover, if errors had arisen in two different bit positions of the word, this situation could not even be detected. For example, in an 8-bit machine, addition of the check bit would extend 0110 1100 to 0110 1100 1, and 1110 0101 to 1110 0101 0. Now, if the 1110 0101 0 were to become 0110 0101 0, or 1110 0111 0, or 1110 0101 1, we would know that an error had arisen, but if it had changed to 0111 0101 0, then the parity would still be odd, and the error would go undetected. These simple codes are called single-error detecting codes.

DEFINITION 4.9 Consider $a, b \in \{0, 1\}^n$. The *Hamming distance* between a and b, denoted $d(a, b)$ is the number of coordinates in which the n-tuples a and b differ. The *minimal distance* of a code is the minimum of the Hamming distances between all pairs of distinct words in the code. The *weight* of a, denoted $w(a)$, is the number of coordinates in a that are ones.

Examples

1. Hamming distances have the following properties:

   (i) $d(a, b) \geq 0$ for all a and b, with equality holding if and only if $a = b$;

(ii) $d(a, b) = d(b, a)$ for all a and b;

(iii) $d(a, b) \leqq d(a, c) + d(c, b)$ for all a, b, c.

2. Consider the code displayed as Table 4.2. Here all Hamming distances are 3 or 4. For example, $d(x_0, x_6) = d(x_3, x_5) = 4$, $d(x_1, x_5) = d(x_5, x_7) = 3$. The minimal distance of the code is 3. Some weights: $w(x_0) = 0$, $w(x_2) = w(x_4) = 3$, $w(x_6) = 4$. The first three coordinates of each code word in the table represent the actual information; the remaining three coordinates are check bits. The set of eight triples obtained by extracting the first three coordinates from all eight code words is $\{0, 1\}^3$.

TABLE 4.2

A Group Code

$$
\begin{aligned}
x_0 &= \langle 0, 0, 0, 0, 0, 0 \rangle \\
x_1 &= \langle 0, 0, 1, 1, 0, 1 \rangle \\
x_2 &= \langle 0, 1, 0, 0, 1, 1 \rangle \\
x_3 &= \langle 0, 1, 1, 1, 1, 0 \rangle \\
x_4 &= \langle 1, 0, 0, 1, 1, 0 \rangle \\
x_5 &= \langle 1, 0, 1, 0, 1, 1 \rangle \\
x_6 &= \langle 1, 1, 0, 1, 0, 1 \rangle \\
x_7 &= \langle 1, 1, 1, 0, 0, 0 \rangle
\end{aligned}
$$

3. In what follows the zero-weight n-tuple $\langle 0, 0, \ldots, 0 \rangle$ will be written as just 0, and we shall write 010011 for $\langle 0, 1, 0, 0, 1, 1 \rangle$, say.

Suppose that a word a' received at the destination is not a legitimate code word. What should it be decoded to? We use a rule based on Hamming distances: Find a legitimate code word a such that $d(a', a) \leqq d(a', b)$ for all b in the code; then decode a' as it if were a. Consider the code of Table 4.2, and let $a' = 001110$. The legitimate code word closest to it in terms of Hamming distance is $x_3 = 011110$ with $d(a', x_3) = 1$. The next closest words are x_1 and x_4 with $d(a', x_1) = d(a', x_4) = 2$. Here a' would be decoded as if it were x_3.

We shall now find a rationale for the decoding rule. Hamming distance $d(a', b)$ is equal to the number of changes that have to be made to b to convert it into a'. The word a' started out as a legitimate code word, but we do not know which code word it was. A single error would have sufficed to change x_3 into a', but two errors would have been necessary to change x_1 or x_4 into a', and an even greater number in the case of any other code word. The probability of a single error arising is much higher than the probability of two errors, i.e., a' is much more likely to have started out as x_3 than as x_1 or x_4. Therefore, if we decode a' as x_3 rather than as x_1 or x_4, we are much more likely to have made the correct choice. We must however realize that if there is a nonzero probability of a single error, then there are also nonzero probabilities, however small, of two or more errors, i.e., there is always a nonzero probability that our choice has been incorrect. Suppose $a' = 111111$. The least Hamming distance to a legitimate code word in Table 4.2 is now 2, i.e., at least two errors have arisen, and this distance is realized by x_3, x_5, and x_6. We would arbitrarily select one of the three codes, and decode a' as if it were this code. In this case the probability of an incorrect choice is very high (close to $\frac{2}{3}$ in any realistic situation). Th. 4.3 characterizes the error detecting and error correcting capabilities of codes.

THEOREM 4.3   A code can *detect* k or fewer errors in a transmitted word if and only if its minimal distance is at least $k + 1$, it can *correct* all such errors if and only if the minimal distance is at least $2k + 1$.

Proof. Exercise 4.21.

Th.4.3 tells that the minimal distance of a single-error correcting code must be at least 3, and that a code having a minimal distance of 3 can detect two errors. Our task now will be to design single-error correcting codes, and we shall see that group theory can be put to good use in this task.

DEFINITION 4.10   Let A_n be the set of n-tuples (code words) of a code. Set A_n is a *group code* if it forms a group under the n-tuple operation $\oplus$ defined for all $a, b \in A_n$ by

$$a \oplus b = \langle a_1 \oplus b_1, a_2 \oplus b_2, \ldots, a_n \oplus b_n \rangle,$$

where operation $\oplus$ in $\{0, 1\}$ is defined by $0 \oplus 0 = 1 \oplus 1 = 0$, $0 \oplus 1 = 1 \oplus 0 = 1$.

Examples

1. The code of Table 4.2 is a group code. Write the group formed by this code as $\langle A_6, \oplus, e \rangle$, where $A_6 = \{x_0, x_1, \ldots, x_7\}$ and the identity element e is x_0, i.e., $e = 0$.

2. Clearly $a \oplus a = 0$, and $a \oplus b = c$ implies $c \oplus a = b$ and $b \oplus c = a$.

3. It is easy to show that the minimal distance of a group code A_n is equal to the least weight of the words in $A_n - \{0\}$. Define the minimal distance by $d(a, b)$. Then $a \oplus b \in A_n$, but $a \oplus b \neq 0$ because a and b are distinct. By the definition of $\oplus$, $a \oplus b$ contains a 1 only in those coordinate positions in which a and b differ. Hence $d(a, b) = w(a \oplus b)$. Thus there exists a word $a \oplus b \in A_n - \{0\}$ such that $w(a \oplus b)$ is equal to the minimal distance. If $w(a \oplus b)$ were not minimal, then there would exist some $c \in A_n - \{0\}$ with $w(c) < w(a \oplus b)$, but $w(c) = d(c, 0)$, and this would imply $d(c, 0) < d(a, b)$,

which contradicts the initial assumption that $d(a, b)$ defines the minimal distance.

Encoding and decoding may be performed with the aid of a matrix H, which is a matrix of zeros and ones having n rows and r columns, where $r = n - m$. The problem is to find an appropriate H. First we shall define the meaning of an operation $a * H$ for $a \in \{0, 1\}^n$. We write this as

$$\langle a_1, a_2, \ldots, a_n \rangle * \begin{bmatrix} h_{11} & h_{12} \cdots h_{1r} \\ h_{21} & h_{22} \cdots h_{2r} \\ \vdots & \vdots & \vdots & \vdots \\ h_{n1} & h_{n2} \cdots h_{nr} \end{bmatrix} = \langle b_1, b_2, \ldots, b_r \rangle.$$

The r-tuple $\langle b_1, b_2, \ldots, b_r \rangle$ belongs to $\{0, 1\}^r$, and its coordinates are given by

$$b_i = (a_1 * h_{1i}) \oplus (a_2 * h_{2i}) \oplus \cdots \oplus (a_n * h_{ni}), \qquad i = 1, 2, \ldots, r,$$

where the operation $*$ in $\{0, 1\}$ is defined by $0 * 0 = 0 * 1 = 1 * 0 = 0$, $1 * 1 = 1$ (i.e., the operation is conventional multiplication).

It can be shown that the set of n-tuples $\{a \mid a * H = 0\}$ is a group under the $\oplus$ of D.4.10 (Exercise 4.23). In case this set is a group code, H is called a *parity check matrix*, e.g., for the group code of Table 4.2 the parity check matrix is

$$H_c = \begin{bmatrix} 1 & 1 & 0 \\ 0 & 1 & 1 \\ 1 & 0 & 1 \\ 1 & 0 & 0 \\ 0 & 1 & 0 \\ 0 & 0 & 1 \end{bmatrix}$$

Matrix H can be used to generate a group code. We shall prove that if an $n \times r$ matrix H does not contain a row of all zeros, and no two rows in H are identical, then H is a parity check matrix of a single-error correcting code. In such a matrix the difference between the number of rows and columns, $m = n - r$, determines how many different words the code can contain. We state without proof that this number is 2^m. All possible words having length m can then be encoded. The number of check bits that are added to a word in the encoding process to convert it from a member of $\{0, 1\}^m$ to a member of $\{0, 1\}^n$ is r (from $m = n - r$), and this is the number of columns in H. The maximal m for a given value of r is then easily determined: H can have at most $2^r - 1$ distinct rows, and $m = n - r$ becomes $m = 2^r - r - 1$. Values of the maximal m are given in Table 4.3. This table shows that a single-error correcting code for computer words of the popular lengths of 32 (IBM 360 or 370) or 36 (PDP-10) requires that each word be extended by at least six check digits.

TABLE 4.3

NUMBER OF CHECK DIGITS
AND WORD LENGTH FOR
SINGLE-ERROR CORRECTING
CODES

r	m
1	0
2	1
3	4
4	11
5	26
6	57

We need the concept of a *canonical* parity check matrix for what follows. If the submatrix defined by the bottom r rows of $n \times r$ parity check matrix H is the identity matrix, then H is said to be canonical. (An $n \times n$ matrix A is the identity matrix of order n if $a_{ii} = 1$ for $i = 1, 2, \ldots, n$, and all other elements of A are zero. In H, rows $m + 1, m + 2, \ldots, m + r$ define the identity matrix, and this can be expressed as $h_{m+i,j} = 1$ if and only if $i = j$ for $i = 1, 2, \ldots, r$.) Matrix H_c defined above is canonical.

The number of different computer words that can arise in a 36-bit machine is 2^{36}. Obviously encoding by means of a table such as Table 4.2 is then out of the question. The parity check matrix, however, has only $36 + 6 = 42$ rows and 6 columns in this case, and encoding can be done using this matrix. Given a word $a \in \{0, 1\}^m$, the corresponding code word $b \in \{0, 1\}^n$ is constructed using the *canonical* parity check matrix H as follows:

(i) Set $b_i = a_i$ for $i = 1, 2, \ldots, m$;
(ii) Set $b_{m+i} = \bigoplus_{k=1}^m a_k * h_{ki}$ for $i = 1, 2, \ldots, r$.

Let us encode $a = 110$ using H_c. We have $b = 110b_4 b_5 b_6$, where

$$b_4 = (a_1 * h_{11}) \oplus (a_2 * h_{21}) \oplus (a_3 * h_{31}) = 1 \oplus 0 \oplus 0 = 1,$$
$$b_5 = (a_1 * h_{12}) \oplus (a_2 * h_{22}) \oplus (a_3 * h_{32}) = 1 \oplus 1 \oplus 0 = 0,$$
$$b_6 = (a_1 * h_{13}) \oplus (a_2 * h_{23}) \oplus (a_3 * h_{33}) = 0 \oplus 1 \oplus 0 = 1.$$

The result, $b = 110101$, is the x_6 of Table 4.2, as expected. Only the first m rows of the parity check matrix are used in the encoding process, but the entire matrix is needed for decoding.

THEOREM 4.4 Let H be a parity check matrix of n rows and $r = n - m$ columns. Then H defines a group code of minimal distance at least 3 if and only if no row of H consists of all zeros and no two rows are identical.

Proof. Assume that a row h_i in H consists of all zeros, and take an n-tuple a such that $a_i = 1$ and all other coordinates are zero. Then $w(a) = 1$, and since $a * H$ is clearly zero, a belongs to the code defined by H. Hence the existence in H of a zero row implies existence of a code word of weight 1. Next take two distinct rows h_{i_1} and h_{i_2}, and assume $h_{i_1} \oplus h_{i_2} = 0$, which can arise only if $h_{i_1} = h_{i_2}$. Then the n-tuple b with $b_{i_1} = b_{i_2} = 1$ and all other coordinates zero satisfies $w(b) = 2$ and $b * H = 0$, i.e., a code word of weight 2 exists. The equivalence of least weights and minimal distances established in Example 3 of D.4.10 permits us to conclude that the code has minimal distance of at least 3 only if no row of H is zero and no two rows are identical. Conversely, assumptions of existence of code words having weights 1 and 2 lead to conclusions that H contains a zero row or that two rows of H are identical.

The received message has to be decoded. If we know that all code words were transmitted without error, there would be no problem: decoding would be simply the throwing out of all check bits. As it is, even if a code word arrives without having picked up any errors, there is no way of telling that this is so just by looking at the word. Consequently, every word has to be subjected to a procedure that ascertains whether a received word is a valid code word, and if it is not, finds the valid code word that should take its place. This is done by finding an appropriate *corrector* n-tuple that is added to the word to make it a valid code word. If the received word is already a valid code word the corrector that the procedure finds is zero.

A systematic decoding procedure for single-error correcting codes is provided by group theory. The set of all n-tuples is obviously a group under $\oplus$, and this group contains the code A_n as a subgroup. We must find a corrector n-tuple c that would convert a received word a' to the $a \in A_n$ that is closest to a' in terms of Hamming distance: $a = a' \oplus c$. Given a', we could determine for all code words $w_i \in A_n$ the corresponding correctors c_i that satisfy $w_i = a' \oplus c_i$. Then the c_i having the least weight is the c of $a = a' \oplus c$. We know that $w_i = a' \oplus c_i$ implies $c_i = a' \oplus w_i$ (Example 2 of D.4.10), and from the latter expression we see at once that all c_i belong to coset $a'A_n$, and a' belongs to this coset as well (Example 1 of D.4.6). The problem thus reduces to finding the coset to which a' belongs, finding the n-tuple of least weight in this coset (this n-tuple, which is called the *coset leader*, is c), and generating the proper code word by means of $a' \oplus c$. Theorem 4.5 indicates a simple method of finding the coset leader of the coset to which a' belongs.

THEOREM 4.5 Two n-tuples a and b belong to the same coset if and only if $a * H = b * H$.

Proof. Assume that a and b both belong to coset cA_n. Then we can write $a = c \oplus d_1$ and $b = c \oplus d_2$, where $d_1, d_2 \in A_n$. Then $a * H = (c \oplus d_1) * H = (c * H) \oplus (d_1 * H) = (c * H) \oplus 0 = c * H$. Similarly, $b * H = c * H$. Hence $a * H = b * H$. Conversely, if $a * H = b * H$, then $(a * H) \oplus (b * H) = 0$, or $(a \oplus b) * H = 0$. This means that $a \oplus b \in A_n$, which we express as $a \oplus b = c$. Then $c \in A_n$, and $a \oplus b = c$ implies $b = a \oplus c$. From this it follows that b and a both belong to the same coset, namely aA_n.

By Th.4.1 the distinct cosets aA_n constitute a partition of $\{0, 1\}^n$. Th.4.5 tells us how many cosets there are: $a * H$ is an r-tuple, and there are 2^r distinct r-tuples; hence there are at most 2^r distinct cosets. The coset leader of the coset to which an observed n-tuple a' belongs is found as follows. Compute $a' * H$ and interpret the resulting r-tuple $b_1 b_2 \cdots b_r$ as an integer (e.g., interpret the 5-tuple 11101 as 29). If $b_1 b_2 \cdots b_r = 0$, then a' is a valid code word. Otherwise interpret the integer as a subscript to an array in which the appropriate coset leaders have been stored beforehand. The storage requirements for this array are moderate. Even for $r = 6$ there are only $2^6 = 64$ cosets, and an array of 63 locations is sufficient.

Table 4.4 holds the nonzero coset leaders for the group code of Table 4.2. Note that the coset characterized by $b_1 b_2 b_3 = 7$ contains no 6-tuples of weight 1, but that there are three 6-tuples of weight 2 in this coset, namely 100001, 010100, and 001010. The choice of 100001 for the coset leader has been arbitrary. Consider decoding of $x = 110011$, $y = 011010$, $z = 111111$

TABLE 4.4

COSET LEADERS

$a' * H_c =$ Subscript		Coset leader
001	1	000001
010	2	000010
011	3	010000
100	4	000100
101	5	001000
110	6	100000
111	7	100001

with the aid of Table 4.4. In the first stage find $x * H_c = 110$, $y * H_c = 100$, $z * H_c = 111$. These values give access to the appropriate coset leaders in Table 4.4. They are, respectively, 100000, 000100, 100001, and they are used to compute the valid group code words corresponding to the observed 6-tuples: $110011 \oplus 100000 = 010011 = x_2$, $011010 \oplus 000100 = 011110 = x_3$, $111111 \oplus 100001 = 011110 = x_3$.

A vexing problem remains: How does one find the coset leaders in the first place? In principle there is no difficulty. Compute $a * H$ for all $a \in \{0, 1\}^n$, and assign a to the appropriate coset. Then find an n-tuple of least weight in each coset. This approach is impracticable for large n. For example, a single-error correcting code for 36-bit computer words has $n = 42$, but $\{0, 1\}^{42}$ has $2^{42} = 4,398,046,511,104$ elements. It would take an impossibly long time to examine them all. The way out of this difficulty is to find characteristics that coset leaders must possess, and thus reduce the number of n-tuples that could possibly qualify as coset leaders. In general this is still a very difficult problem.

However, for a code defined by an $n \times r$ parity check matrix H it can be shown that the weight of no coset leader exceeds 2 if n and r are related by $2^{r-1} \leq n < 2^r$, and the rows of H, when interpreted as integers, are valued $1, 2, \ldots, r - 1, r$ (Exercise 4.31). Hence, in determining the nonzero coset leaders, only n-tuples having weight 1 or 2 have to be examined. The number of such n-tuples is $C(n, 1) + C(n, 2) = \frac{1}{2}n(n + 1)$. Our H_c satisfies the requirements: $2^{r-1} \leq n < 2^r$ holds when $n = 6$ and $r = 3$, and the row values are 6, 3, 5, 4, 2, 1, reading from top to bottom.

4c. Algebra of Strings

DEFINITION 4.11   An *alphabet* is a finite set of symbols. An alphabet will always be denoted by the letter V.

Example

The set $\{a, b, c, \ldots, z\}$ can be an alphabet, and so can the set $\{apple, pear, banana, carrot\}$, but, if the second set is used for an alphabet, every element in the set must be considered a single indivisible object.

DEFINITION 4.12   A *string* over V of length $m \, (m \geq 0)$ is an m-sample of V. The string of length 0 is distinguished as the *empty string*; we write Λ for it. A string $\langle x_1, x_2, \ldots, x_m \rangle$ will be written $x_1 x_2 \cdots x_m$ for convenience, possibly enclosed in quotes, "$x_1 x_2 \cdots x_m$". The set of all strings over V is denoted by V^*. Members of V^* will be denoted by Greek letters: α, β, γ, ... The length of string α will be denoted by $|\alpha|$.

Example

Let $V = \{a, b\}$. We have $V^* = \bigcup_{i \in N} S_i(V)$, where N is the set of non-negative integers, and $S_0(V) = \{\Lambda\}$, $S_1(V) = \{a, b\}$, $S_2(V) = \{aa, ab, ba, bb\}$, and so on. It is meaningless to talk of strings of infinite length, but obviously no bound can be set on the length of a string.

In linguistics the term *vocabulary* is sometimes used as a synonym for our *alphabet*, and its members are called *words*. In logic, on the other hand, *word* is sometimes used to denote our *string*.

DEFINITION 4.13 Let α be the string $x_1 x_2 \cdots x_m$ and β the string $y_1 y_2 \cdots y_n$. The *concatenation* (*complex product*) of α and β, written $\alpha \cdot \beta$ or simply $\alpha\beta$, is the string $x_1 x_2 \cdots x_m y_1 y_2 \cdots y_n$.

Example

Let $\alpha = ter$, $\beta = ra$. Then $\alpha\beta = terra$, $\beta\alpha = rater$.

Sometimes one has to consider samples of V^* as strings. Let $V = \{e, g, i, m, n, r, s, t\}$. Then $semi \in V^*$ and $string \in V^*$, and one 2-sample of V^* is $\langle semi, string \rangle$. We shall call the taking of a 2-sample and the 2-sample itself *juxtaposition*, and use the symbol $+$ for it (making sure that $+ \notin V$). Then $\langle semi, string \rangle$ becomes the string $semi + string$. Juxtaposition must not be confused with concatenation. Since $+ \notin V$, juxtaposition cannot be an operation in V^*.

THEOREM 4.6 The algebra of strings $\langle V^*, \cdot, \Lambda \rangle$ is a semigroup (with identity).

Proof. Obvious.

DEFINITION 4.14 If $A \subseteq V^*$ and $B \subseteq V^*$, then the *complex product* of A and B is the set of strings $A \cdot B = AB = \{\alpha\beta \mid \alpha \in A, \beta \in B\}$.

DEFINITION 4.15 Let $A \subseteq V^*$. Then the powers of A are defined by $A^0 = \{\Lambda\}$, $A^n = A^{n-1}A$ ($n \geq 1$). We put $A^* = \bigcup_{i \in N} A^i$, where N is the set of non-negative integers, and call A^* the *star* of A. If $A = \{a\}$, where $a \in V$, we write $a^0 = \Lambda$, $a^n = a^{n-1}a$.

Examples

1. $\{a\}^* = \{\Lambda, a, aa, aaa, \ldots\}$.
2. If $A \supseteq V$ holds, then $A^* = V^*$.

If $\langle A, * \rangle$ is a semigroup, then the smallest subset of A from which every element of A can be generated by repeated application of the operation $*$ is called the set of *generators* of A. In the case of $\langle V^*, \cdot, \Lambda \rangle$ the set of generators is V. The algebra $\langle V^*, \cdot, \Lambda \rangle$ is sometimes referred to as a *free* semigroup. It is very difficult to explain the difference between a free algebra and one that is not free. The definition itself is straightforward. Let A be a semigroup with generators B, and let F be the set of functions $\phi: B \to M$, where M denotes any semigroup. Then A is a free semigroup if and only if every member of F possesses an extension $f: A \to M$ that is a homomorphism. Other free algebras are defined analogously. The definition suggests that the elements of a free algebra are as unrestricted as they can possibly be, and still have the structure of this algebra; i.e., only properties that follow from the axioms can be of any consequence in a free algebra. Consider a semigroup V^* with generators $\{a, \ldots, z\}$, say. If V^* is to be free, we can accept only the following definition of equality in V: $a_1 a_2 \cdots a_n = b_1 b_2 \cdots b_m$ if and only if $n = m$ and $a_i = b_i$ for $1 \leq i \leq n$. This is simply the definition of equality of samples. If we were to extend the meaning of equality by rules such as *two · tens = twenty*, say, which cannot be derived from the axioms, V^* would cease to be a *free* semigroup.

DEFINITION 4.16   String β is a *substring* of string σ if there are strings α and γ (possibly empty) such that $\sigma = \alpha\beta\gamma$. If at least one of α and γ is nonempty, then β is a *proper substring* of σ.

Examples

1. Let $\sigma = {*}{*}{*}a{*}{*}{*}bbcd{*}{*}{*}cbdee$. Then $***bbcd$ is a substring of σ, and so is $***a*$, and so forth.
2. The string *aabb* has nine substrings. They are Λ, *a*, *b*, *aa*, *ab*, *bb*, *aab*, *abb*, *aabb*.
3. Consider strings *semi* and *tone*. Their concatenation is *semitone*, their juxtaposition *semi + tone*. The concatenation has *emit* for a substring, but not the juxtaposition. The string *one* is a substring of both *semitone* and *semi + tone*.

Concatenation is the only operation in a semigroup of strings. If two strings are concatenated, the length of the resulting string cannot be smaller than the length of the longer of the two arguments. Obviously concatenation can operate on strings only as indivisible entities. In most practical situations, however, substrings have to be extracted, or deleted, or rearranged into new patterns. We need, therefore, to define a process of substitution.

DEFINITION 4.17   If $\sigma = \alpha\beta\gamma$ and $\sigma' = \alpha\beta'\gamma$ are strings, then σ' is the result of a *substitution* of β' for β in σ. If, moreover, $\alpha\beta$ cannot be expressed as $\alpha'\beta\gamma'$, where γ' is nonempty, the substitution is *canonical*. Substitution is a function in a given V^*. We use the notation $f(\sigma, \alpha, \beta, \beta')$. In the case of canonical substitution only three arguments are needed, and we write $f_c(\sigma, \beta, \beta')$. (The functions are defined only when β is a substring of σ.)

Examples

1. $f(ararat, ar, ara, \Lambda) = art$ and $f(ararat, ar, ara, den) = ardent$, but $f_c(ararat, ara, \Lambda) = rat$. Note that canonical substitution is simply a substitution for the leftmost occurrence of the specified substring in the string.

2. $f_c(tun, \Lambda, s) = stun$. This is an example of a canonical substitution for the null string. We can say that σ' is the result of a canonical substitution for the null string if and only if $\sigma' = \beta'\sigma$. If $\sigma = \Lambda$, this becomes $\sigma' = \beta'$.

4d. Markov Algorithms

Any manipulation of a string can be formulated as a sequence of canonical substitutions. In this section we define a notation for specifying sequences of canonical substitutions for particular tasks, give examples of such sequences, and discuss general properties of the formalism.

DEFINITION 4.18   Let V be an alphabet $\{a, b, c, \ldots\}$ and V' an *auxiliary* alphabet $\{a', b', c', \ldots\}$ such that $V \cap V' = \varnothing$. Let $\rightarrow$ and . be symbols that are not members of $V \cup V'$. If $\beta, \beta_1 \in (V \cup V')^*$, then the string $\beta \rightarrow \beta_1$ is a *simple (Markov) production* and the string $\beta \rightarrow . \beta_1$ is a *terminal (Markov) production*. In these productions β is the *antecedent* and β_1 the *consequent*.

DEFINITION 4.19   A production with antecedent β and consequent β_1 is *applicable* to a string σ if and only if the canonical substitution $f_c(\sigma, \beta, \beta_1)$ is defined (i.e., if and only if β is a substring of σ). The image of $\langle \sigma, \beta, \beta_1 \rangle$ is then the *result* of the production.

Example

Productions $ara \rightarrow \Lambda$ and $ara \rightarrow den$ are both applicable to the string *ararat*. The results are *rat* and *denrat*, respectively. Neither production is applicable to either of strings *rat* and *denrat*. Production $\Lambda \rightarrow s$ is applicable to the string *tun*. The result is *stun*.

DEFINITION 4.20   A *Markov algorithm* (*normal algorithm*) is a finite sequence of productions $P_1, P_2, \ldots, P_n$ applied to a string $\sigma_0 \in V^*$ or to a string $\sigma_i \in (V \cup V')^*$, $i > 0$, according to the following procedure.

1. Set $i = 0$.
2. Set $j = 1$.

   3. If P_j is applicable to σ_i, go to 5.

   4. Set $j = j + 1$. If $j \leqq n$, go to 3. Else algorithm is *blocked*.

   5. Apply P_j to σ_i and obtain σ_{i+1}. Set $i = i + 1$. If P_j was simple, go to 2. Otherwise algorithm *terminates*.

DEFINITION 4.21   A Markov algorithm is *applicable* to a string σ_0 if and only if it stops (by termination or blocking) after a finite number of steps.

Examples

   1. The algorithm $\Lambda \to .\ \Lambda$ is applicable to every string. It corresponds to the identity function. The algorithm $\Lambda \to \Lambda$, since it never stops, is not applicable to any string.

   2. Let $V = \{a, b, c, d\}$. The following Markov algorithm removes the first d and every symbol following it from any string over V.

$$da \to d$$
$$db \to d$$
$$dc \to d$$
$$dd \to d$$
$$d \to .\ \Lambda$$

Applied to the string *aabdcbdda*, the algorithm produces in turn *aabdcbdd*, *aabdbdd*, *aabddd*, *aabdd*, *aabd*, *aab*. If the first four productions were written in some other order, then the strings produced at intermediate stages could differ from the ones above, but the final string would still be *aab*. We shall abbreviate the algorithm by writing a single expression for the first four productions. In this notation the algorithm becomes

$$dx \to d \qquad (x \in V)$$
$$d \to .\ \Lambda$$

Although the composite production $dx \to d$ represents the four separate productions in some *definite* order, one can, for convenience, give a different interpretation: Take *da* for the antecedent if the first d in the string is followed by a, take *db* if it is followed by b, take *dc* if it is followed by c, and take *dd* if it is followed by another d. Under this interpretation the abbreviated algorithm changes *aabdcbdda* to *aabdbdda* (instead of to *aabdcbdd*). If the production $d \to .\Lambda$ were changed to $d \to \Lambda$ the algorithm would stop by blocking.

   Some authors consider a Markov algorithm inapplicable if it stops by blocking. Whether or not one agrees with this view is largely a matter of aesthetics. On the one hand, a formalism that permits only one type of stop has greater simplicity. On the other hand, it is sometimes possible to shorten an algorithm (by one line) if blocking is a legitimate mode of stopping.

We should distinguish two types of applicability. That of D.4.21 is concerned only with stopping. The other type, external to the formalism, is concerned with the proper completion of a specified task, and in this sense a particular Markov algorithm is applicable only if it produces the string that we expect it to produce. Applicability in the sense of D.4.21 is, of course, a pre-condition for applicability in the narrower sense. The distinction is analogous to that between a computer program that is free of syntactic errors, but may still contain "logical bugs," and a completely debugged program.

We have not used an auxiliary alphabet this far. Let us therefore take as our next example an algorithm for duplicating strings. Auxiliary symbols have to be used. In the first stage of the algorithm a copy is made of every symbol in the string; an auxiliary symbol a' moves along the string pointing to the symbol that is to be copied next. In the second stage all copies are moved to one end of the string. To make sure that only the copies are moved, they must be suitably marked; auxiliary symbol b' is the marker.

$$a'x \rightarrow xb'xa' \qquad (x \in V)$$
$$b'xy \rightarrow yb'x \qquad (x, y \in V)$$
$$b' \rightarrow \Lambda$$
$$a' \rightarrow . \Lambda$$
$$\Lambda \rightarrow a'$$

The pointer is introduced by the last production to ensure that it will not be produced more than once. Let us apply the algorithm to a string over $V = \{a, b, c\}$, say *acbcc*. We have

$$acbcc \rightarrow a'acbcc$$
$$\rightarrow ab'aa'cbcc$$
$$\vdots$$
$$\rightarrow ab'acb'cbb'bcb'ccb'ca'$$
$$\rightarrow acb'ab'cbb'bcb'ccb'ca'$$
$$\vdots$$
$$\rightarrow acbccb'ab'cb'bb'cb'ca'$$
$$\rightarrow acbccab'cb'bb'cb'ca'$$
$$\vdots$$
$$\rightarrow acbccacbcca'$$
$$\rightarrow acbccacbcc$$

Our examples of Markov algorithms have corresponded to mappings from V^* into V^*, but this is not an essential feature of Markov algorithms. The string produced by an applicable algorithm may belong to $(V \cup V')^*$ without belonging to V^*. The following algorithm, which counts occurrences of a specified substring, is a case in point. The symbol $+$ $(+ \in V')$ is appended to the string for every occurrence of the substring. We shall write the specified substring α as $\beta\gamma$, where β stands for the first symbol in α. The general form of the algorithm is

$$a'\beta\gamma \to \beta + a'\gamma$$
$$a'x \to xa' \qquad (x \in V)$$
$$+x \to x+ \qquad (x \in V)$$
$$a' \to . \Lambda$$
$$\Lambda \to a'$$

If $\alpha = ara$, say, then the first production is

$$a'ara \to a + a'ra.$$

Apply the algorithm to the string $ararat$:

$$ararat \to a'ararat$$
$$\to a + a'rarat$$
$$\to a + ra'arat$$
$$\to a + ra + a'rat$$
$$\vdots$$
$$\to a + ra + rata'$$
$$\to ar + a + rata'$$
$$\vdots$$
$$\to ararat + + a'$$
$$\to ararat + +$$

The next algorithm converts a string of tallies, $+ + \cdots +$, to a decimal count.

$$b'0+ \to b'1$$
$$b'1+ \to b'2$$
$$b'2+ \to b'3$$
$$\vdots$$
$$b'8+ \to b'9$$
$$b'9+ \to +b'0$$
$$+b' \to b'+$$
$$b'+ \to b'0+$$
$$b' \to . \Lambda$$
$$\Lambda \to b'0$$

Let the counting algorithm and the tally converter be denoted by M_1 and M_2, respectively. The two algorithms can be combined into an algorithm M_3, which carries out the process of M_1 until M_1 would terminate and then carries out the process of M_2 on the result. M_3 is constructed as follows:

1. Change M_1 to M_1' by substituting

$$+a' \to a' +$$
$$a' \to b'0$$

for the production

$$a' \to . \, \Lambda$$

2. Change M_2 to M_2' by deleting the last production ($\Lambda \to b'0$).
3. The combined algorithm is

$$M_2'$$

$$M_1'$$

A general algorithm for combining two algorithms is much more complicated. The segment that carries out the process of the second algorithm has to come first in the combined algorithm, and a string has to be "protected" from its productions while the first process is being applied to the string.

ALGORITHM 4.1   Algorithm for combining two Markov algorithms M_1 and M_2 into a single algorithm M_3. Alphabet V_3 of M_3 is $(V_1 \cup V_1') \cup (V_2 \cup V_2')$, where V_1 and V_2 are the alphabets of M_1 and M_2, respectively, and V_1' and V_2' are the auxiliary alphabets. $V_3' = \{a', b', c', d', e'\}$.

1. Convert M_1 to M_1' by changing every terminal production $\alpha \to . \beta$ to $\alpha \to a'\beta$, and adding $\Lambda \to a'$ as the last production of M_1' (to take care of a stop by blocking).

2. Change the antecedent and the consequent of every production of M_2 as follows:

    change Λ to c',
    change $s_1 s_2 \cdots s_n$ to $c' s_1 c' s_2 c' \cdots c' s_n c'$
(e.g., $\Lambda \to ab$ becomes $c' \to c'ac'bc'$). The modified productions are inapplicable to a string while the process of M_1 is carried out on it.

3. Convert the modified M_2 to M_2' by changing every terminal production $\alpha \to . \beta$ to $\alpha \to d'\beta$, and adding $c' \to d'$ as the last production of M_2'.

4. Introduce productions that change the string produced by M_1' to a form suitable for M_2' and do the final cleaning up. The complete M_3 is

$$
\begin{array}{ll}
xa' \to a'x & (x \in V_1 \cup V_1') \\
a' \to b' & \\
b'x \to c'xb' & (x \in V_1 \cup V_1') \\
b' \to c' & \\
c'xd' \to d'c'x & (x \in V_2 \cup V_2') \\
d' \to e' & \\
e'c'x \to xe' & (x \in V_2 \cup V_2') \\
e'c' \to . \, \Lambda & \\
\quad M_2' & \\
\quad M_1' &
\end{array}
$$

Our final example is a Markov algorithm that appends either T or F to a string depending on whether or not the string is a K-formula. Symbol F is appended to the string at the start, and a pointer is moved along the string. The difference between the number of K-operators and the number of node symbols in the substring to the left of the pointer is given by tallies. If the number of tallies becomes zero before the pointer reaches the last symbol, or the number is nonzero when the last symbol is reached, then the string is not a K-formula. Otherwise the string is a K-formula, and the F is then changed to T. Here $V = N \cup \{*\}$, where N is the set of node symbols.

$$Fx \to xF \qquad (x \in V)$$
$$+x \to x+ \qquad (x \in V)$$
$$a'* \to *+a'$$
$$+a'x \to xa' \qquad (x \in N)$$
$$a'xF \to . xT \qquad (x \in N)$$
$$+ \to \Lambda$$
$$a' \to . \Lambda$$
$$\Lambda \to a'F$$

At this point we digress, and try to come to an understanding of what is meant by a *recursively solvable* (or *decidable*) *problem*. We define a problem as a function, and we say that a problem is recursively solvable if and only if the function is computable, i.e., if and only if there exists a mechanical procedure, which, applied to *any* member of the domain of the function, computes its image within a finite length of time. Take, for example, the problem of deciding whether or not a string is a K-formula. This is a function on the set of all strings into a set of two elements, say $\{T, F\}$. All K-formulas have the image T, all strings other than K-formulas map onto the element F. The Markov algorithm given above is the required mechanical procedure. The problem is therefore decidable.

A well-known abstract device for specifying mechanical procedures is the Turing machine, and it can be shown that a problem is recursively solvable if and only if there exists a Turing machine that computes the function. A mechanical device more powerful than the Turing machine, i.e., one that would compute a function that cannot be computed by a Turing machine, is not known and does not appear to exist. It can be shown also that the Turing machine for computing a function exists only if a Markov algorithm for computing the function exists. The two formalisms are therefore equivalent. Turing machines, important though they are in theoretical studies, are quite impracticable when it comes to describing procedures for solving practical problems. The usefulness of Markov algorithms, on the other hand, extends beyond the theory of decidability. They can provide reasonably efficient characterizations of operations on strings. Programs written in Snobol and

Comit, which are programming languages for processing strings, are very similar to Markov algorithms.

There are unsolvable problems relating to Turing machines and Markov algorithms themselves. For example, the problem of whether or not a Markov algorithm is applicable to a string is recursively unsolvable. It must be stressed that particular solutions can be found. Only the general procedure, which would work for *any* Markov algorithm and *any* string, cannot be devised.

4e. Languages and Grammars

There is very little that is interesting about a set V^* itself. We shall now look at subsets of V^* that we find interesting for some reason or other, and at ways of specifying rules for generating precisely those strings that are members of such subsets. Collections of rules that define subsets of V^* are known as grammars.

Traditionally we think of a grammar of a language as a set of rules a speaker of the language is supposed to obey. A grammar in the traditional sense defines "correct" usage. The modern approach is different. Instead of attempting to prescribe usage, the linguist accepts a language as used, and seeks a description of the language. He looks for a theory that specifies or predicts all sentences in the language, excluding strings that are not sentences. In other words, instead of defining a particular subset of the set of all strings over a vocabulary as *the* language, he takes a particular subset as given, and looks for rules that will generate precisely the members of this subset.

Natural languages, because of their complexity, have defied attempts at their complete specification. This is understandable. The use of a rich language is what makes us human beings, and a description of our linguistic competence would come close to a description of our existence. The methodology has, nevertheless, made significant contributions to important advances in other fields, particularly in computer science. One important source of our improved knowledge of programming languages has been the classification of subsets of V^* according to the form of the rules used in their generation. The classificatory approach has contributed also to a better understanding of the relation between languages and automata. Increased familiarity with linguistic techniques in the computing community has led to the investigation of a variety of structures by linguistic means. Analysis of pictures is an example; it no longer seems strange to speak of picture languages.

DEFINITION 4.22   Let V be an alphabet. Subsets of V^* are *languages* over V (generally denoted by L, possibly with subscripts). If $\alpha \in L$, then α is a *sentence* of L.

Definitions D.4.14 and D.4.15 are, of course, still applicable when sets A and B are interpreted as languages. In particular, if $L \subseteq V^*$, then $L^* = cl(L)$, the *closure* of language L.

DEFINITION 4.23   A *grammar* is a finite system of rules determining a language. The language determined by a grammar G will be denoted by $L(G)$. If $L(G_1) = L(G_2)$, then G_1 and G_2 are *equivalent*.

In D.4.23 the term *grammar* is left too vague to be of much use. We strengthen the term in the next definition, which introduces a specific class of grammars.

DEFINITION 4.24   A *constituent structure grammar* (or *phrase structure grammar*) is a quadruple $G = \langle V, V', P, S, \rangle$, where V and V' are an alphabet and an auxiliary alphabet, respectively, $S \in V'$, and $P \subseteq (V \cup V')^{*2}$ is a finite relation.

Members of P are called *production rules*. A rule $\langle \alpha, \beta \rangle$ is usually written as $\alpha \to \beta$. Members of V are called *terminal* symbols. Members of V' are called *nonterminals*, or *syntactic categories*, or *metalinguistic variables*, or simply *variables*. The term *constituent structure grammars* implies that these grammars, by means of variables, impose structure on constituents of sentences in their languages. We use *constituent structure* in preference to *phrase structure*, despite the wider acceptance of the latter term. Our reason is that *phrase*, because of its traditional place of importance in the terminology of linguistics as a study of natural languages, would evoke the false impression that natural languages will be our concern here. We will be concerned with formal languages or—to use a picturesque quote—chunks carved out of the free monoid V^*.

DEFINITION 4.25   Let $G = \langle V, V', P, S \rangle$ be a constituent structure grammar. We write $\sigma_i \Rightarrow \sigma_{i+1}$ if there exist $\sigma_i = \alpha \beta \gamma$ and $\sigma_{i+1} = \alpha \beta' \gamma$ in $(V \cup V')^*$ and $\beta \to \beta'$ is a member of P, and we write $\sigma_0 \overset{*}{\Rightarrow} \sigma_t$ if either $\sigma_0 = \sigma_t$ or there exists a sequence $\sigma_0, \sigma_1, \ldots, \sigma_t$ such that $\sigma_i \Rightarrow \sigma_{i+1}$ for all $0 \leq i < t$. The sequence is called the σ_0-*derivation* of σ_t; we denote it also by $\sigma_0 \Rightarrow \sigma_1 \Rightarrow \cdots \Rightarrow \sigma_t$.

DEFINITION 4.26   If $G = \langle V, V', P, S \rangle$ is a constituent structure grammar, then

$$L(G) = \{\alpha \,|\, \alpha \in V^* \text{ and } S \overset{*}{\Rightarrow} \alpha\}$$

is the *constituent structure language generated* by G. (The distinguished metalinguistic variable S represents the class of sentences.)

Examples

1. Let N be a set of node symbols $\{a, b, c, \ldots, k\}$. Then $G_1 = \langle\{*\} \cup N,$ $\{S\}, P_1, S\rangle$, where P_1 is the set of rules $\{S \to n \mid n \in N\} \cup \{S \to *SS\}$, is a grammar of K-formulas. We have, for example, $S \Rightarrow *SS \Rightarrow *S*SS \Rightarrow$ $*S*bS \Rightarrow **SS*bS \Rightarrow **bS*bS \Rightarrow **ba*bS \Rightarrow **ba*bc$, and $S \overset{*}{\Rightarrow} **ba*bc$ is an S-derivation of the K-formula $**ba*bc$.

2. Let N be the set of Example 1. Then $G_2 = \langle\{*\} \cup N, \{K, node\},$ $P_2, K\rangle$, where P_2 is the set of productions $\{K \to node, K \to *KK\} \cup$ $\{node \to n \mid n \in N\}$, is another grammar of K-formulas. G_1 and G_2 are equivalent: $L_1(G_1) = L_2(G_2)$. Obviously G_1 is the simpler grammar, but G_2 has the advantage that it differentiates explicitly between node symbols and the K-operator by assigning the node symbols to their own syntactic category.

3. Let $V = \{a, apple, ate, bought, child, green, man, pear, the\}$, $V' =$ $\{S, A, N, NP, T, V, VP\}$, and let $G = \langle V, V', P, S\rangle$ be a grammar in which P contains the following rules:

$$
\begin{array}{lll}
S \to NP.VP & N \to apple & T \to a \\
NP \to T.N & N \to child & T \to the \\
VP \to V & N \to man & V \to ate \\
VP \to V.NP & N \to pear & V \to bought \\
N \to A.N & A \to green &
\end{array}
$$

Let us derive a sentence of $L(G)$.

$$
\begin{array}{l}
S \Rightarrow NP.VP \\
\quad \Rightarrow T.N.VP \\
\quad \Rightarrow the.N.VP \\
\quad \Rightarrow the.child.VP \\
\quad \Rightarrow the.child.V.NP \\
\quad \Rightarrow the.child.V.T.N \\
\quad \Rightarrow the.child.V.a.N \\
\quad \Rightarrow the.child.V.a.A.N \\
\quad \Rightarrow the.child.V.a.green.N \\
\quad \Rightarrow the.child.ate.a.green.N \\
\quad \Rightarrow the.child.ate.a.green.pear
\end{array}
$$

It is only an accident that this sentence "makes sense." The string *a.apple.* *bought.the.green.green.green.pear* is also a sentence in $L(G)$. The symbol . indicates concatenation.

4. G is a grammar that generates all permutations of $\{a, b, c\}$: $G =$ $\langle\{a, b, c\}, \{\pi, A, B, C\}, P, \pi\rangle$, where P consists of the productions $\pi \to ABC,$ $AB \to BA$, $AC \to CA$, $BC \to CB$, $A \to a$, $B \to b$, $C \to c$. Then, for example,

cba may be derived as follows: $\pi \Rightarrow ABC \Rightarrow BAC \Rightarrow BCA \Rightarrow CBA \Rightarrow cBA \Rightarrow cbA \Rightarrow cba$. Alternatively, we can define the simpler $G' = \langle \{a, b, c\}, \{\pi\}, P', \pi \rangle$, where now the productions are $\pi \rightarrow abc$, $ab \rightarrow ba$, $ac \rightarrow ca$, $bc \rightarrow cb$.

5. We can have a grammar $G = \langle V, V', P, S \rangle$ that contains no production of the form $S \rightarrow \alpha$, but the grammar is of little interest; $L(G)$ is vacuous. Likewise, there is no point in having a production rule whose consequent contains a nonterminal that does not appear in the antecedent of any other production of the grammar.

Production rules can be written in a compressed form, which has become known as the *Backus normal form* (*Bnf*). All productions with the same antecedent are written in a single line, the consequents being separated by vertical slashes. The sign $::=$ separates an antecedent from its consequents. To avoid ambiguity, members of V' are enclosed in angular brackets. In Bnf the productions of the grammar of Example 3 are written

$$\langle S \rangle ::= \langle NP \rangle \langle VP \rangle$$
$$\langle NP \rangle ::= \langle T \rangle \langle N \rangle$$
$$\langle VP \rangle ::= \langle V \rangle | \langle V \rangle \langle NP \rangle$$
$$\langle N \rangle ::= \langle A \rangle \langle N \rangle | apple | child | man | pear$$
$$\langle A \rangle ::= green$$
$$\langle T \rangle ::= a | the$$
$$\langle V \rangle ::= ate | bought$$

The grammars defined by D.4.24 are known as *unrestricted* grammars. The definition is sufficiently general in a sense that we shall now clarify. It can be shown that any Turing machine can be represented directly as an unrestricted grammar, and conversely. Therefore, since the Turing machine is the most powerful mechanical device we know, any grammar that can be specified must be equivalent to some unrestricted grammar.

In order to facilitate the proof of equivalence of Turing machines and unrestricted grammars, definitions of the latter are usually tighter than our D.4.24. As an example of the constraints imposed, a definition might require that, for every $\langle \alpha, \beta \rangle \in P$, some substring of α be a member of V'. Under this constraint G' of Example 4 above is not a constituent structure grammar. Other constraints would exclude the grammars discussed in Example 5. The set of languages generated by the grammars of D.4.24 is, however, equal to the set generated by grammars subjected to the more usual constraints, and this is our justification for having opted for the simplest possible formulation in D.4.24.

Unrestricted grammars are too general to be of any practical use. All the more important questions about these grammars are undecidable. We shall now introduce restrictions on the production rules, which are not to be confused with the constraints of the paragraph above, that will define grammars of greater interest. These grammars are known as being of Type 1, Type 2, and Type 3; unrestricted grammars are of Type 0 under this classification. The languages generated by grammars of Type i are known as Type i languages. Every grammar of Type $i + 1$ is also of Type i, but the set of grammars of Type $i + 1$ is a proper subset of the set of grammars of Type i. Sets of the corresponding languages, too, obey the proper subset relation. It is reasonable to hold the opinion that Type 0 grammars are too amorphous to be called grammars. It is, indeed, preferable to call them unrestricted *rewriting systems*, and to reserve the term *grammar* for the restricted systems.

DEFINITION 4.27   A constituent structure grammar is of *Type 1* if the consequent of every production of the grammar contains at least as many symbols as the antecedent.

Example

G_2 of Example 2 of D.4.26 contains the production *node* $\to n$, but *node* is a single symbol, and G_2 is a Type 1 grammar. On the other hand, a system that contains the rule $\langle n \rangle + \langle n \rangle ::= \langle addition \rangle$, say, is not a Type 1 grammar; the antecedent contains three symbols, the consequent only one.

DEFINITION 4.28   A Type 1 grammar is of *Type 1'* only if each production of the grammar has the form $\alpha A \beta \to \alpha \gamma \beta$, where $\alpha, \beta \in (V \cup V')^*$, $A \in V'$, $\gamma \in (V \cup V')^* - \{\Lambda\}$.

Example

If we want to generate all permutations of n objects, it is, of course, possible to do so by means of a grammar that contains as many rules as there are permutations. The G of Example 4 of D.4.26 is an example of how one constructs a grammar with $\frac{1}{2}n(n + 1) + 1$ rules (i.e., fewer than $n!$ when $n > 3$). It is not a Type 1' grammar, but a Type 1' grammar can be constructed that generates all permutation and still contains fewer than $n!$ rules (except for small n). In this grammar every rule that has the form $AB \to BA$ in G is replaced by a set of four rules $\{AB \to AB', AB' \to A'B', A'B' \to BB', BB' \to BA\}$. The number of auxiliary symbols increases from n to n^2; each of the $\frac{1}{2}n(n - 1)$ sets of four rules requires two additional auxiliaries.

Grammars of Type 1' are called *context-sensitive* (or *context-dependent*) grammars. Although there exist Type 1 grammars that are not Type 1', in one sense the two types are equivalent: If G is a Type 1 grammar, then there exists a Type 1' grammar equivalent to G. Far too many problems in the theory of context-sensitive grammars are undecidable. Therefore these grammars are only slightly more interesting than the unrestricted rewriting systems.

DEFINITION 4.29   A grammar is of *Type 2* only if all of its rules take the form $A \to \gamma$, where $A \in V'$ and $\gamma \in (V \cup V')^* - \{\Lambda\}$.

Examples

1. The grammars of Examples 1, 2, and 3 of D.4.26 are of Type 2.

2. The major part of a definition of Algol or Fortran can be expressed in the form of Type 2 production rules. The following Type 2 grammar defines Fortran integers and real numbers. The definition is rather abstract in that there are no limits on the sizes of the numbers, and rightly so. Limits should only be imposed when the language is related to a particular computer; they would be determined by the size of the computer word.

$$\langle\text{digit}\rangle ::= 0\,|\,1\,|\,2\,|\,3\,|\,4\,|\,5\,|\,6\,|\,7\,|\,8\,|\,9$$
$$\langle\text{sign}\rangle ::= +\,|\,-$$
$$\langle\text{unsigned integer}\rangle ::= \langle\text{digit}\rangle\,|\,\langle\text{unsigned integer}\rangle\langle\text{digit}\rangle$$
$$\langle\text{integer}\rangle ::= \langle\text{unsigned integer}\rangle\,|\,\langle\text{sign}\rangle\langle\text{unsigned integer}\rangle$$
$$\langle\text{unsigned F-number}\rangle ::= .\langle\text{unsigned integer}\rangle\,|\,\langle\text{unsigned integer}\rangle.\,|$$
$$\langle\text{unsigned integer}\rangle.\langle\text{unsigned integer}\rangle$$
$$\langle\text{F-number}\rangle ::= \langle\text{unsigned F-number}\rangle\,|$$
$$\langle\text{sign}\rangle\langle\text{unsigned F-number}\rangle$$
$$\langle\text{exponent}\rangle ::= E\langle\text{integer}\rangle$$
$$\langle\text{real}\rangle ::= \langle\text{F-number}\rangle\,|\,\langle\text{F-number}\rangle\langle\text{exponent}\rangle\,|$$
$$\langle\text{integer}\rangle\langle\text{exponent}\rangle$$

Type 2 grammars are known as *context-free* grammars. They have been widely studied, and a lot is known about them. For example, the problem whether the language generated by a grammar is empty, finite, or infinite is decidable for Type 2 grammars, but not for Type 1 grammars. However, the important problem of whether two Type 2 grammars are equivalent is undecidable.

DEFINITION 4.30   A grammar is of *Type 3* only if all of its productions are of the forms $A \to \alpha$ or $A \to \alpha B$, where $A, B \in V'$ and $\alpha \in V^* - \{\Lambda\}$, or, alternatively, they are all of the forms $A \to \alpha$ or $A \to B\alpha$.

Example

$G = \langle\{a, b, c\}, \{S, A\}, P, S\rangle$, where P consists of the productions

$$\langle S\rangle ::= ab\langle S\rangle\,|\,c\langle A\rangle$$
$$\langle A\rangle ::= ba\langle A\rangle\,|\,a$$

is a Type 3 grammar. $L(G)$ is the complex product $(ab)^*c(ba)^*a$. Type 3 grammars are called also *one-sided linear*, or *finite state*, or *regular* grammars. Languages generated by Type 3 grammars are called *regular sets*. G is a *right-linear* grammar because the nonterminal is written to the right of terminals in every consequent containing a nonterminal. Every right-linear grammar has an equivalent *left-linear* grammar. In the case of G, an equivalent left-linear grammar has the following productions:

$$\langle S \rangle ::= \langle A \rangle a$$
$$\langle A \rangle ::= \langle A \rangle ba \,|\, \langle B \rangle c \,|\, c$$
$$\langle B \rangle ::= \langle B \rangle ab \,|\, ab$$

(B is an additional nonterminal symbol). The language $\{(ab)^k c(ba)^k a \,|\, k \geq 0\}$, which is a proper subset of $L(G)$, cannot be produced by a Type 3 grammar.

It is possible to determine whether or not a given string belongs to a given language. This is what A.4.2 does. Proof of validity of the algorithm would take us too far afield in the theory of languages. It is therefore omitted.

ALGORITHM 4.2   Given a Type 1 grammar $G = \langle V, V', P, S \rangle$, and a string $\alpha \in V^* - \{\Lambda\}$, where $|\alpha| = k$. The algorithm determines whether $\alpha \in L(G)$.

1. Set $i = 0$, $Q_0 = \{S\}$.
2. Set $i = i + 1$.
3. Set $Q_i = Q_{i-1} \cup \{\gamma \,|\, \beta \Rightarrow \gamma$ and $\beta \in Q_{i-1}$, and $|\gamma| \leq k\}$.
4. If $Q_i = Q_{i-1}$, stop. String α cannot be generated by G. (Note that $Q_i = Q_{i-1}$ holds for some finite i.)
5. If $\alpha \notin Q_i$, go to 2.
6. Stop. String α has been generated by G.

Example

Since a Type 3 grammar is also of Type 1, we can use A.4.2 with the left-linear grammar of the example of D.4.30. We shall test strings *abca* and *abba*. The length of each string is 4. Hence, only strings that do not exceed this length will become members of the Q_i. Start with $Q_0 = \{S\}$, and apply production $\langle S \rangle :: = \langle A \rangle a$. This gives $Q_1 = \{S, Aa\}$. Next apply productions $\langle A \rangle :: = \langle A \rangle ba \,|\, \langle B \rangle c \,|\, c$ to string Aa to obtain $Q_2 = \{S, Aa, Abaa, Bca, ca\}$. Productions $\langle A \rangle :: = \langle A \rangle ba \,|\, \langle B \rangle c \,|\, c$ are applied to *Abaa*, and productions $\langle B \rangle :: = \langle B \rangle ab \,|\, ab$ to *Bca*. Three of the resulting strings, namely *Ababaa* *Bcbaa*, and *Babca*, are too long. Consequently, $Q_3 = \{S, Aa, Abaa, Bca, ca, cbaa, abca\}$. We have generated *abca*, but not *abba*. However, in generating Q_3 from Q_2 we have added only strings that consist entirely of terminals. Hence $Q_4 = Q_3$, i.e., *abba* cannot be generated by G.

4f. Languages and Automata

Type 3 grammars are called finite state grammars because they are related to *finite state automata*. Let us consider a finite state *acceptor*. This is a device that can be in one of a finite number of distinct *internal states* at any one time. It is equipped with a reading head, and under the reading head we pass a tape on which a string has been written. Depending on the state the automaton is in, and the symbol that it reads, it can remain in the same state or switch to a different state. In more formal terms, we have a set of states Q and a set of symbols S. The machine is described by a function f from $Q \times S$ into Q. One of the states is distinguished: $q_1 \in Q$ is the state in which the machine starts the scan of the tape and to which it should return after it has read the entire string presented to it. We then say that the automaton has *accepted* or *recognized* the string. Assume that the string contains a substring $s_{j-1}s_j$. If, on reading s_{j-1}, the machine goes into state q_i and $\langle q_i, s_j \rangle$ is not in the domain of f, the machine has to stop for lack of further instructions. We interpret this stop as nonacceptance of the string. The significant link between Type 3 languages and finite state acceptors is that for every Type 3 language there exists a finite state acceptor that will accept all sentences of the language and fail to accept strings that are not sentences. Moreover, if a language cannot be described by a Type 3 grammar, there exists no finite state acceptor for the language.

For every unrestricted rewriting system we can produce a Turing machine that will accept strings generated by this system, and no others. A Turing acceptor also has a finite number of internal states. It also reads from a tape, and the next action of the machine is a function from the Cartesian product of states and symbols. How then does it differ from a finite state acceptor? The difference is that a Turing machine has a tape of unbounded length on which it can write as much as it wants to, and that it can read what *it* has previously written. Therefore, in contrast to a finite state acceptor, a Turing acceptor has an infinite memory, i.e., the *finite* refers to memory capacity rather than to the number of internal states.

An automaton is very conveniently represented by a weighted digraph: Nodes represent internal states; arcs represent transitions from state to state. The digraph has an arc $\langle q_i, q_j \rangle$, with weight s_k, if and only if $\langle q_i, s_k, q_j \rangle$ is a member of the function describing the automaton. These digraphs are called *state graphs*. Figure 4.3 shows the digraph of a finite state automaton that accepts the language $(ab)^*c(ba)^*a$. The symbol # is a delimiter. When a

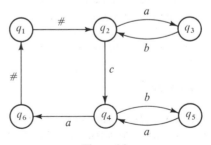

Figure 4.3

string is presented to an automaton, we use the # as special end markers. Thus, the string *ababcbaa* is written #*ababcbaa*# on the tape.

Instantaneous descriptions of an automaton help one understand the process by which an automaton accepts or rejects a string. An instantaneous description consists of the string and, in addition, a pointer to the symbol that is currently under the reading head. The description is not complete unless the current state of the automaton is indicated as well, and this is done by making the state symbol the pointer; it is placed on the left of the symbol being scanned. An initial instantaneous description is, for example, q_1#*ababcbaa*#. For the automaton of Figure 4.3 $f(q_1, \#) = q_2$, and the transition to state q_2 is accompanied by a shift of the tape to the left. The next instantaneous description is therefore #q_2*ababcbaa*#. The complete sequence of instantaneous descriptions depicting acceptance of *ababcbaa* by the automaton of Figure 4.3 is

$$q_1 \# ababcbaa \# \rightarrow \# q_2 ababcbaa \#$$
$$\rightarrow \# a q_3 babcbaa \#$$
$$\rightarrow \# ab q_2 abcbaa \#$$
$$\rightarrow \# aba q_3 bcbaa \#$$
$$\rightarrow \# abab q_2 cbaa \#$$
$$\rightarrow \# ababc q_4 baa \#$$
$$\rightarrow \# ababcb q_5 aa \#$$
$$\rightarrow \# ababcba q_4 a \#$$
$$\rightarrow \# ababcbaa q_6 \#$$
$$\rightarrow \# ababcbaa \# q_1.$$

The automaton halts in state q_1; i.e., the string is accepted. The next sequence of instantaneous descriptions illustrates nonacceptance of a string:

$$q_1 \# acabab \# \rightarrow \# q_2 acabab \#$$
$$\rightarrow \# a q_3 cabab \#.$$

Since there is no $\langle q_3, c \rangle$ in the domain of *f*, the automaton stops.

Figure 4.4, our second example, shows an automaton that accepts the language a^*bc^*.

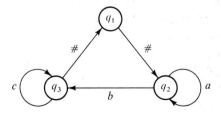

Figure 4.4

An alternative description of an automaton is in terms of a variable adjacency matrix. However, a more convenient way of representing an acceptor is by a *state-symbol matrix*. Let $Q = \{q_1, q_2, \ldots, q_n\}$ be the set of states of an automaton, and let $S = \{s_1, s_2, \ldots, s_m\}$ be its set of symbols (S includes the string end marker). The state-symbol matrix M is an $n \times m$ matrix in which the (i, j)th element is q_k if $f(q_i, s_j) = q_k$, or zero if $f(q_i, s_j)$ is undefined. A.4.3, a program that simulates finite state acceptors, is based on the use of the state-symbol matrix.

ALGORITHM 4.3   Finite state acceptor simulation program.

```
        INTEGER M(..,..),TAPE(..),STATE,SYMBOL,S,Q1,Q2
C1   SET UP MATRIX M - IN TRIPLES (Q1,S,Q2)INTEGERS
C1   1,2,3,... REPRESENT SYMBOLS
        DO 10  I = 1,...
        DO 10  J = 1,...
    10  M(I,J) = 0
        READ (5,100) N
        DO 15  J = 1,N
        READ (5,100) Q1, S, Q2
    15  M(Q1,S) = Q2
C2   READ TAPE AND PRINT IT FOR REFERENCE - PROGRAM
C2   STOPS WHEN THERE ARE NO MORE TAPES TO BE READ (A
C2   FEATURE PROVIDED BY MOST OPERATING SYSTEMS)
    20  READ (5,101) LENGTH, (TAPE(K), K = 1,LENGTH)
        WRITE (6,102)  (TAPE(K), K = 1,LENGTH)
C3   ACCEPTANCE TEST
        STATE = 1
        DO 25  NOW = 1,LENGTH
        SYMBOL = TAPE(NOW)
        STATE = M(STATE,SYMBOL)
        IF (STATE.EQ.0) GO TO 30
    25  CONTINUE
C4   BY CONVENTION AUTOMATON MUST STOP IN STATE 1
        IF (STATE.NE.1) GO TO 30
        WRITE (6,103)
        GO TO 20
    30  WRITE (6,104)
        GO TO 20
   100  FORMAT (3I4)
```

```
101   FORMAT (I4/(40I2))
102   FORMAT (1H0, 50I2/(1H ,50I2))
103   FORMAT (1H0, 15HSTRING ACCEPTED)
104   FORMAT (1H0, 15HSTRING REJECTED)
      END
```

Accepting power intermediate to those of Turing machines and finite state automata is provided by a pushdown store automaton. There is a very close relation between the abstract pushdown store automaton and a pushdown store. The latter has great practical importance in programming, and we shall discuss it in Section 5b. Discussion of the abstract pushdown store is outside the scope of this book.

Notes

The many worked examples and exercises of [Fa63] make it an excellent supplementary text for pursuing the subject of algebraic structures further. In our context the classic [Bi41] may be too thorough a text, but should be consulted for reference. For a basic introduction to the theory of groups see [Le 49]. The relevant sections of [Bi70] and [St73] provide an introduction to coding theory; [In71] is an intermediate text. The standard reference work is [Pe61]; it contains an extensive bibliography. Error-correcting codes in computer arithmetic are discussed in [Ma72c]. A fundamental early paper by Hamming [Ha50] did much to stimulate interest in the design of codes.

Introductions to the theory of Markov algorithms can be found in [Cu63, Gl64, Ko66]—[Cu63] is the more advanced. Our A.4.1 is adapted from [Cu63]. References to the programming languages Comit and Snobol can be found in the Notes to Chapter 10. Decidability problems are discussed in [Mi67, Ho72a, Ni72, Jo73]. [Dr72] is a philosophical analysis of the limitations of machines. After reading this book one should also read its reviews in *Computing Reviews* for balance.

[Ba64] is a good basic introduction to grammars in general; it is addressed to linguists and deals mainly with natural languages. Formal languages and their relation to automata are studied in [Ho69, Ka72a, Ma72a] (Chapters 8 and 9 of [Ka72a] survey decision problems related to grammars and automata). Our classification of grammars follows that of [Ch63]. Th.2.2 of [Ho69] is the basis for our A.4.2. The Bnf notation was introduced in [Ba 59a]; it has become widely known primarily because of its use in the specification of Algol, see, e.g., [Na63].

The relevance of automata theory to computer science is discussed in simple terms in [Ba72c]. After reading this paper one can study the relevant sections of [Mi67], and then turn to the more advanced [Ho69, Ka72a, Ma72a]. [Le71] describes the application of automata theory to the design of a compiler.

Exercises

4.1   (a)   Let R be the set of real numbers, and consider M_2: the set of all 2×2 matrices whose elements belong to R. Show that $\langle M_2, \cdot \rangle$, where $\cdot$ is matrix multiplication, is a semigroup with identity.

4.2   (a)   Show that $\langle \mathscr{P}(A), +, \varnothing \rangle$, where A is a nonempty set and $+$ is the symmetric difference operation, is a semigroup. Is this algebra a group? Is it Abelian?

4.3   (a)   Identify the inverses x' of all elements x in the dihedral group D_4.

4.4   (a)   Perform an analysis analogous to that of Example 3 of D.4.3 for an equilateral triangle and a regular pentagon. Find the "multiplication" tables of the two groups (they are the dihedral groups D_3 and D_5).

4.5   (a)   The rigid motions of a regular polygon of n sides form the dihedral group D_n. Investigate the feasibility of writing a computer program that generates the "multiplication" table of D_n for any given n.

4.6   (a)   Identify all subgroups of the dihedral group D_4.

4.7   (a)   Let G be a group, G_1 a subgroup of G, aG_1 and bG_1 left cosets of G in G_1. Prove that $aG_1 = bG_1$ if and only if $a' * b \in G_1$.

4.8   (a)   Prove that every permutation can be expressed as a product of disjoint cycles.

4.9   (a)   What are the 8-tuples that result when the permutation $p =$ (2 3 7 1)(4 5 8) is applied to 8-tuples $\langle 1, 2, 3, 4, 5, 6, 7, 8 \rangle$ and $\langle 8, 7, 6, 5, 4, 3, 2, 1 \rangle$? Express p as a product of transpositions. Is p even or odd?

4.10   (a)   Express the elements of the symmetric permutation groups $P(\{1, 2, 3\})$ and $P(\{1, 2, 3, 4\})$ as products of disjoint cycles. Then find all proper subgroups of the two groups.

4.11   (a)   Th.4.1 holds also for right cosets. Verify that the left and right decompositions of $P\{(1, 2, 3)\}$ with respect to $G_1 = \{(1), (12)\}$ are not equal.

4.12   (a)   Write a computer program that determines from a "multiplication table" such as Table 4.1 whether or not the structure represented by the table is a group.

4.13   (a)   What pattern do the even and odd permutations follow in A.1.6?

4.14   (a)   Write a subroutine that generates only the odd permutations of a given set.

4.15 (a) An element $a \in B$ has different inverses in the Boolean algebra and the ring of Example 2 of D.4.7. Characterize the inverses of elements of the ring.

4.16 (a) Prove that the algebras $\langle I, +, \cdot, 0, 1 \rangle$ and $\langle B, +, *, 0, 1 \rangle$ in Examples 1 and 2 of D.4.7 are rings.

4.17 (a) Show that $\langle [0, 1], max, \cdot, 0, 1 \rangle$, where $[0, 1]$ is the closed unit interval on the set of real numbers and $\cdot$ is arithmetic multiplication, is a Q-semiring.

4.18 (a) In Q-semiring $\langle Q, +, \cdot, 0, 1 \rangle$ define relation $\geq$ by saying that $a \geq b$ if and only if $a + b = a$. Show that

  (i) Q is partially ordered by $\geq$,
  (ii) $a \geq a \cdot b$,
  (iii) $a \geq b$ and $c \geq d$ imply $a \cdot c \geq b \cdot d$.

4.19 (b) Why is it impossible to devise an error detecting code that detects every possible error when the code contains more than one code word?

4.20 (b) If a code contains a word with zero weight, and the maximal weight of any word in the code is k, what is the maximal Hamming distance between any two words in the code?

4.21 (b) Prove Th.4.3.

4.22 (b) Find the inverses of all elements of the $\langle A_6, \oplus, e \rangle$ in Example 1 of D.4.10. Verify that A_6 is closed under $\oplus$.

4.23 (b) Let H be an $n \times r$ binary matrix. Prove that $\{a \mid a \in \{0, 1\}^n$ and $a * H = 0\}$ is a group under the $\oplus$ of D.4.10.

4.24 (b) Let H be an $n \times r$ binary matrix, and let $a, b \in \{0, 1\}^n$. Prove $(a \oplus b) * H = (a * H) \oplus (b * H)$.

4.25 (b) Let $h_{i_1}, h_{i_2}, \ldots, h_{i_d}$ be d distinct rows of parity check matrix H. Prove that $h_{i_1} \oplus h_{i_2} \oplus \cdots \oplus h_{i_d} = 0$ if and only if the code defined by H contains a code word of weight d. (Note that this is a generalization of Th.4.4.)

4.26 (b) Design a single-error correcting code for the encoding of the set of words $\{0, 1\}^4$.

4.27 (b) Find a canonical parity check matrix with 5 columns that defines a single-error correcting code for the encoding of the set of words $\{0, 1\}^{16}$. How many such parity check matrices is it possible to have? How many different codes are defined by these matrices?

4.28 (b) Generate a table of coset leaders for the code of Exercise 4.26.

4.29 (b) Let A_n be a group code such that $|A_n| = 2^m$. Is it possible that the number of distinct cosets of A_n in $\{0, 1\}^n$ is not a power of 2?

4.30   (b)   Let H be a parity check matrix of n rows. Prove that the coset defined by $a' * H$, where $a' \in \{0, 1\}^n$, contains an n-tuple of weight d if and only if there exist d distinct rows $h_{i_1}, h_{i_2}, \ldots, h_{i_d}$ in H such that $h_{i_1} \oplus h_{i_2} \oplus \cdots \oplus h_{i_d} = a * H$.

4.31   (b)   Let A_n be a group code defined by $n \times r$ parity check matrix H. Prove that the weight of no coset leader of the cosets of A_n in $\{0, 1\}^n$ exceeds 2 if n and r are related by $2^{r-1} \leq n < 2^r$, and the rows of H, interpreted as integers, are valued $1, 2, \ldots, r$.

4.32   (b)   Write a computer program that accepts a parity check matrix as input and generates an array of coset leaders as output.

4.33   (c)   Let f and f_c be the functions of D.4.17. Find

    (i) $f(America, A, me, f)$,   (ii) $f(average, \Lambda, a, o)$,

  (iii) $f_c(average, vera, \Lambda)$,   (iv) $f_c(average, Vera, \Lambda)$,

    (v) $f_c(assassin, n, nation)$,   (vi) $f_c(f_c(assassin, sass, \Lambda), as, moccas)$.

4.34   (c)   Let V be an alphabet, $A = (V^*)^3$, and $B = V^* \times \{\Lambda\} \times V^*$. Let $f_c : A \to V^*$ be a canonical substitution function (see D.4.17). Why is $\langle V^*, f_c \mid B \rangle$ not a semigroup?

4.35   (d)   Given $V = \{u, v\}$ and the two composite Markov productions:

$$a'x \to xb'xa' \qquad (x \in V),$$
$$b'xy \to yb'x \qquad (x, y \in V).$$

Write the composite productions out in full.

4.36   (d)   Give an example of a Markov algorithm that can never be blocked.

4.37   (d)   Let $V = \{a, b\}$ and let S be any string on V. Let α, β, γ be *given* strings on V. Depending on whether $S = \alpha$ or $S \neq \alpha$, the following Markov algorithm gives a different result. What are the two results?

$$
\begin{aligned}
am &\to ma \\
bm &\to mb \\
ma &\to m \\
mb &\to m \\
m &\to . \gamma \\
\alpha a &\to m \\
\alpha b &\to m \\
a\alpha &\to m \\
b\alpha &\to m \\
\alpha &\to . \beta \\
\Lambda &\to m
\end{aligned}
$$

(Here, m is a marker.)

4.38 (d) Design a Markov algorithm that removes *all* occurrences of a specified substring from a given string. Test it on the string *ararat* for substring *ara*.

4.39 (d) Design Markov algorithms that change a string $a_1 a_2 \cdots a_n$ on $V = \{u, v\}$ to

(i) $a_n a_{n-1} \cdots a_1$,
(ii) $a_1 a_2 \cdots a_n a_n a_{n-1} \cdots a_1$.

4.40 (d) Combine the two algorithms of Exercise 4.39 by means of the technique of A.4.1.

4.41 (d) Given two *binary* integers $a_1 a_2 \cdots a_n$ and $b_1 b_2 \cdots b_m$ as the string $a_1 a_2 \cdots a_n + b_1 b_2 \cdots b_m$. Design a Markov algorithm that finds the sum of the two integers as a binary integer.

4.42 (d) Design a Markov algorithm that converts Roman numerals to decimal integers.

4.43 (d) Design a Markov algorithm for the insertion of delimiting commas in an integer, i.e., an algorithm that changes, for example, 1500 to 1,500 and 1356782 to 1,356,782.

4.44 (d) Design a Markov algorithm that converts a Boolean form to its arithmetic representation (see Exercise 2.41).

4.45 (d) What facilities should be added to the formalism of Markov algorithms to convert the formalism into a programming language?

4.46 (e) Which of the following strings are sentences in $L(G)$ of Example 3 of D.4.26 ?

(i) *the.child.ate*
(ii) *The.child.ate.the.apple*
(iii) *the.child.bought.an.apple*
(iv) *the.green.pear.ate.a.apple*

4.47 (e) Rewrite the production rules of G_1 of Example 1 of D.4.26 in Bnf.

4.48 (e) Write grammars for the following languages:

(i) $a*bcc*$,
(ii) $\{a^k b a^k \mid k \geq 0\}$,
(iii) $\{n \mid n$ is a Fortran variable name$\}$,
(iv) $\{a^k b^k a^k \mid k \geq 1\}$,
(v) $\{n \mid n$ is a Boolean form$\}$.

What are the types of these grammars?

4.49 (e) Describe the languages generated by grammars that have the following production rules:

(i) $\langle S \rangle ::= \langle B \rangle \langle A \rangle \,|\, b$
$\langle A \rangle ::= a$
$\langle B \rangle ::= \langle C \rangle \langle S \rangle$
$\langle C \rangle ::= c$

(ii) $\langle S \rangle ::= a \langle A \rangle c \,|\, b$
$\langle A \rangle ::= a \langle S \rangle c \,|\, b$

(iii) $\langle S \rangle ::= \langle A \rangle \langle A \rangle$
$\langle A \rangle ::= \langle A \rangle \langle B \rangle \,|\, a$
$\langle B \rangle ::= b$

(iv) $\langle S \rangle ::= ad \langle A \rangle da \,|\, a \langle S \rangle a \,|\, aca$
$\langle A \rangle ::= b \langle A \rangle b \,|\, bd \langle S \rangle db$

4.50 (e) At times it is convenient to introduce grammars in which some production rules have the null string as consequent. One such grammar is defined by the following production rules:

$$\langle S \rangle ::= a \langle A \rangle b \langle S \rangle \,|\, b \langle B \rangle a \langle S \rangle \,|\, \Lambda$$
$$\langle A \rangle ::= a \langle A \rangle b \langle A \rangle \,|\, \Lambda$$
$$\langle B \rangle ::= b \langle B \rangle a \langle B \rangle \,|\, \Lambda$$

Characterize the language generated by this grammar.

4.51 (e) Find right- and left-linear grammars equivalent to the Type 2 grammar $\langle \{a, b, c\}, \{A, S\}, P, S \rangle$, where P consists of the productions

$$\langle S \rangle ::= a \langle A \rangle c$$
$$\langle A \rangle ::= \langle A \rangle bb \,|\, b$$

4.52 (e) Consider a Type 1 grammar $\langle V_i, V_i', P_i, S \rangle$ that generates all permutations of a set of i symbols ($i \geq 2$), and in which the antecedent of every production belongs to the star of V_i'. Show that P_i need contain at most $\frac{1}{2}i(i + 1) + 1$ production rules. (See Example 4 of D.4.26.)

4.53 (e) Does the language generated by the grammar specified below contain the string $aaabbcc$?

$$\langle S \rangle ::= a \langle S \rangle \langle B \rangle \langle C \rangle \,|\, a \langle B \rangle \langle C \rangle$$
$$\langle C \rangle \langle B \rangle ::= \langle B \rangle \langle C \rangle$$
$$a \langle B \rangle ::= ab$$
$$b \langle B \rangle ::= bb$$
$$b \langle C \rangle ::= bc$$
$$c \langle C \rangle ::= cc$$

4.54 (e) Characterize the language generated by the grammar of Exercise 4.53.

4.55 (e) If Step 3 of A.4.2 is changed to

3'. Set $Q_i = \{\gamma \,|\, \beta \Rightarrow \gamma$ and $\beta \in Q_{i-1}$, and $|\gamma| \leq k\}$,

and the stopping condition in Step 4 to $Q_i = \varnothing$, then the algorithm is still valid for Type 3 grammars. With Type 2 grammars, however, the stopping condition $Q_i = \varnothing$ is never satisfied in some cases, i.e., the algorithm does not terminate. Provide an example of this.

4.56 (f) Draw state graphs of acceptors for the following languages:

    (i) a^*bcc^*;

    (ii) $\{ab^{2n+1}c \mid n \geq 0\}$;

    (iii) $(ab)^* \cup \{bc, a\}^*b$.

4.57 (f) Implement A.4.3 and test the acceptor for the language of Part (iii) of Exercise 4.56 on the following strings:

(i)	#*ababab*#	(v)	#*bcbcaaabcb*#
(ii)	##	(vi)	#*abb*#
(iii)	#*b*#	(vii)	#*bcababb*#
(iv)	#*abcb*#	(viii)	#*bcabab*#

Strings (i)–(v) alone belong to the language.

4.58 (f) It is possible to devise a finite state acceptor for K-formulas when it is known that the number of symbols in a K-formula will never exceed a definite limit, say 50. Give an outline of the structure of this automaton. Why is it not possible to construct a finite state acceptor for K-formulas of unlimited length?

PART II

APPLICATIONS OF STRUCTURES

CHAPTER 5

Trees

5a. Trees as Grammatic Markers

Let us turn back to Example 3 of D.4.26 and look at the derivation of *the.child.ate.a.green.pear.* If, instead of the derivation

$$S \Rightarrow NP.VP \Rightarrow T.N.VP \Rightarrow the.N.VP \Rightarrow \cdots,$$

we followed the sequence

$$S \Rightarrow NP.VP \Rightarrow NP.V.N \Rightarrow T.N.V.N \Rightarrow \cdots,$$

we could still arrive at the same sentence. There are in fact 32 different S-derivations of this sentence in the given grammar G, but the derivations are not *essentially* different. Equivalence of derivations is brought out very clearly when derivations are represented by directed trees. Figure 5.1 shows the derivation tree for our sentence. Each node carries a label—the label is a terminal symbol if the node is terminal; otherwise it is an auxiliary symbol. Here order is important. The labels on the terminal nodes, taken in a left-to-right sequence, must give *the.child.ate.a.green.pear* and not, for example, *ate.green.pear.a.the.child.*

In constructing a derivation tree we start with an isolated node labeled S. Application of $S \rightarrow NP.VP$ corresponds in the construction process to two arcs being dropped from the isolated node, the terminal nodes of these arcs

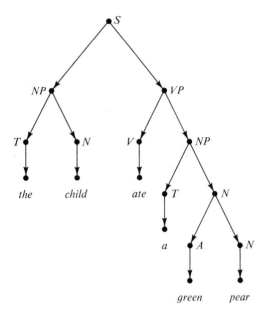

Figure 5.1

receiving labels *NP* and *VP*. If next we apply $NP \to T.N$, then arcs are suspended from the node labeled *NP*. If, on the other hand, rule $VP \to V.NP$ is used next, arcs are suspended from the node labeled *VP* and nothing happens at the node labeled *NP*. In general, if a derivation has produced at some point a string $c_1 c_2 \cdots a \cdots c_n$, then in the construction of the tree we have at this stage a structure in which the terminal nodes carry labels $c_1, c_2, \ldots, a, \ldots, c_n$, reading from left to right. If the derivation now proceeds with application of a production $a \to b_1 b_2 \cdots b_m$, then the corresponding action in the construction of the tree consists of suspending *m* arcs from the terminal node labeled *a*, and labeling the terminal nodes of these arcs (from left to right) $b_1, b_2, \ldots, b_m$. The important thing is that all 32 derivations of our example ultimately result in the same tree; i.e., a derivation tree displays the structure of a sentence without reflecting minor details of the derivation process. Note, however, that the representation of structure by derivation trees is effective only with context-free grammars (Types 2 and 3).

It is possible that a sentence has two or more essentially different derivations. We say then that the grammar is *ambiguous*. A context-free grammar is ambiguous if and only if at least one sentence generated by the grammar has more than one derivation tree. Consider grammar $G = \langle \{a, b\}, \{S, A, B\},$ $P, S \rangle$, where *P* is the set of rules,

$$\langle S \rangle ::= \langle A \rangle \langle B \rangle$$
$$\langle A \rangle ::= a \langle A \rangle \mid \langle A \rangle b \mid a$$
$$\langle B \rangle ::= \langle B \rangle b \mid b.$$

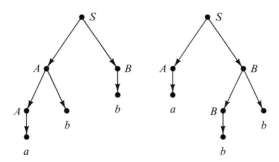

Figure 5.2

Figure 5.2 shows that the sentence *abb* has two derivation trees. Grammar *G* is therefore ambiguous.

Can one tell whether a grammar is ambiguous? Unfortunately, as regards the grammars we defined in Section 4e, the ambiguity problem is recursively solvable only for Type 3 grammars. This means that even in the case of Type 2 grammars there exists no algorithm that will decide for every grammar of this type whether it is ambiguous.

Undecidability of the ambiguity problem has very important effects on the design of programming languages. Type 3 grammars are too primitive for programming languages, and grammars of most programming languages approximate to Type 2 grammars. The best known example is Algol. The major part of the document defining Algol consists of production rules; they are productions of a Type 2 grammar. Examples of essentially different derivations have been found in Algol, and the set of derivations has been changed to remove essential ambiguities (with no absolute guarantee, however, that the grammar is unambiguous as it now stands). We have a very good reason for a preoccupation with ambiguity. In some contexts it is sufficient merely to recognize a string as a sentence in the language defined by the grammar. Not so with programming languages. A compiler is not only a recognizer; it also generates code. The code generated depends on the derivation tree, and two different structural interpretations of a sentence could give rise to two different sequences of instructions. A programmer who wants one of the sequences is not happy when the compiler inserts the other in his object program.

Undecidability of the ambiguity problem in general does not exclude the possibility of being able to find procedures that could test *particular* grammars for ambiguity, but search for the particular is bad scientific practice. It is easy to prove that a given language has an infinite number of grammars generating it. Frequently only some of the grammars are ambiguous, and then the language is said to be essentially unambiguous. A language is *essentially ambiguous* if and only if every grammar that generates it is ambiguous. The designer of a programming language should design an essentially unambiguous language and an unambiguous grammar to go with it. In the past languages have been specified first, and grammars fitted to the languages afterward in a manner that has been *ad hoc* to a greater or lesser extent. Instead, we should look for classes of grammars of sufficient power (subclasses of Type 2 grammars, but not as restrictive as Type 3) for which algorithmic tests for ambiguity exist. If we have such tests, then the design of a language can proceed side by side with the specification of its grammar in an iterative manner, until the language satisfies the requirements put on it, and its grammar is unambiguous.

Unfortunately the difficulty of finding algorithms for anything that has to do with grammars increases very rapidly as the power of the grammar increases. Consider a very simple class of grammars known as *parenthesis grammars*. A parenthesis grammar is a context-free grammar in which all productions have the form $A \to (\alpha)$, where α contains no occurrences of (or of). If no two productions in a grammar have the same consequent, the grammar is said to be *backward-deterministic*. A backward-deterministic parenthesis grammar is unambiguous. Let $G' = \langle \{a, b, (,)\}, \{S, A, B\}, P, S \rangle$ be a parenthesis grammar with production rules,

$$\langle S \rangle ::= (\langle A \rangle \langle B \rangle),$$
$$\langle A \rangle ::= (a\langle A \rangle) \,|\, (\langle A \rangle b) \,|\, (a),$$
$$\langle B \rangle ::= (\langle B \rangle b) \,|\, (b).$$

Under G' derivations analogous to those of Figure 5.2 produce two distinct sentences: $(((a)b)(b))$ and $((a)((b)b))$. This is so because the sentences carry the structure of their derivation trees with them as patterns of parentheses. A decision procedure for telling whether two parenthesis grammars are equivalent exists, but, although parenthesis grammars are rather simple, derivation of this procedure is very involved.

The strings produced by parenthesis grammars suggest a linear representation for derivation trees. Let us write $\langle A, a_1 \rangle$, $\langle A, a_2 \rangle$, $\ldots$, $\langle A, a_n \rangle$ for the arcs originating at a node labeled A, and terminating at nodes labeled a_1, a_2, $\ldots$, a_n. This sequence of arcs is represented by $A(a_1 a_2 \cdots a_n)$. The linear string that represents the derivation tree of Figure 5.1 is

$$S(NP(T(the)N(child))VP(V(ate)NP(T(a)N(A(green)N(pear))))).$$

A *syntactic chart* displays the entire set of productions of a grammar. This is a structure resembling a directed tree in that the order of arcs is sometimes important. Nonterminal nodes are labeled either & or *OR*; terminal nodes have terminal symbols for labels. Some arcs are labeled with auxiliary symbols; others carry no labels. To see how the chart is constructed, consider the productions

$$\langle VP \rangle ::= \langle V \rangle \,|\, \langle V \rangle \langle NP \rangle$$

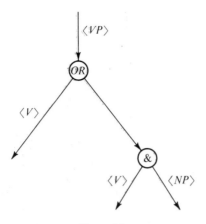

Figure 5.3

of Example 3 of D.4.26. They are represented by the structure shown in Figure 5.3. The arc labeled ⟨*VP*⟩ terminates at a node that carries the label *OR*. This label indicates choice: ⟨*VP*⟩ can be rewritten in as many ways as there are arcs originating from this node. Here their number is 2. The first of the arcs carries the label ⟨*V*⟩, and the path through the node and down this arc represents the production *VP* → *V*. The other arc carries no label. Its sole purpose is to lead to the node labeled &. The label & symbolizes necessity: If the second production is chosen, then all symbols carried by the arcs originating from the & node must be used in the rewriting of *VP*. This is where the need for order comes in. The left-to-right order of the arcs specifies the order that the labels carried by the arcs have in the production rule. Here the left-to-right order is ⟨*V*⟩⟨*NP*⟩. This branch therefore represents the production *VP* → *V.NP*.

Figure 5.4 shows the complete syntactic chart of the grammar of Example 3 of D.4.26. Let us see how the chart is used. On entering the chart, we come at once to an & node, and we are told that ⟨*S*⟩ must be rewritten as ⟨*NP*⟩⟨*VP*⟩. No choice is given in the rewriting of ⟨*NP*⟩ either, and the string becomes ⟨*T*⟩⟨*N*⟩⟨*VP*⟩. With the rewriting of ⟨*VP*⟩ we are given a choice: It can be rewritten as ⟨*V*⟩ or as ⟨*V*⟩⟨*NP*⟩ but, if the second alternative is taken, there is no choice in the rewriting of ⟨*NP*⟩. We take the second alternative, and the complete string to this stage becomes

$$⟨T⟩⟨N⟩⟨V⟩⟨T⟩⟨N⟩.$$

Every auxiliary in this string can be rewritten in more than one way. For the first ⟨*N*⟩ we choose ⟨*A*⟩⟨*N*⟩, and rewrite the ⟨*N*⟩ in this string as a further

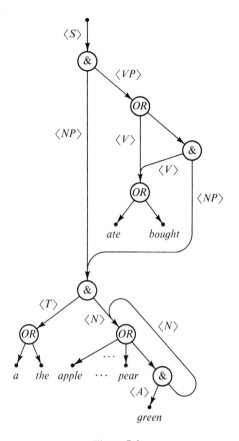

Figure 5.4

$\langle A\rangle\langle N\rangle$, giving $\langle A\rangle\langle A\rangle\langle N\rangle$. The complete string is now

$$\langle T\rangle\langle A\rangle\langle A\rangle\langle N\rangle\langle V\rangle\langle T\rangle\langle N\rangle.$$

We can replace every auxiliary in this string by a terminal symbol: For the $\langle T\rangle$ we can choose *a* or *the*, the $\langle A\rangle$ must be rewritten as *green*, as must the second $\langle A\rangle$; the $\langle N\rangle$ can be rewritten as *apple*, or *child*, or *man*, or *pear*; and so on. One sentence in the language specified by the grammar is *a.green.green.apple.bought.the.child*. If a chart contains a cycle, as it does in our example $(N \rightarrow A.N)$, no bound can be put on the longest sentence. Here we can make the substring *green.green.green.* $\cdots$ as long as we wish.

For a second example we take the right-linear grammar of the example of D.4.30. Its syntactic chart is shown in Figure 5.5.

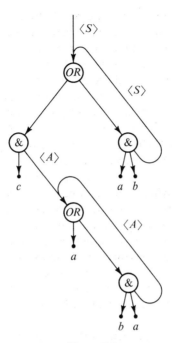

Figure 5.5

5b. Pushdown Stores

In Section 5a trees were used as a display device that helped us understand certain features of grammars. Trees, in particular the B-trees of D.3.25, are also very effective as computational tools, and in the sections that follow they will be used to represent data on which a program is to operate. As a preliminary we interpose here a discussion of pushdown stores without which it would be very difficult to devise efficient algorithms for working on trees.

Basically a pushdown store is a set of storage locations, which are initially empty. As data are stored in the pushdown store, the store "remembers" the order in which they were stored. When a datum is to be fetched from a conventional store, a copy of the datum is actually moved. The datum itself remains in the store and can be fetched again and again. In the case of a pushdown store a fetch instruction moves a datum right out of the store. Only one datum is accessible in a pushdown store at any one time; in the case of a *last in–first out* (LIFO) store this is the most recently stored item.

We can picture a LIFO store as a stack of buttons on which information is inscribed. LIFO stores are in fact very often called *stacks*. Putting a button on an empty table constitutes the first storing operation in our illustration.

The next storing operation places a second button on top of the one already on the table. Each subsequent storing operation increases the height of the stack of buttons. To get a datum from the stack we must take the topmost button, i.e., the one that was stored last. There is no direct access to the first button stored; pulling it out would collapse the stack. The only way of getting at this button is by removal of the buttons above it, one by one, until the last button is exposed. Its removal leaves the stack empty. The term *pushdown store* originates from a similar illustration. In some parts of the world bus conductors are provided with coin dispensers that operate as follows. The dispenser is a hollow tube closed at the bottom and partly closed by a semicircular rim at the top. In an empty dispenser a disk is held against the rim by a spiral spring occupying the entire tube. The dispenser is filled by pushing coins in under the rim, thus pushing down the disk. The pressure of the spring behind the disk holds the stack of coins in place between the rim at the top and the disk at its bottom. A coin being pushed into the dispenser pushes down the coins already there and becomes the topmost coin. In dispensing the topmost coin is slid out from under the rim. Since it is at the top, the coin that went in last comes out first. The remaining coins are pushed upward by the spring and the coin that was immediately below the dispensed coin pops into the topmost position.

One advantage that a stack has over a conventional store is that its user does not have to worry about addresses. Only two instructions are needed: a storing instruction, which we shall designate PUSH, and a fetching instruction to which we give the name IPOP. When stacks are considered in the context of the theory of automata they have unlimited depth, but in practice we must decide on a workable limit. Let us take 100 for the limit here. Then an array, say N(1) $\cdots$ N(100), can be set up as a stack simply by providing a pointer, which we shall call IP, and by making sure that IP points at all times to the topmost datum in the stack. Initially IP is given the value zero. Instruction PUSH increments the value of IP and inserts a datum in the location to which IP then points. Instruction IPOP fetches the item to which IP points and then decrements IP. Figure 5.6 gives a trace of the changes in the appearance of the array N during execution of a sequence of PUSH and IPOP instructions. The appearance of the array and the value of IP *after* execution of an instruction are given in the same row as the instruction. The contents of the stack are indicated by shading.

It is very easy to set up a Fortran array as a working stack. All that is needed is an initiating routine that sets IP to zero, and two routines that take the functions of PUSH and IPOP, respectively.

```
SUBROUTINE SKOPEN
COMMON N(100), IP
IP = 0
```

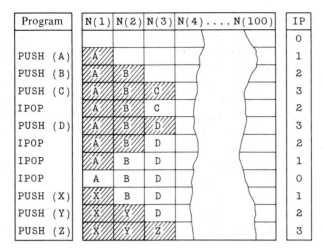

Figure 5.6

```
      RETURN
      END

      SUBROUTINE PUSH (IN)
      COMMON N(100), IP
      IF (IP.EQ.100) GO TO 999
      IP = IP + 1
      N(IP) = IN
      RETURN
999   WRITE (6,100)
      STOP
100   FORMAT (1H1, 28HSTACK OVERFLOW — TERMINATION)
      END

      FUNCTION IPOP (IT)
C     BOTH IPOP AND IT RETURN THE DATUM
      COMMON N(100), IP
      IF (IP.EQ.0) GO TO 999
      IT = N(IP)
      IPOP = IT
      IP = IP - 1
      RETURN
999   WRITE (6,100)
      STOP
100   FORMAT (1H1, 29HSTACK UNDERFLOW — TERMINATION)
      END
```

Note that the main program must have access to IP to enable it to test the stack for emptiness. Access is through COMMON. Therefore, initiation can be performed in the main program itself; i.e., we can make do without a separate initiating routine. Whether we should terminate execution on stack overflow or underflow is a debatable point. These exceptional conditions indicate that the program is misbehaving, but the user of the program may still be interested in having the program continue to run so as to accumulate more output. The output data could help determine the program error that caused the exceptional condition.

Perhaps the simplest example of the use of the stack is the inversion of the order of elements in a vector. Suppose that we are given an unknown non-zero number of nonzero elements (<100) in the low end of an array LOT, delimited by a zero value. The elements are to be stored in reverse order in the same array. The following sequence of Fortran statements will do the job:

```
      DO 20 K = 1,100
      IF (LOT(K).EQ.0) GO TO 25
  20  CALL PUSH (LOT(K))
C   EXIT FROM THE DO LOOP IS ALWAYS VIA THE GO TO 25.
C   HENCE K IS DEFINED ON REACHING STATEMENT 25.
  25  K = K - 1
      DO 30  J = 1,K
  30  LOT(J) = IPOP (IT)
```

The order in which data go into the stack determines the order in which they will come out, and this is the reverse of the input order. Therefore, the ease with which the stack can be made to deal with the reversal problem should cause no surprise. Indeed, all applications that involve the use of stacks are concerned with change of order.

In another type of restricted access device, which can still be called a pushdown store, data are pushed down at one end, but access to the stored data is only from the other end of the store. This type of store has come to be known as a *queue*. It is called also a *first in–first out* (FIFO) store. A Fortran implementation of a queue is more difficult than the implementation of a stack. Still more difficult to implement is a scheme in which storage and access is at either end of the data area (see Exercise 10.6).

We shall now discuss an interesting application in which extensive use is made of stacks. Given a string α, it is required to find in α substrings of given length d that occur at least twice (possibly overlapping), and to determine the position in α of each such repeated substring. Suppose repeated substrings of length 5 are to be looked for in the string

$$abbaabaabab. \qquad (5.1)$$

The only repeated substring of length 5 is *baaba*, with the two occurrences of this substring overlapping:

$$\overline{ab\overline{baaba}abab}.$$

Positions of symbols in string α will be numbered consecutively 1, 2, 3, ..., n for reference purposes. For (5.1) the positions are

a	b	b	a	a	b	a	a	b	a	b
1	2	3	4	5	6	7	8	9	10	11

Now define E_k-equivalence of substrings: iE_kj when substrings of length k starting in positions i and j are identical. The algorithm for detecting repeated substrings will be based on the following observation:

$$iE_kj \quad \text{and} \quad (i+m)E_k(j+m) \quad \text{imply} \quad iE_{k+m}j \quad \text{for} \quad m \le k. \quad (5.2)$$

In string (5.1) $3E_26$ and $5E_28$. Hence $3E_46$. We also have $6E_29$, but then $m = 3$, i.e., $m > k$, and we may *not* draw the conclusion $3E_56$ (although this equivalence does in fact happen to hold).

Let us first devise a procedure for constructing equivalence relation E_{k+m} from E_k. Equivalence relation E_k partitions all substrings of length k of α into equivalence classes, which we label 1, 2, ..., t. Relation E_k is represented by a vector $E^{(k)}$ with elements $E^{(k)}(1)$, $E^{(k)}(2)$, ..., $E^{(k)}(n - k + 1)$, where $E^{(k)}(i)$ contains the label of that equivalence class to which the substring of length k starting at i belongs. For example, in (5.1) there are four equivalence classes of substrings of length 2: *aa*, *ab*, *ba*, *bb* define the classes, and we use labels 1, 2, 3, 4, respectively. Then

$$\alpha = a \quad b \quad b \quad a \quad a \quad b \quad a \quad a \quad b \quad a \quad b$$
$$E^{(2)} = (2 \quad 4 \quad 3 \quad 1 \quad 2 \quad 3 \quad 1 \quad 2 \quad 3 \quad 2) \quad (5.3)$$
$$i = 1 \quad 2 \quad 3 \quad 4 \quad 5 \quad 6 \quad 7 \quad 8 \quad 9 \quad 10 \quad 11$$

In constructing E_{k+m} from E_k we shall use $2t$ stacks, all initially empty, where t is the number of E_k-equivalence classes:

$$P(1), P(2), \ldots, P(t);$$
$$Q(1), Q(2), \ldots, Q(t).$$

The construction procedure will be described somewhat informally to permit us to study how the procedure deals with string (5.1), or more precisely its representation (5.3), as we go along.

Stage 1   [*Distribute* $E^{(k)}$ *over stacks* P]: For each $E^{(k)}(i)$, $i = 1, \ldots,$ $n - k + 1$, push down i in $P(E^{(k)}(i))$. In terms of representation (5.3) we produce the following configuration:

$P(1)$	$P(2)$	$P(3)$	$P(4)$
4	1	3	2
7	5	6	
	8	9	
	10		

Stage 2   [*Distribute stacks* P *over stacks* Q]: Pop up numbers from $P(1)$ until it is empty, then from $P(2)$ until it is empty, etc. The number q that is popped up from $P(i)$ is pushed down in $Q(E^{(k)}(q + m))$ if $q + m \leq n - k + 1$, or discarded otherwise. This produces E_k-equivalence classes "shifted" so that numbers q and r go into the same pushdown store Q precisely when $(q + m)E_k(r + m)$. Continuing with the example, take $m = 2$ (the largest number that satisfies $m \leq k$). The condition that q has to satisfy for it to be pushed down is $q \leq 8$ (from $q + 2 \leq 11 - 2 + 1$). Disposition of the first q in detail: pop up 7; then $E^{(2)}(7 + 2) = 3$; hence push the 7 down in $Q(3)$. We get:

$Q(1)$	$Q(2)$	$Q(3)$	$Q(4)$
5	8	7	
2	6	4	
	3	1	

Stage 3   [*Construct* $E^{(k+m)}$]:

1. Set $c = 0$, $i = 0$.
2. Set $i = i + 1$. If $i > t$, stop.
3. If $Q(i)$ is empty, go to 2; else set $c = c + 1$, pop up q from $Q(i)$, set $E^{(k+m)}(q) = c$.
4. If $Q(i)$ is empty, go to 2; else pop up r from $Q(i)$.
5. If $E^{(k)}(r) \neq E^{(k)}(q)$, set $c = c + 1$.
6. Set $E^{(k+m)}(r) = c$, $q = r$, go to 4.

Again returning to our example, vector $E^{(4)}$ produced in Stage 3 is

$$E^{(4)} = (5 \quad 1 \quad 3 \quad 6 \quad 2 \quad 3 \quad 6 \quad 4)$$

$$\alpha = a \quad b \quad b \quad a \quad a \quad b \quad a \quad a \quad b \quad a \quad b$$

$$i = 1 \quad 2 \quad 3 \quad 4 \quad 5 \quad 6 \quad 7 \quad 8 \quad 9 \quad 10 \quad 11$$

$E^{(4)}$ tells us that identical substrings of length 4 begin at 3 and 6 (label 3), and at 4 and 7 (label 6).

A note is now in order. In terms of (5.2), the purpose of Stage 2 is to get all i and j such that $(i + m)E_k(j + m)$ in the one place (the same Q-stack). Then in Stage 3 we check whether, when $(i + m)E_k(j + m)$ holds, iE_kj holds as well. If it does, then $iE_{k+m}j$ holds, and $E^{(k+m)}(i)$ and $E^{(k+m)}(j)$ receive the same equivalence class label (the c is the equivalence class "counter"), It remains to specify the actual algorithm.

ALGORITHM 5.1 An algorithm for finding in string α all occurrences of substrings of given length d that occur at least twice.

1. Scan α to construct equivalence relation E_1.
2. Use the construction procedure given above to construct, in turn, E_2, E_4, E_8, ..., E_r, where $r = 2^{\lfloor \log_2 d \rfloor}$ ($\lfloor x \rfloor$ is the *floor function*: its value is the greatest integer not greater than x).
3. If d is a power of 2, stop (with $d = r$); otherwise have d $< 2r$, and the construction procedure is applied once more to construct E_d from E_r.

Each equivalence relation is derived from an earlier equivalence relation with time dependence n (in fact, E_k is derived with time dependence $n - k$), and there are $\lceil \log_2 d \rceil$ constructions of equivalence relations ($\lceil x \rceil$ is the *ceiling function*: its value is the least integer not smaller than x; note that $\lceil x \rceil = -\lfloor -x \rfloor$). Hence the time dependence of A.5.1 is of the order of $n \log d$. The number of E_r-equivalence classes determines the number of stacks required. There are at most $min(n, |V|^r)$ E_r-equivalence classes, where V is the alphabet over which the string α ranges, and the maximal number of stacks is twice this.

5c. Traversal of B–Trees

In this section we shall be primarily concerned with the B-trees of D.3.25. First we have to find a computer representation of a B-tree. This is provided by a two-dimensional array with two columns and as many rows as there are nodes in the B-tree. Consider the B-tree of Figure 5.7 in which the nodes have been given identifying numbers 1, 2, ..., 11. Node k is represented by row k in array P of Figure 5.7: P(k, 1) holds the identifying number of the left successor of k, P(k, 2) that of the right successor. If node k does not have one or other of the successors, then the appropriate entry in P is zero. For example, node 5 has only a left successor, namely node 6. Hence P(5, 1) = 6,

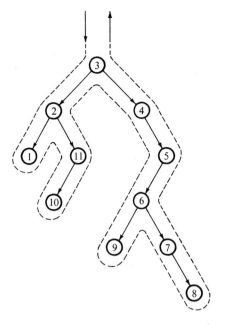

ROOT: [3]

$$P: \begin{array}{c} 1 \\ 2 \\ 3 \\ 4 \\ 5 \\ 6 \\ 7 \\ 8 \\ 9 \\ 10 \\ 11 \end{array} \left[\begin{array}{cc} 0 & 0 \\ 1 & 11 \\ 2 & 4 \\ 0 & 5 \\ 6 & 0 \\ 9 & 7 \\ 0 & 8 \\ 0 & 0 \\ 0 & 0 \\ 0 & 0 \\ 10 & 0 \end{array} \right]$$

Figure 5.7

and P(5, 2) = 0. Since node 9 has no successors, P(9, 1) = P(9, 2) = 0. The identifying number of the root is held in a separate location, which we have named ROOT. A broken line surrounds the B-tree in Figure 5.7. It has been drawn to indicate that we shall be tracing round the B-tree in a left to right direction.

We stipulate that in tracing round the B-tree we shall carry out some well-defined action once at every node, and we shall say that we "process" the node when we carry out this action. Note, however, that a node may be visited three times in the course of the traversal. For example, node 6 of Figure 5.7 is first visited on the down swing from node 5, visited for the second time in upward motion from node 9, and for a third time on return from node 7. The node can be processed at any one of these three opportunities. This leads us to recognize three basic types of traversal. The three different sequences of events that are possible at a node characterize the three types of traversal:

    A. *Preorder* traversal
        • Process node
           Proceed to left successor
           Proceed to right successor

B. *Inorder* traversal
    Proceed to left successor
  • Process node
    Proceed to right successor

C. *Postorder* traversal
    Proceed to left successor
    Proceed to right successor
  • Process node

The order in which the nodes of the B-tree of Figure 5.7 are processed under the tree types of traversal is:

Preorder— 3,	2,	1,	11,	10,	4,	5,	6,	9,	7,	8;
Inorder— 1,	2,	10,	11,	3,	4,	9,	6,	7,	8,	5;
Postorder—1,	10,	11,	2,	9,	8,	7,	6,	5,	4,	3.

Let us examine in detail what happens in the subtree rooted at node 6. Under preorder traversal node 6 is processed as soon as it is first reached. Then we proceed to node 9, and process this node. Since node 9 has no successors, we return to node 6. The first two events in the preorder sequence for node 6 have already taken place. Therefore we now proceed to its right successor, which is node 7, and process it. This node has no left successor, so the right successor is next. This is node 8, which we process. On return from node 8 we pass node 7, which has already been processed, and node 6, which also has been processed, and are then out of the subtree rooted at node 6. The order in which the nodes of this subtree were processed is 6, 9, 7, 8.

Under inorder traversal, on reaching node 6 we proceed to its left successor, which is node 9. This node has no left successor, so the processing of node 9 takes place next. There is no right successor either, and we return to node 6, which can now be processed. Then we proceed to the right successor of node 6. This is node 7, and it has no left successor. Hence we process it, and the traversal then takes us to node 8. Node 8 is processed, and we move upwards in the tree past nodes 7 and 6, which have both already been processed. Under inorder, then, the order of processing the nodes of the subtree is 9, 6, 7, 8.

Postorder traversal takes us straight from node 6 to node 9, and node 9 is processed because it has no successors. We return to node 6, but move out again to node 7. This node has no left successor, but it has a right successor, and processing of node 7 is postponed as well. We move to node 8, which we process, move back to node 7, process it, move back to node 6, at long last process it, and then move out of the subtree. Here the order is 9, 8, 7, 6.

ALGORITHM 5.2   Algorithm for preorder traversal of a B-tree. The input to the algorithm is ROOT, which holds the identifying number of the root of the B-tree, and array P, which represents the B-tree in the manner defined at the beginning of this section.

1. Set NODE = ROOT.
2. Process NODE.
3. If P(NODE, 2) ≠ 0, push down P(NODE, 2).
4. Set NODE = P(NODE, 1).
5. If NODE ≠ 0, go to 2.
6. If stack empty, stop; else pop up NODE and go to 2.

ALGORITHM 5.3   Algorithm for inorder traversal of a B-tree. The input is as for A.5.2.

1. Set NODE = ROOT.
2. ...
    ⋮

Specification of the rest of the algorithm is left as Exercise 5.17.

ALGORITHM 5.4   Algorithm for postorder traversal of a B-tree. The input is as for A.5.2. This algorithm is more complicated than A.5.2 or A.5.3 because a node number may have to be pushed down into the stack twice. To distinguish between the two cases, the node number is pushed down either as it is, or is negated before being pushed down.

1. Set NODE = ROOT.
2. Push down NODE.
3. If P(NODE, 2) ≠ 0, push down − P(NODE, 2).
4. Set NODE = P(NODE, 1).
5. If NODE ≠ 0, go to 2.
6. If stack empty, stop; else pop up NODE.
7. If NODE < 0, set NODE = −NODE and go to 2; else process NODE and go to 6.

Examples

1. We have already defined digraph isomorphism in Section 3g. The definition given at the end of that section will be useful here: Digraphs $\langle A_1, R_1 \rangle$ and $\langle A_2, R_2 \rangle$ are isomorphic if there exists a total one-to-one function $h: A_1 \rightarrow A_2$ such that $\langle a, b \rangle \in R_1$ implies $\langle h(a), h(b) \rangle \in R_2$ and

$\langle c, d\rangle \in R_2$ implies $\langle h^{-1}(c), h^{-1}(d)\rangle \in R_1$ for all members of R_1 and R_2. This definition can be extended to B-trees $\langle A_1, R_1, f_1\rangle$ and $\langle A_2, R_2, f_2\rangle$ by further requiring that $f_1(a, b) = f_2(h(a), h(b))$ for all $\langle a, b\rangle \in R_1$. Isomorphism of B-trees can be very easily established: two B-trees are isomorphic if and only if, on application of one of A.5.2, A.5.3, or A.5.4 to both B-trees, the algorithm goes through the same actions in precisely the same sequence in the two cases.

2. Given a B-tree $T = \langle A, R, f\rangle$, it is required to find the roots of full trees of order k that are subtrees of T. A procedure can be devised on the basis of the observation that for a node a to be the root of a full subtree of order k both $l(a)$ and $r(a)$ must be roots of full subtrees of order $k - 1$, where l and r are the successor functions of Example 2 of D.3.25. We define the function $t : A \rightarrow N$, where N is the set of non-negative integers, as follows: $t(a) = 0$ if $l(a)$ or $r(a)$ is undefined; otherwise $t(a) = 1 + min(t(l(a)), t(r(a)))$. In this context the "processing" of a node $a \in A$ is the computation of $t(a)$, and a node cannot be processed before its successors have been processed. Postorder traversal is therefore the appropriate mechanism for putting the nodes in proper order for processing. At the end of the traversal $\{x \mid t(x) \geq k\}$ is the set of roots of full trees of order k in T. Figure 5.8 shows a B-tree with each node x carrying $t(x)$ as a label. Nodes 1, 2, 4, and 5 are roots of full trees of order 2; node 2 is the root of a full tree of order 3 as well.

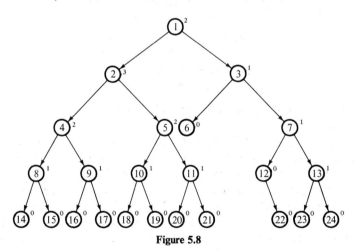

Figure 5.8

3. The following algorithm for postorder traversal uses a shallower stack than A.5.4, but it may be more difficult to understand. It makes use of a temporary location ITEMP.

1. Set NODE = ROOT.

2. While $P(NODE, 1) \neq 0$, push down NODE and set $NODE = P(NODE, 1)$.
3. If $P(NODE, 2) \neq 0$, push down NODE and set $NODE = P(NODE, 2)$ and go to 2.
4. Process NODE.
5. If stack empty, stop; else set $ITEMP = NODE$ and pop up NODE.
6. If $P(NODE, 1) = ITEMP$, go to 3; else go to 4.

5d. Subtree Isomorphism

An interesting application of preorder traversal arises with the following problem: given B-trees $T = \langle A_t, R_t, f_t \rangle$ and $S = \langle A_s, R_s, f_s \rangle$, find in T all nodes that are roots of subtrees isomorphic to S. One approach is to find for each $x_s \in A_s$ the set of all nodes a_t in T such that a path originating at a_t exactly replicates the path from the root to x_s in S. Let this set of nodes be $Q(x_s)$. Then, if some node in T belongs to sets $Q(x_s)$ of *all* the *terminal* nodes of S, this node has paths originating from it that constitute a complete replica of S, i.e., it is the root of a subtree isomorphic to S. Hence the set of all nodes of T that are roots of subtrees isomorphic to S is simply the intersection $\bigcap_{x_s \in X_s} Q(x_s)$, where X_s is the set of the terminal nodes of S. For the B-trees of Figure 5.9 we can establish by visual inspection that

$$Q(a) = \{1, 2, 3, \ldots, 16\},$$
$$Q(b) = \{1, 2, 5, 6, 10, 12, 14\},$$
$$Q(c) = \{1, 2, 3, 5, 9, 10, 12, 14\},$$
$$Q(d) = \{2, 3, 9, 10, 12\},$$
$$Q(e) = \{1, 2, 9, 10, 12\}.$$

Then the set of roots of subtrees isomorphic to S is given by $Q(b) \cap Q(d) \cap Q(e) = \{2, 10, 12\}$.

Let x_0 be the root of S. Then clearly $Q(x_0) = A_t$, and $Q(x_i) \subseteq Q(p(x_i))$ for all $x_i \in S - \{x_0\}$. The indicated procedure is to generate each $Q(x_i)$ from $Q(p(x_i))$, but this is not all that straightforward. Consider the path (a, c, d) in the S of Figure 5.9, and suppose that we are currently processing node d. Then $Q(c)$ contains all those nodes in T from which originate paths having the same structure as path (a, c). Here this is just the set of initial nodes of all arcs having right orientation. One such arc is $\langle 3, 6 \rangle$, node 3 is in $Q(c)$, and node 3 becomes a member of $Q(d)$ as well if and only if node 6 has a left successor, but $Q(c)$ does not tell us that it is node 6 that has to be investigated to determine the eligibility of node 3 for membership in $Q(d)$.

One way out of this difficulty is to make members of sets $Q(x_i)$ ordered pairs. We define sets $Q'(x_i)$, where $\langle a_u, a_v \rangle \in Q'(x_i)$ if and only if there exists

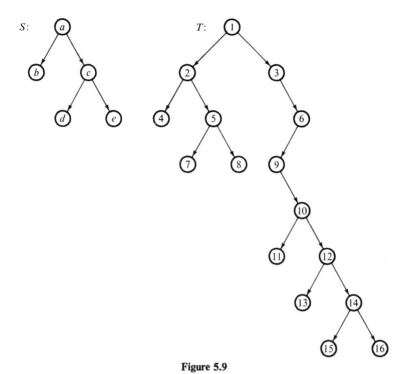

Figure 5.9

in T a path $(a_u, \ldots, a_v)$ that is a replica of path $(x_0, \ldots, x_i)$ in S. We then have the following algorithm.

ALGORITHM 5.5   Algorithm for subtree isomorphism. Given B-trees $T = \langle A_t, R_t, f_t \rangle$ and $S = \langle A_s, R_s, f_s \rangle$. Let x_0 be the root and X_s the set of terminal nodes in S. The algorithm finds set $T(S)$, which is the set of all nodes in T that are roots of subtrees isomorphic to S.

   1.   Traverse S in preorder, processing nodes $x_i \in A_s$ as follows:

      a.   If $x_i = x_0$, generate $Q'(x_0) = \{\langle a_t, a_t \rangle \,|\, a_t \in A_t\}$.

      b.   If x_i is a left successor, i.e., if $l(p(x_i)) = x_i$, generate $Q'(x_i)$ such that $\langle a_u, a_w \rangle \in Q'(x_i)$ if and only if $\langle a_u, a_v \rangle \in Q'(p(x_i))$ and a_w is the left successor of a_v.

      c.   If x_i is a right successor, generate $Q'(x_i)$ such that $\langle a_u, a_w \rangle \in Q'(x_i)$ if and only if $\langle a_u, a_v \rangle \in Q'(p(x_i))$ and a_w is the right successor of a_v.

2. For all $x_i \in X_s$ generate $Q(x_i) = \{a_u \,|\, \langle a_u, a_w \rangle \in Q'(x_i)\}$, i.e., in the sets corresponding to terminal nodes of S reduce the ordered pairs to just their first coordinates.
3. Compute $T(S) = \bigcap_{x_i \in X_s} Q(x_i)$ and stop.

Example

A.5.5 applied to the B-trees of Figure 5.9 finds

$Q'(a) = \{\langle 1, 1 \rangle, \langle 2, 2 \rangle, \ldots, \langle 16, 16 \rangle\}$,
$Q'(b) = \{\langle 1, 2 \rangle, \langle 2, 4 \rangle, \langle 5, 7 \rangle, \langle 6, 9 \rangle, \langle 10, 11 \rangle, \langle 12, 13 \rangle, \langle 14, 15 \rangle\}$,
$Q'(c) = \{\langle 1, 3 \rangle, \langle 2, 5 \rangle, \langle 3, 6 \rangle, \langle 5, 8 \rangle, \langle 9, 10 \rangle, \langle 10, 12 \rangle, \langle 12, 14 \rangle,$
$$\langle 14, 16 \rangle\},$$
$Q'(d) = \{\langle 2, 7 \rangle, \langle 3, 9 \rangle, \langle 9, 11 \rangle, \langle 10, 13 \rangle, \langle 12, 15 \rangle\}$,
$Q'(e) = \{\langle 1, 6 \rangle, \langle 2, 8 \rangle, \langle 9, 12 \rangle, \langle 10, 14 \rangle, \langle 12, 16 \rangle\}$.

Consider in detail how $\langle 2, 7 \rangle$ becomes a member of $Q'(d)$. Set $Q'(d)$ is generated from $Q'(c)$ and, since arc $\langle c, d \rangle$ has left orientation, we are interested only in left successors. First look at $\langle 1, 3 \rangle \in Q'(c)$. This pair has 3 as its second coordinate, but node 3 has no successor, and we look at $\langle 2, 5 \rangle$ next. Node 5 has a left successor, namely 7. Consequently, we take the 2 from $\langle 2, 5 \rangle$, and this 7, and the resulting ordered pair $\langle 2, 7 \rangle$ goes into $Q'(d)$. Sets $Q(x_i)$ are generated in Step 2:

$$Q(b) = \{1, 2, 5, 6, 10, 12, 14\},$$
$$Q(d) = \{2, 3, 9, 10, 12\},$$
$$Q(e) = \{1, 2, 9, 10, 12\}.$$

Finally, $T(S) = Q(b) \cap Q(d) \cap Q(e) = \{2, 10, 12\}$.

5e. Prefix, Postfix, and Infix Formulas

The order of evaluation of an arithmetic expression such as

$$a + bc + d/e - f \tag{5.4}$$

is determined by convention. Evaluation proceeds from left to right, but multiplication or division is performed before addition or subtraction. The precedence imposed by the hierarchy of operations can be overruled by means of parentheses: The whole expression enclosed in a pair of parentheses is considered a single operand. For example, we can use parentheses to enforce strict left-to-right evaluation:

$$((a + b)c + d)/e - f. \tag{5.5}$$

If every expression of the form operand–operator–operand is enclosed in parentheses, and we stipulate that evaluation proceeds outward from the innermost parentheses, then the hierarchy of operations does not have to be specified—it is implicit in the structure. An example of a completely parenthesized expression:

$$(((a + b)(c + d))/(e - f)). \qquad (5.6)$$

In completely parenthesized form expressions (5.4) and (5.5) become $(((a + (bc)) + (d/e)) - f)$ and $(((((a + b)c) + d)/e) - f)$, respectively.

Arithmetic expressions can be represented by trees. Every operation corresponds to a labeled nonterminal node. The label specifies the operation, and arcs originating from the node lead to the operands. Figure 5.10 shows the trees corresponding to the three expressions (5.4), (5.5), and (5.6).

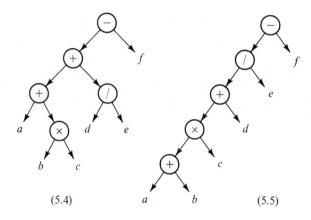

(5.4)   (5.5)

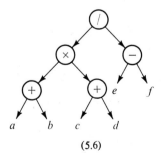

(5.6)

Figure 5.6

Now, starting from the top and keeping to the left, we trace round a tree, stringing together the symbols as they are encountered, see Figure 5.11. This procedure generates the expression,

$$- + + a \times bc/def. \tag{5.4a}$$

From the other trees of Figure 5.10 we obtain

$$-/ + \times + abcdef, \tag{5.5a}$$

$$/ \times + ab + cd - ef. \tag{5.6a}$$

These expressions are *prefix* forms of (5.4), (5.5), and (5.6). Each operator precedes its two operands. Take the multiplication operator in (5.4a). It needs two operands. The $+$ cannot be an operand; it is itself an operator. Therefore, in order to obtain the first operand for the multiplication, we have to evaluate $+ab$ before we can perform the multiplication. The second operand of $\times$ is c.

The trees of Figure 5.10 are labeled B-trees, and the operation of stringing together the symbols to generate a prefix form is preorder traversal in which the processing of a node is taken to mean the appending of the label of the node to the prefix form generated that far. Prefix expressions have the same advantage that completely parenthesized expressions have; one does not have to specify a hierarchy of operations. Their further advantage over the

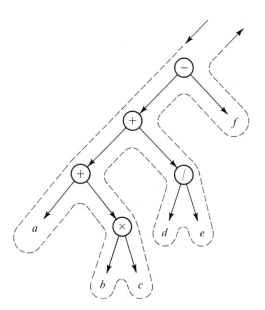

Figure 5.11

completely parenthesized expressions is that they are shorter; their disadvantage is that we are not as used to the prefix form operator–operand–operand as to the *infix* sequence operand–operator–operand. Inorder traversal of a B-tree representing an arithmetic expression produces an *infix* form, but, since parentheses are not inserted, the infix expressions produced by such traversal do not specify the intended order of execution of the operations unambiguously. For example, inorder traversal of the B-trees of Figure 5.10 produces $a+b\times c+d/e-f$ in all three cases. Postorder traversal, however, provides another unambiguous specification of the intended order of execution. Postorder traversal of the three trees of Figure 5.10 generates the *postfix* forms

$$abc\times +de/+f-,\qquad(5.4b)$$
$$ab+c\times d+e/f-,\qquad(5.5b)$$
$$ab+cd+\times ef-/.\qquad(5.6b)$$

In a postfix form each operator is preceded by its two operands.

The hierarchy of operations in arithmetic is so well established that there is no real danger that the intentions of the writer of an arithmetic expression will be misinterpreted by the reader. When we turn to expressions in the statement calculus the situation is not as satisfactory. The functionally complete set of operations $\{\vee, \wedge, \neg\}$ comprises all the logical operations available in Fortran (as .OR., .AND., and .NOT.). In logic the usual convention requires evaluation of $\wedge$ before $\vee$, with parentheses again being used to override the precedence imposed by this convention. The unary operator $\neg$ takes precedence over both $\wedge$ and $\vee$, but parentheses are important: The forms $\neg p \wedge q$ and $\neg(p \wedge q)$ require different evaluation sequences. In the first case $\neg p$ is evaluated first, and then $\neg p \wedge q$. In the second case $p \wedge q$ is evaluated first; the truth value of the whole expression is then the complement of the truth value of $p \wedge q$. In Standard Fortran the expression

.NOT. A1 .AND. A2.OR. A3 .AND. A4

is interpreted to correspond to the tree of Figure 5.12 but the Fortran compiler supplied with the CDC 3200 computer interprets the formula as having the structure in Figure 5.13; i.e., the conventions of logic are not universally accepted. This emphasizes the need for an unambiguous representation, such as the one provided by prefix notation. The prefix formulas corresponding to the two trees are distinct. Using conventional symbols for the logical operations, they are

$$\vee\ \wedge\ \neg\ A1\ A2\ \wedge\ A3\ A4,\qquad(5.7)$$

$$\wedge\ \vee\ \wedge\ \neg\ A1\ A2\ A3\ A4.\qquad(5.8)$$

In the interpretation of formulas (5.7) and (5.8) it is still necessary to know that $\neg$ is a unary operation, and that $\vee$ and $\wedge$ are binary operations. If the

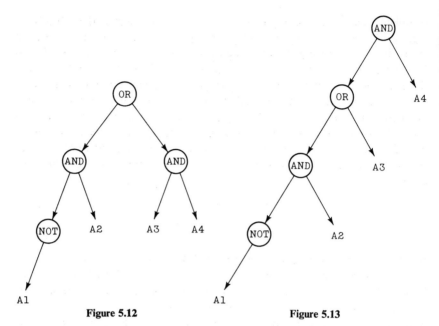

Figure 5.12   Figure 5.13

same symbol can stand for a unary and a binary operation, as, for example, + and − do in arithmetic, prefix formulas can be ambiguous. Both of the trees in Figure 5.14 correspond to the prefix formula $--ab$, but the first tree represents $-(a - b) = -a + b$, while the second stands for $(-a) - b = -a - b$. We had similar difficulty with the tree of Figure 5.1. In writing down the linear string corresponding to the tree (and this linear string is a prefix formula) we had to use parentheses to avoid ambiguity.

If a data structure can be represented as a tree, then the choice between leaving it in this form and converting it to a prefix formula is a matter of convenience, largely determined by the programming language that is to be

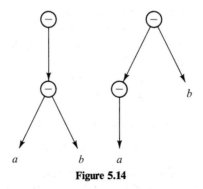

Figure 5.14

used in implementing the processing algorithms. We shall now deal with the compilation of arithmetic expressions, and in this application prefix or postfix formulas are more convenient than their tree representations.

We shall make extensive use of stacks. Indeed, the use of stacks in this context has achieved the distinction of a classic in computer science. We described above what is meant by a completely parenthesized expression. For example, the Fortran statement

$$A = B*C + D*(E-F)$$

becomes

$$(A=((B*C)+(D*(E-F))))$$

when completely parenthesized. The purpose of the parentheses is to avoid having to specify a hierarchy of operations. At the other extreme we have parenthesis-free notations. The above statement becomes

$$=A+*BC*D-EF$$

in prefix notation, or

$$ABC*DEF-*+=$$

in postfix notation. Again the hierarchy of operations does not have to be specified.

Let us now see how a postfix formula would be compiled. A.5.6 sets up a table of entries $n_1 \# n_2$, where n_1 and n_2 stand for variable names (or locations) and $\#$ stands for an operator. The result of the operation of row i is stored in an auxiliary location $T.i$.

ALGORITHM 5.6 Write the statement to be converted to an operand–operator–operand table as $s_1 s_2 \cdots s_k$.

1. Set $i = 1$; set $J = 1$.
2. Set $S = s_i$. If S is an operator, go to 4.
3. Push down S; set $i = i + 1$; go to 2.
4. Pop up n_2; pop up n_1; enter $n_1 S n_2$ in row J of table.
5. If stack is empty, stop.
6. Set $S = T.J$; set $J = J + 1$; go to 3.

Example

Applied to $ABC*DEF-*+=$ the algorithm produces Table 5.1. It is then easy to compile the statement: Simply replace each line of the table by an appropriate "chunk" of machine code. There is really no need to generate the table as such. In Step 4, instead of entering $n_1 S n_2$ into a table, the appropriate machine commands can be generated and put out directly.

TABLE 5.1

OPERAND–OPERATOR–OPERAND TABLE

Row	Operand–operator–operand		
1	B	*	C
2	E	−	F
3	D	*	$T.2$
4	$T.1$	+	$T.3$
5	A	=	$T.4$

There still remains the question: How does one get the statements into postfix form? We observe that the order of the variable names is the same in all notations. Only the order of the operators and their locations change. We shall see that the reordering of the operators can be performed by a stack with the aid of a table of priorities.

ALGORITHM 5.7   The following algorithm for converting an infixed arithmetic statement to postfix form uses a priority table:

Operator—   ( )   =   + or −   * or /   **
Priority—   0   1   2   3   4   5

The priority of a symbol s will be denoted by $p(s)$, e.g., $p(+) = 3$. Write the statement as $s_1 s_2 \cdots s_k$. We assume that the statement does not contain + or − as unary operators.

1. Set $i = 1$.
2. Set $S = s_i$. If S is (, then go to 9.
3. If S is a variable name, transfer it to the output string and go to 10.
4. If stack is empty, go to 9.
5. Pop up symbol n from the stack.
6. If $p(n) \geq p(S)$, transfer n to output string and go to 4.
7. If S is) and n is (, then go to 10.
8. Push down n.
9. Push down S.
10. Set $i = i + 1$. If $i \leq k$, then go to 2.
11. Empty stack into output string and stop.

Examples

1. Table 5.2 illustrates the conversion of the statement

        A = B*C + D*(E - F)

to postfix form. In the table the stack status and the additions to the output string refer to the state of affairs on reaching Step 10.

TABLE 5.2

GENERATION OF POSTFIX FORMULA

s_i	Stack status	Addition to output string
A		A
=	=	
B	=	B
*	=*	
C	=*	C
+	=+	*
D	=+	D
*	=+*	
(	=+*(	
E	=+*(	E
−	=+*(−	
F	=+*(−	F
)	=+*	−
	Emptying of stack	*
		+
		=

2. Symbol n, which is popped up in Step 5 of A.5.7 may have to be pushed down again in Step 8. Therefore, we would like a facility for examining the contents of a stack without actually popping up data. This facility could be provided by a function subprogram LOOK(K) that returns as its value the Kth datum in the stack, counting from the top. For example, in Step 5 of A.5.7 the value of LOOK(1) would be n.

5f. Sort Trees and Dictionaries

Quite often a computer program has to generate a list of all distinct words in a text. This can be accomplished by reading in the entire text, and producing the list by normal sorting procedures. There are, however, serious objections to this approach. First, if the number of distinct words (types) is small compared with the number of all words (tokens), memory space is wasted in storing redundant information. Sometimes, particularly when the length of the input text is unknown, this results in an unnecessarily complicated program; provision has to be made for transfer of data to and from auxiliary storage when, if some other approach were taken, all relevant data could be accommodated in core storage. Second, total processing time improves when input operations are made to overlap with straight computing. It is therefore desirable to generate the list of types while the text is being read. This becomes essential rather than just desirable when reduction of processing time is a major concern of the programmer, e.g., in writing nonexperimental compilers. In many assemblers, compilers, and interpreters the creation of tables of variable names (symbol tables) is one of the most important activities. Third, the table may have to go into full use before it is completed. This is the case with symbol tables in incremental compilers.

The simplest table of types is an unordered list. A word is simply adjoined to the end of the list if it is not already in the list. In the worst case, i.e., when a word is not in the list, the word has to be compared against every listed word. Alternatively, the list can be kept in alphabetic order. Then the time required to establish whether or not a word is already in the list is greatly reduced (see Section 11a), but insertion of a new word requires shifting of all words that come after it. The simplest arrangements are therefore the least economical. We need a structure that can be searched through in less time than an unordered list, but one that also permits new words to be readily added to it. A sort tree is one such structure.

ALGORITHM 5.8   Algorithm for creating a sort tree. A *sort tree* is a labeled binary tree. The labels make up a table of types. If a node is labeled, it is called *filled*; if not, it is called *free*. Let w_i stand for the ith word in the text, and assume that the text contains n words.

1. Initiate the tree as a single free node (this remains the root of the tree throughout), and set $i = 0$.
2. Set $i = i + 1$. If $i > n$, stop.
3. Enter the tree at the root.
4. If the node reached is free, make w_i the label of this node, drop two arcs from the node, thus creating two new free nodes, and go to 2.
5. A filled node has been reached. If w_i is equal to the label, go to 2.
6. If w_i is "smaller" than the label, proceed to the next node by taking the left arc down; if "larger", take the right arc down. Go to 4.

Example

Figure 5.15 shows the tree generated from the text,

> *Friends, Romans, countrymen, lend me your ears;*
> *I come to bury Caesar, not to praise him.*

The tree contains many arcs that terminate at free nodes, and are, therefore, superfluous. This is a minor technical detail. The algorithm can be made to suppress creation of redundant arcs, but the reformulated algorithm would not show the salient features of the procedure quite as clearly as A.5.8. On removal of the superfluous arcs the tree becomes a B-tree.

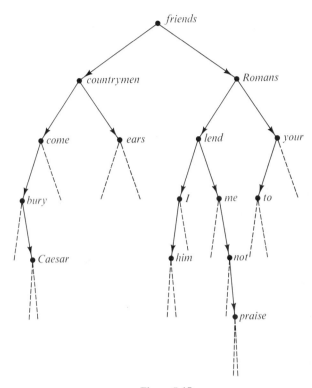

Figure 5.15

For simplicity we have made the labels single items of data. In most practical applications of sort trees labels are ordered pairs $\langle s_k, a_k \rangle$, but only the first coordinates (the symbols s_k) enter the comparisons of A.5.8. The set of labels is then a function f, with $a_k = f(s_k)$. Assume that the tree is used to generate frequency counts of words in a text. Then, at Step 4 of A.5.8, $\langle w_i, 1 \rangle$ instead of just w_i is made the label, and at Step 5, if w_i is equal to the first coordinate of the label, the second coordinate is incremented by 1. After the algorithm has stopped, the a_k of each $\langle s_k, a_k \rangle$ is the number of occurrences of the type s_k in the text. For example, with the short text of the example of A.5.8, all labels, except the label $\langle to, 2 \rangle$, would have the form $\langle s_k, 1 \rangle$. If the tree is a symbol table of an incremental compiler, then the second coordinates of labels might be addresses assigned to the variables (first coordinates).

Sort trees can be easily implemented using Fortran or a similar language. In our example the input will be a string of N integers. For simplicity it will be assumed that the integers are already in store, in array D. An array of pointers P will be generated by A.5.2. Element P(J,1) is a pointer to the node reached by following the left arc originating from J, and element P(J,2) is

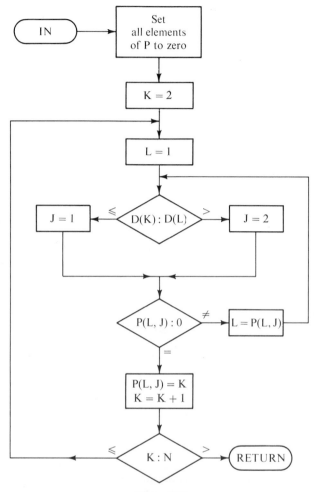

Figure 5.16

a pointer to the node reached by taking the right arc. If a pointer is zero, the corresponding arc would lead to a free node, i.e., would be redundant. Duplication will be permitted. In terms of A.5.8 this means deletion of Step 5 and change of *smaller* in Step 6 to *less than or equal*.

ALGORITHM 5.9   Figure 5.16 is an algorithm for implementation of a sort tree.

Example

Let the input string (array D) be

26   23   26   27   22   25   28   26   21   28   23   24.

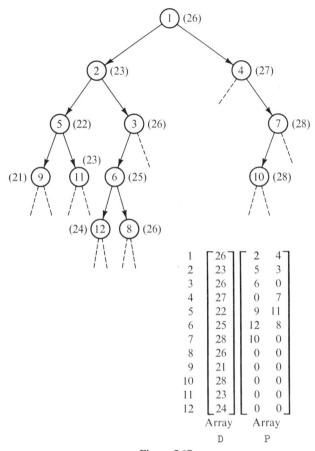

Figure 5.17

Then array P of Figure 5.17 is the array generated by A.5.9. The sort tree is an exact representation of the arrays D and P, and vice versa. The nodes have been given identifying numbers 1, 2, ..., 12, which correspond to subscripts in D. The numbers in parentheses are the labels; the label of node J is D(J).

If the B-tree of Figure 5.17 were subjected to inorder traversal, with the processing of a node being the printing of the label associated with the node, then we would produce a listing of the elements of D in ascending order. A.5.10 defines inorder traversal of sort trees. When applied to the tree of Figure 5.17 it produces the sorted string

    21   22   23   23   24   25   26   26   26   27   28   28.

ALGORITHM 5.10   Figure 5.18 is a flowchart of a program for the output of elements in a sort tree in ascending order. D is the array of data, and P is the array of pointers (see Figure 5.17).

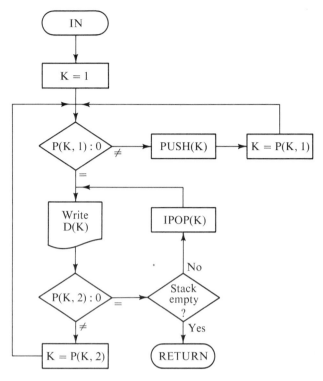

Figure 5.18

Inorder traversal of the sort tree of Figure 5.15 produces an alphabetized (sorted) list of the data stored in the tree: *bury, Caesar, come, countrymen, ears, friends, him, I, lend, me, not, praise, Romans, to, your.*

The trees of Figures 5.15 and 5.19 are equivalent in the sense that inorder traversal produces the same sorted list with both of them. The tree of Figure 5.19 is balanced, that of Figure 5.15 is not. Assume that we continue processing more text, and that the words in the text have an equal probability of occurrence. Then the expected number of comparisons that the next word of input has to undergo is $(1 \times 1 + 2 \times 2 + 4 \times 3 + 4 \times 4 + 3 \times 5 + 1 \times 6)/15 = 3.6$ for the unbalanced tree and $(1 \times 1 + 2 \times 2 + 4 \times 3 + 8 \times 4)/15 = 3.27$ for the balanced tree. Processing efficiency can be improved if a sort tree is converted to the equivalent balanced tree after 15 or 31 nodes have been filled. However, if the text is short, the subsequent gains in processing time may be too small to justify the time spent on rearranging the tree. An input text that is already in alphabetic order is a calamity. Note that an algorithm for balancing a B-tree must take into account the type of traversal. If the B-trees of Figures 5.15 and 5.19 were traversed in preorder, say, then the word lists derived from the two trees would differ. The B-tree of Figure

5.19 is equivalent to the B-tree of Figure 5.15 *only* under inorder traversal.

We shall now consider the effect of balancing on a sort tree. Let the tree contain N nodes, and let n_i be the number of nodes located on level i of the tree. We are interested in the expected number of comparisons required to find a given datum in the tree. Denote this number by C_N for the general case, and by C'_N for the special case of the tree being in balance. The meaning of C_N needs some explanation. In building a tree of N nodes, N items of data are entered. The N items can be entered in $N!$ different sequences, giving rise to $N!$ trees (which need not all be distinct). For a given tree the total number of comparisons required to find all N items of data divided by N is the expected number of comparisons for finding any one item in that tree. This expected number of comparisons averaged over all $N!$ trees is C_N.

We have

$$C'_N = \frac{1}{N} \sum_{i=0}^{M} (i + 1)n_i,$$

where $M = \lfloor \log_2 N \rfloor$. But

$$n_i = 2^i, \quad i < M;$$
$$n_M = N - (2^M - 1).$$

Hence

$$C'_N = \frac{1}{N}(M + 1)(N + 1 - 2^M) + \frac{1}{N} \sum_{i=0}^{M-1} (i + 1)2^i$$

$$= (M + 1)\left(1 + \frac{1}{N} - \frac{2^M}{N}\right) + \frac{(M - 1)2^M}{N} + \frac{1}{N}$$

$$= (M + 1)\left(1 + \frac{1}{N}\right) - \frac{2^{M+1}}{N} + \frac{1}{N}$$

$$\simeq M, \quad \text{for large } N.$$

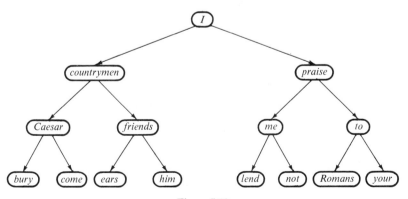

Figure 5.19

Thus, the expected number of comparisons in a balanced tree tends to $\log_2 N$ as N increases.

In the general case we shall find an expression for C_N in terms of C_{N-1}. When the sort tree contains $N - 1$ nodes, the number of positions that can be occupied by an Nth node on level i is

$$2n_{i-1} - n_i, \qquad i > 0.$$

Note that the result of summing this quantity over all levels of the tree is N. Hence, if we assume that the new node has equal likelihood of occupying any one of the N positions, the expected " number " of nodes to be added to level i when the new Nth node is added to the tree is

$$\frac{1}{N}(2n_{i-1} - n_i).$$

Hence

$$C_N = C_{N-1} + \frac{1}{N}\sum_{i=1}^{N-1}\frac{i+1}{N}(2n_{i-1} - n_i),$$

and, noting that

$$\sum_{i=0}^{N-2}n_i = N - 1,$$

we have

$$N^2(C_N - C_{N-1}) = \sum_{i=1}^{N-1}(i+1)(2n_{i-1} - n_i)$$

$$= \sum_{i=1}^{N-1}in_{i-1} + 2\sum_{i=1}^{N-1}n_{i-1}$$

$$+ \sum_{i=1}^{N-1}(in_{i-1} - in_i) - \sum_{i=1}^{N-1}n_i$$

$$= NC_{N-1} + 2(N-1) + \sum_{i=0}^{N-2}n_i - \sum_{i=1}^{N-1}n_i$$

$$= NC_{N-1} + 2(N-1) + (n_0 - n_{N-1}).$$

Since $n_0 = 1$ and $n_{N-1} = 0$ in a tree with $N - 1$ nodes,

$$C_N = \left(1 + \frac{1}{N}\right)C_{N-1} + \frac{2}{N} - \frac{1}{N^2}$$

after some simple algebraic manipulation. This recurrence relation can be shown to have the solution

$$C_N = 2 \left(1 + \frac{1}{N} \right) H_N - 3,$$

where $H_N = 1 + \frac{1}{2} + \frac{1}{3} + \cdots + \frac{1}{N}$. There exists a series expansion

$$H_N = \log_e N + \gamma + \frac{1}{2N} - \frac{1}{12N^2} + \frac{1}{120N^4} - \cdots,$$

where $\gamma = 0.577216$ is Euler's constant. Hence, for large N,

$$C_N \simeq 2 H_N \simeq 2 \log_e N.$$

Thus, for large N,

$$\frac{C_N}{C_N'} \simeq 2 \log_e 2 = 1.386.$$

The H_k are called *harmonic numbers.*

The analysis shows that the expected average number of comparisons required to find a datum in a tree that is created in a totally random manner is on the average 39 % higher than in a balanced tree. For small N the exact ratio is even smaller, e.g., it is 1.33 for $N = 1024$, and 1.18 for $N = 10$. Nevertheless, trees that are excessively out of balance can arise in practice due to lack of randomness in the input, and an algorithm for converting an unbalanced sort tree to its balanced equivalent may have to be applied.

ALGORITHM 5.11   The Martin and Ness algorithm for balancing B-trees. The input is an array P of pointers that represents the structure of a B-tree (see Figure 5.17), the number of the row in P that corresponds to the root of this tree (in ROOT), and the number of nodes N in the tree. The algorithm transforms P so that this array represents a balanced tree equivalent to the original tree in terms of inorder traversal, and returns in ROOT the number of the row of P that represents the root of the balanced tree. Two stacks are required: stack DOWN of maximal depth N and stack BACK of maximal depth $3\lfloor \log_2 N \rfloor$. The algorithm makes an inorder traversal of the tree, the traversal being controlled by DOWN. We shall say that a node has been updated when it has been provided with the pointers it will have in the balanced tree. Nodes that will be terminal nodes in this tree are identified as such as soon as they are encountered in the traversal, and they are updated by having their pointer values set to zero. A node that will be nonterminal in the balanced tree is updated as soon as all nodes that will be reachable from this node in the balanced tree have been updated. Data are saved in BACK relating to nodes that have been visited, but cannot yet be updated.

1. [Initialize.] Set TRACER = ROOT, SIZE = N, TYPE = 1.
2. [Determine subtree sizes.] Set ROOT = 0. While SIZE > 1, do the following: push TYPE on stack BACK, push ⌊SIZE/2⌋ on stack BACK, set SIZE = ⌊(SIZE − 1)/2⌋, TYPE = 2.
3. If SIZE = 1, set SWITCH = 0 and go to 6.
4. [Completion test.] If TYPE = 1, stop; else if TYPE = 2, pop up SIZE from stack BACK, push ROOT on BACK, set SWITCH = 1, go to 6.
5. [TYPE = 3; update nonterminal node.] Pop up SIZE from stack BACK, pop up the pointer value P(SIZE, 1) from stack BACK, set P(SIZE, 2) = ROOT, ROOT = SIZE, pop up TYPE from stack BACK, go to 4.
6. [Traverse B-tree.] While TRACER ≠ 0, push TRACER on stack DOWN and set TRACER = P(TRACER, 1).
7. Pop up ROOT from stack DOWN, set TRACER = P(TRACER, 2).
8. [Update terminal node.] If SWITCH = 0, set P(ROOT, 1) = P(ROOT, 2) = 0 and go to 4; else push ROOT on stack BACK, set TYPE = 3, go to 2.

Example

There are no shortcuts for coming to an understanding of an algorithm as complicated as A.5.11: one must apply the algorithm to several actual B-trees and follow through step by step how the algorithm transforms the trees. In other words, one must play at being a computer. It may help to express A.5.11 as a flowchart and to work on a drawing of a B-tree to see properly how the structure of the tree is changed. The algorithm converts the B-tree of Figure 5.17 to that of Figure 5.20. In a sort tree generated by A.5.9,

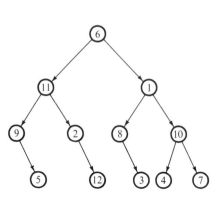

	Array D	Array P	
1	26	8	10
2	23	0	12
3	26	0	0
4	27	0	0
5	22	0	0
6	25	11	1
7	28	0	0
8	26	0	3
9	21	0	5
10	28	4	7
11	23	9	2
12	24	0	0

ROOT [6]

Array D   Array P   ROOT

(Unchanged)

Figure 5.20

which permits duplication, equal integers lie on just one path from the root to some terminal node. This is not necessarily so after the tree has been balanced.

Our discussion has shown that A.5.9 can be used as first stage of a sorting procedure, with the second stage being A.5.10. Some gain is to be had in going through the second stage if the sort tree is to be used extensively after its construction. Search efficiency is improved in the case of an unbalanced tree, and array P is made available for storing other data. The extravagant storage requirements do, however, detract from the usefulness of the algorithm as a sorting technique. Therefore, unless there is a special reason for constructing a sort tree to begin with, other sorting procedures can be found that are more practicable. One such procedure follows.

ALGORITHM 5.12 Subroutine TREEUP sorts an array of N elements. In the worst case approximately $2N(log_2 N - 1)$ comparisons and $N(log_2 N - 1)$ interchanges have to be made. The algorithm is most easily followed if array A is *pictured* as a directed tree rooted at A(1) with *imaginary* arcs joining elements. An arc terminating at A(J) originates from A(JHALF), where JHALF = J/2, and the operation is Fortran integer division; e.g., arcs terminating at A(4) and A(5) originate from A(2). Figure 5.21 shows the structure of an array with six elements.

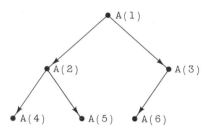

Figure 5.21

The segment starting with statement 20 (the shift procedure) is the mainstay of the program. The first loop (ending with statement 5) uses it to rearrange the elements so that the relation A(JHALF) ≧ A(J) holds for JHALF = 2, 3, . . . , N/2. When the shift procedure is entered with the elements so ordered, the largest element of a subtree specified by I and L is shifted to the root node of the subtree. In the loop ending with statement 15 the shift procedure is used to shift the largest of the N elements into A(1). This element is then interchanged with A(N). Then the largest of the remaining N-1 elements is shifted into A(1) and interchanged with A(N-1), and so on. After N-1 iterations the array is sorted.

```
      SUBROUTINE TREEUP (A,N)
      DIMENSION A(N)
      ITOP = N/2
      ASSIGN  5 TO NN
      L = N
      DO  5  K = 2,ITOP
      I = ITOP + 2 - K
      GO TO 20
    5 CONTINUE
      ASSIGN 10 TO NN
      DO 15  K = 2,N
      I = 1
      GO TO 20
   10 COPY = A(1)
      A(1) = A(L)
      A(L) = COPY
   15 L = L - 1
      RETURN
C  THE SHIFT PROCEDURE THAT FOLLOWS CAN BE WRITTEN
C   AS A SEPARATE SUBROUTINE
   20 COPY = A(I)
   25 J = 2 * I
      IF (J - L) 28, 30, 35
   28 IF (A(J+1).GT.A(J)) J = J + 1
   30 IF (A(J).LE.COPY) GO TO 35
      A(I) = A(J)
      I = J
      GO TO 25
   35 A(I) = COPY
C  SOME COMPILERS MAY OBJECT TO THE FOLLOWING TRANSFER
C  ALTHOUGH ANSI STANDARD FORTRAN PERMITS IT
      GO TO NN, (5,10)
      END
```

A sort tree can function as a dictionary. Then the s_k of a label $\langle a_k, s_k \rangle$ may be an English word, and the a_k its equivalent in some other language, e.g., $\langle$ *friends, amis* $\rangle$ in an English–French dictionary, or $\langle$ *Freunde, friends* $\rangle$ in a German–English dictionary. Another way in which trees can be used in the construction of dictionaries is exemplified by the following scheme. For simplicity we shall assume that the entries are single words rather than pairs. We construct a tree with 27 arcs originating from the root, the first 26 arcs leading to nodes labeled $a, b, c, \ldots, z$. From each of these 26 nodes we suspend another tree having exactly the same structure; i.e., we have a tree with

27 + 26 × 27 arcs. Each terminal node has a list attached to it, which consists of words whose first two letters are the labels of the nodes in the path
from the root to the list. For example, by going from the root to the node
labeled *c*, and then to the node labeled *o*, we reach a list of words that begin
with *co*: *come, countrymen*, ... (see Figure 5.22). Since this list is reached by
a unique path, the first two letters of every word are superfluous, and can be
chopped off to give *me, untrymen*, ... The loss of the first letters presents
difficulties with short words, such as *a, an, me*. This is where the 27th arc
(the *ω*-arc) comes in. Words only one letter long are stored at the node
reached by taking the *ω*-arc from the root. In the case of a word that consists
of two letters we go from the root to the node indicated by the first letter of
the word, and take the *ω*-arc from there, e.g., *me* is stored as *e* at the node
reached by first taking the *m*-arc from the root, and then the *ω*-arc.

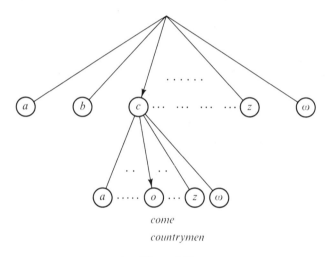

come

countrymen

Figure 5.22

A similar application arises with arrays. A multidimensional array can be
stored as a linear sequence of elements, and the position of an element in the
array computed from the declared bounds of the array (Section 9b). Alternatively, the array can be set up as a tree in which the number of arcs originating from a node on level *i* is equal to the (*i* + 1)th bound. For example, if a
3-dimensional array has bounds ⟨5, 4, 10⟩, the array is represented by a tree
with 5 arcs originating from the root, and 4 arcs originating from each of the
5 nodes on level 1. The 20 nodes on level 2 are terminal nodes, and a vector
of 10 elements is attached to each of them. Let us see now how a particular
element in this array is reached, say ⟨2, 3, 5⟩. The second of the arcs from the
root leads to the appropriate node on level 1, and the third arc originating
from this node terminates at a node that has the vector containing element

$\langle 2, 3, 5 \rangle$ attached to it. The required element is the fifth element in the vector; it is accessed by the machine language technique of indexing.

5g. Decision Trees and Decision Tables

Flowcharts have undeniable merits as devices for displaying the logic of computer programs. Sometimes, however, a situation can become too complex for flowcharts. The greater the number of conditional statements in a program, the more confusing the corresponding flowchart. Finally, it can become so abstruse that the tracing of a particular execution sequence is no better than running a maze. This is where decision tables can restore clarity. Note, however, that only a very limited class of programs, arising mainly in business applications, and only parts of programs in this class, can be represented by decision tables.

Let us take a simple example based on a check being presented to a bank. The bank asks a number of questions:

q_1—*Is the check covered?*
q_2—*Is the account blocked?*
q_3—*Is the new balance greater than* $300?

Answers to the questions form triples of yeses and noes. The triple $\langle Y, N, Y \rangle$ causes the bank to take an action different from that elicited by $\langle N, N, N \rangle$. The possible actions are:

A1—*Do not accept the check.*
A2—*Accept unconditionally.*
A3—*Accept, but charge a handling fee.*

There are eight possible triples. If the triples are tabulated, together with the appropriate actions, the result is an *extended-entry decision table*. The decision table for our example is Table 5.3. Each triple and the corresponding action, i.e., each column in the table, is a *decision rule*.

TABLE 5.3

EXTENDED-ENTRY DECISION TABLE

Rule		1	2	3	4	5	6	7	8
Condition	q_1	Y	Y	Y	Y	N	N	N	N
	q_2	Y	Y	N	N	Y	Y	N	N
	q_3	Y	N	Y	N	Y	N	Y	N
Action		A1	A1	A2	A3	A1	A1	A1	A1

Here we selected a very simple example to keep explanation of techniques simple. It is not unknown to have situations involving as many as 100 conditions. The extended-entry table for 100 conditions has 2^{100} rules! Fortunately we can combine rules to arrive at a *limited-entry* decision table. The conversion of an extended-entry table to a limited-entry table is best followed in a *sequential decision tree*. This is a binary tree in which arcs carry labels Y and N, nonterminal nodes have the conditions for labels, and the terminal nodes are labeled with the appropriate actions. Figure 5.23 shows the sequential decision tree corresponding to Table 5.3. The tree is, of course, a flowchart in an unfamiliar guise.

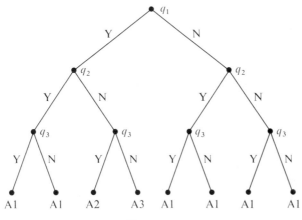

Figure 5.23

From the tree we can see at once that if q_1 and q_2 have both brought the response Y, then q_3 does not have to be asked; the outcome is independent of the response to this question. If the answer to q_1 is N, then the action is independent of the other conditions. We can therefore prune the tree down to that of Figure 5.24. The latter can be converted back to a decision table. This table, Table 5.4, is of the limited-entry variety. There are only four rules. The absence of an entry in a limited-entry table signifies a "don't care" condition.

TABLE 5.4

LIMITED-ENTRY DECISION TABLE

Rule	1	2	3	4
Check covered?	Y	Y	Y	N
Account blocked?	Y	N	N	–
Balance > \$300?	–	Y	N	–
Action	A1	A2	A3	A1

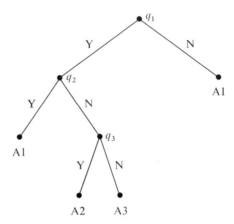

Figure 5.24

When there are 100 conditions one cannot very well construct the complete sequential decision tree. Pruning away of redundant branches has to take place while the tree is being constructed. For instance, in our rather over-simplified situation (we have not allowed for overdrafts for one thing) we know from the start that an uncovered check must evoke action A1.

In a computer a decision table is set up as a matrix of bits and a vector of addresses, called *table matrix* and *transfer vector*. In the table matrix 1 stands for Y, and 0 for N or a "don't care" condition. Decision rule n is represented by the nth column of this matrix and the nth element of the transfer vector. Table 5.3 becomes

$$\begin{bmatrix} 1 & 1 & 1 & 1 & 0 & 0 & 0 & 0 \\ 1 & 1 & 0 & 0 & 1 & 1 & 0 & 0 \\ 1 & 0 & 1 & 0 & 1 & 0 & 1 & 0 \end{bmatrix}$$

[A1   A1   A2   A3   A1   A1   A1   A1]

In processing a particular check we first set up a *data vector* of three elements (or, in general, as many elements as there are conditions). If, for this particular check, q_1 is answered with a *yes*, the first element of the data vector is 1; otherwise it is 0. The second element is 1 if q_2 is answered with *yes*, and 0 otherwise; and so forth. The data vector is compared with successive columns of the table matrix. If the vector matches a column, then the corresponding address in the transfer vector is used to transfer control to the program segment that performs the required action. Assume that a check has given rise to the data vector

$$\begin{bmatrix} 0 \\ 1 \\ 0 \end{bmatrix}.$$

It matches the sixth column of the table matrix, and the sixth element of the transfer vector is therefore used to transfer control to the program segment that prints a message "Check cannot be accepted" or performs some similar action.

The limited-entry decision table of our example becomes

$$\begin{bmatrix} 1 & 1 & 1 & 0 \\ 1 & 0 & 0 & 0 \\ 0 & 1 & 0 & 0 \end{bmatrix}$$

$$[A1 \quad A2 \quad A3 \quad A1]$$

but

$$\begin{bmatrix} 0 \\ 1 \\ 0 \end{bmatrix}$$

does not match any column in this table matrix. The way out of the impasse is to suppress a 1 in the data vector whenever the 1 would be compared with a 0 that stands for a "don't care." The masking out is done by means of a *mask matrix* in which every Y or N entry of the decision table is represented by 1, and a "don't care" by 0. In our case the mask matrix is

$$\begin{bmatrix} 1 & 1 & 1 & 1 \\ 1 & 1 & 1 & 0 \\ 0 & 1 & 1 & 0 \end{bmatrix}.$$

Now, before the data vector is compared with column n in the table matrix, it is modified by use of the nth column of the mask matrix. If an element in the data vector is 1, but the corresponding element in the nth column of the mask matrix is 0, the entry in the data vector is made 0. This modification is achieved by taking the $\wedge$ of each element of the data vector and the corresponding element of the mask matrix ($1 \wedge 1 = 1$, $1 \wedge 0 = 0 \wedge 1 = 0 \wedge 0 = 0$). In our case this means that

$$\begin{bmatrix} 0 \\ 1 \\ 0 \end{bmatrix}$$

remains unchanged for the first three comparisons (in the first three columns of the mask matrix the second element is 1), but that it is changed to

$$\begin{bmatrix} 0 \\ 0 \\ 0 \end{bmatrix}$$

for the comparison with the fourth column. This procedure is called the *rule mask technique*.

If the cost of setting up the data vector is high, then an *interrupted* rule mask technique should be used. Let us rearrange the mask matrix and the table matrix with its associated transfer vector so that the numbers of zeros in columns of the mask matrix are in descending order. The result is Table 5.5. Applicability of the first rule in the rearranged table (Rule 4) is determined by condition q_1, and applicability of the second rule (Rule 1) by conditions q_1 and q_2 alone. Evaluation of the data vector can therefore be interrupted after its first element is computed (and the remaining elements set to zero). No more is needed for comparison with the first rule. If a match results, action A1 is performed. If not, evaluation of the data vector resumes, and the second element is computed. This partial data vector is then compared with the second column of the table matrix. The third element is computed only if there is still no match.

TABLE 5.5

REPRESENTATION OF A DECISION TABLE

	Mask matrix				Table matrix			
q_1	1	1	1	1	0	1	1	1
q_2	0	1	1	1	0	1	0	0
q_3	0	0	1	1	0	0	1	0
					[A1	A1	A2	A3] Transfer vector
					4	1	2	3 Rule number

A concise representation of the sequence of interruptions is provided by a $2 \times (c + r)$ *sequencing matrix*, where c is the number of conditions and r the number of rules. The top row contains numbers representing conditions; the bottom row numbers of rules. The conditions follow the order of their evaluation. One element in each column is the number of either a condition or a rule; the other is zero. In our example the matrix is

$$\begin{bmatrix} 1 & 0 & 2 & 0 & 3 & 0 & 0 \\ 0 & 4 & 0 & 1 & 0 & 2 & 3 \end{bmatrix}$$

A sequencing matrix is interpreted as follows: Starting with element $\langle 1, 1 \rangle$, one moves along the top row evaluating conditions until a zero is reached; then one switches to the bottom row and tests rules until a zero is encountered in this row; then switches back to the top row and resumes evaluation of conditions until a further zero is encountered; and so on. The sequencing matrix of the original limited-entry table is

$$\begin{bmatrix} 1 & 2 & 0 & 3 & 0 & 0 & 0 \\ 0 & 0 & 1 & 0 & 2 & 3 & 4 \end{bmatrix}.$$

In practice there is no need to rearrange the mask and table matrices bodily. The arrangement of columns in the sequencing matrix gives enough information for the process to be performed as if the matrices were rearranged.

If the mask matrix is, for example,

$$\begin{bmatrix} 1 & 0 & 1 & 1 & 1 & 1 & 1 \\ 0 & 1 & 1 & 0 & 1 & 1 & 1 \\ 0 & 1 & 1 & 1 & 0 & 1 & 1 \\ 1 & 0 & 0 & 1 & 1 & 1 & 1 \end{bmatrix},$$

the order of evaluation of the first three conditions can be q_1 and q_4 followed by q_2, or q_1 and q_4 followed by q_3, or q_2 and q_3 followed by q_1. If the cost of evaluation is the same for all conditions, then it would not seem to matter which order of evaluations is adopted. If, however, the costs differ, they should be taken into account.

Evaluation costs are not alone in affecting the efficiency of a program derived from a decision table. One must also consider the probabilities associated with the conditions. Returning to the example of Table 5.5, let us associate with each q_i a cost c_i and a probability of success (*yes* answer) p_i. To make the probabilities realistic we shall leave undefined the context in which the table is used. A set of values is given in Table 5.6. The interrupted rule mask procedure illustrated by Table 5.5 is exactly equivalent to the

TABLE 5.6

Costs and Probabilities of Conditions

Condition q_i	Cost c_i	Probability p_i
q_1	40	0.85
q_2	15	0.25
q_3	25	0.60

sequential decision tree of Figure 5.24. We have redrawn the tree as Figure 5.25, adding costs and probabilities. The expected cost of interrupted processing of a data vector can be easily computed by reference to the tree. It is $40 + 0.85(15 + 0.75 \times 25) = 68.6875$. By contrast, if the interrupting procedure were not followed, the cost would be $40 + 15 + 25 = 80$.

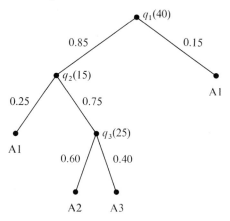

Figure 5.25

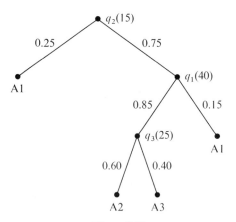

Figure 5.26

In the tree of Figure 5.25 we see that if q_1 is answered with a *yes*, and q_2 is answered with a *yes*, action A1 is taken. If q_1 is answered *no*, A1 is again taken, irrespective of what the answer to the unasked q_2 might be. In other words, A1 is taken if q_2 is answered with a *yes*, no matter how q_1 is answered. This means that we can rearrange the tree, putting q_2 at the root. Figure 5.26 shows the rearranged tree. Here the expected cost is $15 + 0.75(40 + 0.85 \times 25) = 60.9375$, which is a further reduction.

In a practical application one would rarely be able to assume that the probabilities associated with the conditions q_i are independent of each other. For example, if our conditions were

$$q_1\text{—}Older\ than\ 40\ years?$$
$$q_2\text{—}Older\ than\ 50\ years?$$

then the probability that an individual is older than 50 is greater for people over 40 than for the total population, and it is zero for people whose age does not exceed 40. Therefore, the optimization of decision tables should be based on the probabilities of applicability of the rules rather than on the probabilities associated with conditions.

Decision tables have some definite advantages as a form of documentation over sequential decision trees. Unless conditions are reduced to simple symbols, a tree is in danger of being overcluttered. Just the opposite holds for a table; spelling out the conditions actually enhances the readability of the table. Moreover, on account of the geometry, the information content of a rectangular table inscribed in the rectangle of a page of a document is greater than the information carried by a triangular tree inscribed in a page of the same size. If the document is generated by a computer, then the printer is adequate for producing tables. The program for generating trees is more complex, and has to use a plotter for output. Nevertheless, as some of our examples have shown, trees can sometimes be very useful for gaining insight in the structure of decision tables.

A further advantage of decision tables is that a small extended-entry table can be directly coded in Fortran or some other higher-level language. Conversion of a tree to a Fortran program would be a much more devious process. Assume that every Y in an extended-entry table and the data vectors is coded as 1, and every N as 0. In every row of the table substitute 2^{m-1} for every 1, where m is the number of the row. Then compute the column totals. In the case of Table 5.3 they are 7, 6, ..., 1, 0, i.e., column totals identify rules uniquely. Now, given a data vector of n elements, perform the same valuation, and obtain a value between 0 and $2^n - 1$, which is equal to the column total of the column that the data vector matches. This value (increased by 1) can therefore be used in a computed GO TO to effect a transfer of control to the program segment in which the appropriate action is performed. The program for Table 5.3 is simply

```
INDEX = 1 + D(1) + 2*D(2) + 4*D(3)
GO TO (N1,N1,N2,N3,N1,N1,N1,N1), INDEX
```

where D is the data vector and N1, N2, N3 stand for statement numbers associated with program segments in which actions A1, A2, A3, respectively, are performed.

Notes

Hardware implementation of stacks in the KDF9 and B5000 computers is described in [Ha62b] and [Ca63], respectively (see also [Sa62] for the drawing of a stack machine that was patented as early as 1957). A more recent hardware implementation of a stack is reported in [Ha68a].

The use of a stack in the compilation of arithmetic expressions is described in the classic [Ba59b]. Algol permits recursive procedure calls, i.e., a procedure may call itself, and the structure of the language is such that recursive programming can be used extensively in the compilation of an Algol program. The storage problems associated with recursive programming are elegantly solved by the use of a stack (see [Di60]), and the main reason for the stack in the B5000 is that the designers envisaged Algol as the major programming language to be used on this computer. [Go67] is a good introduction to recursive methods for the solution of problems in general. For a more detailed presentation of applications of recursive programming see [Ba68].

In practice one is not interested in generating all sentences of a language. Rather, one wants to know whether a given sentence belongs to a particular language. This requires a parser. In [In66], which deals with the writing of compilers for programming languages, the syntactic chart of a grammar is used in the construction of a parser. Other techniques for parsing of programming languages are described in, for example, [Gr71]. Parsing of natural languages is surveyed in [Sa67]. [Ha67b] is a text on computational linguistics; it contains parsing algorithms. [Wo70] is a later paper of fundamental importance. Automated natural language processing in general is surveyed in various reviews in *Annual Review of Information Science and Technology*. McNaughton has shown that a backward-deterministic parenthesis grammar is unambiguous, see [Mc67], and Knuth proves in [Kn67] that the problem of whether a Type 2 language has a parenthesis grammar can be decided. Another class of unambiguous grammars (precedence grammars) is discussed in Section 12a.

Traversal of B-trees is discussed in [Kn68] (where they are called *binary* trees). Our algorithms for subtree isomorphism and substring matching are based on [Ka72b]. See [Wa74] for a different approach to substring matching.

The sort tree of Figure 5.15 is adapted from [Bo60], which contains a thorough analysis of search efficiency in the sort tree. Balancing algorithm A.5.11 derives from [Ma72b]. Numerous variants of the basic sort tree are surveyed in [Kn73a]. In some later work on AVL trees (see Example 3 of D.3.25) the conditions for balance are being relaxed in order to reduce the time spent on restructuring the trees, see [Fo73a, Ni73]. Algorithm 5.12 is adapted from [Fl64]; for an interesting proof of the algorithm see [Lo70b, Re71]. See [Ni71] on how trees are used in artificial intelligence research.

The literature on decision tables is surveyed in [Po74]. [Mc68] is an expository monograph that contains several very interesting examples; [Po71a] is a more extensive text. [Mu70] presents an important elegant algorithm for the conversion of decision tables to computer programs (see also [Po71b]); ambiguity in decision tables is discussed in [Ki73]; the application of information theory to the conversion of decision tables to computer programs is described in [Ga73a]. The technique of the computed GO TO described in the final paragraph of Section 5g is taken from [Ve66].

Exercises

5.1 (a) Write a program that determines, given the adjacency matrix of a digraph D, whether or not D is a directed tree, and, if it is, finds its root.

5.2 (a) Sentence *a.green.man.bought.the.green.apple* has been generated by the grammar of Example 3 of D.4.26. Draw the derivation tree of this sentence and represent the tree by a linear string.

5.3 (a) Show that $G = \langle \{a, b\}, \{S, A\}, P, S \rangle$, where P consists of

$$\langle S \rangle ::= ab\langle S \rangle b \,|\, a\langle A \rangle b \,|\, a$$
$$\langle A \rangle ::= b\langle S \rangle$$

is an ambiguous grammar. What is $L(G)$? Find an unambiguous grammar G_1 such that $L(G) = L(G_1)$.

5.4 (a) Draw syntactic charts of the grammars of Exercises 4.49 and 4.51.

5.5 (a) Find a Type 3 grammar that generates the language of Part (iii) of Exercise 4.56 and draw the syntactic chart of the grammar. Would you find the syntactic chart of assistance in the design of an acceptor for the language?

5.6 (b) Consider the Fortran implementation of a stack as described in Section 5b. What does the stack contain after execution of the following program segment?

```
        CALL SKOPEN
        DO  5  K = 1,10
5       CALL PUSH (K)
        DO  6  K = 1,5
6       NEX(K) = IPOP (IT)
        CALL PUSH (IT)
        DO  7  K = 1,5
7       CALL PUSH (NEX(K))
```

5.7 (b) Consider the Fortran implementation of a stack as described in Section 5b. Assuming that 20 numbers have been stored in the stack, write a program that removes the element that is just below the topmost element in the stack, and every second element thereafter. (This leaves 10 elements in the stack at the end of the operation.)

5.8 (b) Write PUSH and IPOP routines for a *first in–first out* store. (An IPOP routine that shifts every item that remains in the store to an adjacent location after an item has been extracted is not acceptable.)

5.9 (b) Consider a computer program that reads in n integers, $n/2$ of which are the distinct nonzero integers 1, 2, ..., $n/2$, and the remaining $n/2$ are zeros. If an integer is nonzero, it is pushed down in a stack; if it is zero, a number is popped up from the stack and printed. For example, the input 123004056000 generates the output 324651, the input 506120030040 generates 521364, the input 100023004506 is invalid. Write this program.

5.10 (b) The program of Exercise 5.9 is a permutation generator: it generates 324651 from 123456, and 521364 from 561234. In general, given an input permutation $a_1a_2\cdots a_k$ of $\{1, 2, ..., k\}$, suitably interlaced with k zeros, the program is capable of generating some permutations of $\{1, 2, ..., k\}$, but not all. For example, it cannot generate 312645 from 123456. How many permutations can it generate? Hint: Count the number of ways $a_1 a_2\cdots a_k$ can be interlaced with k zeros, and the number of such sequences that are *not* valid for the purposes of the program. (Direct counting of the valid sequences is too difficult.)

5.11 (b) Given two permutations $a_1a_2\cdots a_k$ and $b_1b_2\cdots b_k$ of $\{1, 2, ..., k\}$, e.g., 561234 and 521364, write a program that accepts the two permutations for its input, and determines the sequence of push and pop operations that transforms the first into the second by the program of Exercise 5.9, or indicates that the transformation is not possible.

5.12 (b) Use A.5.1 to find all occurrences of substrings of length 5, then substrings of length 7, and then substrings of length 10 that occur more than once in the string

abccbaccbaccbaccbaccbabbac.

5.13 (b) How would you apply A.5.1 to the finding of all occurrences of a *specific* substring in a given string? Apply A.5.1 to the finding of all occurrences of *ccbabb* in the string of Exercise 5.12.

5.14 (c) Consider traversal of a B-tree in right to left direction. Define three types of traversal for this case, and indicate how they are related to preorder, inorder, and postorder traversal.

5.15 (c) In what order are the nodes in the B-tree of Figure 5.8 and the B-tree T of Figure 5.9 processed under preorder, inorder, and postorder traversal?

5.16 (c) Characterize the B-trees in which the nodes are processed in exactly the same order under (a) preorder and inorder traversal and (b) inorder and postorder traversal. In what order are the nodes in such B-trees processed under postorder traversal for case (a) and under preorder traversal for case (b)?

5.17 (c) Complete the specification of A.5.3.

5.18 (c) Prove that A.5.2 does in fact process the nodes of a B-tree in the order required for preorder traversal.

5.19 (c) Prove that A.5.4 does in fact process the nodes of a B-tree in the order required for postorder traversal.

5.20 (c) Find an array representation like that of Figure 5.7 for the B-tree of Figure 5.8 and B-tree T of Figure 5.9.

5.21 (c) Prove that knowledge of the order in which the nodes of a B-tree are processed under preorder and under inorder traversal is sufficient for the construction of the B-tree. Specify the construction algorithm.

5.22 (c) Specify an algorithm for the determination of isomorphism of two B-trees. Apply the algorithm to the B-tree of Figure 5.7 and a B-tree specified by

$$\text{ROOTA: [7]} \qquad \text{PA:} \begin{bmatrix} 0 & 0 \\ 0 & 1 \\ 0 & 0 \\ 3 & 2 \\ 4 & 0 \\ 0 & 5 \\ 8 & 6 \\ 11 & 9 \\ 10 & 0 \\ 0 & 0 \\ 0 & 0 \end{bmatrix}$$

Then apply it to the B-tree of Figure 5.7 and a B-tree specified by ROOTA and PA as above, but with the two entries in row 7 of PA reversed, i.e., reading 6,8 instead of 8,6.

5.23 (d) Apply A.5.5 to B-tree S of Figure 5.9 and the B-tree of Figure 5.8 (as the T of A.5.5).

5.24 (d) To each node of a B-tree a string can be assigned that represents a specification of the path from the root of the tree to that node. Consider B-tree $\langle A, R, f \rangle$ with $a \in A$ the root. For each node of the tree define a string σ over $\{0, 1\}$, called the *sequence* of the node, as follows:

$$\sigma(a) = \Lambda,$$
$$\sigma(x) = \sigma(p(x)) \cdot f(p(x), x), \qquad x \in A - \{a\},$$

where p is the predecessor function. With reference to node 11 in B-tree T of Figure 5.9, we generate in succession $\sigma(1) = \Lambda$, $\sigma(3) = \sigma(1) \cdot f(1, 3) = \Lambda \cdot 1 = 1$, $\sigma(6) = \sigma(3) \cdot f(3, 6) = 1 \cdot 1 = 11$, $\sigma(9) = 110$, $\sigma(10) = 1101$, $\sigma(11) = 11010$. The sequences of the terminal nodes of a B-tree T constitute an unambiguous specification of T in that we can find a procedure that constructs precisely T from these sequences. Find the sequences of all other terminal nodes of B-tree T.

5.25 (d) Given a B-tree T in which the terminal nodes are defined by their sequences 100, 101, 0010, 0011, 0100, 1100, 1101, 01100, 01111, 011010, 011011, 011101, 0101010, 0101011. Use A.5.5 to determine subtrees in T that are isomorphic to a B-tree S in which the terminal nodes are defined by sequences 00, 01, 101.

5.26 (d) How many full trees of order 2 does the B-tree T of Exercise 5.25 contain? Should one use A.5.5 or the method given as Example 2 of A.5.4 for this determination?

5.27 (e) Given infix formula $R = ((A+B)*(A+C))/X + Y$. Draw the tree corresponding to this formula and use the tree to write down the corresponding prefix formula.

5.28 (e) Write down infix formulas corresponding to the following prefix expressions:

$$= X + + A*BCD$$
$$= X * + AB + CD$$
$$= X**ABC$$
$$= X*A*BC$$

5.29 (e) Define a parenthesis grammar that generates completely parenthesized arithmetic expressions in variables a, b, ..., z, and binary operators $+$, $-$, $/$, $\times$, $=$.

5.30 (e) Although multiplication in the set of real numbers is an associative operation, it is not associative in the set of computer representations of real numbers. For example, $A*(B*C)$ and $(A*B)*C$ may have very different values if floating point underflow occurs. Therefore, it may be quite realistic to have to write an extended product as $((A*(B*C))*(D*E))*F$. Draw the tree of this expression, and find its prefix form. Then draw the tree of the K-formula $***a*bc*def$, and rewrite the K-formula in infix form. Find infix forms of the following K-formulas:

(i) $**a***c*bc**dcbef$;
(ii) $***a***bbcd***cbdee$;
(iii) $*a**d*b*cd*ea$.

Does the prefix or the infix form afford a better insight in the structure of the digraphs represented by the formulas? What effect does change in the left-to-right order of arcs in the tree of a K-formula have?

5.31 (e) Develop an algorithm that converts an infixed arithmetic statement to prefix form.

5.32 (e) In compiling arithmetic assignment statements unary plus (+) or minus (−) can be distinguished from the corresponding binary operator by means of a type indicator. Initialize the indicator to 1 for the leftmost symbol of the statement, and alternate it between 1 and 0 as each succeeding symbol, excluding parentheses, is scanned. Then, assuming that the statement is well formed, a + or − is binary if the indicator is 0, but unary if the indicator is 1. The indicator is made to remain 1 for the symbol following the unary operator. For example, in scanning

$$X = A - (- (- B)) + C$$

the indicator assumes values

$$1 \quad 0 \ 1 \ 0 \quad 1 \quad 1 \ 1 \quad \ 0 \ 1$$

Write a program that identifies unary + and − operators in arithmetic assignment statements.

5.33 (e) An alternative to the method used in A.5.7 for dealing with parentheses is to push down not just the operator, but the operator and its adjusted priority. A parenthesis counter is kept. The counter is incremented by 1 for each opening parenthesis, and decremented by 1 for each closing parenthesis encountered in the scan of the statement. The adjusted priority of an operator is then the sum of its priority value from the priority table and the count in the parenthesis counter at the time the operator is being processed. Opening parentheses do not have to be pushed down now. Incorporate the counter technique in A.5.7, and implement this revised algorithm.

5.34 (e) Combine A.5.6 and A.5.7 into a single algorithm that uses two stacks (an operator stack and an operand stack) concurrently.

5.35 (e) Develop an algorithm that converts a representative set of K-formulas (see Section 3f) to a list of arcs and a list of isolated nodes. Implement the algorithm as a Fortran program and apply it to the set

$$\{**a***a*bc**dcbef, **bf**e**bad*ac\}.$$

Use the program to show that

$$*a*a*bc*****dcbef$$

is not a K-formula.

5.36 (e) Develop an algorithm that tests a Boolean form for well-formedness (see D.2.8 and its example).

5.37   (e)   Develop an algorithm that tests whether a given sequence of K-operators and node symbols is a valid K-formula (see Section 3f).

5.38   (f)   Construct tree dictionaries for the following passages:

  (i) The only problem to be faced in using the foregoing algorithm to obtain a solution to the traveling salesman problem for an arbitrarily large number of cities is a storage problem.

  (ii) Assuming that subsequent text will be composed entirely of words from this dictionary and that all words will occur with equal probability, compute the average number of comparisons for this dictionary and for an equivalent balanced tree dictionary.

Apply Part (ii) to both trees.

5.39   (f)   Set up array P (see the example of A.5.9) for the sort tree of Part (i) of Exercise 5.38.

5.40   (f)   The two trees of Exercise 5.38 are to be combined into a single sort tree. One way would be to send the first passage down the second tree. Since a considerable effort has gone into the construction of the first tree, it may be possible to find a more efficient procedure that utilizes the structure of this tree. Investigate.

5.41   (f)   Implement A.5.10 as a Fortran program and apply it to the tables of Figure 5.17.

5.42   (f)   In Example 3 of D.3.25 three definitions of a balanced B-tree are discussed. Which of the three definitions do the B-trees as restructured by A.5.11 satisfy?

5.43   (f)   A.5.11 is applied to a set of B-trees, where all trees belonging to the set have the same number of nodes N. Is there just one restructured B-tree in all these cases? If so, draw the restructured trees for $N = 4, 5, 6, 7$.

5.44   (f)   Figure 5.27 is a Venn diagram showing 11 elements, which belong to five sets. Devise a tree representation of the situation depicted by the diagram. What structure would you need to represent the situation if a sixth set $F = \{b, c, k, m\}$ were introduced?

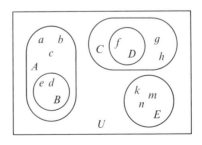

Figure 5.27

5.45 (g) In Exercise 2.27 consider the inputs as conditions, and the presence or absence of an output signal as actions A and B, respectively. Set up extended-entry decision tables corresponding to Parts (ii) and (iv) of Exercise 2.27, and find limited-entry tables equivalent to the extended-entry tables.

5.46 (g) In processing driving 'license applications of drivers who hold licenses from other states all applicants are given a quiz on road rules. In addition, a driving test is given to applicants under the age of 21, or over the age of 65, and to applicants who have had licenses suspended. Moreover, applicants over 65 have to undergo a medical examination, and applicants under 21 who have had licenses suspended have to attend a course on road safety. Tabulate the data as an extended-entry table, and convert this to a limited-entry table.

5.47 (g) Table 5.7 is an extended-entry decision table in which the top row gives the probability of a data vector matching the corresponding decision rule. Draw a sequential decision tree that corresponds to the table and reduce it to two different trees of four terminal nodes each (rooted at q_1 and q_3, respectively). Assuming that the data vector is passed across the table matrix from the left, arrange the columns in the table matrices of the corresponding limited-entry tables in such a way that the expected number of comparisons is minimized. Which arrangement is the more efficient in this sense?

TABLE 5.7

	0·10	0·25	0·15	0·20	0·05	0·05	0·05	0·15
q_1	Y	Y	Y	Y	N	N	N	N
q_2	Y	Y	N	N	Y	Y	N	N
q_3	Y	N	Y	N	Y	N	Y	N
Action	A1	A3	A1	A2	A1	A1	A1	A1

5.48 (g) Set up interrupted rule mask procedures to correspond to the two reduced decision trees of Exercise 5.47. If the evaluation costs of conditions q_1, q_2, and q_3 are, respectively, 1.5, 4, and 2 units, what is the cost of producing a data vector when the interrupted rule mask technique is not used? Which of the interrupted rule mask procedures is more efficient?

5.49 (g) Assume that each probability in Table 5.7 is $\frac{1}{8}$ (this assumption would have to be made if actual probabilities were not known). Which of the interrupted rule mask procedures of Exercise 5.48 is now the more efficient?

5.50 (g) Consider the procedure that you selected as the more efficient in Exercise 5.49. With each of the three conditions there is associated an estimate of the probability that the condition will have to be evaluated. If for a sufficiently long time counts are kept of the number of times each condition is in fact evaluated, one might find that the assumption of Exercise 5.49 is wrong. It is even possible that the other interrupted rule mask procedure is more efficient. Can any conclusion be made about the relative efficiencies of the two procedures from the counts?

CHAPTER 6

Paths and Cycles in Digraphs

6a. Shortest Path Problems

A road map is a labeled graph. Towns are nodes and roads between towns edges (or, if we want to interpret the map as a digraph, pairs of arcs); mileages are weights. If two towns in a densely populated area are three or four hundred miles apart, very many routes lead from one to the other. The one with the least total mileage is the shortest path. To a motorist setting out from town A, and wishing to reach town B as early as possible, finding the shortest path is a very real practical problem.

Still keeping to the example of roads, the path that is shortest in the sense of least traveling time is not always the path of shortest distance; it may take twice as long to cover 10 miles on a country lane as to go 20 miles on a freeway. Traveling times can therefore be more suitable weights than distances. Costs can also function as weights. In fact, we can take any nonnegative number (under certain conditions even a negative number) for a weight, and define the shortest path problem as the problem of finding a path for which the sum of weights is a minimum. Solutions of the problem are independent of physical interpretation of the weights. The unweighted digraph is merely a special case, interpreted as a weighted digraph with every weight equal to 1. The shortest path given by the general algorithm must then be the path of fewest arcs.

The general shortest path algorithm is itself a special case of an even more general algorithm for paths that are extremal in some sense. The latter is a generalization of the Roy–Warshall algorithm (A.3.1) to Q-semirings. The generalized algorithm will be called the RF algorithm in recognition of Robert and Ferland, who established its general nature. In the specification of the algorithm it will be necessary to introduce conventional arithmetic and the integer 1. To avoid confusion we substitute the notation $\langle Q, \oplus,$ $*, e_1, e_2 \rangle$ for the $\langle Q, +, \cdot, 0, 1 \rangle$ of D.4.8.

ALGORITHM 6.1   The RF algorithm. Let $\langle Q, \oplus, *, e_1, e_2 \rangle$ be a Q-semiring, and define operations $C = A * B$ and $D = A \oplus B$ in the set of square matrices of order n whose elements are members of Q as follows:

$$c_{ij} = (a_{i1} * b_{1j}) \oplus (a_{i2} * b_{2j}) \oplus \cdots \oplus (a_{in} * b_{nj}),$$
$$d_{ij} = a_{ij} \oplus b_{ij}.$$

Let X be a square matrix of order n with elements in Q, and define $X^k = X^{k-1} * X$. The algorithm stops with

$$X^* = X \oplus X^2 \oplus \cdots \oplus X^n.$$

1. Set $X^* = X$.
2. Set $j = 1$.
3. Set $i = 1$.
4. If $x_{ij}^* \neq e_1$, then set $x_{ik}^* = x_{ik}^* \oplus (x_{ij}^* * x_{kj}^*)$ for all k from 1 to n.
5. Set $i = i + 1$. If $i \leqq n$, go to 4.
6. Set $j = j + 1$. If $j \leqq n$, go to 3; else stop.

Examples

1. Consider $\langle R_+^\infty, min, +, \infty, 0 \rangle$, the Q-semiring of Example 2 of D.4.8. In this case the algorithm can be expressed as the following program:

```
SUBROUTINE PATHLS (X, N, RINF)
DIMENSION X(N,N)
DO 10   J = 1,N
DO 10   I = 1,N
IF (X(I,J).EQ.RINF) GO TO 10
DO  5   K = 1,N
5    X(I,K) = AMIN1(X(I,K), X(I,J)+X(J,K))
10   CONTINUE
RETURN
END
```

The subroutine is entered with a matrix of weights (for example, mileages) associated with the arcs. If no arc joins nodes i and j, then the element

X(I , J) is set to RINF, which is a very large number, say 10^{15}. RINF is our "infinity." On return X(I , J) is still equal to RINF if there is no path from i to j; otherwise X(I , J) contains the length of the shortest path from i to j. X(I , I) contains the length of the shortest cycle through node i; If there is no cycle of nonzero length through i, then X(I , I) = RINF.

2. In the case of the Q-semiring (Boolean algebra) $\langle \{0, 1\}, \vee, \wedge, 0, 1 \rangle$ A.6.1 becomes A.3.1.

3. All applications of the RF algorithm relate to a weighted digraph $\langle A, R, Q, W \rangle$, where A is the set of nodes, $R \subseteq A \times A$ is the set of arcs, and function $W : R \rightarrow Q$ associates weights $w_{ij} \in Q$ with all arcs $\langle i, j \rangle \in R$. The status of $\langle i, j \rangle \in A \times A$ determines matrix X of A.6.1: $x_{ij} = w_{ij}$ if $\langle i, j \rangle \in R$; $x_{ij} = e_1$ otherwise. Set Q is defined separately for each application, but every Q is partially ordered by $\oplus$, with $a \geq b$ defined by $a \oplus b = a$ (Exercise 4.18), and this enables us to find a general interpretation of what the x_{ij}^* generated by A.6.1 are. With every path $(i, s, t, \ldots, z, j)$ in the digraph we can associate a *composite* weight $W^{ij} = w_{is} * w_{st} * \cdots * w_{zj}$. Now, if there are m paths from i to j, let the composite weights of these paths be $W_1^{ij}, W_2^{ij}, \ldots, W_m^{ij}$. A.6.1 computes as x_{ij}^* the supremum of the composite weights: $x_{ij}^* \geq W_k^{ij}$ for all $k = 1, 2, \ldots, m$. This means that x_{ij}^* is the composite weight of that path from i to j that is extremal in a sense determined by the particular application. Of course, if there is no path from i to j, then x_{ij}^* remains e_1 (but see Example 4 in which the nonexistence of the path does not imply $x_{ij}^* = e_1$). It is important to note that if $(i, \ldots, u, \ldots, j)$ is extermal, then $x_{ij}^* = x_{iu}^* * x_{uj}^*$.

4. A communications network can be represented by a weighted digraph. The arcs in this digraph represent communications links along which messages are sent, but a link may be subject to failure. Thus, at a particular time, some of the links may be out of action, and no messages get through those links. Here the weights are probabilities: w_{st} is the probability that a message can get through $\langle s, t \rangle$. The appropriate Q-semiring for this application is $\langle [0, 1], max, \cdot, 0, 1 \rangle$, where $[0, 1]$ is the closed unit interval, and $\cdot$ is conventional multiplication (see Exercise 4.17). The extremal path from i to j is the path along which a message originating at i has the greatest likelihood of getting to j. This is called the path of maximal reliability, and x_{ij}^* is the probability of the message getting through *along this path*.

Knowledge of the length alone of a shortest path is rarely sufficient; one has to know the path explicitly. A.6.2 specifies all simple paths and cycles in a digraph. It would seem that it is then an easy matter to find the shortest paths. We shall see that this is not so, but the algorithm is included here anyway because it is interesting in its own right. The algorithm is based on a matrix operation which we shall call symbolic multiplication. Let a square matrix of order n have strings for its elements. The symbolic product $C = AB$ in a set of such matrices is defined by $c_{ij} = a_{i1}b_{1j} + a_{i2}b_{2j} + \cdots + a_{in}b_{nj}$, where $+$ denotes juxtaposition and $a_{ik}b_{kj}$ denotes concatenation if neither a_{ik} nor b_{kj} is null, but $a_{ik}b_{kj} = \Lambda$ if $a_{ik} = \Lambda$ or $b_{kj} = \Lambda$. Juxtaposition is associative; it distributes over concatenation as follows: $\alpha(\beta + \gamma) = \alpha\beta + \alpha\gamma$, $(\beta + \gamma)\alpha = \beta\alpha + \gamma\alpha$. The null string is neutral in juxtaposition: $\Lambda + \alpha = \alpha + \Lambda = \alpha$.

ALGORITHM 6.2   Let the arcs of a digraph with n nodes be identified by symbols a, b, c, ..., and let the symbols be assembled into a variable adjacency matrix V, in which nonexistence of an arc is indicated by the null string Λ.

1.   Define the matrix V_1: for $i, j = 1, 2, \ldots, n$ set $(v_{ii})_1 = \Lambda$ and, if $i \neq j$, set $(v_{ij})_1 = v_{ij}$.
2.   Define the vector D_1 by $(d_i)_1 = v_{ii}$, $i = 1, 2, \ldots, n$.
3.   Set $q = 1$.
4.   If $q = n$, stop; else form the symbolic matrix products $V_L = V_1 V_q$ and $V_R = V_q V_1$.
5.   Define V_{q+1}: for $i, j = 1, 2, \ldots, n$ set $(v_{ii})_{q+1} = \Lambda$ and, if $i \neq j$, make $(v_{ij})_{q+1}$ the juxtaposition of the terms that occur in *both* $(v_{ij})_L$ and $(v_{ij})_R$.
6.   Define D_{q+1} by $(d_i)_{q+1} = (v_{ii})_L = (v_{ii})_R$, $i = 1, 2, \ldots, n$.
7.   Set $q = q + 1$; go to 4.

Element $(v_{ij})_t$, $i \neq j$ represents all simple paths of length t from node i to node j, and $(d_i)_t$ represents all simple cycles of length t through i.

Example

Figure 6.1 shows a digraph and the matrix V associated with the digraph. The sequence of matrices and vectors that follows illustrates application of A.6.2 to this digraph.

$$
V_1 = \begin{bmatrix} \Lambda & a & \Lambda & b \\ \Lambda & \Lambda & c & \Lambda \\ \Lambda & \Lambda & \Lambda & e \\ f & g & h & \Lambda \end{bmatrix} \qquad D_1 = \begin{bmatrix} \Lambda \\ \Lambda \\ d \\ \Lambda \end{bmatrix}
$$

$$
(V_L)_2 = (V_R)_2 = \begin{bmatrix} bf & bg & ac + bh & \Lambda \\ \Lambda & \Lambda & \Lambda & ce \\ ef & eg & eh & \Lambda \\ \Lambda & fa & gc & fb + he \end{bmatrix}
$$

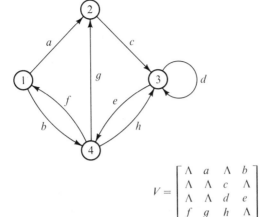

$$V = \begin{bmatrix} \Lambda & a & \Lambda & b \\ \Lambda & \Lambda & c & \Lambda \\ \Lambda & \Lambda & d & e \\ f & g & h & \Lambda \end{bmatrix}$$

Figure 6.1

$$V_2 = \begin{bmatrix} \Lambda & bg & ac+bh & \Lambda \\ \Lambda & \Lambda & \Lambda & ce \\ ef & eg & \Lambda & \Lambda \\ \Lambda & fa & gc & \Lambda \end{bmatrix} \qquad D_2 = \begin{bmatrix} bf \\ \Lambda \\ eh \\ fb+he \end{bmatrix}$$

$$(V_L)_3 = \begin{bmatrix} \Lambda & bfa & bgc & ace \\ cef & ceg & \Lambda & \Lambda \\ \Lambda & efa & egc & \Lambda \\ hef & fbg+heg & fac+fbh & gce \end{bmatrix}$$

$$(V_R)_3 = \begin{bmatrix} \Lambda & \Lambda & bgc & ace+bhe \\ cef & ceg & ceh & \Lambda \\ \Lambda & efa & egc & efb \\ \Lambda & \Lambda & fac & gce \end{bmatrix}$$

$$V_3 = \begin{bmatrix} \Lambda & \Lambda & bgc & ace \\ cef & \Lambda & \Lambda & \Lambda \\ \Lambda & efa & \Lambda & \Lambda \\ \Lambda & \Lambda & fac & \Lambda \end{bmatrix} \qquad D_3 = \begin{bmatrix} \Lambda \\ ceg \\ egc \\ gce \end{bmatrix}$$

$$
(V_L)_4 = \begin{bmatrix} acef & \wedge & bfac & \wedge \\ \wedge & cefa & \wedge & \wedge \\ \wedge & \wedge & efac & \wedge \\ gcef & hefa & fbgc & face \end{bmatrix} \qquad (V_R)_4 = \begin{bmatrix} acef & aceg & aceh & bgce \\ \wedge & cefa & \wedge & cefb \\ \wedge & \wedge & efac & \wedge \\ \wedge & \wedge & \wedge & face \end{bmatrix}
$$

$$
V_4 = \begin{bmatrix} \wedge & \wedge & \wedge & \wedge \\ \wedge & \wedge & \wedge & \wedge \\ \wedge & \wedge & \wedge & \wedge \\ \wedge & \wedge & \wedge & \wedge \end{bmatrix} \qquad D_4 = \begin{bmatrix} acef \\ cefa \\ efac \\ face \end{bmatrix}
$$

Since there can be no simple paths of length n, the purpose of the final iteration is merely to detect Hamiltonian cycles. For this it is sufficient to evaluate just the diagonal elements of $(V_L)_n$ or $(V_R)_n$. Since $(V_L)_2 = (V_R)_2$, the first iteration can be treated as a special case also. In all other iterations it is necessary to compute both products in order to eliminate nonsimple paths.

Undesirable features that make A.6.2 next to useless for the explicit specification of shortest paths should now be noted. First, the algorithm has to be programmed in a language with string processing capabilities. This is not bad in itself, but in most languages that provide string processing capabilities the string operations tend to be significantly slower than arithmetic operations. Secondly, and more importantly, there is the sheer magnitude of the task for larger digraphs. Consider a total digraph on n nodes. In such a digraph there are $1 + \sum_{r=1}^{n-2} P(n-2, r)$ paths from node i to node j, which already amounts to 1957 paths for the rather small $n = 8$. Setting aside questions of time and storage requirements for the generation of the paths, the finding of the shortest path among all these paths is a far from easy matter.

Fortunately, the RF algorithm needs to be modified only slightly to provide enough information for rapid specification of extremal paths. The input to the modified algorithm consists of the matrix X of A.6.1, and a matrix of nodes M that has the same dimensions as X. When the algorithm stops, m_{ik} contains the name (identifying number) of the first intermediate node on an extremal path from i to k, e.g., if this path is $(i, t, \ldots, k)$, then $m_{ik} = t$. Further, m_{tk} contains the first intermediate node on an extremal path from t to k, and so forth. Hence an extremal path from i to k is defined in a reasonably explicit fashion. If more than one extremal path $(i, \ldots, k)$ exists, matrix M specifies just one of the paths, but usually this is all one needs.

ALGORITHM 6.3   RF algorithm with path specification. Let X be a matrix of weights as in A.6.1. A matrix M that has the same dimensions as X is initialized as follows:

$$m_{ik} = k, \quad \text{if } x_{ik} \neq e_1;$$
$$m_{ik} = 0, \quad \text{if } x_{ik} = e_1.$$

We assume that M is supplied for the algorithm as input. Then the algorithm is as A.6.1, with Step 4 changed to

4.   If $x_{ij}^* \neq e_1$, then set $x_{ik}^* = x_{ik}^* \oplus (x_{ij}^* * x_{jk}^*)$ and if x_{ik}^* actually changes value, also set $m_{ik} = m_{ij}$, for all k from 1 to n.

Example

For the shortest path problem A.6.3 can be implemented as subroutine SHORTP. The RINF has the same purpose as in Example 1 of A.6.1, NODES is the M of A.6.3, and NODES is initialized in the subroutine.

```
      SUBROUTINE SHORTP (X,XSTAR,NODES,N,RINF)
      DIMENSION X(N,N), XSTAR(N,N), NODES(N,N)
      DO  5  I = 1,N
      DO  5  J = 1,N
      XSTAR(I,J) = X(I,J)
      NODES(I,J) = 0
    5 IF (X(I,J).NE.RINF) NODES(I,J) = J
      DO 15  J = 1,N
      DO 15  I = 1,N
      IF (XSTAR(I,J).EQ.RINF) GO TO 15
      DO 10  K = 1,N
      T = XSTAR(I,J) + XSTAR(J,K)
      IF (T.GE.XSTAR(I,K)) GO TO 10
      XSTAR(I,K) = T
      NODES(I,K) = NODES(I,J)
   10 CONTINUE
   15 CONTINUE
      RETURN
      END
```

Let the arcs of the digraph of Figure 6.1 be assigned weights according to the following scheme:

a	b	c	d	e	f	g	h
1.0	0.2	0.4	0.2	0.6	0.3	0.7	1.5

Then the input to SHORTP is

$$X = \begin{bmatrix} \infty & 1.0 & \infty & 0.2 \\ \infty & \infty & 0.4 & \infty \\ \infty & \infty & 0.2 & 0.6 \\ 0.3 & 0.7 & 1.5 & \infty \end{bmatrix},$$

and in the loop ending with Statement 5 SHORTP initializes NODES to

$$NODES = \begin{bmatrix} 0 & 2 & 0 & 4 \\ 0 & 0 & 3 & 0 \\ 0 & 0 & 3 & 4 \\ 1 & 2 & 3 & 0 \end{bmatrix}.$$

Subroutine SHORTP returns

$$XSTAR = \begin{bmatrix} 0.5 & 0.9 & 1.3 & 0.2 \\ 1.3 & 1.7 & 0.4 & 1.0 \\ 0.9 & 1.3 & 0.2 & 0.6 \\ 0.3 & 0.7 & 1.1 & 0.5 \end{bmatrix}, \qquad NODES = \begin{bmatrix} 4 & 4 & 4 & 4 \\ 3 & 3 & 3 & 3 \\ 4 & 4 & 3 & 4 \\ 1 & 2 & 2 & 1 \end{bmatrix}.$$

The RF algorithm gives appropriate results, e.g., lengths of shortest paths, for all pairs of nodes in a given network. Frequently, however, one is not interested in all this information. A traveler wishing to go from place a to place b is not concerned with the shortest path from c to d. A.6.3 is an uneconomical procedure for solving the traveler's problem, and we shall now discuss a procedure that is more efficient than the general algorithm for finding shortest paths from a given node to every other node that is reachable from this node.

Let $A = \{a_1, a_2, \ldots, a_n\}$ be the nodes of a network. The problem is to find shortest paths from node a_1 to all other nodes in A that are reachable from a_1. In this preliminary discussion we shall assume that the lengths of the shortest paths are all different. This will prevent introduction of minor technical detail that could obscure the main argument. Two algorithms for this problem will be described, one known as Dantzig's algorithm, the other due to Dijkstra. Although the two algorithms are essentially equivalent, a seemingly minor modification introduced by Dijkstra makes his algorithm significantly faster. Both algorithms will be discussed here to emphasize the importance of rather small details in the design of algorithms.

Let set A be partitioned into sets A_i and $A - A_i$ in such a way that all a_k for which the lengths of the shortest paths $(a_1, \ldots, a_k)$ are already known are in set A_i. Denote the length of the shortest path $(a_1, \ldots, a_k)$ by $c(a_k)$. The basic procedure is to define $A_1 = \{a_1\}$, set $c(a_1) = 0$, and generate A_2, A_3, ... iteratively until an A_m is generated such that $od(A_m) = 0$. Nodes in $A - A_m$, if there are any, are not reachable from a_1. In the $(i - 1)$th iteration the length of the shortest path $(a_1, \ldots, a_k)$ is established in the manner described below for some a_k in $A - A_{i-1}$, and this node is transferred to A_{i-1}, which thus becomes A_i. At the beginning of the ith iteration we compute for all arcs $\langle a_k, a_t \rangle$ that originate at this node a_k and terminate at nodes in $A - A_i$ the values $d_{kt} = c(a_k) + x_{kt}$. This is where the two algorithms begin to differ.

In Dantzig's algorithm the important quantities are the d-values, which are saved from iteration to iteration. Hence in Dantzig's algorithm we now already have from previous iterations the values d_{ik} for all arcs $\langle a_i, a_k \rangle$ such that $a_i \in A_{i-1}$ and $a_k \in A - A_i$, i.e., at this point we have a d-value for every arc that crosses the boundary that surrounds set A_i in the outward direction. Let the smallest of these d-values be d_{uv}. It is easy to prove that this smallest value defines the length of a new shortest path $(a_1, \ldots, a_v)$. We set $c(a_v) = d_{uv}$ and generate A_{i+1} by setting $A_{i+1} = A_i \cup \{a_v\}$.

In Dijkstra's algorithm the d-values are less important. At the very start every node $a_k \in A - \{a_1\}$ is given a label $c(a_k) = \infty$, and the label values are reduced throughout the process until they become the lengths of shortest paths $(a_1, \ldots, a_k)$. The value remains as ∞ only if a_k is not reachable from a_1. We take up from the point at which $d_{kt} = c(a_k) + x_{kt}$ are computed. In Dijkstra's algorithm each d_{kt} is at once compared with the current value $c(a_t)$ and if $d_{kt} < c(a_t)$, then we set $c(a_t) = d_{kt}$. In any case, the d_{kt} is discarded. After all d_{kt} have been found, and the c-values adjusted, the smallest of the c-values labeling nodes in $A - A_i$ is the length of the shortest path from a_1 to the node that carries this label. This is the same a_v that Dantzig's algorithm finds in the ith iteration, and as before we set $A_{i+1} = A_i \cup \{a_v\}$.

ALGORITHM 6.4 Dantzig's algorithm. Given a node a_1 in a weighted digraph $D = \langle A, R \rangle$ with $|A| = n$, and the weights, which must all be nonnegative, defined by matrix X. Let A_m be the set of all nodes reachable from a_1. For each $a_j \in A_m$ the algorithm finds $c(a_j)$, the length of the shortest path from a_1 to a_j, by iteration. Digraph T defines the shortest paths explicitly.

1. Set $A_1 = \{a_1\}$, $c(a_1) = 0$, $i = 1$. Construct a digraph T consisting of a single node a_1.
2. If $od(A_i) = 0$, stop.

3.   For every arc $\langle a_k, a_t \rangle$ such that $a_k \in A_i$ and $a_t \in A - A_i$ compute $d_{kt} = c(a_k) + x_{kt}$.
4.   Set $A_{i+1} = A_i$ and determine $d = min\ d_{kt}$. For every arc $\langle a_u, a_v \rangle$ for which $d_{uv} = d$ (there may be more than one such arc):
   a.   Set $c(a_v) = d$.
   b.   Set $A_{i+1} = A_{i+1} \cup \{a_v\}$.
   c.   In T draw arc $\langle a_k, a_v \rangle$. (T already contains node a_k; node a_v may also be already in T.)
5.   Set $i = i + 1$ and go to 2.

Example

We apply the algorithm to the digraph of Figure 6.2.

$i = 1.$ $A_1 = \{1\}$, $c(1) = 0.0$.
   $d_{12} = 0.0 + 0.1 = 0.1$,
   $d_{13} = 0.0 + 0.7 = 0.7$.
   $d = 0.1$, $c(2) = 0.1$, $A_2 = \{1, 2\}$.

$i = 2.$ $d_{13} = 0.7$,
   $d_{24} = 0.1 + 0.2 = 0.3$,
   $d_{25} = 0.1 + 0.2 = 0.3$.
   $d = 0.3$, $c(4) = c(5) = 0.3$, $A_3 = \{1, 2, 4, 5\}$.

$i = 3.$ $d_{13} = 0.7$,
   $d_{46} = 0.3 + 0.8 = 1.1$,
   $d_{47} = 0.3 + 0.4 = 0.7$,
   $d_{53} = 0.3 + 0.5 = 0.8$,
   $d_{57} = 0.3 + 0.5 = 0.8$.
   $d = 0.7$, $c(3) = c(7) = 0.7$, $A_4 = \{1, 2, 3, 4, 5, 7\}$.

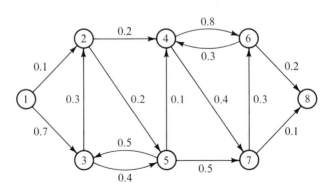

Figure 6.2

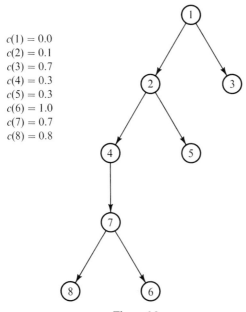

$c(1) = 0.0$
$c(2) = 0.1$
$c(3) = 0.7$
$c(4) = 0.3$
$c(5) = 0.3$
$c(6) = 1.0$
$c(7) = 0.7$
$c(8) = 0.8$

Figure 6.3

$i = 4.$ $d_{46} = 1.1,$
$d_{76} = 0.7 + 0.3 = 1.0,$
$d_{78} = 0.7 + 0.1 = 0.8.$
$d = 0.8,\ c(8) = 0.8,\ A_5 = \{1, 2, 3, 4, 5, 7, 8\}.$

$i = 5.$ $d_{46} = 1.1,$
$d_{76} = 1.0.$
$d = 1.0,\ c(6) = 1.0,\ A_6 = A.$

The results are displayed in Figure 6.3. The tree is a partial subdigraph of the digraph of Figure 6.2.

For the implementation of A.6.4 as a computer program we would need a computer representation of T. If T is a directed tree, with nodes $1, 2, \ldots, n$, then it can be unambiguously specified by just a vector of n elements. Let this vector be t. Then, for all arcs $\langle i, j \rangle$ in the tree, set $t(j) = i$, i.e., set the jth vector element to the name (identifying number) of the predecessor of node j in T. Every node in a directed tree has a unique predecessor except the root. Therefore, setting the vector element corresponding to the root equal to zero completes construction of the representation. The vector representation of the directed tree of Figure 6.3 is

$$t = [0, 1, 1, 2, 2, 7, 4, 7].$$

The path from the root of T to a node i is defined in reverse order by i, $t(i)$, $t(t(i))$, ... For example, the path from the root to node 8 is built up success-ively as $(\ldots, 8)$, $(\ldots, 7, 8)$, $(\ldots, 4, 7, 8)$, $(\ldots, 2, 4, 7, 8)$, $(1, 2, 4, 7, 8)$, at which point we stop because $t(1) = 0$ indicates that the root has been reached.

In general, the T of A.6.4 need not be a directed tree. If there are two or more shortest paths from a_1 to a_j in D, then there are two or more paths from a_1 to a_j in T. However, it is an easy matter to suppress the specification of all but one such path for each node, and then T is a directed tree. In terms of vector t this is done by replacing Step 1 of A.6.4 with

 1'. Set $A_1 = \{a_1\}$, $c(a_1) = 0$, $i = 1$. Set $t(a_j) = 0$ for $j = 1, 2, \ldots, n$.

and Part c of Step 4 with

  c'. Set $t(a_v) = a_k$.

All elements of t are initialized to zero. Then, if a_i is a node that is not rea-chable from a_1, $t(a_i)$ is still zero when the modified A.6.4 stops.

If a digraph contains n nodes, then in the ith iteration of A.6.4, at most $i(n - i)$ values of d_{kt} have to be searched through for a minimum; i.e., there are at most $i(n - i) - 1$ comparisons. The greatest total number of com-parisons that can arise (for a complete symmetric digraph) is therefore $\sum_{i=1}^{n-1} [i(n - i) - 1]$, and it can be shown that this is approximately equal to $n^3/6$. By contrast, the number of comparisons in A.6.3 is n^3 in the worst case.

ALGORITHM 6.5 Dijkstra's algorithm. Given node 1 in a weighted digraph $\langle A, R \rangle$ with $A = \{1, 2, \ldots, n\}$, and the weights, which must be nonnegative, defined by matrix X. When the algorithm stops, B is the set of all nodes reachable from node 1, for each $i \in B$ the value $c(i)$ is the length of the shortest path from 1 to i, and t permits the shortest paths to be explicitly specified in the manner described above.

 1. Set $B = \{1\}$, $c(1) = 0$, $c(2) = c(3) = \cdots = c(n) = \infty$, $t(1) = t(2) = \cdots = t(n) = 0$, $k = 1$.
 2. For every arc $\langle k, j \rangle$ such that $j \in A - B$ set $c(j) = min(c(j), c(k) + x_{kj})$ and, if $c(j)$ actually changes value, also set $t(j) = k$.
 3. Find $k \in A - B$ such that $c(k) \neq \infty$, and $c(k) \ngtr c(i)$ for all $i \in A - B$. If no such k exists, stop; else set $B = B \cup \{k\}$ and go to 2.

Examples

1. For the weighted digraph of Figure 6.2 the algorithm goes through seven iterations.

$i = 1.$ $c = (0, 0.1, 0.7, \infty, \infty, \infty, \infty, \infty)$,
   $t = (0, 1, 1, 0, 0, 0, 0, 0)$,
   $B = \{1, 2\}$.

$i = 2.$ $c = (0, 0.1, 0.7, 0.3, 0.3, \infty, \infty, \infty)$,
$\quad\quad t = (0, 1, 1, 2, 2, 0, 0, 0)$,
$\quad\quad B = \{1, 2, 4\}$.

$i = 3.$ $c = (0, 0.1, 0.7, 0.3, 0.3, 1.1, 0.7, \infty)$,
$\quad\quad t = (0, 1, 1, 2, 2, 4, 4, 0)$,
$\quad\quad B = \{1, 2, 4, 5\}$.

$i = 4.$ Vectors c and t do not change,
$\quad\quad B = \{1, 2, 3, 4, 5\}$.

$i = 5.$ Vectors c and t do not change,
$\quad\quad B = \{1, 2, 3, 4, 5, 7\}$.

$i = 6.$ $c = (0, 0.1, 0.7, 0.3, 0.3, 1.0, 0.7, 0.8)$,
$\quad\quad t = (0, 1, 1, 2, 2, 7, 4, 7)$,
$\quad\quad B = \{1, 2, 3, 4, 5, 6, 7\}$.

$i = 7.$ Vectors c and t do not change,
$\quad\quad B = \{1, 2, 3, 4, 5, 6, 7, 8\}$.

2. One application of A.6.5 is in the design of a distribution network for some utility (gas, water, etc.). If node a_1 stands for a supply station, and nodes a_2, a_3, ... represent localities to which the utility is to be supplied, then A.6.5 can be used to produce the most economical layout of supply lines.

In the ith iteration of A.6.5 at most $n - i$ d-values have to be compared against existing c-values, and at most $n - i$ c-values have to be searched for a minimum, i.e., the greatest number of comparisons that can arise for the entire algorithm is $\sum_{i=1}^{n-1} 2(n - i) - 1 = (n - 1)^2$. Thus the speed of A.6.5 depends on n^2, while A.6.4 has an n^3 time dependence. However, for some digraphs with few arcs A.6.4 may be faster.

Dijkstra's algorithm, too, can be generalized to Q-semirings. We shall define the generalized algorithm and prove its validity.

ALGORITHM 6.6   Generalized Dijkstra algorithm. Given node i in a weighted digraph with the node set $A = \{1, 2, \ldots, n\}$, and a matrix of weights X, the elements of which are in Q-semiring $\langle Q, \oplus, *, e_1, e_2 \rangle$. The algorithm computes as $c(j)$ the composite weights of extremal paths from node i to all other nodes j in A. If the algorithm stops with a $c(j)$ equal to e_1, then there is no path from i to j. Vector t gives an explicit specification of the extremal paths in the manner described above.

1.   Set $B = \{i\}$, $c(i) = e_2$, $c(1) = \cdots = c(i - 1) = c(i + 1) = \cdots = c(n)$
$\quad = e_1$, $t(1) = t(2) = \cdots = t(n) = 0$. Select node i for the k of Step 3.
2.   If $B = A$, stop.

3. For all $j \in A - B$ set $c(j) = c(j) \oplus (c(k) * x_{kj})$, and if $c(j)$ actually changes value, also set $t(j) = k$.
4. Set $v = e_1$.
5. For all $j \in A - B$ set $v = v \oplus c(j)$.
6. Set $B = B \cup \{k\}$, where k is a node in $A - B$ such that $c(k) = v$. Go to 2.

THEOREM 6.1   The $c(j)$ found by A.6.6 are indeed the quantities defined in the preamble of A.6.6.

Proof. The proof is by induction, with the induction step as follows. On reaching Step 4 in a particular iteration of the algorithm the nodes are partitioned in sets B and $A - B$. Suppose that the c-values of nodes in B are composite weights of extremal paths from i to these nodes, i.e., that $c(j) = x_{ij}^*$ for all $j \in B - \{i\}$, where x_{ij}^* are elements of the ith row of matrix X^* as computed by A.6.1. Consider all sets of paths $(i, \ldots, u)$ that terminate at nodes $u \in A - B$, but otherwise pass entirely over nodes in B. We suppose further that $c(u)$ is the composite weight of the extremal path in a set of such paths $(i, \ldots, u)$. Steps 4 and 5 find the supremum of the c-values of nodes in $A - B$, and, on the basis of this determination, node k is transferred to B in Step 6. If the extremal path is $(i, \ldots, j, k)$, where all $i, \ldots, j \in B$, then $c(k) = x_{ik}^*$ on the basis of the second assumption above. Suppose, however, that the extremal path is $(i, \ldots, j, \ldots, k)$, where j is still in $A - B$, but all nodes preceding it on the path are in B. Then $x_{ik}^* = x_{ij}^* * x_{jk}^* = c(j) * x_{ik}^*$. But, since $c(j) \geqq c(j) * b$ for all $b \in Q$ (Exercise 4.18), then $c(j) \geqq c(j) * x_{jk}^*$ in particular. Thus we have $c(j) \geqq x_{ik}^*$, and, since $c(k)$ is the supremum of the c-values of nodes in $A - B$, also $c(k) \geqq c(j)$, giving $c(k) \geqq x_{ik}^*$. However, since x_{ik}^* is the supremum of the composite weights of all paths from i to k, $x_{ik}^* \geqq c(k)$. Thus again $c(k) = x_{ik}^*$, i.e., the property assumed above for nodes in B is established. Subsequent execution of Step 3 restores to set $A - B$ the property assumed for the $c(u)$.

The list of nodes that remain in $A - B$ can be maintained in two ways. The simplest is to initialize all elements of a vector u by setting $u(i) = 0$, $u(1) = \cdots = u(i - 1) = u(i + 1) = \cdots = u(n) = 1$. Element $u(k)$ is set to zero when node k is transferred to set B in Step 6 of A.6.6. Set $A - B$ is then defined by subscripts of the elements in u that have value 1. In the second method u is initialized by setting $u(j) = j$ for $j = 2, \ldots, n$ and then $u(i) = 1$ [it does not matter what $u(1)$ is]. The first time Step 3 is reached, $A - B$ is defined by values of $u(2), \ldots, u(n)$. Assume that the nodes selected in Step 6 are $k_2, k_3, \ldots$ in successive iterations $(k_1 = i)$. During selection of k_t, one determines $s \in \{t, t + 1, \ldots, n\}$ such that $u(s) = k_t$, and then $u(s)$ is set to the value of $u(t)$. Set $A - B$ is then defined by values of $u(t + 1), u(t + 2), \ldots, u(n)$.

If one is merely interested in finding a single extremal path $(i, \ldots, j)$, then the generalized Dijkstra algorithm can be applied from node i and also, in a "backward" sense, from node j. For a network with many nodes and few arcs this two-ended algorithm may be more efficient than A.6.6. However, since the extremal path may be Hamiltonian, in which case the extremal path $(i, \ldots, j)$ necessarily specifies extremal paths from i to *every* other node in the network, we would not expect that the efficiency of the algorithm could be improved further in general. Indeed, in the worst case, the number of times operations $\oplus$ and $*$ are performed in the two-ended algorithm is about 50% higher than in A.6.6.

ALGORITHM 6.7 Two-ended generalized Dijkstra algorithm. Given nodes i and j in a weighted digraph with the node set $A = \{1, 2, \ldots, n\}$ $(n \geq 2)$, and a matrix of weights X, the elements of which are in Q-semiring $\langle Q, \oplus, *, e_1, e_2 \rangle$. The algorithm computes the composite weight x_{ij}^* by application of A.6.6 in forward and backward directions. In the forward direction the algorithm builds up set B; in the backward direction it builds up B'. In each iteration the direction is chosen on the basis of the test in Step 2.

1. Set $B = \{i\}$, $B' = \{j\}$. Set $c(k) = c'(k) = e_1$ for all $k = 1, 2, \ldots, n$, and then set $c(i) = c'(j) = e_2$. Select node i for the k of Step 3, and node j for the m of Step 5.
2. If $od(B) > id(B')$, then go to Step 5.
3. For all $t \in A - B$ set $c(t) = c(t) \oplus (c(k) * x_{kt})$.
4. Find the supremum of the c-values of all nodes in $A - B$, and let any node whose c-value is the supremum be k (see Steps 4 and 5 of A.6.6). If $k \in B'$, go to 7; else set $B = B \cup \{k\}$ and go to 2.
5. For all $t \in A - B'$ set $c'(t) = c'(t) \oplus (c'(m) * x_{tm})$.
6. Find the supremum of the c'-values of all nodes in $A - B'$, and let any node whose c'-value is the supremum be m. If $m \notin B$, set $B' = B' \cup \{m\}$ and go to 2.
7. For all $s \in B$, $t \in B'$, compute $d_{st} = c(s) * c'(t) * x_{st}$. The supremum of the d-values is x_{ij}^*.

The algorithm terminates when a node q is found that should be made a member of one of the sets B or B', but already belongs to the other of the sets. The quantity $c(q) * c'(q)$ need not be the composite weight of the extremal path from i to j; it is merely the composite weight of the extremal path from i to j *through* q. However, it is easy to show that the procedure of Step 7 is sufficient for finding x_{ij}^*. There is no loss of generality in assuming that Step 7 is reached from Step 4. Then we have a path $(i, \ldots, k, \ldots, j)$. Suppose that the extremal path is $(i, \ldots, s, \ldots, u, \ldots, t, \ldots, j)$, where only the nodes defining subpath $(i, \ldots, s)$ are in B, and only nodes defining $(t, \ldots, j)$ are in B'.

Since u belongs to neither B nor B', we have $x_{ik}^* \geqq x_{iu}^*$ and $x_{kj}^* \geqq x_{uj}^*$. Consequently (Exercise 4.18), $x_{ik}^* * x_{kj}^* \geqq x_{iu}^* * x_{uj}^*$, and, by the assumption that $(i, \ldots, u, \ldots, j)$ is extremal, $x_{iu}^* * x_{uj}^* \geqq x_{ik}^* * x_{kj}^*$, i.e., $x_{ik}^* * x_{kj}^* = x_{iu}^* * x_{uj}^*$. Hence either $(i, \ldots, k, \ldots, j)$ is extremal, or, if $(i, \ldots, s, \ldots, u, \ldots, t, \ldots, j)$ is in fact extremal, u belongs to B or B', so that the extremal path is $(i, \ldots, s, t, \ldots, j)$. In either case Step 7 does find x_{ij}^*.

Another interesting problem is that of finding a *longest* simple path from one node to another. Although the problem appears to be related to the shortest path problem, the RF algorithm cannot be used to solve it in the general case. The minimization process of the algorithm for shortest paths necessarily produces simple paths. Suppose now that a try is being made to derive a longest path by maximization. If there exists a simple path $(a, \ldots, c, \ldots, b)$, but there is a cycle through c, then the " length " of the path $(a, \ldots, b)$ can be made arbitrarily large by going round and round the cycle (this is the reason why we have not formally defined the length of a nonsimple path, see D.3.7). Another difficulty is this: In the shortest path problem, if $(a, c, \ldots, b)$ is a shortest path from a to b, then the subpath $(c, \ldots, b)$ is a shortest path from c to b, a property on which the shortest path algorithm is based; if, on the other hand, $(a, c, \ldots, b)$ is a longest simple path from a to b, there may well exist a simple path $(c, a, \ldots, b)$ that is longer than the subpath $(c, \ldots, b)$ of $(a, c, \ldots, b)$.

Acyclic digraphs provide an exception. In matrix X of the example of A.6.3 make all weights greater than zero, letting $x_{ij} = 0$ indicate nonexistence of arc $\langle i, j \rangle$. Define semigroups $\langle R_+, max, 0 \rangle$ and $\langle R_+, \perp \rangle$, where R_+ is the set of non-negative real numbers and operation $\perp$ is defined as follows: $a \perp b = a + b$ if neither a nor b is zero, but $a \perp 0 = 0 \perp a = 0$. We can find no identity element for $\langle R_+, \perp \rangle$, i.e., R_+ cannot be a semiring. This is a consequence of the difficulties mentioned in the paragraph above. But, if the digraph with adjacency matrix X is acyclic, then, with operations $\oplus$ and $*$ interpreted as *max* and $\perp$, respectively, A.6.1 gives lengths of longest paths, and a program similar to A.6.3 can be used to find these paths (Exercise 6.16).

6b. Cycles

A.3.1 is an algorithm for detecting the presence of cycles in a digraph: Node i lies on a cycle if $x_{ii}^* = 1$ in the path matrix. Computation of an $n \times n$ path matrix by A.3.1 may, however, take as many as n^3 operations. A faster method to determine for just one node a_i whether or not this node lies on a cycle derives from A.6.7. Let A.6.7 be used as a shortest path algorithm with $B = B' = \{a_i\}$ initially. Eventually the algorithm finds explicitly a simple cycle of shortest length through a_i, but, since B and B' are not disjoint in this application, A.6.7 has to be subjected to several minor modifications (Exercise 6.20).

One application of the set of cycles through a given node arises with K-formulas. Let $\{k_1, k_2, \ldots, k_m\}$ be a minimal set of K-formulas of a digraph. The leading nodes of these K-formulas define a node base of the digraph. Let a_i be the leading node of k_i, and let A_i be the set of nodes that lie on cycles through a_i (we assume that a_i lies on a cycle of zero length in any case, i.e., that A_i contains at least a_i). Set A_i can be generated by taking the subdigraph defined by k_i, and applying the procedure based on A.6.7 to leading node a_i. Let us generate $A_1, A_2, \ldots, A_m$. These sets define all node bases of the digraph. The number of different node bases is $\prod_{i=1}^{m} |A_i|$, and a node base is found by taking exactly one node from each A_i.

Suppose there is a fast algorithm for finding the strong components of a digraph. Then Th.3.10 suggests a procedure for generating all node bases of a digraph more readily. One way of finding the strong components is given by the solution of Exercise 3.30. The composite algorithm suggested there generates path matrices, and the time dependence of A.3.1 for path matrices is n^3, where n is the number of nodes in the digraph. Hence the time dependence of the composite algorithm cannot be better than n^3. A faster algorithm for finding strong components, based on K-trees, has only n^2 time dependence. To be able to use this algorithm we first need an algorithm for merging atomic K-trees of all nodes of a digraph into a single K-tree or a set of K-trees.

ALGORITHM 6.8   An algorithm for merging atomic K-trees. Let the atomic K-trees of nodes 1, 2, ..., n of a digraph $D = \langle A, R \rangle$ be collected into a list $L: t_1, t_2, \ldots, t_n$. Note that if node $k \in A$ has no arcs originating from it, then t_k consists of just a root node.

1.   Set $i = 1$.
2.   Take the leftmost atomic tree that is still in L, name it T_i, and delete it from L.
3.   If L is now empty, stop with K-trees $T_1, T_2, \ldots, T_i$ ($i \leqq n$) representing D.
4.   Select the leftmost unprocessed terminal node of T_i for processing. For the purposes of Step 5 assume that this terminal node is labeled k.
5.   If t_k is in L, replace the terminal node k by the atomic tree t_k, delete t_k from L, and go to 3.
6.   Traverse T_i in a left to right direction from the terminal node that has just been processed until another terminal node is

reached. Select this node for processing, i.e., assume that it is labeled k for the purposes of Step 5 and go to Step 5. If no more terminal nodes are encountered in the traversal, set $i = i + 1$ and go to 2.

Examples

1. The labels carried by nonterminal nodes of any K-tree produced by A.6.8 are distinct, but more than one terminal node may carry the same label, and more often than not this label is associated with a nonterminal node as well.

2. Figure 6.4 shows a digraph and the atomic K-trees of its nodes, and Figure 6.5 displays the stages in the construction of a K-tree that represents this digraph. Consider the construction of (d) from (c). K-tree (c) was produced by attaching the atomic K-tree of node 3 to the leftmost node carrying label 3 in K-tree (b) in Step 5 of A.6.8. We go to Step 3, and since L is not empty, to Step 4. The leftmost unprocessed terminal node in K-tree (c) is now the node 1 introduced as part of the atomic tree of node 3. There is no longer a t_1 in L, and we go to Step 6. Terminal node 4 is reached next, and we return to Step 5. Atomic tree t_4 is degenerate, so all we have to do is delete t_4 from L and go to Step 3. Set L is still not empty, and when we now move into Step 4, the terminal node selected for processing carries label 5. Hence, in Step 5, t_5 is attached to this node to produce K-tree (d). In this instance T_1 is the only K-tree generated. Th.3.13 tells us that the number of K-trees T_i generated by A.6.8 is at least equal to the number of nodes in a node base of the digraph. We prove below that the arcs belonging to any one strong component of the digraph are all to be found in the one K-tree.

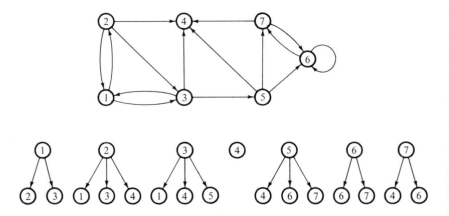

Figure 6.4

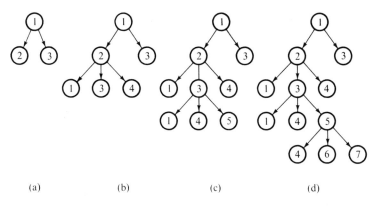

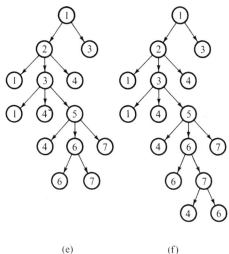

Figure 6.5

THEOREM 6.2 Let A.6.8 generate a representation of a digraph D in terms of K-trees T_i. If S is a strong component of D, then the entire representation of S is confined to a single K-tree T_k, i.e., T_k contains all arcs of S.

Proof. Every arc is of S in some K-tree or other. Let T_k be the first K-tree to be constructed that contains at least one arc of S, and denote this arc by $\langle a_1, a_j \rangle$. We have as a simple consequence of Th.3.9 that all nodes of S lie on a cycle. Then, in particular, node a_1 lies on this cycle, and we write the cycle as $(a_1, a_2, \ldots, a_i, \ldots, a_m, a_1)$. Now, if $\langle a_1, a_j \rangle$ is in T_k, then so is $\langle a_1, a_2 \rangle$ because T_k must contain the entire atomic K-tree of node a_1. For the induction step assume that $\langle a_1, a_2 \rangle, \langle a_2, a_3 \rangle, \ldots, \langle a_{i-1}, a_i \rangle$ of the cycle are in T_k, and prove that $\langle a_i, a_{i+1} \rangle$ is also in T_k. A nonterminal node a_i must exist because of the fact that node a_i lies on a cycle. This node cannot belong to a tree constructed before T_k is constructed because no arc of S, in particular $\langle a_i, a_{i+1} \rangle$, can be in such a tree. Further, the nonterminal a_i cannot be in a tree constructed after T_k has been constructed because then the a_i of the $\langle a_{i-1}, a_i \rangle$ in T_k would have been a terminal node at the time the construction of T_k was completed, with the atomic tree of a_i still in list L. The specification of A.6.8 precludes such a possibility. Hence the nonterminal node a_i is in T_k, and arc $\langle a_i, a_{i+1} \rangle$ is then in T_k. This implies that every node of S is in T_k as a nonterminal node, and hence all arcs orginating from nodes in S are in T_k.

   In discussing the K-tree representation of a digraph on nodes $A = \{1, 2, \ldots, n\}$ a clear distinction must be made between the identifying names of the nodes of the K-tree, which must be all distinct, and the labels associated with the nodes, which are the identifying names of the nodes of the digraph, and which need not be distinct in the K-tree. We shall use letters $a, b, c, \ldots$ for the identifying names of nodes of the K-tree, and denote the set of these names by T. Figure 6.6 illustrates this distinction. We define a function $G : T \to A$ such that $G(x)$ is the label assigned to node x of the K-tree. Then, with regard to Figure 6.6, $G(a) = G(n) = 1$, $G(h) = G(l) = G(o) = 7$, $G(b) = 2$, etc.

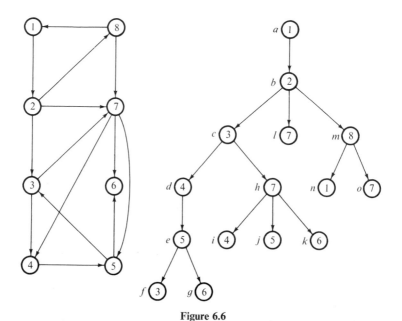

Figure 6.6

For the purposes of A.6.9 we introduce three partial functions from T into T. They are, respectively, the leftmost successor function $L(x)$, the predecessor function $P(x)$, and the right neighbor function $N(x)$. Function $L(x)$ is defined for nonterminal nodes alone, function $P(x)$ for all nodes except the root, and function $N(x)$ for those nodes that have neighbors on the right in the K-tree. Both L and N depend on how the tree is drawn, i.e., on the left to right order of the sets of neighbors. With respect to Figure 6.6 we have $L(a) = b$, $L(b) = c$, $L(e) = f$, but $L(f)$ and $L(n)$ are undefined; $P(a)$ is undefined, but $P(c) = P(l) = P(m) = b$, and $P(e) = d$; $N(a)$ is undefined, and so are $N(g)$ and $N(h)$, but $N(i) = j$ and $N(j) = k$, and $N(f) = g$.

ALGORITHM 6.9　A fast algorithm for the strong components of a digraph $D = \langle A, R \rangle$ with $A = \{1, 2, \ldots, n\}$. The input to the algorithm is the K-tree representation of D as generated by A.6.8. For clarity it is assumed that the digraph is represented by a single K-tree; it is not difficult to rephrase it for the general case (Exercise 6.21). The algorithm makes use of a vector S of n elements, and of a stack of maximal depth n. When the algorithm stops S defines the strong components: Nodes $i, j \in A$ belong to the same strong component if and only if $S(i) = S(j)$. Functions G, L, P, and N are defined above.

1. Set $S(J) = 0$ for $J = 1, 2, \ldots, n$. Set $I = 0$. Let the root of the K-tree be node a for the purposes of Step 2.
2. Set $K = G(a)$. If $S(K) \neq 0$, go to 4; else set $I = I + 1$, $S(K) = I$.
3. If $L(a)$ is defined, set $a = L(a)$, push down K, and go to 2.
4. If K is in the stack, set $x = P(a)$, $Q = G(x)$, $S(Q) = min(S(Q), S(K))$.
5. If $N(a)$ is defined, set $a = N(a)$ and go to 2.
6. Set $a = P(a)$, $K = G(a)$. If a is now the root of the K-tree, empty the stack and stop; else set $x = P(a)$, $Q = G(x)$, $S(Q) = min(S(Q), S(K))$.
7. If $S(Q) < S(K)$, pop up labels from the stack until a label equal to K is popped up. In any case go to 5.

Examples

1. A.6.9 applied to the K-tree of Figure 6.6 produces

$$J = 1 \quad 2 \quad 3 \quad 4 \quad 5 \quad 6 \quad 7 \quad 8$$
$$S(J) = 1 \quad 1 \quad 3 \quad 3 \quad 3 \quad 6 \quad 3 \quad 1$$

Hence the strong components are defined by the node sets $\{1, 2, 8\}$, $\{3, 4, 5, 7\}$, and $\{6\}$. The basic action of A.6.9 is the left to right traversal of the K-tree that the algorithm receives as input. There is only one way of gaining an understanding of what happens during the traversal. One must take paper and pencil, apply the algorithm to an actual K-tree, and follow through the processing of that K-tree step by step.

2. While a K-tree is being constructed by A.6.8 it is in effect being traversed. Consequently appreciable processing time would be saved if A.6.8 and A.6.9 were combined into a single algorithm in which there would be just the one traversal of the K-tree.

3. If A.6.9 is to be implemented as a computer program, we need a computer representation of a K-tree. Note that A.6.9 makes no reference to the K-tree as such, but rather to the functions G, L, P, and N. In fact, functions G, L, and N provide a complete specification of a K-tree. Consider how the function L can be represented by a vector L of m elements, where m is the number of nodes in the K-tree (which is one more than the number of arcs in the digraph from which the K-tree derives). We associate nodes a, b, c, ... of the K-tree with elements 1, 2, 3, ... of vector L. In effect, we are changing the identifying names a, b, c, ... to identifying names 1, 2, 3, ... In the K-tree of Figure 6.6 we have, for example, $L(a) = b$ and $L(h) = i$, or, under the renaming, L(1) = 2 and L(8) = 9. If L is undefined for some node, as for example $L(f)$ is undefined, the appropriate element of L is made zero. Here f becomes 6 in the renaming, and L(6) = 0. A vector N, representing function N, is constructed similarly. Figure 6.7 shows vectors G, L, and N for the K-tree of Figure 6.6. There is no need for an explicit specification of the predecessor function for all m nodes. As the K-tree is traversed, we hold in vector P the nodes that define the path from the root of the K-tree to the predecessor of the node we have reached. Entries in P

		G	L	N
a	1	1	2	0
b	2	2	3	0
c	3	3	4	12
d	4	4	5	8
e	5	5	6	0
f	6	3	0	7
g	7	6	0	0
h	8	7	9	0
i	9	4	0	10
j	10	5	0	11
k	11	6	0	0
l	12	7	0	13
m	13	8	14	0
n	14	1	0	15
o	15	7	0	0

Figure 6.7

change during the traversal, but P needs to have only n elements, where n is the number of nodes in the original digraph. Thus, when we are at node $f(=6)$, P is [1 2 3 4 5 0 0 0], and when we have reached node k ($=11$), P is [1 2 3 7 0 0 0 0]. By keeping count of how many node names there are currently in P we can always determine the predecessor of the node that we have just reached. Vector P is in effect a stack. Finally, in Step 4 of A.6.9 we have to know whether a particular K is in the stack. This can always be established by reference to a logical vector YES of n elements. Initially all elements of YES are made .FALSE.. When K is pushed down, we set YES(K) = .TRUE., and when it is popped up, we set YES(K) = .FALSE.. Then YES(K) is .TRUE. if and only if K is in the stack.

We are now ready to deal with the generation of all simple cycles in a digraph. A list of all simple cycles may assist in the testing of pairs of digraphs for isomorphism by the heuristic method of Section 3g. For another example, the structure of the flow of control in a computer program may be represented by a digraph. The loops of the program become cycles in the digraph model, and it is necessary to have a list of all the simple cycles when program optimization, program segmentation, or related problems are studied with the aid of the model. These problems will be discussed in Chapter 7. Note also that an algorithm for finding cycles can be used to find the longest simple path from node a to node b. If the digraph does not contain arc $\langle b, a \rangle$ already, add it to the digraph. Simple cycles $(a, \ldots, b, a)$ then define simple paths $(a, \ldots, b)$, and the longest of the cycles defines the longest simple path from a to b. However, as we noted in our discussion of A.6.2, there may be many simple paths $(a, \ldots, b)$, and the determination of the longest of them is then by no means trivial.

In an algorithm for finding cycles it is not necessary to process the entire digraph. Instead, each strong component of a digraph can be processed on its own. This may substantially reduce the time requirement of the algorithm. A.6.9 can be looked upon as a valuable preprocessing algorithm for a cycle finding algorithm. Of course, if the digraph is strongly connected, the preprocessing time becomes pure overhead. Since A.6.9 produces the strong components as K-trees, our first algorithm for finding cycles is based on K-trees. A.6.10 is an informal, but precise statement of this algorithm.

ALGORITHM 6.10 A K-tree algorithm for the simple cycles of a digraph. Suppose that K-trees $T_1, T_2, \ldots, T_m$ represent the strong components of a digraph D that consist of more than one node. The following procedure is to be applied to *each* of the trees $T_1, T_2, \ldots, T_m$. Enter the K-tree representing the strong component at the root and initiate a left to right traversal of the tree. Interrupt the traversal when a terminal node is reached. Assume that the terminal node is k. If the path from the root of the

K-tree to this node contains a subpath $(h, \ldots, k)$ such that $G(h) = G(k)$ and neither node h nor any node preceding it on the path from the root carries a marker, then output the G-values associated with the subpath $(h, \ldots, k)$, namely $(G(h), \ldots, G(k))$. Else, if there exists a nonterminal node d such that $G(d) = G(k)$ that is not on the path from the root to k, detach the subtree rooted at d from its present position ("prune" it, leaving d where it is, as a terminal node now), replace node k by this subtree ("graft" it on), and attach a marker to k (all nodes are assumed to be unmarked initially). In any case resume the traversal until the next terminal node is encountered, in which case again carry out the interrupt procedure defined above. Stop when the traversal has been completed, i.e., when the root of the K-tree is reached, and all arcs leading out of the root have already been traversed.

Examples

1. If the only criterion for the selection of the G-values associated with a subpath $(h, \ldots, k)$ for output as a cycle were that $G(h) = G(k)$, then the same cycle could get put out more than once. It will be proven as Th.6.4 that elimination of duplicates is ensured if it is further required that at least one arc of $(h, \ldots, k)$ still occupies its initial position in the K-tree, i.e., has not been moved by pruning and grafting at the time node k is reached. The markers permit it to be established whether or not this additional requirement is satisfied. If a node sequence $(h, \ldots, k)$ is a path in a K-tree, then the sequence of labels $(G(h), \ldots, G(k))$ is always a path in the original digraph. Therefore there is no great loss of precision if we identify paths in the K-tree as well by sequences of labels attached to the nodes of the K-tree rather than by sequences of the identifying names of these nodes. We shall do so in what follows.

2. Figure 6.8 shows a digraph, and K-tree (a) of Figure 6.9 is the representation of this digraph produced by A.6.8. The K-trees of Figure 6.9 illustrate successive stages in the traversal. In tree (a) traversal takes us from the root along the leftmost path to terminal node 1. Path (1, 2, 1) defines a cycle, and is put out. On resumption of traversal, nonterminal node 2 is revisited, and

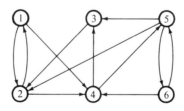

Figure 6.8

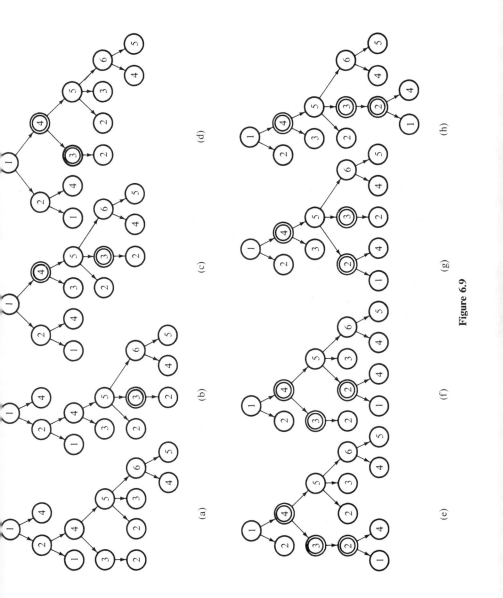

Figure 6.9

293

from there downward travel takes us to terminal node 2. The path from the root to this node contains subpath (2, 4, 3, 2), which defines a cycle. This cycle is put out, and traversal is resumed. In similar fashion cycle (2, 4, 5, 2) is generated, and then we arrive at terminal node 3. The path (1, 2, 4, 2, 3) does not contain a subpath of the form (3, ..., 3), but there is a nonterminal node 3 not on path (1, 2, 4, 5, 3). The pruning and grafting that now ensues produces tree (b). Note that node 3 is marked as part of this operation; marking is indicated by double circles in Figure 6.9. From our node 3, which has now become nonterminal, we reach terminal node 2. The path to be examined is (1, 2, 4, 5, 3, 2). It contains subpath (2, 4, 5, 3, 2), which defines a cycle for output. At the next terminals to be visited we put out cycles (4, 5, 6, 4) and (5, 6, 5). From terminal node 5 we back up in the tree, ultimately returning to the root. Arc $\langle 1, 4 \rangle$ then leads to terminal node 4, and pruning and grafting now produces K-tree (c). After traversal of arc $\langle 4, 3 \rangle$ in this tree further pruning and grafting is called for, and the result is (d). In this tree, too, pruning and grafting takes place after traversal of just one arc, and tree (e) is produced. Traversal in K-tree (e) results in output of cycle (1, 4, 3, 2, 1), and then node 4 is reached. Here the path from the root is (1, 4, 3, 2, 4), and it contains a subpath of the form (4, ..., 4), but there is no output because the nonterminal 4 is marked. Pruning and grafting again takes place when the next terminal is reached, and the result is (f). Traversal of this K-tree produces output (1, 4, 5, 2, 1). Next tree (g) is generated, no cycles are produced in the traversal of this tree, and it is transformed into K-tree (h). After output of cycle (1, 4, 5, 3, 2, 1), which occurs after traversal of just one arc in tree (h), the final interrupt occurs at terminal node 5. Here the path from the root is (1, 4, 5, 6, 5), and it contains subpath (5, 6, 5), but we suppress output because of the marked node 4 preceding the nonterminal 5 in (1, 4, 5, 6, 5). From terminal node 5 we back up to the root, and traversal is complete on reaching the root.

We shall now prove the validity of A.6.10. There are three parts to the validity proof of an algorithm. It has to be proven that the algorithm does what it is supposed to do, that it does only what it is supposed to do, and that it terminates. In most cases one or other of these three parts is trivial. A.6.10 provides an interesting exception. It is not at all obvious that A.6.10 outputs all cycles of a digraph, and that no cycle is duplicated in the output. Even that A.6.10 stops is not all that obvious.

THEOREM 6.3   Algorithm 6.10 finds every simple cycle of digraph D.

Proof. If A.6.10 finds every simple cycle in a particular strong component S of D, then it must find all simple cycles of D. Hence it suffices to show that for any simple cycle C belonging to S the algorithm establishes a path defining this cycle in the K-tree of S. Write the cycle as $(c_1, c_2, \ldots, c_k, c_1)$, where $\langle c_1, c_2 \rangle$ is that arc of C that is first reached in the traversal of the K-tree. Clearly the path defined by arc $\langle c_1, c_2 \rangle$ exists in the tree at all times, but it has to be shown that when this arc is first traversed, there has been no opportunity to disturb node c_1 by pruning and grafting, i.e., that arc $\langle c_1, c_2 \rangle$ has not been moved prior to this time. This is ensured by A.6.8, which requires that every atomic tree be introduced into the partially constructed tree as far to the left as possible. Our K-tree S is a K-tree generated by A.6.8, or it has been obtained from such a K-tree by removal of arcs without otherwise disturbing it, and thus every atomic tree is initially in S as far to the left as possible. Hence, for every nonterminal node c_i on the path from the root of the K-tree of S to nonterminal node c_1, no terminal nodes labeled c_i can exist in the part of the tree traversed in getting to the nonterminal c_i. Further, since any terminal c_i that is reached in the traversal from nonterminal node c_i to nonterminal node c_1 is in the subtree rooted at the nonterminal c_i, there is no opportunity for pruning and grafting that would disturb nonterminal node c_1 in this stage of the traversal **either**. Similarly, no such opportunity presents itself in the traversal from the c_1 to the c_2 of $\langle c_1, c_2 \rangle$. This is the base for an induction proof. For the induction step assume that subpath $(c_1, c_2, \ldots, c_m)$ of C can be established by A.6.10, and that the traversal of the tree has taken us to node c_m on this subpath. It will now be shown that subpath $(c_1, c_2, \ldots, c_m, c_{m+1})$ of C can be established. Either the c_m of the subpath is nonterminal, in which case we already have $(c_1, \ldots, c_m, c_{m+1})$, or c_m is a terminal node. In the latter case we know that the nonterminal c_m does not lie on the path from the root of the tree to our terminal c_m. Hence the subtree rooted at the nonterminal c_m can be pruned from its present location and grafted on in place of our terminal c_m. This produces $(c_1, \ldots, c_m, c_{m+1})$. The earlier argument makes it obvious that traversal from c_m to c_{m+1} does not disturb any node on the path from the root to this c_{m+1}. It follows that the path $(c_1, c_2, \ldots, c_k, c_1)$ can be produced, and that terminal node c_1 is reached without disturbing any node on the path from the root to this terminal node.

THEOREM 6.4   Algorithm 6.10 finds a simple cycle of digraph D no more than once.

Proof. The key to the proof is that at least one arc of every cycle found has not been disturbed by pruning and grafting, and that the nonterminal nodes in a K-tree have unique labels. Clearly, if a cycle of D is found twice, then this must happen in the traversal of the K-tree of just one strong component of D. Assume that cycle $C_2 = (c_1, c_2, \ldots, c_k, c_1)$ is presently being found, but that it has already been found as $C_1 = (c_t, c_{t+1}, \ldots, c_t)$. First consider the case $c_t \neq c_1$. Then the path defining C_2 must contain a subpath $(c_t, \ldots, c_1, c_2)$. Since $\langle c_1, c_2 \rangle$ has not been disturbed by pruning and grafting, the entire subpath cannot have been so disturbed. Hence we would now have a path $(c_t, \ldots, c_1, \ldots, c_t, \ldots, c_1)$ in the K-tree, but this is impossible on account of the repeated c_t. Next consider $c_t = c_1$. When the generation of the path defining C_2 is started, arc $\langle c_1, c_2 \rangle$ has remained undisturbed, and node c_2 must have been already passed in the traversal at the time C_1 was found. Now assume that subpath $(c_1, c_2, \ldots, c_m)$ of C_2 has not been disturbed since C_1 was found. This implies that c_m must have been passed in the traversal at the time C_1 was found, and, because of this, that subpath $(c_1, c_2, \ldots, c_m, c_{m+1})$ of C_2 has been undisturbed since C_1 was found. From this we conclude that $(c_1, c_2, \ldots, c_k, c_1)$ cannot have been disturbed since C_1 was found, and it was traversed in its entirety at that time, i.e., at a later time there is no way of traversing $\langle c_k, c_1 \rangle$ again. Hence C_1 cannot be found for a second time.

THEOREM 6.5   Algorithm 6.10 terminates.

Proof. Construct a "traversal tree" by first making a copy of a K-tree that is to be traversed. Each time pruning and grafting takes place in the original K-tree, a copy of the pruned subtree is grafted on at the appropriate place in the traversal tree, but pruning is carried out in this tree only if the subtree that is to be grafted on is located in the part of the K-tree that has not yet been traversed. Thus the traversal tree provides a complete history of the traversal of the original K-tree. It is easy to show that the traversal tree is finite. Since a finite number of K-trees form the input to A.6.10, the algorithm must terminate.

For our second algorithm assume that we are given the adjacency matrix A and the path matrix P of a digraph with n nodes. Now, if $a_{ik} p_{ki} = 1$, then there exist paths (i, k) and $(k, \ldots, i)$; i.e., there exists a cycle $(i, k, \ldots, i)$. If, however, $a_{ik} p_{ki} = 0$ for all $k = 1, 2, \ldots, n$, then node i does not lie on any cycle. In principle the algorithm makes use of the products $a_{ik} p_{kj}$ to construct something similar to the level trees of K-formulas. The process is initiated by drawing a node and labeling it 1. Then an arc is drawn for every i such that $a_{1i} p_{i1} = 1$ ($i = 1, 2, \ldots, n$), and the terminal node of the arc is labeled i. For the purposes of the argument assume that $a_{1i} p_{i1} = 1$ for some i; i.e., assume that we have a nontrivial tree. Take any terminal node labeled k, say, where $k \neq 1$. Draw an arc from this node for every j such that $a_{kj} p_{j1} = 1$ ($j = 1, 2, \ldots, n$), and assign label j to the terminal node of the arc. Note, however, that the arc is *not* drawn if $j \neq 1$ and j is already the label of some node on the path from the root of the tree to the node labeled k. Continue this process until all terminal nodes carry the label 1. There is now a path from the root of the tree to a terminal node for every elementary cycle through node 1 in the digraph. The cycles are defined by labels on nodes in the paths. Next generated submatrices A_2 and P_2 by deleting the first row and column of A and of P. An analogous procedure now finds cycles that go through node 2, but not through node 1. In the third stage delete the first two rows and columns of A and P, and use the resulting submatrices A_3 and P_3 to find cycles through node 3, etc. In effect this, is what A.6.11 does.

ALGORITHM 6.11 Algorithm for finding all cycles in a digraph, given the adjacency and path matrices of the digraph. The program, as written, can cope with a digraph having at most 50 nodes.

```
      SUBROUTINE CYCLES (A,P,N)
      LOGICAL A(N,N), P(N,N)
      LOGICAL USED(50)
      INTEGER ROOT, REACHJ(50), PATH(51)
      DO 35 ROOT = 1,N
C   INITIATE TREE
      DO  5 K = ROOT,N
      REACHJ(K) = ROOT
    5 USED(K) = .FALSE.
      LEVEL = 1
      PATH(1) = ROOT
      I = ROOT
C   TEST WHETHER PATH CAN BE EXTENDED
   10 JMIN = REACHJ(I)
      IF (JMIN.GT.N) GO TO 20
      DO 15 J = JMIN,N
      IF (A(I,J).AND.P(J,ROOT).AND..NOT.USED(J))
     X      GO TO 30
   15 CONTINUE
C   BACKTRACK IN TREE, RESETTING REACHJ AND USED
   20 REACHJ(I) = ROOT
   25 USED(I) = .FALSE.
      LEVEL = LEVEL - 1
      IF (LEVEL.EQ.0) GO TO 35
      I = PATH(LEVEL)
      GO TO 10
C   EXTEND PATH
   30 USED(J) = .TRUE.
      REACHJ(I) = J + 1
      LEVEL = LEVEL + 1
      PATH(LEVEL) = J
      I = J
      IF (J.NE.ROOT) GO TO 10
```

```
C   PRINT PATH
        WRITE (6,100) (PATH(NODES), NODES = 1,LEVEL)
  100   FORMAT (1H , 40I3 / 1H , 15X, 11I3)
        GO TO 25
C   END OF MAIN LOOP - REACHED WHEN LEVEL=0
   35   CONTINUE
        RETURN
        END
```

Example

Figure 6.10 shows a digraph, its adjacency matrix, and the trees constructed by the algorithm for nodes 1, 3, and 4. Since the first rows in A_2 and A_5 are zero, there are no trees for nodes 2 and 5. The trees for nodes 3 and 4 illustrate a phenomenon that we shall discuss in detail further on; it suffices to note here that the constructions do not represent cycles. Since the digraph contains a Hamiltonian cycle, $p_{ij} = 1$ for all $i, j = 1, 2, \ldots, n$. The program outputs the cycles in lexicographic order:

$$1 \quad 3 \quad 4 \quad 5 \quad 1$$
$$1 \quad 3 \quad 4 \quad 5 \quad 2 \quad 1$$
$$1 \quad 3 \quad 5 \quad 1$$
$$1 \quad 3 \quad 5 \quad 2 \quad 1$$
$$1 \quad 4 \quad 5 \quad 1$$
$$1 \quad 4 \quad 5 \quad 2 \quad 1$$
$$1 \quad 5 \quad 1$$
$$1 \quad 5 \quad 2 \quad 1.$$

Note that in the tree for node 1 the four subtrees rooted at the nodes labeled 5 are identical. So are the two subtrees rooted at the nodes labeled 4. Processing speed can be greatly improved if the program takes identity of subtrees into account. The improved program would be more complicated, and would require much additional storage.

One can become sidetracked in the second and subsequent stages of A.6.11. Assume that in the second stage of the process some $a_{ik}p_{k2}$ is equal to 1, but that $p_{k2} = 1$ by virtue of the existence of a path $(k, \ldots, j, 1, \ldots, 2)$ alone. In the tree this means that time is wasted on the construction of a path, with nodes labeled $2, \ldots, i, k, \ldots, j$, which, because it cannot be extended any further, does not give rise to a cycle. The trees for nodes 3 and 4 in Figure 6.10 illustrate this phenomenon.

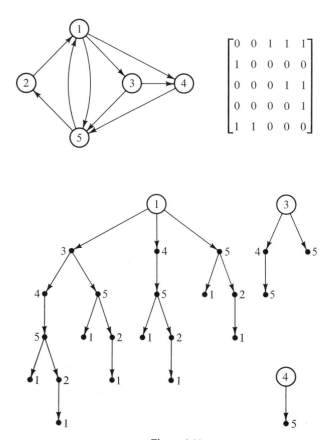

Figure 6.10

The sidetracking is avoided if the process is modified. Instead of working with ever smaller submatrices of A and P in successive iterations of the algorithm, we start with A_1 consisting of just the element a_{11}, and for $k = 2$, 3, ..., n generate A_k from A_{k-1} by augmenting the latter with the first k elements of row k and of column k of the adjacency matrix A. The idea is to find first the cycle through node 1 in the subdigraph on node 1 alone [if it exists, it is the sling $(1,1)$], then the cycles through node 2 in the subdigraph on nodes $\{1, 2\}$, then the cycles through node 3 in the subdigraph on nodes $\{1, 2, 3\}$, and so forth. Recall now that in A.3.1 the matrix X^* is initially A, that after the iteration with $j = 1$ element $x_{ij}^* = 1$ if and only if there is a path from node i to node j involving nodes $\{i, j, 1\}$ alone, that after the iteration with $j = 2$ element $x_{ij}^* = 1$ if and only if there is a path from i to j involving nodes $\{i, j, 1, 2\}$ alone, and so forth. Hence, if the generation of the path matrix is done in stages in A.6.11 itself, and we take P_1 to be just a_{11}, P_2 to be the 2 × 2 submatrix in the upper left corner of X^* after the iteration with $j = 1$, and, in general, P_k to be the $k \times k$ submatrix in the upper left corner of X^* after the iteration with $j = k - 1$, then the sidetracking is avoided.

6c. A Scheduling Problem

All but the most trivial production processes are composed of a number of separate activities. The activities are not independent, and in most practical cases their interdependence can be very complicated indeed. Perhaps the most effective visual aid to the understanding of a schedule of activities is a display of the activities and their relations in the form of a network. But the network of a complicated process can itself be very complicated. Mechanical procedures have therefore been developed for highlighting certain critical sections of the network. Proper managerial supervision of the project is then much easier to achieve. The information derived from the network by the analysis program enables management to allocate resources to a better effect.

The analysis techniques have become very important tools in operations research. Some very sophisticated systems have been developed: PERT (Program Evaluation Review Technique), CPA or CPM (Critical Path Analysis or Critical Path Method), RAMPS (Resource Allocation and Multi-Project Scheduling), and so forth. Here we can only introduce the basic terminology and some of the more fundamental principles.

Instead of choosing an impressive example and showing how to save a few million dollars, we shall consider a very simple task, the writing and mailing of a letter. The decomposition of this "production process" might be as follows:

A.   Get paper and envelopes.
B.   Get pen.
C.   Write letter.
D.   Address envelope.
E.   Put letter into envelope and seal envelope.
F.   Get stamp.
G.   Affix stamp.
H.   Mail letter.

Let us assume that three members of a family are involved in these activities. Mrs. S. is the instigator of the project, she has a letter to write. Since her writing is not as legible as her husband's, she has Mr. S. addressing the envelope. Mrs. S. also has trouble remembering where she last put her pen. Mrs. S. then assigns activities B and D to her husband, keeping activities A, C, and E for herself. Junior is called in for the more strenuous activities; he is

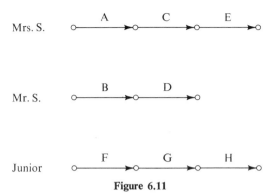

Figure 6.11

made responsible for F, G, and H. Figure 6.11 shows the sequence of activities for the three persons involved.

Figure 6.11 shows some of the relations between activities, but it does not describe the process completely. The following relations are not made explicit:

(a) Activities A, B, and F can be concurrent.

(b) One of C or D must be completed before the other is started (assuming that there is only one pen). Assume that D precedes C.

(c) Activities A and B must both be completed before D can be started.

(d) Activity G should not be started before D is completed (if writing of the address is not successful at first try, and G has been completed, then a stamp is lost); activities E and G cannot be concurrent, but C and G can.

(e) Activity E must precede activity H.

The five drawings of Figure 6.12 show successive stages in the construction of the network. For example, Drawing (c) represents the network after Conditions (a), (b), and (c) have been incorporated. Dependence of the start of D on completion of A is indicated by a *dummy activity*, represented by the broken line. Another dummy activity is introduced in Stage (d); it indicates that G cannot start before D is finished. The convention adopted throughout is that an activity represented by an arc originating from a node *a* cannot start before all activities represented by arcs terminating at *a* have been completed.

Let us now identify the nodes. Then we can dispense with activity symbols in the network itself (as long as we keep a reference list of arcs and the corresponding activities). Finally let us estimate durations of activities. The duration of an activity is an estimated time difference between the finish and the start of the activity. Dummy activities have zero durations. The duration of an activity is assigned as a weight to the arc representing the activity. In Figure 6.13, which shows the complete network, durations are given in minutes.

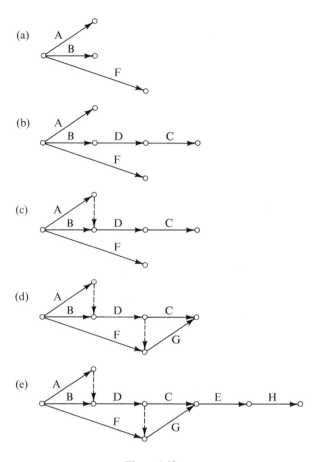

Figure 6.12

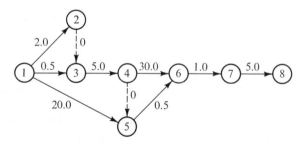

Figure 6.13

6d. Critical Path Scheduling

Let us now give a rigorous definition of what we mean by a scheduling network.

DEFINITION 6.1   A *scheduling network* is a 6-tuple $\langle E, e_s, e_t, A, D, W \rangle$, where

E is a set of numbered nodes—$E = \{ 1, 2, \ldots, n \}$,
e_s is the only node with zero indegree,
e_t is the only node with zero outdegree,
A is a subset of $E \times E$,
D is a set of values (weights),
W is a function $W: A \to D$,

and the digraph defined by $\langle E, A \rangle$ is acyclic. Members of E, A, and D are called, respectively, *events*, *activities*, and *durations*. If $W(i, j) = 0$, then $\langle i, j \rangle$ is a *dummy activity*. Events e_s and e_t are called *start* and *termination*, respectively. If, for every $\langle i, j \rangle \in A$, the relation $i < j$ holds, then the activities are said to be in *topological order*.

The network of Figure 6.13 is in topological order; a network constructed from the digraph of Figure 6.2 by removing arcs $\langle 5, 3 \rangle$ and $\langle 6, 4 \rangle$ is not. The requirement that the node with zero indegree or zero outdegree be unique is not unduly restrictive. If there is more than one node having zero indegree to begin with, one simply selects one of these nodes for the start and joins the others to it by dummy activities. Multiple terminations are dealt with similarly. If a network is in topological order, then $e_s = 1$ and $e_t = n$.

Scheduling networks cannot contain cycles because of the interpretation of activities incident with an event; an activity originating from a node cannot start before all activities terminating at the node are completed. This is best seen in the case of a sling. Then we have the absurd situation that an activity cannot start before it is completed! In a small network cycles can be detected by visual inspection, but in a practical problem involving hundreds or even thousands of events and activities the network has to be checked for absence of cycles mechanically. Note that a scheduling network is acyclic if all activities are in topological order; i.e., an algorithm that orders the activities also detects cycles.

Normally construction of the network proceeds from a *precedence table* of activities. Table 6.1 is a precedence table for the example of Section 6c. Generation of precedence tables is a highly skilled operation requiring intimate knowledge of the production process. In our example the choice of C as a successor of D is determined by knowledge of availability of machinery (only one pen) and manpower (overall performance is made more efficient

TABLE 6.1

PRECEDENCE TABLE FOR CONSTRUCTION OF
FIGURE 6.12(e)

Activity	Immediate successors
A	D
B	D
C	E
D	C, G
E	H
F	G
G	E
H	–

if the addresser of the envelope is released to some other project as early as possible). The scheduling network itself does not contain all the information that has gone into its construction. Therefore, if a preliminary analysis of the network suggests that it should be rearranged, the rearrangements that are made are only partly determined by the results of the analysis. Whether or not one has to rearrange depends greatly on the skill with which the original table was constructed.

Construction of precedence tables and their possible rearrangement will remain a manual activity for some time to come. The data that have to be taken into account are often qualitative rather than quantitative, and they vary greatly in type. Our techniques for dealing with such data in a computer are as yet too crude to justify mechanization of this stage. The next stage, the drawing of the network with dummy activities included and events numbered, or, what is equivalent to actually drawing it, numbering of events and setting up of a table of arcs, can be programmed, but is still most often done manually. Assume that we have constructed a network as far as Stage (e) in the particular example of Figure 6.12. The manual algorithm A.6.12 numbers events in such a way that activities are in topological order.

ALGORITHM 6.12   (Fulkerson's rule) X is the set of nodes numbered at any particular stage in the application of the algorithm to an acyclic digraph.

1. Set $i = 1$.
2. If there is no unnumbered node with zero indegree, then go to 5.
3. Assign number i to an unnumbered node with zero indegree.
4. Set $i = i + 1$; go to 2.
5. If all nodes are numbered, restore all removed arcs and stop.
6. If $od(X) \neq 0$, remove all arcs originating from X and go to 2.
7. Error condition: Existence of an unnumbered node and $od(X) = 0$ imply existence of a cycle in the network.

DEFINITION 6.2   Let $\langle E, 1, n, A, D, W \rangle$ be a topologically ordered scheduling network. With each node $i \in E$ there are associated two times, the *earliest event time* $t^-(i)$ and the *latest event time* $t^+(i)$, defined as follows:

(a) $t^-(1) = 0$.
(b) $t^-(k) = max_{i \in E}[t^-(i) + W(i, k)]$, $k \neq 1$.
(c) $t^+(n) = t^-(n)$.
(d) $t^+(i) = min_{k \in E}[t^+(k) - W(i, k)]$, $i \neq n$.

Example

Table 6.2 is a list of earliest and latest event times for the network of Figure 6.13. Let us look at the computations for $t^-(5)$ and $t^+(1)$. $W(1, 5)$ and $W(4, 5)$ are defined in the case of $t^-(5)$. The maximum of $t^-(1) + W(1, 5) = 0 + 20.0$ and $t^-(4) + W(4, 5) = 7.0 + 0$ is 20.0. In the case of $t^+(1)$ we have $W(1, 2)$, $W(1, 3)$, and $W(1, 5)$ defined. The values of $t^+(k) - W(1, k)$ are, respectively, $2.0 - 2.0 = 0$, $2.0 - 0.5 = 1.5$, and $36.5 - 20.0 = 16.5$. The minimum is 0. The network does not have to be topologically ordered for the purposes of D.6.2, but topological order helps in the processing of the nodes in a practical sense. Earliest event times can then be assigned to the nodes in the order 1, 2, ..., n, and latest event times in the order n, $n - 1$, ..., 1.

TABLE 6.2

EARLIEST AND LATEST EVENT TIMES FOR THE
NETWORK OF FIGURE 6.13

Event	Earliest event time	Latest event time
1	0	0
2	2.0	2.0
3	2.0	2.0
4	7.0	7.0
5	20.0	36.5
6	37.0	37.0
7	38.0	38.0
8	43.0	43.0

DEFINITION 6.3   Let $\langle E, 1, n, A, D, W \rangle$ be a topologically ordered scheduling network. With each activity $\langle i, j \rangle \in A$ we associate a time, called the *float* of the activity, defined

$$float(i, j) = t^+(j) - t^-(i) - W(i, j).$$

An activity with zero float is called a *critical activity*, and a path $(1, ..., n)$ consisting entirely of critical activities is a *critical path*.

Example

Table 6.3 lists the floats of all activities in the network of Figure 6.13. The path (1, 2, 3, 4, 6, 7, 8) is critical. Every scheduling network contains at least one critical path; there may be more than one.

TABLE 6.3

FLOATS OF ACTIVITIES IN THE
NETWORK OF FIGURE 6.13

Activity	Float
$\langle 1, 2 \rangle$	0
$\langle 1, 3 \rangle$	1.5
$\langle 1, 5 \rangle$	16.5
$\langle 2, 3 \rangle$	0
$\langle 3, 4 \rangle$	0
$\langle 4, 5 \rangle$	29.5
$\langle 4, 6 \rangle$	0
$\langle 5, 6 \rangle$	16.5
$\langle 6, 7 \rangle$	0
$\langle 7, 8 \rangle$	0

THEOREM 6.6   A critical path in a scheduling network is a longest path from start to termination.

Proof. Exercise 6.37.

We shall now examine the significance of critical path analysis. First we note that the total time to complete the project is 43.0 min in our example. Let us look at Event 5, the only event for which $t^- \neq t^+$. The earliest event time, 20.0 min, is the earliest time by which we *can* reach the event. The latest event time is the time by which we *may* reach the event without upsetting the schedule. There is, therefore, nothing gained by urging Junior to hurry up in getting to and from the post office. Indeed, Junior may as well have an ice cream on his way, and he may spend up to 16.5 minutes at the drug store. If, however, he stays there for 18 minutes, say, then the duration of activity $\langle 1, 5 \rangle$ becomes 38 minutes, the new critical path is (1, 5, 6, 7, 8), and the project completion time jumps to 44.5 minutes. (Activities $\langle 1, 2 \rangle$, $\langle 2, 3 \rangle$, $\langle 3, 4 \rangle$, $\langle 4, 6 \rangle$ are then no longer on the critical path. If the duration of $\langle 1, 5 \rangle$ is exactly 36.5 minutes, then both (1, 2, 3, 4, 6, 7, 8) and (1, 5, 6, 7, 8) are critical.)

But the purpose of critical path analysis is not to give Junior a reason for indulging. Rather it is to reduce the task completion time. If the letter has to be in the mailbox in less than 43 minutes, then critical path analysis tells us not to worry about activities $\langle 1, 3 \rangle$, $\langle 1, 5 \rangle$, and $\langle 5, 6 \rangle$. The efficiency of the *critical* activities must be improved. In a realistic large-scale network with perhaps 5000 activities, only 10%, perhaps, of the activities would be found on critical paths. By concentrating on these 500 activities, rather than all 5000, and reallocating resources so that the critical activities are completed in shorter time, the project completion time can be greatly reduced.

We must always remember that the initial durations are only estimates, and that the network has to be periodically reviewed. A drastic difference between an actual duration and its estimate may significantly change the pattern of critical paths.

The method dates from about 1957, and its success has been spectacular right from the start. The Polaris missile program was one of the earliest applications. It has been estimated that this program, which took 5 years to complete, would have taken 7 years without critical path analysis.

Notes

Generalization of the Roy–Warshall algorithm to Q-semirings is due to Robert and Ferland [Ro68], but Floyd discovered the particular application described in Example 1 of A.6.1 much earlier—[Fl62] is an Algol procedure for finding lengths of shortest paths. For a somewhat dated survey of shortest-path problems see [Dr69]. Algorithms for finding shortest paths between all pairs of nodes in a digraph on n nodes are reported in the following papers: [Hu68] describes a decomposition strategy for finding shortest paths in very large digraphs, and [Hu69] is an improvement over it for digraphs with few arcs (see also [Ye71]); [Ye72] contains an algorithm that requires $\frac{1}{2}n^3$ additions and n^3 comparisons (see [Wi73] for a correction); [Ho72b] contains an algorithm that is theoretically faster than Floyd's algorithm, but is not expected to outperform the latter except when n is very large because of the very complex structure that the "faster" algorithm has; [Sp73] reports an algorithm with expected time dependence $O(n^2 \log^2 n)$, but a worst time of $O(n^3 \log n)$ (see Section 11d for an explanation of the O-notation). [Pa74] discusses the effect that changing the weights of some arcs has on the lengths of shortest paths.

A.6.2 is due to Ponstein [Po66]; A.6.3 is suggested by [Ro68]; A.6.4 is described in [Bu65]. The technique of A.6.7 is described in [Ni66, Po71c]; [Bo67] is an Algol program corresponding to [Ni66]. An algorithm for finding kth shortest paths is described in [Fo73b], but for finding k shortest paths in [Mi74]. The problem of finding a spanning tree of a graph such that the sum of the weights of the edges making up the spanning tree is a minimum is related to shortest-path problems; algorithms for minimal spanning trees can be found in [Wh72, Ke72]. An entire chapter (Chapter 5: "Juggling Jugs") of [Be70] is devoted to a discussion of questions relating to our Exercise 6.13. A.6.9 is adapted from [Ta72]; see [Pu70a, Mu71] for algorithms that find the path matrix rapidly when the strong components of a digraph are known. The longest-path problem is closely related to the traveling salesman's problem, see [Ha62a, Pa64]. An approach to the solution of the traveling salesman's problem based on man–machine interaction is described in [Kr71]; [Kr72] surveys man–machine interaction as an aid to the solution of problems in a number of contexts.

A.6.11 is adapted from Figure 7 of [F167]. A more efficient algorithm for enumerating the cycles of a digraph is to be found in [Ta73].

To a computer scientist, publications that deal specifically with computers in critical path scheduling have greater relevance than the more general works, but one is well advised to look at a few of the latter: [Ob69] surveys scheduling problems in general; [Wi69] is an elementary introduction addressed to managers; [Lo64] is somewhat more technical, and its companion volume [Lo66] is a good source of exercises; [Ba67] is a more advanced work (its bibliography contains 197 items, and our A.6.12 is adapted from it). Algorithms for topological ordering are given in [La61, Ka62]. The RAMPS system is described in [Mo63], and the critical path algorithm built into RAMPS in [K167] (the program of [K167] accepts input that is not topologically ordered; another example of this is the program of [La65a]). [Mo67] contains a detailed description of internal representation of data in a program for very large problems. [Ho63b] deals with the somewhat similar problem of assembly line balancing (a Fortran program is included; the procedure is based on the adjacency matrix of a digraph representation of the assembly line).

Exercises

6.1 (a) Apply subroutine PATHLS of Example 1 of A.6.1 to the digraphs of Figure 3.6 and Figure 6.2.

6.2 (a) Write a subroutine for finding composite weights of extremal paths for the case described in Example 4 of A.6.1, and apply it to the digraph of Figure 3.2.

6.3 (a) Interpret the weight x_{ij} associated with arc $\langle i, j \rangle$ of a weighted digraph as the greatest amount of some commodity that can be moved along $\langle i, j \rangle$ in unit time. Assume that the x_{ij} belong to the Q-semiring $\langle R_+^\infty, max, min, 0, \infty \rangle$ of Example 2 of D.4.8, and apply A.6.1 to X. Give an interpretation of the composite weights generated by A.6.1 and of the extremal paths with which these composite weights are associated.

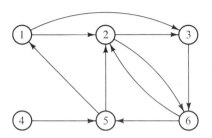

Figure 6.14

6.4 (a) Define a variable adjacency matrix for the digraph of Figure 6.14 and apply A.6.2 to it. (If you are familiar with a programming language that has string processing capabilities, then you should use a computer for this. If not, then the drudgery of this exercise should provide incentive to learn such a language.)

6.5 (a) Given matrix NODES, as generated by A.6.3, write a subroutine that returns the shortest path (I, ..., J) for specified I and J as a vector of node numbers.

6.6 (a) Devise an algorithm that constructs from matrix NODES, as generated by A.6.3, a digraph containing only those arcs that belong to extremal paths in the original digraph.

6.7 (a) Express A.6.4 as a Fortran subroutine. Test the subroutine on the digraph of Figure 6.2.

6.8 (a) Given a directed tree with nodes {1, 2, ..., n} in which the left to right order of the terminal nodes has no significance, i.e., the directed tree is an ordinary digraph. The tree can be specified by a vector t of n elements in which $t(k)$ contains the predecessor of node k, or, in the case of the root, the value zero. Prove that t contains sufficient information for the construction of the directed tree.

6.9 (a) Implement A.6.5 as a Fortran subroutine, and test it on the digraph of Figure 6.2.

6.10 (a) Write a program to find the composite weight and the explicit specification of the extremal path from node i to another node j for the application described in Example 4 of A.6.1. Use the program to find the extremal path from node 1 to node 8 in the digraph of Figure 6.2.

6.11 (a) Devise an algorithm that finds the shortest paths to a given node from all other nodes in a weighted digraph.

6.12 (a) Construct a weighted digraph that represents the maze of Figure 6.15 and use A.6.7 to find the shortest path from A to B.

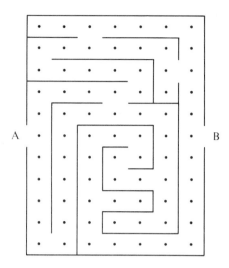

(The distance between adjacent dots is 1 unit)

Figure 6.15

6.13 (a) You have a 16 gallon drum of gasoline, and you have promised a friend half of it. For measuring you have only two containers capable of holding 10 and 6 gallons, respectively. Through what sequence of pouring actions do you have to go to measure off 8 gallons? Construct a labeled digraph in which arcs represent pouring actions, and the label associated with the terminal node of an arc is an ordered triple representing the contents of the three containers after the pouring action has been completed. The start node is labeled $\langle 16, 0, 0 \rangle$. You have to find the shortest path from this node to a node labeled $\langle 8, 8, 0 \rangle$.

6.14 (a) Repeat Exercise 6.13 with containers having capacities 19, 13, and 7 gallons, respectively. Find the shortest path from the node labeled $\langle 0, 13, 7 \rangle$ to a node labeled $\langle 10, 10, 0 \rangle$.

6.15 (a) Prove that A.6.1 is valid.

6.16 (a) Write a program similar to A.6.3 to define longest paths in an acyclic digraph. Use this program and the program of Exercise 6.5 to find the longest path from node 1 to node 8 in the digraph of Figure 6.2 with arcs $\langle 5, 3 \rangle$ and $\langle 6, 4 \rangle$ removed.

6.17 (a) One would expect that a maximization procedure analogous to A.6.4 would find the longest paths from a given node in an acyclic digraph. Show that this is not always the case. Could a maximization procedure analogous to A.6.5 be used to find longest paths in an acyclic digraph?

6.18 (a) Devise an algorithm that finds the shortest chains from node i to all other nodes in an undirected graph.

6.19 (b) The number of cycles in a digraph can be quite large. Evaluate

$$\sum_{i=2}^{n} (\sum_{j=1}^{n} (\prod_{k=1}^{i-1} (j - k)))$$

for $n = 5$, and show that this expression gives the number of elementary cycles (excluding slings) in a complete symmetric digraph on n nodes.

6.20 (b) Modify A.6.7 so that it finds the shortest cycle through a given node of a digraph. Apply this algorithm to nodes 2 and 4 in the digraph of Figure 6.2.

6.21 (b) Rephrase A.6.9 for the case in which digraph D is represented by more than one K-tree.

6.22 (b) Use A.6.9 to find the strong components of the digraphs represented by K-formulas

   (i)   ***a*b*c*d***eabdcd*;
   (ii) ***a***bb***ebdedce*;
   (iii) ***11*2***312*5*6**77*86***4139*;
   (iv) ***11*2**312***4139, **53*6**77**869*.

6.23 (b) Combine A.6.8 and A.6.9 into a single algorithm that merges the atomic K-trees and determines the strong components in a single traversal.

6.24 (b) Implement A.6.9 as a Fortran program and apply the program to the digraphs of Exercise 6.22.

6.25 (b) Apply A.6.10 to the digraphs of Exercise 6.22.

6.26 (b) Write a program for the simple cycles of a digraph, incorporating in A.6.11 the modification suggested at the end of Section 6b. Apply the program to the digraphs of Figures 6.5, 6.6, 6.8, and 6.10.

6.27 (c) A production process comprises activities a, b, c, and d. Activity c cannot start before a is completed, and d cannot start before a and b are both completed. Give a graphical representation of the process.

6.28 (c) Smith, Jones, and Brown are gathering information separately at three production plants; it takes them 8, 6, and 7 days, respectively, to complete this task. Smith and Brown pass their data to Jones, who then proceeds to work out a feasible production schedule for all three plants. It takes Jones 6 days to draw up the schedule. Meanwhile Brown is contacting suppliers and collating data on availability of supplies; this takes 10 days. Both the production schedule and the report on supplies are needed by Jones to work out delivery dates, and by Brown to advise suppliers of the dates on which supplies should reach the production plants. These activities take 2 and 3 days, respectively. Jones hands his schedule of deliveries to Smith, who then organizes transport, taking 3 days to do so. The planning is completed when Smith and Brown have completed their respective tasks. Give a graphical representation of this planning process.

6.29 (d) Write a program that checks, given the adjacency matrix of a digraph, that there is exactly one node with zero indegree and exactly one node with zero outdegree in the digraph. (In CPA parlance the program checks for "holes" in the activity network.)

6.30 (d) Find the critical path or paths in the network of Figure 6.16.

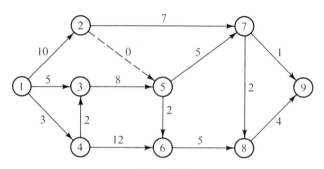

Figure 6.16

6.31 (d) In what respects does the network of Figure 6.16 change when durations of activities ⟨4, 6⟩ and ⟨5, 6⟩ are halved?

6.32 (d) Find the critical path or paths in the network of Exercise 6.28.

6.33 (d) It is discovered that Smith is supposed to take a holiday after he finishes gathering information at his plant and before he starts organizing transport. Amend the network of Exercise 6.28 so that it contains Smith's holiday as a new activity. What is the greatest number of days that Smith can be away without affecting the completion time of the planning process?

6.34 (d) A driver D arrives at a service station, and his car is serviced by employees A, B, C. This process is defined by Table 6.4. Some of the durations may be unrealistic. If this bothers you, disregard the descriptions of the activities. Use the information of Table 6.4 to construct a scheduling network, and carry out a critical path analysis of the network. The network should contain at most 11 nodes and at most 2 dummy activities. (Note that B can fill the gas tank while performing other tasks at the same time.)

6.35 (d) An examination of the analyzed network of Exercise 6.34 will show that C's activities can be taken over by A and B without an increase in the overall time required to service the car. Assign C's activities to employees

TABLE 6.4

Activity	Participants	Description of activity	Duration	Predecessors
a	D	Select grade of gas	10	—
b	D	Have a soda pop	75	a
c	B	Fill gas tank	120	a
d	A	Prepare bill	45	c, j
e	A, D	Make payment	25	b, d
f	B	Clean windshield	35	—
g	B	Check and inflate tyres	120	a, f
h	A	Open hood	15	—
i	A	Check oil	30	a, h
j	A	Add oil	35	i
k	C	Check battery	5	h
l	C	Add water to battery	40	k
m	C	Check radiator	5	l
n	C	Top up radiator	40	m
o	C	Close hood	5	j, n

A and B, construct the new network, and perform a critical path analysis of this network. The new network should contain at most 13 nodes and 3 dummy activities.

6.36 (d) Assign the n numbers $1, 2, \ldots, n$ to nodes in a network. Write a program based on A.6.12 that takes the set of arcs in the network for its input and renumbers the nodes in such a way that the arcs are topologically ordered.

6.37 (d) Prove Th.6.6.

6.38 (d) A network has been checked and found to contain no holes (see Exercise 6.29) and no cycles. The program of Exercise 6.16 is used to find a longest path $(1, \ldots, n)$. How can one tell whether this longest path is a unique longest path from 1 to n?

6.39 (d) Use the matrix of lengths and the matrix of nodes generated when the procedure of Exercise 6.16 is applied to an activity network to find *all* critical paths in the network.

6.40 (d) In what respects is A.3.4 superior to A.6.12 for detecting cycles in a network?

CHAPTER 7

Digraphs of Programs

7a. Flowchart Digraphs

Normally an algorithm comprises a preamble, which defines the objects that are to be operated on, and a list of operations, presented in such a manner that the order of their execution is unambiguously prescribed. A computer program that performs the way one wants it to perform is, of course, an algorithm. In a program one finds three types of statements. Declarations are statements of the first type. They are the preamble. Statements of the second type have to do with the actual computation, and statements of the third type effect transfers of control.

Every statement, regardless of type, is just a sequence of symbols, and normally one defines a computer program as a string or a sequence of strings, well formed according to a set of rules, which constitute the syntax of the language in which the program is written. Syntax alone, however, leaves a language unintelligible, and semantic rules must be added to turn a language into an effective medium of communication. In the case of a programming language some of the semantic rules deal with the sequence in which execution of the program is to proceed. They give an interpretation to statements of Type 3, but, since these statements look very much like statements of the other types, it is not easy to visualize the flow of control in a program by just looking at its listing.

If a grid of transfers of control specifying the execution sequence is superimposed on a program, our understanding of the program is greatly aided. Flowcharting provides the grid, but a flowchart is both a digraph of flowlines and a specification of the statements of the program (except Type 1 statements). In the next two sections we shall be interested in the digraph alone. Therefore we want a definition of a program in which the digraph is considered part of the program, but abstraction of the digraph is made easy.

DEFINITION 7.1   A computer program is a quintuple $\langle S, A, E, T, N \rangle$, where $S = \{s_1, s_2, \ldots, s_n\}$ is a nonempty set of executable statements, N is a set of declarative statements (possibly empty), $E \subseteq S$ is a nonempty set of entry points, $T \subseteq S$ is a nonempty set of terminal statements, and A is a square matrix of order n satisfying the following conditions:

(a) $a_{ij} = 1$ if control may pass from s_i to s_j;
      $a_{ij} = 0$ otherwise.

(b)   Column i of A is zero if and only if $s_i \in E$; row j of A is zero if and only if $s_j \in T$.

(c)   For every element s_i in $(S - E)$ there exists a sequence of non-zero elements of A, $a_{k_1 k_2}, a_{k_2 k_3}, \ldots, a_{k_u k_{u+1}}$, such that $s_{k_1} \in E$, $s_{k_{u+1}} \in T$, and one of $k_2, k_3, \ldots, k_{u+1}$ is i.

At first sight this looks like a case of excessive formalization for its own sake, but the appearance changes when we interpret the s_i as nodes in a digraph having A for its adjacency matrix. By taking A on its own we have abstracted the digraph of possible transfers of control. We call this the *flowchart digraph* of the program. In terms of the flowchart digraph, Condition (b) of D.7.1 becomes $E = \{s_i \mid id(s_i) = 0\}$ and $T = \{s_i \mid od(s_i) = 0\}$, and Condition (c) states that every executable statement in the program must be reachable from an entry point and that a terminal statement must in turn be reachable from this statement.

Let us now look at the forms particular Fortran statements take in a flowchart digraph. Formats, dimension statements, and other nonexecutable statements are ignored in the construction of a flowchart digraph. Every executable statement must be given an identification number. We shall find it necessary to introduce auxiliary nodes; i.e., a flow chart digraph will contain more nodes than there are statements in the corresponding program. Figure 7.1 shows subdigraphs of the program segments that follow. The 5, 6, 5a, SUB5, etc. in Figure 7.1 are unique identifying names of nodes. They are not labels in the sense of labels in labeled digraphs.

(a)   (5)   X = T
             (6)   T = Y

(b)   (5)   IF (X.NE.Y) X = Y
             (6)   ...

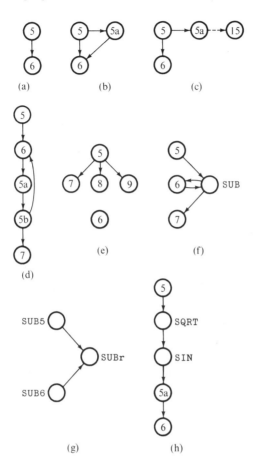

Figure 7.1

Here an auxiliary node 5a has to be introduced. It corresponds to the statement X = Y.

(c)   (5) IF (X.NE.Y) GO TO 15
             (6) ...

The GO TO 15 is an executable statement. Therefore, for the sake of consistency, we have introduced the auxiliary node 5a, although here we could have drawn the direct pointer ⟨5, 15⟩ instead.

(d)   (5) DO   6   K = 1,N
              6   A(K) = 0
             (7) ...

Two auxiliary nodes are required. It does not matter whether they are named 5a and 5b, or 6a and 6b, or something else altogether. The first stands for the incrementation of K, the second for the test of K against N.

    (e)   (5) `GO TO (7,7,8,9), J`
                      6   ...

Node 6 is isolated only as far as our subdigraph is concerned. There must be some statement transferring control into 6, and some way out of 6 as well.

    (f)   (5) `CALL SUB (A,B)`
                  (6) `CALL SUB (C,D)`
                  (7) ...

A decision has to be made whether to consider every routine as a separate program or to draw a single program flowchart for the entire program comprising a main routine and its subprograms. Since one is not normally interested in the structure of library routines, the former approach appears to be more sensible. We introduce an auxiliary node carrying the name of the subprogram. Then, if the structure of the subprogram is of interest, its flowchart digraph is produced, but separately, and we assume that this digraph *can* be substituted in place of the auxiliary node.

    (g) Assume that in subroutine SUB we have the program segment

                  (5) `RETURN`
                        :
                  (6) `RETURN`

Note now that there are only single arcs ⟨SUB, 6⟩ and ⟨SUB, 7⟩ in digraph (f). Therefore, to permit substitution of digraph SUB for the node SUB in digraph (f), we must have a single terminal node in SUB, and we introduce the auxiliary collective return node SUBr. Then, if we make the substitution, ⟨SUB, 6⟩ and ⟨SUB, 7⟩ are replaced by ⟨SUBr, 6⟩ and ⟨SUBr, 7⟩, respectively.

    (h)   5   `X = SIN(SQRT(X)) + Y`
                (6)   ...

A node named 5 has to precede nodes that stand for function subprograms in case some GO TO statement in the program transfers control to 5. Node 5a represents the computation steps that remain to be done after the function calls.

7b. Detection of Programming Errors

Some programming errors and irregularities can be detected in the flowchart digraph on its own. Others require the flowchart digraph to be used in conjunction with the program or, at least, to have a naming convention for the nodes that assigns particular significance to certain nodes in the flowchart digraph.

Discontinuities can be detected with great ease. Consider the program segment

```
       GO TO 15
   20  ...
```

where the program contains no Type 3 statement giving access to statement 20. By D.7.1 we require that every executable statement be reachable from some entry node. Let us first find the path matrix P of the program digraph (as a logical array). Then, assuming that $E = \{1\}$ and that the digraph contains N nodes,

```
       I = 1
       DO 50   K = 2,N
       NOPATH(K-1) = 0
       IF (P(1,K)) GO TO 50
       NOPATH(I) = K
       I = I + 1
   50  CONTINUE
```

assembles in vector NOPATH numbers of nodes that are not reachable from the entry node. If, on exit from the loop, NOPATH(1) is zero, then every node is reachable from the entry node. An analogous procedure detects nodes from which no terminal statement can be reached.

A less frequent error condition arises when a Type 3 statement transfers control to a nonexecutable statement, e.g., a format statement. This type of error can be detected during construction of the flowchart digraph. If, for example, the Type 3 statement is

```
   64  GO TO (69,69,70,71), J
```

where 70 is the number of a format statement, and a list of numbers of executable statements has already been generated, then the setting up of arc $\langle 64, 70 \rangle$ is prevented by 70 not being in the list. If, on the other hand, nodes are numbered while the flowchart digraph is being set up, then the arc is generated, but there is no arc originating from 70, and the error is detected in the search for nodes from which there is no path to a terminal node.

Next let us consider DO-loops. If node numbers corresponding to the incrementation step and the exit test are distinguished in some manner (e.g., nodes representing exit tests, and only those nodes, have numbers from a given range, say 100–199, assigned to them), then cycles corresponding to DO-loops can be distinguished from other cycles. Assume that cycle $(a_1, a_2, \ldots, a_1)$ represents a DO-loop, that b_k is the DO-statement and a_1 the statement following it, and that there exists an arc $\langle b_j, a_i \rangle$ ($\neq \langle b_k, a_1 \rangle$) such that a_i is on the cycle, but b_j is not. The DO-loop is then entered from outside. Unless there exists another cycle $(a_1, \ldots, b_j, a_i, \ldots, a_1)$, in which case b_j represents a statement belonging to a legitimate extension of the DO-loop, this is an error condition.

Superfluous transfers, such as

```
GO TO 43
   ⋮
43 GO TO 47
```

can be detected if names of nodes corresponding to Type 3 statements are distinguished. Then, if nodes a and b on a path (a, b, c) represent Type 3 statements, the program is simplified if arcs $\langle a, b \rangle$ and $\langle b, c \rangle$ are replaced by $\langle a, c \rangle$. The greatest significance of this example is that it shows the limited practical utility of simplification schemes. Transfers of control during execution of a program take very little time; search for the paths (a, b, c) uses a lot of it. The net result of this " simplification " is an increase in total processing time.

Detection of programming errors is an essential part of compilation. Although techniques that are not explicitly based on the digraph representation may in general be faster and use less storage than the digraph techniques, the latter would be the faster if a flowchart of the program were to be constructed as well. Then the flowchart digraph and a list of its cycles would have to be generated in any case, and the error detection techniques described above could be implemented at little additional cost.

7c. Segmentation of Programs

At times a computer program cannot be accommodated in its entirety in the main store of the computer. The program has to be segmented, and there arises the problem of selecting cutting points to minimize the number of segment interchanges between different levels of storage.

The segmentation problem is extremely difficult. Let the executable statements (and auxiliary statements) in a program be numbered consecutively $1, 2, \ldots, n$. If a cut is made between statements i and $i + 1$, the cut produces two segments, comprising, respectively, statements $1, 2, \ldots, i$ and $i + 1, \ldots, n$. In the simplest approach to the problem cuts are made at points in the program that are spanned by the least number of program loops.

Let us call the two segments A and B. In the flowchart digraph there may be more than one arc $\langle i, j \rangle$ such that the statements associated with i and j are in A and B, or in B and A. The natural representation of a segment is a subdigraph of the flowchart digraph defined on the set of nodes representing statements in the segment *and* nodes that do not belong to this set, but lie at the other end of arcs originating or terminating in the set. If the subdigraph is looked upon as a flowchart digraph in its own right, then these latter nodes are entry or terminal nodes of the digraph. Figure 7.2 illustrates segmentation of the following skeleton program, with the cut having been made between statements 9 and 10.

```
 1   IF ( ... ) GO TO 15
 3   ... = ...
 4   ... = ...
 5   IF ( ... ) GO TO 19
 7   DO 10 ...
 8   DO 10 ...
 9   ... = ...
10   ... = ...
15   ... = ... .
16   ... = ...
17   IF ( ... ) GO TO 4
19   STOP
```

A few terms have to be defined now. If two distinct paths $(a, \ldots, b)$ in a flowchart digraph have only nodes a and b in common, then the two paths are *parallel*. If P and Q are paths from an entry node to a terminal node, P is simple and $P \subset Q$, and Q does not contain a path that is parallel to a sub-path of P, then every maximal path in $(Q - P)$, i.e., every path that is not the subpath of some other path in $(Q - P)$, is a *return path*. By Th.3.1 every cycle in a flowchart digraph contains a return path. The return path of a cycle corresponding to a DO-loop contains just one arc. Return paths of other cycles may contain more than one arc. Paths $(5, 7, \ldots, 19)$ and $(5, 6, 19)$ are parallel in the complete flowchart digraph of our example; return paths are $(12, 9)$, $(14, 8)$, and $(17, 18, 4)$. If $(a, \ldots, b, c)$ represents a return path, then $\langle b, c \rangle$ is the *final arc* of the return path.

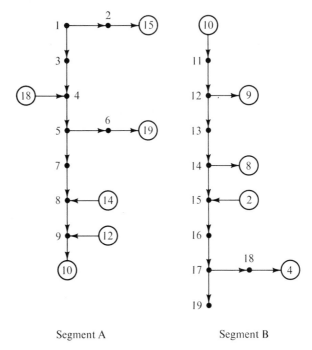

Segment A   Segment B

Figure 7.2

The criterion that a cut should be made at a point spanned by the least number of loops becomes, in terms of the flowchart digraph, that the segmentation process should sever the least number of return paths. Let us take adjacency matrix C of the cycle digraph of a program (A.3.4). Then

$$L_i = \sum_{j=1}^{i} \sum_{k=i+1}^{n} c_{kj}$$

seems to define the number of return paths severed by a cut after statement i. This is not strictly true, as the following skeleton program shows.

```
1   DO   5 . . .
2   GO TO 4
3   GO TO 5
4   GO TO 3
5   . . . = . . .
8   STOP
```

Here $L_3 = 2$, although there is only the one cycle (2, 4, 3, 5, 6, 7, 2). The L_i become reliable counts if the flowchart digraph is made acyclic by removing the final arc of every return path, the remaining arcs are put into topological order, and the removed arcs restored.

Even when the L_i give the true number of severed return paths there is the difficulty that one must have a knowledge of the iteration counts of the loops for optimal segmentation. These will rarely be available. Segment interchanges depend also on the location of data. Flow of data across a cut has as much importance as the flow of control. Significant work on this aspect of segmentation has barely started. Summarizing, we are quite far from having sound procedures for optimizing segmentation. It would appear that the selection of cutting points will have to be a dynamic process, the cuts being selected during execution of the program on the basis of information gathered while the program is being executed.

7d. Automatic Flowcharting

In trying to understand a program one is primarily interested in the flow of control. We have already seen that a listing of the program is of little help because one string of symbols looks to us very much like any other. In a flowchart sequencing of statements for execution is indicated by flowlines, and the statements themselves by boxes. A line is one dimensional, a box two dimensional, and this difference we can discern at a glance. The use of flowcharts as aids to the design of programs and for documentation has been with us since the very earliest days of electronic computing. Here we shall consider the use of the theory of digraphs in the automatic preparation of flowcharts from programs. The utility of automated documentation should be obvious. Flowcharts prepared while a program is still being debugged can be equally important—for drawing attention to unintended irregularities in the flow of control.

It is easy enough to write a procedure that encloses statements of a program in boxes, superimposes a grid of arbitrarily intersecting flowlines on the column of boxes, and writes *flowchart* at the bottom. To deserve this name, however, the drawing must enable one to trace the flow of control readily, and identify with ease points at which decisions are made. Therefore a flowchart must be two dimensional, with the order of statements of the original program rearranged where rearrangement simplifies the pattern of flowlines. In quite a normal program we may well find a hundred statements interposed between statements x and y, where statement x tells that control may next go to y. A two-dimensional disposition of the boxes allows boxes for statements that are executed one after the other to be placed near each other. For the sake of clarity the number of intersections of flowlines should be kept as low as possible.

Moreover, particularly if the flowchart is being generated as a documentation record to be filed, it must be separated into pages of standard size by making cuts at fixed intervals of 10.5 or 12.5 in., say. The product will hardly be acceptable unless the flowchart generator has already segmented the flowchart into pages of the required size. The paging requirement imposes a limit on the width of the flowchart as well (generally the width is limited in any case by the nature of the output device).

The quality of output of existing automatic flowchart generators varies greatly, and is far from perfect even with the better generators. This is probably due to the approaches to the problem having been largely *ad hoc*, the inherent lack of generality of such approaches preventing a continuous growth of knowledge. If a problem is formulated in sound mathematical terms, then an existing store of knowledge can be put to use, and partial solutions, instead of being isolated achievements, add to this store. The appropriate mathematical formulation of the flowcharting problem should proceed from some definition similar to our D.7.1.

The paging problem in flowchart generation is related to the segmentation problem for programs, but the two problems are distinct. In both cases one operates on a flowchart digraph. Ideally segments should be generated by cutting arcs that do not lie on cycles. Unfortunately this solution is inadequate when the segments turn out too large. A cut across a loop can have a very serious effect on the execution time of the program, and it is therefore necessary to exercise great care in selecting cuts.

In the preparation of a flowchart one's main concern is that the logical pattern of the program should be easy to follow, and it is as important to draw parallel paths originating from a decision node side by side on the same page as it is to avoid cutting loops. In the first instance the flowchart digraph has to be segmented in such a way that all arcs belonging to a cycle are confined to a single segment, and also all paths that are parallel to each other. Segments that are too small can be reassembled into page-sized segments without difficulty. Unfortunately, compared to an admissible program segment in most multilevel storage systems, a page of a flowchart, which cannot take more than 25 or so flowchart symbols (nodes), is quite small; and, too frequently for one's liking, flowchart segments have to be subdivided further. We have no adequate theory to guide us in this process, but cutting of loops is not as critical as in the case of program segmentation, and the lack of a theory is not much of a handicap. Despite this, a list of all cycles in the flowchart digraph is still needed, for guidance in the subdivision of segments that are too large and for designing the layout of a page.

We call an arc of a digraph a *separator* of the digraph if it does not lie on a cycle or on a path that is parallel to some other path. It is easy to see that deletion of separators produces a partial digraph whose connected components are the segments of the flowchart digraph. Exercise 7.8 requires one to find the separators in a flowchart digraph that has a single entry node and a single terminal node. The solution to this exercise suggests the approach that can be taken in designing an algorithm for the much more difficult case of multiple entry and terminal nodes (Exercise 7.9).

Assume now that the nodes to go on a page have been selected. The next problem relates to layout. An axis has to be selected within a page of the flowchart. This will be called the main flowpath. Other paths are drawn either side of the main flowpath. An automatic flowchart generator cannot be expected to identify the main flowpath with the path having greatest logical significance (often even the writer of the program would find this a difficult task), and some other criterion has to be used. In the program segment corresponding to the subdigraph that is being fitted to the page there will be one or more points at which control passes into the segment or out of it. The corresponding nodes are entry nodes and terminal nodes, respectively. An empirical main flowpath is obtained by finding the longest elementary path originating at an entry node. Preferably the path should originate at an entry node that is the last node of the main flowpath relative to the page immediately preceding this page, and it should end at a terminal node, but there is little loss of clarity if the flowpath originates at some other entry node and ends at a node that is not terminal. The reason is that an automatic flowcharter should produce flowcharts on at least two levels of detail. On the lower level the output is a conventional flowchart, separated into pages. On the higher level a chart is generated that represents the logical sequence and interrelation of the pages.

If A.6.2 was used to find the cycles, then we have now also a list of all simple paths in the flowchart digraph, and one of these paths is the longest simple path in the subdigraph that we are fitting to the page. If, on the other hand, the cycles were found by the more accessible A.6.11, then the longest simple path still remains to be found. We break all cycles by removing final arcs of return paths. Then the longest simple path in the page can be found by the procedure of Exercise 6.16, and the removed arcs restored.

The return path in a cycle need not be unique. The digraph of Figure 7.3 contains just the one cycle (c, d, e, f, g, c). Taking $P = (a, b, c, d, h)$ the return path is (d, e, f, g, c), but taking $P = (a, f, g, c, d, h)$ it is only (d, e, f). One result of this is that removal of final arcs does not necessarily produce a longest simple path in the absolute sense. In the digraph which results when final arc $\langle g, c \rangle$ is removed the longest simple path is (a, b, c, d, e, f, g), but the longest simple path in the digraph with final arc $\langle e, f \rangle$ removed is (a, f, g, c, d, h), which is shorter by one arc.

Finally there remains the problem of minimizing the number of intersections of flowlines in the drawing. One could analyze the undirected graph

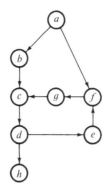

Figure 7.3

corresponding to the flowchart digraph; the layout problem then becomes the planarity problem (Section 3h). A practical algorithm for finding how near a graph is to being planar does not appear to have been discovered. This certainly means that we do not have a good general algorithm that will rearrange edges in the geometrical representation of the graph until the number of intersections is a minimum, but, since paging reduces the number of flowlines (explicit flowlines are replaced by connectors), the problem becomes tractable when a page is considered on its own. As the longest elementary path is the axis of the page and all cycles are known, a trial-and-error procedure is then probably as efficient as any other that could be discovered.

Notes

A survey of applications of graph theoretical models of programs made prior to 1960 can be found in [Ma60]. [Ka60] is an early paper describing the use of properties of digraphs in the detection of programming errors and elimination of redundancies. Later work on optimization of programs is reported in [Al69, Ea72, Sc73, Ea74]. The decision of what an optimizing compiler for a programming language is to optimize should be based on the characteristics of programs written in that language, established by empirical study of a sufficiently large sample of actual programs. Knuth [Kn71] has carried out such a study for Fortran (see also [Ho73]).

Ramamoorthy applies graph theory to analysis of programs in a number of papers: [Ra66a] establishes the terminology and gives some basic algorithms (a variant of the algorithm of Exercise 7.3 is an example), [Ra66b] deals with segmentation of programs for a multiprogrammed computer, and [Ra67] extends the work to maintenance of hardware; [Ra71] deals with models of computer programs in general. The indices L_i were introduced by Schurmann [Sc64]. Estimation of running times for specific sections of a program is an important precondition for effectiveness of segmentation. Because of its difficult nature, little work has been done on this problem, but some results may be found on pp. 364–369 of [Kn68], and in [Ha66, Ma67, Kr68, Kn73b]. Efficiency of program segmentation depends also on data flow across segment boundaries; [Ku67] deals with optimization of programs with respect to data flow. A selection of other works dealing with program segmentation: [Lo70a] (see also [Sa70]), [Ve71], [Ke71] (see [Lu74] for a follow-up), and [Ba72a].

Analysis of time sharing and multiprogramming by means of graph theoretical models is carried out in a number of papers; we recommend, in rough order of increasing difficulty, [Lo69b, Re68, Ka66].

For background information on flowcharting see [Ch70a]. A survey of automatic flowchart generators can be found in [Wa73b]. Automatic construction of flowcharts specifically for debugging of programs is discussed in [St65]. [Pr71b, Ma73] contain highly theoretical discussions of the place of flowchart digraphs in programming theory.

Exercises

7.1 (a) Draw flowchart digraphs of the programs of A.1.5 and A.5.12.

7.2 (b) Write a program that detects in a flowchart digraph nodes from which no terminal statement can be reached. Assume that there may be more than one terminal statement. (The algorithm should be similar to that given in Section 7b for finding nodes that are not reachable from an entry node.)

7.3 (b) Assume that nodes n, $n - 1$, ..., $n - k$ represent terminal statements in a flowchart digraph. The following algorithm detects nodes from which no terminal statement can be reached:

1. Transfer column n of adjacency matrix A of the flowchart digraph to vector T.
2. For $j = n - 1$, ..., $n - k$ and for $i = 1, 2, ..., n$ set $t_i = t_i \lor a_{ij}$ (for definition of operation $\lor$ see A.3.1).
3. For $j = 1, ..., n - k - 1$ and for $i = 1, 2, ..., n$: if $a_{ij} = 1$, then set $t_i = t_i \lor a_{ij}$.
4. Repeat Step 3 until no more changes take place in T.

If now a t_i is zero ($1 \leq i < n - k$), then no terminal statement can be reached from node i. Discuss the relative efficiencies of this algorithm and that of Exercise 7.2.

7.4   (c)   Use A.3.4 to find the cycle digraph of the program of A.5.12 and compute the loop indices L_i defined in Section 7c.

7.5   (c)   Consider the following definition of a return path in a flowchart digraph: " Every arc that lies on a simple path from an entry node to a terminal node (a forward path) is a forward arc; an arc that is not forward is a return arc. The return arcs define return paths: A path $(b, \ldots, a)$ made up entirely of return arcs, such that nodes a and b lie on a forward path, is a return path." Show by an example that this definition is *not* equivalent to our definition in Section 7c.

7.6   (c)   Is the number of return paths in a flowchart digraph necessarily equal to the number of cycles? Is the number of final arcs of return paths necessarily equal to the number of cycles?

7.7   (c)   Identify return paths in the flowchart digraph of the program of A.5.12 by visual inspection and remove the final arcs of these paths. Write a program (or use a program that you may have already written) to find the longest path in the resulting structure.

7.8   (d)   If a flowchart digraph has a single entry node and a single terminal node, then the finding of separators is a relatively easy matter. Develop an algorithm that finds the separators in this special case.

7.9   (–) (major project)   Write a subroutine that finds the separators in a flowchart digraph.

7.10   (–) (major project)   Given an adjacency matrix of order 25 or less that defines a subdigraph of a flowchart digraph. Develop an algorithm that places nodes of the subdigraph in such a way relative to each other that the flowchart boxes corresponding to the nodes would be properly laid out on a page of the flowchart. The output might be a matrix D, defined as follows:

$$d_{ij} = a \times 3^0 + b \times 3^1,$$

where $a = -1$ if node i is below node j,
           $= 0$ if the nodes are on the same horizontal level,
           $= 1$ if i is above j,
and $b = -1$ if node i is to the left of node j,
           $= 0$ if the nodes are on the same vertical level,
           $= 1$ if i is to the right of j.

7.11   (–) (research project)   Computer programs are nearly always such that the procedure of Exercise 7.9 gives segments that are much too large to fit on a page. Develop (in outline) a complete solution of the paging problem.

7.12   (–) (research project)   Write an algorithm that finds final arcs of all return paths in a flowchart digraph. (The definition of a return path given in

Section 7c will be of little use in this endeavor. However, the purpose of Exercises 7.5 and 7.7 has been to give an intuitive understanding of what a return path is, and the constructive definition of Exercise 7.5 is, in fact, equivalent to the definition of Section 7c in most cases. One approach to the solution of the problem would be to find a constructive definition that is equivalent to our definition in all cases, but the possibility that a useful definition of final arcs could be found without having to define return paths should not be ignored.)

CHAPTER 8

Other Applications of Graphs

8a. Flow Problems

DEFINITION 8.1   A *capacitated network* (*capacitated transportation network*) is a quadruple $\langle A, Q, c, R_+ \rangle$, where $\langle A, Q \rangle$ is a digraph, R_+ is the set of nonnegative real numbers, and $c: Q \to R_+$ is a function. We denote $c(i, j)$ by c_{ij}, and call it the *capacity* of arc $\langle i, j \rangle$.

Example

The weighted network of Figure 8.1 is a capacitated network. Only the interpretation given to weights c_{ij} distinguishes the capacitated network of Figure 8.1 from other weighted digraphs. A capacity c_{ij} can be thought of as the greatest amount of some commodity that can be moved along $\langle i, j \rangle$ in a unit of time. A fundamental problem in the theory of networks is to find the greatest amount of a commodity that can be conveyed from one given node to some other given node in the network. This is the maximal flow problem.

DEFINITION 8.2   Let $\langle A, Q, c, R_+ \rangle$ be a capacitated network. A *flow* f of value v from node s to node t is a function $f: Q \to R_+$ such that

(a) $0 \leqq f(i, j) \leqq c_{ij}$ for all $\langle i, j \rangle \in Q$,

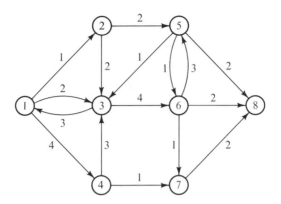

Figure 8.1

(b) $\sum_{Q^+_{\{p\}}} f(p, i) - \sum_{Q^-_{\{p\}}} f(i, p) = v$ for $p = s,$
$= -v$ for $p = t,$
$= 0$ for $p \in A - \{s, t\}.$

Nodes s and t are called, respectively, *source* and *sink* of the network with respect to flow f. (Q^+ and Q^- are defined by D.3.6.)

Conditions (a) of D.8.2 state that nowhere can the flow along an arc exceed the capacity of the arc. Conditions (b) are conservation equations. A commodity is pumped into the network by way of the source at some set rate. At t as much of the commodity must come out as goes in at s. At all intermediate points the inflow is equal to the outflow. The problem is to find the greatest value of v that is consistent with the conditions.

DEFINITION 8.3   Let $\langle A, Q, c, R_+ \rangle$ be a capacitated network with source s and sink t. Let X be a subset of A such that $s \in X$, $t \notin X$. Then the set of arcs Q^+_X is a *cut* in the network, and the sum of capacities of all arcs in Q^+_X is the *capacity of the cut*, denoted $C(X)$.

Example

In the capacitated network of Figure 8.1 let node 1 be the source and node 8 the sink. The cut corresponding to $X = \{1, 2, 4, 7\}$ is the set of arcs $\{\langle 1, 3\rangle, \langle 2, 3\rangle, \langle 2, 5\rangle, \langle 4, 3\rangle, \langle 7, 8\rangle\}$. The cut corresponding to $\{1, 2, 3, 4\}$ is $\{\langle 2, 5\rangle, \langle 3, 6\rangle, \langle 4, 7\rangle\}$. Capacities of the two cuts are $2 + 2 + 2 + 3 + 2 = 11$ and $2 + 4 + 1 = 7$, respectively.

THEOREM 8.1   If X defines a cut in a capacitated network $\langle A, Q, c, R_+ \rangle$, and v is the value of a flow in the network, then $v \leqq C(X)$.

Proof. Let f' be an extension of f to the domain $A \times A$, defined by

$$f'(i,j) = f(i,j) \quad \text{for} \quad \langle i,j \rangle \in Q,$$
$$= 0 \quad \text{for} \quad \langle i,j \rangle \notin Q.$$

From Conditions (b) of D.8.2, in terms of the extension f', we obtain

$$\sum_{i \in A} f'(p,i) - \sum_{i \in A} f'(i,p) \begin{array}{l} = v \quad \text{for} \quad p = s, \\ = 0 \quad \text{for} \quad p \in A - \{s,t\}. \end{array}$$

Hence, summing over all members of X,

$$\sum_{p \in X, i \in A} f'(p,i) - \sum_{i \in A, p \in X} f'(i,p) = v.$$

But, by symmetry,

$$\sum_{p \in X, i \in X} f'(p,i) - \sum_{i \in X, p \in X} f'(i,p) = 0.$$

Hence

$$\sum_{p \in X, i \in A-X} f'(p,i) - \sum_{i \in A-X, p \in X} f'(i,p) = v,$$

and, dropping the zero terms,

$$v = \sum_{Q_X^+} f(p,i) - \sum_{Q_X^-} f(i,p).$$

Hence

$$v \leqq \sum_{Q_X^+} f(p,i) \leqq \sum_{Q_X^+} c_{pi} = C(X).$$

THEOREM 8.2 (Ford and Fulkerson's max-flow min-cut theorem) Let $\langle A, Q, c, R_+ \rangle$ be a capacitated network with v_{max} the greatest possible flow from source s to sink t. Let C_{min} be the smallest capacity of a cut in the network. Then $v_{max} = C_{min}$.

Proof. Let the maximal flow v_{max} from s to t be defined by function f'. Define a set X' recursively as follows:

(i) $s \in X'$;
(ii) if $p \in X'$, and $f'(p,q) < c_{pq}$ or $f'(q,p) > 0$ (or both), then $q \in X'$.

We show that making t a member of X' leads to the contradiction that the flow can be improved. From the definition of X', if $t \in X'$, then there exists a semipath $S = (s, \ldots, t)$. Now, if $\langle p,q \rangle \in S$ is in the direction from s to t, define $f_{pq} = c_{pq} - f'(p,q)$. If $\langle p,q \rangle$ is in the reverse direction, put

$f_{pq} = f'(p, q)$. Finally set $v' = min_s f_{pq}$. Now the flow in each "forward" arc can be increased by v' and the flow in each "backward" arc decreased by v' without affecting the conditions of D.8.2. But then the maximal flow becomes $v_{max} + v'$, and this is an obvious contradiction. Hence $t \notin X'$, i.e., set X' defines a cut. An arc with only one node in X' cannot have satisfied Part (ii) of the definition of X', and we must have

$$f'(p, q) = c_{pq} \quad \text{for every} \quad \langle p, q \rangle \in Q_{X'}^+,$$
$$f'(q, p) = 0 \quad \text{for every} \quad \langle q, p \rangle \in Q_{X'}^-.$$

But then, from the proof of Th.8.1, putting v_{max} for the v there,

$$v_{max} = \sum_{Q_{X'}^+} f'(p, q) - \sum_{Q_{X'}^-} f'(q, p)$$
$$= \sum_{Q_{X'}^+} c_{pq} - 0$$
$$= C(X').$$

Since $v_{max} \leqq C(X)$ in general, $C(X') = C_{min}$.

Direct use of the theorem is not feasible. Let $|A| = n$. Then the number of candidates for the subset of A that would define a min-cut set is

$$\sum_{k=0}^{n-2} C(n - 2, k) = 2^{n-2}.$$

Even for a relatively small network with 30 nodes 2^{28} still amounts to 268,435,456. But the *proof* of Th.8.2 is constructive in that it defines a min-cut set, and this definition is the basis for the following algorithm.

ALGORITHM 8.1   (Ford–Fulkerson algorithm)   Given a capacitated network $\langle A, Q, c, N_+ \rangle$, where N_+ is the set of nonnegative integers and c is now a function into N_+. Flow function f is integer valued also. The following algorithm finds a set $X' \subset A$ that defines a minimal cut. Labels are attached to the nodes as part of the procedure.

1.   Assign arbitrary flows $f(p, q)$ that are consistent with D.8.2 to all arcs; e.g., make the flows all zero.
2.   Make $h(s) = \infty$ and attach label $\langle -, h(s) \rangle$ to s. Select node s for the p of Steps 3 and 4.
3.   For every arc $\langle p, q \rangle$ such that q is not labeled compute $d(p, q) = c_{pq} - f(p, q)$, and, if $d(p, q) > 0$, attach to q the label $\langle p^+, h(q) \rangle$, where $h(q) = min[h(p), d(p, q)]$.
4.   For every arc $\langle q, p \rangle$ such that q is still not labeled and $f(q, p) > 0$ attach to q the label $\langle p^-, h(q) \rangle$, where $h(q) = min[h(p), f(q, p)]$. Node p is now processed.
5.   If t is labeled, then go to 7.
6.   Select a labeled node p that has not been processed and go to 3.

If none remain to be processed, stop. Then the labeled nodes constitute set X' and the $f(p, q)$ define the greatest flow.

7. The algorithm has produced a semipath on labeled nodes $(s, \ldots, t)$, where the first coordinate of the label on a node names the node that precedes it in the semipath. Adjust the flow: Working backward from t, until s is reached, for every labeled node q on semipath $(s, \ldots, t)$ set $f(p, q) = f(p, q) + h(t)$ or set $f(q, p) = f(q, p) - h(t)$, depending on whether the label of q is $\langle p^+, h(p)\rangle$ or $\langle p^-, h(q)\rangle$, respectively.

8. Discard all labels and go to 2.

Example

Tables 8.1 and 8.2 summarize computation of the greatest flow from node 1 to node 8 in the capacitated network of Figure 8.1. Initially all flows are assumed zero; final flows are as shown in Figure 8.2 (where arcs in which the

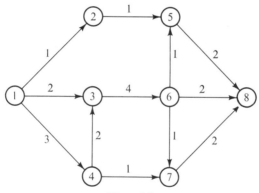

Figure 8.2

TABLE 8.1

Node Labels

Node	Iteration					
	1	2	3	4	5	6
1	$\langle -, \infty\rangle$	$\langle -, \infty\rangle$	$\langle -, \infty\rangle$	$\langle -, \infty\rangle$	$\langle -, \infty\rangle$	$\langle -, \infty\rangle$
2	$\langle 1^+, 1\rangle$		$\langle 5^-, 1\rangle$	$\langle 5^-, 1\rangle$	$\langle 5^-, 1\rangle$	
3	$\langle 1^+, 2\rangle$	$\langle 1^+, 2\rangle$	$\langle 4^+, 3\rangle$	$\langle 4^+, 2\rangle$	$\langle 4^+, 2\rangle$	$\langle 4^+, 1\rangle$
4	$\langle 1^+, 4\rangle$	$\langle 1^+, 4\rangle$	$\langle 1^+, 4\rangle$	$\langle 1^+, 3\rangle$	$\langle 1^+, 2\rangle$	$\langle 1^+, 1\rangle$
5	$\langle 2^+, 1\rangle$	$\langle 6^+, 2\rangle$	$\langle 6^+, 2\rangle$	$\langle 6^+, 1\rangle$	$\langle 6^+, 1\rangle$	
6	$\langle 3^+, 2\rangle$	$\langle 3^+, 2\rangle$	$\langle 3^+, 2\rangle$	$\langle 3^+, 1\rangle$	$\langle 3^+, 1\rangle$	
7	$\langle 4^+, 1\rangle$	$\langle 4^+, 1\rangle$	$\langle 4^+, 1\rangle$	$\langle 4^+, 1\rangle$	$\langle 6^+, 1\rangle$	
8	$\langle 5^+, 1\rangle$	$\langle 6^+, 2\rangle$	$\langle 5^+, 1\rangle$	$\langle 7^+, 1\rangle$	$\langle 7^+, 1\rangle$	

TABLE 8.2

ADJUSTED FLOWS

Arc	Iteration					
	1	2	3	4	5	6
$\langle 1, 2 \rangle$	1	1	1	1	1	
$\langle 1, 3 \rangle$		2	2	2	2	
$\langle 1, 4 \rangle$			1	2	3	
$\langle 2, 3 \rangle$						
$\langle 2, 5 \rangle$	1	1	1	1	1	
$\langle 3, 1 \rangle$						
$\langle 3, 6 \rangle$		2	3	3	4	
$\langle 4, 3 \rangle$			1	1	2	
$\langle 4, 7 \rangle$				1	1	
$\langle 5, 3 \rangle$						
$\langle 5, 6 \rangle$						
$\langle 5, 8 \rangle$	1	1	2	2	2	
$\langle 6, 5 \rangle$			1	1	1	
$\langle 6, 7 \rangle$					1	
$\langle 6, 8 \rangle$		2	2	2	2	
$\langle 7, 8 \rangle$				1	2	

flow is zero have been omitted). Here $X' = \{1, 3, 4\}$, but note that this is not the only set defining a minimal cut. In Step 6 the node having the smallest number for its name was always selected.

If the capacities are not all integers, then it may happen that A.8.1 does not stop, or that it produces an erroneous solution. However, the requirement that all capacities be integers is not unduly restrictive. In all *practical* applications it should be possible to scale nonintegral capacities so that they become integers. For example, if the capacities in some network were 1.5, 0.75, 1.25, 0.9, 1.25, say, we would convert them to 150, 75, 125, 90, 125 by scaling.

A.8.1 is a prescription for pencil and paper computation. If this algorithm is to be implemented on a computer, a more suitable formulation is required. A.8.1a is one such formulation.

ALGORITHM 8.1a   An algorithm for maximal flow in a capacitated network $\langle A, Q, c, N_+ \rangle$. The algorithm uses matrices C and F, where C is initially the matrix of capacities of the arcs in the network, and the flow is built up in F. Initially F defines any feasible flow, i.e., a flow consistent with D.8.2. It is common practice to make the initial flow values all zero. If the initial flow is not zero, matrix C has to be adjusted by setting $c_{ij} = c_{ij} - f_{ij}$, $c_{ji} = c_{ji} + f_{ij}$ for all $f_{ij} \neq 0$. Vectors M and D define a flow path and the flow in it.

1. Set $m_i = d_i = 0$ for all $i = 1, 2, \ldots, n$. Set $m_s = d_s = \infty$. Set $B = \varnothing$. Select node s for the k of Steps 2 and 3.
2. For all i such that $m_i = 0$ set $d_i = min(d_k, c_{ki})$ and, if $d_i > 0$, set $m_i = k$.
3. Set $B = B \cup \{k\}$. If $m_t \neq 0$, go to 6.
4. If one exists, select any node k such that $k \in A - B$ and $m_k \neq 0$, and go to 2. (If no such node exists, Step 5 is taken next.)
5. For $i = 1, \ldots, n$, and for $j = i + 1, \ldots, n$:
   If $f_{ij} > f_{ji}$, then set $f_{ij} = f_{ij} - f_{ji}, f_{ji} = 0$;
   else set $f_{ji} = f_{ji} - f_{ij}, f_{ij} = 0$.
   Stop: Matrix F defines maximal flow.
6. Set $j = t, i = m_t$,
7. Set $f_{ij} = f_{ij} + d_t$, $c_{ij} = c_{ij} - d_t$, $c_{ji} = c_{ji} + d_t$.
8. If $i = s$, go to 1; else set $j = i, i = m_i$, and go to 7.

A network that contains multiple sources $s_1, s_2, \ldots, s_k$ can be converted to a network with a single source by adding a collective source node s' and augmenting the network with arcs of infinite capacity from s' to each of the s_i. The problem becomes one of finding the maximal flow from s' to t. Multiple sinks can be dealt with in a similar fashion. Another generalization involves capacities. So far we have assumed that the lower bound on the flow in any arc is zero. In the general case two explicit flow bounds c_{low} and c_{high} ($c_{low} \leqq c_{high}$) are assigned to each arc, and a flow in the arc is required to lie in the interval $[c_{low}, c_{high}]$. The bounds can be negative, a negative $f(p, q)$ being interpreted as a flow from q to p of magnitude $|f(p, q)|$. In the most common situation $c_{low} = -c_{high}$ for every arc; flow in an arc can be in both directions, a common bound restricting its magnitude in either direction. One way of dealing with this special case is to add arc $\langle q, p \rangle$ for every $\langle p, q \rangle$ in the network. Both pairs of bounds can then be set to $[0, c_{high}]$, and we have again the capacitated network of D.8.1. If both $\langle p, q \rangle$ and $\langle q, p \rangle$ are already in the network, having bounds $[-c_1, c_1]$ and $[-c_2, c_2]$, respectively, simply assign capacity $c_1 + c_2$ to each of the two arcs. (In the general case it is possible to construct a network that supports no flow, e.g., a network with $Q = \{\langle s, 2 \rangle, \langle 2, t \rangle\}$, where the bounds are $[1, 2]$ and $[3, 4]$.)

A maximal flow need not be unique, and one may be required to select a particular maximal flow that satisfies some additional criterion. Consider a function $m: Q \to R_+$ that assigns to each arc $\langle p, q \rangle \in Q$ a value $m(p, q)$, which we interpret as the cost of sending one unit of a commodity through $\langle p,q \rangle$. The total cost associated with a flow f is $\sum_{\langle p, q \rangle \in Q} m(p,q) \cdot f(p,q)$ and the problem is to find a maximal flow for which the total cost is a minimum. This is known as the minimal cost problem. Investigation of the general bounded network and minimal cost problems is beyond the scope of this book.

The max-flow min-cut theorem is related, rather unexpectedly, to a very important result of combinatorial mathematics concerning the existence of distinct representatives of subsets of a set.

DEFINITION 8.4   Let S be a set, and let $\mathscr{S} = \{S_1, S_2, \ldots, S_m\}$ be a family of subsets of S (not necessarily disjoint). A set of *distinct* elements $\{a_1, a_2, \ldots, a_m\}$ such that $a_i \in S_i$ is a *system of distinct representatives* for $\mathscr{S}$.

THEOREM 8.3   (P. Hall's theorem)   Let

$$\mathscr{S} = \{S_i \mid i \in I\}, \qquad \text{where} \quad I = \{1, 2, \ldots, m\},$$

be a family of subsets of a set S. A system of distinct representatives for $\mathscr{S}$ exists if and only if $|\bigcup_{i \in I_k} S_i| \geq k$ for every I_k, where I_k is a subset of I having k elements, and for every $k = 1, 2, \ldots, m$.

Proof. Necessity is obvious. To prove sufficiency construct a network with nodes s and t, and a node for each element $x_j \in S$ and each subset $S_i \in \mathscr{S}$, i.e., a total of $2 + |S| + m$ nodes. Draw arc $\langle s, S_i \rangle$ for every node S_i, arc $\langle x_j, t \rangle$ for every node x_j, and arc $\langle S_i, x_j \rangle$ whenever $x_j \in S_i$. Complete the construction by assigning capacity 1 to each arc. Now construct a flow f. If (s, S_i, x_j, t) is a path, then $x_j \in S_i$, and x_j can be a representative of S_i. Now, if this path carries a nonzero flow, we interpret the flow in the path as making x_j the representative of subset S_i. Since the inflow at S_i cannot exceed 1, only one of the arcs originating from S_i can carry the flow out. Moreover, the outflow from x_j cannot exceed 1 either. Therefore, the only flow into x_j must come from S_i. Every f selects representatives of some of the subsets, and a maximal flow selects representatives of the greatest possible number of subsets. Therefore, $\mathscr{S}$ has a system of distinct representatives if and only if the value of the maximal flow from s to t is m. Suppose now that $\mathscr{S}$ has no system of distinct representatives. Then the value of the maximal flow from s to t must be less than m, and by Th.8.2 the capacity of a minimal cut is less than m. Now assume that the cut contains k_1 arcs that originate at s. Therefore, the set X' of Th.8.2 contains exactly $m - k_1$ nodes of type S_i. Denote the set of these nodes by S', and let X be the set of elements in the union of all the members of $\mathscr{S}$ that belong to S'. Partition X into

$X_1 = \{x_j \mid x_j \in X'\}$ and $X_2 = \{x_j \mid x_j \notin X'\}$, and assume that $|X_1| = k_2$. Then the cut contains k_2 arcs that terminate at t. Consequently, arcs originating from S' and terminating in X_2, which make up the rest of the cut, must be fewer than $m - k_1 - k_2$ in number. This means that $|X_2| < m - k_1 - k_2$. But then $|X| = |X_1| + |X_2| < m - k_1$, and, since $|S'| = m - k_1$, we have shown that the nonexistence of a system of distinct representatives implies the existence of a collection of k subsets the union of which has fewer than k elements, i.e., the theorem has been proven by proving its contrapositive.

Example

An association has a number of committees; a member of the association may serve on any number of them. At the end of the year each committee selects one of its members to report on its activities. The problem is to choose the reporters in such a way that no individual reports on more than one committee. This problem can be solved by setting up a network as in the proof of Th.8.3. The S_i stand for committees, the x_j for members of committees. If there are k committees, and the maximal flow in the network has the value k, then the problem has a solution, and the flow defines the solution. If more than one flow is maximal, there is more than one solution.

8b. Graphs in Chemistry

There is probably no science in greater need of mechanized information retrieval than chemistry. Millions of chemical compounds are known; new ones are produced at an ever faster rate. The chemist has two main problems: First, he wants to find out whether the substance in his test tube is already known; second, given a substance, he wants to know the properties of similar substances. Both problems reduce to a matching process; a description of the given substance has to be matched against descriptions of substances that make up the data base of the retrieval system. A precondition for a satisfactory retrieval system is a standard representation of chemical compounds. The representation must be unambiguous, amenable to classification so as to facilitate search, and reasonably compact. Quite a number of systems of representation are in use. The great diversity of possible search requests ensures that almost any system has some feature that makes it superior to others for dealing with some particular aspect of the retrieval problem.

Chemical formulas are very compact, but they are ambiguous. Consider the hydrocarbons of the paraffin series. Their general formula is $C_k H_{2k+2}$ (e.g., CH_4, C_2H_6). Each carbon atom is linked to four other atoms; a hydrogen atom can be linked to only one other atom, which has to be carbon.

The total number of links in C_kH_{2k+2} is $\frac{1}{2}(4k + 2k + 2) = 3k + 1$. Let us interpret the links as edges in a graph having the atoms for nodes. Then the theory of Section 3h tells us that the graph contains no circuits ($m - n + 1 = 3k + 1 - 3k - 2 + 1 = 0$), i.e., that the graph is a tree. The subgraph of carbon atoms must be a connected tree, and more than one tree of the carbon atoms can be constructed for every $k \geqq 4$. Each distinct tree on the k carbon atoms represents an *isomer* of C_kH_{2k+2}. Since isomers have different properties, the formular representation is inadequate. For example, when $k = 6$, there are 5 isomers, all corresponding to the single formula C_6H_{14}. Enumeration of isomers is an important problem. Cayley (1875) interpreted the isomerism problem for the paraffin series as an enumeration problem for trees, and solved it in this form; his solution is one of the classics of graph theory.

In a diagrammatic representation each isomer has a different structural diagram. Figure 8.3 shows the structural diagrams of isomers of C_4H_{10}.

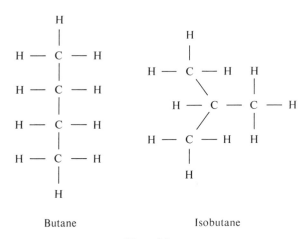

Butane   Isobutane

Figure 8.3

Structural diagrams are very often drawn with the hydrogen atoms stripped off. Then, if, for example, there are b edges incident with a carbon atom, we know that $4 - b$ is the number of hydrogen atoms bonded to the carbon atom. Sometimes two atoms are linked by more than one bond. Either diagram of Figure 8.4 is an example. (In these diagrams, knowing that oxygen has 2 bonds and nitrogen 3, we can easily work out that the molecules contain three hydrogen atoms.) Structural diagrams are labeled graphs with parallel edges; such graphs are known as *multigraphs*. Labeled multigraphs give a reasonably adequate description of chemical substances. It must be remembered, however, that the graphs are projections of three-dimensional structures into the plane. For stereochemistry, which distinguishes different arrangements of the atoms of a molecule in space as stereoisomers, the planar representation is still inadequate.

The matching problem can be dealt with very well in terms of chemical structures. It becomes the graph isomorphism problem, considerably simplified by the labels carried by the nodes. The procedure that we are going to describe, Sussenguth's algorithm, is based on two principles. First, if graphs G and G^* are isomorphic, then the subset of nodes of G that exhibit some property must correspond to the subset of nodes of G^* that exhibit this same property. Second, if the subsets of nodes of G and G^* that are characterized by some property do not have the same number of elements, then the two graphs cannot be isomorphic.

Consider the structural diagrams of Figure 8.4 in which subscripts are node identifiers. The matching procedure starts with generation of subsets of nodes that represent the same type of atom; nodes that represent oxygen

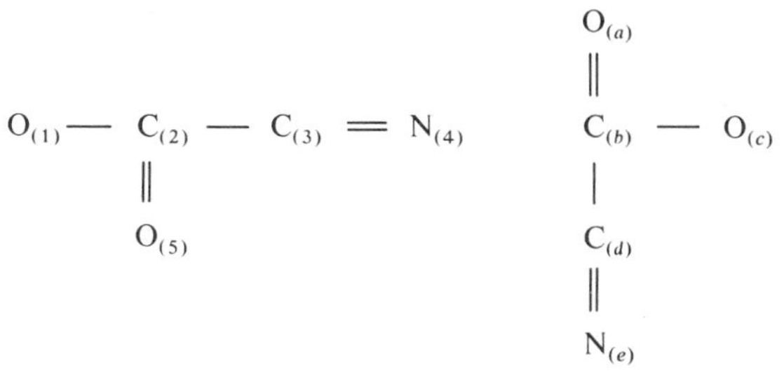

$$O_{(1)} - C_{(2)} - C_{(3)} = N_{(4)} \qquad \begin{array}{c} O_{(a)} \\ \| \\ C_{(b)} - O_{(c)} \\ | \\ C_{(d)} \\ \| \\ N_{(e)} \end{array}$$

$$\begin{array}{c} \| \\ O_{(5)} \end{array}$$

Graph G Graph G^*

Figure 8.4

atoms, say, in graph G must correspond to nodes representing oxygen atoms in G^*. These correspondences are shown by lines 1 to 3 in Table 8.3. Next the subsets of nodes that are joined by the same type of bond are made to correspond (lines 4 and 5). At this point a partitioning procedure takes over. The purpose of partitioning is to reduce the number of nodes of G^* to which a node of G can correspond. The purpose is achieved by taking intersections. For example, from the correspondence of $\{1, 5\}$ and $\{a, c\}$ (line 3), we know merely that node 1 of G corresponds to one of a or c in G^*, but

$$\{1, 5\} \cap \{1, 2, 3\} = \{1\} \quad \text{and} \quad \{a, c\} \cap \{b, c, d\} = \{c\},$$

implying that 1 corresponds to c. Partitioning gives lines 6 and 7 in the table. Three of the nodes are now matched, but correspondence of elements in sets $\{2, 3\}$ and $\{b, d\}$ is still unresolved. We define the *degree* of a node as the number of edges incident with it (counting sets of parallel edges linking two nodes as a single edge), and generate subsets of nodes that have the same degree (lines 8 to 10). There is no need to resume the partitioning procedure; all nodes are matched. The correspondence of nodes in the two graphs is

$$\text{Graph } G: \qquad 1 \quad 2 \quad 3 \quad 4 \quad 5$$

$$\text{Graph } G^*: \qquad c \quad b \quad d \quad e \quad a$$

TABLE 8.3

MATCHING OF CHEMICAL STRUCTURES

Basis for subset generation		Subset of G	Subset of G^*	Line
Node label:	C	$\{2, 3\}$	$\{b, d\}$	1
	N	$\{4\}$	$\{e\}$	2
	O	$\{1, 5\}$	$\{a, c\}$	3
Bond:	single	$\{1, 2, 3\}$	$\{b, c, d\}$	4
	double	$\{2, 3, 4, 5\}$	$\{a, b, d, e\}$	5
Partition:	lines 3, 4	$\{1\}$	$\{c\}$	6
	lines 3, 5	$\{5\}$	$\{a\}$	7
Degree:	1	$\{1, 4, 5\}$	$\{a, c, e\}$	8
	2	$\{3\}$	$\{d\}$	9
	3	$\{2\}$	$\{b\}$	10
Neighbors:	line 2	$\{3\}$	$\{d\}$	8a
	line 6	$\{2\}$	$\{b\}$	9a

If some nodes were still not matched, new subsets would have to be generated. Let us define the *order* of a node as the number of edges in the smallest circuit through this node. Subsets of nodes having the same order would be put in correspondence. (All nodes in the graphs of Figure 8.4 have the same order, namely 0, and the concept of order is of no value here.) Another concept that can be used is one of neighborhood. If a node of G is already matched to a node of G^*, then nodes that are the immediate neighbors of the identified nodes form corresponding subsets. If, instead of using the degrees of nodes to generate subsets, we had made use of neighborhoods, the matching procedure would have continued as shown in Table 8.3 below the dividing line.

In general, the algorithm terminates when every node in G has been paired off with a node in G^*, or when two corresponding subsets of nodes of G and G^* are found to differ in the number of nodes they contain. If the former is the case, graphs G and G^* are isomorphic; if the latter, isomorphism is impossible. Occasionally, however, the algorithm exhausts all subset generating properties before either of the two conditions is satisfied. This happens when more than one isomorphism is possible between the two graphs, or when the subset generating properties are incomplete in the sense that some property that would establish isomorphism or the lack of it has been neglected in the design of the algorithm.

For the sake of the argument assume that the algorithm cannot take us beyond line 7 of Table 8.3. Nodes in subset $\{2, 3\}$ have remained unmatched, but we know that their possible correspondents must belong to $\{b, d\}$. Therefore we postulate the two correspondences

$$A(1) = \begin{bmatrix} 1 & 2 & 3 & 4 & 5 \\ c & b & d & e & a \end{bmatrix} \quad \text{and} \quad A(2) = \begin{bmatrix} 1 & 2 & 3 & 4 & 5 \\ c & d & b & e & a \end{bmatrix}$$

and carry out a node-by-node comparison of the two graphs. If both assignments are valid, there are two isomorphisms; if only one is valid, there is a single isomorphism; if both assignments result in contradictions, then the graphs are not isomorphic.

After the nodes have been partitioned according to their labels (lines 1 to 3 of Table 8.3), only the structure of the graphs determines validity of the arrangements. The structure can be represented by a *connectivity matrix* C in which $c_{ij} = n$, where n is the number of times edge $\{i, j\}$ is drawn in the multigraph. We have

$$C_G = \begin{bmatrix} 0 & 1 & 0 & 0 & 0 \\ 1 & 0 & 1 & 0 & 2 \\ 0 & 1 & 0 & 2 & 0 \\ 0 & 0 & 2 & 0 & 0 \\ 0 & 2 & 0 & 0 & 0 \end{bmatrix} \quad \text{and} \quad C_{G^*} = \begin{bmatrix} 0 & 2 & 0 & 0 & 0 \\ 2 & 0 & 1 & 1 & 0 \\ 0 & 1 & 0 & 0 & 0 \\ 0 & 1 & 0 & 0 & 2 \\ 0 & 0 & 0 & 2 & 0 \end{bmatrix}.$$

(In C_{G^*} subscripts $1, \ldots, 5$ refer to nodes $a, \ldots, e$, respectively.) From C_{G^*} generate the connectivity matrices corresponding to the two assignments. They are

$$C_{A(1)} = \begin{bmatrix} 0 & 1 & 0 & 0 & 0 \\ 1 & 0 & 1 & 0 & 2 \\ 0 & 1 & 0 & 2 & 0 \\ 0 & 0 & 2 & 0 & 0 \\ 0 & 2 & 0 & 0 & 0 \end{bmatrix} \quad \text{and} \quad C_{A(2)} = \begin{bmatrix} 0 & 0 & 1 & 0 & 0 \\ 0 & 0 & 1 & 2 & 0 \\ 1 & 1 & 0 & 0 & 2 \\ 0 & 2 & 0 & 0 & 0 \\ 0 & 0 & 2 & 0 & 0 \end{bmatrix}.$$

Since $C_G = C_{A(1)} \neq C_{A(2)}$, there exists a single isomorphism.

A structure diagram is completely specified by its connectivity matrix and a vector of labels E. In our example the vectors are

$$E_G = [\text{O} \quad \text{C} \quad \text{C} \quad \text{N} \quad \text{O}] \quad \text{and} \quad E_{G^*} = [\text{O} \quad \text{C} \quad \text{O} \quad \text{C} \quad \text{N}].$$

For the input of chemical structures one can use a special chemical typewriter. The typewriter produces a paper tape, and a conversion program uses the information on the tape to set up the connectivity matrix and label vector.

An analogous procedure can be used to identify a given graph G as a subgraph of another graph G^*. Defining properties are again used to generate corresponding subsets. Denote by S and S^* the subsets of nodes of G and G^*, respectively, that are generated by the same defining property. The two principles on which the matching algorithm is based now become: If G is a subgraph of G^*, then $S \subseteq S^*$; if $|S| > |S^*|$, then G cannot be a subgraph of G^*.

8c. Graphs in Information Retrieval

Information retrieval consists of two disciplines: document retrieval and fact retrieval. A scientist, before he sets out to perform some piece of research, wants a list of references to all work in his chosen problem area. The literature search is done by a document retrieval system. If his examination of the retrieved publications shows that what he wants to do is unlikely to have been done before, then the scientist starts on his project. Soon he finds that he needs answers to highly specific questions; e.g., he may want to know the number of isomers of $C_{10}H_{22}$. For this information he turns to a fact retrieval system. If the system cannot supply the answer (Answer: $C_{10}H_{22}$ has 75 isomers), then he has to appeal again to the document retrieval system for a list of references on enumeration of isomers.

A retrieval system can mean many things. It may mean the scientist and his personal file of index cards, or the scientist and a few bibliographies, or the scientist and a roomful of handbooks, or a little request card and a computer with a huge data base and a battery of complex document and fact retrieval procedures. The fully automatic system of the last example does not exist. Semiautomatic document retrieval systems, which require the scientist to do some work himself, are, however, in existence. Automatic fact retrieval systems also exist, and in some narrow areas, e.g., retrieval of stock market quotations and chemical retrieval, they are fully automatic; but these systems do rarely more than search through a few lists of data. A system with a *wide* data base, capable of making *complex* inferences, is still only a hope for the future. This is due partly to the sheer size of the required data base, partly to linguistic problems. We shall discuss only the simpler, but still very difficult, problem of document retrieval.

With a primitive semiautomatic system the user supplies a set of key words, e.g. {*graph, network, tree*}, and the system retrieves documents that have one or other of these words or some derivative of it in the title. The *semi* refers to the work that is likely to go on afterwards. First, the set of titles retrieved may contain " Programming *graphic* devices," " Handbook of mathematical functions with formulas, *graphs*, and mathematical tables," " The place of a small library in the national *network*," etc. These references have to be weeded out manually, but one has to be careful not to assume offhand, for example, that " The enumeration of *trees* by height and diameter " deals with forestry. Second, the system will fail to retrieve documents that are relevant, but do not have one of the given key words in their titles, e.g., " The four-color problem."

Both types of shortcomings can be dealt with reasonably effectively. One takes a dictionary of concepts, known as a *thesaurus*, and selects terms from this dictionary that will describe a particular document. They become the *index terms* associated with the document; their selection is the process of *indexing*. The user of the system selects words or phrases from the same thesaurus to define the categories of documents that he wants retrieved. These we shall call *search terms*. The number of elements in the intersection of the sets of index and search terms determines the relevance of a document. Both index and search terms can be weighted, and the system can use the weights to evaluate a finer measure of relevance of a document with respect to the search request. The retrieved documents are graded in order of relevance. Under this scheme " The four-color problem " and " The enumeration of trees by height and diameter " are assigned high relevance; the other titles quoted above sink to the bottom of the list. The system is still semiautomatic in that the selection of index terms has to be done manually, or, at best, semiautomatically.

This has been an exceedingly naïve account of the retrieval problem. Continuing in the same naïve vein, let us take a superficial look at the structure of a thesaurus. The semantic value of a word is unknown unless we have some idea how this word is related to other words. A concept is not a single word (or phrase), but a word and other words related to it, words that are, in turn, related to the words to which the first word is related, and so on, to any suitable distance. A thesaurus is a dictionary in which related words are grouped into clusters. Consider *Roget's Thesaurus*, which contains 1000 clusters, each cluster defining a particular concept. For example, cluster No. 792 defines the concept *thief*; 65 terms are listed in this cluster. A conventional thesaurus does not, however, indicate the strength of the relation between two words in a cluster. The cluster of our example contains the terms *fence* and *viking*. It is hard to see any relation between the terms, let alone define its strength, until other terms of the cluster are used to set up a relational chain *fence —receiver of stolen goods—thief— robber—pirate— viking*. The length of the chain between two terms can be used as a measure of the relatedness between the terms. This suggests that a graph gives a more effective representation of a concept than an unstructured list. The concept graphs can be combined into a single graph representing the entire thesaurus; it is connected because each term that belongs to more than one cluster is still represented by a single node. The term *fence* alone, because it occurs in 6 of the 1000 clusters, connects 6 concept graphs.

Let us now take a new approach to the retrieval problem. With an effectively constructed thesaurus it is possible to permit the user to supply only a few search terms. The system then uses the thesaurus to generate a larger internal set for the comparisons with index sets of documents. The internal set could be the union of clusters in which more than one or two, say, of the supplied terms have been found. If the thesaurus defines few concepts, as is the case with *Roget's Thesaurus*, the concepts are very broad, and the internal set is much too large. Moreover, to conserve storage, redundancy should be eliminated by making the entire thesaurus a single graph, but then the individual concepts lose their identity. In this single thesaurus graph a procedure for constructing the internal set could be based on the following, or some similar, definition: The internal set contains all the search terms supplied, and every term that is joined by an edge to at least four other terms in the set, of which at least two must belong to the initial search set. Figure 8.5 shows a subgraph in which the term *arc* is represented in three conceptual senses (as in *arc light, arc in a network, arc of a circle*). In terms of the search set {*arc, path*} and this graph, the only internal set consistent with the

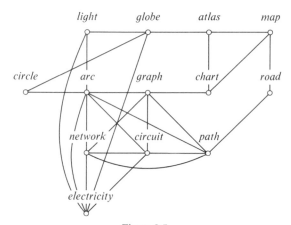

Figure 8.5

definition is $\{arc, graph, network, circuit, path\}$. The probability that all relevant documents will be retrieved is much greater with this set than with the original set $\{arc, path\}$.

Another graph that can be of interest in the retrieval of documents is the *citation digraph* $\langle D, R \rangle$, where D is a set of documents and R is the set $\{\langle d_i, d_j \rangle \mid d_i \text{ cites } d_j\}$. If we have already selected a subset X of D that consists of relevant documents, and we have a document $d_k \notin X$, then the number of arcs in the intersection $R_X^+ \cap R_{\{d_k\}}^-$ (see D.3.6) is the number of documents in X that cite the document d_k. This number can be used in the evaluation of the relevance of d_k to the search request.

A further use of the citation digraph is in establishing the absolute importance of a document. Libraries are becoming very short of space. It is, therefore, important to determine the importance of documents in their collections. Documents that are in little demand can be cleared from the open shelves to give readier access to those for which a strong demand exists. One measure of the importance of a document d_k is the number of other documents that cite it, directly or indirectly. In terms of the citation digraph this is the number of nodes from which node d_k is reachable.

Notes

For further study of flow problems one can turn to Chapter 7 of [Bu65], Chapter 14 of [De74b], the classic [Fo62], and [Ed72]. Our formulation of the Ford–Fulkerson algorithm (A.8.1) follows closely the exposition given in [Be64a]. Our proof of Th.8.3 derives from that given in [Ha65b].

Sussenguth's matching procedure for chemical structures is described in [Sa64] and, in greater detail, in [Su65]. References to chemical notations, and to the part they play in the retrieval of chemical information can be found in [Ta67, Ly71]. One should consult the *Annual Review of Information Science and Technology* for up-to-date surveys of various aspects of mechanized information retrieval. Salton's SMART system is perhaps the most advanced operational system for experimentation with automated information retrieval procedures. Salton's textbook on information retrieval [Sa68a] describes retrieval principles in relation to this existing system. For this reason it has a sustained vitality that warrants a very warm recommendation of the book. [Sa71] is a collection of technical papers relating to the SMART system; [Sa73] is also relevant.

The graph of our Figure 8.5 relates words in the simplest possible way. For an indication of further possibilities inherent in this approach one should study the sophisticated relational scheme devised by Quillian, see [Qu67]. Quillian's work has influenced Simmons and his co-workers in the design of their question answering system Synthex—see [Sc70]. [Si70] is a survey of question answering systems. With reference to Figure 8.5 again, the effectiveness of a retrieval system in which internal representation of data is in the form of graphs depends on algorithms for detecting cliques in such graphs. [Au70] should be read for general background; [Br73] contains a very efficient algorithm for finding cliques.

Exercises

8.1 (a) Interpret the networks of Figures 3.6 and 6.13 as capacitated transportation networks and find, respectively, the value of maximal flow from node c to node f and from node 1 to node 8.

8.2 (a) If all capacities in the network of Figure 8.1 are (i) doubled, and (ii) halved, what is the value of the maximal flow from node 1 to node 8?

8.3 (a) If in the network of Figure 8.1 we change c_{58} to 3, then the value of the maximal flow can be increased to 7 by altering the capacity of any one of two other arcs. Identify these arcs.

8.4 (a) In the network of Figure 8.1 let nodes 1 and 2 be two sources and node 8 the sink. Find the maximal flow from the sources to the sink.

8.5 (a) Implement A.8.1a as a computer program, and apply it to the networks of Figures 3.6 and 6.2.

8.6 (a) An alternative to the method used in A.8.1a for computing flow paths is to use A.6.6 with the Q-semiring $\langle R_+^\infty, max, min, 0, \infty \rangle$ (see Exercise 6.3). Modify A.8.1a accordingly, and apply the modified algorithm to the networks of Exercise 8.5.

8.7 (a) The maximal flow in an antisymmetric transportation network, i.e., a network in which the presence of an arc $\langle i, j \rangle$ implies the absence of arc $\langle j, i \rangle$, can be found by a variant of A.8.1a that uses only one matrix, namely the matrix of capacities C. Ultimately this matrix defines a maximal flow. Design such an algorithm, implement it, and apply it to the network of Figure 3.6. Hint: The initial adjustment of matrix C, in case the initial flow is nonzero, now consists of setting $c_{ij} = c_{ij} - f_{ij}$, $c_{ji} = -f_{ij}$, for all $f_{ij} \neq 0$.

8.8 (a) One generalization of the capacitated network is a network in which (some or all) nodes are capacitated as well. For example, although the sum of capacities of arcs terminating at a node may be 15, say, and the sum of capacities of arcs originating from this node may also be 15, the total flow through the node may be restricted to values not exceeding 12, say. A node-capacitated network may be converted to an equivalent network in which arcs alone are capacitated by the addition of dummy nodes and arcs. Describe the conversion process.

8.9 (a) Committees of an association are composed as follows: $A = \{a, b, d\}$, $B = \{b, d, e, g\}$, $C = \{c, d\}$, $D = \{a, b, c\}$, $E = \{a, f, g\}$, $F = \{c, d, g\}$, $G = \{a, b, c, f\}$. Show that it is possible to choose reporters from all committees in such a way that no individual reports on more than one committee. Although it is possible to solve this problem by inspection, you should use the Ford–Fulkerson algorithm for practice.

8.10 (a) A Department of Computer Science wants to give the following courses in Spring Term: CS1, CS12, CS13, CS248, CS293, CS31, CS328. Faculty members are qualified to teach the courses as follows:

Brown	CS1, CS13, CS248;
Douglas	CS1, CS31;
Evans	CS1, CS248, CS31;
Harris	CS12, CS293;
Jones	CS1, CS13;
Kelly	CS12, CS293, CS328;
Smith	CS1, CS13, CS31.

Show that the department cannot give all seven courses if each faculty member is to teach only one course.

8.11 (b) Graph S of Figure 8.6 is a subgraph of Graph G. Use the matching procedures described in Section 8b to prove this. (The leftmost line in the drawing of S, which is not an edge, serves to indicate the degree of the node to the right of it.)

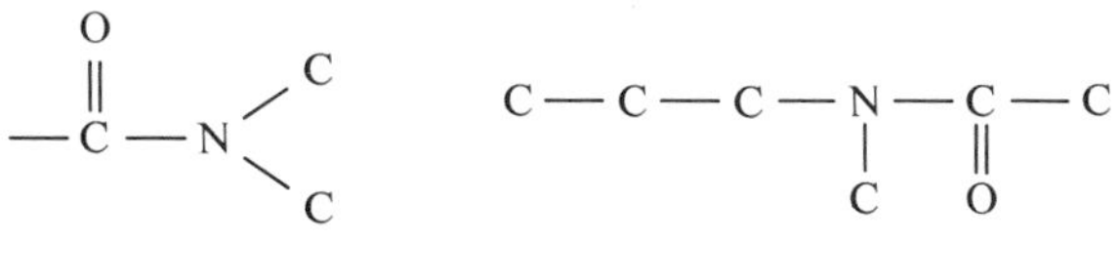

Subgraph S Graph G

Figure 8.6

8.12 (b) (nontrivial project) Implement Sussenguth's algorithm for matching chemical structures as a computer program.

PART III

COMPUTER REPRESENTATION OF STRUCTURES

CHAPTER 9

Arrays

9a. Storage Media and Their Properties

In this section, which serves for an introduction to the remainder of the book, we shall endeavor to come to a limited understanding of some storage media used in modern computers. It is not our purpose to delve into the physical principles underlying the different storage mechanisms; we shall consider only those properties that may have direct relevance to programming. Moreover, only storage media that are in wide use will be discussed.

The most important storage unit in a modern computer is its magnetic core store. The cores, each of which stores one bit, are arranged in planes with 32, or 64, or 128, or 256 cores in both directions (the numbers are powers of 2 to enable full use to be made of the bits assigned to specification of addresses in machine language commands), and the planes are stacked one on top of the other. Usually the number of cores in a plane determines the number of words in the memory unit, and the number of planes determines the length of a word. For example, a 128 by 128 unit 36 planes deep stores 16 384 (or 16 K for short) 36-bit words. The time of access to a word, called the *cycle time*, is the time required to enter an address in the address register, read the information from the selected location, and, if the reading operation is destructive, write the information back into the same location. The IBM 360, Model 50 is a typical modern computer of moderate size. Depending on the model, the number of 32-bit words in its core memory can vary from 16K to 131K; the cycle time is 2 μsec. The important feature of core memory is that access time is independent of the location of a word. The time to access 100 words stored sequentially is the same as the time to access 100 words that have their addresses selected at random. For this reason core memory is called a *random access memory*.

Sometimes core storage is arranged on two levels. There is a *main* store and a slower *mass* or *bulk* store. The fast main store of the IBM 360, Model 50 can be supplemented with a bulk store having a cycle time of 8 μsec and a capacity of 262K or 524K 32-bit words. Access is still fully random, and a word in the mass core store functions exactly like a word in the main store. Therefore, the mass store is simple an extension of the main store. A different approach is taken by CDC with their 6000 series machines, which have a cycle time of 1 μsec and main core memory ranging in size from 32K to 131K 60-bit words. Here information has to be transferred from the bulk store into the main store before it can be operated on, but transfer is very fast. Most efficient transfer is in blocks of 8 60-bit words, and transfer rates of 0.1 to 0.8 μsec for a word can be achieved (these figures depend on the sizes of the main store and the bulk store—the latter can vary in size from 126K to 2015K words).

The accessing mechanism of a magnetic core store is electronic. This means that the storage unit and the components that give access to it remain stationary during reading and writing. In the other storage devices that we shall consider the storage medium is a thin surface layer of magnetic material. Information passes between the computer proper and the storage device through a *read–write head*. Access to a particular region of the surface is gained by bringing the head in near contact with the region by mechanical means. Consequently access times for magnetic surface storage are longer than for core storage.

A magnetic *disk store* consists of a number of disks, their flat surfaces coated with magnetic material, in continuous rotation about an axis through their centers. The surfaces are divided into annular regions, called *tracks*. Some manufacturers divide a track into *sectors*. The unit of information being transferred to or from the disk store is then equal in size to the storage capacity of a sector, and access is by selection of the particular surface, track, and sector on which data are to be written, or from which they are to be read. IBM does not use the sectoring approach. Instead, instructions are provided that give access to the precise location in the disk store that one is interested in.

Two read–write heads are attached to an access arm that is free to move in the space between two adjacent disks; one of the heads is assigned to the lower surface of the disk above the arm, the other to the upper surface of the disk below it. There is an access arm for every pair of such surfaces. The topmost and bottommost surfaces of the entire assembly are not used for recording data. A *seek* instruction positions the appropriate read–write head over the track one wants to access, and data transfer occurs when the motion of the disk assembly carries the appropriate section of the track past the head. The head positioning time is known as the *seek time*. Note that the entire set of access arms moves together as a unit, i.e., that the seek operation positions a read–write head over the same track of every recording surface in the assembly. If, after finishing with a particular track, one wished to access an adjoining track on the same surface, a repositioning of the head would have to take place, but the same track on a different surface can be accessed without a further seek. This explains the emphasis given in data processing to the concept of the *cylinder*, which is the set of all tracks accessed by a single movement of the access assembly. Note that some disk devices have several independent access assemblies to reduce the amount of mechanical motion.

There are two main types of disk stores. In one the disks are permanently fixed in the disk drive, in the other the set of disks constitutes a disk pack that can be removed from the disk drive for off-line storage. For our example of the former we take the CDC 821 disk store. It provides storage for 8.38×10^8 6-bit characters on a total of 65,536 tracks, each track consisting of 20 sectors, and each sector holding 640 characters. The seek time varies from 21 to 140 msec, depending on how far the read–write head has to travel. There is also a *latency time* to consider. This is the time one has to wait for the required storage locations to move up to the head after the head is in position. The maximal latency time is the time for one revolution of the disk. For the 821 this is 35 msec. The maximal rate of transfer of data to and from the 821 is 416K characters per sec.

The IBM 2311 is an example of a removable disk pack unit. The pack consists of 6 disks that provide 10 recording surfaces. There are 203 tracks to each surface, 200 for regular use and 3 held in reserve as replacements of the regular tracks should any of them develop faults. Each track can hold 3625 8-bit characters, and total capacity of a pack is 7.25×10^6 characters. The seek time is 21–140 msec, the maximal latency time 35 msec. Maximal transfer rate is 156K characters per sec.

Both access times and costs of *magnetic drums* are intermediate to those of bulk core and disk stores. The magnetic material is carried by the curved surface of a rigid rotating cyclinder. The geometry permits read–write heads to be permanently fixed in position, and more heads can be made to transmit information simultaneously. Hence waiting times and transfer rates are better than for movable head disk stores. A typical drum (CDC 863) has a capacity of 4×10^6 6-bit characters; the average waiting time is 17 msec, and a maximal transfer rate of 2×10^6 characters per sec can be achieved. Some early computers, e.g., the IBM 650, had drums for their main stores, and were called "drum computers." Those drums, however, were very slow by modern standards. Because disks and drums are provided with addressing mechanisms they are sometimes called *random access devices*, but they are not as "random" as core memory. It is more appropriate to call them *direct access devices*. Other examples of direct access devices are fixed head disk stores, which are functionally indistinguishable from drums, and *magnetic card* or *strip* devices. The latter have not been able to withstand the competition of disk stores.

The storage medium of a *magnetic tape* is supported by a flexible ribbon, up to about 2400 ft long. A typical tape unit, the IBM 2420, Model 7, moves tape at 200 in. per sec, and a 1-in. strip of tape can accommodate 1600 rows of information, each row storing an 8-bit character. The standard way of expressing this is to say that the tape has a *recording density* of 1600 bpi (bits per inch). A maximum of 4.6×10^7 characters could be stored with this recording density on a reel 2400 ft long, and the entire reel could be read in about 144 sec. However, the maximal capacity cannot be achieved because information is stored in *blocks*, and gaps some 0.6 in. long must be left between blocks to allow for stopping and starting between blocks. With large blocks, comprising, for example, 8000 characters (or 2000 IBM 360/370 words), the effect of the gaps on either capacity or transfer rate is barely noticeable (10% decrease in capacity, and a similar decrease in the maximal transfer rate of 320K characters per sec).

In contrast to disks and drums, magnetic tape devices have no addressing mechanism. One simply sets the tape in motion and identifies a required block by counting the blocks that pass the reading head, or by reading identifying data stored within the blocks themselves. In either case this is a matter of programming, and the access time is determined by the sequence in which the blocks were originally stored on the tape. For this reason magnetic tape storage is called *sequential storage*. If data have to be accessed in more or less random manner, latency times of the order of minutes make tapes completely useless, but they serve very well as an inexpensive medium for permanent storage of bulky records and for some types of temporary storage. Another drawback of conventional magnetic tapes is that data stored on a tape cannot be altered in a localized fashion. The contents of the entire tape have to be copied onto a new tape to alter the contents of just one block.

A multiprogramming system processes several programs at the same time, and each of these programs may individually require more storage space than the main core store can provide. The users of the system certainly cannot be expected to cope with the intricate details of transfers between the main store and auxiliary storage devices in this environment, and the transfers must be scheduled and carried out by the system. There is, therefore, no obstacle to improving the well-being of the user by letting him assume that he has the computer all to himself, and that the main store at his disposal is nearly unlimited in size. Multiprogramming systems support this illusion by some variant of the *paging concept*. The entire memory of the computer is divided into pages of, say, 512 words, and the programmer can use a large number of these pages. The pages go in and out of core memory as required, but there cannot be too much of a delay between the request for a page and its arrival in core storage. The illusion would soon be shattered if magnetic tapes were used for the auxiliary memory.

9b. Storage of Arrays

Consider a function f with domain $A_1 \times A_2 \times \cdots \times A_t$. Let $|A_k| = n_k$, and denote the members of A_k by $a_{k1}, a_{k2}, \ldots, a_{kn_k}$. The $1, 2, \ldots, n_k$ are *subscripts* or *indices*, and we denote $f(a_{1i}, a_{2j}, \ldots, a_{tw})$ in terms of indices by $f_{ij\cdots w}$. Take a very simple case, a function f defined on $A \times B$, where $|A| = n$ and $|B| = m$. This function can be represented by an $n \times m$ matrix of its values, i.e., by an array of nm "boxes" arranged in the plane:

$$
\begin{bmatrix}
f_{11} & f_{12} & \cdots & f_{1m} \\
f_{21} & f_{22} & \cdots & f_{2m} \\
\vdots & \vdots & \vdots & \vdots \\
f_{n1} & f_{n2} & \cdots & f_{nm}
\end{bmatrix}.
$$

The indices determine the position of the box that stores f_{ij}; we find it at the intersection of the ith row and the jth column. The function with values $f_{ij\cdots w}$ has $n_1 n_2 \cdots n_t$ members, and it is represented by a t-dimensional array in t-space. The box that contains $f_{ij\cdots w}$ in this space is found at the intersection of vectors defined by subscripts $i, j, \ldots, w$ parallel to the axes of the space.

Fortran does permit us to refer to f_{ij} by the name F(I, J), but all conventional computers still require a multidimensional array to be stored as a linear sequence of elements. The compiler must, therefore, contain a procedure that computes the actual address of an element in an array from its specification in terms of indices. The mapping from the multidimensional array to the linear array is not unique; here we shall quite arbitrarily assume that elements of the multidimensional array are stored in lexicographic order of their indices, e.g., $f_{111}, f_{112}, \ldots, f_{11n_3}, f_{121}, \ldots, f_{n_1 n_2 n_3}$ (the ANSI Fortran Standard actually requires the order to be $f_{111}, f_{211}, \ldots, f_{n_1 11}, f_{121}, \ldots, f_{n_1 n_2 n_3}$). We want a *storage mapping function, loc*, defined on the indices as follows:

$$loc(i, j, \ldots, w) = loc(1, 1, \ldots, 1) + c_0 + c_1 i + c_2 j + \cdots + c_t w,$$

where the $c_0, c_1, \ldots, c_t$ are constants. The problem is to find the constants. To see how it is done let us consider an array A, dimensioned (10, 15, 7), where we want the address of element A(5,7,4). This element comes fourth in the seventh row of the fifth plane of the array; i.e., it is preceded by 4 planes, 6 rows, and 3 elements. But a plane contains 15×7 elements, and a row 7 elements. Hence

$$loc(5, 7, 4) = loc(1, 1, 1) + 4(15 \times 7) + 6(7) + 3,$$

and for three-dimensional arrays in general we have

$$\begin{aligned} loc(i, j, k) &= loc(1, 1, 1) + n_2 n_3(i - 1) + n_3 (j - 1) + (k - 1) \\ &= loc(1, 1, 1) - (n_2 n_3 + n_3 + 1) + n_2 n_3 i + n_3 j + k. \end{aligned}$$

It is now easy to see that in the general case of a t-dimensional array

$$\begin{aligned} c_0 &= -(n_2 \cdots n_t + n_3 \cdots n_t + \cdots + n_t + 1), \\ c_1 &= n_2 \cdots n_t, \\ c_2 &= n_3 \cdots n_t, \\ &\vdots \\ c_{t-1} &= n_t, \\ c_t &= 1. \end{aligned}$$

The part played by array bounds $n_1, n_2, \ldots, n_t$ in storage mapping is one reason why most programming languages that provide subscripted variables require the actual dimensions of arrays to be declared. Fortran permits up to three dimensions; in Algol the number of dimensions is unlimited, but implementations of the language do, in effect, set some limit on this number. Some compilers, e.g., the Watfor Fortran compiler, generate a code that tests during execution of a program whether a reference to a subscripted variable lies outside the declared array bounds. If it does, and were to remain undetected, information might get written into locations that house other data or even the program itself, and the result would be a rather erratic behavior of the program. The increase in execution time due to these tests is well worth it in a compiler that is used mainly for program testing.

The standard higher-level languages (Fortran, Algol, PL/I) require all arrays to have a rectangular structure. Very often this results in considerable waste of storage space. For example, if a matrix A is *upper triangular*, i.e., if $a_{ij} = 0$ whenever $j < i$, then only elements with $j \geqq i$ need to be stored. Similarly, nearly half the information contained in a *symmetric* matrix A is redundant because $a_{ij} = a_{ji}$, and again only the upper (or lower) triangle of the values has to be stored. Another example is the *tridiagonal* matrix in which only the elements a_{ij} such that $j = i$ or $j = i \pm 1$ are nonzero:

$$
\begin{bmatrix}
a_{11} & a_{12} & 0 & 0 & 0 & \ldots \\
a_{21} & a_{22} & a_{23} & 0 & 0 & \ldots \\
0 & a_{32} & a_{33} & a_{34} & 0 & \ldots \\
& \vdots & \vdots & \vdots & \vdots &
\end{bmatrix}.
$$

Nonzero elements of an upper triangular matrix A, dimensioned (N,N), can be stored in vector UPT of dimension M = N*(N+1)/2 as follows:

UPT(1)	UPT(2)	UPT(3)	UPT(4)	...	UPT(M)
A(1,1)	A(1,2)	A(2,2)	A(1,3)	...	A(N,N)

Element A(I,J) is in location UPT(K), where K = J*(J-1)/2 + I. A tridiagonal matrix T, dimensioned (N,N), can be stored in vector TRD of dimension M = 3*N - 2 as follows:

TRD(1)	TRD(2)	TRD(3)	TRD(4)	TRD(5)	...	TRD(M)
T(1,1)	T(2,1)	T(1,2)	T(2,2)	T(3,2)	...	T(N,N)

Element T(I,J) is in location TRD(K), where K = 2*J + I - 2. Alternatively, a tridiagonal matrix can be stored in three vectors:

$$
\begin{array}{lllll}
[\text{T}(1,2) & \text{T}(2,3) & \text{T}(3,4) & \ldots & \text{T}(N-1,N)] \\
[\text{T}(1,1) \quad \text{T}(2,2) & \text{T}(3,3) & \text{T}(4,4) & \ldots & \text{T}(N,N)] \\
[\text{T}(2,1) & \text{T}(3,2) & \text{T}(4,3) & \ldots & \text{T}(N,N-1)]
\end{array}
$$

Two upper triangular matrices A and B, both dimensioned (4, 4), say, can be stored as a single matrix AWITHB, dimensioned (5, 4), as follows:

$$
\text{AWITHB} =
\begin{bmatrix}
\text{A}(1,1) & \text{A}(1,2) & \text{A}(1,3) & \text{A}(1,4) \\
\text{B}(1,1) & \text{A}(2,2) & \text{A}(2,3) & \text{A}(2,4) \\
\text{B}(1,2) & \text{B}(2,2) & \text{A}(3,3) & \text{A}(3,4) \\
\text{B}(1,3) & \text{B}(2,3) & \text{B}(3,3) & \text{A}(4,4) \\
\text{B}(1,4) & \text{B}(2,4) & \text{B}(3,4) & \text{B}(4,4)
\end{bmatrix}.
$$

Then A(I,J) = AWITHB(I,J), but B(I,J) = AWITHB(J+1,I).

9c. Sparse Matrices

In Example 3 of D.3.4 we represented a matrix X by a network. The network can be represented, in turn, by a different matrix, which we call Q (to make the example more interesting we have added elements $x_{51} = 7$ and $x_{54} = 3$):

$$Q = \begin{bmatrix} 1 & 1 & 2 & 2 & 3 & 4 & 4 & 5 & 5 & 5 & 5 \\ 1 & 2 & 1 & 3 & 5 & 1 & 4 & 1 & 3 & 4 & 5 \\ 4 & 3 & 2 & 4 & -1 & 8 & -2 & 7 & 1 & 3 & 2 \end{bmatrix}.$$

The first two elements of a column in Q define an arc, the third is the weight associated with the arc, or, in the terminology of arrays, a column stores the indices and the value of a nonzero element of X. Generalizing, let a matrix X have n rows and m columns, and let k be the number of nonzero elements in X. Normally the matrix would be stored in nm locations, but when $3k < nm$, a matrix such as Q gives a more economical representation. We call a matrix with many zero elements a *sparse* matrix. The sparseness of a matrix is measured by its *density*, which is the ratio of the number of nonzero elements of the matrix to its total number of elements. Unfortunately the representation could prove rather awkward for some operations on sparse matrices stored in this fashion. It is reasonably easy to find all elements belonging to a given row of X because they occupy contiguous columns in Q, but the elements belonging to a given column are scattered throughout Q.

Therefore, instead of the representation of Figure 3.7, we shall consider a digraph in which there is a node for every nonzero element of the sparse matrix, and triples ⟨*row number, column number, value*⟩ are assigned as labels to the nodes. All nonzero elements belonging to the same row or column in the matrix are represented by adjoining nodes on a path in the digraph. Figure 9.1 shows the matrix of our example under this representation.

Now we can represent matrix X (or the digraph of Figure 9.1) by a 4×11 matrix QQ in which the first three rows are a copy of Q, but a fourth row contains pointers linking elements that belong to the same column in X:

$$QQ = \begin{bmatrix} 1 & 1 & 2 & 2 & 3 & 4 & 4 & 5 & 5 & 5 & 5 \\ 1 & 2 & 1 & 3 & 5 & 1 & 4 & 1 & 3 & 4 & 5 \\ 4 & 3 & 2 & 4 & -1 & 8 & -2 & 7 & 1 & 3 & 2 \\ 3 & 0 & 6 & 9 & 11 & 8 & 10 & 0 & 0 & 0 & 0 \end{bmatrix}.$$

We shall call this the four-row representation of the matrix. Let us look at column 1 of X. Elements that belong to this column are identified by a 1 in the second row of QQ. They are stored in columns 1, 3, 6, and 8 of QQ, and the entries in the fourth row of QQ do send us from the first column to the third, then to the sixth, and finally to the eighth column. The zero in QQ(4,8) indicates that the element stored in QQ(3,8) is the last nonzero element

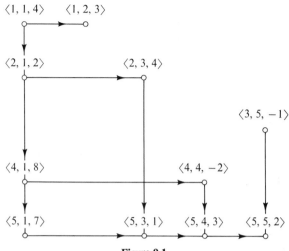

Figure 9.1

belonging to column 1 of X. We supplement QQ with two "entry" vectors NC and NR:

$$NC = [1 \quad 2 \quad 4 \quad 7 \quad 5]$$
$$NR = [1 \quad 3 \quad 5 \quad 6 \quad 8 \quad 12].$$

The value in NC(J) points to the column of QQ that contains the first non-zero element of column J in X; if NC(J) = 0, then all elements of column J are zero. NR(I) contains the number of the column in QQ that stores the first nonzero element of row I in X and, since NR(I+1) contains a pointer to the first nonzero element of row I+1, there are NR(I+1) - NR(I) contiguous columns storing elements of row I. If all elements of row I are zero, then NR(I) = NR(I+1). This convention makes it necessary for NR to contain one more element than there are rows in X; this last element contains a number that is 1 greater than the number of columns in QQ.

The normal procedure for forming a matrix product C = AB is

```
      DIMENSION A(N,K),  B(K,M),  C(N,M)
         :
         :
      DO  5   I = 1,N
      DO  5   J = 1,M
      C(I,J) = 0.
      DO  5   L = 1,K
   5  C(I,J) = C(I,J) + A(I,L)*B(L,J)
```

We shall now give a program for finding C = AB when matrices A and B have four-row representation.

ALGORITHM 9.1   Formation of the matrix product $C = AB$. The N × K matrix A with KA nonzero elements is specified by arrays QA, NCA, NRA. The K × M matrix B with KB nonzero elements is specified by QB, NCB, NRB. Matrix C has the conventional representation. Values of NP and KP are greater by 1 than those of N and K, respectively. For convenience elements of the matrices are assumed integers. Note that NCA and NRB, K, and KP are not referenced in the text of the subroutine. These arguments are listed merely to emphasize the representation used for A and B.

```
      SUBROUTINE ABYB (QA,NCA,NRA,QB,NCB,NRB,C,KA,KB,
     1                 N,NP,K,KP,M)
      INTEGER QA(4,KA), QB(4,KB), C(N,M)
      DIMENSION NCA(K), NCB(M), NRA(NP), NRB(KP)
      DO 50  I = 1,N
      DO 10  J = 1,M
   10 C(I,J) = 0
C   TEST FOR EMPTY ROW IN A
      IF (NRA(I).EQ.NRA(I+1)) GO TO 50
      DO 40  J = 1,M
      KANOW = NRA(I)
      KBNOW = NCB(J)
C   TEST FOR EXHAUSTED COLUMN IN B OR ROW IN A
   15 IF (KBNOW.EQ.0.OR.KANOW.EQ.NRA(I+1)) GO TO 40
C   FIND K SUCH THAT A(I,K), B(K,J) BOTH NONZERO
      IF (QA(2,KANOW)-QB(1,KBNOW)) 20,25,30
   20 KANOW = KANOW + 1
      GO TO 15
   25 C(I,J) = C(I,J) + QA(3,KANOW)*QB(3,KBNOW)
      KANOW = KANOW + 1
   30 KBNOW = QB(4,KBNOW)
      GO TO 15
   40 CONTINUE
   50 CONTINUE
      RETURN
      END
```

Multiplication of sparse matrices is quite easy even when the matrices have the three-row representation exemplified by the array Q discussed at the beginning of this section. Let the representations of matrices A and B be QA and QB, respectively, and let the respective numbers of columns in QA and QB be QACOL and QBCOL. Then the code for generating $C = AB$ is

```
      DO 10 I = 1,N
      DO 10 J = 1,N
```

```
10   C(I,J) = 0
     DO 50 I = 1,QACOL
     DO 40 J = 1,QBCOL
     IF (QA(2,I) - QB(1,J)) 50,20,40
20   KA = QA(1,I)
     KB = QB(2,J)
     C(KA,KB) = C(KA,KB) + QA(3,I)*QB(3,J)
40   CONTINUE
50   CONTINUE
```

This procedure is simpler than that of A.9.1, but A.9.1 should be considerably faster. Speeds of the two algorithms would come more in line if QB were provided with a row entry vector, and this vector used to prevent the loop on J from being started with 1 each time (Exercise 9.11), but A.9.1 would still retain an edge over the three-row algorithm.

Next let us consider what happens in the four-row representation of a matrix when a nonzero element becomes zero, or an element that was previously zero acquires a nonzero value. The first case is easily dealt with: simply change the appropriate value in the third row of the representation to zero. Four memory locations are taken up unnecessarily, but this is not too serious. In the second case a new column has to be added to the four-row representation QQ. To cope with this, QQ has to be dimensioned at the very start to have more columns than there are nonzero elements. Assume that x_{22} changes from 0 to 6. In terms of QQ this calls for the insertion of a new column between columns 3 and 4. The new data go into column 4, and the old columns 4 through 11 have to be shifted to the right. Hence the need for a reserve of empty columns at the high end of QQ. In addition, all entries greater than or equal to 4 in the fourth row of QQ, and in all of NC and NR have to be increased by 1, and we have to set $QQ(4,2) = 4$. The resulting representation is

$$
QQ = \begin{bmatrix}
1 & 1 & 2 & 2 & 2 & 3 & 4 & 4 & 5 & 5 & 5 & 5 & \cdots \\
1 & 2 & 1 & 2 & 3 & 5 & 1 & 4 & 1 & 3 & 4 & 5 & \cdots \\
4 & 3 & 2 & 6 & 4 & -1 & 8 & -2 & 7 & 1 & 3 & 2 & \cdots \\
3 & 4 & 7 & 0 & 10 & 12 & 9 & 11 & 0 & 0 & 0 & 0 & \cdots
\end{bmatrix},
$$

$$
NC = \begin{bmatrix} 1 & 2 & 5 & 8 & 6 \end{bmatrix},
$$

$$
NR = \begin{bmatrix} 1 & 3 & 6 & 7 & 9 & 13 \end{bmatrix}.
$$

All in all, updating is a very expensive operation in the four-row representation. As an alternative, let us take QQ as it stands, and add a fifth row to it so as to create a five-row representation QQQ. The fifth row consists of pointers linking elements that belong to the same row in the original matrix X.

There is complete analogy between the interpretation of the entries in the new row and those in the fourth row. In addition, the format of the row entry vector NR is changed to make NR analogous to NC. We have

$$
QQQ = \begin{bmatrix}
1 & 1 & 2 & 2 & 3 & 4 & 4 & 5 & 5 & 5 & 5 & \cdots \\
1 & 2 & 1 & 3 & 5 & 1 & 4 & 1 & 3 & 4 & 5 & \cdots \\
4 & 3 & 2 & 4 & -1 & 8 & -2 & 7 & 1 & 3 & 2 & \cdots \\
3 & 0 & 6 & 9 & 11 & 8 & 10 & 0 & 0 & 0 & 0 & \cdots \\
2 & 0 & 4 & 0 & 0 & 7 & 0 & 9 & 10 & 11 & 0 & \cdots
\end{bmatrix},
$$

$$
NC = [1 \quad 2 \quad 4 \quad 7 \quad 5],
$$

$$
NR = [1 \quad 3 \quad 5 \quad 6 \quad 8].
$$

Note that QQQ has more columns than are necessary at this time. A small reserve of empty columns has been provided to allow for addition of new data should this become necessary.

Let us see what now happens when x_{22} changes from 0 to 6. Instead of squeezing in the representation of the new nonzero element between representations of the other nonzero elements, we append it at the high end of QQQ as column 12. Other changes are minimal: the zero from QQQ(4,2) goes into QQQ(4,12) and QQQ(4,2) is set to 12; the 4 from QQQ(5,3) goes into QQQ(5,12) and QQQ(5,3) is set to 12. In this particular instance there are no changes to NC or NR. The result:

$$
QQQ = \begin{bmatrix}
1 & 1 & 2 & 2 & 3 & 4 & 4 & 5 & 5 & 5 & 5 & 2 & \cdots \\
1 & 2 & 1 & 3 & 5 & 1 & 4 & 1 & 3 & 4 & 5 & 2 & \cdots \\
4 & 3 & 2 & 4 & -1 & 8 & -2 & 7 & 1 & 3 & 2 & 6 & \cdots \\
3 & 12 & 6 & 9 & 11 & 8 & 10 & 0 & 0 & 0 & 0 & 0 & \cdots \\
2 & 0 & 12 & 0 & 0 & 7 & 0 & 9 & 10 & 11 & 0 & 4 & \cdots
\end{bmatrix}.
$$

One could now step through the nonzero elements of row 2 of X as follows: Pick up NR(2). Since it is 3, go to column 3 in QQQ. This column represents $x_{21} = 2$. The 12 in QQQ(5,3) tells that the next nonzero element of row 2 of X is represented by column 12. This element is $x_{22} = 6$, and QQQ(5,12) $= 4$ sends one to column 4. This column represents $x_{23} = 4$, and, since QQQ(5,4) $= 0$, there are no other nonzero elements in row 2 of X.

Neither the four-row nor the five-row representation can be conveniently implemented when we lack a prior knowledge of the number of nonzero elements in a matrix. In the next section we shall develop techniques that will enable us to store arrays without dimensioning them.

9d. Storage Allocation at Execution Time

Fortran requires constant array bounds to be specified before execution of a program. Adjustable dimensions are permitted in subprograms, but the actual arrays that take the place of the dummy "place holders" during execution of a subprogram must have been given constant dimensions. For example, if the program contains the statement

```
CALL SUB (X,5)
```

and the definition of SUB starts with

```
SUBROUTINE SUB (ARRAY,N)
DIMENSION ARRAY(N,N)
```

then somewhere X must have been given constant bounds X(5,5). In A.9.1 matrix C was stored in the conventional form because we did not have the information that would have enabled us to declare a four-row array to take this matrix. In Algol and PL/I programs array bounds can be specified and storage allocated to the arrays during execution of a program, but this facility still does not solve our problem. We want to avoid declaring some arrays altogether.

One way of solving the problem is to store all arrays of unknown dimensions in a large vector, and to use a second array for bookkeeping. For example, if we declare the arrays by

```
DIMENSION STORE(10000), INFO(100,2)
```

then we have 10,000 locations reserved for storing arrays, and the 100 rows of INFO can be used to store information about 100 arrays at a time. We do not refer to an array by a name, but by the number K of the row in INFO that contains information pertaining to it. INFO(K,1) contains the subscript of the element of STORE at which the stored array begins, and INFO(K,2) contains its size. Further, there is a location INDEX, which contains a pointer to the first element in STORE that has not been used up.

To see how the scheme works assume that two arrays are to be read from cards and put into STORE in the conventional representation of matrices, that their product is to be formed, also in STORE, and that finally the product is to be converted to the four-row representation. We assume that the first card of the input contains two numbers, which specify the number of rows and columns, respectively, of the first matrix, and that this card is followed by cards containing the elements of the matrix punched in lexicographic order of the indices. This set of cards is followed by a second set that defines the second matrix. We have to assume that the number of columns in the first matrix is equal to the number of rows in the second (otherwise the product would be undefined). The program that follows reads the two matrices and forms their product, but the conversion to the four-row representation is left as an exercise (Exercise 9.15).

```
        COMMON INDEX, STORE(10000), INFO(100,2)
        DIMENSION NSTORE(10000)
        EQUIVALENCE (STORE(1), NSTORE(1))
C   THE EQUIVALENCE PERMITS US TO REFER TO THE STORAGE
C   ARRAY BY TWO NAMES.  THIS GETS AROUND THE
C   DIFFICULTY CREATED BY THE FORTRAN NAMING
C   CONVENTION FOR INTEGERS AND REALS.
        INDEX = 1
        CALL READER (N,K,1)
        CALL READER (K,M,2)
        INFO(3,1) = INDEX
        INFO(3,2) = N*M
        DO 10  I = 1,N
        DO 10  J = 1,M
        INOW = INFO(1,1) + (I-1)*K
        JNOW = INFO(2,1) + (J-1)
        STORE(INDEX) = 0.
        DO  5  L = 1,K
        STORE(INDEX) = STORE(INDEX)
      X                     + STORE(INOW)*STORE(JNOW)
        INOW = INOW + 1
    5   JNOW = JNOW + M
   10   INDEX = INDEX + 1
        :
```

(Conversion to four-row representation)

```
        :
        SUBROUTINE READER (I,J,K)
        COMMON INDEX, STORE(10000), INFO(100,2)
        READ (5,100) I,J
        INFO(K,1) = INDEX
        INFO(K,2) = I*J
        IHI = INDEX + INFO(K,2) - 1
        READ (5,101) (STORE(II), II = INDEX, IHI)
        INDEX = IHI + 1
        RETURN
  100   FORMAT (2I5)
```

```
101  FORMAT (8F10.0)
     END
```

Assume that N=10, K=5, M=20, and that there are 15 nonzero elements in the product matrix. Then, after the four-row representation has been found, STORE and INFO appear as shown in Figure 9.2.

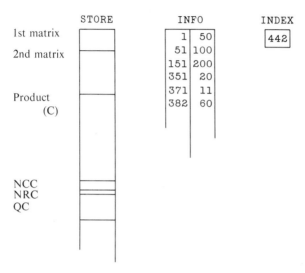

Figure 9.2

Assume now that we no longer require the first three matrices in STORE. The storage space occupied by these arrays can be used again. We leave as an exercise (Exercise 9.17) the writing of the program that deletes the three arrays and shifts the remaining arrays to the beginning of STORE. Figure 9.3 shows the appearance of the storage regions after the deletions.

The dynamic storage allocation scheme described above is too specific. We would prefer to relegate much of the processing to general subprograms. For example, we would like to have a subroutine that compacts STORE by deleting all arrays that are no longer required. This subroutine could be called by other routines whenever the storage capacity of STORE is exceeded. A second unsatisfactory feature of the present scheme is that arrays are specified by row numbers of INFO instead of mnemonic names.

Let us analyze the compaction problem. Assume that a third column is added to INFO, and that INFO(k, 3) contains 1 if array k is still required, -1 if it is no longer in use, and 0 if there is no such array. The programmer has the responsibility of putting -1 in the appropriate location in INFO when he has finished with an array. The compaction subroutine, which we shall call

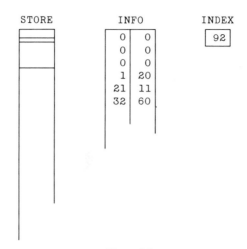

Figure 9.3

GRBAGE, can then compact STORE by deleting arrays marked -1, moving all arrays marked 1 to the head of the store, and making appropriate changes in INFO. Looking again at the situation depicted in Figure 9.3, assume that a new array has been read into STORE. The first row of INFO was empty, and we assume that the information pertaining to the new array has been stored there. The first row of INFO then corresponds to the fourth array in STORE. But, if the order of arrays in STORE differs from the order in which information about them is stored in INFO, we are in serious difficulties with the design of GRBAGE; the compacting procedure cannot then simply go down INFO, compacting as it moves from row to row. The easiest solution is to require that each row of INFO be used only once, and that one cannot use row I+1 before row I has been used. Under this scheme information about the new array would be put into row 7 of INFO. Another solution is for GRBAGE to shift rows of INFO as well, so that the position of an array in STORE always agrees with the number of the row in INFO that contains information about it. But how will the main program and the other routines know what changes have been made to INFO?

We take the second alternative. However, instead of worrying how to pass information about changes made to INFO out of the subroutine, we change the whole scheme so that the main program is no longer concerned with INFO. This is done by introducing mnemonic names for the dynamically stored arrays, and specifying all operations on these arrays by means of subprograms. The main program then becomes just a sequence of calls to the subprograms. We shall use integer variables for naming arrays in STORE. If variable NN refers to an array, then it is made to contain the number of the row in INFO that contains information about this array. INFO is augmented with yet another column; this column contains references to the names of arrays. Assume that array NN is the 27th array in STORE. Then the location NN contains the value 27, and INFO(27,4) contains a reference to location NN. Now assume that the markers in INFO(25,3) and INFO(26,3) are both −1, and that GRBAGE is called. If all the other 24 arrays preceding NN are still in use, then GRBAGE makes NN the 25th array in STORE, transfers contents of the 27th row of INFO to the 25th row, and changes the value in location NN to 25. Establishing access to variable NN is the trickiest part in the design of the scheme because Fortran does not provide the address of NN. This part of the problem is solved by asking the programmer to put names of all arrays that at some time will occupy STORE into COMMON, as in the following example:

```
INTEGER A, B, C, XA, XB, ......
COMMON A, B, C, N1, N2, N3, XA, XB, ......
```

Let us now write an initiating routine START, which is to be called by the main program before anything else is done:

```
SUBROUTINE START
COMMON NAMES(250)
COMMON/INTERN/INDEX, INFROW, STORE(10000),
X                 INFO(100,4)
    DO  1  K = 1,250
1   NAMES(K) = −K
    DO  2  I = 1,100
    DO  2  J = 1,4
2   INFO(I,J) = 0
    INDEX = 1
    INFROW = 1
    RETURN
    END
```

Variable N3 has the same location as NAMES(6), and, after return from START, this location contains the value −6. Straight after the call to START we may decide to make a call to a subroutine that reads in an array from cards. Assume that the array has size 50, and that we have decided to call it N3. Then the input routine puts (1, 50, 1, 6) into the first row of INFO and changes the −6 in NAMES(6) to 1. After N3 has been stored INDEX contains the value 51, and INFROW, which points to the row of INFO that is to be used next, contains 2. If next we read matrix N1 (size 64) from cards, the second row of INFO is made (51, 64, 1, 4), and NAMES(4) receives the value 2. INDEX and INFROW become 115 and 3, respectively. Taking this example still further, indicate that array N3 is not to be saved by making INFO(N3,3) equal to −1, and then call GRBAGE. This subroutine takes the 6 from INFO(1,4) and restores it as −6 to NAMES(6); after this the name N3 may be used to refer to another array. Then it shifts array N1 to locations STORE (1) to STORE(64), sets INDEX equal to 65 ánd INFROW equal to 2, puts (1, 64, 1, 4) into the first row of INFO, clears the second row to zero, and changes the 2 in NAMES(4) to 1.

An important consideration in the design of the system is what to do with dimensions of arrays. They could be stored with the arrays themselves— the block occupied by an array in STORE then contains several locations additional to those that store the elements of the array; these locations contain the dimensions of the array. In what follows we shall assume that this course has been taken. Of course, some implementers may prefer to transmit dimensions in argument lists of calls. The processing routines are then simpler, and this may outweigh the inconvenience of having to clutter up argument lists with dimension data.

For our final example we assume that the calls

```
CALL CONVRT (C,C4)
NUMBER = KOUNT (C4)
CALL DELETE (C)
```

convert a matrix C to its four-row representation C4, determine the number of nonzero elements in the matrix, and indicate that C need not be saved after this. Under the scheme we have been discussing so far, after it is indicated that an array identified by NAMES(K) is not to be saved, the name of this array may not be used before GRBAGE has been called. This would be the case with array C here. The reason is that the task of restoring the value −K to NAMES(K) has been assigned to GRBAGE. A more satisfactory solution is to have this restoring done by DELETE instead. Then the name C may be used as the name of a new array at once. Function KOUNT and subroutine DELETE are simply

```
FUNCTION KOUNT(NNN)
COMMON/INTERN/INDEX,INFROW,STORE(10000),
X               INFO(100,4)
KOUNT = INFO(NNN,2)/4
RETURN
END

SUBROUTINE DELETE(NNN)
COMMON/INTERN/INDEX,INFROW,STORE(10000),
```

```
X                 INFO(100,4)
  INFO(NNN,3) = -1
  NNN = -INFO(NNN,4)
  RETURN
  END
```

GRBAGE has to be called whenever the value in INDEX exceeds 10,000, or
the value in INFROW exceeds 100. Therefore, before a start is made on the
actual conversion, subroutine CONVRT calls GRBAGE if INFROW exceeds 100:

```
      IF (INFROW.GT.100) CALL GRBAGE
      IF (INFROW.GT.100) GO TO 111
      :
111   WRITE (6,100)
      STOP
100   FORMAT (30H TOO MANY ARRAYS - TERMINATION)
      :
```

Assume that we build up the final value of INDEX by adding 4 whenever a nonzero element is transferred from C to C4. If the value exceeds 10,000, then
one calls GRBAGE, tests INDEX again and terminates if it still exceeds 10,000,
adjusts some parameters (C4 has certainly been shifted to a new region in
STORE, and C may also have been shifted), and resumes the conversion process. It is probably more convenient to have the error exits in GRBAGE itself.

This sketchy introduction to the implementation of dynamic storage
allocation facilities in Fortran has taken us from a relatively simple technique
to a complex system of subprograms. We have given only a few examples of
the subprograms that a complete system would contain. Although the system
can be written entirely in Fortran, and the calls to the subprograms are
Fortran statements, we have, in effect, a new programming language. The
system extends the power of Fortran by giving a non-Fortran interpretation
to the variables that refer to arrays in STORE. In Fortran I, J, and K are
integer variables, and K = I + J is a meaningful statement. If, however,
we use I, J, and K to represent dynamically stored arrays, then the variables
are no longer integer variables in the usual sense (K = I + J is then
meaningless). The powerful technique for creating new programming languages by assigning new interpretations to certain constituents of an existing
language is known as *embedding*.

Calls to subprograms are the statements of our new language; the language is, in fact, defined by the subprograms. Once the representation of data
and the mechanism for access to the data have been decided on, and a few
basic routines that implement the access mechanism have been written, one
is at liberty to write as few or as many additional subprograms as one wishes.
Even a fairly complex system of some 30 subprograms should not take an

experienced programmer more than a few days to write. It is a simple matter to add new facilities; one simply writes a few new subprograms.

Efficiency is the chief advantage that embedding has over independent special purpose languages. A special purpose language can be considered as made up of two components: the facilities specific to the problem area in which the language is used and general facilities, such as input and output, arithmetic capability, and sequencing of the computational process. A general purpose language provides all these facilities, and, since many people are involved in the design and improvement of the language, these facilities are generally excellent. Moreover, by being able to spread the cost over a large number of users, the compiler can be optimized to produce highly efficient machine code. The designers of an independent special purpose language have to provide the general facilities and a compiler or interpreter, and they lack the resources to do as good a job. With embedding the general facilities already exist, and all available resources can be directed to the implementation of just those facilities that relate to the special problem area.

Notes

The first edition of this book carried the following: "Apart from the highly technical [Ri67] (with a bibliography of some 1000 entries), I know of no book that I would be prepared to recommend for reference on storage media and their properties. This is so because in the rapidly advancing science and technology of computing the fastest changes take place in the technology of storage devices." I still recommend [Ri67], but not for the reason given above. The fact that this book is still current is an indication that the technology has slowed down, at least as regards basic principles. Of course, improvements to existing device types continue to be made, and the reader is referred to *Datamation, Computer Decisions*, and *Computer* to keep up with the changes in performance figures.

Addressing of elements in multidimensional arrays is discussed in [He62, Hi62]. [Po73] is a survey of sparse matrix compression techniques, and [Mc71] is a package of Fortran subroutines that constitutes a system for operating with sparse matrices. The ANSI Fortran standard requires that matrices be stored in column order. However, all better-known methods for matrix inversion and the solution of simultaneous linear equations access the elements of matrices in row order. This combination can lead to intolerably long execution times for large problems in a paging environment. [Mc69b, Mo72, E174] address themselves to the resolution of this problem.

A Fortran-embedded system that constitutes one solution of the dynamic storage allocation problem is described in [Sa68b]. The rationale of embedding is spelled out in [Bo64]. For examples of embedding see [Co66, Sa68b].

The ingenious system of subroutines for semi-analytic differentiation described in [We64] provides a particularly simple but effective illustration of the power of embedding.

Exercises

9.1 (b) A Fortran array X is dimensioned (10, 10, 10). Assuming that elements of arrays are stored in lexicographic order of their indices, find displacements of the locations of X(5,6,7), X(10,9,8), and X(1,5,9) relative to the location of X(1,1,1).

9.2 (b) Devise a storage mapping function for the storage order required by the ANSI Fortran Standard. Repeat Exercise 9.1 using this storage mapping function.

9.3 (b) An array X is dimensioned (K,L,M). How many elements of X have identical displacements under the storage mapping functions of Exercises 9.1 and 9.2?

9.4 (b) In the definition of the storage mapping function we assumed that every subscript has 1 for its lower bound. In Algol the lower bound of a subscript can be any integer. Define the storage mapping function for this general case.

9.5 (b) Assume that we have a computer in which the word size is 36 bits, and that an array A of dimensions (L, M, N), which has all of its elements belonging to $\{0, 1\}$ is stored in a compact form, 36 elements to a word, in a linear array LOGIC. LOGIC(1), LOGIC(2), LOGIC(3) contain the dimensions, and the remaining words of LOGIC contain the elements of A. Assembler language subprograms for storing and fetching elements of A can be written, and these subprograms can be referenced by a Fortran program:

```
CALL STORE (NUMBER,LOGIC,I,J,K)
```

causes NUMBER to be stored as a_{ijk}, and the function reference

```
NFETCH (LOGIC,I,J,K)
```

supplies the value of a_{ijk}. Both these subprograms require a subroutine PLACE, which, given arguments LOGIC, LDIM, I, J, K, where LDIM is the dimension of LOGIC, returns the subscript of the element of LOGIC in which a_{ijk} is to be found, and its bit position. Write this subroutine in Fortran. What should be stored in the first three words of LOGIC in preference to the dimensions for more efficient performance of PLACE?

9.6   (b)   Given matrices

$$A = \begin{bmatrix} 1 & 2 & 3 & 4 \\ 0 & 3 & 4 & 5 \\ 0 & 0 & 5 & 6 \\ 0 & 0 & 0 & 7 \end{bmatrix} \quad \text{and} \quad B = \begin{bmatrix} 1 & 1 & 3 & 5 \\ 0 & 3 & 3 & 5 \\ 0 & 0 & 5 & 5 \\ 0 & 0 & 0 & 7 \end{bmatrix},$$

write a program that reads the two matrices into a compact 5×4 array and finds the matrix products AB and BA, which are also upper triangular matrices, in two vectors (each of dimension 10).

9.7   (b)   Apply the principle illustrated by Figure 5.22 to the design of a storage scheme for arrays. Describe your scheme fully, and give a detailed analysis, with reference to a particular computer with which you are familiar, of its advantages and disadvantages as compared to a scheme based on the storage mapping function.

9.8   (c)   Give four-row representations, including the entry vectors, for matrix X of Example 1 of D.3.12 and for matrix X^3 (see the example of Th.3.6).

9.9   (c)   Given four-row representations of matrices A and B, subroutine ABYB of A.9.1 finds the product of the two matrices. Write similar routines for finding

   (i)   the sum $A + B$,
   (ii)   the transpose A', where $(a')_{ij} = a_{ji}$, in place, i.e., without creating a new four-row representation.

9.10   (c)   Given an N × M matrix MAT with K nonzero elements. Write a subroutine that converts MAT to its four-row representation. The subroutine starts as follows:

```
SUBROUTINE FORROW (MAT,N,M,MATFOR,K,NC,NR,NP)
DIMENSION MAT(N,M), MATFOR(4,K), NC(M), NR(NP)
```

9.11   (c)   It was pointed out in the text that the algorithm for finding the matrix product AB, given three-row representations of A and B, could be made faster if the representation of B were provided with a row entry vector. Devise this faster algorithm. The format of the row entry vector should be selected to suit your convenience.

9.12   (c)   Write a subroutine for multiplying two sparse matrices, given their five-row representations.

9.13   (c)   Write a subroutine that converts a matrix to its five-row representation.

9.14 (c) Consider the three-row representation Q displayed at the beginning of Section 9c. Each pair of row and column subscripts can be replaced by a single value:

$$Q = \begin{bmatrix} 1 & 2 & 6 & 8 & 15 & 16 & 19 & 21 & 23 & 24 & 25 \\ 4 & 3 & 2 & 4 & -1 & 8 & -2 & 7 & 1 & 3 & 2 \end{bmatrix}.$$

How was this value computed? Find formulas for the row and column subscripts in terms of this value and the dimensions of the matrix represented by Q.

9.15 (d) Incorporate the conversion procedure of Exercise 9.10 in the matrix multiplication program of Section 9d.

9.16 (d) In the matrix multiplication program of Section 9d the product matrix is first generated in its conventional form, and a four-row representation derived afterwards. Alter the program so that it builds up the product in four-row representation from the start.

9.17 (d) With reference to the storage scheme depicted in Figure 9.2, write a subroutine that deletes the first K arrays stored in STORE, shifts all remaining arrays to the head of STORE, and adjusts INFO and INDEX accordingly.

9.18 (d) Explain why the statement labeled 1 in subroutine START of Section 9d is NAMES(K) = —K rather than NAMES(K) = K.

9.19 (d) (major project) Write a set of subprograms to provide Fortran with dynamic storage allocation facilities. (The proper design of the system is more important than the coding of the routines.)

CHAPTER 10

Lists and List Structures

10a. Lists—Introductory Concepts

Very often the storage needs of a program cannot be predicted in advance. Consider the implementation of a stack, with an array functioning as the stack. In Fortran the size of the array has to be decided on before execution of the program begins. Algol and PL/I, which are more flexible, permit the size of the array to be specified during execution of the program, but storage allocation must still be made before the first datum is pushed down into the stack. Even as late as this it is sometimes impossible (or, if not theoretically impossible, so impracticable as to be impossible in an operational sense) to estimate the maximal depth that the stack will attain. Underestimation then results in stack overflow; overestimation in inefficient utilization of storage space.

One solution to this problem was advanced in Section 9d. However, implicit in the design of the system of Section 9d is the assumption that only one array is "active" at any one time. If, then, we wished to make use of more than one stack simultaneously, as in A.5.1, this dynamic storage arrangement would not be applicable.

One way of making the dynamic storage allocation scheme of Section 9d work when multiple stacks are in use simultaneously is to utilize STORE merely as a backup facility. Each stack is implemented as a conventional array of, say, 50 elements. Then, if a PUSH instruction would cause overflow, the 25 items of data at the bottom of the " fixed " stack are transferred

377

as a block to STORE. The remaining 25 items are then moved to the area just vacated and the pointer adjusted accordingly. If at some other time an IPOP instruction finds the fixed stack empty, the most recently stored overflow block associated with this stack is returned from STORE. This at once releases the 25 locations in STORE for other use. We have suggested a block size of 25 locations rather than 50 to avoid excessive shifting of blocks to and from STORE.

We shall not discuss here how the overflow blocks are linked together in STORE because this system is not very satisfactory either. Assume that we are going to have at most *n* stacks in use at any one time. Then we could set aside a matrix of 50 rows and *n* columns for a stack storage area, and instead of having a single pointer, provide a vector of *n* pointers for the *n* stacks. The permanent assignment of 50 × *n* locations to the stacks is rather wasteful of space. Our purpose now is to look at more economical schemes for organizing an area of store in such a way that on demand more storage space can be assigned to any one of a number of sets of data at any stage of execution of a program.

For inspiration we look to the IBM 650, a rather antique computer. In most present day computers instructions have in general the format

(Operation code)(Address of operand),

and normally instructions are executed in the order in which they are stored unless explicit transfer instructions override the normal sequence. The IBM 650 format of instructions was

(Op. code)(Addr. of operand)(Addr. of next instruction).

The storage medium was a rotating magnetic drum. Since the address of the next instruction was always given explicitly, the instructions could be distributed over the drum in any order. The purpose was optimization: The instructions were to be so placed that, by the time the current instruction had been executed, the drum would have brought up the next instruction.

To give another illustration of the concept let us look at the Fortran program segment

```
IT = N(IP)
IPOP = IT
IP = IP - 1
```

Here the results depend on the order of the instructions. If, however, we rewrite the segment as in Figure 10.1, i.e., if we provide statement labels and pointers (the GO TO statements), then the boxed statement pairs can be shuffled at will without affecting the results of the program.

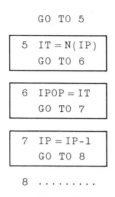

Figure 10.1

It does not take long to realize that if a program can be stored in non-consecutive locations, the same can be done with data, i.e., that a scheme of pointers can represent the logical ordering of data just as well as the conventional interpretation that consecutive memory locations contain consecutive items of data. A data storage scheme in which the logical order of data is determined by pointers is known as a *list storage* scheme, and a vector of data stored under such a scheme is called a *list*.

To see how a list storage scheme works let us take an array of dimensions 100×2, say. We shall call the first cell in a row the *data cell,* and the second by inserting in the pointer cell of each row the number of the row that follows it. The last row, of course, has nothing following it. Here a zero is inserted in the pointer cell. This structure is a list (Figure 10.2). At the start all data cells are empty; i.e., the list is a *list of available space* (LAVS list) or *free list*. We also have a *list name* (here it is LAVS), which contains the number of the first row occupied by the list (here this number is 1).

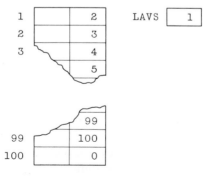

Figure 10.2

I	21	(17321)
J	73	(17322)
	5	(17323)
	29	(17324)
	84	(17325)
K	89	(17326)

Figure 10.3

Consider now a set of data I = 21, J = [73, 5, 29, 84], K = 89. Under a conventional static storage scheme these data might be stored as shown in Figure 10.3. Throughout the program every instruction referring to the datum I then contains the address 17321 in its address field. Similarly K is referred to by the address 17326, and J(3) by a base address 17322 and an increment of 2.

Let us now set up *lists* I, J, and K. Lists in isolation are useless; the whole purpose is to have them operated on by programs, which must know where to find them. Therefore, each list must have a name, which will contain the number of the first row occupied by the list.

ALGORITHM 10.1   The following algorithm stores a vector of values $[d_1, d_2, \ldots, d_n]$, where n need not be known in advance, as list L. The list storage area is the 2-column matrix LIST.

1. Set L = LAVS.
2. Set $i = 1$.
3. Set LIST(LAVS,1) = d_i.
4. Set ITEMP = LAVS.
5. Set LAVS = LIST(LAVS,2).
6. If d_i is the last element of a vector, set LIST(ITEMP,2) = 0 and stop.
7. Set $i = i + 1$, go to 3.

In Step 1 of A.10.1 lists L and LAVS are made to coincide. This is the only place where L is explicitly referred to. In Step 3 a datum is inserted in the list. Note that the sequence of pointers is not changed except at the very end. In Step 6 the end of list L is marked by placing 0 in the last pointer cell. This breaks the sequence of pointers; i.e., list L is separated from LAVS.

Figure 10.4 shows the list store after lists I, J, and K have been stored in it by A.10.1. At first sight there does not seem to be any advantage to this scheme. The first six elements of the first column of LIST look exactly like Figure 10.3. What, then, is the purpose of the pointers? To show their purpose assume that I does not contain a conventional piece of data, but, instead, that I is a stack. Assume now that a datum IDATUM is to be pushed down.

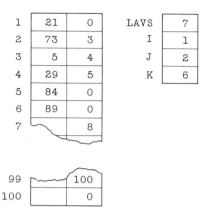

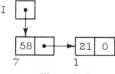

Figure 10.4

The following Fortran subroutine will do the job.

```
      SUBROUTINE PUSH (STACK,IN)
      COMMON LIST(100,2), LAVS
      INTEGER STACK
C     CHECK FOR LIST STORE OVERFLOW
      IF (LAVS.EQ.0) GO TO 999
      LIST(LAVS,1) = IN
      ITEMP = LAVS
      LAVS = LIST(LAVS,2)
      LIST(ITEMP,2) = STACK
      STACK = ITEMP
      RETURN
999   WRITE (6,100)
      STOP
100   FORMAT (1H1,28HLAVS EXHAUSTED - TERMINATION)
      END
```

Assume that I DATUM contains the value 58. Figure 10.5 gives a schematic representation of the list (stack) I after execution of

```
      CALL PUSH (I,IDATUM)
```

Row 7 now contains the topmost element of the stack in its data cell.

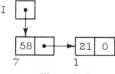

Figure 10.5

Next, assume that I, J, and K are all made to function as stacks, and that the following sequence of calls is executed

```
CALL PUSH (J,38)
CALL PUSH (I,17)
CALL PUSH (K,46)
```

The schematic configuration of the three stacks and the appearance of the list store are shown in Figure 10.6.

Under this arrangement for stacks function IPOP becomes

```
      FUNCTION IPOP (STACK)
      COMMON LIST(100,2), LAVS
      INTEGER STACK
C   CHECK FOR STACK UNDERFLOW
      IF (STACK.EQ.0) GO TO 999
      IPOP = LIST(STACK,1)
      ITEMP = STACK
      STACK = LIST(STACK,2)
      LIST(ITEMP,2) = LAVS
      LAVS = ITEMP
      RETURN
  999 WRITE (6,100)
      STOP
  100 FORMAT (1H1,29HSTACK UNDERFLOW - TERMINATION)
      END
```

Note that each row of LIST is returned to LAVS when it is released by the IPOP operation. When the last datum is removed from the stack, the pointer in its name (e.g., location I for stack I) is made 0. A list with 0 in its name is an *empty* or *undefined* list.

A PUSH operation consists of the storing of a datum and the adjustment of certain pointers; in an IPOP operation a datum is retrieved from the list, and again there is an adjustment of pointers. Under PUSH these adjustments have the effect of detaching an element from LAVS and making it an element of STACK; under IPOP an element is detached from STACK and returned to LAVS. The pointers do not change value; they are merely sent from location to location in a cyclic pattern. Figure 10.7 illustrates their movements. It should be apparent that LAVS too functions as a stack.

List storage schemes have their disadvantages as well as advantages. One of the disadvantages is that access to a specified datum is slow. Since the kth datum is found by tracing through a sequence of k pointers, the average access time increases with k. In an array the access time is independent of k. Another disadvantage is that a list store can accommodate much less data

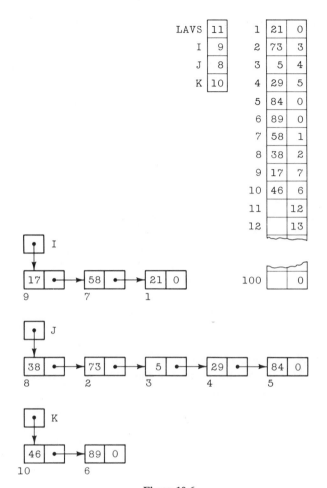

Figure 10.6

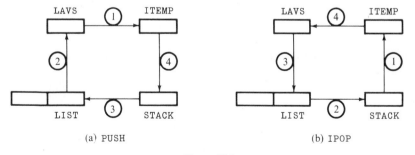

(a) PUSH (b) IPOP

Figure 10.7

than a conventional store of the same size. We shall look at list storage schemes that have better storage utilization characteristics in Section 10c, but there is no list storage scheme as efficient as a conventional store in this respect. Conventional storage arrangements have, however, the disadvantage of being static.

In some applications, however, a list storage scheme may be at an advantage over a conventional storage arrangement in all respects. Exercise 5.8 asks for the implementation of a queue using a conventional one-dimensional Fortran array. This task, while not all that difficult, is still nontrivial. The implementation of a queue as a list is actually more straightforward. Moreover, although two words are used for each datum in the queue, they are used for just those data that are actually in the queue at a given time. In the conventional arrangement an array of fixed size is reserved to hold the queue for the entire time the queue is in existence, and many elements of this array may, in fact, be unnecessary. One possible list representation of a queue is shown schematically in Figure 10.8. Elements are pushed down at the head of the list; they are popped up from its end. The PUSH routine for stacks can be used here unchanged. However, IPOP has to trace through the entire sequence of pointers to find the end of the list. The broken lines in Figure 10.8 show the movement of pointers when IPOP removes an element from the representation of the queue. Note that we have to know where the secondlast element of the list is located. This means that in stepping through the list we have to save the pointer to the element we are leaving when we pass from this element to the next. Note further that there is no need for ITEMP here because we know that the pointer field of the last element of a list contains zero, i.e., the pointer movements can be simplified to the following: (i) from LAVS to last element of Q; (ii) from secondlast element of Q to LAVS; (iii) zero to secondlast element of Q. The more complex scheme is shown in Figure 10.8 to stress its essential identity with Scheme (b) of Figure 10.7.

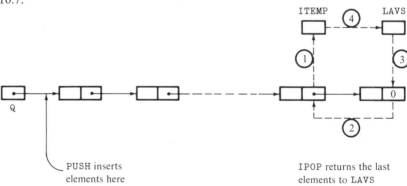

PUSH inserts   IPOP returns the last
elements here   elements to LAVS

Figure 10.8

Let us try to improve the speed of IPOP by providing immediate access to the end of the list. We do so by making Q a vector of two elements, where Q(1) points to the first, and Q(2) to the last element of the list, as in Figure 10.9, but this does not seem to solve the problem. Look again at the pointer movements in Figure 10.8: in order to return the last element of the list to LAVS, IPOP must know the location of the secondlast element, and Q(2) is of no help there.

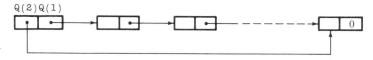

Figure 10.9

However, if the "direction" of the queue is reversed, i.e., IPOP applied to the head and PUSH to the end of the list, then the new scheme works, and it should be comparable in speed to a scheme based on a conventional array. Figure 10.10 shows the new configuration, with broken lines again indicating movement of pointers. Note that Q(2) needs to be updated whenever PUSH is invoked. This is done by moving the pointer from ITEMP to Q(2). Again, the pointer movements at the end of the list can be executed without a temporary location: (i) LAVS to last element of list and to Q(2); (ii) new element to LAVS; (iii) zero to new element.

In lists functioning as stacks or queues insertion of new elements and removal of existing elements occurs only at the extremities of the list. In a more general context insertion and removal of elements may have to take

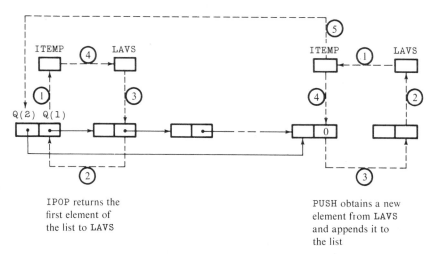

IPOP returns the first element of the list to LAVS

PUSH obtains a new element from LAVS and appends it to the list

Figure 10.10

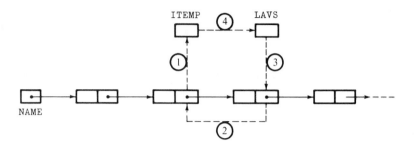

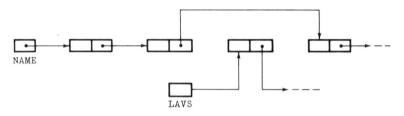

Figure 10.11

place anywhere in a list. Figure 10.11 shows a list before an element is removed from its middle, after it has been removed, and, superimposed on the "before" picture, the pointer movements that bring about this change. Again observe that the pattern of pointer movements is essentially identical to that shown as Scheme (b) in Figure 10.7.

Let us write Fortran code for retrieving (as IDATA) the datum from the Kth element as the list NAME, deleting this element from NAME, and returning it to LAVS:

```
      J = NAME
      KK = K - 1
      DO 10 I = 1,KK
      JJ = J
   10 J = LIST(J,2)
      IDATA = LIST(J,1)
      ITEMP = LIST(JJ,2)
      LIST(JJ,2) = LIST(J,2)
      LIST(J,2) = LAVS
      LAVS = ITEMP
```

There are two flaws in the code. First, we should test for K being larger than the number of elements in the list. This case can arise very easily, and the program should print an error message when it does. It is easily detected:

the error condition exists if the value of J becomes zero during execution of the loop.

The second flaw is more annoying. Every element of a list except the first is pointed to by its predecessor in the list. The pointer to the first element, however, is not in another list element; instead, it is in the list name, which is external to the list storage area. Because of this difference our Fortran code is invalid for K = 1. One solution is to make a special case of K = 1. An alternative is to redesign the lists so that the first element of a list no longer differs from the others. This can be done by providing a special list *header* that resides in the list storage area, and is interposed between the list name and the first proper element of the list. The external name of the list then points to the header, and the header points to the first element of the list. The data cell of the header can be left undefined, or it can be made to contain a pointer to the last element of the list, or a count of the elements in the list, etc. Every list should have a header, even an empty list. This means that all variables that are going to be used as list names have to be "declared" in some fashion, and a header must be created for each list during initialization of the list storage scheme. Recall how COMMON was used to "declare" array names for the purposes of the dynamic storage allocation system for arrays in Section 9d. A similar technique can be used for the list names here.

Figures 10.12 and 10.13 illustrate the interchange of two elements of a list. The top diagram of Figure 10.12 shows how the pointers are to be moved to interchange the elements containing *B* and *E*. The two lower diagrams show the list after the interchange has been made. The diagram in the middle emphasizes that only pointers have been moved; the interchange has been effected

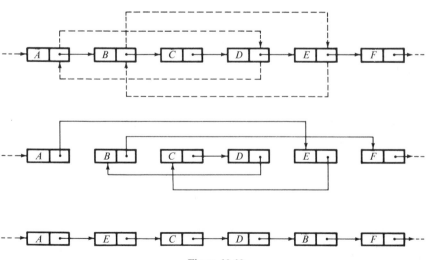

Figure 10.12

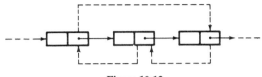

Figure 10.13

with no movement of data. The bottom diagram emphasizes the logical structure of the list after the interchange. Figure 10.13 shows the movement of pointers for the special case in which adjacent list elements are interchanged. Although it is not shown in the diagram, a temporary location is necessary in both the general and the special case.

Operators can be grouped into two classes according to the type of data they operate on. The operators of arithmetic operate on numbers and belong to the first class. Rearrangement operators operate on symbolic data and belong to the second class. There is some overlap of the two classes; comparison operators can belong to either class. It is important to realize that numerals can function as numbers and as symbols. Thus, when we add two numerals, we are adding numbers, but when we sort a set of numerals, or insert a numeral in a sequence of numerals, or push a numeral into a stack, then we operate on the numerals as symbols. We speak of two branches of computation: numerical and symbolic. For numerical computation conventional static storage is normally more efficient. Symbolic computation, which involves extensive rearrangement of data, is often performed more effectively if the data are stored as lists.

10b. Sparse Matrices and Cross-Lists

Figure 9.1 is the drawing of a digraph representing a matrix X. The nodes are laid out and joined in such a way that there are sets of horizontal and vertical lines. The former correspond to rows, the latter to columns of the matrix. A representation of the matrix now suggests itself in which each row and each column is represented by a list. Then, as regards the five lists representing rows, they will contain, respectively, 2, 2, 1, 2, and 4 elements. Consider matrix element x_{41}. It would be represented by elements in the lists of row 4 and of column 1, which we shall denote NR(4) and NC(1). In list NR(4) the list element corresponding to x_{41} would consist of the data $\langle 4, 1, 8 \rangle$ and a pointer to the list element representing x_{44}; in NC(1) the data in the list element representing x_{41} would again be $\langle 4, 1, 8 \rangle$, but now the pointer would be to the representation of x_{51}.

Should we create two separate list elements for x_{41} in which the data are identical, and only the pointer values differ? Such a design would waste computer storage space. Instead, we should recognize that it is quite in order to have one list element belonging to more than one list. In the present context we make every list element belong to two lists, a row list and a column list. The list element of x_{41} then consists of the data $\langle 4, 1, 8 \rangle$ and two pointers, one relating to its membership in NR(4), the other to its membership in NC(1). A particular row list consisting of k elements is thus " crossed " by k column lists, and we have a precise correspondence to what is displayed in Figure 9.1. A structure in which each element belongs to m lists will be called a *cross-list structure of order m*. A sparse matrix is represented by a cross-list structure of order 2. A sparse three-dimensional array would require a cross-list structure of order 3 for its representation.

The five-row representation QQQ of Section 9c is in fact a cross-list structure. Entry vectors NR and NC are the names of the row lists and column lists, and QQQ itself is a list storage area very much like the one we discussed in Section 10a. A schematic representation of the cross-list structure representing the sparse matrix of Figure 9.1 is shown as Figure 10.14.

Compared to conventional representation of an $n \times n$ matrix, the design of Figure 10.14 brings about a reduction in storage requirements only if the density of the matrix is less than $(n - 2)/(5n)$. Can we do any better? The pointers and the values of the nonzero matrix elements are essential, but reduction in storage requirements can be achieved at the expense of the subscripts. As we trace through list NC(3), say, we know that every element

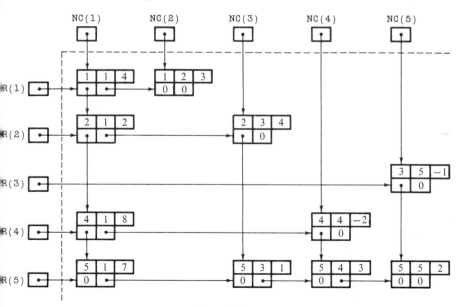

Figure 10.14

encountered belongs to column 3 of the matrix. Hence it would seem that the column subscripts, which do no more than reaffirm this fact, could be eliminated. Similarly for the row subscripts.

Consider, however, matrix multiplication. In computing the matrix product $C = AB$, where A and B are $n \times n$ matrices, element c_{ij} is the sum of the products $a_{ik} b_{kj}$ over $k = 1, 2, \ldots, n$. To compute c_{ij} with A and B represented by cross-list structures we would enter row list i in the representation of A and column list j in the representation of B. We would come to an element a_{is} and an element b_{tj}. The product $a_{is} b_{tj}$ contributes to the value of c_{ij} if $s = t$. However, unless the column subscript is part of the representation of a_{is}, we do not know which column a_{is} actually belongs to, i.e., we do not know s. Similarly, in the absence of row subscripts, we do not know which row of B the element b_{tj} belongs to.

Consequently it must be made possible to establish the subscript values of the matrix element represented by an arbitrary list element even when the only thing known about this list element is its location in the list storage area. For this one does not necessarily have to associate explicit row and column subscript values with every list element. A composite index from which these values can be computed when the need arises is sufficient (see Exercise 9.14).

A different design makes use of the row pointer field of the last list element of a row, and the column pointer field of the last element of a column. If the zeros in these fields are replaced by appropriate row and column subscripts, then the row and column subscripts of an element can be determined by following the row pointers to the end of the row list, and the column pointers to the end of the column list, respectively. One problem remains, that of telling when the last element of a row (or column) has been reached. Instead of 0, the row pointer field of the last element of row 5 now contains 5, but there is nothing to distinguish this 5 from a possible pointer to another list element. The ambiguity may be resolved by storing the subscripts negated, e.g., a -5 in a pointer field represents the subscript 5, but a 5 in this field is a proper pointer. Figure 10.15 shows the cross-lists of Figure 10.14 under the new design, and in Figure 10.16 one possible actual configuration of the list store corresponding to the schematic representation of Figure 10.15 is displayed.

A cross-list structure exemplified by Figure 10.15 has lower storage requirements than the conventional representation of a matrix if the density of the matrix is less than $(n - 2)/(3n)$. A sparse matrix with the average number of elements in each row and in each column no greater than 5 is typical. If the average number of elements in a row is 5, then the expected number of pointer references one has to make to determine the row subscript is $(5 + 4 + 3 + 2 + 1)/5 = 3$. This should take less time than the determination of the row subscript from the composite index as in Exercise 9.14.

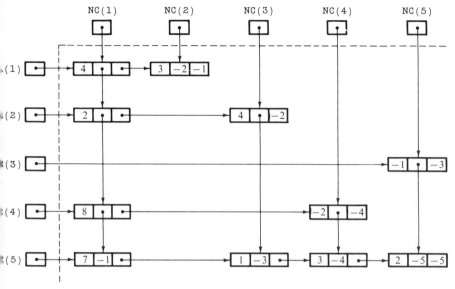

Figure 10.15

$$
\begin{array}{c c}
1 \\
2 \\
3 \\
4 \\
5 \\
6 \\
7 \\
8 \\
9 \\
10 \\
11 \\
\dots \\
\dots
\end{array}
\quad
\begin{bmatrix}
4 & 7 & -2 \\
8 & 5 & 10 \\
-1 & 8 & -3 \\
4 & 11 & 6 \\
7 & -1 & 7 \\
3 & -2 & -1 \\
1 & -3 & 9 \\
2 & -5 & -5 \\
3 & -4 & 8 \\
-2 & 2 & 1 \\
2 & 2 & 1 \\
& & \\
& &
\end{bmatrix}
\quad
\begin{bmatrix}
4 \\
6 \\
1 \\
10 \\
3
\end{bmatrix}
\quad
\begin{bmatrix}
4 \\
11 \\
3 \\
2 \\
5
\end{bmatrix}
$$

LIST   NC   NR

Figure 10.16

10c. Formats of List Elements

A list element is composed of one or more data fields, one or more pointer fields, and, possibly, one or more marker fields. Markers are used to distinguish between types of list elements, and the scheme of Figure 10.15 provides an example of where such use is called for. A pointer field in Figure 10.15 may contain a legitimate pointer or a subscript value. The problem is to tell which is which, and one solution is to provide a marker bit (flag bit) that is 0, say, in the case of a pointer, and 1 in the case of a subscript value. Since each list element in the example contains two pointer fields, two markers would be necessary. Because the addition of explicit marker fields would have increased the storage requirements of the scheme, the actual solution in our example was to make the sign of the datum occupying the pointer field function as the marker.

Under the schemes developed in Sections 10a and 10b a list element occupies one row in a two-dimensional array, and each pointer and data field of this list element occupies one complete cell in that row. We shall now see how we can save some space by compacting the fields of a list element. These schemes have to be implemented at assembler language level. To start with, we shall take a retrospective look to the time when all list processing was implemented in assembler language, and the pointers were machine addresses rather than row subscripts of an array. The basic techniques of list processing evolved on the IBM 704 and related machines, of which the IBM 7090 is perhaps the best known, and we shall therefore briefly consider some formats of list elements for such machines.

A word in the IBM 7090 and related machines was 36 bits long, and, since their core memories consisted of at most 32,768 words, only 15 bits were needed for a pointer. This left 21 bits for other uses, of which 3 bits could be assigned to a marker field, and the remaining 18 bits for storage of symbols. The 7090 character code used 6 bits for the representation of a character. These 18 bits could then be used to store a string of three characters or a numerical symbol in the range 0–262,143 ($262,143 = 2^{18} - 1$). This "packed" representation could be used on any machine that had a similar word structure, but the details were determined by the instruction set of the particular machine considered. For example, IBM 7090 and 7040 were very similar computers, but, while the 7040 had instructions giving direct access to character fields, access to individual characters in the 7090 was by means of the shifting operations. In the 7090 best efficiency resulted when a word in the list store was formatted as shown in Drawings (a) or (b) of Figure 10.17. In the 7040, on the other hand, Formats (c) or (d) could lead to better execution times. Of course, these formats show only a few of the possibilities.

Machine addresses are no longer important because assembler language as a *dominant* programming tool is dead. It is generally accepted that for large programming projects the average productivity of programmers is just 8–10 lines of code per man-day. This figure represents the length of the checked out program as delivered to the user, divided by the total number of man-days put into the project by its active participants, and it is *independent* of the language in which the programs are written. Clearly, one can in general put much more computing power into 10 lines of Fortran or PL/I than in

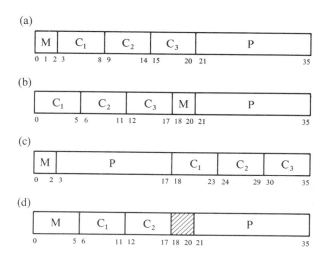

Figure 10.17 M, marker; C, character; P, pointer. In (d) bits 18–20 are not used; they may be used for a second marker field.

10 assembler language instructions. Moreover, it has now been proven in the field that structured programming can greatly increase productivity, to 35 lines of code per man-day or more, but structured programming makes real sense only in the context of higher level languages.

On occasion speed and storage economy are of so great a concern that the use of assembler language is justified, but it should be used sparingly and selectively. List processing is an example. We know that packing separate fields of a list element into a single computer word greatly reduces storage requirements, but this requires routines for generating the compact representations, and for extracting specific fields from these representations. Although the packing and unpacking can be done in a higher level language (see below), the time may be prohibitive. Therefore, most programming *of* a list processing system, and all programming *in* the system should be in a higher level language, but field insertion and extraction should be performed by assembler language routines.

The list storage area is then still a Fortran array, just as in Sections 10a and 10b, but we may now have more than one field in one cell. If all fields of a list element can be accommodated in a single computer word, the array is a vector. If more than one word is needed, then the list storage area can be a two-dimensional array of k columns, where k is the number of words required for a list element. Alternatively, the storage area can be a vector, which we picture as broken up into parcels of k contiguous words, each parcel being an element of LAVS or of an active list. The pointer values are row subscripts, where, under the latter variant, only multiples of k are valid pointer values.

Let us assume a list processing application on a PDP-10 in which a need for at most 2500 list elements at any one time is envisaged. A datum would be a string of three characters, consisting of numerals and capital letters, or an integer in the range 1–2500. Most of the time the three-character strings would be treated as single units, but occasionally the characters would have to be accessed individually. A marker is required to distinguish between the two types of data. Since $2500_{10} = 100,111,000,100_2$, the pointer field requires 12 bits. The PDP-10 has a word length of 36 bits, and internal representation of character data is either in ASCII (American Standard Code for Information Interchange), which is a 7-bit code, or a 6-bit code. Hence, even if ASCII is used rather than the 6-bit code, there are still $36 - 12 - 3 \times 7 = 3$ bits left over for the marker field. As a first try, we propose Design (a) of Figure 10.18.

(a)

(b)

Figure 10.18

Let us, however, examine some features of the PDP-10 that might suggest an improved design. The instruction set of this computer permits fast access to halfwords (bits 0–17, or 18–35) and tests on the sign bit (bit 0). To gain access to other fields, "byte" instructions have to be used, which give access to any number of consecutive bits in a word with comparable ease, irrespective of where these bits are located, but the "byte" instructions are appreciably slower and more complicated than halfword instructions. Now, if we were to use 6-bit representation for the characters, then the three characters would fit exactly into a half-word, and we would have faster access to the character string as a whole. A change to 6-bit representation is therefore worthwhile, and Drawing (b) of Figure 10.18 shows the revised design. The relative order of the fields has been changed to make the sign bit part of the marker field. We need only one bit for the marker, and if this is the sign bit, then a sign test can be used to establish the type of data stored in the data field of the list element. If we were to find that the list store has to be made larger, the 12-bit pointer field would remain sufficient for up to 4095 elements, but a wider pointer field would be required if the size of the list store were to exceed 4095 (13 bits for up to 8191, 14 bits for up to 16,383, etc). The pointer field can easily be extended to the left, with a corresponding reduction in the width of the marker field.

Next consider our design problem in the context of IBM 360/370 computers. Basic storage units in these machines are individually addressable 8-bit bytes. Whereas the PDP-10 "byte" is a group of bits of variable size, the 360/370 byte is fixed in size. Two IBM bytes form a *half-word*, and four bytes a *full-word*. An interesting feature of Fortran for these computers is that one may declare an array of half-words. We shall find this feature useful. A full-word is now 32 bits, and since we still need 12 bits for the pointer field, there are 20 bits left over. However, in the 360/370 characters are represented in an 8-bit code. Although we could introduce our own "private" 6-bit character code, access to a group of bits that straddles byte boundaries is considerably more difficult and slower than access to a byte holding an 8-bit representation of a character. Therefore, unless there is severe shortage of storage space, we should use a set of three half-words for a list element. Figure 10.19 shows one possible design based on the three half-words.

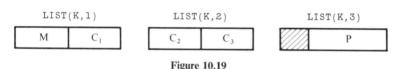

Figure 10.19

Although it was stated above that accessing of fields inside a word should be the task of assembler language routines, there can be exceptions to this general rule. If most of the bookkeeping associated with a subprogram call is performed in the calling program, then the cost of going through a calling sequence may become very high. It could then become more ecomical to avoid making a subprogram call part of an accessing operation, and to use the higher level language throughout. We illustrate how Fortran can be used to extract specific fields from a word. Consider a 36-bit word IW, and assume that the four bits 0–3 of IW are not in use (and are set to zero). Then, for example, bits 4–18 are extracted by $IW/131072$, bits 21–35 by $MOD(IW,32768)$, and bits 19–20 by $MOD(IW,131072)/32768$. In all insertions and extractions one must watch the sign bit. In most computers 2's complement representation is used for negative integers, and this is what complicates matters. The sign bit is a convenient choice for a marker, and the easiest way to change the sign bit from 0 to 1 would be simply to negate IW, but in 2's complement representation negation changes the other bits as well. The safest way to proceed when negation is used to change the sign bit value is to test the sign of IW prior to any extraction or insertion, to set $IW = -IW$ if IW is found to be negative, and to use $IW = -IW$ again to reset the sign after the operation has been completed.

10d. List Structures

In Section 5a we saw that derivation trees can be represented by parenthesized linear strings. For example, the tree of Figure 5.1 can be represented by

$$S(NP(T(the)N(child))VP(V(ate)NP(T(a)N(A(green)N(pear))))).$$

Similarly, the tree of Figure 10.20 can be represented by $a(bc(fg(j))d(hi)e)$.

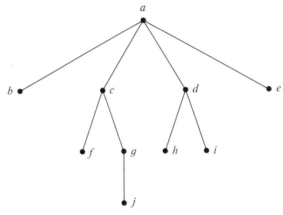

Figure 10.20

However, often it is more convenient to have a representation that corresponds more directly to the way we picture a tree. A tree structure can be represented in this more explicit fashion by a set of linear lists if the lists are provided with a mechanism for branching from one list to another. Since anything at all can be put in the data field of a list element, the datum can be a pointer to another list, *designated as such by the setting of a marker*. A set of lists can then be linked by inserting pointers in the data fields and setting markers. If we have lists X and Y, and there exists a link *from* list X *to* list Y, then Y is a *sublist* of X. Unless sublists have to be independently referenced they need not have their own names.

The tree of Figure 10.20 can be represented by linked lists as in Figure 10.21. We have assumed Format (a) of Figure 10.17, with the convention that the first bit of the marker field, which is the sign bit of a 7090 word, is 1 (minus) if the data field contains a pointer and 0 (plus) if it contains a symbol. Bits 1 and 2 are not used. If the datum is a pointer, i.e., an address, it is stored in bit positions 3–17. This field, called the *decrement field* in the 7090 terminology, was directly accessible to some machine instructions. The representation of Figure 10.21 contains 10 lists, one for each node in the tree of

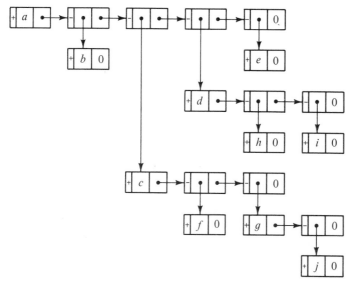

Figure 10.21

Figure 10.20. Since the marker of a list element is 0 if and only if the element is the first element in a list and is 1 otherwise, and the determination of whether or not an element is first in a list can be made without reference to markers, the markers are redundant.

A different representation of the tree of Figure 10.20 is shown in Figure 10.22. Here there are only four lists, one for each nonterminal node of the tree, and the total number of list elements is reduced from 19 to 13. In this more economical representation markers are essential. We shall refer to the two conventions, exemplified by Figures 10.21 and 10.22, as A and B, respectively. For some purposes convention A may be more to the point in

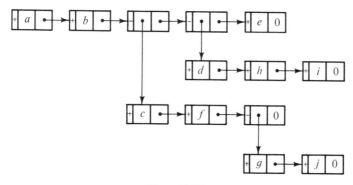

Figure 10.22

that every element with the marker 1 (minus), i.e., every element with a pointer in its data field, stands for an arc. There is no counterpart under convention B to this very natural representation of arcs by pointers.

Lists can be used to represent more complicated structures than trees. Convention A generalizes very easily to digraphs. Figure 10.23 shows two digraphs and their representation by lists under this convention. These two digraphs could be represented under convention B as well. In Case (b) this would result in the saving of one list element: the element containing the symbol *d* would be eliminated, with the *d* transferred to the data field of the

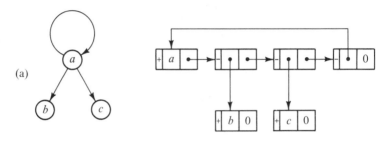

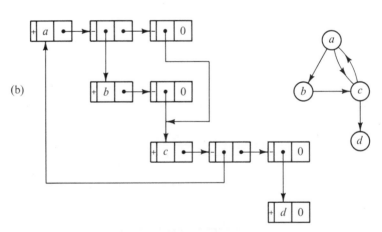

Figure 10.23

element that contains a pointer to the element being eliminated. However, if an arc ⟨*b, d*⟩ were now added to the digraph, then under representation B we would have to add a third element to the list representing node *b*, and have a pointer from the data field of this element to the element that now contains the symbol *d* (the third element in the list representing node *c*). In general there is little if any difference in the number of list elements needed to represent a digraph under the two conventions (Exercise 10.14), but there are good reasons to avoid pointers in data fields to elements other than first elements of lists. For example, such pointers would greatly complicate the discussion of the next paragraph. The use of convention B should therefore be limited to trees alone.

Just as a digraph can be represented by a set of linked lists, so, conversely a set of linked lists can be represented by a digraph in which each list is represented by a node and each element that contains a pointer in its data field by an arc. A set of linked lists is a *list structure* if its digraph is connected. It is a *reentrant* list structure if its digraph contains cycles. In particular, a list that is a sublist of itself, i.e., that contains a pointer to itself, is a *reentrant list*. The digraph of a reentrant list is a sling. If two lists have the same list as a sublist, then they are said to *share* the sublist. In the digraph the indegree of a node representing a shared list is equal to at least 2.

Let us now suppose that we have stored a tree as a list structure and that we want to produce a parenthesized string from it. As we traverse the list structure we may come to a pointer to a sublist. We have to go down the sublist, but we have to mark in some way how far down the main list we have come; in other words, we have to remember the address of the next element in the main list. The remembering is done by a stack.

ALGORITHM 10.2   Figure 10.24 shows an algorithm for generating a parenthesized expression from a tree stored as a list structure under convention A. It is assumed that an entire list element occupies just one computer word: E refers to a list element, and E_i has location i (array element i in the array functioning as the list store); S(E) is the sign bit of list element E, D(E) is the data field, A(E) is the pointer field. The list name (LN) contains a pointer to the first element of the list (the subscript of the array element occupied by the list element). The algorithm makes use of a stack.

Let us consider the three types of traversal of B-trees discussed in Section 5c. Of these, preorder and postorder traversal generalize in an obvious way to arbitrary trees in which the order of terminal nodes is important. Let the "processing of a node" for both types of traversal be the output of the symbol associated with the node. Then preorder and postorder traversal of the tree of Figure 10.20 would result in the output of the strings *abcfgjdhie* and *bfjgchidea*, respectively. The first of these outputs is identical with the output from A.10.2 after removal of parentheses.

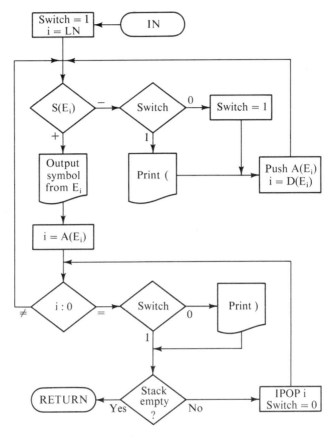

Figure 10.24

Every tree has an equivalent B-tree, which can be constructed by means of A.10.3. The motivation for wishing to find the equivalent B-tree is that sometimes the representation of a tree in this form requires less storage.

ALGORITHM 10.3   An algorithm for constructing a B-tree equivalent to a given tree T with ordered terminal nodes.

1. Draw a node that corresponds to the root of T. For the purposes of Step 2 let this node be named s.
2. Process node s: If s is nonterminal in T, then add to the B-tree, with left orientation, arc $\langle s, u \rangle$, where u is the leftmost successor of s. Further, if s has a neighbor on the right in T, then add, with right orientation, arc $\langle s, v \rangle$, where v is the closest neighbor on the right of s.

3. Select in the B-tree a node *s* that has not been processed, and go to Step 2. If all nodes have been processed, stop.

Example

Figure 10.25 shows the result of applying A.10.3 to the tree of Figure 10.20. Drawing (a) shows the B-tree, and Drawing (b) is a schematic representation of how the B-tree could be stored in a list store. The particular representation is possible only because 2 is the greatest number of arcs that originate from any node of a B-tree. If the overall specifications permit the three fields of each list element to be compacted into a single computer word, then the B-tree representation has lower storage requirements than either of the schemes shown in Figures 10.21 and 10.23 (10 words against 19 or 13), but not if two computer words are required for each list element. Note that in preorder traversal of the B-tree the nodes are processed in the order *abcfgjdhie*, which is exactly the order of processing under preorder traversal of the tree of Figure 10.20. Under postorder traversal the orders differ: the order is *jgfihedcba* for the B-tree, but *bfjgchidea* for the tree from which the B-tree derives.

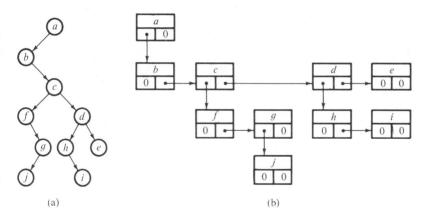

(a)   (b)

Figure 10.25

We are interested in an algorithm that, applied to a B-tree, would process the nodes in the order in which they would be processed under postorder traversal of the tree from which the B-tree derives. In the case of the B-tree of Figure 10.25 the algorithm should process the nodes in the order *bfjgchidea*, but this, of course, is the order of processing under inorder traversal. Hence we have already obtained the algorithm in solving Exercise 5.17, and it is spelled out here as A.10.4 for the benefit of just those who did not do Exercise 5.17.

ALGORITHM 10.4   An algorithm for inorder traversal of a B-tree, which is equivalent to postorder traversal of the (nonbinary) tree from which the B-tree derives. E refers to a list element and E_i has location i (i is the subscript of the row that holds the list element in the array functioning as the list store); LL(E) and RL(E) are, respectively, the left and right pointer fields of the list element. The list name (LN) contains a pointer to the element representing the root of the B-tree. The algorithm makes use of a stack.

1. Set i = LN.
2. While LL(E_i) ≠ 0, push down i and set i = LL(E_i).
3. Process E_i, set i = RL(E_i).
4. If i ≠ 0, go to 2.
5. If stack empty, stop; else pop up i and go to 3.

Let us turn again to the sort tree of Figure 5.17 and consider implementation of the sort tree as a list structure. As a matter of fact, arrays D and P are already an implicit list structure, but, since they are fixed arrays, the structure cannot be extended. For extensibility we have to make use of a reasonably sizeable list storage area, and bring in the concept of the list of available space. The form an extensible list structure corresponding to the tree of Figure 5.17 would take in this list storage area is shown schematically in Figure 10.26. The storage requirements could be as low as 12 words (one for each list element), or they could be 24 (two words for each list element). One additional word is required for the list name. In either case, the requirements are lower than the 36 words required for arrays D and P.

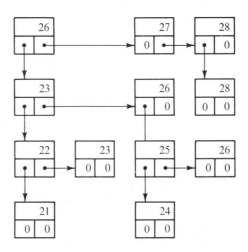

Figure 10.26

It could well be that a reverse transformation that generates a tree *T* similar to that of Figure 10.20 from a sort tree would result in more efficient utilization of storage. Note that when A.10.3 is used to generate a B-tree from a tree *T*, the root of the B-tree cannot have an arc of right orientation originating from it because the root of *T* is, of course, without neighbors. Since arcs of both orientations may originate from the root of a sort tree, a dummy root node has to be created in the nonbinary tree. Figure 10.27 shows the nonbinary tree that corresponds to the sort tree of Figure 5.17; X is the dummy root node. In a list representation of this tree the dummy node X could be represented by the list name, which is external to the list storage area. Figure 10.28 shows the tree of Figure 10.27 as a list structure (under convention B). This representation consists of 18 elements of 2 fields each (with an additional bit for the marker), while the representation of Figure 10.26 consists of 12 elements of 3 fields each. If it is possible to accommodate the 2 fields into a single computer word, but it becomes necessary to use two words for each list element when there are 3 fields, the transformation of a B-tree to the equivalent nonbinary form may be worthwhile. Of course, the B-tree itself can be given a representation analogous to that of Figure 10.28.

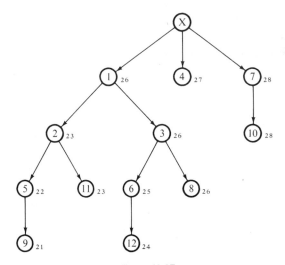

Figure 10.27

Note that the data stored in the tree of Figure 10.27 can be collected in sorted order by postorder traversal of the tree. There is a price to be paid for the lesser storage needs. Although it is not difficult to devise the equivalent of A.5.9 for implementation of a sort tree in its nonbinary form, traversal of the nonbinary structure is slower. The element containing the datum

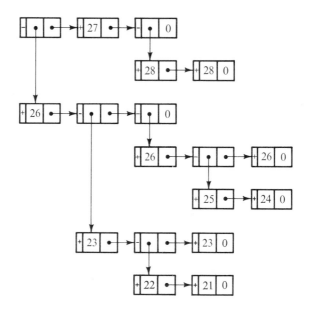

Figure 10.28

24 is furthest from the root in both representations. While the path to this element in Figure 10.26 is over only 5 elements, it is over 8 elements in Figure 10.28.

10e. Threaded and Symmetric Lists

If, instead of putting a zero in the pointer field of the last element of a list, we point back from this element to where the list starts, then we have a *threaded* list (also called a *circular* list). We shall call the pointers in the last elements *return addresses*. Figure 10.29 shows a threaded list structure, which represents the tree of Figure 10.20. To avoid making Figure 10.29 incomprehensible by too many lines, return lines have not been drawn, but are implied by return addresses in the appropriate pointer fields. In the case of the main list the return address is still zero, and this zero indicates the end of the structure; the return address of a sublist refers to the element that establishes a link to this sublist in the list of which it is a sublist. Because of the return addresses a threaded list structure can be traversed without the aid of a stack. Marker fields are essential: Not only do we have to differentiate between data elements and elements that represent structural features of the list structure; now the last element of a list has to be distinguished as well. Note that Figure 10.29 is a threaded counterpart of Figure 10.21 rather than of 10.22,

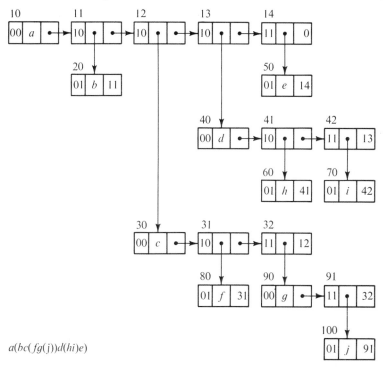

$a(bc(fg(j))d(hi)e)$

Format of marker: Bit 1 — 0 indicates a data element;
                     1 indicates a pointer element.

Bit 2 — 0 indicates that the element is not last in the list;
         1 indicates the last element.

Figure 10.29

i.e., that convention A is in use here. We have already discussed in Section 10d that under this convention the marker bit that distinguishes between data elements and pointer elements is not really essential; it is essential only under convention B.

ALGORITHM 10.5   Figure 10.30 shows an algorithm for generating a parenthesized expression from a tree stored as a threaded list structure. The notation convention is the same as in A.10.2. However, since now the marker field occupies two bit positions, the first bit is called $S_1(E)$, and the second $S_2(E)$. The switch indicates whether a particular pointer element is reached for the first or second time.

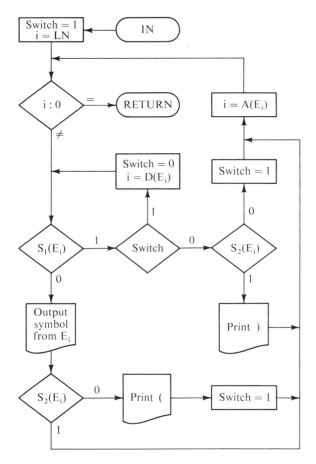

Figure 10.30

The convention adopted in Figure 10.29 does not allow for sharing of sublists. Although it is quite easy to make sharing possible by a change in the format of the marker fields to permit more than one "last" element, and, consequently, more than one return address, nothing is gained. The one good feature of threaded list structures is that they can be traversed without having to use a stack. Multiple return addresses would make it again necessary to keep a record of the history of a traversal; i.e., a stack would have to be used. This means that threaded list structures cannot represent structures that are more general than trees.

Consider now the special case of B-trees. In a B-tree of n nodes $n + 1$ pointer fields contain zeros; they are effectively going to waste. Threading puts these fields into use. In the first instance, threading of the type described above changes the representation of a B-tree from that shown in Figure 10.26 to the partially threaded form of 10.31. The threading is only partial in that all left pointer fields that were zero still remain zero. The structure of Figure 10.31 is called a *right-threaded B-tree* because only the right pointer fields may contain return addresses. The markers distinguish between forward and return addresses. Right-threading is adequate for preorder and inorder traversal without the aid of a stack, and, with A.5.2 and A.10.4 to refer to, the specification of algorithms for these two types of traversal should not give any difficulties. Note that in a right-threaded B-tree the thread (return address) associated with .a node N points to the node that is processed immediately after node N under inorder traversal. This property is shared by some of the regular right pointers, *but not by all*. Nevertheless, inorder traversal of a B-tree should be faster when it is guided by threads than when it is under the control of a stack.

Postorder traversal is a different matter. Under this type of traversal the nodes of the B-tree of Figure 10.31 are processed in the order 9, 11, 5, 12, 8, 6, 3, 2, 10, 7, 4, 1. With some ingenuity an algorithm could be devised that does not use a stack and processes the first ten nodes correctly. Then, however, a way has to be found for getting from node 7 to nodes 4 and 1, and this is impossible without major changes in either the representation of the B-tree or the basic structure of the traversal algorithm. A mechanism for implementing postorder traversal without a stack is provided by the addition of left threads: wherever the left pointer field of a node is zero, the zero

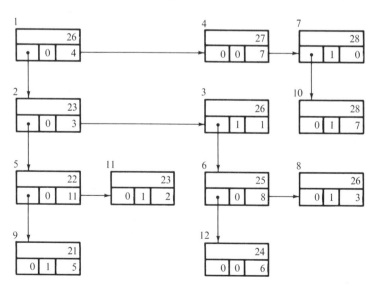

Figure 10.31

is replaced by a pointer to the data node that is processed immediately before the node in question under inorder traversal. However, even with full threading, postorder traversal is very complicated, and, should a stack be inconvenient to use, an algorithm based on the reversal of pointers technique (see A.10.8) should be easier to implement, and faster to run. There is no great practical utility to full threading.

The usefulness of even the right-threaded representation would diminish if the insertion of a new element into the threaded structure, or the deletion of an existing element were to become inordinately difficult. In fact, the algorithms for these operations are rather easy, but some difficulty is to be expected with the deletion algorithm due to the threads.

ALGORITHM 10.6   An algorithm for inserting a new datum in a sort tree, where the sort tree has a right-threaded representation. Duplication of elements is permitted. It is assumed that elements in the list of available space (LAVS) are linked by pointers in their left pointer fields. Denote the datum to be inserted by N. The notation follows that of A.10.4, with these additions: the marker field of element E is denoted by $M(E)$, the data field by $D(E)$. Some of the operations are duplicated in Steps 4 and 6 to put emphasis on the substance of the process; they could be shifted into Step 1.

1. Set $i = LN$, $j = LAVS$, $D(Ej) = N$, $LAVS = LL(Ej)$.
2. If $N > D(E_i)$, go to 5.
3. If $LL(E_i) \neq 0$, set $i = LL(E_i)$ and go to 2.
4. Insertion on the left: Set $LL(Ej) = 0$, $RL(Ej) = i$, $M(Ej) = 1$; $LL(E_i) = j$. Stop.
5. If $M(E_i) = 0$, set $i = RL(E_i)$ and go to 2.
6. Insertion on the right: Set $LL(Ej) = 0$, $RL(Ej) = RL(E_i)$, $M(Ej) = 1$; $RL(E_i) = j$, $M(E_i) = 0$. Stop.

The basis for an algorithm that deletes a node k from a sort tree in such a way that the remaining structure is still a sort tree is this: (a) If k is terminal, return k to LAVS and stop. (b) Else if k has exactly one successor, coalesce k with its successor, i.e., make the predecessor of k point to the successor of k instead of to k itself, return k to LAVS and stop. (c) Else k has two successors. In this case move to the right successor of k and from there go down the tree following left pointers until a node is reached that has no left successor; transfer the datum from this node to the data field of k, and apply the algorithm again with this node the new k. Since the new k has at most one successor, only Cases (a) and (b) can apply.

In a right-threaded tree Case (b) is more complicated than in an unthreaded tree. There is no difference if k has a right successor, but, if the successor is a left successor, then k contains a thread in its right pointer field. Moving out from the successor of k, right links must be followed until a node is reached that has no right link. The thread from k must be transferred to this node.

The deletion process is illustrated by Figure 10.32. The drawing on the left is of a threaded B-tree from which nodes F and E are to be deleted. With node F we have Case (c). Here the right pointer leads to node H, and the left pointer from there leads to node G. Since node G has no left successor, the datum G is transferred to element 12. The old G (element 14) is now to be deleted. Since it is terminal, Case (a) applies, and element 14 is returned to LAVS. Node E satisfies the condition for Case (b). Its predecessor, namely element 12, is made to point to its successor, which is node B. Since node E contains a thread, we trace through right pointers out of B, coming first to C, and then to D, which has no right successor. The right pointer field of this node receives the thread from node E, and node E is returned to LAVS. The result of these two deletion operations is shown by the drawing on the right in Figure 10.32. Note that if a header node were interposed between the list name and the root of the tree, then the right pointer field of node J (element 7) would indicate the header node instead of being zero.

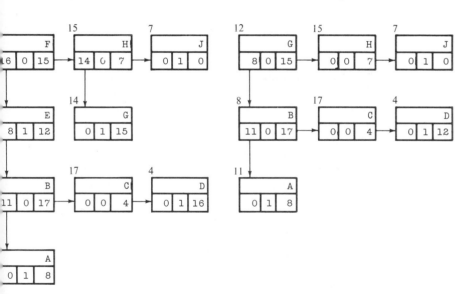

Figure 10.32

ALGORITHM 10.7 An algorithm for deleting a node k from a sort tree in right-threaded representation in such a way that the remaining structure is still a sort tree. For simplicity it is assumed that a header node is interposed between the list name and the root. It is further assumed that the predecessor p of k is known, and that the orientation of $\langle p, k \rangle$ is supplied by means of a parameter *switch*, which has the value 0 for left orientation and 1 for right orientation. Symbols p, k, and the like are used inter-changeably to denote nodes in the B-tree and the locations in the list store corresponding to these nodes. Otherwise the notation is the same as for A.10.6.

1. Set $i = k$.
2. Select case: If $LL(E_i) = 0$ and $M(E_i) = 1$, go to 11; else if $LL(E_i) = 0$, go to 7; else if $M(E_i) = 1$, go to 8.
3. Two links originate at node that is to be deleted: Set $p = i$, *switch* = 1, $i = RL(E_i)$.
4. While $LL(E_i) \neq 0$, set $p = i$, *switch* = 0, $i = LL(E_i)$.
5. Set $D(E_k) = D(E_i)$.
6. If $M(E_i) = 1$, go to 11.
7. Only link from the node is to the right: Set $LL(E_i) = LAVS$. If *switch* = 0, set $LAVS = LL(E_p)$, $LL(E_p) = RL(E_i)$; else set $LAVS = RL(E_p)$, $RL(E_p) = RL(E_i)$. In any case stop.
8. Only link from the node is to the left: Set $k = LL(E_i)$, $LL(E_i) = LAVS$. If *switch* = 0, set $LAVS = LL(E_p)$, $LL(E_p) = k$; else set $LAVS = RL(E_p)$, $RL(E_p) = k$.
9. Steps 9 and 10 are necessitated by threading: While $M(E_k) = 0$, set $k = RL(E_k)$.
10. Set $RL(E_k) = RL(E_i)$. Stop.
11. Delete terminal node: Set $LL(E_i) = LAVS$. If *switch* = 0, set $LAVS = LL(E_p)$ $LL(E_p) = 0$; else set $LAVS = RL(E_p)$, $RL(E_p) = RL(E_i)$, $M(E_p) = 1$. In any case stop.

The reorganization of a B-tree occasioned by the deletion of a node is specific to the type of traversal one has in mind. Thus, with reference to Figure 10.32, under inorder traversal the nodes in the B-tree on the left are processed in the order ABCDEFGHJ, and in the order ABCDGHJ in the B-tree on the right, i.e., the relative order of processing of the remaining nodes is unaffected by deletion of nodes E and F. Under preorder traversal, on the other hand, the nodes in the two trees are processed in the order FEBACDHGJ and GBACDHJ, respectively, i.e., the relative position of node G in the pro-cessing sequence has been changed.

Both conventional and threaded lists can be traversed in one direction only. This is not always convenient, as the following examples show. In Exercise 10.8 we shifted the largest of a set of numbers that were stored in the form of a list to the end of the list. If we wished to bring this element by the selfsame technique to the front of the list, then the comparisons of $A(I)$ and $A(I + 1)$ would have to be carried out in reverse order, specified by the sequence $I = N - 1, N - 2, \ldots, 2, 1$, and we would need a mechanism for tracing through the list from its last to its first element. The other two examples concern deletions. An element may have to be removed from the end of a list when the list serves as a deque (see Exercise 10.6), and a pointer adjustment then has to be made in the element p that precedes this element in the list. The only way of establishing the location of p under the designs considered this far is by traversal of the entire list. An even more serious problem can arise with cross-lists. Assume that we have been traversing list L of a cross-list system, and that we decide to delete element k that we have just reached. The deletion is an easy matter as regards L itself, but other lists may cross L at k, and k may have to be deleted from these lists as well. In this case we are unlikely even to know the list names of these lists. This latter problem can be solved by threading: in turn follow each list that crosses L at k to its last element, then, assuming that the last element contains a pointer to the list name (or to the header element of the list if headers are in use), to the list name (or the header), and from there back to element k, establishing the location of its predecessor along the way. Threading thus saves us from having to trace through every list belonging to the cross-list system, but the cost of deleting an element is still high.

All these problems are solved when every element in a list is provided with two pointers: a forward pointer and a backward pointer. The list is then a *symmetric* list or a *two-way* list. The second set of pointers adds to the cost in terms of storage space, and the adjustments of pointers associated with insertions and deletions are now more in number, but in many applications the benefits gained from the symmetric representation more than balance the disadvantages.

In most computers an element of a symmetric list has to occupy at least two words. One of the words is used for storing a symbol or a pointer to a sublist. The other contains the forward and backward pointers, and a marker field. Examples of symmetric list structures are shown in Figures 10.33 to 10.35. Since any one of a number of feasible designs is as good as another,

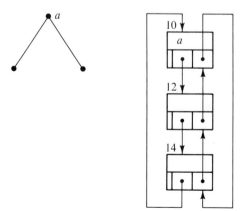

Figure 10.33

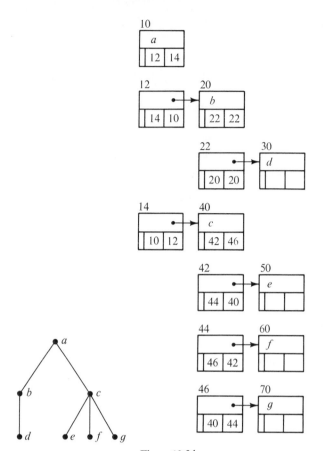

Figure 10.34

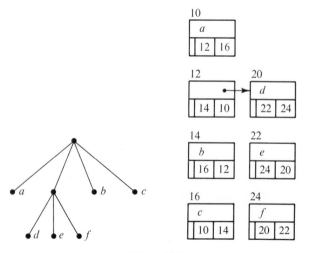

Figure 10.35

the format of marker fields and, in Figure 10.34, the contents of the pointer fields of elements representing terminal nodes of the tree have been left unspecified.

10f. Representation of Digraphs as List Structures

We have already seen digraphs represented as list structures; notably in Figure 10.23. A feature of this representation is that lists are shared, and this means that threaded list structures cannot in general represent digraphs.

An alternative representation to that of Figure 10.23 keeps symbols and structure separate, and the digraph is represented by a set of lists. In this representation some lists consist entirely of pointers, others entirely of symbols. A marker *in the list name* indicates the type of the list, and—since all elements in the one list are of the same type—it is not necessary to provide individual elements with markers. A set of lists that represents the labeled digraph of Figure 10.36 is shown in Figure 10.37. SYMBOL is the list of all

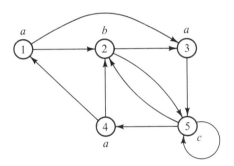

Figure 10.36

node labels. Each node is represented by a list of addresses of the names of lists representing other nodes. These lists indicate the nodes to which there are arcs from the given node; i.e., the list associated with a node is, in effect, a list of arcs originating from this node. Since each of the lists has its own name, we have a set of independent lists rather than a list structure.

Changes that affect structure alone or symbols alone are somewhat easier to make when there is separation of symbols and structure than when the two are intermingled. This advantage, however, is insignificant compared to that brought about by elimination of markers. At the end of Section 5f (Figure 5.22) we considered dictionaries arranged as trees. The important data in this design are the lists of dictionary entries suspended from terminal nodes, and the success of the system depends on the speed with which an entry can be retrieved. Unless structure is separated from data, too much time would be

Names of lists:

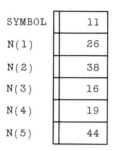

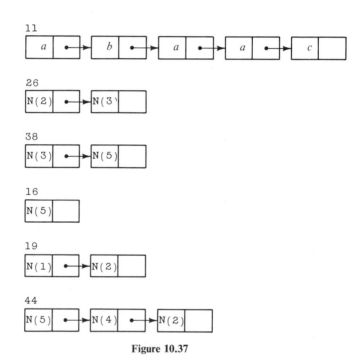

Figure 10.37

spent examining markers. In general, one should try to keep symbols and structure separate whenever one of these types of information dominates the other.

Referring again to Figure 10.37, one may object to this representation on the grounds that in contrast to a list structure, which may be specified by a single external name, the set of lists requires as many external names as there are lists in the set. If the number of nodes of the digraph is large, a considerable block of static storage has to be set aside for list names. This becomes awkward when the representation of a digraph is being generated without prior knowledge of the number of nodes (we then have precisely the situation that made us investigate list storage schemes in the first place). The only solution is to do away with the block of static storage and store the names themselves as a list, with a single external name referring to this list. The implementation of such an indirect addressing scheme presents a number of technical problems, but they are fairly easy to solve.

10g. Variable Length List Elements

In processing symbols the main operations are insertion, deletion, and rearrangement. Each of these operations calls for changes in structure, and these changes are best made when each symbol is linked into a list as a separate entity, i.e., wholly occupies a single list element. For such applications the schemes that we have been discussing are very good. But there are other application areas requiring dynamic storage in which these schemes do not function as well. In Section 10a we discussed a stack in which the active part is in a static storage region and inactive deeper sections have been transferred to a dynamic store in blocks of 25. The blocks can be stored in a list store that has pairs of words for its elements, but this arrangement is very inefficient, in terms of both time and space. Since each of the 25 symbols has to be transferred separately, the transfer rate is low. On the other hand, while the block is in the list store, no changes are made to it. This means that the pointer words paired to the data words have no functional use.

Efficiency is improved by use of multiword elements. Presume that the list store is divided into 26-word elements. As in the 2-word element, one of the words contains pointers, but now a single pointer word services 25 words of data. However, the list store will probably be used for a variety of purposes, and it would not be good policy to divide the entire list store into elements of the same size. One possibility is to use elements whose size may be one of a restricted set of possible sizes, say {2, 4, 8, 16, ..., 256}. Then the 25 symbols of a background block can be stored in a 32-word element, with 6 words going to waste, or they may be distributed over a set of linked smaller elements: a 16-word element, an 8-word element, and a 4-word element, reducing the number of words wasted. Under this scheme the size of the block must be stored in the pointer word of the block (external directories holding the sizes of blocks have been used as well, but they reduce the flexibility of the scheme). Available space can be arranged as a set of lists, one for each size, or as a single list. Greater efficiency is achieved with a set of lists. If no element of a required size is available, it is created by splitting a larger element; this is the reason for making each size half the next larger size. Periodically all unused elements are shifted to one end of the list store and restructured into larger elements.

An alternative is a scheme in which the sizes of elements are completely unrestricted. Initially the entire list store is a single element of available space. If a stack block has to be stored, 26 cells are taken from this element, reducing its size by this amount. Again, if a list structure representation of the tree $a(bc(fg(j))d(hi)e)$ is to be created, then 19 elements of size 2 are taken from the element of available space. As lists are erased, they are returned to available space, and the available space region now becomes a multielement list. If at some later stage a stack block is to be stored, and a search through the list of available space fails to produce an element of size 26 or larger, all unused elements are shifted to one end of the list store and merged to form a single element of available space from which the 26-word element can then be sliced off.

10h. Management of List Stores

In several places we have written in passing that lists and list structures are erased and then returned to the list of available space (LAVS). Let us now discuss mechanisms for their return. Consider the tree of Figure 10.20 and its representation in Figure 10.21. The tree, as a list structure, has an external name containing a pointer to the first element of the structure (the element containing the symbol a). The complete tree is erased by setting the pointer in its name to zero. If this is done, then all list elements that make up the tree become *inaccessible*. One might, on the other hand, merely delete the subtree rooted at d. This would be done by shifting the second pointer from the fourth element in the first row of Figure 10.21 to the second pointer field of the third element in this row, and then the six elements that represent the subtree would become inaccessible.

Sharing of sublists makes it difficult to return elements to LAVS after each erasure because a deleted sublist may belong to some other structure or part of the same structure in which it should be retained, and in general it is very difficult to tell whether or not this is the case. Moreover, the original storage reserves in LAVS may be sufficiently large to enable a program to run to proper completion even if no erased elements are returned to LAVS. The return of elements to LAVS does take time, and this time is then spent unnecessarily. Even single elements that are deleted from a list, as by A.10.7, for example, need not be immediately returned to LAVS. Therefore, most list processing systems postpone the retrieval of inaccessible elements until LAVS is nearly or completely exhausted. A procedure that retrieves all inaccessible elements, called the *garbage collector*, is then brought into action. Garbage collection proceeds in two stages. First, the external names are examined. Whenever a name contains a pointer, all paths that have their origin defined by this pointer are traced through, and every element encountered in tracing the paths is marked. After this has been done for every name all accessible elements are marked and all inaccessible elements remain unmarked. The marked elements define lists that are *active* at this time. In the second stage the unmarked elements are strung together to form a new list of available space, and the markers removed from the accessible elements.

Sharing of sublists presents no difficulty. If two structures have shared a sublist, and the sublist has been deleted from one of the structures, the elements of the sublist are still accessible in the other structure. The requirement that at least one bit in the marker field of every element has to be set aside for exclusive use in garbage collection is generally of minor consequence. There is, however, one major difficulty. We have seen that the traversal of list structures requires one to use a stack (except in the case of threaded list structures). Unfortunately, there is no available space for the stack in the list store when garbage collection takes place. One solution is to provide the system with a stack external to the list store and inaccessible to the programmer. A more attractive solution is to use a reversal-of-pointers technique, which enables one to retrace paths to their origins. The following marking algorithm makes use of this technique.

ALGORITHM 10.8   Marking algorithm for a garbage collector.   The algorithm marks all elements that belong to a list structure defined by a nonzero pointer in its name (LN). NPLACE is the address of LN. In each element we assume a marker field comprising locations S_1, S_2, and S_3—S_1 is 0 if the list element contains data and 1 if it contains a pointer to a sublist; S_2 is used to keep track of the reversal of pointers; the algorithm sets $S_3 = 1$ in all elements accessible from LN. The pointers $A(E)$ and $D(E)$ have the same interpretation as in A.10.2. Note that the algorithm works for reentrant list structures, and that the lists may consist of multiword elements. It is assumed that all S_2 and S_3 are initially zero; they should be reset to zero in the second phase of garbage collection.

1. Set $I = LN$, $J = NPLACE$.
2. If $S_3(Ei) = 0$, go to 3. Else, if $J \neq NPLACE$, go to 9, but if $J = NPLACE$, then stop.
3. Set $K = A(E_I)$, $A(E_I) = J$, $S_3(E_I) = 1$, $J = I$, $I = K$.
4. If $I \neq 0$, go to 3.
5. If $S_1(E_J) = 0$, go to 8.
6. If $S_2(E_J) = 1$, go to 9.
7. Set $K = D(E_J)$, $D(E_J) = A(E_J)$, $A(E_J) = I$, $S_2(E_J) = 1$, $I = K$; go to 2.
8. Set $K = A(E_J)$, $A(E_J) = I$; go to 10.
9. Set $K = D(E_J)$, $D(E_J) = I$.

10.   Set I $=$ J, J $=$ K; if K $\neq$ NPLACE, go to 5.
11.   Stop.

Comments. If a list is already marked—it may be a sublist of another structure that has already been processed, or it may belong to a reentrant structure—then the processing of the list is bypassed (Step 2). In Steps 3 and 4 one moves down the list, marking elements and reversing pointers, until the end of the list is reached. Then the path along the list is retraced backwards, pointers being restored to their original settings (Steps 8 to 10). Sublists are dealt with in this stage. An element containing a pointer to a sublist is visited twice during the backward traversal. Step 6 distinguishes between the two instances. The first time S_2 (E) is 0, and one interrupts the restoring of pointers to move into the sublist. The action shifts to Step 2 via Step 7, but Step 6 is reached again after processing of the sublist, all of its sublists, and so forth has been completed. This time S_2 (E) is 1, and restoring of pointers in the list is resumed. The algorithm is more general than implied above. It can be employed for traversal of list structures in general, not just for purposes of garbage collection. In the case of traversal of B-trees, the order of traversal that is to be followed may necessitate some changes in the strategy of the algorithm.

If all list elements have the same size, the creation of the new list of available space in the second stage of the garbage collection process is very simple. Complications arise when multiword elements of various sizes have to be compacted into a single element of available space. Active list structures must be relocated, and this involves updating of pointers. As part of the process one may wish to do some compacting of the active lists as well. This is an extremely difficult task, and an intermediate transfer of the list structures to auxiliary storage (disk, drum, tape) appears to give the only feasible solution. The mere transfer of the active structures to one end of the list store is still fairly difficult, particularly when sublists are shared.

An alternative to garbage collection is the *reference counter* approach. We recommend it for systems that keep structure and symbols separate (see Section 10f). In this approach an empty list has a reference count of 0 to start with. A nonempty list starts with a count of 1. Whenever the list is made a sublist of another list the reference count is increased by 1; when the list ceases to be the sublist of a list the count is decreased by 1. In terms of Figure 10.37, the reference counts of N(1), N(2), ..., N(5) are, respectively, 2, 4, 3, 2, 4; that of SYMBOL is 1. A field can be set aside in the list name for the reference counter. Whenever an erasure is called for, or a list is removed from a structure, the appropriate reference count is adjusted. A list is returned to available space when its count drops to zero. Looking at Figures 10.36 and 10.37, let us remove arc $\langle 5, 4 \rangle$. This means removing the second element of N(5) (it becomes part of the available space list), and decreasing the reference count in N(4) by 1. Next, let node 4 be removed; i.e., let N(4) be erased. Since the reference count in N(4) now becomes 0, list N(4) is returned to available space. At the same time counts in N(1) and N(2) are decreased. Next consider what happens when the two operations are performed in reverse order. Now the erasure of N(4) results merely in a decrease of the reference count. Next, when ⟨5, 4⟩ is removed, the reference count in N(4) becomes 0, return of N(4) to available space takes place, and the reference counts of N(1) and N(2) are decremented at this stage.

In our example the reference counter approach seems to lead to an unnatural situation: Why should the removal of a node result in the removal of arcs originating from the node when the indegree of the node is zero, but not when it is nonzero? This perplexing state of affairs has nothing to do with reference counters, but is a consequence of the peculiar interpretation we have given to "removal of a node." When a node is removed we must remove *all* arcs incident with it. Therefore, node 4 is not properly removed before the removal of arc ⟨5, 4⟩, and it is meaningless to comment on the situation before this has taken place.

The problem of reentrant structures is much more serious. One should be able to return the whole digraph to available space by erasing N(1), N(2), ..., N(5) in turn. Actually what happens is that the counts in the list names decrease by 1 in each instance, without any one decreasing to zero! Consider the erasure of N(1). Since the reference count in N(1) decreases only to 1, the list is not returned to available space. We can, however, revise our approach, and decrease the reference counts in N(2) and N(3) at this point, instead of waiting until the return of N(1) to available space. Then all five counts ultimately reduce to zero, but they do so at rather awkward times. The count in N(1) becomes zero while N(4) is being erased: We move along list N(4), see the reference to N(1) in the first element, and decrement the counter of N(1). Since the count is now zero, processing of N(4) has to be interrupted so that list N(1) can be returned to available space. This type of interrupt is fairly easy to deal with, but things become rather chaotic when a list refers to itself, as N(5) does. When we come to the processing of N(5) its counter holds the value 2. This is reduced to 1, and processing of the list begins. The first element of N(5) contains a reference to N(5), and the count is decreased again. Now it becomes 0, and N(5) should be returned to available space, but if we do so at once, then N(2) and N(4) are left up in the air. The solution of the problem requires some delicate programming.

One of our aims in separating data and structural information was to eliminate markers. Since garbage collection depends on the use of markers, we recommend the reference counter technique for "separated" lists, even when they form reentrant structures, despite the greater complexity of this scheme. An exception is provided by lists in which the elements are all of the same size, but they rarely are in systems of the type considered here. Then markers for a garbage collector can be arranged in external tables of bits, the nth bit in a table being associated with the nth element in the list store.

10i. PL/I-Type Data Structures

The *structures* of Cobol and PL/I are more complicated than arrays. The PL/I declaration

    DECLARE 1U(2), 2V, 2W, 3Y, 3Z(2,2), 2X;

generates a data structure that has the form

$$
U(1)\ \begin{bmatrix} V \\ W \begin{bmatrix} Y \\ Z(1,1) \\ Z(1,2) \\ Z(2,1) \\ Z(2,2) \end{bmatrix} \\ X \end{bmatrix}
\qquad
U(2)\ \begin{bmatrix} V \\ W \begin{bmatrix} Y \\ Z(1,1) \\ Z(1,2) \\ Z(2,1) \\ Z(2,2) \end{bmatrix} \\ X \end{bmatrix}
$$

A prefix in the declaration indicates the *level* of the variable in the structure; numbers in parentheses indicate that the variable represents an array of the given dimensions. The first V is referenced by writing $U(1).V$, or, if no ambiguity can arise, simply $V(1)$. The second $Z(1,2)$ is referenced by $U(2).W.Z(1,2)$, or by $U(2).Z(1,2)$, or by $W(2).Z(1,2)$, or by $Z(2,1,2)$, and this list does not exhaust all the possible forms. Structure U contains 14 *simple* data elements: $V(1)$, $Y(1)$, $Z(1,1,1)$, $Z(1,1,2)$, $Z(1,2,1)$, $Z(1,2,2)$, $X(1)$, $V(2)$, $Y(2)$, $Z(2,1,1)$, $Z(2,1,2)$, $Z(2,2,1)$, $Z(2,2,2)$, $X(2)$. Names U and W refer to the data collectively: U names the main structure, W a substructure of U.

Let us now generate a second structure of identical form by

    DECLARE 1UU(2), 2VV, 2WW, 3Y, 3ZZ(2,2), 2XX;

Since Y now appears in two declarations, every reference to it must be *qualified*; i.e., we must specify the structure in which the particular Y we want resides.

The "simple" PL/I statement,

$$U = U + UU;$$

is equivalent to

$$U(1) = U(1) + UU(1);$$
$$U(2) = U(2) + UU(2);$$

The second of these is, in turn, equivalent to the three statements

$$V(2) = V(2) + VV(2);$$
$$W(2) = W(2) + WW(2);$$
$$X(2) = X(2) + XX(2);$$

and $W(2) = W(2) + WW(2)$ is equivalent to

$$U.Y(2) = U.Y(2) + UU.Y(2) ;$$
$$Z(2,1,1) = Z(2,1,1) + ZZ(2,1,1);$$
$$Z(2,1,2) = Z(2,1,2) + ZZ(2,1,2);$$
$$Z(2,2,1) = Z(2,2,1) + ZZ(2,2,1);$$
$$Z(2,2,2) = Z(2,2,2) + ZZ(2,2,2);$$

The collective assignment statement $U = U + UU$ is equivalent to 14 normal assignment statements in all.

These structures differ from list structures in that their structural features cannot be altered once they have been declared. Nevertheless, a compiler has to use a system of pointers in setting up the structures so as to achieve efficiency in the compilation of statements that refer to the structures. Representation of structures by trees can greatly assist one in coming to an understanding of the concepts involved. The labeled tree of Figure 10.38 represents structure U.

Let us consider how a compiler would deal with the two declarations of our example. We need two tables: a *symbol table* and a *structure table*. An entry in the symbol table consists of a symbol and a pointer to an entry in the structure table. In compiling the declaration of U an entry is generated in the symbol table for every node of the tree corresponding to U. When the declaration of UU is compiled, entries are generated for symbols that are

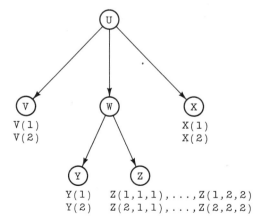

Figure 10.38

not already in the symbol table, i.e., for UU, VV, WW, ZZ, and XX, but not for Y.

The structure table contains an entry for *every* node. In our example there are 11 entries in the symbol table, but 12 in the structure table. This means that all entries in the structure table corresponding to the one entry in the symbol table must be chained by means of pointers. Another set of pointers is needed to conserve the structural features established by the declarations. Moreover, in the case of terminal nodes, the structure table must contain information relating to the memory locations reserved for storage of the data elements associated with these nodes. If a single data element is associated with a node, then the information is simply the address of the location assigned to this datum. If the data elements form an array (in our example they do so at every terminal node), dimensions of the array may have to be stored in addition to the address of its first element. Storage assignment does not interest us here, and we shall ignore all parts of the structure table that relate to this aspect of the problem.

For our example the tables are as shown in Figure 10.39. The first column in STRUCT contains pointers linking entries that correspond to the same symbol. For a given node the second column contains a pointer to the right-most terminal node in the structure that can be reached from this node. In the case of a terminal node this is a reference to itself. We shall now see that this information is sufficient for the location of a given terminal node.

ALGORITHM 10.9 Given specification $E_1 . E_2 . --- . E_N$, the algorithm finds the entry in the structure table STRUCT corresponding to this specification.

Symbol table SYMBOL   Structure table STRUCT

1	U	1		1	0	6	
2	V	2		2	0	2	
3	W	3		3	0	5	
4	Y	10		4	0	4	
5	Z	5		5	0	5	Information
6	X	6		6	0	6	relating to
7	UU	7		7	0	12	storage
8	VV	8		8	0	8	assignment
9	WW	9		9	0	11	
10	ZZ	11		10	4	10	
11	XX	12		11	0	11	
				12	0	12	

Figure 10.39

If the specification is ambiguous or improperly written, then an error return is taken (Step 17). An auxiliary array NREF of size N is used to store row numbers of STRUCT. All symbols in the *one* structure are assumed distinct.

1. Set $J = 1$, FIRST = .TRUE..
2. Look up E_J in SYMBOL—assuming that E_J = SYMBOL($K,1$), set NREF(J) = SYMBOL($K,2$).
3. Set $J = J + 1$.
4. If $J \leq N$, go to 2.
5. Set $J = 1$.
6. Set K = NREF(J). If $K = 0$, go to 18.
7. If $J = N$, go to 12.
8. If $K \geq$ NREF($J+1$), set NREF(J) = STRUCT($K,1$) and go to 5.
9. Set KK = NREF($J+1$). If $KK = 0$, go to 18.
10. If STRUCT($KK,2$) > STRUCT($K,2$), set NREF($J+1$) = STRUCT($KK,1$) and go to 5.
11. Set $J = J + 1$ and go to 6.
12. If FIRST = .FALSE., go to 17.
13. Set $J = 1$, FIRST = .FALSE., INDEX = NREF(N).
14. Set K = NREF(J).
15. If STRUCT($K,1$) = 0, go to 19.
16. Set NREF(J) = STRUCT($K,1$), $J = J + 1$. If $J \leq N$, go to 14; else go to 5.
17. Return—error condition.
18. If FIRST = .TRUE., go to 17.
19. Return—INDEX contains the number of the required row of STRUCT.

Comments. Array NREF is initiated in Steps 1 to 4. Steps 5 to 11 locate a region of STRUCT that the given specification refers to. Changes are made to NREF if the row numbers stored in NREF are not in strictly ascending order (Step 8), or if two row numbers in NREF refer to two different structures (Step 10). If the given specification does not refer to any declared structure, then K or KK becomes zero, and an error return is taken. If no inconsistency is detected, a check is carried out in Steps 13 to 16, and if the check indicates a possibility that there might be a second structure that could be described by the given specification, then Steps 5 to 11 are executed again. This time an inconsistency indicates that the given specification is unambiguous; if J attains the value N (Step 7), then there are at least two structures to which the given specification might refer, and the error return is taken. In Cobol the same symbol may be used more than once in the one structure, with some limitations. PL/I has fewer such limitations in that all structures that allow unambiguous specifications are permitted. However, even experienced PL/I programmers have some difficulty understanding what "unambiguous" means in the PL/I context, and in determining what a particular specification refers to in a structure that is declared by 1X, 2Y, 3X, 3Y, 2X, 5Y, 6X, 6Y; say. A.10.9 is meant merely to convey the flavor of the processing of structures; it is far from being a working algorithm for a Cobol or PL/I compiler. The latter would necessarily have to be more complicated.

Next let us consider how we would locate all the simple data elements denoted by U.W, say. A.10.9 would be used to find the entry corresponding to U.W in STRUCT. In terms of Figure 10.39, the relevant entry would be in row 3. Note that STRUCT(3, 2) = 5. This value is used to delimit the relevant section of STRUCT; we look for a row K farther down the table such that STRUCT(K, 2) is 5, and use the information relating to storage assignments in rows 3 to K to gain access to the data. Here K = 5, and, since only rows 4 and 5 refer to terminal nodes, the information contained in these rows would be used.

Notes

[Kn68] is a good general reference that covers much of the material of this chapter in greater detail. Note that the exercises are a most important part of this text. [Fo67] is a general work to consult on lists and their processing; [Br72] emphasizes the use of the Waterloo Fortran dialects in list and string processing. [Wi71a] surveys representations for graphic data. [Wi64, Wi65] contain examples of applications of list structures; further references to examples can be easily extracted from [Sa66], an excellent annotated and indexed bibliography of 297 items on the use of computers for nonnumerical mathematics.

List processing begins with the work of Newell, Shaw, and Simon on their "logic theory machine," see [Ne57]. Threaded lists were introduced by Perlis and Thornton [Pe60], and symmetric lists by Weizenbaum [We63]. [Co64] is a survey of the organization and use of list structures with multiword elements. Storage allocation when list elements are restricted in size to 2^n ($n = 0, 1, 2, 3$) words is described in [Kn65] (see also [Is71]); [Pu70b] is a thorough analysis of this system. For a list storage scheme with multiword elements of arbitrarily variable size see [Ro67b]. In string processing it is sometimes advantageous to make a distinction between a logical element (a string) and a list element, where it is permissible to have a logical element distributed over several list elements. In [Wo65] a formula is derived for the optimal number of words in multiword list elements of constant size in terms of the average number of words in a logical element. A string storage scheme with list elements of variable size is described in [Be65].

Garbage collection based on the marking of the accessible list elements was first described by McCarthy [Mc60]; the reversal-of-pointers technique of A.10.8 is taken from [Sc67]; for other traversal procedures see [Th72, Li73]. A garbage collection scheme for the case when lists occupy two levels of storage is described in [Co67]. Reference counters were introduced by Collins [Co60]. The inadequacy of the basic technique when it comes to recovery of erased reentrant list structures was pointed out in [Mc63b]. Nevertheless, the technique has been used quite effectively in two Fortran-embedded list processing languages, see [We63, Co66]. A hybrid scheme that uses a marking procedure in addition to the counter technique to get around the difficulty of reentrant list structures is described in [We69]. Alternatively, one can use the recursive scheme outlined at the end of Section 10h; note that the effectiveness of this scheme does *not* depend on the separation of structural information from symbolic data. Compaction of storage blocks of variable size is discussed in [Ha67c]. Copying of list structures is discussed in [Li74].

Facilities for structuring data along the lines of Section 10i are provided in Cobol and PL/I (see [Sa68c], pp. 330–381 for a description of Cobol and pp. 540–582 for PL/I). [Kn68] contains a very useful section on structures (pp. 423–434, see in particular p. 432 where the system of tables of Figure 10.39 is ascribed to Dahm); [Ga73b] is a more recent reference dealing with the implementation of PL/I structures.

List and string processing languages are surveyed in [Ab68, Ra68a]. Chapter 6 (pp. 382–470) of [Sa68c] is devoted to list and string processing languages; a very good feature of this book is the clear way the significant contributions made to technology in the design and implementation of a language are pointed out. [Wa73a] deals with the implementation of various facilities that a list or string processing language should provide; [Bo72] is a thoughtful analysis of features one would expect to find in an advanced list processing language. One of the hardest problems confronting the designer of a list or string processing language is how to deal with null objects. A very valuable discussion of this problem can be found on pp. 185–186 of [Mo68].

LISP has been the most influential list processing language. The LISP philosophy is set out by McCarthy in [Mc60]; [Mc62] is the manual; [Ma72d] is a primer. The LISP literature is quite extensive: [Be64b] is a book that alone contains 20 papers on LISP, ranging from exposition to implementation and applications. Addition of Fortran-like features to LISP is the subject matter of [Kn69]. A number of papers in [Be64b] deal with applications; in addition one may consult [Ra64]. While LISP is a high level language, L^6 is a low-level list processing language (L^6 stands for the six occurrences of L in " Bell Telephone Laboratories' Low-Level Linked List Language "). It is defined in [Kn66]. Weizenbaum's SLIP is a list processing language embedded in Fortran. It is defined in [We63]; [Sm67] is a good introduction. Applications of SLIP are discussed in [La65b, Ra68b]. Weizenbaum's own application papers, [We66b, We67], do not give programming details, but they should be read for a discussion of the type of problems list processing languages are designed for, and for Weizenbaum's elegant style. Instead of embedding one can permit statements written in a list processing language to be intermingled with statements in an established general purpose language, and submit a program consisting of this mixture to a preprocessor that converts the list processing statements to statements in the general purpose language. The resulting program can then be compiled by a compiler for the general purpose language. [Cl74] provides an example of this approach, PL/I being the general purpose language in this instance.

Comit is the oldest string processing language; it is as old as Fortran. It has been largely supplanted by the newer language Snobol. [Yn72] is a Comit primer. [Gr68] is the manual for Snobol. Languages designed for the processing of graphs and digraphs are defined in [Cr70, Pr71a, Ki72, Rh72].

[Ax67, De67, Sm67] constitute a comparison study: They contain, respectively, LISP, Snobol, and SLIP programs for an expression recognition problem. Annotated sample programs can be found also in [Ra68a].

Structured programming was mentioned in Section 10c. Structured programming leads to the creation of correct programs by means of a systematic approach to their design. For examples see [Wi71b, He72, Na72, Le74a]. The benefits that resulted from the use of structured programming in the production of a very large system have been documented in [Ba72b]. Further reading on costs in large programming projects is provided by [Wo74].

Exercises

10.1   (a)   Elements in the first 10 rows of a 500×2 array LIST (and only these locations) are to be used for list names, and the remaining elements of LIST are to function as a list store. Taking LIST(1,1) for the name of the list of available space, write a routine INITIO that initializes LIST.

10.2   (a)   Assuming that a list store is arranged as described in Exercise 10.1, write the following subprograms:

    (i) KOUNT—to find the number of elements in a given list.
    (ii) LAST—to find the value of the last element in a given list.
    (iii) NTHOFF—to delete the last element in a given list.
    (iv) KTHOFF—to delete the kth element in a given list.
    (v) KTHADD—to introduce a given datum into a given list so that the new

element becomes the kth element of the list, the old kth element becomes the $(k + 1)$th element, etc.

(vi) ALLOFF—to delete an entire given list.

(vii) MCHOFF—to delete every element in a given list that matches a given value.

10.3 (a) Assuming that a list store is arranged as described in Exercise 10.1, make appropriate changes to subprograms PUSH and IPOP of Section 10a so that they will function for this arrangement. What is the appearance of the array LIST after execution of the following program segment?

```
      CALL INITIO
      DO  5   K = 1,10
      DO  5   J = 1,2
  5   CALL PUSH (LIST(J,2),K+J)
      DO  6   K = 1,5
      DO  6   J = 1,2
  6   NEX(J,K) = IPOP (LIST(J,2))
      CALL PUSH (LIST(1,2),NEX(1,5))
      CALL PUSH (LIST(2,2),NEX(2,5))
      DO  7   J = 1,2
      DO  7   K = 1,5
  7   CALL PUSH (LIST(J,2),NEX(J,K))
```

10.4 (a) Write PUSH and IPOP routines for a queue analogous to the ones of Exercise 10.3 for a stack. A system of two external pointers as shown in Figure 10.9 should be used.

10.5 (a) Under the assumptions of Exercise 10.1, write a subroutine DUPLY that duplicates a list A as list B, i.e., creates a list B that has as many elements as A, these elements containing in their data cells the same data that are contained in A, and in the same logical sequence. Although you may use the routines of Exercise 10.2, DUPLY would be faster if these routines were not used.

10.6 (a) The most general pushdown store is one in which data can be added and taken off at both ends. Such a pushdown store is called a *deque* (*d*ouble *e*nded *que*ue). An implementation of a deque requires four routines: PUSH and IPOP for operations at one end, and PUT and IGET, say, for operations at the other end. Write these routines assuming that the list store is arranged as in Exercise 10.1.

10.7 (a) Rewrite the routines of Exercises 10.1 and 10.2 under the assumption that all lists are provided with headers. Make your own decision as to what the data cell of the header is to contain.

10.8 (a) Given a vector of numbers A(1),...,A(N), go through the vector looking in turn at all pairs of elements A(I) and A(I+1) for I = 1,2,...,N − 1, and interchange A(I) and A(I + 1) whenever A(I) > A(I + 1). This procedure moves the largest element of the vector into location A(N). Suppose that A(1),...,A(N) are elements of a list. Implement this procedure as a list processing routine in such a way that all interchanges are performed by movements of pointers alone (see Figure 10.13). A note on the practicability of the suggested method: If the A(I) are just single numbers, then it is much easier to interchange the data rather than adjust pointers. However, if each of the numbers has some 20 words, say, of additional information associated with it, and these blocks of data have to be interchanged, then movement of pointers becomes the better solution.

10.9 (b) Write routines for inserting and deleting a matrix element in the representation of Figure 10.14.

10.10 (b) Repeat Exercise 10.9 for the representation of Figure 10.15.

10.11 (b) Write a routine for multiplying two matrices that have the representation of Figure 10.14, where the product is also to be generated in this representation.

10.12 (b) Repeat Exercise 10.11 using the representation of Figure 10.15.

10.13 (d) Represent the tree of Figure 13.13 and the digraph of Figure 3.1 by list structures.

10.14 (d) Characterize the digraphs that are represented by identical list structures under the two conventions A and B.

10.15 (d) Modify A.10.2 for the case where the list elements are not provided with markers.

10.16 (d) Design an algorithm equivalent to A.10.2 for generating a parenthesized expression from a tree stored as a list structure under convention B.

10.17 (d) Develop an algorithm that generates a list structure from a parenthesized string. You may select the convention that you find easier to work with.

10.18 (d) Design an algorithm that generates a parenthesized expression from a B-tree representation of a nonbinary tree, where this parenthesized expression is to be identical to that which would be generated by A.10.2 if this algorithm were applied to the nonbinary tree from which the B-tree has been derived.

10.19 (d) Design an algorithm for traversing a digraph in terms of a list structure representation of the digraph. Each node is to be "processed" as part of the traversal, and the algorithm is to stop when all nodes have been processed. (The form that the processing is to take is left to your discretion.)

10.20 (d) Design an algorithm for postorder traversal of a nonbinary tree that is stored as a list structure under convention B.

10.21 (d) Devise an algorithm that generates a nonbinary tree equivalent to a given B-tree in the sense of Figures 5.17 and 10.27.

10.22 (d) Assume that the tree of Figure 10.27 is functioning as a sort tree. Develop a procedure for inserting a new datum in the tree.

10.23 (d) Devise the equivalent of A.5.9 for implementation of a sort tree in a nonbinary form, e.g., as exemplified by Figure 10.27.

10.24 (d) Design list representations of the following structures: (i) binary trees in which only terminal nodes are labeled, (ii) weighted digraphs, (iii) weighted labeled digraphs, (iv) trees that have the form shown in Figure 6.10, allowing for the sharing of sublists.

10.25 (d) Devise a list structure representation of finite state acceptors (see, e.g., Figure 4.4), and, hence, the equivalent of A.4.3 for this representation.

10.26 (e) Redraw the list structures of Exercise 10.13 using threaded list representation.

10.27 (e) Modify A.10.5 to take for its input a threaded list structure obeying convention B, i.e., a list structure with return addresses that derives from the representation of Figure 10.22 in just the same way that Figure 10.29 derives from Figure 10.21.

10.28 (e) Specify algorithms for inorder and preorder traversal of a right-threaded B-tree that do not use a stack.

10.29 (e) Redraw Figure 10.31, making the B-tree fully threaded.

10.30 (e) Reformulate A.10.7 for the simpler representation of a B-tree exemplified by Figure 10.26.

10.31 (e) Reformulate A.10.7 to delete a node in such a way that the relative order of processing of the remaining nodes under preorder traversal is unchanged by the deletion. Is it possible to write a deletion algorithm that preserves relative processing order under both inorder and preorder traversal?

10.32 (e) Devise a balancing algorithm for sort trees in right-threaded representation (cf. A.5.11).

10.33 (e) If an algorithm for inorder traversal of a threaded B-tree is applied to an unbalanced tree of n nodes and an equivalent balanced tree of n nodes, which tree do you expect to be traversed faster?

10.34 (e) Redraw the list structures of Exercise 10.13 using symmetric list representation.

10.35 (e) In the structure of Figure 10.35 only terminal nodes carry labels. Redraw the structure of Figure 10.34 to make it conform to this convention, and generate the corresponding symmetric list representation. Find general formulas for the numbers of list elements required for symmetric list representation of parenthesized strings under the two conventions. Find also a general formula for the number of list elements required for threaded list representation of a parenthesized string.

10.36 (e) Design algorithms for processing of symmetric lists that correspond to subprograms KOUNT, LAST, NTHOFF, KTHOFF, and MCHOFF of Exercise 10.2.

10.37 (e) Let a FIFO store be represented by a symmetric list. Develop PUSH and IPOP procedures for this representation.

10.38 (e) Design algorithms for symmetric lists that correspond to the routines of Exercise 10.6, i.e., use a symmetric list for the implementation of a deque.

10.39 (h) Repeat Exercise 10.16 using now the reversal-of-pointers technique to keep track of the traversal.

10.40 (h) Repeat Exercise 10.28 using now the reversal-of-pointers technique instead of threading to keep track of the traversal.

10.41 (h) A reference counter technique for recovering reentrant list structures is outlined at the end of Section 10h. Expand the outline to an explicit detailed algorithm.

10.42 (i) Draw a tree that represents the data structure declared by the PL/I statement

DECLARE 1X, 2Y, 3Z(3), 3YY(2), 2XX, 3XY;

10.43 (i) Develop an algorithm for the creation of table SYMBOL and the first two columns of table STRUCT (see Figure 10.39) from declarations of data structures.

CHAPTER **11**

Organization of Files

11a. Records and Files

Let us start with a quote: "Data management problems are what the Internal Revenue Service has when it receives 65 million income tax returns every April 15." The returns are records in an extremely large file. Another example of a file is a telephone directory in which the triples {*name, address, telephone number*} are the records. The information kept by a computer installation on the jobs it has run, which may be a set of quintuples of the form {*job number, name, department, phone, cumulative total of money spent on computer use*}, is another example. The bibliography at the end of this book is a file of modest size; its records are the quintuples {*code, author(s), title, publishing data, reference data*}. A *file*, then, is a set of *n*-tuples, the *n*-tuples are *records* in the file, and we shall call the coordinates of an *n*-tuple the *fields* of a record. Large or small, files have to be organized and managed, and the purpose of this chapter is to provide some insight in the problems associated with these activities.

A considerable effort has gone into the formalization of file processing concepts, but, although we must be ready to recognize the benefits that can derive from a formal approach, we should be cautious not to become too pedantic. Most formal theories of files propounded so far do not appear to satisfy significantly the requirement set down in another quote: "The

431

mathematical system serving as a model must yield theorems whose interpretation affords some deeper insight or knowledge." For this reason, apart from giving a sound definition of the objects that we shall talk about, we shall adopt an informal approach.

DEFINITION 11.1   A *file* is a collection of data, each datum consisting of three elements:

(a)   a *unit*—an entity (object, person, concept, etc.) that may be considered, for data processing purposes, in terms of a finite number of properties;

(b)   a *property*—a characteristic to which measures can be assigned;

(c)   a *measure*—a value capable of being expressed in a finite number of information units (bits, characters, etc.).

The set of data in a file associated with the one unit is a *unit record* or simply a *record*.

The values are the fields of a record, and in most files only values are explicitly represented. Such files are called *homogeneous*. It is then essential to have the values ordered so that they can be correlated with the appropriate properties as and when required. Let $P = \{p_1, p_2, \ldots, p_n\}$ be a set of properties, and let V_i be the set of values that property p_i can take. A homogeneous file on P is a subset of $V_1 \times V_2 \times \cdots \times V_n$, and the members of the subset are the records. A V_i may have to include a special null value in case p_i is inapplicable to a given unit, or its measure is unknown. A case in point: In the bibliography of this book references that carry a Zz code have anonymous authors, and, if we consider the bibliography as a subset of $V_1 \times V_2 \times V_3 \times V_4 \times V_5$, then V_2 must contain the special null value, which is assigned to the Zz entries.

The decision of whether or not to make a file homogeneous is determined by the characteristics of the unit records and by the purpose behind the setting up of the file, i.e., by what is to be done with the file afterwards. In many instances homogeneous design is natural. For example, the population census of a country produces a unit record for each resident of the country. Here $P = \{name, address, date of birth, place of birth, \ldots\}$. The file can be stored on magnetic tapes. Since the properties for each unit record are the same, there is no need to give an explicit representation of the properties in any one record. The file is homogeneous, with each record occupying a block of fixed size on a tape. The representation of the measures within a record adheres to a fixed format, so that a particular measure, say *date of birth*, occupies a well-defined field in each block.

Next consider a fact retrieval system based on a file of Nobel Prize winners, with the records having the format Name/date of birth/date of death/Peace/

Literature/Chemistry/Physics/Medicine/Economics. A record in the file might be

Watson, James Dewey/1928/ $\emptyset$ / $\emptyset$ / $\emptyset$ / $\emptyset$ / $\emptyset$ /1962/ $\emptyset$

On the other hand, the record could be stored in a nonhomogeneous file as

Watson, James Dewey/B1928/M1962

Although the homogeneous file would take up more space, retrieval of, say, all winners of the Medicine Prize after 1950 would be faster, and this consideration could lead one to the adoption of the homogeneous design.

The design of a file should not be hurried into. Even the small file of Nobel Prize winners demonstrates how easily the unwary designer may get into difficulties, particularly if a homogeneous design has been selected. The homogeneous design here does not provide for a prize to be awarded more than once in the one category to the same person or organization, but the International Red Cross has received the Peace Prize a number of times. There is also the minor matter that dates of birth and death do not apply to organizations, but this can be easily taken care of by leaving the appropriate fields blank.

A file may be designed so that every record in the file occupies the same amount of storage space, or the size of individual records may be permitted to vary. We speak then of *fixed length records* and *variable length records*, respectively. A homogeneous file generally consists of fixed length records. In a nonhomogeneous file the amount of information that makes up a record may greatly vary from record to record, and the greater storage efficiency achieved with variable length records may outweigh the benefits deriving from the greater simplicity of a file in which all records have the same length.

A file must give reasonably fast access to a specified item of information contained in it. This calls for organization. The most common organization of records in a file is the *sequential* organization. Although there are exceptions (for example, the sequential order in a file of incoming messages in a message-switching system may be determined by the order of arrival of the messages), generally the records in a sequential file are in lexicographic order of the values in some particular field or fields within the records. The fields that determine the sequential order are called *keys*. In a telephone directory the key is the property *name*. In our bibliography the key is the code field; since the names of the authors have been used in the construction of the codes, the names are also very nearly in lexicographic order, but not quite.

When the key of a number of records has the same value, the use of a single key may be inadequate, and a second key may have to be used to establish the sequence of records for which the first key has the same value. In some bibliographies the field *name of author* is the first key, and *publication year* the second.

The records are put into sequential order by *sorting* on the key or keys. Some sorting procedures will be given in Section 11d. When the values of a key are in lexicographic order, *logarithmic search* (also called *binary search*) can be used to gain access to a record specified by a given value of the key. This value is called the *search key*.

Logarithmic search is based on the following observation. Assume that A is a vector of n elements, and that the elements are in lexicographic order, i.e., that $a_k \leqq a_{k+1}$ for $k = 1, 2, \ldots, n - 1$. Further assume that a given datum d, if it is in A, is one of $a_i, a_{i+1}, \ldots, a_j$. Compute $k = \lfloor (i + j)/2 \rfloor$, where $\lfloor x \rfloor$ is the floor function of x, and compare d with a_k. If $d = a_k$, the search is over; if $d < a_k$, then d can only be one of $a_i, \ldots, a_{k-1}$; if $d > a_k$, it can only be one of $a_{k+1}, \ldots, a_j$. Logarithmic search starts with $i = 1$ and $j = n$, and the search region is successively reduced. The total number of comparisons is at most $\lfloor \log_2 n \rfloor + 1$; it is $\lfloor \log_2 n \rfloor$ if one can assume that d is in A. By contrast, if the elements of A were unordered, one would have to go down A, comparing d against each element in turn. If d were in A, the expected number of comparisons would be $n/2$; if it were not, then one would have to go through all n elements before one could be sure.

ALGORITHM 11.1   A program for finding a given datum KEY in the first column of a matrix M by logarithmic search. It is assumed that the first column of M contains integers in ascending order. SEARCH returns the number of the row in which KEY is found; it returns 0 if KEY is not in the first column of M.

```
      INTEGER FUNCTION SEARCH (KEY,M,N,K)
      DIMENSION M(N,K)
      INTEGER HI
      LO = 1
      HI = N
      SEARCH = 0
    5 IF (LO.EQ.HI .AND. KEY.NE.M(LO,1)) RETURN
      MID = (LO+HI)/2
      IF (KEY - M(MID,1)) 6,10,7
    6 HI = MID
      GO TO 5
    7 LO = MID + 1
      GO TO 5
   10 SEARCH = MID
      RETURN
      END
```

Examples

1. Binary search in an ordered sequential file of n records requires the same number of comparisons as search in a balanced sort tree of n nodes, both in the average case and the worst case. The sort tree has the advantage that it is easier to add new records to it than it is to insert new records in the sequential file in such a way that the sequential file remains ordered, but this advantage is offset by a deterioration in performance when the sort tree becomes unbalanced as more records are added to it, and by the need to provide each record with two pointer fields.

2. A very small file is best left unordered, and searched record by record. We cannot go just by the number of comparisons, $n/2$ against $\log_2 n$; what matters are the times to perform these operations. Since the program for binary search has a more complex structure than the program for sequential search, the break-even point for these two methods can range from $n = 20$ to $n = 40$, depending on the computer, the programming language, and the compiler for the language.

3. A.5.1 finds in a string α all occurrences of substrings of given length d that occur at least twice. An interesting problem is to find the longest duplicated substrings in α. The procedure is to perform Steps 1 and 2 of A.5.1, but to let the r in Step 2 be the least power of 2 such that each equivalence class of E_r contains just one substring, i.e., E_r is trivial. Then we have $r/2 \leq d_{\max} < r$, and the solution is completed using binary search: Use $E_{r/2}$ to get $E_{3r/4}$. If $E_{3r/4}$ is nontrivial, use it to get $E_{7r/8}$; else use $E_{r/2}$ to get $E_{5r/8}$, and so forth.

11b. Indexed Files

The registers kept by motor registration authorities are files. Assume that records in the file of one such authority are divided into the fields *name/ address/registration number/date of expiry/model of car*. The file might serve a variety of purposes. The primary purpose should be to provide information for sending out renewal notices, but the file might be used in crime detection as well. As far as the primary purpose is concerned, the appropriate sort key is *date of expiry*. However, sorted this way, the file is not properly ordered for finding the name and address corresponding to a given registration number—an application that could arise in crime detection.

One solution is to arrange the file in 12 *blocks*, one for each month of expiry, and to have each block sorted on the *registration number*. The block starting addresses are kept in an external directory of 12 entries. Then, given a registration number, one applies logarithmic search to each block in turn.

Assuming that the blocks are approximately equal in size and that the total number of records in the file is n, the expected number of comparisons for locating a record is approximately $6 \log_2 (n/12)$.

A more drastic solution would be to keep two complete files: one sorted on *date of expiry*, the other on *registration number*. This design would squander memory; the only information that we really need in the second file is the set of registration numbers and pointers to records in the first file. Let us, therefore, generate the second file as follows: (a) from each record in the first file copy the registration number and attach to it the address of the record, and (b) sort these ordered pairs on the registration numbers. The second file is now an *index* of the first. An index can be prepared using any of the fields. A file that has a set of indexes associated with it is known as an *indexed file*.

Let us turn again to document retrieval, which was introduced in Section 8c. Assume that we have a set of documents, and that the documents have index terms associated with them. The index terms might be:

> Document 1—memory protection, monitor, operating system, time-sharing;
> Document 2—integer programming, operations research, zero–one variables;
> Document 3—data structures, file handling, paging, storage allocation, storage organization, time-sharing;
> ⋮

An indexed document file is set up by storing the bibliographic information in order of document numbers (preferably with all entries made the same size), and by creating a sorted list of index terms in which each term is followed by identifying numbers of all documents with which it is associated. Let us call the two components of the indexed file document register and index, respectively. A user might make a request for documents that carry all of the following index terms: memory protection, operating system, time-sharing. The three terms would be looked up in the index, and the intersection of the three sets of document numbers computed. The resulting set of document numbers then identifies all documents satisfying the request, and the bibliographic information relating to these documents is extracted from the document register.

The nature of the document file differs somewhat from that of the motor registration file. The basis of the indexed motor registration file is a sequential file containing all the information that is stored in the system, and this sequential file remains intact throughout; the indexes are *additions* to it. Searches are made in the sequential file and in the indexes. Imagine that the indexed document file, too, is generated from a sequential file, one in which each record consists of bibliographic data and the index terms, i.e., of more than one field. Now, however, each record is reduced to a single field, and *all* other data are placed in the index; i.e., a separation of the data takes place. Searches are made in the index alone. A file of this type is called *inverted*. The distinction between indexed and inverted files can become very blurred. For instance, if it is considered worthwhile to supply the user of the document retrieval system with additional information that would help him come to a finer appreciation of the relevance of the retrieved documents, then the full sets of index terms associated with the retrieved documents should be incorporated in the output, and this means that the index terms should be part of the register entries. Then the document register carries too much information for the file to be a pure inverted file. On the other hand, since there is no direct interrogation of the register, the file is not a pure indexed file.

The process of making changes to a file is called *updating* of the file. The document file has to be updated when new documents come to hand, and the ease or difficulty of updating is determined by the original design of the file. No complex system is perfect, and sooner or later an existing system ought to be scrapped and replaced by a new system designed on the basis of operational experience with the existing system. Therefore, one can decide on the greatest number of documents that the file will be permitted to contain, taking the view that when this number is in danger of being exceeded the time will have come to redesign the system anyway. One may also be able to decide in advance on a set of permissible index terms, and, having a bound on the number of documents, one would have a fair idea of how many locations should be assigned to each index term for storing document numbers. We shall call these locations the *reference vector* of the index term. With this design updating of both the document file and the index is trivial. When a new document is brought into the system, the bibliographic data are simply appended to the existing document register. The index terms associated with the document are looked up in the index, and, for each index term, the number of the new document is inserted in the first free location of its reference vector.

If the set of index terms cannot be fixed in advance, then the document register is still easy to update, but updating of the index becomes difficult. Assume that an index term for which there is no entry in the index is associated with the new document. One cannot just append the entry for the new index term to the end of the index, because then the index is no longer ordered and logarithmic search becomes inapplicable. Therefore, storage has to be found for the new entry at its rightful place within the index, and this involves shifting of all entries that come after it. A file or a component of a file organized sequentially in lexicographic order can be efficiently searched, but the efficiency of updating is very poor.

Efficiency of updating improves when the index is set up as a list structure. Consider the index of the document file arranged as a binary sort tree. The tree is stored as a list structure (Figure 10.26 shows an example of a list structure corresponding to a sort tree) in which an element consists of left and right pointers, the index term, and locations for storing document numbers. Search in a *balanced* binary sort tree is as efficient as binary search in the corresponding sequentially organized sorted index, but, since the sort tree is unlikely to be balanced, we can expect some loss of search efficiency. Because of the left and right pointers there is some loss of storage efficiency as well.

A change in the design of the list structure eliminates the need to estimate in advance the number of documents that will be indexed by a particular index term. Instead of representing a node in the sort tree by an element, let us represent it by a list. We now need two types of list elements. An element of the first type carries left and right pointers and an index term as before, but, in place of the locations for storing document numbers, there is a pointer to a list of these numbers. Document numbers are stored in elements of the second type. These elements consist of two fields: one for a document number, the other for a pointer to the next element containing a document number. The document numbers are stored in ascending order. Figure 11.1 shows the list corresponding to a node of the sort tree.

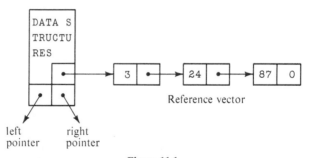

Figure 11.1

11c. Scatter Storage Techniques

Logarithmic search locates a record in a sorted sequential file fairly rapidly, but even better search times are achieved when the design of a file is based on scatter storage techniques. Moreover, updating efficiency matches the search efficiency. Although a scatter file occupies more storage than a sequential file containing the same amount of information, the additional locations required may be fewer than the locations taken up by pointers in a sort tree.

Let us take the compilation of Fortran programs for the context of our discussion. A compiler has to keep track of locations assigned to variables in the program that is being compiled; i.e., a file with records of the form ⟨*variable name, location*⟩ has to be maintained. If A is the set of permissible Fortran variable names, then $|A|$ is approximately equal to 1.6×10^9 (Exercise 1.41), but in a particular program only a comparatively small number of possible names will be encountered. Let T be a vector in which we store names as they are encountered. (We also need a vector in which to store the assigned locations, but this vector is irrelevant to our discussion.) Consider a function $f: A \rightarrow I$, where I is the set of subscripts of the elements of T, and the restriction $f \mid N$, where N is the set of variable names actually appearing in the program. Now, $f \mid N$ cannot be one to one, i.e., cannot associate all names in N with unique subscripts (otherwise, for T of any reasonable size, the computation of values of the function would take so long that the purpose for having the function would be lost), but it is possible to define functions f such that the number of elements in the range of $f \mid N$ is not much smaller than $|N|$, i.e., the restriction is close to being one to one, and the number of elements in the range of f is not much greater than $|N|$, i.e., the storage requirements are modest. Moreover, the subscripts can be computed very rapidly.

In general terms, we take a record, and apply a function f, called the *scatter function* or *hash function*, to a key in the record to arrive at an address in a scatter file storage area. Several different scatter functions have been devised. We shall consider the three most commonly used. To simplify our discussion we shall continue with the example of the Fortran compiler, and describe the operations in terms of variable names and subscripts defining locations in the table T (which is our *scatter table* or *hash table*).

a. Square the name and extract n bits from the middle of the result. The value of this field (the *hash address*) defines a location in T. Since the middle bits of the square of a word depend on every bit in the word, the probability that different variable names will give rise to different addresses is nearly the same for LOCA and LOCB, XARRAY and YARRAY, ABCDEF and ZYXWUV. Unless one employs a scaling procedure, the size of T must be 2^n, where n is the number of bits extracted. This can prove rather annoying: If a table of, say, 2048 locations is too small, then the table having the next possible size of 4096 may be much too large.

b. Compute the hash address by separating the name into n-bit fields, adding the fields, and taking the n lowest bits of the sum. Whether this method is preferable to squaring depends entirely on the speed with which the computer performs the operations. A variant of this method is to split the name in half, and to apply the fast logical *exclusive or* operation on the two halves, e.g., from GORSE (represented by octal integer 475762634500_8 in the PDP-10 sixbit code) and HORSE (505762634500_8) derive 241232_8 and 331232_8, respectively. The n bits are extracted from the result. Unfortunately, nearly equal names will tend to give the same hash address. Here the same hash address is obtained if one takes the low bits. If the high bits were taken, then the same hash address would be obtained for names differing only in the last character.

   c. Divide the name by the size of the table and take the remainder for the hash address. The method is more effective if the size of the table is an odd number. Otherwise the datum and the hash address have the same lowest bit. When a variable name does not occupy an entire word, the spare character positions are normally filled with blanks. All short names will then give rise to even hash addresses, and the result will be a heavier use of the even locations in the table. It has been suggested that a prime number as the divisor (the size of the table) would give the most even distribution of the hash addresses over their range. In theory this is so, but in experimental studies the uniformity of the distribution has been found to be effectively independent of whether the divisor is a prime or an arbitrary odd number. Experimental comparison of the remainder with other hash functions has shown the division–remainder method to be the most reliable, i.e., the one most likely to give a uniformly distributed set of hash addresses. This method has two additional advantages: One does not have to go below the level of a computer word in the computation of the hash address, and the size of the table is not restricted to powers of 2. If a key consists of more than one computer word, then the separate words can be added together, and the division–remainder method applied to the sum. However, since addition can result in fixed-point overflow, it is best to write an assembler language routine that combines the separate words by means of the exclusive or, and to apply the division–remainder method to this result.

   In nearly all practical situations one has to deal with multifield records. Quite often the key is not as important as the other fields. For example, in symbol tables of compilers and assemblers the addresses assigned to variables, rather than the variable names, are the important data, and the names may actually be discarded at some stage of the process. It would be to our advantage to discard the names as early as possible, and store in T the locations assigned to variables instead of their names. However, if we discard keys while the file is being added to, then we cannot deal with situations in which a hash address refers to a location that is already occupied. If the computed hash address refers to an empty location, or the location is found to be occupied, but the key agrees with the stored key, the job is done. If, however, the key and the stored key differ, then we have a *collision*. We shall now consider a number of methods for dealing with collisions.

The simplest technique is to look for a free location (or for agreement of the key with a stored key) in the neighborhood of the location to which the hash address points. One examines location after location in the forward direction until the job is done. If the end of the table is reached, the search shifts to the head of the table. This linear search procedure leads to clustering of entries and is rather inefficient as a consequence.

Figure 11.2 illustrates how forward linear search works. We consider input of keys 97, 49, 88, 76, 64 to a hash table of size 11, and division–remainder as the method for computing hash addresses. Division by 11 yields remainders 9, 5, 0, 10, 9, respectively. Keys 97, 49, 88, 76 are stored in the table without difficulty, but when an attempt is made to enter key 64 into its rightful location (location 9), this location is found to be already occupied. Location 10 is therefore tried, and it is found to be occupied as well. The table ends here, so the search for a free location is taken up again with location 0, which is also found to be occupied. Key 64 is finally stored in the vacant location 1. Let us now try to determine whether key 32 is in the table. Division by 11 results in the remainder 10. Hence location 10 is tried, and, since 32 is not equal to the key found in this location ($32 \neq 76$), location 0 is tried next ($32 \neq 88$), then location 1 ($32 \neq 64$), and finally location 2, which is empty. Since we have pushed through to an empty location without having found the key 32, we know that this key cannot be in the table.

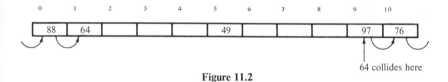

Figure 11.2

To investigate how clusters arise we make use of Figure 11.2 again. Consider a key K, and an arbitrary hash function f. Function f is applied to K, and we assume that all 11 possible hash addresses 0, 1, ..., 10 are equally likely values of $f(K)$, but this assumption does not imply that the 6 locations that are still free are equally likely to be occupied by K. The key goes into location 2 if $f(K) \in \{9, 10, 0, 1, 2\}$, but into 3 only if $f(K) = 3$. Hence insertion into location 2 is five times as likely as insertion into location 3. If the key is then in fact inserted into 2, the situation is further aggravated. With linear search clusters form, and there is a snowballing effect associated with the clusters. This phenomenon is called *primary clustering*.

The clustering effect is reduced by making the search procedure cover the table in jumps of varying magnitude. With a table of size N, if collision occurs at the kth location, compute a pseudorandom integer r on the interval $[1, N - 1]$, and make a new try at the $(k + r)$th location, or at the location given by the remainder of $(k + r)/N$ in case $k + r > N$. The pseudorandom number generator must produce every integer on $[1, N - 1]$ exactly once. The table is full when repetition sets in. The same sequence of integers r must be produced for every new key; i.e., every insertion or look-up operation involving collisions must start with a new initialization of the pseudorandom number generator. The generator may, for example, generate the sequence 1, 6, 31, 13, ... Then, if the hash address is 18, say, and a collision occurs, one tries location 19. If this probe results in a collision as well, one tries 24, then 49, and so on. If the table size is 161 and the hash address 153, say, collisions would make one try in turn locations 154, 159, 23, and so forth. There is still clustering, although not as obvious, and we speak of a *secondary clustering* effect. It arises because the sequence of pseudorandom numbers is exactly the same for all keys, i.e., in terms of the last example, locations 153, 154, 159, 23, ... are tried for *all* keys K such that $f(K) = 153$. Most of the time only a few probes will be needed to retrieve a record or reach a free location. Therefore considerable savings in computer time are achieved if the first few numbers in the sequence are stored permanently in a small table (of size 5, say), the pseudorandom number generator being entered only when the sequence has to be extended beyond the numbers stored in this table.

An alternative method for generating a search sequence rapidly requires N to be a prime number. Define a secondary hashing function f^*:

$$f^*(K) = 1 \qquad (f(K) = 0),$$
$$= N - f(K) \qquad (f(K) > 0).$$

Then, for a given key K, setting $s = f(K)$ and $r = f^*(K)$, the set of addresses $s, s + r, s + 2r, \ldots, s + (N - 1)r$ is equal to the set $\{0, 1, \ldots, N - 1\}$ if addition is performed modulo N, i.e., the entire table is covered by this set of addresses. Secondary clustering has not been eliminated in that the same path through the table is still followed with keys K_1 and K_2 whenever $f(K_1) = f(K_2)$. Moreover, this method reduces to linear search when $f(K) = 0$ or $f(K) = N - 1$, and this can lead to the growth of a sizeable primary cluster at the head of the hash table.

The ideal is a truly uniform hashing situation: a key selected at random is equally likely to go into any one of the locations that are still empty, irrespective of how many locations in the hash table are occupied. The uniform hashing situation can be approached by making f^* independent of f. With the f^* defined above, if $f(K_1) = f(K_2)$, then the probability that $f^*(K_1) = f^*(K_2)$ holds as well is of course 1. We want this latter probability to be $1/N$. One function that satisfies the independence criterion is

$$f^*(K) = 2 + r(K),$$

where $r(K)$ is the remainder of the division $K/(N-2)$. Alternatively $r(K)$ can be the remainder of the division $\lfloor K/N \rfloor /(N-2)$. This latter form is particularly useful for assembler language programming because $\lfloor K/N \rfloor$ is already available in a register as a byproduct of the computation of $f(K)$ by the division–remainder technique. Experimental tests show that the use of an f^* that is independent of f gives a very close approximation to the uniform hashing situation.

Analysis of uniform hashing is quite easy. We deal first with the expected number of probes necessary to enter the $(k+1)$th record in the hash table. One probe is always required. An additional probe is required if location $f(K)$ is occupied, yet another if $f(K) + f^*(K)$ (modulo N) is occupied as well, and so forth. The probability of $f(K)$ being occupied is k/N; given that $f(K)$ is occupied, the probability that location $f(K) + f^*(K)$ is occupied is $(k-1)/(N-1)$; and so forth. Hence the expected number of probes to enter the $(k+1)$th record is given by

$$E_k = 1 + \frac{k}{N}\left(1 + \frac{k-1}{N-1}\left(1 + \frac{k-2}{N-2}(1 + \cdots) \cdots\right)\right)$$

$$= 1 + \sum_{i=1}^{k} \frac{P(k,i)}{P(N,i)}$$

$$= 1 + \frac{k}{N-k+1}$$

$$= \frac{1}{1 - k/(N+1)}.$$

We define the *load factor* α of a hash table as $\alpha = k/N$, where k is the number of occupied locations in the table, and note that E_k very nearly depends on α alone, i.e., that the subscript k can be dropped. Then we have

$$E_k \simeq \frac{1}{1-\alpha} = E.$$

The average number of probes R that must be made to look up an item is equal to the average of $E_0, E_1, \ldots, E_{k-1}$, and this is (approximately)

$$R = \frac{1}{\alpha}\int_0^\alpha \frac{dx}{1-x} = -\left(\frac{1}{\alpha}\right)\ln(1-\alpha).$$

Some representative values:

α:	0.50	0.75	0.90	0.95
R:	1.39	1.85	2.56	3.15
E:	2.00	4.00	10.0	20.0

Analysis of linear search as a method for resolving collisions is very difficult. Approximations E and R for the expected number of probes in this case are therefore presented here without even an attempt at an explanation:

$$R = \frac{1}{2}\left(1 + \frac{1}{1 - \alpha}\right),$$

$$E = \frac{1}{2}\left(1 + \frac{1}{(1 - \alpha)^2}\right).$$

Representative values:

α:	0.50	0.75	0.90	0.95
R:	1.50	2.50	5.50	10.5
E:	2.50	8.50	50.5	200

All the above methods for resolving collisions are called *open addressing* methods. A different approach is to chain together all records having the same hash address in a list. The hash address is computed, and, if the location indicated by this address is empty, the new record is inserted there. If the hash address points to the first element of a list, the sequence of pointers is followed until the keys agree or the end of the list is reached. In the latter case a free location is found by some means or other, the record is inserted in this location, and the location joined to the list. A difficulty arises when the hash address points to a location occupied by an element that is not the *first* element of a list, i.e., belongs to the list corresponding to some other hash address. In this case the old entry must be moved to a new location so that the record can become the first element of a new list. The relocation involves changing the pointer in the list element preceding the element that has to be moved, and there arises the problem of finding this element (Exercise 11.11).

Before an analysis of the chaining scheme is attempted it has to be decided what a *probe* means in this context. The number of probes will be taken to be the number of times the key fields of records in the lists are examined. Let $f(K) = s$ for some key K. If location s is "empty," i.e., is truly unoccupied *or* contains a record with key K_1 such that $f(K_1) \neq s$, then it will be assumed that one probe is required to establish this fact. If s contains the first element of a list of t records, then insertion will be assumed to require t probes because each of the t key fields has to be examined before it can be said that K is not in the list.

The probability that a key hashes to a particular location in the hash table is $1/N$, and the probability that not one of the k keys already in the table has hashed to this location, i.e., that it is "empty," is $(1 - 1/N)^k$. Hence the probability that a location is not "empty," i.e., that it contains the first element of a list is $p = 1 - (1 - 1/N)^k$. The expected number of such locations is pN, and, since this is the expected number of lists, the expected number of elements in a list is $k/(pN)$. The expected number of probes required to enter a record in the hash table is the sum of two terms. One is the probability that a location is "empty" multiplied by the number of probes, which then is 1; the other is the probability p that a location is not "empty" multiplied by the expected length of the lists, namely $k/(pN)$. Hence the expected number of probes is

$$E_k = \left(1 - \frac{1}{N}\right)^k + \frac{k}{N}.$$

A good approximation is provided by

$$E = e^{-\alpha} + \alpha.$$

A rather advanced knowledge of probability theory is required for the derivation of

$$R = 1 + \frac{\frac{1}{2}(k - 1)}{N}$$

$$\simeq 1 + \tfrac{1}{2}\alpha.$$

The expected numbers of probes are significantly smaller than for the other schemes:

α:	0.50	0.75	0.90	0.95	1.00
R:	1.25	1.38	1.45	1.48	1.50
E:	1.11	1.22	1.31	1.34	1.37

Here retrieval requires more probes than insertion because the "empty" locations, which help keep down the average number of probes for insertion, are, of course, disregarded in the analysis of retrieval. These values do not tell the whole story. Relocation of elements can be quite costly in terms of time, the actual overheads depending greatly on the skill of the programmer. Moreover, additional space is taken up by the pointers. It is therefore misleading to use the same value of α when comparing the chaining method with an open addressing method. If the pointer field takes up $v\%$ of the record, then the value $\alpha = a$ in the chaining case corresponds to a value $\alpha = (1 - v/100)a$ under open addressing.

A modification of the method eliminates relocation. In this variant, if a key hashes to location s, and s contains a record, no attempt is made to determine whether this record is the first element of a list, or some other element. The new record is simply added to the end of the list of which the record occupying location s is some element. The difference between the two schemes is illustrated by Figure 11.3, where the hash table is a Fortran array. Hence row numbers start with 1 rather than with 0 as in our earlier examples, and the remainders have to be converted to hash addresses by adding 1 to them. A pointer value of zero indicates the end of a list. Elements other than first elements of lists are stored in empty locations at the low end of the array. Assume that (a) shows the configuration of the table for both variants just before key 154 is entered. Division of 154 by 17 gives the remainder 1, and the hash address is 2. However, location 2 is already occupied by a member of the list originating at hash address 11. In the original scheme this list is rearranged, as shown by (b). In the new variant the entering word is simply appended to the end of the list reached by following pointers from location 2, and the result is shown as (c).

	(a)		(b)		(c)	
1	136	0	136	0	136	0
2	61	5	154	0	61	5
3	115	0	115	0	115	0
4	156	0	156	0	156	0
5	146	0	146	0	146	6
6			61	5	154	0
7						
8						
9						
10						
11	95	2	95	6	95	2
12						
13						
14	149	3	149	3	149	3
15						
16						
17						

Figure 11.3

The analysis leading to the expected number of probes for insertion is more complicated for this variant. We have

$$E_\kappa = 1 + \frac{1}{4}\left[\left(1 + \frac{2}{N}\right)^k - 1 - \frac{2k}{N}\right],$$

and the approximation

$$E = 1 + \tfrac{1}{4}(e^{2\alpha} - 1 - 2\alpha).$$

The expected number of probes for retrieval is

$$R_k = \sum_{i=0}^{k-1} \frac{E_i + i/N}{k} ,$$

which approximates to

$$R = 1 - \tfrac{1}{4}(1 - \alpha) + \frac{\tfrac{1}{8}(e^{2\alpha} - 1)}{\alpha} .$$

Some numerical values:

α:	0.50	0.75	0.90	0.95	1.00
R:	1.30	1.52	1.68	1.74	1.80
E:	1.18	1.50	1.81	1.95	2.10

These values do not greatly differ from those obtained for the chaining method in which lists are not permitted to overlap. Which one of these chaining methods is given preference depends on the usage characteristics of the file. In some applications each record is retrieved only a few times, in others it may be retrieved over and over again. In the latter instance the cumulative potential savings in retrieval time may be large enough to warrant expenditure of more time at the insertion stage, and the first of our two variants should then be implemented in the interests of overall efficiency. However, in many instances it is next to impossible to carry out a *meaningful* analysis. The symbol table of a compiler is one example. Somewhere in the specifications of a compiler one will find a limit on the number of variable names a programmer is permitted to use. The size of the hash table may be fixed at this limit. Then, if the number of variable names in a program is close to the permitted maximum, the appreciable difference in the number of probes for the two variants at high loads does have a significant effect. But load factors close to 1.0 should arise only very rarely, much smaller load factors being the norm. Moreover, even if the load factor does ultimately become 1.0, this value is reached over a period of time, and many of the lookups take place while the load factor is far from its ultimate value.

Still keeping to the example of symbol tables, a consequence of making the size of the hash table equal to the greatest number of variable names permitted to occur in a program is that the hash table operates at uneconomically low load levels for most of the time. An alternative would be to select a smaller table size to start with, and expand the table only if it becomes necessary. Changing the size of a standard hash table during a run is very difficult, but there is a further variant of the chaining method that does permit effective expansion of the table while it is in use. The total storage region is divided into two segments. One is the scatter storage area itself; the other is an overflow area, arranged as a list of available space. Only the first element of a list is located in the scatter storage area. All other elements go into the overflow area. Then a hash address must always point either to a free location or to the first element of a list. Consider the second alternative and assume that the key of the new record does not agree with the stored key. If the pointer is zero, then an element is taken from the list of available space, the new record is inserted in this overflow element, and a pointer to the element put in the pointer field of the element in the scatter storage area. If the pointer is not zero, then one follows pointers until the end of the list is reached (assuming that the keys do not agree anywhere along the way). Then the record is stored in an element taken from the list of available space, and this element is added to the list. If now the overflow area becomes full, the system is asked to give the compiler an additional block of storage space to be used as an extension of the overflow area. In a multiprogramming environment the use of only as much space as is actually needed at a particular time results in more efficient operation of the entire computer system.

When a separate overflow table is used, the load factor with respect to the primary hash table can become greater than 1. Let the *entire* hash table contain k records, and let the size of the primary hash table be N. The numbers of probes are the same as in the case of a single undivided hash table and nonoverlapping lists:

$$E = e^{-\alpha'} + \alpha',$$

$$R = 1 + \tfrac{1}{2}\alpha',$$

where $\alpha' = k/N$ is the load factor in terms of the size of the primary hash table. However, since total storage requirements are $k + N(1 - 1/N)^k$, where the second term is the number of unoccupied locations in the primary hash table, the true overall load factor is

$$\alpha = \frac{k}{k + N(1 - 1/N)^k}$$

$$\simeq \frac{\alpha'}{\alpha' + e^{-\alpha'}}$$

Here representative values are presented in two tables. The first permits comparison of search and insertion efficiencies with the other methods on the basis of equal load factors:

α:	0.50	0.75	0.90	0.95
α':	0.57	1.05	1.68	2.17
R:	1.28	1.52	1.84	2.08
E:	1.13	1.40	1.87	2.28

The numbers of probes for search and insertion in the second table are the same as for chaining with no overlap and no separate overflow area:

$$\alpha': \quad 0.50 \quad 0.75 \quad 0.90 \quad 0.95 \quad 1.00$$

$$\alpha: \quad 0.45 \quad 0.61 \quad 0.69 \quad 0.71 \quad 0.73$$

$$R: \quad 1.25 \quad 1.38 \quad 1.45 \quad 1.48 \quad 1.50$$

$$E: \quad 1.11 \quad 1.22 \quad 1.31 \quad 1.34 \quad 1.37$$

An examination of this second table shows that equivalent search and insertion efficiency can be achieved only at the cost of a decrease in the true load factor.

Sometimes storage space can be saved by a separation of keys from their records. Consider a hash table with load factor $\alpha = 0.5$ that contains 500 records, where each record is 5 computer words long, the key occupies a single word, and an open addressing method has been used to resolve collisions. Here the file occupies 5000 words, but we can do better. Instead of storing entire records in the hash table, the records can be stored sequentially in a compact storage area, and the hash table made to contain just key-pointer pairs, the pointer indicating where the corresponding vector is stored. Now the storage requirements are 2000 words for the hash table, and 2500 words for the file. For long records the savings are, of course, much greater. There may be no real need to store the keys in both the hash table and with the records, in which case 500 additional words can be saved. The general concept is illustrated in Figure 11.4 for a small file. A.11.2 is an

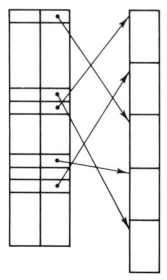

Figure 11.4

algorithm for insertions and searches in a hash table that follows the suggested design. Separation of keys from records permits hashing to be used with
files containing variable length records. A.11.2 requires very little modification to become applicable in this situation.

ALGORITHM 11.2   A program for operations in a hash table. Given a hash
   table IHASH of 503 locations, and a file storage area IFILE of L locations.
   The hash table contains just pointers. If IHASH(K) = J (J ≠ 0), then
   the corresponding record is assumed to be located at IFILE(J),...,
   IFILE(J + N − 1), where IFILE(J),...,IFILE(J + M − 1) are
   assumed to contain the key. Division–remainder is used to compute hash
   addresses, and linear search to resolve collisions. Input to subroutine
   HASHER consists of IFILE, L, N, M, and an array IREC of N locations in
   which IREC(1),...,IREC(M) contain a key. If IFILE contains no
   record with the same key as contained in IREC, then IREC is inserted in
   the file; otherwise the record corresponding to the given key is retrieved
   from IFILE and returned in IREC. The subroutine returns in INSERT
   the value 0 if insertion was performed, the value 1 if retrieval took place;
   a negative value signals an error condition (IHASH overflow if INSERT =
   −1, IFILE overflow if INSERT = −2). IHASH is assumed to be initialized to zero, and IP, a pointer for IFILE, to contain the value 1 initially.
   It is assumed that an assembler language routine IEXOR is available that
   takes the exclusive or of IREC(1), IREC(2),...,IREC(M), and returns
   the absolute value of the result.

```
            SUBROUTINE HASHER (IFILE,L,IREC,N,M,INSERT)
            DIMENSION IFILE(L), IREC(N)
            COMMON IHASH(503), IP
            INSERT = 0
C COMPUTE HASH ADDRESS
            IH = MOD(IEXOR(IREC,M),503) + 1
C SEARCH IHASH. SOME COMPILERS MAY OBJECT TO EXTENDED
C DO LOOPS ALTHOUGH ANSI STANDARD FORTRAN PERMITS THEM
            ASSIGN 10 TO NN
            DO 10 J = IH,503
            IF(IHASH(J).EQ.0) GO TO 25
            GO TO 45
   10       CONTINUE
            ASSIGN 20 TO NN
            DO 20 J = I,IH
            IF (IHASH(J).EQ.0) GO TO 25
            GO TO 45
   20       CONTINUE
```

```
C ERROR CONDITION - - IHASH FULL
      INSERT = -1
      RETURN
C INSERT RECORD
  25  IHASH(J) = IP
      JJ = IP
      IP = IP + M
      IF (IP.LE.L+1) GO TO 27
C ERROR CONDITION - - IFILE FULL
      INSERT = -2
      RETURN
  27  DO 30 J = I,N
      IFILE(JJ) = IREC(J)
  30  JJ = JJ+1
      RETURN
C TEST KEY AGAINST KEY IN IFILE
  45  II = IHASH(J)
      DO 50 I = 1,M
      IF (IREC(I).NE.IFILE(II)) GO TO NN, (10,20)
  50  II = II+1
C RETRIEVE RECORD
      INSERT = 1
      MM = M+1
      DO 60 I = MM,N
      IREC(I) = IFILE(II)
  60  II = II+1
      RETURN
      END
```

Let us summarize the techniques for resolving collisions. No general recommendations will be made because there can always be peculiar circumstances that make any one of the methods superior to the others.

A. Linear search. This method requires the greatest number of probes for insertion and retrieval, but the cost of a probe is less than for any other method. It is the only open addressing method that permits deletion of records, and deletion is reasonably easy.

B. Search for an empty location along a path defined by a function $f^*(K)$ that is related to $f(K)$ [e.g., $f^*(K) = N - f(K)$], or by a fixed sequence of pseudorandom numbers. This method requires fewer probes than Method A, but secondary clustering is present. Deletion of records is effectively impossible.

C. Search path defined by a function $f^*(K)$ independent of $f(K)$ [e.g., $f^*(K) = \lfloor K/N \rfloor \bmod (N - 2) + 2$]. There is neither primary nor secondary clustering. Deletion of records is effectively impossible.

D. Chaining of records into nonoverlapping lists. Retrieval is fast. Insertion of new records may require some rearrangement of existing records. Deletion of a record is also fast, but there is some difficulty in making the spaces occupied by the deleted records available for insertion of new records.

E. Chaining of records into lists that may overlap. Retrieval is somewhat slower than under D, but insertion may be faster because there is no rearrangement of records. Deletion is slightly less efficient than with Method D because the lists are longer on the average.

F. Chaining of records to an overflow area. More probes are required for retrieval and insertion than with Method D for the same load level. This method permits the fastest deletion of records, with the possible exception of Method A. The overflow area can be easily expanded. A variant: Use D or E until the primary hash table is full; then chain to the overflow area (see Exercise 11.12).

The summary contains several references to deletion. Let us first consider this process in the context of open addressing. The deletion of a record has to be more than just a removal of the record from the location it has occupied. Otherwise, at a later time, searches might be improperly terminated on reaching this location. Improper termination arises if a search path is followed to the location in question, and should be followed beyond it, but is not because the location is now empty. The difficulty with hash tables created by the more sophisticated open addressing schemes (Methods B and C) is that there exists no procedure for establishing whether or not a given record is an intermediate point on some search path, i.e., whether it may be safely removed from the location it occupies. Consequently, the gap created by a deletion must always be filled with some other record, but there is no record that can be moved from its existing location without creating the same problem over again at that location. Deletion is therefore impossible under Methods B and C. An acceptable alternative is to delete a record, but to flag the location it occupied in some special way to distinguish the empty locations at which searches should not be terminated from those at which they should be.

Deletions are possible with Method A because there each search path is confined to a well defined region of the hash table. Assume that a record located at $s = s'$ has just been deleted, that locations $s' + 1, \ldots, s' + t$ are occupied, and that $s' + t + 1$ is not. For records in locations $i = s + 1$, $s + 2, \ldots$ compute $f(K)$. If $f(K) \leq s$, shift the record from i to s, let the location so vacated become the new s, and iterate until the record at $i = s' + t$ has been processed. This, in broad terms, is the substance of A.11.3.

ALGORITHM 11.3   An algorithm for deleting a record in a hash table in which linear search is used to resolve collisions. Denote the contents of the key field of location i by K_i ($i = 1, \ldots, N$), let the record occupying location i be denoted by R_i, and assume that R_s is the record to be deleted. The adjustments in Steps 5 and 6 take into account the cyclic ("wrap-around") organization of the hash table in which the head of the table is considered a continuation of its end.

1.   Delete R_s and set $i = s$, *wrap* $= 0$.
2.   Set $i = i + 1$. If $i > N$, set $i = 1$ and *wrap* $= 1$.
3.   If $K_i = 0$, stop.
4.   Set $k = f(K_i)$. If *wrap* $= 0$, go to 7.
5.   If $k \leq i$, set $k = k + N$.
6.   If $s < i$, set $k = k - N$.
7.   If $k > s$, go to 2.
8.   Move R_i to s and delete R_i.
9.   Set $s = i$ and go to 2.

Deletion is straightforward with the chaining methods, although one minor problem is created for Methods D and E. In these methods a pointer is set to the lowest location in the hash table. When a new record is to be added to an existing list, or an existing record shifted to a new location, as occasionally required by Method D, the table is examined sequentially, beginning with the location indicated by the pointer, until an empty location is found. The record under consideration is inserted in this location. When the pointer indicates location k, locations $1, 2, \ldots, k - 1$ have all been filled; the table is full when the pointer reaches the last element. When deletions are possible, a new free location may be created in the section of the table that has already been scanned with the aid of the pointer. Obviously it would be an inefficient policy to set the pointer back to the head of the table when the end of the table has been reached. Therefore, if deletion of records is anticipated, the free locations should be linked together in a list of available space. This list should be a two-way list.

Let us examine again a file in which retrieval is to be on more than one set of keys. We saw in Section 11b that indexing is a solution. Assume that a file has a set of indexes associated with it. Each of the indexes can be held in a separate hash table, or all the indexes can be combined into a single hash table. Our analysis showed that search efficiency depends on the load factor alone, and the load factor remains the same when just the one hash table is used. However, underlying the analyses were the customary randomness assumptions. The larger the table, the less of an overall deviation from randomness would we expect. On the other hand, a set of smaller tables is easier to handle in storage. Also, while the keys in one set would not be expected to differ much in length, there could be considerable difference in the lengths of keys between sets, e.g., all social security numbers are of the same length, and all years of birth are of the same length, but a social security number contains twice as many characters as a year of birth.

Hybrid schemes may be employed in which several different methods are used in the organization of the indexes associated with a file: one index may be hashed, another may be set up as a sort tree; the records themselves may be kept in sequential order determined by yet another set of keys, with new records being simply appended to the end of the sorted portion of the file. This particular design could work very well in a case where few new records are added to the file, but certain fields in the records have to be updated to new values fairly frequently. An example: a company maintains a file on the products it manufactures, where a record may have the format *Product code / Description / Sales volume / Manufacturing cost / Selling price / Quantity on hand / Current production rate / Production capacity* (maximal rate at which the product could be manufactured) */ Suppliers of parts / . . . .*

Hard copy summaries of the file have to be produced for management at regular intervals. For this reason the file is kept in sorted order of the product codes. Frequently it is required to access individual records with the product code as the key for updating purposes or for retrieval of specific facts regarding particular products. Binary search has been rejected as too slow, and consequently the set of product codes is stored in two places: in the sequential file storage area with the records themselves, and as a separate index in a hash table. In our company, management is obsessed with the relative standing of the products as regards their contributions to the profits of the company. From time to time a complete listing of the products is demanded, ranked on a profitability value, defined by *Sales volume* × (*Selling price* − *Manufacturing cost*). More frequently a manager would ask for a list of just the top 50 products, or of the worst 50, depending on his mood at the time. The profitability values constitute another index. This index cannot be maintained in sequential order of rank because of frequent drastic changes in the relative standing of the products, and a hash table cannot be used because output is required in ranked order of profitability values. The binary sort tree provides an efficient solution here. Whenever a change in a sales volume, manufacturing cost, or selling price alters the profitability of a product, the old profitability value is deleted from the tree (see A.10.7), and the new value is entered in the standard manner (see A.5.9 and A.10.6). Only for these operations does it matter how well the tree is balanced. The ranked listing of the products is generated in an inorder traversal of the tree, and the efficiency of the traversal depends very little on whether the tree is or is not balanced. However, if the tree is traversed with the aid of a stack, storage requirements for the stack are determined by the length of the longest path from the root to a terminal node, and this length is a minimum when the tree is balanced.

For a different example let us take a personnel file in which records have the format *Name | Social security number | Plant location | Department | Job classification | ....* . This file is to be used fairly frequently for the identification of all employees with a particular job classification, or all employees belonging to a particular department. The design of the file should make these determinations easy. Assume that the file is stored in a hash table with employee names used as keys. Let us add two pointer fields to each record, and link together the records of all employees having the same job classification and all employees belonging to the same department. A list is thus created for each job classification and each department. All these lists have to be provided with external names. This is unlikely to introduce too great an overhead because, compared to the number of employees the number of job classifications and departments ought to be small. The result is a system of cross-lists superimposed on the hash table.

A sort tree can be superimposed on a hash table in a similar manner. Figure 11.5 shows a hash table that contains records having two fields. Consider the record in row 8. The two fields of the record occupy the first two cells in this row. The hash function is computed using the value in the field on the left; the sort tree is constructed using the field on the right for a key. The other two cells hold pointers: the element in row 8 has no left successor; its right successor is located in row 3. The root of the tree is indicated by the external pointer ROOT. Here the root occupies row 13.

1	697	369	15	10	ROOT	13
2						
3	767	158	0	0		
4						
5	361	294	0	0		
6						
7						
8	670	156	0	3		
9	484	136	0	8		
10	483	572	0	0		
11	688	305	0	0		
12						
13	573	284	9	1		
14						
15	847	297	5	11		
16						
17						

Figure 11.5

This section has been devoted to the demonstration that hashing is a very powerful method of file organization. Let us compare hash tables, sort trees, and sequential files with respect to their storage requirements and retrieval efficiency. If no new records are to be added to a file once it has been created, and records do not have to be retrieved while it is being created, then all three organizations could be used. However, since a sequential file has the lowest storage requirements, and its retrieval efficiency matches that of a sort tree, the sort tree is without any advantage in this context. The choice thus reduces to hashing and sequential organization. Retrieval is expected to be faster in the hash table, but the sequential file has lower storage requirements. Moreover, the order imposed on the records by the sequential organization may be very useful in some applications.

If a file is still growing while records are already being retrieved from it, then hashing and the sort tree alone are feasible. Except under very unusual circumstances, the storage requirements of a sort tree exceed those of a properly designed hash table whenever the load factor of the hash table exceeds $\frac{2}{3}$, but even with load factors as high as this the hash table should be much more efficient for retrieval than the sort tree.

Why then have we been discussing sort trees at all? The important advantage that the sort tree has over all variants of hashing is that the data stored in a sort tree are effectively in sequential order. This was the reason for selecting the sort tree as one component in the design of the file of products manufactured by a company that we studied earlier in this section. Similarly, if the symbol table of a compiler is maintained as a sort tree, then an alphabetic listing of the variable names used in a program can be produced at no appreciable additional cost. A hash table would have to be explicitly sorted, but it should be kept in mind that the hash table may be so much more efficient for retrieval that there may be a net gain in time even with the time for sorting it taken into account. Still on the same subject, the records that precede or come after a given record in a sequential file may be significant in some retrieval applications. These neighboring records can be fairly easily retrieved in the equivalent sort tree, but they would be impossible to find in a hash table.

Although the average number of probes to retrieve a record is generally much smaller for a hash table than for a sort tree, in the worst case the number of probes may be as high as k for the hash table (k is the number of records in the file), while for a *balanced* sort tree the number of probes is at most $\lfloor \log_2 k \rfloor + 1$. In some real-time applications excessive search times cannot be tolerated, even if they arise very rarely, and in these applications one is forced to use a sort tree. One instance in which fast response is critical is the control of a complex process or device by a computer. When an anomaly is sensed, corrective action has to be taken at once, and the selection of an appropriate action may well be a retrieval process.

11d. Sorting

Although file organization is becoming more dependent on scatter storage techniques, the importance of sorting is not diminishing. Files are maintained for the sake of providing us with information, and we expect to receive the information that we request in what we call a "natural" order. Therefore, irrespective of how files are organized inside a computer, records of an output file must be in lexicographic order of the values of some key or another.

The algebra of sets provides another context in which we depend on order. Set operations, such as union or intersection, take much longer when the operations are carried out on sets with unordered elements than when the elements are ordered. Assume that vector A contains the N elements of a set A, and that B contains the M elements of set B. A.11.4 is a procedure that merges elements of A and B into C. It is easy to modify the procedure so that it finds $A \cup B$, i.e., removes duplicates.

ALGORITHM 11.4 A procedure for merging numbers stored in order of magnitude in arrays A and B.

```
      SUBROUTINE MERGE (A,N,B,M,C,NPLUSM)
      DIMENSION A(N), B(M), C(NPLUSM)
      I = 1
      J = 1
      K = 1
  1   C(K) = A(I)
      IF (B(J).LT.C(K)) GO TO 3
      I = I + 1
      K = K + 1
      IF (I.LE.N) GO TO 1
      DO 2 II = J,M
      C(K) = B(II)
  2   K = K + 1
      RETURN
  3   C(K) = B(J)
      IF (A(I).LT.C(K)) GO TO 1
      J = J + 1
      K = K + 1
      IF (J.LE.M) GO TO 3
      DO 4 II = I,N
      C(K) = A(II)
  4   K = K + 1
      RETURN
      END
```

ALGORITHM 11.5 Let arrays A and B contain *distinct* elements of sets A and B in order of magnitude. Subroutine DIFF finds in C the K elements of

$A - B$. Note that

```
CALL DIFF (A,N,B,M,A,K)
```

is permitted.

```
    SUBROUTINE DIFF (A,N,B,M,C,K)
    DIMENSION A(N), B(M), C(N)
    J = 1
    K = 0
    DO 15  I = 1,N
 3  IF (A(I) - B(J))  10, 15, 5
 5  J = J + 1
    IF (J - M)  3, 3, 17
10  K = K + 1
    C(K) = A(I)
15  CONTINUE
    RETURN
17  DO 20  J = I,N
    K = K + 1
20  C(K) = A(J)
    RETURN
    END
```

   Perhaps *selection sort* is the sorting method that is easiest to understand. Assume that an array $[a_1, a_2, \ldots, a_n]$ is to be sorted. One selects the largest of $a_1, a_2, \ldots, a_n$ and interchanges this number with a_n, then selects the second largest number in a scan of elements $a_1, a_2, \ldots, a_{n-1}$ and interchanges it with a_{n-1}, and so on. This method requires $(n - 1) + (n - 2) + \cdots + 1 = \frac{1}{2}(n^2 - n)$ comparisons. Next we consider *exchange sort*. In principle this method does not greatly differ from selection sort. In the first pass of the exchange sort one compares a_i with a_{i+1} for $i = 1, 2, \ldots, n - 1$, and exchanges the elements whenever $a_i > a_{i+1}$. This shifts the largest element into position a_n, and a_n is not involved in subsequent comparisons. The exchanges of the second pass shift the second largest element into a_{n-1}, and so on. The process is stopped when no exchanges have been made in a pass. This can reduce the number of comparisons below the maximal value of $\frac{1}{2}(n^2 - n)$ in certain cases. Exchange sort is sometimes called *bubble sort*. This designation finds its inspiration in the imagery of elements bubbling up, so to speak, to their final positions in a sequence of exchanges of neighboring elements. The imagery is somewhat spoiled in A.11.6 because it is the "heaviest" (largest) element that gets "bubbled" into position a_n.

ALGORITHM 11.6   Exchange sort. Array A has been declared INTEGER because the comparisons of A(L) with A(L + 1) may take less time in integer than in real arithmetic. Assume, however, that we make the call

CALL EXSORT (ARRAY, 100)

where ARRAY is REAL. Most systems do not check whether the actual argument ARRAY agrees in type with the dummy argument A. Moreover, representation of real numbers in many computers is such that, for real a and b, $a \leq b$ if and only if $a \leq b$ when a and b are *interpreted as integers*. Such a representation permits the use of the one subroutine for sorting both integer and real arrays.

```
      SUBROUTINE EXSORT (A,N)
      INTEGER A(N), TEMP
      LOGICAL FINISH
      DO 6 K = 2,N
      FINISH = .TRUE.
      LP = N - K + 1
      DO 5 L = 1,LP
      IF (A(L).LE.A(L+1)) GO TO 5
      TEMP = A(L+1)
      A(L+1) = A(L)
      A(L) = TEMP
      FINISH = .FALSE.
    5 CONTINUE
      IF (FINISH) RETURN
    6 CONTINUE
      RETURN
      END
```

Example

The array [3, 2, 1, 6, 4, 5] is sorted in three passes (no exchanges are made in the third pass). On the other hand, sorting of [2, 3, 4, 5, 6, 1] requires the maximal five passes to get the 1 into the first location. A.11.6 sorts a set of numbers, and the interchanges are interchanges of pairs of single numbers. In most practical applications the items to be placed in order by sorting are entire records. Comparisons are made of keys, but entire records are interchanged. In what follows we shall continue to refer to movement of keys rather than records, but movement of a key will be assumed to imply the movement of the entire record associated with this key.

Selection and exchange sorts are based on an algorithm $A(k)$ that moves the largest of k keys into its final location. After $A(n)$ has been applied to a set of n keys, only $n - 1$ keys remain to be sorted and $A(n - 1)$ is applied to this set of keys, then $A(n - 2)$ is applied to the remaining $n - 2$ unsorted keys, and so forth. Let c_k be the number of comparisons that $A(k)$ performs, and let $S_A(k)$ be the total number of comparisons required to sort k keys by a sequence of applications of algorithms A. We have

$$S_A(n) = S_A(n - 1) + c_n,$$

which we interpret as saying that $A(n)$ has reduced the problem of sorting n keys to the "smaller" problem of sorting $n - 1$ keys.

Suppose now that there exists an algorithm $B(k)$ that selects a key on a basis other than that it be the largest of the k keys, moves this key into its final location, does it in such a way that all keys to one side of it are smaller and all keys to the other side of it are larger, and performs the same number of comparisons, namely c_k. Let us apply $B(n)$ to a set of n keys, and assume that the final position into which the selected key is moved is location a_{m+1}, i.e., that $B(n)$ has split the set of n keys into a block of m unsorted keys in locations $a_1, \ldots, a_m$, the single key at a_{m+1}, and a second block of unsorted keys in locations $a_{m+2}, \ldots, a_n$. Algorithm $B(n)$ reduces the problem to the two "smaller" problems of sorting m and $n - m - 1$ keys. Stipulating that the smaller problems will now be solved by applying algorithms A, we have

$$S_A^*(n) = S_A(m) + S_A(n - m - 1) + c_n.$$

Making use of $S_A(k) = \frac{1}{2}k(k - 1)$ it is easy to prove that

$$S_A(n - 1) \geqq S_A(m) + S_A(n - m - 1), \qquad 0 \leqq m \leqq n - 1,$$

where equality holds only if $m = 0$ or $m = n - 1$. Hence

$$S_A^*(n) \leqq S_A(n).$$

It is somewhat more tedious to prove that

$$S_B(n) \leqq S_A(n),$$

where $S_B(n)$ is the total number of comparisons required to sort n elements if algorithms B are used throughout to produce ever smaller unsorted blocks.

Algorithm $B(k)$ exists, and Figure 11.6 illustrates the application of this algorithm to the array of numbers

$$12 \quad 3 \quad 16 \quad 8 \quad 4 \quad 15 \quad 5 \quad 14 \quad 6 \quad 21$$

Extract the leftmost element (12), and mark its position (1). Move into the array from the right, comparing elements against 12 in turn; when a *smaller* number is encountered, transfer it to the marked position (6 to position 1), and mark the position whence it came (9). Then move from the left, starting with location 2, and compare these elements against 12; in this left to right

	1	2	3	4	5	6	7	8	9	10	
	—	[3	16	8	4	15	5	14	6	21]	←
→	6	[3	16	8	4	15	5	14]	—	21	
	6	3	—	[8	4	15	5	14]	16	21	←
→	6	3	5	[8	4	15]	—	14	16	21	
	6	3	5	8	4	—	15	14	16	21	
	6	3	5	8	4	(12)	15	14	16	21	

Figure 11.6

scan transfer a number that is *larger* than 12 to the marked position (16 to position 9), and mark the position from which the element came (3). Now take up the right to left scan again, starting from position 8. This leads to the transfer of element 5 from location 7 to location 3. Resume left to right scan from location 4, and transfer 15 from location 6 to location 7. The right to left scan would have to be resumed from location 6, but this location has already been examined in the left to right scan; in fact it is the location that was the last to be marked. Element 12 is moved into this marked location, and it is now in its final position. Every element on its left is smaller than 12; every element on its right is larger.

Algorithm $B(k)$ is the basis of a sorting procedure known as *Quicksort*. In terms of our example this algorithm can next be applied to the block (6, 3, 5, 8, 4), and the leftmost element of this block moved into its final position, and to the block (15, 14, 16, 21). At this stage there may be four blocks to process. The necessity to remember which blocks remain to be processed is a detrimental feature of Quicksort. It is not a *minimal storage* sort, where by minimal storage is meant storage for just the array and one additional temporary location that makes interchanges possible. Quicksort requires a stack to keep track of the blocks as they are generated and saved for future processing. One pushes down the limits of the *larger* of the two blocks generated, and processes the smaller block. For the example of Figure 11.6 the limits of the larger block are defined by the ordered pair of subscripts $\langle 1, 5 \rangle$. It can be shown that the depth of the stack cannot exceed $\lfloor 1 + \log_2 \frac{1}{3}(n + 1) \rfloor$.

ALGORITHM 11.7   Quicksort, an algorithm for sorting keys $K(1), K(2), \ldots,$
$K(N)$ into ascending order. Dummy keys $K(0)$ and $K(N + 1)$ are presumed, such that $K(0) \leq K(I) \leq K(N + 1)$ for all $I = 1, 2, \ldots, N$. This is to avoid having to treat the boundary elements as special cases.

1. Initialize: Set $LO = 1, HI = N$.
2. Process new block $[K(LO), \ldots, K(HI)]$: If $HI - LO \leq 0$, go to 6; else set $I = LO, J = HI, KREF = K(LO)$.

3. Right to left scan: While KREF < K(J), set J = J - 1. If J ≤ I, set K(I) = KREF and go to 5; else set K(I) = K(J), I = I + 1.
4. Left to right scan: While K(I) < KREF, set I = I + 1. If J ≤ I, set K(J) = KREF, I = J, and go to 7; else set K(J) = K(I), J = J - 1, and go to 3.
5. Push down: If (HI - I) < (I - LO), then push down ⟨LO, I - 1⟩ and set LO = I + 1; else push down ⟨I + 1, HI⟩ and set HI = I - 1. In any case go to 2.
6. Pop up: If stack empty, stop; else pop up ⟨LO, HI⟩ and go to 2.

We shall now find the *average* number of comparisons of keys that Quicksort makes in sorting a file of n records. This number will be denoted by $S(n)$. In the first phase it takes $n - 1$ comparisons to split the initial block of n records into two blocks of sizes m and $n - m - 1$, respectively, where $0 \leq m < n$. The average number of comparisons to sort these two blocks is $S(m)$ and $S(n - m - 1)$, respectively, and there are n possible values of m, all equally probable. Hence

$$S(n) = \frac{1}{n} \sum_{m=0}^{n-1} [(n - 1) + S(m) + S(n - m - 1)]$$

$$= (n - 1) + \frac{1}{n} \sum_{m=0}^{n-1} S(m) + \frac{1}{n} \sum_{m=0}^{n-1} S(n - m - 1)$$

$$= (n - 1) + \frac{2}{n} \sum_{m=0}^{n-1} S(m). \tag{A}$$

Actually, while Quicksort can be defined in such a way that it partitions a block of n keys using only $n - 1$ comparisons of keys, in A.11.7 some overlap of the left to right and right to left scans has been permitted in the interests of reducing the overall time for the algorithm. The actual number of comparisons is closer to $n + 1$ than it is to $n - 1$. A more detailed analysis specifically of A.11.7 gives

$$S^*(n) = \left(n + 1 - \frac{1}{n}\right) + \frac{2}{n} \sum_{m=0}^{n-1} S(m).$$

Expressing (A) as

$$nS(n) = n(n - 1) + 2 \sum_{m=0}^{n-1} S(m),$$

and as

$$(n - 1)S(n - 1) = (n - 1)(n - 2) + 2 \sum_{m=0}^{n-2} S(m),$$

and subtracting, we obtain after some rearrangement

$$\frac{S(n)}{n+1} = \frac{S(n-1)}{n} + \frac{2}{n+1} - \frac{2}{n(n-1)}.$$

Now use this formula to express $S(n-1)$ in terms of $S(n-2)$, $S(n-2)$ in terms of $S(n-3)$, and so forth. The result is

$$\frac{S(n)}{n+1} = \frac{S(1)}{2} + 2 \sum_{k=3}^{n+1} \frac{1}{k} - 2 \sum_{k=2}^{n} \frac{1}{k(k+1)}$$

$$= 0 + 2 \sum_{k=1}^{n} \frac{1}{k} - 2 \sum_{k=1}^{n} \frac{1}{k(k+1)} - \frac{2n}{n+1}$$

$$= 2H_n - \frac{2n}{n+1} - \frac{2n}{n+1}.$$

Hence

$$S(n) = 2(n+1)H_n - 4n. \tag{B}$$

An expansion for H_n was given in Section 5f. Using the first three terms of the expansion, namely,

$$H_n \simeq \log_e n + 0.577216 + \frac{1}{2n},$$

we finally obtain

$$S(n) \simeq 2n \log_e n - 2.8456n + 2 \log_e n + 2,$$

in which only the first term really matters when n gets large, e.g., $S(1000) = 13,816 - 2,846 + 14 + 2$.

The worst input to A.11.7 would be a file that is already sorted. Then the performance of Quicksort would be no better than that of selection or exchange sorts.

We shall now describe a sorting procedure based on the merging operation of A.11.4. There are fewer comparisons than with selection or exchange, but $2n$ locations are now needed to sort n numbers. The numbers are paired, and placed into "arrays" of length 2, the smaller number of a pair becoming the first element of the "array." Next pairs of "arrays" of length 2 are merged to produce "arrays" of length 4, pairs of these "arrays" are merged to produce "arrays" of length 8, and so on. The method is most effective when $n = 2^m$, but usually n is not an exact power of 2. For all n satisfying $2^{m-1} < n \le 2^m$ the number of passes is m, i.e., the number of passes is given by $\lceil \log_2 n \rceil$ where $\lceil x \rceil$ denotes the ceiling function of x. The method is illustrated by Figure 11.7. Actually one uses only the two arrays A and B, both of size n,

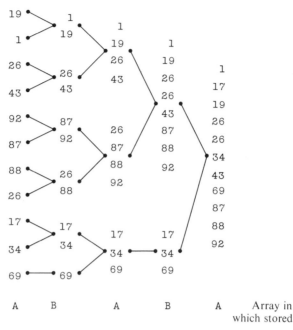

Figure 11.7

and the "arrays" of the discussion above correspond to sequences of elements in A or B.

The procedure that we have described is known as a *two-way merge* because pairs of arrays are merged. If, instead of merging two arrays, we produced the new arrays by merging q arrays at a time, then we would have a *q-way merge*. The number of passes in a q-way merge is $\lceil \log_q n \rceil$, and the total number of comparisons is less than $(q - 1)n\lceil \log_q n \rceil$.

When n is about 1000, two-way merge makes about 10,000 comparisons. Exchange sort makes about 50 times as many, but is minimal as far as storage requirements are concerned. Our objective is to find a sorting procedure that combines the speed of two-way merge with minimal storage requirements. One minimal storage procedure that does not make the excessive number of comparisons of exchange sort is *Shellsort* (after D. L. Shell), in which, instead of always comparing adjacent keys, one compares and exchanges keys that may be far apart to begin with. Let us define the *disorder* of a file to be the average distance that a record is from the location it will ultimately occupy in the sorted file. One approach to the design of a sorting algorithm is to aim at a reduction of this measure to its ultimate value of zero in a *systematic* manner. Shellsort exemplifies this approach. Let $[a_1, a_2, \ldots, a_n]$ be the array to be sorted. Define the numbers

$$d_1 = 2^{\lfloor \log_2 n \rfloor} - 1;$$
$$d_k = \lfloor \tfrac{1}{2} d_{k-1} \rfloor, \qquad k = 2, \ldots, m-1;$$
$$d_m = 1.$$

In the first stage of the process strings $a_i \, a_{i+d_1}$ ($i = 1, 2, \ldots, n - d_1$) are sorted by exchange, and, in general, in the kth stage strings $a_i \, a_{i+d_k} \, a_{i+2d_k} \cdots$ ($i = 1, 2, \ldots, d_k - 1$) are sorted by exchange. For the array of Figure 11.7, since $n = 11$, have $d_1 = 7$ and $m = 3$. The first stage sorts strings $a_1 a_8$, $a_2 a_9$, $a_3 a_{10}$, $a_4 a_{11}$. We find, however, that in our example these strings are already in order. In the second stage, since $d_2 = \lfloor 7/2 \rfloor = 3$, exchange is applied to strings $a_1 a_4 a_7 a_{10}$, $a_2 a_5 a_8 a_{11}$, $a_3 a_6 a_9$. For example, string 19 43 88 34 becomes 19 34 43 88. At the end of the second stage the array is in rather good order: [19, 1, 17, 34, 26, 26, 43, 69, 87, 88, 92]. Therefore, the sort is completed with very few exchanges in the third stage.

ALGORITHM 11.8   Shellsort. (For reasons of efficiency the sequence of operations is not exactly as described above—there is some overlap in the sorting of the strings in stages 2, 3, ..., $m - 1$.)

```
       SUBROUTINE SHELL (A,N)
       INTEGER A(N), TEMP, D
       D = 1
  1    D = 2 * D
       IF (D.LE.N) GO TO 1
  2    D = (D-1)/2
       IF (D.EQ.0) RETURN
       ITOP = N - D
       DO  4  I = 1,ITOP
       J = I
  3    L = J + D
       IF (A(L).GE.A(J)) GO TO 4
       TEMP = A(J)
       A(J) = A(L)
       A(L) = TEMP
       J = J - D
       IF (J.GT.0) GO TO 3
  4    CONTINUE
       GO TO 2
       END
```

Throughout this book we are emphasizing that a high-level language, such as Fortran, which was designed primarily for coding numerical algorithms, can be applied to problems of a nonnumerical nature. We have seen that Fortran can deal with such problems quite effectively, provided the data of the problems can be translated to numbers. Difficulty begins when the data cannot be interpreted as numbers. Consider alphabetic data read into the computer under A-conversion. In IBM 360/370 machines the trouble is minimal. Characters are stored in 8-bit fields (bytes), and 4 such fields make up a word. For example, we would have the representation,

BATE	11000010	11000001	11100011	11000101
ABET	11000001	11000010	11000101	11100011
BAT	11000010	11000001	11100011	01000000

where the code 01000000 in the last word represents a blank. Negative integers are represented by a 1 in the leading bit position and the 2's complement of the integer in the remaining 31 bit positions. Interpreted as integers our data become

-111101	00111110	00011100	00111011
-111110	00111101	00111010	00011101
-111101	00111110	00011100	11000000

Clearly, when these data are sorted as integers, we get the proper order

ABET
BAT
BATE

But, if the words to be sorted contain both upper and lower case letters, then the words beginning with lower case letters precede *all* words beginning with upper case letters, and we would get, for example, a "sorted" list

abet
bat
bate
Adam

The position is more difficult with some other codes. For example, the code for internal representation of alphabetic data in the IBM 7040 used 6 bits (or 2 octal digits) to represent a character, and there were 6 characters to a word. With this code, interpreting the representations as integers, we have

| GORSE | 2746516225608 |
| HORSE | 3046516225608 |

MORSE	-44651622560_8
MORSEL	-44651622543_8
MORSES	-44651622562_8

and an impossible "sorted" list is obtained:

MORSES
MORSE
MORSEL
GORSE
HORSE

Other than going to assembler language, there is no solution. A Fortran program interprets the 36-bit word (6 characters) as a number composed of a sign bit and 35 other bits, and the sign bit causes part of the trouble. Assembler language provides "logical" comparison, which, in effect, treats all 36 bits as a positive integer, and this facility should be used whenever the Fortran procedure would make an arithmetic comparison. Then the sorted list is

GORSE
HORSE
MORSEL
MORSE
MORSES

Only MORSE is out of place in this list. If, moreover, blanks are translated to zeros before sorting, and translated back to blanks afterward, the proper order is obtained.

Fortunately the difficulty one had with the IBM 7040 does not arise in all computers that have a 36-bit word length and use a 6-bit character code. We give now the octal representation of our set of words in the PDP-10, and the values the octal codes have when interpreted as integers:

GORSE	475762634500_8	-302015143300_8
HORSE	505762634500_8	-272015143300_8
MORSE	555762634500_8	-222015143300_8
MORSEL	555762634554_8	-222015143224_8
MORSES	555762634563_8	-222015143215_8

Here sorting results in the properly ordered list

GORSE
HORSE
MORSE
MORSEL
MORSES

The proper order is a consequence of the use of 2's complements to represent negative integers. In the PDP-10 negative numbers of type real (floating point numbers) are also stored in 2's complement representation, and this enables one to use the same subroutines to sort both integer and real arrays (see the preamble of A.11.6).

A more common PDP-10 practice is to represent characters by their ASCII 7-bit codes, with 5 characters stored in bit positions 0–34, and bit position 35 remaining unused. Again character strings consisting entirely of upper case or entirely of lower case letters are sorted into their proper order when they are interpreted as integers, but the same difficulty one has in IBM 360/370 machines arises here when upper and lower case letters are intermixed. (The character set represented by the 6-bit codes does not include lower case letters.)

Some assembler languages give access to individual characters, and this facility is used in *radix sort*, which is a popular sorting procedure for mechanical card sorters, but is not widely used on computers because of very high storage requirements. In this method, to sort words over an alphabet of k characters, $k + 1$ "bins" are used. If d is the length of the longest word in the set to be sorted, then every word in the set is assumed to be d characters long; the extra characters are assumed to be blanks at the right-hand end of the word. The dth character is examined first, and the word is assigned to the bin associated with that character. Then the words are collected and distributed again on the $(d - 1)$th character, and so on. Table 11.1 shows how the procedure works. Storage requirements come to $(k + 2)n$, but there are only nd comparisons. The $(k + 1)$-way comparisons can be executed very rapidly by making use of assembler language indexing techniques. Storage requirements can be significantly reduced if the bins are set up as lists. For a more detailed discussion regarding implementation of a radix sort see Section 12b.

A refinement of the method, which requires only $2n$ storage locations, can be implemented when individual bits are accessible. Examine the lowest bit position: Going through the array from top to bottom first transfer all items with a 0 in this position to an auxiliary array; then transfer all items with a 1 in this bit position. Next examine the second lowest bit position, again transferring first all items with a 0, then items with a 1 in this position (these transfers are back to the original array), and so on. Figure 11.8 illustrates the procedure with 5-bit numbers. Although the method involves bn transfers, where b is the number of bits in an item, and $2bn$ individual bits are examined, the method, which we call *binary radix sort*, can be quite fast.

Another method that has greater than minimal storage requirements is *sorting by address calculation*. In order to be able to apply this method one has to know the range of the numbers to be sorted, and—for efficient performance—something must be known about their distribution. To illustrate

TABLE 11.1

RADIX SORT

	A	B	C	D	E	G	H	blank
BEACH CAB ACE ADAGE BEAD					ADAGE		BEACH	CAB ACE BEAD
ADAGE BEACH CAB ACE BEAD			BEACH	BEAD		ADAGE		CAB ACE
BEACH BEAD ADAGE CAB ACE	BEACH BEAD ADAGE	CAB			ACE			
BEACH BEAD ADAGE CAB ACE	CAB		ACE	ADAGE	BEACH BEAD			
CAB ACE ADAGE BEACH BEAD	ACE ADAGE	BEACH BEAD	CAB					

17	10001	01100	01100	11000	10001	00110	6
9	01001	00110	11000	10001	10001	01001	9
12	01100	11000	10001	01001	10011	01100	12
6	00110	10001	01001	10001	00110	10001	17
24	11000	01001	10001	10011	11000	10001	17
19	10011	10011	00110	01100	01001	10011	19
17	10001	10001	10011	00110	01100	11000	24

Pass   1   2   3   4   5

Figure 11.8

the *principle* of the method assume that 90 distinct unordered integers in the range [1, 100] occupy array N, and that a second array M, of dimension 100, is available. The numbers can be sorted by the following procedure:

```
      DO   4   K = 1,100
   4  M(K) = 0
      DO   5   K = 1,90
      I = N(K)
   5  M(I) = I
      I = 0
      DO 10   K = 1,90
   7  I = I + 1
      IF (M(I).EQ.0) GO TO 7
  10  N(K) = M(I)
```

Of course, the sort is not nearly as neat in a practical situation. First, the calculation of the address, i.e., of subscript I of the location in M that an item having value t is to occupy, can take considerable time. If n numbers have uniform distribution and range in value from k_1 to k_2, and M has dimension D, then an estimate of I is given by $(t - k_1)c$, where $c = D/(k_2 - k_1)$. The formula would be more complicated for nonuniformly distributed items. Secondly, the same address may be computed for more than one item, e.g., when there is duplication. Then we may find M(I) already occupied, and another location has to be found for the new item. All items in M at any particular stage must be in their correct order. Therefore, insertion of the new item may involve some shifts. To avoid having to shift too many items, D has to be made greater than n. When $D = 1.5n$, then, assuming that the formula for the address calculation reflects the distribution of the data reasonably well, the method requires about $1.33n$ comparisons. One must, of course, include address calculations in time estimates.

There is a well-known result, usually obtained using an information theoretical argument, that an *optimal* algorithm for sorting n records is an $O(n \log n)$ process, where the O can be interpreted as shorthand for "of the order of." More precisely: An actual number $F(n)$ can be represented by $O(f(n))$ if there exists a positive constant k such that $|F(n)| \leq k|f(n)|$ for all positive integers n. For example, we say that the average number of comparisons made by Quicksort is $O(n \log n)$, although the actual approximation we obtained for this number was

$$S(n) \simeq 2n \log_e n - 2.8456n + 2 \log_e n + 2.$$

Since, as n increases, $n \log_e n$, grows more rapidly than either n or $\log_e n$, we say that the term in $n \log_e n$ is the *dominant* term of the expression, and we know from mathematical analysis that a constant k can be found such that

$$2n \log_e n - 2.8456n + 2 \log_e n + 2 \leq kn \log_e n.$$

Moreover, since the conversion of logarithms from one base to another requires the introduction of just a constant multiplier, and this constant multiplied by k is still a constant, it does not matter what the base of the logarithm in $O(n \log n)$ is.

Commonly analysis of a sorting algorithm proceeds by estimating the number of comparisons of keys that an algorithm makes, and we say that an algorithm that makes $O(n^2)$ comparisons is not as good as one that makes $O(n \log n)$ comparisons. We actually say that an algorithm that makes $O(n \log n)$ comparisons is optimal, and that no "faster" algorithm can be found, e.g., one that requires say $O(n \log \log n)$ or just $O(n)$ comparisons, but this seems to be contradicted by radix sort, in which the number of comparisons of keys is zero. Here we have a classical difficulty in the analysis of algorithms. It is proper to compare algorithms on the basis of a particular measure, say the number of comparisons of keys, and it is proper to speak of optimality in terms of this measure, but one must be careful to restrict the discussion to the class of algorithms for which this measure is meaningful. For radix sort it clearly is not. The class of algorithms for which $O(n \log n)$ comparisons is an appropriate measure of optimality is defined to consist of just those algorithms that are capable of ranking a set of objects into order of weight, where comparisons are interpreted as weighings. Radix sort and sorting by address calculation do not satisfy this criterion.

A sorting algorithm may be $O(n \log n)$, but still require more comparisons than an $O(n^{3/2})$ algorithm, say, unless n is very large. Consider

$$5n \log_2 n + n = O(n \log n)$$

and

$$\tfrac{1}{2} n^{3/2} - n = O(n^{3/2}).$$

Equating the two left-hand sides, and solving for n, we get the rather high break-even value $n = 21{,}973$.

Having established what we mean in saying that an algorithm is $O(f(n))$, let us state the efficiencies of the sorting algorithms that we have been considering. Both selection sort and exchange sort are $O(n^2)$ in the average and worst cases, but exchange is $O(n)$ in the best case. Quicksort is $O(n \log n)$ on the average, but $O(n^2)$ in the worst case (which is the best case for exchange sort). The tree sort of Section 5f (A.5.12) is $O(n \log n)$ in both average and worst cases, and so is two-way merge. Shellsort is $O(n^{3/2})$, and there is no difference in the number of comparisons between best, worst, and average cases.

Evaluation of sorting procedures has to be approached with great caution. The size of the coefficient of a dominant term, and terms neglected in going from a reasonably accurate estimate of the number of comparisons to $O(f(n))$ are of considerable importance when n is small. Even when accurate estimates of numbers of comparisons are available, they do not tell the full story. Efficiency depends on the quality of coding and the complexity of programs as well: a much larger proportion of the total execution time is spent sequencing the actual computation steps in a complicated program than in a program having a simple structure. Efficiency depends also on the language in which the program is written, on the compiler, and on the peculiarities of the computer. A test on Algol versions of A.5.12 and A.11.8 run on the CDC 1604A has shown that with $n = 10,000$ Shellsort takes 1.33 times as long as the tree sort for integer arrays, but 1.38 times as long for real arrays. The difference in these ratios should be due to causes unrelated to the algorithms themselves.

Let us describe sorting as follows: In sorting of a file we compare values of a *key* and interchange *records*. This description applies equally well to a file of multifield records and a file in which the key is the entire record. Despite the identity of the processes in principle, sorting of multifield records may create its own particular problems. Consider matrix Q of Section 9c. It is a very simple file; its columns are records. If the first element in a column is taken for the key, then the file is already sorted. We may, however, decide to sort on the second element of a column, and, to make things more difficult, on the first element within each group of columns having the same second element. But the file is already sorted on the first element, and this should be taken into account in selecting the sorting procedure. We want a procedure that keeps records having the same second element in their existing relative order. Then, at the end of the sort on the second element, the records are in order on the secondary key as well. A procedure that has this property is called a *stable* sort. A single pass radix sort, with five bins for the five values of the key, is obviously one such method.

Shifting of records during a sort is inconvenient when the file consists of long records. The situation is aggravated when the records are of varying length, or the file is too large to fit in core memory. The usual procedure then is to extract values of the key, and to have a record identifier associated with each value (the identifier may be the address of the first location occupied by a record). The ordered pairs $\langle key, identifier \rangle$ are sorted, and after the sort the sequence of record identifiers defines the ordered file; i.e., the sorted ordered pairs constitute an index of the file. If we can afford the space for permanent retention of the index, then we have now an indexed file, and there is no need for physical rearrangement of the records. If the file is in core memory, a vector of identifiers is all that we require. The identifiers are used to gain access to values of the key in the file itself when a comparison has to be made, and only the identifiers are ever exchanged. This variant is slower, and the records have to be rearranged at the end of the sort.

11e. Magnetic Tape Files

A few years ago some of the experts who know about such things were predicting that magnetic tape was soon to be displaced by magnetic disks in all applications except archival storage. However, major advances in the technology of tape drives have resulted in data transfer rates between core and tape that are better than transfer rates between core and removable disk packs. The low cost of magnetic tapes has also helped this storage medium maintain its overall superiority for applications in which an entire file has to be processed in a sequential fashion.

Let us take the customer sales file of a company for our example. We shall distinguish between a *master file*, which constitutes a substantially complete source of information regarding sales by the company, and a temporary *transaction file*. Every working day the company makes sales and receives payments. Information relating to these transactions goes into the transaction file, each new transaction record being simply appended to the end of the file. At fixed intervals of time, say at the end of each week, the transaction file is used to update the master file. It has then served its purpose, but the next transaction thereafter begins a new transaction file. This file is built up over the next week and used to update the master file again at the end of that week.

There are several activities associated with the sales file. (1) An invoice has to be prepared for each sales order. This can be done at the time the sales order is processed for inclusion in the transaction file. (2) Overdue accounts have to be identified once a week. This requires inspection of every record in the file. (3) Monthly statements have to be prepared, which are sent out to the customers. Again every record in the file has to be accessed. (4) Monthly sales reports have to be prepared for management. This activity, too, requires examination of the entire file. (5) Credit ratings and account balances of specified accounts have to be supplied at once on request.

The first activity has no effect on file design or selection of the appropriate storage medium. Magnetic tape is a very suitable medium as far as the next three activities are concerned, but the checks on credit ratings and account balances require direct access to specific individual records, and a search for these records on a magnetic tape is out of the question. Let us therefore examine what is involved if the entire master file is held on magnetic disk. The system can make adequately fast responses to the queries. Moreover, there is no need for a separate transaction file: the appropriate record in the master file can be updated as soon as a transaction is made. Let us now make some assumptions regarding the size of the file. We shall assume that there are about 8000 accounts, and that each record in the master file consists of somewhere around 1000 characters. A record would have numerous fields, including *Account number*, *Company name*, *Address*, *Credit rating*, *Sales orders executed*, *Payments received*, *Account balance* (difference between Payments and Sales), *Sales to date*, etc. However, the fields that one is interested in for purposes of the credit checks are just the *Account number*, *Company name*, *Credit rating*, and *Account balance*, which would add up to a total of no more than 30–40 characters. If a separate file is split off from the master file for the purposes of credit checks, this file would consist of just $0.24 - 0.32 \times 10^6$ characters, which is much less than the 8×10^6 characters of the entire master file.

The appropriate solution then is to keep the master file on tape, and the transaction and credit check files on disk. We shall assume that the transaction file never exceeds 100,000 characters. The credit check file would require at most 500,000 characters of space, even if it were organized as a very fanciful hash table with both company names and account numbers serving as keys. Thus, in the very worst case, the total disk storage requirements under the proposed design (and our assumptions) are only about 8% of those for the entire master file.

What is the schedule of activities for this system? Throughout the day, as part of the execution of a sales order or the processing of a payment, an appropriate record is added to the end of the transaction file. The record would consist of *Account number*, *Company name*, and other information as appropriate. At this same time the *Account balance* field of the record corresponding to the *Account number* and *Company name* is updated in the credit check file. Both fields should be compared as a check on the accuracy of the input. As a further check on the input, payment values that are out of line with the previous account balance should be detected, unit prices in the input should be checked against tables of unit prices stored in the computer (also on disk), feasibility checks should be run on quantities ordered, etc. Unexpected inputs should generate warning messages. It is essential to build such checks into the system to prevent occurrences of the absurd situations that newspapers delight in reporting, and that help generate fear and mistrust of computers in the general population.

At the end of the week the master file is updated. Assume that records in the master file are stored in order of account numbers. Then, prior to the updating run, the transaction file must be sorted so that it too is ordered on account numbers. Two tape drives are required for the updating activity because records on tape cannot be altered by overwriting. If any changes are to be made, the entire file has to be copied out on a second tape, with the changes incorporated in the output. In our context a record is read from the input tape, updated if necessary, and a check is made to determine whether the account is overdue. The record is then written out, possibly modified, on the output tape.

Finally, at the end of a month, statements have to be prepared and a sales report generated. A single tape scan is sufficient for both activities. There is no updating. Hence just the one tape drive is in use.

It would seem that the tape system is particularly unsuited to dealing with customer queries relating to the statements they have received. This is not so. The response to a customer query should not be another sheet of computer output. The query should be handled on a manual basis using information from hard-copy files. This activity should not be regarded as defeating the purpose of automation; rather, it should be looked upon as a safeguard against perpetuation of errors due to program bugs and erroneous data inputs.

Nevertheless, there is no question that greater flexibility can be achieved with a disk-based master file, particularly in a time-sharing environment. Instead of having to rely on a sales report that may be close to a month old, and the rather limited set of data in the credit check file, sales personnel could gain access to any specific record in the master file in next to no time. However, one has to balance costs. If another disk drive has to be added to the system to attain the flexibility, then one has to ask whether the benefits do in fact justify the additional outlay of capital. We cannot give any detailed attention to such questions because the economics of computing is clearly outside the scope of this book.

11f. Tape Sorting

Let us assume that the sales file is to be reorganized. Instead of emphasis being put on account numbers, greater prominence is to be given to the names of the companies that purchase from us. As a first step we want to change the order of the records in the master file so that the records are ordered on company names rather than account numbers. Sorting the entire file in core is out of the question. If just the company names were extracted from the file, and an appropriate sequential record identifying number attached to each company name, then these pairs could be sorted in core, but the sorted list would be of no help to us here. We would still have to rearrange the actual records, and there is no way the sorted list could be used to bring about significant improvement in the efficiency of this task. Consequently, we have to resort to tape sorting.

We shall look at merge sort again, this time transferring records between tapes rather than between arrays in core. Of course, the tape-to-tape transfers have to go through core. Assume that we have four tape drives at our disposal, named A, B, C, and D. The file to be sorted is presumed to reside on tape C, with keys $c_1, c_2, \ldots, c_k$.

In terms of the key set of Figure 11.7 we have

$$C: \quad 19 \quad 1 \quad 26 \quad 43 \quad 92 \quad 87 \quad 88 \quad 26 \quad 17 \quad 34 \quad 69$$

The first stage is to distribute the records to tapes A and B:

1. Set $i = 1$.
2. Let $T = A$, output c_i to tape T.
3. Set $i = i + 1$. If $i > k$, stop.
4. If $c_i \geq c_{i-1}$, output c_i to tape T and go to 3.
5. If $T = B$, go to 2; else let $T = B$, output c_i to T and go to 3.

At the end of the initial distribution we have

$$A: \quad 19 \quad 87 \quad 88 \quad 17 \quad 34 \quad 69$$

$$B: \quad 1 \quad 26 \quad 43 \quad 92 \quad 26$$

If tape B were now empty, we would be finished.

Denote the keys of the records on A by $a_1, a_2, \ldots, a_n$, and the keys of the records on B by $b_1, b_2, \ldots, b_m$. The next stage is to merge records from tapes A and B onto tapes C and D:

1. Set $i = j = k = 1$.
2. Let $T = C$.
3. Let $f = min$.
4. Set $c_k = f(a_i, b_j)$.
5. Output c_k to tape T. If $c_k = a_i$, set $i = i + 1$, and if $i > n$, go to 10; if $c_k \neq a_i$, set $j = j + 1$, and if $j > m$, go to 11.
6. Set $k = k + 1$.
7. Set $c_k = f(a_i, b_j)$. If $c_k \geq c_{k-1}$, go to 5.
8. If $f = min$, let $f = max$ and go to 7.
9. If $T = C$, let $T = D$ and go to 3; else go to 2.
10. Output $b_j, \ldots, b_m$ to tape T and stop.
11. Output $a_i, \ldots, a_n$ to tape T and stop.

If now D is empty, we are finished. Otherwise records are merged from tapes C and D onto A and B using the same procedure with obvious changes in the tape names. If now B is empty, we are finished; otherwise the next merge is again from A and B onto C and D, and so forth. In terms of our example the first application of the merging procedure results in

$$C: \quad 1 \quad 19 \quad 26 \quad 43 \quad 87 \quad 88 \quad 92$$
$$B: \quad 17 \quad 26 \quad 34 \quad 69$$

and the next in

$$A: \quad 1 \quad 17 \quad 19 \quad 26 \quad 26 \quad 34 \quad 43 \quad 69 \quad 87 \quad 88 \quad 92$$
$$B:$$

At this point the sorted file is on tape A.

There is a difference between the merge sort we have considered here and the merge sort of Section 11d. We have two variants of the basic merge sort: *balanced merge* and *natural merge*. Here we have been discussing natural merge sort, which is called *natural* because it takes advantage of the natural order that may already exist in the keys. In our input we can distinguish five blocks of keys that are already in order: (19), (1, 26, 43, 92), (87, 88), (26), (17, 34, 69). After the initial distribution there are two blocks on A and two on B: (19, 87, 88), (17, 34, 69), and (1, 26, 43, 92), (26), respectively. Only two applications of the merge procedure are now required to complete the sort. We cannot continue to use the term *block* to denote an ordered sequence of records because in tape terminology *block* already has a different well-established meaning (see Section 9a). In the literature of sorting the ordered blocks are usually called *strings*, but because of the very general meaning assigned to the term *string* by D.4.12 we should not use this term either. We shall therefore settle on the term *run* to denote a sequence of ordered keys.

A balanced merge for tapes would be a strict translation of the algorithm we considered in Section 11d. In the initial distribution we would read two records at a time from the input tape C, and write the pairs of records alternately on A and B, interchanging the two records when they are not in order. The result would be

$$A: \quad (1, 19) \quad (87, 92) \quad (17, 34)$$
$$B: \quad (26, 43) \quad (26, 88) \quad (69)$$

The first merging pass would result in

$$C: \quad (1, 19, 26, 43) \quad (17, 34, 69)$$
$$D: \quad (26, 87, 88, 92)$$

and the second in

$$A: \quad (1, 19, 26, 26, 43, 87, 88, 92)$$

$$B: \quad (17, 34, 69)$$

One additional pass would be required to complete the sort. Balanced merge typically requires at least one more merging pass than natural merge, but for sorting in core, balanced merge has the advantage that the size of runs is always fixed in advance, and balanced merge is therefore easier to implement.

Instead of two-way merges on may use p-way merges, where $p > 2$, as long as $2p$ tape drives are available. In balanced merging all input tapes for a merge pass contain approximately the same number of runs, and all runs except one are of the same size. Hence the term *balanced*. Natural merge is still balanced with respect to the number of runs, deviations from balance being brought about by variability in the sizes of the runs. Tape-sorting methods have been devised that deliberately create an unbalanced distribution of runs on the tapes. This permits a p-way merge to be carried out with fewer than $2p$ tapes, and consequently there is a reduction in the number of merge passes. Let us consider an unimaginative straightforward approach to p-way merging with $p + 1$ tapes. The records are initially distributed from the input tape to the other p tapes. A p-way merge is then made back to the original input tape, the runs that have grown on this tape in the merging pass are distributed over the other tapes, and another merging pass is made. The distribution phases consist of nothing but copying, which is time consuming and unproductive, and the deliberate creation of imbalance aims at eliminating all this copying. As one would expect, the strategies are rather complicated.

Here we shall consider only one of a class of methods in which creative use is made of imbalance, namely *polyphase merge sort*. This is considered to be the most effective method when the number of available tape drives is six or less. With a larger number of tape drives *oscillating merge sort* is more efficient, but the days of large banks of tape drives are gone. Installations that supported twelve or more tape drives were quite common in the early sixties; nowadays it is unusual to see more than four tape drives in one place. Oscillating merge has therefore lost its importance.

In polyphase merge with three tapes the contents of the tapes are determined by the Fibonacci numbers defined in Exercise 11.4: 1, 1, 2, 3, 5, 8, 13, 21, 34, 55, ... Assume that we have 34 runs on the input tape (tape A). The first task is to distribute them 21 to tape B and 13 to tape C, where 13 and 21 are the two numbers preceding 34 in the Fibonacci sequence. Now merge from tapes B and C, taking one run from each tape, merging the two runs, and writing the merged run out on tape A. When the 13 runs from C

have all been used up, this tape is empty, but there are now 13 larger runs on
A and 8 runs *are still on B*, and this is what the method is all about. Instead of
having to go through an intermediate copying phase we are at once ready to
merge the 8 runs that are still on *B* with 8 of the 13 runs on *A* to produce an
output of 8 runs on *C*, with 5 runs remaining on *A*. In general, at the beginning of each merge pass we have c_k and c_{k+1} runs on two tapes, and the third
tape is empty. The merge pass generates c_k runs on the previously empty
tape, and the tape that contained c_{k+1} runs now contains $c_{k+1} - c_k = c_{k-1}$
runs. Consequently, we are ready for another merge pass from the tapes with
c_{k-1} and c_k runs. Returning to our example, we have initially

A:

B:

C: 19 1 26 43 92 87 88 26 17 34 69

Distribute the keys to tapes *A* and *B* using a variant of the initial distribution
procedure for the natural merge sort (the numbers of runs on *A* and *B* have
to be two successive members of the Fibonacci sequence):

A: (19) (87, 88) (17, 34, 69)

B: (1, 26, 43, 92) (26)

C:

Now merge from *A* and *B* to *C*:

A: (17, 34, 69)

B:

C: (1, 19, 26, 43, 92) (26, 87, 88)

Next merge from *A* and *C* to *B*:

A:

B: (1, 17, 19, 26, 34, 43, 69, 92)

C: (26, 87, 88)

The next merge pass completes the sort.

Let us generalize the procedure to $p + 1$ tapes, where $p > 2$. Let there be
$n_1, n_2, \ldots, n_p$ runs on p of the tapes after the initial distribution from the
input tape, and assume $n_1 \geq n_2 \geq \cdots \geq n_p$. We want to take one run from
each of the tapes, merge the p runs into a single run by means of a p-way
merge, and do this n_p times. The distribution of runs on the $p + 1$ tapes after

the initial merge pass is defined by numbers $n_1 - n_p, n_2 - n_p, \ldots, n_{p-1} - n_p,$
$0, n_p$. It is required that there be just a single run on each of p tapes prior to
the final merge pass. Suppose we have 5 tapes and 181 runs on the input
tape. Then the following sequence of run counts is appropriate:

A	B	C	D	E	
0	0	0	0	181	(initial configuration)
56	52	44	29	0	(initial distribution)
27	23	15	0	29	(after first merge)
12	8	0	15	14	(after second merge)
4	0	8	7	6	(after third merge)
0	4	4	3	2	(after fourth merge)
2	2	2	1	0	(after fifth merge)
1	1	1	0	1	(after sixth merge)
0	0	0	1	0	(after seventh merge)

Two questions arise. First, the scheme does not work for an arbitrary
number of input runs. What then are the "proper" numbers for which it
works? What makes 181 one of the proper numbers? Second, given that the
number of input runs is one of the proper numbers, how does one find the
initial distribution numbers $n_1, n_2, \ldots, n_p$? Both questions find answers in a
generalization of the Fibonacci sequence. Given a particular value of p
($p \geq 2$), define two sequences of numbers:

$$c_1^{(p)} = c_2^{(p)} = \cdots = c_p^{(p)} = 1,$$

$$c_k^{(p)} = c_{k-1}^{(p)} + c_{k-2}^{(p)} + \cdots + c_{k-p}^{(p)}, \qquad k > p,$$

and

$$d_1^{(p)} = d_2^{(p)} = \cdots = d_{p-1}^{(p)} = 0, \qquad d_p^{(p)} = 1,$$

$$d_k^{(p)} = d_{k-1}^{(p)} + d_{k-2}^{(p)} + \cdots + d_{k-p}^{(p)}, \qquad k > p.$$

In both sequences a member of a sequence is the sum of its p predecessors,
but the initial values differ. For example, with $p = 4$ (5 tapes) we have

$$c_1^{(4)} = c_2^{(4)} = c_3^{(4)} = c_4^{(4)} = 1,$$

$$c_k^{(4)} = c_{k-1}^{(4)} + c_{k-2}^{(4)} + c_{k-3}^{(4)} + c_{k-4}^{(4)}, \qquad k > 4;$$

$$d_1^{(4)} = d_2^{(4)} = d_3^{(4)} = 0,$$

$$d_4^{(4)} = 1,$$

$$d_k^{(4)} = d_{k-1}^{(4)} + d_{k-2}^{(4)} + d_{k-3}^{(4)} + d_{k-4}^{(4)}, \qquad k > 4.$$

The sequences defined by the two recurrence relations are

$$c_i^{(4)}: \quad 1, 1, 1, 1, 4, 7, 13, 25, 49, 94, 181, 349, \ldots$$

$$d_i^{(4)}: \quad 0, 0, 0, 1, 1, 2, 4, 8, 15, 29, 56, 108, \ldots$$

The proper numbers of input runs are the $c_i^{(p)}$, and, in terms of our example, we find that 181 is $c_{11}^{(4)}$. For our example we have

$$n_1^{(4,11)} = d_7^{(4)} + d_8^{(4)} + d_9^{(4)} + d_{10}^{(4)},$$

$$n_2^{(4,11)} = d_8^{(4)} + d_9^{(4)} + d_{10}^{(4)},$$

$$n_3^{(4,11)} = d_9^{(4)} + d_{10}^{(4)},$$

$$n_4^{(4,11)} = d_{10}^{(4)}.$$

In general, if the number of blocks on the input tape in a $(p + 1)$-tape polyphase merge sort is $c_m^{(p)}$, then the number of runs to be placed on tape i in the initial distribution is

$$n_i^{(p,m)} = \sum_{k=m-1-p+i}^{m-1} d_k^{(p)}, \qquad i = 1, 2, \ldots, p.$$

In the case $p = 2$ the two sequences are

$$c_i^{(2)}: \quad 1, 1, 2, 3, 5, 8, \ldots$$

$$d_i^{(2)}: \quad 0, 1, 1, 2, 3, 5, \ldots$$

i.e., the d-sequence is simply the c-sequence displaced by one position. Hence the very simple relationship between the proper numbers and the distribution numbers for a 3-tape polyphase merge.

There is one snag. What if the number of runs in the unsorted file is not one of the proper numbers? One then makes use of dummy runs. Optimal solutions to this problem are interesting, but unfortunately they are also very complicated. We shall indicate a relatively simple solution that is close to being optimal. The number of runs is to be brought up to the proper number next higher than the actual number of runs by the use of dummy runs. For example, with $p = 4$ and 67 runs, we have to add $94 - 67 = 27$ dummy runs. For 94 runs the initial distribution is defined by 29, 27, 23, 15. We could distribute the 67 runs to all four tapes one at a time until each had received 15 runs, then distribute the remaining 7 runs over the first three tapes. The distribution would be $11 + 18$, $10 + 17$, $6 + 17$, $0 + 15$, where the first number in each sum defines the number of dummy runs that are presumed to be present at the beginning of the tape. This is not a good solution because it does not distribute the dummies uniformly over all four tapes.

The real difficulty is that we do not know how many runs the input tape contains. Consequently we need a procedure that computes the number of dummy runs to go on each tape without prior knowledge of the appropriate distribution numbers, i.e., the distribution numbers are themselves to be computed as part of the process, and their computation and the distribution of runs from the input tape must proceed simultaneously. We shall assume $p + 1$ tapes with the input on tape $p + 1$, i.e., the input runs will have to be distributed over tapes $1, 2, \ldots, p$. Arrays N and NIL will be used, each of $p + 1$ elements; at the end of the initial distribution $N(i)$ will hold the distribution number $n_i^{(p,m)}$, and NIL(i) will hold the number of dummy runs on tape i.

1. For $I = 1, 2, \ldots, p$: Set $N(I) = NIL(I) = 1$.
2. Set $N(p + 1) = NIL(p + 1) = 0, M = 1, K = 1$.
3. If tape $p + 1$ exhausted, stop; else write a run on tape K and set $NIL(K) = NIL(K) - 1$.
4. If $NIL(K) < NIL(K+1)$, set $K = K + 1$ and go to 3.
5. If $NIL(K) \neq 0$, set $K = 1$ and go to 3; else set $KK = N(1)$.
6. For $I = 1, 2, \ldots, p$: Set $NIL(I) = KK + N(I+1) - N(I)$, $N(I) = N(I) + NIL(I)$.
7. Set $M = M + 1, K = 1$, and go to 3.

For our example of 67 runs and 5 tapes ($p = 4$) this distribution algorithm computes

$$N = (29, 27, 23, 15, 0),$$

$$NIL = (\; 6, \quad 7, \quad 7, \quad 7, 0), \text{(handwritten annotation)}$$

and 23, 20, 16, and 8 actual runs are distributed over tapes 1, 2, 3, and 4, respectively. The value of M is 6, and this is the number of merges that will now have to be made.

Let us look at the first merge pass in detail. The records are merged onto tape 5 until tape 4 has been exhausted. First the dummy runs are "processed": in each of the first six iterations $NIL(1), \ldots, NIL(4)$ are decremented by 1, and $NIL(5)$ is incremented by 1. When some of the values in $NIL(1), \ldots, NIL(p)$ have decreased to zero, say q such values, a q-way merge is made from the tapes for which these values are zero, and the $(p - q)$ nonzero elements of $NIL(1), \ldots, NIL(p)$ are decremented by 1. The merged run is written out to tape $p + 1$. In our example this happens when $NIL = (0, 1, 1, 1, 6)$, and we make a "1-way merge," i.e., a block is simply copied from tape 1 onto tape 5. Continuing with this example, at the end of the first pass $NIL = (0, 0, 0, 0, 6)$, and the distribution of the actual runs is

$$14 \quad 12 \quad 8 \quad 0 \quad 9$$

At the end of the second merge all elements of NIL are zero, and the distribution of runs is

$$6 \quad 4 \quad 0 \quad 8 \quad 7$$

In the second merge pass the first six output runs were generated by 3-way merge from tapes 1, 2, and 3, and the next two runs by 4-way merge from tapes 1, 2, 3, and 5. Since NIL is now empty, normal 4-way merge takes over, i.e., the rest of the process is as if we had a proper number of runs to begin with.

In our discussion it has been assumed that in the initial distribution records are transferred directly from the input tape to one of the distribution tapes. An improvement would result if the greatest number of records that could be held in core storage were read from the input tape into core, these records were sorted using one or other of the minimal storage internal sorting methods we discussed in Section 11d, and the sorted records were then written out as a run. The initial merge would then be operating on substantially fewer runs than would otherwise be the case, and the total number of merge passes would be reduced.

We can do even better. Let n be the number of records that can be held in core at any one time. Standard sorting produces a run consisting of just these n records, but a *replacement selection* sort can generate runs of average size $2n$. The basic idea is to read into core a *replacement* from the input tape as soon as a record is written out on the distribution tape. The criterion for writing out a record is that it have the smallest key not smaller than the key of the last record written out. The replacement record is considered as well in the *selection* of the record to be written out according to this criterion. The replacement record will ultimately become part of the run that is being produced if its key is not smaller than the key of the record it is replacing.

Consider the keys

$$19 \quad 1 \quad 26 \quad 43 \quad 92 \quad 87 \quad 15 \quad 27 \quad 88 \quad 34 \quad 69$$

and assume that five records can be held in core. Read in 19, 1, 26, 43, 92 and write out the smallest key, namely 1. Read 87 to replace it and output the smallest of 19, 87, 26, 43, 92, which is 19. Read in 15 to give 15, 87, 26, 43, 92. The smallest key is 15, but 15 is smaller than 19, which was the key last written out. Therefore the next output is 26, and 27 is its replacement. We now have 15, 87, 27, 43, 92 in core, and 27 is written out. Continuing in this fashion until all the input has been read we generate the run

$$1 \quad 19 \quad 26 \quad 27 \quad 43 \quad 87 \quad 88 \quad 92$$

and keys 15, 69, 34 remain in core. They define a second run.

Analysis of replacement selection requires rather advanced mathematics. Hence we merely state the results of such analysis: the expected length of the first run is $1.72n$, that of the second is $1.95n$, and that of subsequent runs $2.00n$ (the expected length approaches $2n$ asymptotically).

The replacement selection algorithm can be based on A.5.12, which is first converted to an algorithm for sorting in descending order by changing statements 28 and 30 to

```
28   IF (A(J + 1).LT.A(J)) J = J + 1

30   IF (A(J).GE.COPY) GO TO 35
```

We shall refer to the shift procedure starting with Statement 20 as if it were a separate subroutine SHIFT with input arguments I and L. In practice this program segment should not be implemented as a separate subroutine, to save the appreciable time that would be spent in transfers to and from a subroutine. In keeping with the way A.5.12 is specified we shall talk of a number A(J), but we shall actually mean a record or a key, whichever is appropriate in the context. It is assumed that N numbers are already in array A. The replacement selection algorithm can then be specified as follows:

1. Order the numbers in array A in such a way that A(JHALF) $\leq$ A(J) holds for JHALF = 2, 3, ..., N/2 by a program segment analogous to that ending with Statement 5 in A.5.12.
2. Call SHIFT with I = 1, L = N. This moves the smallest of the numbers into A(1).
3. Set REF = A(1), write A(1) on the distribution tape, read a new number from the input tape into A(1).
4. Call SHIFT with I = 1 and the current value of L.
5. If A(1) $\geq$ REF, go to 3; else interchange A(1) and A(L) and set L = L − 1.
6. If L = 0, stop; else go to 4.

The algorithm stops with A holding N numbers, and the algorithm can be applied at once to the generation of the next run.

Throughout our discussion we have been neglecting practical matters. For example, consider an input tape from which records are distributed to other tapes in the initial stage of a merge sort. After this initial distribution the input tape has to be rewound before we can start merging records back onto this tape. As far as our program is concerned we are sent into a wait state while the tape is being rewound. However, a tape operation, once initiated, proceeds independently of the central processor, and the latter has therefore potential for performing useful work during the rewind. In a multiprogramming system execution is begun or resumed of a different program that can make use of the central processor while our program is waiting for the tape operation to be completed. When the tape has been rewound, execution of this other program can be interrupted and execution of our program resumed. The overall efficiency of the system will therefore not be greatly improved by attempts on our part to overlap the rewinding time with other activities within our own program. This argument holds as long as there are enough jobs around that can make use of the central processor without generating much input/output themselves, where input/output is understood to include data transfers between core and peripheral storage devices, and support activities associated with such transfers, e.g., rewinding of tapes.

The job mix of a university computer center can be expected to include many jobs with high demands on the central processor and very little input/output (the so called number crunchers). Consequently the central processor should be in use all the time. On the other hand, nearly all jobs run by a commercial data processing installation require extensive input/output. Here the situation can easily arise where all programs that are being processed are in an input/output phase, and the central processor is then forced into idleness. If this is the case, then it does pay to make attempts at overlapping tape activities with internal processing at the level of an individual program. A proper discussion of the techniques one would employ requires a thorough understanding of input/output at the hardware level, and of the input/output component of one's operating system. It is not unreasonable to assume that many readers of this book do not possess such background knowledge. Hence we cannot pursue this discussion any further.

11g. Files and Disks

The management of large files is outside the scope of this book. It is an important topic that keeps growing in importance, and it deserves to be studied thoroughly in its own right, not as an addendum to something else. Nevertheless, we shall look at some aspects of the processing of large files in a very rudimentary fashion, if only to show that there are fundamental differences between the processing of data that are stored in core memory and the processing of data that reside on peripheral storage devices. Moreover, it just does not seem right to leave the topic of files without explaining the terms ISAM and bucket.

The properties of the medium on which a file is stored affect the organization of the file and the procedures used in its processing. If a sequential file is stored in core memory, then logarithmic search is the proper procedure for gaining access to a record, but imagine applying logarithmic search to a file stored on magnetic tape! The tape is spun forward 1000 feet, say, back 500 feet, back 250 feet, again forward 125 feet, and so on. Certainly a fascinating spectacle, but that is about all it would be.

When a file is not in core memory the *page* of a file becomes an important concept. Records are regarded as grouped into a sequence of pages, the size of a page depending on the characteristics of the storage medium. In the case of a magnetic tape the pages are tape blocks. With this sequential storage medium the only way of getting at the nth page is by going through the preceding $n - 1$ pages, and one might as well have the search guided by data on these pages. Therefore, instead of performing logarithmic search on the file, one reads the pages in sequence, inspecting the value of the key in the last record of a page. If the search key exceeds this value, the next page is read; if not, then logarithmic search is applied to the page currently in core memory.

Magnetic disks (and drums) call for a different strategy. Let us interpret the tracks as pages. Nearly all of the time required to access particular records is spent in gaining access to the pages to which they belong, but each page can be accessed independently. The best search time is achieved if one can identify the page that holds the record indicated by a given search key without direct reference to other pages of the file. Suppose we have in core memory a directory or index that holds the value of the key of the last record of every page of the file. Then, given a search key, the page of the file that holds the record corresponding to this key can be identified by something similar to logarithmic search in the directory. This page is brought into core memory, and the page searched for the appropriate record either sequentially or logarithmically. This is the principle on which the popular *Indexed Sequential Access Method* of file management (ISAM for short) is based.

In practice a file to which ISAM is applied will be rather large, occupying perhaps an entire disk pack, and ISAM uses two levels of indexes. A *cylinder index*, which consists of keys of the last records of all cylinders occupied by the file, is kept in core memory throughout the file processing run. Given a particular key, a search through the cylinder index identifies the cylinder in which the record corresponding to this key is located. A seek instruction positions the assembly of read-write heads over the tracks that make up this cylinder, and a *track index* is read into core memory from the first track of the cylinder. The track index holds keys of last records for all tracks in the cylinder. A search through this index identifies the track that holds the desired record, and this track is read into core memory. Note that no further seeks are needed once the cylinder that holds the record we are after has been accessed, i.e., the cost of locating a record is a single seek followed by the reading of two tracks. (Actually one does not necessarily read entire tracks. For example, IBM 360/370 disk instructions enable one to search the track while it moves past the read-write head, and to read into core just the one record corresponding to the given search key.)

Of course, the records of an indexed sequential file must follow a sequential order determined by the sorted order of their keys. The sequential order permits rapid sequential processing of the file; the system of indexes superimposed on the sequence of records gives rapid access to single records. This dual efficiency accounts for the popularity of ISAM.

However, if many new records are added to a file after it has been created, the efficiency may soon be gone. Addition of new records is made possible by reserving certain tracks as overflow areas at the time the file is created, and the added records go into these overflow areas. Normally a programmer does not have to be concerned with the detailed mechanisms for adding new records. Modern operating systems provide file processing programs that look after the detail. To take an actual example, let us see how the file processing programs of the IBM operating system (OS) for its 360/370 computers deal with the addition of new records under ISAM.

These programs permit one to utilize one or other or both of two types of overflow areas: a cylinder overflow area and an independent overflow area. The advantage of having an overflow area in the same cylinder in which overflow occurs is that access to this area does not require an additional seek. However, if additions to a file are unevenly distributed, space in some of the cylinder overflow areas goes to waste. For this reason one may decide to use just the independent overflow area. All new records that are added to the file then go into this area. When both types of overflow areas are being used, new records are normally stored in the cylinder overflow areas. The independent overflow area is used only when the cylinder overflow area in which a record should be stored is full.

Actually the records that are stored in the overflow areas need not be the new records. The new records that would overflow from a particular track are often stored on the track itself, and the old records that are thus displaced are shifted into overflow areas. Let $K_1, K_2, \ldots, K_n$ be the ordered sequence of *all possible* keys that could be used to identify the records of a given file (the keys of records in the file at any given time are a subset of this " universal " set). Just after the file has been created, let K_j be the key of the last record on a track T in the file, and let K_i be the key of the last record on the track that precedes T. When new records are added to the file there must be a clear understanding of where they should go. Under ISAM all records with keys that belong to subsequence $K_{i+1}, K_{i+2}, \ldots, K_j$ of the sequence of possible keys are identified with track T. Let c be the capacity of T, i.e., the number of records that T can hold, and suppose that at a given time records

R_1^T, R_2^T, ..., R_c^T, R_{c+1}^T, ..., R_{c+m}^T are identified with track T. We assume that the records in this sequence are ordered on their keys. Under ISAM records R_1^T, R_2^T, ..., R_c^T are now in this order on track T, and records R_{c+1}^T, ..., R_{c+m}^T constitute the overflow from track T. The overflow records are chained together in a list (each record has a pointer field appended to it). The track index actually holds three entries for each track: the key of record R_c^T, the key of record R_{c+m}^T (which must be K_j), and a pointer to the first record in the overflow list, which is R_{c+1}^T here. These entries permit reasonably efficient retrieval, but, particularly if the overflow chains begin to reach into the independent overflow area, a serious degradation of performance may arise, and the file should then be reorganized so that it again assumes proper sequential order.

Let us now consider hashing in the context of disk storage. When a hash table is stored on disk the number of probes is not the major concern. What matters now is that the number of disk accesses be kept low. Consequently the designer of the hash storage scheme should aim at retrieval of a record by a single access to the disk store, even if the strategy for achieving this aim results in making many probes. If a second access is required, then it should be to the same cylinder in order to eliminate a second seek operation.

One approach toward the reduction of the number of accesses is to use multirecord *buckets*. The result of applying a hash function to a key is an address. In the discussion of Section 11c it was assumed that this address refers to a storage region that holds or is capable of holding just one record. Let the entire hash table be partitioned into N such regions. Then, for example, under the division–remainder method division of the key by N generates a hash address, and there are N possible addresses 0, 1, ..., $N - 1$. However, we may divide the hash table into larger regions, each capable of holding k records. If this is done, then the divisor becomes N/k, and the hash addresses that are generated are 0, 1, ..., $N/k - 1$. More keys are now expected to generate the same hash address, but the storage region identified by this hash address can now hold more than one record. This storage region is called a *bucket*.

There is no advantage in using buckets that hold more than one record when a hash table is in core memory, but a good case can be made for the use of multirecord buckets with disks, where a bucket may be a track, a segment of a track, or some other identifiable section of a track. Suppose we are given a key K, and are required to locate the record corresponding to this key. We compute the bucket address using the division–remainder method, say, and the entire bucket identified by this address is brought into core. The bucket is then searched through for the required record. This search time is very small compared to the times taken by disk operations, certainly much smaller than the time required to access the disk for a second time, even when the same track is being accessed, i.e., when no second seek is required.

For our analysis of the effect that buckets have we shall use a well known model in probability theory. Suppose we are given n balls, and a receptacle made up of t compartments. We distribute the n balls randomly over the t compartments. The expected number of balls to a compartment is n/t, but some compartments will receive more balls than n/t, others fewer. The probability that a given compartment contains exactly i balls belongs to the binomial probability distribution, and it is

$$\binom{n}{i}\left(1 - \frac{1}{t}\right)^{n-i}\left(\frac{1}{t}\right)^{i} = \binom{n}{i}\left(\frac{t-1}{t}\right)^{n}\left(\frac{1}{t-1}\right)^{i}.$$

Now suppose that each compartment is capable of holding no more than k balls, i.e., that all balls in excess of k spill over and roll away. The probability that more than k balls were distributed to a given compartment is

$$p_k = 1 - \left(\frac{t-1}{t}\right)^{n}\sum_{i=0}^{k}\binom{n}{i}\left(\frac{1}{t-1}\right)^{i},$$

and the expected number of compartments from which such spillage has occurred is tp_k. The expected number of balls in the compartments that received exactly 0, or 1, $\ldots$, or k balls is

$$\left(\frac{t-1}{t}\right)^{n}\sum_{i=0}^{k}it\binom{n}{i}\left(\frac{1}{t-1}\right)^{i},$$

and the number of balls that were distributed to the compartments from which spillovers occurred is therefore n reduced by this quantity. Spillovers occurred from tp_k compartments, and these compartments are capable of holding ktp_k balls. Hence the number of balls that are expected to have rolled away is

$$n - ktp_k - \left(\frac{t-1}{t}\right)^{n}\sum_{i=0}^{k}it\binom{n}{i}\left(\frac{1}{t-1}\right)^{i}.$$

Some simple algebraic manipulation transforms this expression into

$$n - kt + t\left(\frac{t-1}{t}\right)^{n}\sum_{i=0}^{k}(k-i)\binom{n}{i}\left(\frac{1}{t-1}\right)^{i}.$$

In our context we take a hash table that is capable of holding N records, assume that n records are to be stored in the table, and propose a bucket size of k. The records correspond to the balls, the bucket size to the compartment limit, and N to the capacity of the entire receptacle, which is kt. The number of records that overflow from full buckets corresponds to the number of balls that roll away in the model. This number of records is

$$n - N + \frac{N}{k}\left(\frac{N-k}{N}\right)^n \sum_{i=0}^{k} (k - i)\binom{n}{i}\left(\frac{k}{N-k}\right)^i .$$

For $N = 500$, $n = 375$, and $k = 5$ this expression evaluates to 32, and the expected number of overflowing buckets is 17.6. This means that 343 of the 375 records can be retrieved by access to a single bucket, and only 32 records would require more than one bucket to be accessed.

Two methods are commonly employed for dealing with records that overflow a bucket. One is an open addressing method in which an overflow record is stored in the next adjacent bucket if the "home" bucket is full, in the next bucket after it if the adjacent bucket is also full, and so forth. The other method is to chain overflow records into lists. Each cylinder is provided with its own overflow region. If records overflow from a particular bucket, then they are stored in this region. There is a pointer from the full "home" bucket to the first such record, a pointer from this record to the second overflow record, and so forth. Each overflow region is on the same cylinder as the "home" bucket to minimize seek times. In addition to these primary overflow regions a single secondary overflow region should be provided to which records are chained from all primary overflow regions that have themselves become full.

In our original model there is a big difference between the case where the balls that spill over roll away and where they drop into adjacent receptacles. It should be clear that our analysis applies only to the chaining method, and not to open addressing. Returning to our example, the expected length of an overflow chain is 32/17.6, and the expected number of disk accesses for retrieval is no greater than $[375 + 32 \times (1 + 32/17.6)/2]/375 = 1.12$.

An extensive study of eight files containing between 500 and 33,575 records has provided valuable experimental results regarding the efficiency of different hash functions, and of chaining and open addressing (see reference [Lu71]). The study showed that division–remainder is the most reliable of eight hash functions investigated. With this hash function, and with the load factor $\alpha = 0.75$, the number of disk accesses for retrieval was found to be 1.11 (with a standard error of 0.05) under chaining, and 1.29 (standard error 0.27) under open addressing. Our value of 1.12 compares well with the experimental value 1.11 ± 0.05. The percentage of overflow records was found to be 8 (standard error 4), which also compares well with our $32 \times 100/375 = 8.5$.

Let us summarize the properties of indexed sequential and hashed files. Take the indexed sequential organization first: (i) At least two disk accesses are required for the retrieval of a record when records are accessed in a random rather than sequential manner. (ii) The sequential organization permits rapid processing of the entire file or of a sequence of records in the file. Moreover, the neighbors of a given record are significant in some applications, and these neighboring records can be easily retrieved. (iii) There is a storage overhead in that space has to be provided for the indexes. (iv) If many new records are added to the file, then a serious degradation of performance is to be expected. Consequently the file has to be reorganized whenever the ratio of overflow records to "normal" records reaches too high a level.

Now for the properties of random organization: (i) On the average fewer disk accesses are required to retrieve a record, but it can happen that very long overflow chains develop. In these rare instances one may have to choose a new hash function and reorganize the file. (ii) Sequential processing is not possible. However, when the entire file has to be processed, at times it does not matter in what order the records are processed. If this is the case, then a hashed file can be processed nearly as rapidly as the equivalent indexed sequential file, simply by stepping through the entire storage region and processing the records in the order they are encountered. (iii) Storage overheads arise as a consequence of the need to keep the load factor in an acceptable range. They may be higher than for an indexed sequential file. (iv) If the ultimate storage needs of the file are properly estimated at the time the file is created, then a need to reorganize the file should arise extremely rarely, but if it does arise, then the reorganization should be considerably costlier than the reorganization of an indexed sequential file.

Notes

The two quotes in Section 11a are, respectively, due to Dodd [*Computing Surveys* **1,** p. 117 (1969)] and Lees [*Language* **35,** p. 300 (1959)].

File organization has a very extensive literature, and a representative selection of sources for additional reading would take up a disproportionately large part of our bibliography. Instead of extending the bibliography by too many pages, we recommend the detailed surveys in the *Annual Review of Information Science and Technology* as guides for further study; to these we add [Ro72]. Many of the references given in the Notes to Chapter 10 are relevant here as well because list structuring methods are often used in the organization of files. The implementation problems that are the subject matter of Chapters 10 and 11 are discussed in [Ri73] in the context of the construction of thesauri (see Section 8c). Reference is made to probability theory in certain sections of this chapter. The first two chapters of [Fe50] should suffice as an introduction to the relevant principles.

An alternative to binary search is Fibonacci search, described in [Fe60]. Fibonacci search avoids division (cf. the statement following statement 5 in A.11.1); it may, therefore, be more efficient than A.11.1, depending on the comparative cost of division in a particular computer. See [Ov73] for an analysis of Fibonacci search. Another alternative is polynomial search, defined in [Sh73a], which requires fewer comparisons than binary search under certain well-defined conditions.

[Kn73a] is an outstanding text on searching and sorting. See this work for a definitive survey of scatter storage techniques, and for detailed derivation of some of the expressions introduced in Section 11c. The effectiveness of a hashing function depends on the characteristics of the key set to which the function is applied. Fortran identifiers collected from actual programs are studied in this context in [Lu73b]. For an empirical large scale study of hashing see [Lu71, Lu72]; the results of this study have been found consistent with a theoretical investigation, see [Lu73a]. Although the primary aim of this very important investigation was to study hashing as a method for organizing large files on disks, the results apply to hash tables stored in core as well.

[Ba62] contains algorithms in the form of flowcharts for set operations on sets stored as lists. A.11.7 (Quicksort) and the polyphase merge algorithm of Section 11f have been adapted from [Kn73a], which is the definitive text on sorting. By comparison, [Ma71b] is a rather elementary survey of sorting algorithms (it has the interesting feature of containing a flowchart that enables one to select the sorting method that best meets one's needs). [Ri72a] is a collection of PL/I programs for internal sorting. [Ri72b] is an extensive bibliography containing 301 items; the more modest [Lo71] contains 100 conventional entries and 37 references to implementations of sorting algorithms as computer programs. An $O(n^{3/2})$ stable sort is described in [De74a]. [Jo70] is relevant to sorting by address calculation. The ratios of times given near the end of Section 11d have been calculated using data from [Bl66]. Additional timing data can be found in [Ch70b, Lo74]. The natural selection variant of replacement selection (see Exercise 11.48) is described in [Fr72]. Hardware solutions to sorting problems are reviewed in [Th74].

Some discussion of the practicalities of tape operations that were alluded to at the end of Section 11h can be found in [Kn73a]. Many tape drives permit tapes to be read in both forward and backward directions, and the backward reading facility can be utilized to eliminate the need for explicit rewinding of tapes between distribution phases of merge sorts. Again one will find the appropriate techniques outlined in [Kn73a].

Reingold provides in [Re72] an elegant proof that sorting of n keys requires at least $O(n \log n)$ comparisons. He first proves that $O(n \log n)$

comparisons are needed to decide whether two sets of n unordered elements are equal. However, if the sets were ordered, then only n comparisons would be needed. Hence, if sorting could be done in less than $O(n \log n)$ comparisons, equality of sets would likewise be decidable in less than $O(n \log n)$ comparisons.

It is well known that natural language texts are highly redundant (an indication of this is our ability to understand abbreviations). [Ba60] is a classic paper giving a systematic abbreviation procedure. A survey of a variety of text compression procedures can be found in Chapter 3 of [Bo63]. [Ru72, Ly73] are more recent publications dealing with the compression of data.

A proper coverage of processing of large files, i.e., files that are stored on disks and similar peripheral storage devices, is outside the scope of this book because of the reasons given in the Preface. However, we shall give a few bibliographic pointers to the literature dealing with this topic.

For general background one can consult the tutorial papers [Ch69a, Ch69b, En72, Ca73]. The "official" CODASYL thinking is formulated in [Zz71]. Processing of sequential files is described in [Gi71]; [Mu72] deals with an interesting variant of the ISAM organization in which overflow is assigned to a hash table.

The literature on large data bases is vast, but it consists in the main of nothing more than rather dull repetitive descriptions of implemented or contemplated systems for processing such data bases. Only in the early 1970s did solid analytic work begin to appear. Of this a sequence of papers by Van der Pool is important: [Va72, Va73a, Va73b]. Also in the analytic vein are [Sh73b, Sh74].

The IBM approach to file organization is characterized by great flexibility, and no other manufacturer has succeeded in providing as extensive a range of services as IBM provides for its 360/370 computer systems. For an introduction to these services, and to how one gains access to them see [Fl70, Fl71] (these texts are somewhat flawed by the absence of references, particularly to the IBM manuals on which they are based). [Lo73] covers much the same ground, but not in as great a technical detail.

Examples of the use of discrete mathematics to provide foundations for file structuring investigations are provided by Codd with his relational data structures [Co70a, Co72a, Co72b], and by Childs with his set-theoretical data structure [Ch68]. [De73] is a very interesting paper on the relational model. It deals with the decomposition of a file into subfiles in such a way that the original file can be reconstructed from the subfiles. The decomposition procedure described in this paper is shown to be equivalent to minimization of Boolean functions.

Exercises

11.1 (a) Is the structure defined by the following PL/I statement a file?

    DECLARE 1U(50), 2V, 2W, 3Y, 3Z(2,2), 2X;

If you have decided that the structure is a file, how many records does it contain? What are the properties (or fields)? How many measures does a record in this file contain?

11.2 (a) Why is statement 6 of A.11.1 $HI = MID$ rather than $HI = MID - 1$?

11.3 (a) The function subprogram of A.11.1 becomes slightly simpler if we make $LO = 0$, $HI = N+1$ initially. Rewrite the subprogram with this modification.

11.4 (a) Fibonacci search is based on the Fibonacci numbers c_k, which are defined as follows:

$$c_0 = 0; \quad c_1 = 1; \quad c_k = c_{k-1} + c_{k-2} \qquad (k \geq 2).$$

Assume that A is a vector of lexicographically ordered elements, and that a value d, if it is in A, belongs to an interval of c_k elements beginning with a_i. Then one starts the Fibonacci search process by comparing d with $a_{i+c_{k-1}}$. If the values match, then the search is finished. If $d < a_{i+c_{k-1}}$, then d can only be in the interval of c_{k-1} elements beginning with a_i, and one repeats the process with k set to $k - 1$. If $d > a_{i+c_{k-1}}$, then d can only be in the interval of $c_k - c_{k-1}$ $(=c_{k-2})$ elements beginning with $a_{i+c_{k-1}}$, and the process is repeated with k set to $k - 2$ and i set to $i + c_{k-1}$. Implement the Fibonacci search algorithm as a Fortran program.

11.5 (a) If the computer system to which you have access provides you with the means to measure execution times of specific program segments, find by experiment the break-even point discussed in Example 2 of A.11.1 for your implementations of sequential search and binary search algorithms.

11.6 (b) What is the purpose of storing the document numbers in the reference vector of Figure 11.1 in ascending order?

11.7 (b) Describe the process of updating an entry in the index of a document file with reference to the scheme illustrated by Figure 11.1. Assuming that the number of a document that is being added to the file is always greater than the number of a document already in the file, suggest improvements to the design of the index entry.

11.8 (b) Assume that the index of a document file is arranged as a sort tree with individual entries having the form shown in Figure 11.1. Give a full description of the procedure for amending the index when a document is deleted from the file.

11.9 (c) Write a Fortran implementation of a scatter table using the division–remainder method for computing hash addresses, and linear search for resolving collisions. (You are free to select any format you wish for the data that this table is to cater for.)

11.10 (c) It has been suggested that retrieval of records would be more efficient if in using linear search all records with the same hash address were kept in adjacent locations in the hash table, instead of being intermixed with records having different hash addresses. For example, assume the input sequence of keys 59, 128, 195, 60, 111, 93, and a table of size 17. Division by 17 produces the remainders 8, 9, 8, 9, 9, 8, and consequently the records occupy locations 9, 10, ..., 14 (assuming that addresses begin with 1) in their original input order. Under the alternative scheme they would occupy these locations in the order 59, 195, 93, 128, 60, 111. Show that the expected number of probes is the same for conventional linear search and the suggested variant. You may prove that the average number of probes to retrieve a record in a table holding keys $K_1, K_2, \ldots, K_m$ is independent of the order of insertion of these keys.

11.11 (c) Do Exercise 11.9 again, using now the method of chaining into nonoverlapping lists to resolve collisions (Method D).

11.12 (c) Do Exercise 11.11 again, using Method D to resolve collisions until the hash table is full, and chaining to an overflow area thereafter.

11.13 (c) A hash table is to be constructed in which chaining to an overflow area (Method F) is to be used to resolve collisions. Ultimately the table is to hold 1500 records, and the total storage area available is sufficient for exactly 1800 records. How large should the primary storage area be to ensure that the system of tables functions properly at all times?

11.14 (c) A variant of Method F for resolution of collisions is to keep all records that occupy the same chain in sorted order of keys. Do you expect a significant improvement in retrieval speed? Discuss in detail the various factors that have to be taken into account in a proper analysis of the overall effectiveness of this scheme.

11.15 (c) Do Exercise 11.14 again, considering now the sorting of records when Method D is used to resolve collisions. Can this approach be used with Method E?

11.16 (c) Generalize A.11.2 to the case where several records have the same key. How would deletion be performed in this case? Discuss in detail.

11.17 (c) The technique of A.11.3 is to be applied to the deletion of records from a file that is organized as described in the preamble of A.11.2. When a record is deleted from IFILE, the released space can be reclaimed either by the use of the LAVS concept, or by filling the gap with the "last" record, i.e., the record occupying locations IFILE(IP − N),...,IFILE (IP − 1), and adjusting the value of IP accordingly. Note that under the latter variant the format of the records in IFILE must be altered: a pointer field has to be added to permit one to establish which location in IHASH points to the "last" record so that the pointer in this location can be altered. Implement both variants and discuss their relative merits.

11.18   (c)   Consider the deletion algorithm A.11.3. Suppose that a sequence of records is entered into the hash table, and that one of the records is then deleted by A.11.3 (e.g., enter A, B, C, D; delete C). Would you expect the hash table to have the same appearance it would have had if the deleted record had not been part of the input sequence in the first place (e.g., if just records A, B, D had been entered)?

11.19   (c)   Under linear search (Method A) deletion can be effected by A.11.3 or by flagging. How do the two alternatives compare with regard to expected retrieval time? Expected insertion time?

11.20   (c)   Implement a deletion algorithm in which collisions are resolved by chaining into nonoverlapping lists (Method D). Why should LAVS be a two-way list here?

11.21   (c)   The text describes a file maintained by a company on the products it manufactures. As part of the total file structure a sort tree is used to store "profitability values" of all the products. How would one retrieve the 50 records corresponding to the 50 products with the lowest profitability values most efficiently? Note that the same sort tree is also to be used to retrieve the 50 products with the highest profitability values, that the total number of products is known, and that it is approximately 300.

11.22   (c)   Design a scatter table to cater for variable length records.

11.23   (c)   Design a scheme for storing sparse matrices in a scatter table. (Points to watch: What is to be the argument of the hash function? Is the hash function going to produce reasonably random distribution of hash addresses?)

11.24   (d)   Modify A.11.4 so that it finds the set union of A and B.

11.25   (d)   Array N of dimension K+L contains a sequence of K numbers sorted in ascending order in locations N(1),N(2),...,N(K), and a second sequence of L sorted numbers in locations N(K+1),N(K+2),..., N(K+L). Write a program that merges the two sequences without the use of a further array.

11.26   (d)   Two sets of numbers $N, M \in \{1, 2, ..., 100\}$ are stored in ascending order in arrays N and M. Write a program that determines whether $N \subseteq M$. (Example: N = [1, 5, 17, 24, 63], M = [1, 3, 5, 16, 17, 25, 63, 78].)

11.27 (d) The set of numbers N of Exercise 11.26 can be represented by a 100-element array NN in which $\text{NN}(k) = 1$ if $k \in N$ and $\text{NN}(k) = 0$ if $k \notin N$. Set M can be represented similarly. These arrays can be stored compactly by means of a scheme similar to that suggested in Exercise 9.5. Assuming that assembler language routines are available for insertion and extraction of elements stored under the compact representation, write a program that determines whether $N \subseteq M$ for this representation. Assembler language programmers should write the appropriate assembler language routines.

11.28 (d) Given N, $M \in \{1, 2, \ldots, 100\}$ in the representation of Exercise 11.27, write routines that compute sets $N \cap M$ and $N \cup M$, also in the compact representation. Assembler language programmers will see that there are very good reasons here for writing the complete routines in assembler language.

11.29 (d) Given sets A, B, C, D such that $|D| = \frac{1}{2}|B|$, $|C| = \frac{1}{2}|B|$, $|B| = \frac{1}{2}|A|$. You are required to find $A \cap B \cap C \cap D$. How would you proceed? If you were required to find just $A \cap B \cap C$, would you compute the intersection as $(A \cap B) \cap C$ or as $A \cap (B \cap C)$? Provide as complete a justification of your answers as you can.

11.30 (d) Consider a symmetric list of n elements in which the first m elements, which are in lexicographic order, and the remaining $n - m$ elements, which are also in lexicographic order, represent two sets. Develop an algorithm (as a flowchart) that replaces the list by a new list representing the intersection of the two sets.

11.31 (d) Consider two symmetric lists A and B. The elements in each list are distinct, and they are in lexicographic order. Design a procedure that replaces list A with the set difference A - B and list B with the set difference B - A.

11.32 (d) A.11.6 can be improved by making FINISH an integer variable. FINISH is set to zero at the beginning of the loop on K, and set to L whenever A(L) and A(L + 1) are exchanged. Then, on exit from the loop on L, the return is taken if FINISH = 0. If FINISH $\neq$ 0, then only elements A(1), ..., A(FINISH) need be considered in the next iteration on L. Use this improvement and your procedure from Exercise 10.8 in a routine for sorting the elements of a list by means of exchange sort.

11.33 (d) Implement A.11.7 as a computer program.

11.34 (d) *Insertion sort* is an extremely simple method for sorting an array A(1), A(2), ..., A(N). We have a loop on I. When I = J, the keys in A(1), ..., A(J − 1) are in their proper order and the key held in A(J) is inserted among them in its proper position. Take I = 4, A(4) = 17, and A(1) = 15, A(2) = 19, A(3) = 72. The 17 is compared against

72, and 17 < 72 is found to hold. Hence 72 is moved into A(4), and 17 is compared against 19. Because 17 < 19 the 19 is moved into A(3). The comparison of 17 against 15 results in 17 > 15, and 17 is placed in its proper position A(2). When the insertion procedure has been carried out for I = 2,3,...,N, the array is sorted. Because of the simplicity of the procedure, insertion sort is very fast for small values of N. It has therefore been suggested that insertion sort should be used in A.11.7 instead of the partitioning procedure to sort a block K(LO),...,K(HI) whenever HI − LO is less than some fixed value M. A value of M = 6 is reasonable. Incorporate this modification in your program of Exercise 11.33. If the computer system to which you have access provides you with the means to measure execution times of programs accurately, find the optimal value of M by experiment.

11.35   (d)   A variant of the basic insertion sort of Exercise 11.34 is *binary insertion sort* in which the location into which A(J) is to go is found by binary search. Implement binary insertion sort as a computer program. (Note that binary insertion sort is slower than the basic insertion sort for small values of N. Therefore binary insertion sort would not serve the purposes of Exercise 11.34.)

11.36   (d)   Implement two-way merge sort as a computer program.

11.37   (d)   Implement two-way merge sort as a procedure for sorting elements of a linked list.

11.38   (d)   Assume that you are given a vector of integers in which the first k elements (k is unknown) are in ascending order. Devise a strategy for sorting the vector that makes use of this.

11.39   (d)   Consider A.5.12 and the sorting algorithms of Section 11d. Which are stable sorts?

11.40   (f)   Implement two-way natural merge sort as a program for sorting an array of N integers. Hint: In tape sorting tape C was first distributed to tapes A and B. Here we have an array A and a second array B. In the present context the keys that would be sent to tape A can be stored in locations B(1), B(2), ..., and the keys that would be sent to tape B in locations B(N), B(N−1), ...

11.41   (f)   Repeat Exercise 11.40, making use of queues this time.

11.42   (f)   Consider a sequence of n random numbers (taken from a set {1, 2, ..., 100}, say). What is the expected number of runs in the sequence? An approximate estimate is sufficient.

11.43   (f)   In a polyphase merge sort with four tapes the input tape contains 1201 runs. How are these runs to be distributed to the other three tapes?

11.44   (f)   Consider the initial distribution algorithm for polyphase merge as given in the text. Let $p = 3$. What will arrays N and NIL hold when the algorithm stops if the input tape contains: (i) 39 runs, (ii) 580 runs, (iii) 15,039 runs?

11.45 (f) For each of the three files of Exercise 11.44, how many merge passes will be required to sort it?

11.46 (f) Assume that the algorithm given in the text has been used to carry out the initial distribution of records for polyphase merge. What is the maximal number of subsequent merge passes in which dummy runs have to be taken into account?

11.47 (f) Determine experimentally the lengths of runs generated by replacement selection sort and thus verify the theoretical results stated in the text. Take $n = 25$. Use tables of random numbers to provide you with input data. Alternatively you may want to use a pseudorandom number generator. If neither is available, take a sequence of telephone numbers from a telephone directory and use the last two digits of these telephone numbers for your keys.

11.48 (f) Under some circumstances the following "natural" variant of replacement selection sort is an improvement over basic replacement selection. Instead of a single core area for holding records, have two areas A and B, each of size n. Let A be the current working area, let K be the key of a record that has just been written out on tape from A, and let K' be the key of the record that replaces it. Now, if $K' \geq K$, proceed as in the basic replacement selection sort. However, if $K' < K$, then the replacement record cannot become part of the run that is currently being generated, and the record is then placed in overflow storage area B, another record is read in, and the process iterated with K' being now the key of the new replacement record. When B has been completely filled, area A is emptied out on the magnetic tape in order of keys, and area B becomes the new working area with A serving as the new overflow area. Determine experimentally that the average length of a run generated by natural replacement selection is en, where e is the base of the natural logarithms. (With core storage for $2n$ records basic replacement selection can generate runs of length $4n$, which is considerably better than en. Therefore, in actual practice, the overflow area should not be in core, but on disk or a second magnetic tape.)

CHAPTER 12

Application Studies

12a. Precedence Grammars

The discussion of grammars and languages in Sections 4e and 5a was largely limited to the generation of sentences. In compiling computer programs one is concerned with the reverse process, that of recognizing a given string as a valid statement in the source language, and generating object code corresponding to this statement. To begin with, there must exist a method for reducing the source language input to the sentence symbol S, and for generating code while the reduction is being carried out. Further, to be of practical use, the method has to be reasonably fast, and no ambiguities can be tolerated. In Section 5 backward-deterministic parenthesis grammars were introduced as an example of unambiguous grammars, but it should be obvious that any language generated by a parenthesis grammar would be a rather awkward programming language. Fortunately there exist grammars that are unambiguous, are suitable for defining programming languages, and have fast reduction techniques to go with them. Backward-deterministic *precedence* grammars are the best known of such grammars; we shall use the abbreviation BDPG.

Readers may safely skip to the next paragraph should they find what now follows hard to take. Given $G = \langle V, V', P, S \rangle$ as in D.4.24, we are concerned with the reduction of a string $\sigma \in V^*$ to the single symbol S. Strings belonging to $(V \cup V')^*$ arise in intermediate stages of the reduction. Consider one such string, $\tau = \alpha x y \beta$, where x and y belong to $(V \cup V')$. If G is a BDPG, then one of four mutually exclusive possibilities must arise: (i) The combination xy cannot validly exist, implying that σ is not a member of $L(G)$; (ii) There exists a production rule $U \to \gamma xy\delta$, in which case we say that x and y have equal precedence, symbolized by $x \doteq y$, meaning that x and y are reduced in the same step; (iii) There exists a $w \in (V \cup V')$ such that $x \doteq w$ and $w \overset{*}{\Rightarrow} y\gamma$, in which case x is said to yield to y, symbolized $x \lessdot y$, meaning that y has to be reduced before x is; (iv) There exists a $w \in (V \cup V')$ such that $w \overset{*}{\Rightarrow} \gamma x$ and $w \doteq y$, or there exist $v, w \in (V \cup V')$ such that $v \doteq w$, $v \overset{*}{\Rightarrow} \gamma x$, $w \overset{*}{\Rightarrow} y\delta$ all hold, in which case x is said to take precedence over y, symbolized $x \gtrdot y$, meaning that x has to be reduced before y is.

To summarize, for all ordered pairs $\langle x, y \rangle \in (V \cup V')^2$, either x is unrelated to y, in which case xy is not a substring of any string arising in the reduction of any string $\sigma \in L(G)$, or exactly one of relations $x \doteq y$, $x \lessdot y$, or $x \gtrdot y$ holds. Note the absence of symmetry. For example, $x \doteq y$ does *not* imply $y \doteq x$, and $x \gtrdot y$ does not imply $y \lessdot x$.

The precedence relations are collected into an $n \times n$ array, where $n = |V \cup V'|$, and the array, which is called the *precedence matrix* for the grammar, is used to drive the compiler for $L(G)$. Consider a BDPG G_p, with the following productions:

$$\langle S \rangle ::= \langle Z \rangle$$
$$\langle Z \rangle ::= \langle Z \rangle \langle A \rangle \langle T \rangle \mid \langle T \rangle$$
$$\langle T \rangle ::= \langle Q \rangle$$
$$\langle Q \rangle ::= \langle Q \rangle \langle M \rangle \langle E \rangle \mid \langle E \rangle$$
$$\langle E \rangle ::= I \mid (\langle S \rangle)$$
$$\langle A \rangle ::= + \mid -$$
$$\langle M \rangle ::= * \mid /$$

The precedence matrix for G_p is shown in Table 12.1.

Despite appearances, this book is not about to become in its final chapter a text on the theory of programming languages and the construction of compilers. Our interest in BDPGs is motivated solely by the circumstance that they have generated two interesting practical problems that may be solved by the use of the Roy–Warshall algorithm (A.3.1).

The first problem relates to the construction of the precedence matrix. It is an easy matter to fill in the $\doteq$ entries, but the determination of the $\lessdot$ and $\gtrdot$ relations is rather involved. Define auxiliary matrices C and D as follows:

$c_{ij} = 1$ if $x_i \to x_j \delta$ is a production of G, and x_i and x_j are, respectively, the symbols corresponding to the ith row and jth column of the precedence matrix;

$c_{ij} = 0$ otherwise;

$d_{ij} = 1$ if $x_j \to \gamma x_i$ is a production of G, and x_j and x_i are, respectively, the symbols corresponding to the jth column and ith row of the precedence matrix;

$d_{ij} = 0$ otherwise.

Application of the Roy–Warshall algorithm to C and D produces C^* and D^*.

TABLE 12.1

PRECEDENCE MATRIX FOR G_p

		1 S	2 Z	3 T	4 Q	5 E	6 A	7 M	8 I	9 (	10)	11 +	12 −	13 *	14 /
1	S										≐				
2	Z					≐					⋗	⋖	⋖		
3	T				⋗						⋗	⋗	⋗		
4	Q				⋗	≐					⋗	⋗	⋗	⋖	⋖
5	E				⋗	⋗					⋗	⋗	⋗	⋗	⋗
6	A		≐	⋖	⋖				⋖	⋖					
7	M			≐					⋖	⋖					
8	I				⋗	⋗					⋗	⋗	⋗	⋗	⋗
9	(	≐	⋖	⋖	⋖	⋖			⋖	⋖					
10	)				⋗	⋗					⋗	⋗	⋗	⋗	⋗
11	+		⋗	⋗	⋗				⋗	⋗					
12	−		⋗	⋗	⋗				⋗	⋗					
13	*				⋗				⋗	⋗					
14	/				⋗				⋗	⋗					

We shall represent relations by their adjacency matrices in the sense of Section 3c. Let B be the adjacency matrix of the $\doteq$ relation. It can be found at once. Let K and R be adjacency matrices of the $\lessdot$ and $\gtrdot$ relations, respectively. It can be shown that

$$K = B \wedge C^*,$$
$$R = D^* \wedge (B \vee K),$$

where the Boolean matrix operations $\wedge$ and $\vee$ are as defined in the paragraph preceding A.3.1. A grammar is a BDPG only if $b_{ij} \wedge k_{ij} = 0$, $b_{ij} \wedge r_{ij} = 0$, and $k_{ij} \wedge r_{ij} = 0$ for all $i, j = 1, 2, \ldots, n$.

The second problem concerns reduction of storage requirements. For some, but not all, BDPGs it is possible to find functions

$$f: \ (V \cup V') \to N,$$
$$h: \ (V \cup V') \to N,$$

where N is the set of natural numbers, such that

$$x \ll y \text{ implies } f(x) < h(y),$$
$$x \doteq y \text{ implies } f(x) = h(y),$$
$$x \gg y \text{ implies } f(x) > h(y).$$

If such functions exist, and for many BDPGs they do, then the storage requirements can be reduced from n^2 locations for the precedence matrix to just $2n$ locations for two vectors F and H. These vectors are called *linearization functions* of the precedence matrix.

The algorithm for finding the linearization functions, if they exist, is very simple. We say that $x \leqq y$ if $x \ll y$ or $x \doteq y$, and $x \geqq y$ if $x \gg y$ or $x \doteq y$. Set up a digraph of $2n$ nodes $f_1, f_2, \ldots, f_n, h_1, h_2, \ldots, h_n$. Draw arcs $\langle f_i, h_j \rangle$ for all $\langle x_i, x_j \rangle \in (V \cup V')^2$ such that $x_i \geqq x_j$. Draw a sling on every node in the digraph. Now find the path matrix for this digraph using the Roy–Warshall algorithm. For $I = 1, 2, \ldots, n$, enter in $F(I)$ the number of nodes reachable from f_i, i.e., the number of ones in the row of the path matrix corresponding to f_i, and enter in $H(I)$ the number of nodes reachable from h_i. Then check that vectors F and H are valid linearization functions by testing the precedence matrix against them. If they are valid, then the precedence matrix may be discarded, and F and H take over its functions. If not, then a linearization does not exist.

Let us now look at how Table 12.1 was derived, and determine whether the precedence matrix for G_p can be linearized. Matrices B, C, and D are derived from the production rules of G_p, where the correspondence between rows and columns of the matrices and symbols of $V \cup V'$ is maintained as in Table 12.1, e.g., row and column 7 correspond to symbol M. These matrices are displayed in Figure 12.1.

Matrix B, and matrices K and R, which can now be rather easily computed from the matrices of Figure 12.1, define the precedence matrix of Table 12.1. From the precedence matrix it is in turn easy to derive vectors F and H. They are

$$S \; Z \; T \; Q \; E \; A \; M \; ; \; (\;) + \; - \; * \; /$$
$$F = [2 \; 4 \; 7 \; 8 \; 11 \; 4 \; 6 \; 11 \; 2 \; 11 \; 10 \; 10 \; 9 \; 9],$$
$$H = [2 \; 3 \; 4 \; 5 \; 6 \; 4 \; 8 \; 7 \; 7 \; 2 \; 5 \; 5 \; 9 \; 9]$$

A check of the entries in the precedence matrix against these vectors will show that F and H do indeed linearize the precedence matrix. For example, $M \doteq E$ and $f(M) = h(E) = 6$, $E \gg M$ and $f(E) > h(M)$, $M \ll I$ and $f(M) < h(I)$, etc. A word of caution. Consider the character sequence $I($. Although $f(I) > h(()$, it does not follow that $I \gg ($. The sequence $I($ is in fact illegal as a reference to the precedence matrix will show. Although a parser

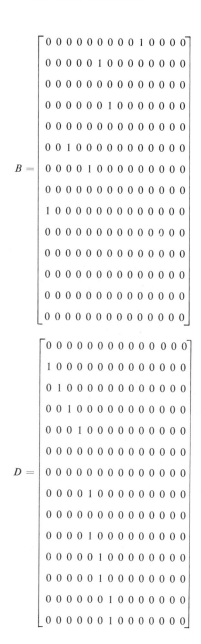

$$B = \begin{bmatrix} 0 & 0 & 0 & 0 & 0 & 0 & 0 & 0 & 1 & 0 & 0 & 0 & 0 \\ 0 & 0 & 0 & 0 & 0 & 1 & 0 & 0 & 0 & 0 & 0 & 0 & 0 \\ 0 & 0 & 0 & 0 & 0 & 0 & 0 & 0 & 0 & 0 & 0 & 0 & 0 \\ 0 & 0 & 0 & 0 & 0 & 0 & 1 & 0 & 0 & 0 & 0 & 0 & 0 \\ 0 & 0 & 0 & 0 & 0 & 0 & 0 & 0 & 0 & 0 & 0 & 0 & 0 \\ 0 & 0 & 1 & 0 & 0 & 0 & 0 & 0 & 0 & 0 & 0 & 0 & 0 \\ 0 & 0 & 0 & 0 & 1 & 0 & 0 & 0 & 0 & 0 & 0 & 0 & 0 \\ 0 & 0 & 0 & 0 & 0 & 0 & 0 & 0 & 0 & 0 & 0 & 0 & 0 \\ 1 & 0 & 0 & 0 & 0 & 0 & 0 & 0 & 0 & 0 & 0 & 0 & 0 \\ 0 & 0 & 0 & 0 & 0 & 0 & 0 & 0 & 0 & 0 & 0 & 0 & 0 \\ 0 & 0 & 0 & 0 & 0 & 0 & 0 & 0 & 0 & 0 & 0 & 0 & 0 \\ 0 & 0 & 0 & 0 & 0 & 0 & 0 & 0 & 0 & 0 & 0 & 0 & 0 \\ 0 & 0 & 0 & 0 & 0 & 0 & 0 & 0 & 0 & 0 & 0 & 0 & 0 \\ 0 & 0 & 0 & 0 & 0 & 0 & 0 & 0 & 0 & 0 & 0 & 0 & 0 \end{bmatrix} \quad C = \begin{bmatrix} 0 & 1 & 0 & 0 & 0 & 0 & 0 & 0 & 0 & 0 & 0 & 0 & 0 \\ 0 & 1 & 1 & 0 & 0 & 0 & 0 & 0 & 0 & 0 & 0 & 0 & 0 \\ 0 & 0 & 0 & 1 & 0 & 0 & 0 & 0 & 0 & 0 & 0 & 0 & 0 \\ 0 & 0 & 0 & 1 & 1 & 0 & 0 & 0 & 0 & 0 & 0 & 0 & 0 \\ 0 & 0 & 0 & 0 & 0 & 0 & 0 & 1 & 1 & 0 & 0 & 0 & 0 \\ 0 & 0 & 0 & 0 & 0 & 0 & 0 & 0 & 0 & 1 & 1 & 0 & 0 \\ 0 & 0 & 0 & 0 & 0 & 0 & 0 & 0 & 0 & 0 & 0 & 1 & 1 \\ 0 & 0 & 0 & 0 & 0 & 0 & 0 & 0 & 0 & 0 & 0 & 0 & 0 \\ 0 & 0 & 0 & 0 & 0 & 0 & 0 & 0 & 0 & 0 & 0 & 0 & 0 \\ 0 & 0 & 0 & 0 & 0 & 0 & 0 & 0 & 0 & 0 & 0 & 0 & 0 \\ 0 & 0 & 0 & 0 & 0 & 0 & 0 & 0 & 0 & 0 & 0 & 0 & 0 \\ 0 & 0 & 0 & 0 & 0 & 0 & 0 & 0 & 0 & 0 & 0 & 0 & 0 \\ 0 & 0 & 0 & 0 & 0 & 0 & 0 & 0 & 0 & 0 & 0 & 0 & 0 \\ 0 & 0 & 0 & 0 & 0 & 0 & 0 & 0 & 0 & 0 & 0 & 0 & 0 \end{bmatrix}$$

$$D = \begin{bmatrix} 0 & 0 & 0 & 0 & 0 & 0 & 0 & 0 & 0 & 0 & 0 & 0 & 0 \\ 1 & 0 & 0 & 0 & 0 & 0 & 0 & 0 & 0 & 0 & 0 & 0 & 0 \\ 0 & 1 & 0 & 0 & 0 & 0 & 0 & 0 & 0 & 0 & 0 & 0 & 0 \\ 0 & 0 & 1 & 0 & 0 & 0 & 0 & 0 & 0 & 0 & 0 & 0 & 0 \\ 0 & 0 & 0 & 1 & 0 & 0 & 0 & 0 & 0 & 0 & 0 & 0 & 0 \\ 0 & 0 & 0 & 0 & 0 & 0 & 0 & 0 & 0 & 0 & 0 & 0 & 0 \\ 0 & 0 & 0 & 0 & 0 & 0 & 0 & 0 & 0 & 0 & 0 & 0 & 0 \\ 0 & 0 & 0 & 0 & 1 & 0 & 0 & 0 & 0 & 0 & 0 & 0 & 0 \\ 0 & 0 & 0 & 0 & 0 & 0 & 0 & 0 & 0 & 0 & 0 & 0 & 0 \\ 0 & 0 & 0 & 0 & 1 & 0 & 0 & 0 & 0 & 0 & 0 & 0 & 0 \\ 0 & 0 & 0 & 0 & 0 & 1 & 0 & 0 & 0 & 0 & 0 & 0 & 0 \\ 0 & 0 & 0 & 0 & 0 & 1 & 0 & 0 & 0 & 0 & 0 & 0 & 0 \\ 0 & 0 & 0 & 0 & 0 & 0 & 1 & 0 & 0 & 0 & 0 & 0 & 0 \\ 0 & 0 & 0 & 0 & 0 & 0 & 1 & 0 & 0 & 0 & 0 & 0 & 0 \end{bmatrix}$$

Figure 12.1

based on linearization functions does not localize errors as well as a parser based on the precedence matrix, it does ultimately detect all errors.

An appropriate laboratory exercise for this section would be the writing of a program that implements the two techniques described above. The first part of the program would find the precedence matrix for a given precedence grammar. The input to this part would consist of matrices B, C, and D. Alternatively, the input could be the actual production rules, and the program would itself generate B, C, and D. The second part of the program would accept the precedence matrix as input, and attempt to linearize it. Vectors F and H can be found in any case, but in some instances the relations defined by the vectors could be inconsistent with the precedence relations. The program would have to check whether or not this is the case for the given grammar.

Economical use of storage should be an important concern in this exercise. It is not unusual to find a precedence grammar such that $|V \cup V'| > 100$. The matrix for computing vectors F and H would then have more than 40,000 elements. Assembler language programmers could utilize bit matrices along the lines suggested by Exercise 9.3. Others could incorporate sparse matrix techniques in their programs. In this instance three lists of ⟨*row number, column number*⟩ pairs would be appropriate to represent the elements having value 1 in matrices B, C, and D. Even if every element of the product matrix were a $\doteq$, $<$, or $>$, the total number of nonzero elements in the three matrices B, K, and R would still be only n^2, i.e., the ⟨*row number, column number*⟩ lists for these three matrices could never require more than $2n^2$ locations. Conventional storage of B, K, and R would require $3n^2$ locations.

In large problems the finding of F and H could become troublesome in that the $2n \times 2n$ matrix used in the computation would become increasingly dense during application of the Roy–Warshall algorithm. Here one solution is to generate the path matrix one row at a time using the generalized Dijkstra algorithm (A.6.6) with Q-semiring ⟨{0, 1}, $\vee$, $\wedge$, 0, 1⟩. A row can be discarded as soon as the number of ones in it has been determined.

12b. Radix Sorting

Many algorithms published in journals are presented in a rather cryptic manner. The main concepts are given, but there is little in way of explanation by means of examples, and even less may be said about implementation. The reader is expected to develop the details on one's own. Our suggestions regarding the implementation of a radix sort procedure will be made deliberately less explicit than they could be to prepare the reader for this uncomfortable reality.

Assume that we have a computer with a 36-bit word length, and we are given 1000 records, where each record consists of three computer words. Assume further that the first word of each record holds a 5-character key, and that the keys are one- to five-character sequences of the letters A, B, C, ..., Z, followed by trailing blanks to make up the five characters where necessary. The file is to be sorted into lexicographic order of the keys, where to start with we assume the lexicographic order to be defined by blank $\leq$ A $\leq$ B $\leq \cdots \leq$ Z. Moreover, the sort is to be stable.

We shall discuss the sorting in terms of the PDP-10 computer, which is a 36-bit machine. It uses ASCII 7-bit code for internal representation of character data. The relevant ASCII bit patterns are as follows:

$$
\begin{array}{cccc}
\text{blank} & 0 & 100 & 000 \\
\text{A} & 1 & 000 & 001 \\
\text{B} & 1 & 000 & 010 \\
\vdots & & \vdots & \vdots \\
\text{Y} & 1 & 011 & 001 \\
\text{Z} & 1 & 011 & 010
\end{array}
$$

Characters KEY followed by two blanks have the ASCII representation

1001011	1000101	1011001	0100000	0100000

The records can be sorted rather rapidly by means of radix sort. We note first that the PDP-10 instruction set contains an instruction that extracts any sequence of a given number of bits from any specified region in a given computer word. Consider an assembler language function subprogram that is referenced in a Fortran program by means of

INDEX (KEY, N)

where KEY refers to a key and N is 1, 2, 3, 4, or 5, depending on which character in KEY is to be looked at. Now, if we extract just the final five bits of the representation of any one of our characters, we get a decimal integer in the range 0–26. We shall make use of a further character, the opening square bracket [, with ASCII representation 1 011 011, or decimal representation 27 if only the final five bits are considered. Decimal integers 0, 1, 2, ..., 26, 27 can thus be made to represent the characters blank, A, B, ..., Z, [. However, since subscripting in all Fortran arrays starts with 1, it is more convenient to have INDEX return as its value the appropriate integer incremented by 1, i.e., a decimal integer in the range 1–28.

It does not take much experience in PDP-10 assembler language programming to write the function subprogram INDEX, and this single assembler language subprogram makes it possible to write the rest of the program for radix sort entirely in Fortran.

Let us investigate a version of radix sort that makes use of two sets of queues

$$IQ(1), IQ(2), \ldots, IQ(27);$$
$$JQ(1), JQ(2), \ldots, JQ(27).$$

The queues themselves are stored as linked lists in a list storage area of 4000 words, in which each list element consists of four computer words, three to hold the record, the fourth to hold a pointer to the next element in the queue.

We read the first record, apply INDEX to the key to determine an integer M that identifies the fifth character in the key, and push the record down in queue IQ(M). This procedure is applied to all records in turn as they are read in, until all 1000 records have been distributed over queues IQ. Next records are popped up from IQ(1) until it is empty, from IQ(2) until it is empty, and so forth, until all IQ queues have been emptied. This time INDEX is used to identify the fourth character of the key, and this character determines the JQ queue into which the record is to be pushed down. The JQ queues are next distributed over the IQ queues on the basis of the third character, and so forth, until the records have finally been distributed over the IQ queues on the basis of the first character. The records are then popped up from IQ(1), IQ(2), ..., IQ(27) and printed. The output is in alphabetical order of the keys.

An alternative design makes do with just the IQ queues. To begin with all records are read into the single queue IQ(1). In addition to IQ(1), IQ(2), ..., IQ(27), there is a queue IQ(28), which is initialized by pushing down 27 dummy records that all have identical keys, namely [[[[[. These dummy records act as separators. The following segment of a Fortran program conveys the gist of the approach.

```
      DO 20 KK = 1,5
      K = 6 - KK
      DO 10 J = 1,27
      CALL POP (IQ(28),RECORD)
10    CALL PUSH(IQ(J),RECORD)
      DO 20 J = 1,27
15    CALL POP (IQ(J),RECORD)
      M = INDEX(RECORD(1),K)
      CALL PUSH(IQ(M),RECORD)
      IF (M.NE.28) GO TO 15
20    CONTINUE
```

Of course, popping up the entire record and placing it into a three element vector RECORD, just to push this record down again at once, consumes much time unnecessarily. Instead of moving the records physically, the transfer of a record from one queue to another should be effected by a change of pointers alone.

Alphabetic order is an artificial concept. It is only by accident that we have settled on the order A, B, C, . . . , Z as a standard. Since everybody is familiar with alphabetic order, such order is convenient, but we could just as well choose a different order. The chain that determines the order produced by a sort is known as the *collating sequence* employed in the sort. The collating sequence for alphabetic sorting is blank $\leq$ A $\leq$ B $\leq$ C $\leq$ $\cdots$ $\leq$ Z. In the collating sequence blank $\leq$ E $\leq$ T $\leq$ A $\leq$ O $\leq$ N $\leq$ I $\leq$ R $\leq$ S $\leq$ H $\leq$ D $\leq$ L $\leq$ U $\leq$ C $\leq$ M $\leq$ P $\leq$ F $\leq$ Y $\leq$ W $\leq$ G $\leq$ B $\leq$ V $\leq$ J $\leq$ K $\leq$ Q $\leq$ X $\leq$ Z the letters are arranged according to the frequency they have in the English language. How could we sort the records into an order determined by this collating sequence? The solution is simple. In addition to the queue names IQ(1), IQ(2), . . . , IQ(27) we would have an array L(1), L(2), . . . , L(27) of pointers. Then, instead of distributing the records from queues IQ(1), IQ(2), . . . , IQ(27) in this order, we would distribute them in the order determined by the pointers, which for the collating sequence blank $\leq$ E $\leq$ T $\leq$ A $\leq$ $\cdots$ $\leq$ X $\leq$ Z would have to be IQ(1), IQ(6), IQ(21), IQ(2), . . . , IQ(25), IQ(27).

The project here is to design and implement an efficient radix sort routine that is reasonably general. The record size and the length of keys would be fixed for a particular application, but would vary from application to application. The preliminary input would consist of the record size, say between 1 and 20 words (or some equivalent number of bytes for IBM 360/370 machines), the key length, say between 5 and 15 characters (or between 4 and 16 characters for the IBM 360/370), and the collating sequence. The keys would consist entirely of capital letters and trailing blanks.

Assembler language programmers should write subprogram INDEX in assembler language. Others should simulate it. The simulation would be rather difficult in Standard Fortran, but in WATFIV or PL/I, which have character handling facilities, it should be quite easy.

12c. Symbolic Differentiation

Most of the early pioneers of computer science were numerical analysts, engineers, or physicists. So, when they realized that the capabilities of computers were not limited to numerical calculations, the nonnumeric applications that they turned to were still closely related to their primary interest in computing with numbers. Among the earliest examples of symbol manipulation by computers were programs for symbolic differentiation. Some were written as early as 1952. Since that time special programming languages have been developed for algebraic manipulation, and it is easy to perform symbolic differentiation if one has access to one or other of these languages. Consequently, the writing of a program for this task no longer has the practical value it had in 1952. Nevertheless, it is good experience in defining appropriate data representations and developing heuristics.

In contrast to numerical integration, which by and large produces very accurate results, the accuracy of results obtained by numerical differentiation leaves much to be desired. For this reason scientists and engineers requiring the derivative of a function often prefer to have it in symbolic form. However, as anyone who has had to find the derivative of a complicated function will readily testify, symbolic differentiation by pencil and paper is perhaps the most error prone activity in algebraic manipulation. Hence the interest in symbolic differentiation by computer.

Let $f(x)$ be a function of the variable x, and let $D(f(x))$ be its derivative with respect to x. The derivative is computed by application of substitution rules from the set given below until all occurrences of the differential operator D have been eliminated. This can be looked upon as a purely mechanical exercise in symbol manipulation, i.e., the application of the rules does not require one to be familiar with the differential calculus. The set of rules is sufficient to differentiate a Fortran arithmetic expression involving the standard operations of addition, subtraction, multiplication, division, and exponentiation, as well as the standard external functions for real valued arguments.

$$D(x) = 1;$$
$$D(a) = 0, \qquad \text{where } a \text{ is a constant or a variable other than } x;$$
$$D(-u) = -D(u);$$
$$D(u + v) = D(u) + D(v);$$
$$D(u - v) = D(u) - D(v);$$
$$D(u * v) = v*D(u) + u*D(v);$$
$$D(u/v) = (v*D(u) - u*D(v))/v**2;$$
$$D(u ** v) = v*D(u)*u**(v - 1) + \log_e(u)*D(v)*u**v;(u)/u;$$
$$D(\exp(u)) = \exp(u) * D(u);$$
$$D(\log_e(u)) = D(u)/u;$$
$$D(\log_{10}(u)) = \log_{10}(e) * D(u)/u = 0.43429448 * D$$
$$D(\sin(u)) = \cos(u) * D(u);$$
$$D(\cos(u)) = -\sin(u) * D(u);$$
$$D(\tanh(u)) = (1 - \tanh(u)**2) * D(u);$$
$$D(\arctan(u)) = D(u)/(1 + u**2).$$

Note that `SQRT(U)` is to be interpreted as $u ** 0.5$, and `ATAN2(U,V)` as arctan(u/v).

Consider a very simple example:

$$f(x) = \texttt{ALOG(X)} + \texttt{5.*X**2}$$

Then

$$
\begin{aligned}
D(f(x)) &= D(\texttt{ALOG(X)} + \texttt{5.*X**2}) \\
&= D(\texttt{ALOG(X)}) + D(\texttt{5.*X**2}) \\
&= D(\texttt{X})/\texttt{X} + D(\texttt{5.*X**2}) \\
&= \texttt{1/X} + D(\texttt{5.*X**2}) \\
&= \texttt{1/X} + \texttt{X**2*}D(\texttt{5.}) + \texttt{5.*}D(\texttt{X**2}) \\
&= \texttt{1/X} + \texttt{X**2*0} + \texttt{5.*}D(\texttt{X**2}) \\
&= \texttt{1/X} + \texttt{X**2*0} + \texttt{5.*(2*}D(\texttt{X})\texttt{*X**(2 - 1)} \\
&\quad + \texttt{ALOG(X)*}D(\texttt{2})\texttt{*X**2}) \\
&= \texttt{1/X} + \texttt{X**2*0} + \texttt{5.*(2*1*X**(2 - 1)} \\
&\quad + \texttt{ALOG(X)*}D(\texttt{2})\texttt{*X**2}) \\
&= \texttt{1/X} + \texttt{X**2*0} + \texttt{5.*(2*1*X**(2 - 1)} \\
&\quad + \texttt{ALOG(X)*0*X**2})
\end{aligned}
$$

The example shows that the designer of a computer program for symbolic differentiation faces several problems. First, definite priorities of the operators were implicitly assumed, e.g., it was assumed that `5.*X**2` is `5.*(X**2)` rather than `(5.*X)**2`. These priorities must be built into the program. Second, the number of symbols in the expression fluctuated while the derivative was being found, with the overall tendency being one of growth. Third, the final result is far from its simplest form, namely

$$D(f(x)) = \texttt{1/X} + \texttt{10.*X}$$

One approach to the solution of the first problem is to change the expression into an unambiguous form, and to generate the derivative in this same form. A priority table could be set up as in A.5.7, and a modified A.5.7 applied to the expression to produce the equivalent postfix form. With the exception of the unary minus, which can be identified by the technique suggested in Exercise 5.32, all arithmetic operators are binary, and all function symbols are unary operators. The modification of A.5.7 is then reasonably straightforward, as long as it is realized that parentheses cannot now be totally avoided. Their purpose would be to distinguish between unary and binary operators, and this purpose would be achieved by enclosing the single operands of the former in parentheses. The algorithm would, for example, transform

$$\texttt{-ALOG(2*X + Y) + X*Y*COS(X)}$$

into

$$\texttt{((2X*Y+)ALOG)-XY*(X)COS*+}$$

There remains the troublesome fact that the output of the original A.5.7 can be ambiguous. This problem was not discussed in Section 5e because there our concern was with principles rather than practical details. Here we are to deal with actual Fortran expressions, and the matter becomes relevant. Given the postfix expression $5.X2***$ it is not clear whether it stands for $5.*X**2$ or $5.**X*2$. The obvious solution is to let a single character represent the exponential operator, but this does not solve all problems. Does $(X)ALOG105*$ represent $ALOG(X)*105$ or $ALOG10(X)*5$? Does $X25*$ represent $X*25$ or $X2*5$? The solution is to regard all symbols as indivisible entities. A compiler breaks down source statements into character groups such that each character group is a single symbol. Each symbol can then be stored in a single computer word of its own. We shall not require our program to identify symbols because an algorithm for this task would be heavily dependent on character handling facilities not provided by Fortran. Instead, the input of a source statement will be done in such a manner that every symbol will occupy its own computer word. This can be achieved by reading in at run time a format that identifies the symbols in the expression to be differentiated, and using this format to read in the expression. For example

$$-ALOG(XY**2+X)$$

is described by the format

$$(A1,A4,A1,A2,A2,A1,A1,A1,A1)$$

We shall use the symbol $\uparrow$ in place of the Fortran exponential operator $**$. Differentiation of $f(x)$ now proceeds as follows:

$$
\begin{aligned}
D(f(x)) &= ((X)ALOG5.X2\uparrow*+)D \\
&= ((X)ALOG)D(5.X2\uparrow*)D+ \\
&= ((X)ALOG)DX2\uparrow(5.)D*5.(X2\uparrow)D*++ \\
&= \ldots \ldots \\
& \ldots \ldots \\
&= 1X/X2\uparrow0*5.21*X21-\uparrow*(X)ALOG0*X2\uparrow*+*+++
\end{aligned}
$$

The result can be converted back to infix, with the insertion of parentheses determined by the table of priorities.

The second problem is the fluctuation in space requirements. Moreover, the postfix expression undergoes internal changes. One way of coping with this is to store the postfix expression as a linear linked list, with each list element consisting of a symbol and a pointer. Structural changes can then be effected very easily, but it is not easy to decide what structural changes are to be made at each stage of the differentiation. This difficulty is removed by storing the expression to be differentiated as a tree. Figure 12.2 shows the tree of $f(x)$.

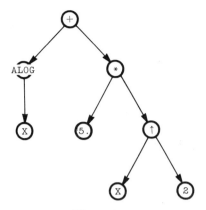

Figure 12.2

The derivative of the expression can now be found in post-order traversal of the tree. In this context the processing of a node is the determination of the derivative of the expression represented by the subtree rooted at the node. All terminal nodes are either variables or constants, and their derivatives can be determined directly $[D(x) = 1$ and $D(a) = 0]$. A nonterminal node s represents either a binary or a unary operation. In case the operation is binary, the subtree rooted at s represents $u \circ v$, where $\circ$ is the operation, and u and v are expressions represented by subtrees rooted at the left and right successors of s. In postorder traversal both the successors have been processed by the time processing of s begins, i.e., $D(u)$ and $D(v)$ are known. Since $D(u \circ v)$ depends on constants, on u and v, and on $D(u)$ and $D(v)$ alone, all the information required for the determination of $D(u \circ v)$ is available. If the operator is unary, then the subtree rooted at s represents a function of u, where u is represented by the subtree rooted at the single successor of s. In this case the derivative depends on constants, and on u and $D(u)$ alone. Again, since s is processed later than its successor, the determination of the derivative of the expression represented by the subtree rooted at s is always possible. The last node to be processed is the root of the entire tree, and the derivative of the entire expression is the result of this processing.

The data element representing a node in the tree has to be provided with two pointer fields in any case. They contain the left and right links. In the present context it becomes necessary to add a third pointer field, which will contain a pointer to the root of the tree representation of the derivative of the expression that the subtree rooted at the node in question represents. We shall call this the D-field of the node.

We shall assume that the substitution rules listed earlier in this section are stored in the program as trees. These trees will be called templates. Templates of three of the rules are shown in Figure 12.3. During construction

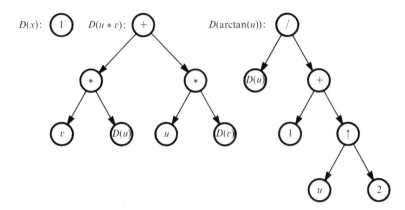

Figure 12.3

of the tree of $f(x)$ a pointer indicating the location of the appropriate template is inserted in the D-field of every node. When the tree is subjected to the postorder traversal, the processing of a node consists of making a copy of the template that the D-field of the node points to, inserting a pointer to this copy in the D-field, and traversing the copy. In this traversal every node that carries a label u, v, $D(u)$, or $D(v)$ is replaced by a copy of the tree that represents the expression denoted by the label, e.g., a node labeled $D(u)$ is replaced by the tree representation of $D(u)$.

Consider the multiplication node in Figure 12.2. The template for multi-

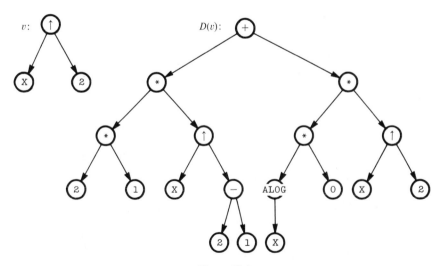

Figure 12.4

plication is one of the trees of Figure 12.3. Here *u* is a single node labeled 5., and *D(u)* is a single node labeled 0. The trees of *v* and *D(v)* are shown in Figure 12.4, and Figure 12.5 shows the tree representing the derivative of the expression rooted at the multiplication node after all appropriate substitutions have been made.

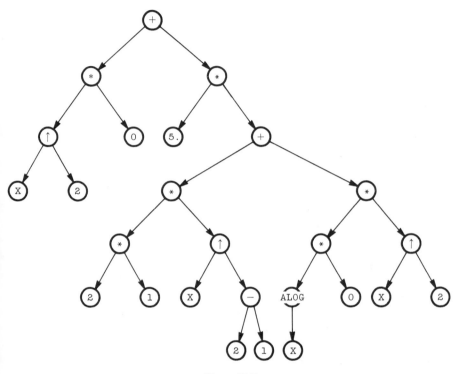

Figure 12.5

The only essential copying is that of the templates. For each node in the tree of $f(x)$ a copy of the template must be made. However, instead of replacing the nodes labeled *u*, *v*, *D(u)*, and *D(v)* in the template with actual copies of the trees representing these expressions, it suffices to replace the labels by pointers to these trees. The pointer structure originating from the template for the root of the tree of $f(x)$ defines a tree representation of $D(f(x))$. Actually, the pointer structure itself is not a tree, but an algorithm can be devised for traversal of the pointer structure that is equivalent to inorder traversal of the tree that the pointer structure represents. The purpose of the inorder traversal would be to generate $D(f(x))$ as an infix expression. Note that the infix expression may have to contain parentheses. A decision procedure regarding insertion of parentheses would have to be devised; it would be based on the table of priorities of the operators.

There remain the problems of simplification and output of the result. The trees that the program builds should be simplified where possible in order to reduce space requirements, improve the readability of the final expression for $D(f(x))$, and reduce the time required to evaluate this final expression for given values of x. Three simplification rules can be implemented very easily. They are:

$$u * 0 = 0,$$
$$u * 1 = u,$$
$$u + 0 = u.$$

Application of just these rules reduces the final expression for $D(\texttt{ALOG(X)}$ + 5.*X**2) derived above to the more acceptable

$$\texttt{1/X + 5.*(2*X**(2 - 1)).}$$

The program can be made to perform arithmetic on constants if input of constants in $f(x)$ is under I- or F-conversion, and integer and floating point constants are identified as such by means of markers. If the program contains such facilities, and the further simplification rule

$$u ** 1 = u$$

is introduced, then $D(f(x))$ can be reduced to $\texttt{1/X + 10.*X}$.

Further simplification rules can be devised, and their implementation in the program carried out. However, an alternative would be to implement just the three basic simplification rules, and to simplify the output of the program by hand. Simplification by hand may, however, introduce errors, and our primary motivation for symbolic differentiation by machine was precisely to prevent this from happening. A simple, but rather effective device for detecting errors is to evaluate both the $D(f(x))$ produced by the program and the simplified $D(f(x))$ for some value of x. If the two results differ, then there is an error. If not, then one has some reassurance that the simplification has been carried out correctly, but there remains a nonzero probability that the two expressions are not equivalent, the agreement in their values being due to chance. This probability becomes much smaller if the two expressions are evaluated with a different value of x, and the two results again agree.

The format for the output of $D(f(x))$ can be built up in an array by the program, and the write statement made to contain the name of this array in place of a reference to a format statement label. Let the name of this array be FMT. The symbols comprising $D(f(x))$ would be stored in another array, named OUTPUT, say. The write statement that makes use of the format defined by FMT must be independent of the form of $D(f(x))$. To achieve the independence, all numerical constants have to be of the same type. We shall assume that all integers are converted to reals prior to being placed in OUTPUT. The expression $1/X+10.*X$ has seven components. These components would be placed in the first seven elements of OUTPUT, with the integer 1 floated along the way. Then the format

$$(5X,F7.3,A1,A1,A1,F7.3,A1,A1)$$

say, would be built up in FMT, and the output statement

$$WRITE(6,FMT)(OUTPUT(K),K = 1,M)$$

with M having the value 7 would produce

$$1.000/X + 10.000*X$$

The project for this section is the implementation of a program for symbolic differentiation. Although a string processing language such as Snobol would be much more suitable for this task, it can be performed reasonably well using Fortran. The only unpleasant feature of a program written entirely in Fortran is that such a program cannot readily separate the input expression into its constituents. A technique was suggested above for coping with this problem. The more satisfactory solution of having the constituents of the expression identified by the program itself would require that a few subprograms be coded in assembler language. Assembler language programmers are urged to try this alternative.

12d. K-Trees and Cycles

Flowchart digraphs of computer programs were discussed in Chapter 7. Analysis of the flow of control in a program, be it for purposes of automatic flowcharting, or program segmentation, or code optimization, requires knowledge of the loop structure of the program. The loops are, of course, cycles in the flowchart digraph. In this section we shall consider an implementation of A.6.10, the K-tree algorithm for simple cycles of a digraph.

A K-tree formulation of the cycle problem gives rather easy answers to certain questions relating to program analysis. As discussed in Sections 7c and 7d, effective program analysis depends on the ability to identify final arcs of return paths in a flowchart digraph. Assume that a program contains a single entry point, and let the node corresponding to the entry point be numbered 1. Then, on account of Condition (c) of D.7.1, a single K-tree that represents the flowchart digraph of the entire program is created by A.6.8. It can be shown further, again on account of D.7.1, that every path defining a cycle in the K-tree has at least one node in common with a path that must exist in the K-tree at that time from the root (entry node) to the node corresponding to a terminal statement. Hence the set of final arcs of the cycles found by A.6.10 is a set of final arcs of the return paths of Section 7c.

Actually A.6.10 may remove the need for a set of final arcs altogether. Both the longest simple path from the entry node in general, and the longest simple path from the entry node to a node representing a terminal statement are generated by A.6.10 as a by-product. It is an easy matter to modify A.6.10 so that it outputs one or other of the paths.

Another advantage to using A.6.10 is that the K-tree retains some of the structure of the original digraph. Solution of layout problems for automatic flowcharting is therefore made easier.

However, if A.6.9 is used to separate a digraph into its strong components, and A.6.10 applied to the individual components, the above remarks lose much of their validity. If one is interested in the cycles for purposes of automatic flowcharting or suchlike, care must be taken that information relevant to the task is not destroyed during application of A.6.9 (or, to be more precise, during preprocessing of the K-tree on the basis of the data generated by A.6.9). One possibility is to save an intact copy of the K-tree of the entire flowchart digraph. Another is to create a representation of the condensation of the flowchart digraph. The most suitable approach would be determined by the nature of the task being undertaken.

Our first objective is to design an appropriate data representation for A.6.10, and in so doing we should consider the requirements of the ancillary algorithms A.6.8 and A.6.9 as well. The same representation should serve all three algorithms. We have to allow for the initial storage of the atomic K-trees, for merging atomic K-trees into composite K-trees, for separating strong components, and for easy pruning and grafting. The last requirement makes it imperative that we should be able to determine rapidly where the K-tree rooted at a particular node is located at any given time. Further, we should be able to prune it away from its current location and graft it on at its new location with very little effort. Since pruning and grafting is expected to be the dominant activity, we should be willing to accept the design we think best for this activity, even though it may not be the most suitable for some other activity. Another basic requirement is that we must be able to tell whether an atomic K-tree is still in the counterpart of list L of A.6.8, or has been incorporated into a composite K-tree.

Let N be the number of nodes and M the number of arcs in the digraph to be processed. One suitable representation consists of an integer vector POINT of N elements, and a 3-column integer matrix TREE of M rows. Figure 12.6 shows the representation of the atomic trees that are ultimately collected into the tree of Figure 6.6. The absolute value of POINT(I) indicates the row in TREE at which storage of the terminal nodes of the atomic tree of node I

	POINT
1	−1
2	−2
3	−5
4	−7
5	−8
6	0
7	−10
8	−13

	TREE		
1	2	0	0
2	3	0	3
3	7	0	4
4	8	0	0
5	4	0	6
6	7	0	0
7	5	0	0
8	3	0	9
9	6	0	0
10	4	0	11
11	5	0	12
12	6	0	0
13	1	0	14
14	7	0	0

Figure 12.6

begins. These nodes are stored consecutively in column 1 of TREE. In column 3 of TREE are links that chain together all the terminal nodes of the one atomic tree. The structure representing the atomic tree of node 2 is shown schematically in Figure 12.7.

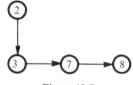

Figure 12.7

Initially all values in POINT are negative or zero. A negative POINT(I) indicates that the atomic K-tree of node I has not yet been incorporated into a composite K-tree; POINT(I) = 0 tells that there is no proper atomic tree of I, i.e., that no arcs originate from node I. One good feature of this representation is that column 1 of TREE remains unchanged throughout the processing of the digraph, and that changes to column 3 are confined to the section of the process that deals with the separation of the digraph into strong components.

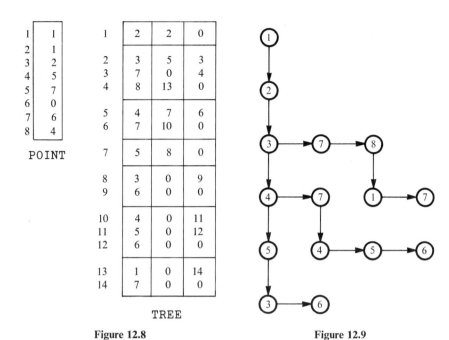

	POINT
1	1
2	1
3	2
4	5
5	7
6	0
7	6
8	4

	TREE		
1	2	2	0
2	3	5	3
3	7	0	4
4	8	13	0
5	4	7	6
6	7	10	0
7	5	8	0
8	3	0	9
9	6	0	0
10	4	0	11
11	5	0	12
12	6	0	0
13	1	0	14
14	7	0	0

Figure 12.8 **Figure 12.9**

Figure 12.8 shows POINT and TREE after A.6.8 has finished building the tree. Figure 12.9 gives a schematic representation of the composite K-tree. The downward links correspond to entries in column 2 of TREE, and the horizontal links to entries in column 3. Consider POINT(2). It points to the row representing nonterminal node 2, namely row 1. TREE(1,2) contains a pointer to the row (row 2) in which the first successor of node 2 is stored. Rows 2, 3, and 4 correspond to the three successors of node 2. These successors are linked by pointers in TREE(2,3) and TREE(3,3).

On the basis of the strong component numbers computed by A.6.9 it is possible to remove from the K-tree arcs that do not belong to any cycle. The removal of such arcs results in changes to columns 2 and 3 of TREE, and in our example the original K-tree is split in two. Five arcs are removed, corresponding to rows 2, 3, 9, 12, and 14 of TREE. Although the entries in column 1 of these rows are not deleted, changes in the pointers make these rows inaccessible. Figure 12.10 shows POINT and TREE after the removal of the arcs, and the two K-trees are displayed as Figure 12.11. Because there are now two K-trees, the roots of these trees have to be explicitly designated. This is the purpose of vector ROOTS in Figure 12.10. Neither of the roots is represented in TREE, but POINT(1) and POINT(3) contain the downward pointers associated with the roots.

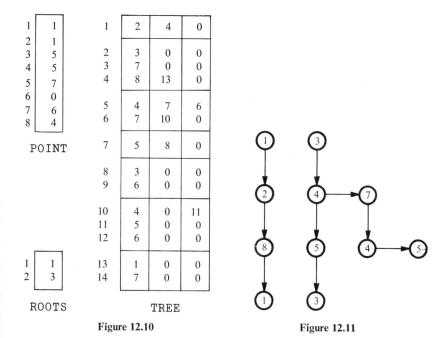

POINT

1	1
2	1
3	5
4	5
5	7
6	0
7	6
8	4

ROOTS

1	1
2	3

TREE

1	2	4	0
2	3	0	0
3	7	0	0
4	8	13	0
5	4	7	6
6	7	10	0
7	5	8	0
8	3	0	0
9	6	0	0
10	4	0	11
11	5	0	0
12	6	0	0
13	1	0	0
14	7	0	0

Figure 12.10

Figure 12.11

The primary activity in A.6.10 is pruning and grafting. Note now what happens when the subtree rooted at nonterminal node 4 is pruned away from its location as shown in Figure 12.11, and attached to the terminal node 4, which now becomes a nonterminal node. This process requires just two pointer changes in TREE, and one in POINT. Figure 12.12 shows the configuration after the pruning and grafting operation has been carried out. The arrows indicate where the pointer changes have been made.

The algorithm requires an integer vector PATH of N + 1 elements in which it stores the sequence of nodes defining the path from the root of the K-tree being traversed to the node that has currently been reached in the traversal of this K-tree. This vector functions somewhat like a stack in that it provides the information necessary to back up in the tree whenever this is called for in the traversal. In addition, output of new cycles would be from this vector. Let us consider what happens when a terminal node J is reached in the traversal. First it has to be determined whether there is a nonterminal node J on the path from the root of the tree to this terminal node. If there is, then the node sequence (J , . . . , J) in PATH defines a cycle. However, if a node on the path from the root to the nonterminal J is marked, then the cycle has already been found before.

A logical vector MARKED of N elements would be a suitable instrument for the marking of nodes. All elements of MARKED would be initialized to

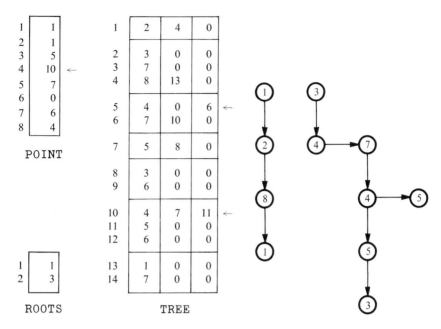

Figure 12.12

.FALSE., and MARKED(I) would be set to .TRUE. when the subtree rooted at node I undergoes pruning and grafting. Determination of whether there is a nonterminal node J in PATH could be made with the aid of another vector, which we shall call ONPATH. This vector would have to be maintained in such a way that ONPATH(J) = K would at all times imply PATH(K) = J, where J is nonterminal, but ONPATH(J) = 0 would imply that J is not on the path, except as the terminal node.

Returning to the discussion of what happens when terminal node J is reached, A.6.10 first determines the value of ONPATH(J). If it is zero, then there can be no cycle, and pruning and grafting would take place. Otherwise, assuming that the value of ONPATH(J) is M, the values of PATH(1), PATH(2),...,PATH(M) are taken in turn, and used as subscripts for gaining access to corresponding elements in MARKED. If all M elements of MARKED that are examined are found to be .FALSE., then output of (J,...,J) takes place. Otherwise output of the cycle is suppressed.

The algorithm may give a poor performance for certain types of digraphs, an example of which is shown in Figure 12.13. In this digraph cycles (s, t, v, s) and (s, u, v, t) would each be traversed 2^{k-1} times. This number of traversals can be sharply reduced by a modification of the algorithm. Assume that a subtree rooted at node J has just been traversed, and that the arc terminating

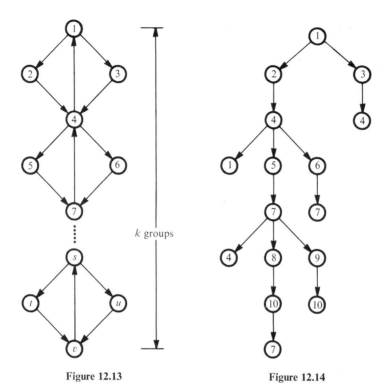

Figure 12.13   **Figure 12.14**

at node J is $\langle$I,J$\rangle$. Arc $\langle$I,J$\rangle$ is deleted from the K-tree provided there exists no path of the form (M, . . . ,I,J, . . . ,M) at this time.

Figure 12.14 shows the K-tree corresponding to the digraph of Figure 12.13 for $k = 3$. In the traversal of the K-tree cycles (1, 2, 4, 1), (4, 5, 7, 4), and (7, 8, 10, 7) are generated before any pruning and grafting takes place. Now, on return to node 8, the conditions are right for deleting arc $\langle 7, 8 \rangle$. Traversal then continues along arcs $\langle 7, 9 \rangle$ and $\langle 9, 10 \rangle$. Note that deletion of arc $\langle 7, 8 \rangle$ has not affected the nature of nonterminal nodes 8 and 10. Hence, on reaching terminal node 10, the subtree rooted at the nonterminal node 10, which consists of just the one arc $\langle 10, 7 \rangle$, is pruned and grafted in the normal fashion. In later stages of the traversal arcs $\langle 7, 9 \rangle$, $\langle 4, 5 \rangle$, and $\langle 4, 6 \rangle$ are deleted.

The exercises that will be suggested here indicate just the beginning of an open ended project that can be taken to any lengths one likes. The first task consists of coming to a thorough understanding of the structure of A.6.9, and hence of adapting the algorithm to the representation of K-trees as described above. For example, a separate vector specifying the right neighbor function N is redundant with this representation in that the pointers in column 3 of TREE constitute an equivalent specification.

The purpose of A.6.9 in our context is to indicate arcs that do not belong to cycles so that these arcs can be deleted from the K-tree. This activity is not specified in A.6.9, the implication there being that such arcs would be removed after A.6.9 has come to a halt. Greater efficiency would result if these arcs were deleted in the same traversal of the K-tree in which the strong component numbers (the elements of vector S) are computed. This traversal can in fact be carried out while the K-tree is being built, i.e., A.6.8 and A.6.9 can be combined into a single algorithm.

It can be argued, however, that the combining of the algorithms would result in loss of clarity, that consequently the likelihood of programming errors in the implementation would be very high, and that debugging of the program would be made difficult by its complexity. As a result there would be no positive real gain in efficiency: a small gain in execution time would be bought at great cost in programming time. The argument is valid, and too much combining is not recommended. It is quite in order to combine A.6.8 and A.6.9 into a single algorithm, but the removal of the arcs that do not belong to cycles should be made a separate process, to be carried out after the strong component numbers have been computed. The second task, then, is the design and implementation of this sequence of processes.

With the preprocessing out of the way, the third task is the implementation of A.6.10 as the third process in the sequence. The modification suggested above to reduce the number of times certain cycles are traversed should be incorporated in the algorithm. The complete program should then be applied to flowchart digraphs derived from actual computer programs.

After this one is on one's own. One possibility would be to design and implement an automatic flowchart generator. But be warned. This is a genuine research project, it is much more difficult than it looks, and it even looks difficult. Relevant references are listed at the end of Chapter 7.

12e. Scheduling Networks

Critical path scheduling, an important activity in operations research, was discussed in Sections 6c and 6d. There it was pointed out that a network for critical path scheduling is usually constructed from a precedence table of activities. Our purpose here is to devise an algorithm for the construction of networks. We are interested in developing a data representation that not only makes the application of the critical path method relatively easy, but can also serve as a suitable input to a routine for drawing the network. Not all pictures are worth a thousand words, but some are worth even more, and in hard currency at that. This is one such instance.

With a large set of activities the original precedence relations are likely to be incomplete, or they may turn out to be inconsistent, i.e., to imply cycles in the network. Debugging then is next to impossible without a drawing of the network. Translation of the precedence relations into the drawing is usually done by hand, and the costs in time may be considerable, particularly if the process has to be put through several iterations before all the bugs have been removed. Automation would save time. Moreover, it is possible that the computer program would generate a network with fewer dummy activities than would otherwise be the case.

There will be no formal specification of an algorithm for deriving a digraph representation from the precedence relations. By going through an example we shall hint at an algorithm, but the detailed specification of this algorithm is left to the reader. Table 12.2 is the input.

From Table 12.2 it is easy to determine the activities with no predecessors. They are the activities not listed anywhere in the immediate successor column, namely a, i, and j. The root of a tree is drawn, and arcs labeled a, i, and j suspended from the root. Further construction of the tree then proceeds in a manner very similar to the construction of a K-tree. Figure 12.15 shows the complete tree, which contains all the information of Table 12.2. The nodes have been given identifying numbers for reference purposes. This tree will be turned into a drawing of the scheduling network by systematic elimination of arcs that carry the same label until all arcs in the structure have unique labels.

TABLE 12.2

Activity	Immediate successors
a	b, d
b	c, e
c	g
d	f, h
e	f, h
f	g
g	o
h	—
i	b, d, l, m, n
j	k
k	m, n
l	o
m	o
n	—
o	—

Note in Figure 12.15 that arcs labeled f and h and originating from node 6 lead to terminal nodes, and that arcs labeled f and h are suspended from node 14 as well. We eliminate node 6 with its subtree, i.e., arcs $\langle 6, 15 \rangle$ and

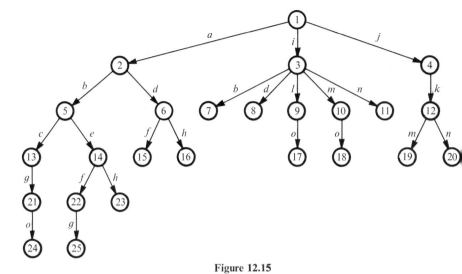

Figure 12.15

⟨6, 16⟩, and shift arc *d* around so that it becomes ⟨2, 14⟩ instead of ⟨2, 6⟩.
Further, arcs *b* and *d* are suspended from both nodes 2 and 3, and both of
these arcs suspended at node 3 lead to terminal nodes. We wish to eliminate
arcs ⟨3, 7⟩ and ⟨3, 8⟩. Arc *i* cannot be changed from ⟨1, 3⟩ into ⟨1, 2⟩
because there already exists an arc ⟨1, 2⟩. In this instance dummy activity
⟨3, 2⟩ has to be introduced. After these two changes the structure has become
as shown in Figure 12.16.

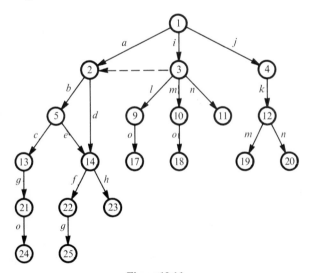

Figure 12.16

The next two steps are: (i) Remove arc ⟨22, 25⟩, and change arc ⟨14, 22⟩ into ⟨14, 13⟩. (ii) Remove ⟨9, 17⟩, and change arc ⟨3, 9⟩ into ⟨3, 21⟩. To make the drawing of ⟨3, 21⟩ easier, rotate the substructure suspended from node 2 so that nodes 13 and 14 change places. The structure after these two steps is shown in Figure 12.17.

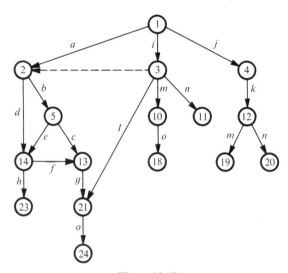

Figure 12.17

One of the two arcs labeled *o* should be removed next. We cannot remove ⟨10, 18⟩ and change ⟨3, 10⟩ into ⟨3, 21⟩ because the structure already contains an arc ⟨3, 21⟩. However, arcs *m* and *n* are also duplicated. This permits us to draw dummy activity ⟨3, 12⟩, transfer the point of attachment of arc *o* from node 10 to node 19 so that arc ⟨10, 18⟩ becomes arc ⟨19, 18⟩, and remove arcs ⟨3, 10⟩ and ⟨3, 11⟩. The next step is to delete arc ⟨19, 18⟩, and change arc *m* from ⟨12, 19⟩ into ⟨12, 21⟩. The final step is to coalesce the remaining three terminal nodes into a single node. Construction of the network is now complete, with the result shown in Figure 12.18.

The first task in the project for this section is to devise a precise specification of the algorithm for generating a network from a precedence table. This algorithm is then to be implemented as a computer program. Table 12.2 is one of immediate successors, but in the early stages of planning the setting up of such a table is difficult. Instead of a table of *immediate* successors one may have at best a table in which each activity is provided with a set of successors, and this set includes all activities that will ultimately be identified as immediate successors, but, in addition, may include successors that will turn out not to

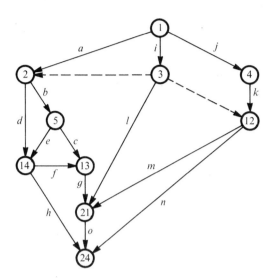

Figure 12.18

be immediate. Table 12.3 is an example. The network construction algorithm must generate the same network irrespective of whether the input is Table 12.2 or Table 12.3, say.

The design of a suitable data representation for the network is an important part of the implementation of the algorithm. The representation should be such that the network is easily put into topological order, and the computation of floats performed efficiently. Still, our main concern should be that the representation be indicative of the geometry of the network, so that a drawing can be created directly from the representation.

It is important to distinguish between two purposes for drawing a network. First, during the initial stages of the analysis, the drawing helps to discover errors in the formulation of the problem. This is the diagnostic purpose. Second, after all floats have been found, a drawing of the network, with the floats superimposed on the drawing, is a compact and forcible means of communicating the results. We shall call this the display purpose.

The most attractive display would be provided by a plotter. If a plotter is not available, a program that uses a line printer to draw the network could be written. As regards the diagnostic purpose, one is not normally interested in producing hard copies of the drawings. Here the primary concern is to get through a number of iterations of the process in as short a time as possible, and the best approach would be to design an interactive program. The drawings could be projected on the screen of a cathode-ray-tube terminal if such a device is available.

TABLE 12.3

Activity	Successors
a	*b, c, d, g*
b	*c, e, h*
c	*g, o*
d	*f, g, h*
e	*f, h*
f	*g*
g	*o*
h	—
i	*b, d, l, m, n*
j	*k, m, n*
k	*m, n*
l	*o*
m	*o*
n	—
o	—

How far the project can be carried will be determined by one's inclination and expertise, and by available resources. The drawing of a large network is in an entirely different category from the drawing of a small network because of the same segmentation problems that make automatic flowcharting so difficult. The design of a program that produces the drawing of a small scheduling network as output from a printer is fairly difficult, but it is easy compared to the implementation of an interactive system centered on a cathode-ray-tube terminal for the initial design and debugging of a large network.

Notes

For background on compiling in general, and precedence grammars in particular, see [Gr71]; [Wi66] is an excellent source of large grammars on which to test your implementations of the algorithms of Section 12a. Our algorithm for the construction of precedence matrices is due to Martin [Ma68]; the technique for constructing linear precedence functions was discovered by Bell [Be69b]. The literature on precedence grammars is surveyed in [Gr71]. For more recent theoretical investigations relating to precedence grammars see [Le70, Ah72, Mc72].

Symbol manipulation in general is surveyed in [To71, Ba72d]; simplification techniques are reviewed in [Mo71, Fi73]. In Section 12c it is pointed out that two expressions may be tested for equivalence by evaluating them with identical sets of parameter values. The very important [Ma71c] contains an analysis of the reliability of this approach. An algorithm for copying trees can be found in [Li73]. It is appropriate for the copying of the templates defined in the text.

The procedure outlined in Section 12e for the construction of scheduling networks is new. For related work see [Ho67, Fi68, Sc68, Co73]. An algorithm for drawing *planar* networks can be found in [Ho71].

Figure 12.13 derives from [Ta73]. Otherwise there are no references relating to Sections 12b and 12d.

Solutions to Selected Exercises

Chapter 1

1.1   Only (iv) presents a clear case of equality. In (ii) there is equality if members of B are interpreted as binary numbers, and if it is assumed that there is no basic difference between binary and decimal numbers. If, however, the elements are interpreted as symbols; i.e., if the base of the number system is considered an important distinguishing feature, then A and B are not equal.

1.2   The basis of the inductive proof is the same as part (i) of the proof in the text. For the induction step assume that $\mathscr{P}(A)$ has 2^{n-1} members when A has $n-1$ members, and consider a set $B = A \cup \{x\}$. $\mathscr{P}(B)$ has all elements of $\mathscr{P}(A)$ and, in addition, each element C of $\mathscr{P}(A)$ gives rise to a new element $C \cup \{x\}$. Hence $\mathscr{P}(B)$ has $2^{n-1} + 2^{n-1} = 2^n$ elements.

1.5   Let $a \in A \cap C$. Then $a \in A$ and $a \in C$. But $a \in A$ implies $a \in B$ (since $A \subseteq B$) and, similarly, $a \in C$ implies $a \in D$. In other words, $a \in B \cap D$. Since $a \in A \cap C$ implies $a \in B \cap D$, $A \cap C \subseteq B \cap D$.

1.9   See Section 11d for hints.

1.11   Let $x \in A$. Since $\mathscr{X}$ and $\mathscr{Y}$ are partitions, there exist precisely one $X_i \in \mathscr{X}$ such that $x \in X_i$ and precisely one $Y_j \in \mathscr{Y}$ such that $x \in Y_j$. Then $x \in X_i \cap Y_j$; i.e., each member of A is a member of some set in $\mathscr{Z}$. Next assume $x \in X_i \cap Y_j$ and $x \in X_m \cap Y_n$. Then $x \in X_i$ and $x \in X_m$, implying $i = m$, and $x \in Y_j$ and $x \in Y_n$, implying $j = n$. Hence the sets comprising $\mathscr{Z}$ are disjoint.

1.13   Example 2 of Th.1.4 gives proof of $\overline{A_1 \cap A_2} = \overline{A_1} \cup \overline{A_2}$. The proof is completed by induction. Take $J = \{1, 2, \ldots, n-1\}$ and assume $\overline{\bigcap_{j\in J} A_j} = \bigcup_{j\in J} \overline{A_j}$. Then

$$\overline{(\bigcap_{j\in J} A_j) \cap A_n} = \overline{(\bigcap_{j\in J} A_j)} \cup \overline{A_n}$$

$$= (\bigcup_{j\in J} \overline{A_j}) \cup \overline{A_n}$$

$$= \bigcup_{i\in I} \overline{A_i}$$

The proof of the other part is similar.

1.15   No. If $A = U$, then $\{A, \overline{A}\} = \{U, \varnothing\}$. If $A = \varnothing$, then $\varnothing \in \{A, \overline{A}\}$. By D.1.9, a partition may not have $\varnothing$ for a member. (However, in some circumstances it may be convenient to change D.1.9 to allow partitions having null sets for members.)

1.20   (i) By D.1.11 and D.1.12, $A + A = (A \cap \overline{A}) \cup (A \cap \overline{A})$ and hence, by Th.1.4, $A + A = \varnothing \cup \varnothing$. But $\varnothing \cup \varnothing$ has no members. It is therefore identical with $\varnothing$.
   (ii) Since $\varnothing$ has no members, $x \in A + \varnothing$ if and only if $x \in A$.
   (iii) By Part (i) of Exercise 1.19,

$$A + B = (A \cup B) \cap (\overline{A} \cup \overline{B}) \text{ and } \overline{A} + \overline{B} = (\overline{A} \cup \overline{B}) \cap (\overline{\overline{A}} \cup \overline{\overline{B}}).$$

But $x \in S$ if and only if $x \notin \overline{S}$, and $x \notin \overline{S}$ if and only if $x \in \overline{\overline{S}}$. Hence $S = \overline{\overline{S}}$. Consequently $\overline{A} + \overline{B} = (\overline{A} \cup \overline{B}) \cap (A \cup B)$, and it is an easy matter to prove $(\overline{A} \cup \overline{B}) \cap (A \cup B) = (A \cup B) \cap (\overline{A} \cup \overline{B})$.
   (iv) The defining formula of $A + B$ (see the example of D.1.12) shows that we can write $(A + B) + B$ as $A + (B + B)$. But $B + B = \varnothing$. Hence $(A + B) + B = A + \varnothing = A$.

1.22 $X = X \cap U$ (Th.1.5, Part 4B)
                                      $= X \cap (A \cup \overline{A})$ (5A)
                                      $= (X \cap A) \cup (X \cap \overline{A})$ (3B)

Similarly, $Y = (Y \cap A) \cup (Y \cap \overline{A})$. Consequently, if $X \cap A = Y \cap A$ and $X \cap \overline{A} = Y \cap \overline{A}$, then $X = Y$.

1.23   By Th.1.6 this is equivalent to proving that $A = A \cap B$ and $C = C \cap D$ imply $A \cap C = (A \cap C) \cap (B \cap D)$. Assuming $A = A \cap B$ and $C = C \cap D$, we have $A \cap C = (A \cap B) \cap (C \cap D)$. Rearrangement gives $A \cap C = (A \cap C) \cap (B \cap D)$.

1.26   See A.11.5 for hints regarding the modification. Since $M + N = (M \cup N) - (M \cap N)$, it is not necessary to have a routine that finds $M + N$ directly. A first call to our routine gives $M \cup N$ and $M \cap N$. A second call, with $M \cup N$ and $M \cap N$ as arguments, gives $(M \cup N) - (M \cap N)$.

1.27   Assuming the principle of duality, we need only prove Part 1 of the theorem. Assume $a \oplus b = a$ for all a. Then, in particular, $0 \oplus b = 0$. But

$$0 \oplus b = b \oplus 0   \quad (1A)$$
$$= b.   \quad (4A)$$

Hence $b = 0$.

1.28   (ii) $a \oplus (a * b) = (a * 1) \oplus (a * b)$ (4B)
                                      $= a * (1 \oplus b)$ (3B)
                                      $= a * 1$ (1A and Part 2 of Th.1.10)
                                      $= a.$ (4B)

1.29   For the proof that $x * z = y * z$ and $x * z' = y * z'$ imply $x = y$ use the method of Exercise 1.22. Then

$$(a \oplus (b \oplus c)) * a = a * (a \oplus (b \oplus c))   \quad (1B)$$
$$= a;   \quad (\text{Th.1.11, Part 3})$$

$$((a \oplus b) \oplus c) * a = a * ((a \oplus b) \oplus c) \qquad \text{(1B)}$$
$$= (a * (a \oplus b)) \oplus (a * c) \qquad \text{(3B)}$$
$$= a \oplus (a * c) \qquad \text{(Th.1.11, Part 3)}$$
$$= a; \qquad \text{(Th.1.10, Part 3)}$$
$$(a \oplus (b \oplus c)) * a' = (a' * a) \oplus (a' * (b \oplus c)) \qquad \text{(1B, 3B)}$$
$$= a' * (b \oplus c) \qquad \text{(1B, 5B, 1A, 4A)}$$
$$= (a' * b) \oplus (a' * c) \qquad \text{(3B)}$$
$$= (a' * (b \oplus a)) \oplus (a' * c) \qquad \text{(4A, 5B, 1B, 3B)}$$
$$= ((a \oplus b) \oplus c) * a'. \qquad \text{(1A, 3B, 1B)}$$

$a * (b * c) = (a * b) * c$ is given by the principle of duality. At this point, however, the more observant readers might have noticed that the "proof" is invalid. Our proof of Part 3 of Th.1.10 (Exercise 1.28) makes use of Part 2 of Th.1.10, and this in turn uses Axiom 2A. Hence we have to prove $a \oplus 1 = 1$ again without resorting to Axiom 2A:

$$a \oplus 1 = (a \oplus 1) * 1 \qquad \text{(4B)}$$
$$= (a \oplus 1) * (a \oplus a') \qquad \text{(5A)}$$
$$= a \oplus (1 * a') \qquad \text{(3A)}$$
$$= a \oplus a' \qquad \text{(1B, 4B)}$$
$$= 1. \qquad \text{(5A)}$$

1.33 The Venn diagrams should suggest that

$$(W \cup X) + (Y \cup Z) \subseteq (W + Y) \cup (X + Z).$$

Show that this condition is equivalent to

$$((W \cup X) + (Y \cup Z)) \cap \overline{(W + Y) \cup (X + Z)} = \varnothing.$$

The rest is tedious algebraic manipulation. (See also Exercise 2.18.)

1.37 Under this definition $\langle a, a, a \rangle = \{\{a\}\} = \langle a, a \rangle$.

1.41 There are 26 letters from which to choose the first character. The rest of the name is an n-sample of a set of 36 elements, where $n \in \{0, 1, \ldots, 5\}$. Hence the number of different names is $26 \sum_{i=0}^{5} 36^i = 1,617,038,306$.

1.45 There are $\frac{1}{2}(n - 1)!$ rosary permutations of n elements.

1.48 The number of such samples is 3×2^5. (What is the general formula, i.e., how many m-samples of a set of n elements are there such that no two adjoining elements in a sample are identical?)

1.50 Let us be given a set of integers stored as array N, say $N = \langle 2, 3, 9, 11, 16 \rangle$. We are required to find M-samples of this set as array SAMPLE. Instead of dealing with N itself, we can find—in array REF—M-samples of the set of subscripts $\{1, 2, 3, 4, 5\}$. Elements of REF are used to extract those elements of N that make up SAMPLE. Thus, if we require 3-samples, we generate, in turn, $\langle 1, 1, 1 \rangle$, $\langle 1, 1, 2 \rangle$, $\ldots$, $\langle 2, 5, 3 \rangle$, $\ldots$, $\langle 5, 5, 5 \rangle$ in REF, and in each instance find the corresponding 3-sample $\langle 2, 2, 2 \rangle$, $\langle 2, 2, 3 \rangle$, $\ldots$, $\langle 3, 16, 9 \rangle$, $\ldots$, $\langle 16, 16, 16 \rangle$ in SAMPLE by means of the program segment

```
      DO 222  K = 1,M
      J = REF(K)
222   SAMPLE(K) = N(J)
```

There is no point in giving a complete solution here; you should test your subroutine by running it on a computer.

1.52 The subroutine performs properly when $NZ = 0$ but not when $M = NZ$. Immediately after statement 102 insert

```
IF (M.LT.KA) RETURN
```

1.53 You are either convinced or not convinced.

Chapter 2

2.1 (i) and (ii).

2.11 The number of one-to-one functions is equal to $n!$, the number of n-permutations of the elements of the set. This is also the number of onto functions. The number of into functions is n^n (by Th.2.2).

2.14 All except (ii). In (ii) the number of opening parentheses exceeds the number of closing parentheses. Since, for example, $(1 \oplus 1) * 0 \neq 1 \oplus (1 * 0)$, the function corresponding to form (i) cannot be unambiguously defined without rules of precedence for the operations. In arithmetic normal evaluation is from left to right with precedence ( ), unary $-$, $\times$ and $/$, $+$ and $-$. In Boolean evaluation the precedence is ( ), $'$, $*$, $\oplus$.

2.15 The Boolean function is $\{\langle 0, 0, 0, 0 \rangle, \langle 0, 0, 1, 0 \rangle, \langle 0, 1, 0, 1 \rangle, \langle 0, 1, 1, 0 \rangle, \langle 1, 0, 0, 1 \rangle, \langle 1, 0, 1, 1 \rangle, \langle 1, 1, 0, 1 \rangle, \langle 1, 1, 1, 1 \rangle\}$.

2.18 Let $h(W, X, Y, Z) = ((W \cup X) + (Y \cup Z)) \cap \overline{(W + Y) \cup (X + Z)}$. One can show that $v(h(m_1, m_2, m_3, m_4)) = \emptyset$ for all 4-samples $\langle m_1, m_2, m_3, m_4 \rangle$ of $\{\emptyset, U\}$ by means of a valuation table.

2.19 $x_1 * (x_1' \oplus x_2) * x_2' = ((x_1 * x_1') \oplus (x_1 * x_2)) * x_2'$
$$= (x_1 * x_2) * x_2'$$
$$= 0.$$

The simplified circuit is an open circuit without any switches.

2.21 In the bridge circuit a signal entering from the left can go along the arm bearing switch x_1, or along the arm bearing switch x_1'. If it passes through x_1, it can next go through x_2', or through x_2 and x_3'. If it passes through x_2', then it cannot continue along the arm bearing switch x_2 because this switch is closed when x_2' is open. Hence the signal continues through x_3 and x_4', or through x_3' and x_4. If, on the other hand, the signal passed through x_1, x_2, and x_3', then it can only go through x_4' next. Thus we have the possible paths x_1—x_2'—x_3—x_4', x_1—x_2'—x_3'—x_4, x_1—x_2—x_3'—x_4'. An open x_1 gives rise to the paths x_1'—x_2—x_3'—x_4, x_1'—x_2—x_3—x_4', x_1'—x_2'—x_3—x_4. But these are the six parallel paths of Figure 2.3.

2.24 (i) The prime implicants are 0-011, 010-1, -1001, 0101-, 1-001, -01-0, 10-0-, 101--, 1-11-; of these 0-011, 0101-, -01-0, 10-0-, 1-11- are essential. The essential prime implicants cover all minterms except 01001 and 11001, and these minterms are covered by -1001. Hence the minimal form is $x_1' x_3' x_4 x_5 \oplus x_1' x_2 x_3' x_4 \oplus x_2' x_3 x_5' \oplus x_1 x_2' x_4' \oplus x_1 x_3 x_4 \oplus x_2 x_3' x_4' x_5$.

2.26 We introduce the notation $f(x_1, x_2) = x_1 \downarrow x_2$. Function f is known as the dagger function. We have

(i) $x_1' = x_1 \downarrow x_1$;
(ii) $x_1 \oplus x_2 = (x_1 \downarrow x_2)' = (x_1 \downarrow x_2) \downarrow (x_1 \downarrow x_2)$;
(iii) $x_1 * x_2 = x_1' \downarrow x_2' = (x_1 \downarrow x_1) \downarrow (x_2 \downarrow x_2)$.

Hence any Boolean function can be represented by a circuit consisting entirely of NOR-gates. Then, since $x_1 \mid x_2 = (x_1 * x_2)'$, we have

(iv) $x_1 \mid x_2 = ((x_1 \downarrow x_1) \downarrow (x_2 \downarrow x_2)) \downarrow ((x_1 \downarrow x_1) \downarrow (x_2 \downarrow x_2))$.

2.31 The definition can be derived from D.2.8 with obvious changes of symbols. It is optional whether or not we permit symbols $\rightarrow$ and $\leftrightarrow$. If we do, the definition ends with

(7) If α and β are statement forms, then $\alpha \rightarrow \beta$ is a statement form.

(8) If α and β are statement forms, then $\alpha \leftrightarrow \beta$ is a statement form.

(9) Only expressions given by (1)–(8) are statement forms.

Although we have not been considering statements containing logical constants F and T in the text (such as $p \vee T$ or $p \wedge \neg p \leftrightarrow F$), any familiarity with logical expressions in Fortran or Algol should convince one that provision for such statements must be made in the definition.

2.33 Statements (i), (ii), and (iii) are shown to be tautologies by means of truth tables. Since (ii) is a biconditional tautology, one can substitute $\neg p \rightarrow \neg q$ for $q \rightarrow p$ in (iii): Statement (iv) results.

2.35 Here one should *not* use truth tables or a computer program. Consider the first implication. This is an argument with premises (1) $p \rightarrow q$, (2) $q \rightarrow r$, (3) $r \rightarrow p$, and conclusion $p \leftrightarrow r$. By laws of detachment and syllogism, (1) and (2) give (4) $p \rightarrow r$. Statements (4) and (3) can be combined into (5) $(p \rightarrow r) \wedge (r \rightarrow p)$. But (5) is the definition of $p \leftrightarrow r$. One proves the other two implications in a similar fashion.

2.36 If $\rightarrow$ is to be associative, then $(p \rightarrow q) \rightarrow r$ must be equivalent to $p \rightarrow (q \rightarrow r)$. Since, for example, $(F \rightarrow F) \rightarrow F$ reduces to F, but $F \rightarrow (F \rightarrow F)$ to T, operation $\rightarrow$ is not associative. By means of a truth table one can show that $(p \leftrightarrow q) \leftrightarrow r$ is equivalent to $p \leftrightarrow (q \leftrightarrow r)$, i.e., that the biconditional is associative.

2.38

(1)	$b \rightarrow i \wedge e$,	(Premise)
(2)	s,	(Premise)
(3)	$s \rightarrow m$,	(Premise)
(4)	$m \rightarrow \neg i \wedge e$,	(Premise)
(5)	m,	(2 and 3)
(6)	$\neg i \wedge e$,	(5 and 4)
(7)	$\neg i$,	(6—$p \wedge q \rightarrow p$ is a tautology)
(8)	$\neg i \vee \neg e$,	(7—$p \rightarrow p \vee q$ is a tautology)
(9)	$\neg(i \wedge e)$,	(8—De Morgan's law)
(10)	$\neg(i \wedge e) \rightarrow \neg b$,	(Contrapositive of 1)
(11)	$\neg b$.	(9 and 10)

2.40 Both conclusions have the same symbolic form, namely $h \rightarrow p$, where h stands for "taxpayers are happy," and p for "prisons are full." (The statements "p is a necessary condition for h," and "h is a sufficient condition for p" are synonymous.)

2.42 Including the null relation, there are $|\mathscr{P}(A \times B)| = 2^{mn}$ relations, irrespective of whether $A \subseteq B$ holds.

2.44 Yes, in some superset of $\{a, b, c, d, \langle a, b \rangle, \langle b, c \rangle\}$.

2.51 Denote the relation by R. Since R is nonempty, there exists some $\langle a, b \rangle \in R$. But then $\langle b, a \rangle \in R$ (by symmetry), and $\langle a, b \rangle \in R$ and $\langle b, a \rangle \in R$ imply $\langle a, a \rangle \in R$ (by transitivity). Hence the relation cannot be irreflexive. Next assume that R is transitive, symmetric, and reflexive in some set A, and consider a set $A \cup \{x\}$ where $x \notin A$. Then relation R is still transitive and symmetric in $A \cup \{x\}$, but $\langle x, x \rangle \notin R$.

2.52 (i) The relation is not transitive.

(ii) Denote the relation by R. Clearly $\langle x_1, x_2 \rangle R \langle x_1, x_2 \rangle$. Next let $\langle x_1, x_2 \rangle R \langle x_3, x_4 \rangle$. Then $x_1 + x_4 = x_2 + x_3$, giving $x_3 + x_2 = x_4 + x_1$ on rearrangement. But then

$\langle x_3, x_4 \rangle\ R\ \langle x_1, x_2 \rangle$. Finally assume $\langle x_1, x_2 \rangle\ R\ \langle x_3, x_4 \rangle$ and $\langle x_3, x_4 \rangle\ R\ \langle x_5, x_6 \rangle$. We have

$$x_1 + x_4 = x_2 + x_3,$$
$$x_3 + x_6 = x_4 + x_5.$$

Add: $x_1 + x_4 + x_3 + x_6 = x_2 + x_3 + x_4 + x_5.$

Subtract $x_3 + x_4$ from both sides:

$$x_1 + x_6 = x_2 + x_5.$$

Hence $\langle x_1, x_2 \rangle\ R\ \langle x_5, x_6 \rangle$.

(iii) Again denote the relation by R and assume $\langle x_1, x_2 \rangle\ R\ \langle x_1, x_2 \rangle$. Then, by definition, $x_1 + x_1 = x_2 + x_2$, which is only true if $x_1 = x_2$. Hence R is not reflexive.

2.55   It is sufficient to show that $S(n, m)$ is the number of ways a set of n elements can be partitioned into m disjoint nonempty subsets. This we do by induction. Clearly, if $n = 1$, there is one partition for $m = 1$ and no partition for $m > 1$. But $S(1, 1) = 1$, and it is easily shown that $S(1, m) = 0$ for $m > 1$. For the induction step assume that $S(n - 1, m)$ is the number of ways a set of $n - 1$ elements can be partitioned into m subsets. Since m is arbitrary, the assumption also gives $S(n - 1, m - 1)$ for the number of ways the $n - 1$ elements can be partitioned into $m - 1$ subsets. Denote the set of $n - 1$ elements by A_{n-1}, and let $A_n = A_{n-1} \cup \{a_n\}$. Partitions of A_n into m subsets are of two types: (i) the set $\{a_n\}$ and a partition of A_{n-1} having $m - 1$ members; (ii) a partition of A_{n-1} having m members, but with a_n merged into one of the members. There are $S(n - 1, m - 1)$ partitions of the first type and $mS(n - 1, m)$ of the second. But $S(n - 1, m - 1) + mS(n - 1, m) = S(n, m)$.

2.57   Let R be an equivalence relation that is not the identity relation. Then there exists some $\langle a, b \rangle \in R$ such that $a \neq b$. Since R is symmetric, also $\langle b, a \rangle \in R$. Now assume that R is a partial ordering, i.e., that it is antisymmetric. Then $\langle a, b \rangle \in R$ and $\langle b, a \rangle \in R$ imply $a = b$, and we have a contradiction.

2.61   Any equivalence relation except the identity relation.

2.63   Denote the partial ordering by $\leq$ and assume that there exist two least elements, b and b'. Then $b \leq a$ and $b' \leq a$ for any element a in the set. In particular $b \leq b'$ and $b' \leq b$; i.e., $b < b'$ or $b = b'$, and $b' < b$ or $b' = b$. But $b < b'$ and $b' < b$ imply $b < b$, which is impossible. Hence $b = b'$. Similarly one shows that there is at most one greatest element. Assume that there exists a least element b and that b is not minimal. Then there exists some a such that $a < b$. But, by D.2.24, $b \leq a$; i.e., $b < a$ or $b = a$. If $b < a$, then $b < a$ and $a < b$ imply $b < b$. If $b = a$, $a < b$ becomes $b < b$. Hence a least element is minimal. Next assume that there exists a least element b and an arbitrary minimal element c. Since b is a least element, $b \leq c$. Since c is minimal, $b < c$ does not hold. Hence $b = c$. The proof for a greatest element is similar.

2.67   None of the sets has a least element.

(i) Minimal elements: 2, 3, 5, 7. Greatest (and maximal) element: 210.

(ii) Minimal elements: 2, 3, 5. Greatest (and maximal) element: 1080.

(iii) Minimal elements: 2, 3, 5. Greatest (and maximal) element: 300.

2.70   One of the order-isomorphic sets is $\{1, 2, 3, 5, 6, 7, 10, 14, 15, 21, 35, 900, 1764,$ $4900, 11{,}025, 85{,}766, 121{,}000{,}000\}$. The diagram turned through 180° represents the partially ordered set $\langle \mathscr{P}(\{a, b, c, d\}), \supseteq \rangle$. In general, there is no definite relation between sets represented by a diagram and the diagram turned through 90°.

2.72   (i) No.   (ii) No.

2.74   Assume $a * b = a$. Then $a = \inf\{a, b\}$; i.e., a is a lower bound of $\{a, b\}$. Hence, by D.2.27, $a \leq b$. Next assume $a \leq b$. Clearly $b \leq b$ as well, and b is an upper bound of $\{a, b\}$.

Assume $b \neq \sup \{a, b\}$; i.e., assume $c = \sup \{a, b\}$ such that $b \neq c$. Then $c \leq b$ (c is the supremum) and $b \leq c$ (c is an upper bound), and, since $b \neq c$, $c < b$ and $b < c$. But this is impossible. Hence $b = \sup \{a, b\}$. Finally assume $a \oplus b = b$. This means that b is an upper bound of $\{a, b\}$, i.e., that $a \leq b$. Since $a \leq a$ as well, a is a lower bound of $\{a, b\}$. Just as the assumption $b \neq \sup \{a, b\}$ led to the impossible $b < b$ above, assumption $a \neq \inf \{a, b\}$ leads to $a < a$. Hence $a = \inf \{a, b\} = a * b$.

2.76   By D.2.27 and D.2.24, $\inf \{a, b\} \leq a \leq \sup \{a, b\}$, or, by D.2.29, $a * b \leq a \leq a \oplus b$. The equivalences of Exercise 2.74 then give

$$(a * b) \oplus a = a = a * (a \oplus b).$$

2.82   Take a system $\langle A, \oplus, * \rangle$ with

(i) $a \oplus b = b \oplus a,$ $a * b = b * a;$
(ii) $a \oplus (b \oplus c) = (a \oplus b) \oplus c,$ $a * (b * c) = (a * b) * c;$
(iii) $a \oplus (a * b) = a,$ $a * (a \oplus b) = a$

as axioms, and define relation $\leq$ such that $a \leq b$ if and only if $a \oplus b = b$ (or $a * b = a$). We can then prove theorems

$$a \oplus a = a,$$
$$a \leq b \text{ and } b \leq a \text{ imply } a = b,$$

etc. Axioms (i) and (ii) form part of the set of axioms of Boolean algebra. In Boolean algebra Statements (iii) can be derived as theorems, but Statements (i) and (ii) do not suffice for this purpose (see Exercise 1.28). Hence Statements (iii) are axioms here. (Distributive complemented lattices are Boolean algebras.)

2.83   (i) Let array LAT contain the elements of X. Then

```
SUBROUTINE SETUP (LAT, LESS, N)
LOGICAL TEST
DIMENSION LAT(N), LESS(N,N)
DO  5  I = 1,N
DO  5  J = 1,N
LESS(I,J) = 0
5   IF (TEST(LAT(I),LAT(J))) LESS(I,J) = 1
RETURN
END
```

Because of the restriction on the order in which elements of the set may be stored in LAT we need not define LESS(I,J) when J is less than I, and the DO 5 J =1,N can be changed to DO 5 J =I,N. For the lattice of Example 1 of D.2.29 TEST can be written as follows:

```
LOGICAL FUNCTION TEST (N,M)
TEST = .FALSE.
IF (MOD(M,N).EQ.0) TEST = .TRUE.
RETURN
END
```

Subroutine TABLE generates the addition–multiplication table in array LESS, and in so doing overwrites its previous contents. Some attention must therefore be given to the order in which the entries are computed. Entries of the addition table must be created first. The computation is based on the observation that if $x_i \leq x_k$ and $x_j \leq x_k$, then x_k is an upper bound of $\{x_i, x_j\}$. Hence the least value of K such that $\text{LESS}(\text{I}, \text{K}) = \text{LESS}(\text{J}, \text{K}) = 1$ gives the least upper bound.

```
        SUBROUTINE TABLE (LAT,LESS,N)
        DIMENSION LAT(N), LESS(N,N)
        DO 10  I = 2,N
        II = I - 1
        DO 10  J = 1,II
        DO  5  K = I,N
        IF (LESS(I,K)*LESS(J,K).EQ.1) GO TO 10
     5  CONTINUE
    10  LESS(I,J) = LAT(K)
        DO 20  I = 1,N
        II = N + 1 - I
        DO 20  J = 1,I
        JJ = N + 1 - J
        DO 15  K = I,N
        KK = N + 1 - K
        IF (LESS(KK,II)*LESS(KK,JJ).EQ.1) GO TO 20
    15  CONTINUE
    20  LESS(II,JJ) = LAT(KK)
        RETURN
        END
```

2.85 (i) Set B is closed under $\oplus$, $*$, and $'$. Hence $x \in B$ and $y \in B$ imply, in turn, $y' \in B$, $x * y' \in B$, $x' \in B$, $x' * y \in B$, $x + y \in B$.

(ii) The most obvious examples are addition and multiplication. Set N is not closed under subtraction (e.g., $5 - 12 \notin N$), but one can have an operation $\dot{-}$ (proper subtraction), defined by

$$x \dot{-} y = x - y, \qquad x \geq y,$$
$$= 0, \qquad x < y,$$

under which N is closed. Out of the multitude of other operations under which N is closed we select a one-argument operation S (successor function), defined by $S(n) = n + 1$.

2.86 The similar algebras are (i), (iii), and (v). Since $\oplus$ and $*$ are both two-argument operations, each operation in a corresponding pair from (i) and (iii) has the same number of arguments. Two algebras need not have the same number of elements for similarity. Hence, even though $|B| \neq |\{0, 1\}|$, (i) and (v) are similar. Algebra (ii) does not have as many operations as the other algebras, and $'$ in (iv) does not have as many arguments as the corresponding operation ($\oplus$ or $*$) in any of the other algebras.

2.87 If X is a sublattice of a distributive lattice L, then, since the identities of D.2.30 hold for any $a, b, c \in L$, they hold, in particular, for any $a, b, c \in X$ ($X \subseteq L$). Hence X is distributive. If Y is a homomorphic image of L under some homomorphism $h: L \to Y$, and x, y, z are arbitrary elements of Y, then, by definition of homomorphism, there may be found in L elements a, b, c such that $h(a) = x$, $h(b) = y$, $h(c) = z$. Consequently, if L is distributive, we have

$$x * (y \oplus z) = h(a) * (h(b) \oplus h(c))$$
$$= h(a) * h(b \oplus c)$$
$$= h(a * (b \oplus c))$$
$$= h((a * b) \oplus (a * c))$$
$$= h(a * b) \oplus h(a * c)$$
$$= (h(a) * h(b)) \oplus (h(a) * h(c))$$
$$= (x * y) \oplus (x * z),$$

and, by Exercise 2.78, the other distributive law holds as well. Hence Y is distributive.

Chapter 3

3.2   A digraph $\langle A, R \rangle$ is bipartite if there exists a partition $\{X, Y\}$ of A such that, for all $\langle a, b \rangle \in R$, $a \in X$ and $b \in Y$.

3.6   Simple cycles: $(a_1, a_2, a_6, a_5, a_1)$, (a_2, a_6, a_2), (a_2, a_6, a_3, a_2), (a_9, a_9). Nonsimple cycle: $(a_1, a_2, a_6, a_3, a_2, a_6, a_5, a_1)$. Note that, for example, node sequences $(a_2, a_6, a_2, a_6, a_2)$ and (a_2, a_6, a_2) correspond to the same cycle.

3.7   The first part is obvious. The second part can be established by means of a counter-example: Consider paths (a, c, d, b) and (b, d, a) in a digraph

$$\langle \{a, b, c, d\}, \{\langle a, c \rangle, \langle b, c \rangle, \langle c, d \rangle, \langle d, a \rangle, \langle d, b \rangle\} \rangle;$$

there exists no simple cycle $(a, \ldots, b, \ldots, a)$.

3.15   Take the path matrix of A_k, adjoin to it the $(k + 1)$th row and column of X, and call this matrix $\mathbf{M}$. First compute the $(k + 1)$th column:

```
      KP = K + 1
      DO  5  J = 1,K
      IF (M(J,KP).EQ.1) GO TO 5
      DO  3  I = 1,K
      IF (M(J,I)*M(I,KP).EQ.1) GO TO 4
   3  CONTINUE
      GO TO 5
   4  M(J,KP) = 1
   5  CONTINUE
```

A possible alternative is

```
      KP = K + 1
      DO  5  J = 1,K
      IF (M(J,KP).EQ.0) GO TO 5
      DO  3  I = 1,K
   3  IF (M(I,J).EQ.1) M(I,KP) = 1
   5  CONTINUE
```

Next deal with the $(k + 1)$th row in a similar fashion:

```
      DO 10  J = 1,KP
      IF (M(KP,J).EQ.1) GO TO 10
      DO  8  I = 1,KP
      IF (M(KP,I)*M(I,J).EQ.1) GO TO 9
    8 CONTINUE
      GO TO 10
    9 M(KP,J) = 1
   10 CONTINUE
```

It is a very common mistake to omit the final part:

```
      DO 15  I = 1,K
      DO 15  J = 1,K
      IF (M(I,J).EQ.1) GO TO 15
      M(I,J) = M(I,KP)*M(KP,J)
   15 CONTINUE
```

3.16   If indices j and k are interchanged, then the entire algorithm has to be iterated $\log_2 n$ times. A study of the second part of the proof of Th.3.7 ($p_{ik} = 1$ implies $x_{ik}^* = 1$) will tell you what happens if j and i are interchanged.

3.20   The antisymmetry test is changed to a symmetry test:

```
C3  SYMMETRY TEST
    IF (MX(I,J).NE.MX(J,I)) RETURN
```

3.25   Use proof by induction, with the induction step as follows: Consider a tournament on n nodes, and select a particular node x. The subdigraph on the other $n - 1$ nodes is also a tournament. Assume that this tournament contains a Hamiltonian path, and write this path as $(a_1, a_2, \ldots, a_{n-1})$. Let us examine the $n - 1$ arcs that are incident with x and with the $n - 1$ nodes $\{a_1, a_2, \ldots, a_{n-1}\}$ in the tournament on n nodes, i.e., the arcs that do not belong to our tournament on $n - 1$ nodes. If there exists some pair of arcs $\langle a_k, x \rangle$, $\langle x, a_{k+1} \rangle$, then we have a Hamiltonian path. If not, then *all* the $n - 1$ arcs must originate at x, or they must *all* terminate at x. In either case there is a Hamiltonian path: $(x, a_1, \ldots, a_{n-1})$ or $(a_1, \ldots, a_{n-1}, x)$, respectively.

3.29   Let **M** be the adjacency matrix. "Symmetrize" it, possibly as follows:

```
      DO 1  I = 1,N
      DO 1  J = 1,N
    1 IF (M(I,J).EQ.1)  M(J,I) = 1
```

Now find **MP**, the path matrix corresponding to the "symmetrized" adjacency matrix and in **MP** set all diagonal elements to 1:

```
      DO 50  J = 1,N
   50 MP(J,J) = 1
```

MP is then the matrix C.

3.31   By the corollary of Th.3.9 the strong components of a digraph are the connected components of its cycle digraph. But connectedness is an equivalence relation. Hence, if the procedure of Exercise 3.29 is applied to the adjacency matrix of the cycle digraph, and the resulting matrix made the input to I SEQUI as modified in Exercise 3.22, then the equivalence classes printed by I SEQUI define the strong components of the digraph.

3.34   For example, a digraph $\langle \{1, 2, 3, 4, 5\}, \{\langle 1, 2 \rangle, \langle 3, 4 \rangle, \langle 4, 5 \rangle, \langle 5, 3 \rangle\} \rangle$.

3.35   By Th.3.3, a node belonging to a node base must have zero indegree, or must lie on a cycle. The node base of a disconnected digraph contains at least two nodes. Therefore, an acyclic digraph with exactly one node having indegree 0 must be connected. Next we show that a connected digraph without slings in which exactly one node has indegree 0 and every other node has indegree 1 is acyclic. Consider a digraph on n nodes that satisfies the conditions. Since all nodes but one have indegree 1, and the remaining node has indegree 0, there are $n - 1$ arcs. It is easy to prove (a) that a connected digraph on n nodes contains at least $n - 1$ arcs, i.e., that our digraph is minimal with respect to the number of arcs, and (b) that a cyclic connected digraph remains connected after removal of an arc belonging to a cycle, i.e., that a cyclic connected digraph is not minimal with respect to the number of arcs. Hence the conditions do imply that the digraph is acyclic.

3.39   The minimal sets contain, respectively, one and four K-formulas.

3.42
```
      LOGICAL FUNCTION ISKFOR (KFORM,M)
      INTEGER  KFORM(M)
C   THE M SYMBOLS OF THE FORMULA ARE SUPPLIED IN ARRAY
C   KFORM — THE K—OPERATOR IS REPRESENTED BY 0.
      ISKFOR = .FALSE.
      K = 0
      N = 0
      J = 0
    5 J = J+1
      IF (J.GT.M) RETURN
      IF (KFORM(J).EQ.0) GO TO 10
      N = N+1
      GO TO 15
   10 K = K+1
   15 IF (K.GE.N) GO TO 5
      IF (J.EQ.M) ISKFOR = .TRUE.
      RETURN
      END
```

3.46   Work with complements of the digraph. Then it is easy to see that the digraphs are isomorphic. The correspondence of the nodes is

$$a \quad b \quad c \quad d \quad e \quad f$$

$$6 \quad 3 \quad 5 \quad 2 \quad 4 \quad 1$$

(For practice one should establish the isomorphism of D_1 and D_2 directly as well.)

3.49   A complete digraph has a sling on every node (see Example 1 of D.3.15). Therefore, if $D = \langle X, R \rangle$ is complete symmetric, then R is the universal relation in X, and the adjacency matrix of D is invariant under permutations of rows and columns, i.e., for all D', D and D' are isomorphic. (Actually, we have a much stronger result: D and D' are identical.)

3.53 We have to show that a connected graph contains no circuits (p) if and only if it becomes disconnected when any one of its edges is removed (q). Assume p, and prove q: In a graph that contains no circuits an edge $\{a, b\}$ is a unique chain between a and b, and after removal of this edge there is no longer a chain between the nodes, i.e., the graph is disconnected. Next assume q and prove p. If removal of an arbitrary edge $\{a, b\}$ has disconnected the graph, then there are now nodes c and d in the graph such that no chain $(c, \ldots, d)$ exists. A chain $(c, \ldots, d)$ must have existed before the removal of the edge, and the removed edge must have belonged to the chain. But, if there had existed a circuit containing $\{a, b\}$, then a chain $(c, \ldots, d)$ would still exist. Therefore, no circuit containing $\{a, b\}$ could have existed, and since $\{a, b\}$ is arbitrary, no circuit at all could have existed.

Chapter 4

4.1 Consider arbitrary matrices

$$A = \begin{bmatrix} a & b \\ c & d \end{bmatrix}, \qquad B = \begin{bmatrix} s & t \\ u & v \end{bmatrix}, \qquad C = \begin{bmatrix} w & x \\ y & z \end{bmatrix}.$$

Then

$$A.(B.C) = (A.B).C = \begin{bmatrix} asw + aty + buw + bvy & asx + atz + bux + bvz \\ csw + cty + duw + dvy & csx + ctz + dux + dvz \end{bmatrix}.$$

The identity element is

$$\begin{bmatrix} 1 & 0 \\ 0 & 1 \end{bmatrix}.$$

4.4 An equilateral triangle ABC can be rotated through 120°, 240°, and 360° in the plane. Let the midpoints of sides AB, BC, CA be denoted by X, Y, and Z, respectively. The triangle can be rotated about axes AY, BZ, and CX. The six rotations form a group, where the rotation through 360° is the identity. Setting up of the "multiplication" table is rather trivial. For the pentagon there are 5 rotations in the plane, and 5 rotations about axes drawn from a vertex to the midpoint of the side opposite it.

4.8 Give a permutation

$$p = \begin{pmatrix} a_1 & a_2 & \cdots & a_n \\ b_1 & b_2 & \cdots & b_n \end{pmatrix},$$

construct a digraph $D = \langle A, R \rangle = \langle \{a_1, \ldots, a_n\}, \{\langle a_1, b_1 \rangle, \ldots, \langle a_n, b_n \rangle\} \rangle$. We shall prove that there exist strong components $\langle A_i, R_i \rangle$ of D such that the R_i constitute a partition of R and each R_i is a simple cycle. Then each digraph cycle defines a permutation cycle and the product of the permutation cycles is p. Since $\{a_1, \ldots, a_n\} = \{b_1, \ldots, b_n\}$, exactly one arc originates from and exactly one arc terminates at each node. This means that every node a_i lies on a path $(\ldots, a_i, \ldots)$. Consider the longest possible path through a_i. If arc $\langle a_i, a_i \rangle$ exists, then, since this arc can be the only one incident with node a_i, the longest path is the simple cycle (a_i, a_i) and $\langle \{a_i\}, \{\langle a_i, a_i \rangle\} \rangle$ is a strong component. Otherwise denote the longest path through a_i by $(c_1, \ldots, c_{k-1}, c_k)$. It must be a simple cycle: Since an arc $\langle c_j, c_1 \rangle$ exists, but the path is not $(c_j, c_1, \ldots, c_k)$, the arc appears elsewhere in the path, and, since $c_1, \ldots, c_{k-1}$ are distinct (otherwise more than one arc would originate from a node), the path is $(c_1, \ldots, c_j, c_1)$. No arc that does not belong to the cycle can be incident with a node on the cycle. Hence the nodes and arcs that define the cycle constitute a strong component and a node that belongs to the strong component cannot belong to any other strong component. Moreover, there is a one-to-one correspondence between nodes $a_i \in A$ and arcs $\langle a_i, \ldots \rangle \in R$, and, if $a_i \in A_i$, then $\langle a_i, \ldots \rangle$ belongs to R_i and to R_i alone. But every $a_i \in A$ belongs to some A_i. Consequently the R_i constitute a partition of R.

4.13 They alternate.

4.17 Obviously the set is closed under *max*; since $0 \leq ab \leq b$ for $0 \leq a \leq 1$ and $b \geq 0$, the set is closed under multiplication. Multiplication and *max* are associative, and $a \cdot 1 = 1 \cdot a = a$ and $max(b, 0) = max(0, b) = b$ when $b \geq 0$. Hence $\langle [0, 1], max, 0 \rangle$ and $\langle [0, 1], \cdot, 1 \rangle$ are semigroups. Also, $max(a, b) = max(b, a)$, $max(a, 1) = 1$ when $a \leq 1$, and $a \cdot 0 = 0 \cdot a = 0$ for all a. It remains to be shown that $a \cdot max(b, c) = max(ab, ac)$ and $max(b, c) \cdot a = max(ba, ca)$, but, since multiplication and *max* are commutative, it suffices to show that $a \cdot max(b, c) = max(ab, ac)$ when $b \geq c$. If $b \geq c$, then $max(b, c) = b$ and $ab \geq ac$ for $a \geq 0$. Consequently $a \cdot max(b, c) = ab$ and $max(ab, ac) = ab$.

4.19 The cases in which transmission errors change code words into other legitimate code words are impossible to detect.

4.21 We shall prove only the second part. Assume that the minimal distance is $2k + 1$, and consider a legitimate code word a that has arrived at the destination as a', having picked up no more than k errors. Let c be any other legitimate code word. We have $d(a, c) \leq d(a, a') + d(a', c)$ [Example 1 of D.4.9], which is equivalent to $d(a', c) \geq d(a, c) - d(a, a')$. But $d(a, c) \geq 2k + 1$, and $d(a, a') \leq k$. Consequently $d(a', c) \geq k + 1$, which means that a' is further from c than it is from a, i.e., that a' can be correctly decoded to a. To prove the converse, assume a minimal distance less than $2k + 1$. Then there exist two code words, a and c, say, such that $d(a, c) \leq 2k$. Now construct a' by letting it differ from a in precisely k of the coordinate positions in which a and c differ. We then have $d(a, a') = k$, but $d(a', c) \leq k$. Consequently a' will not necessarily become a in the decoding process, although it differs from a in only k coordinate positions.

4.34 The domain of f_c is not V^*. Hence f_c and $f_c \mid B$ cannot be operations in V^*.

4.36 Any Markov algorithm that contains a production having the null string for its antecedent.

4.38 The problem is overlap: Removal of all occurrences of *ara* from *ararat* should leave just the *t*. Write the specified substring as $\alpha\beta$, where α is the first character of the substring. Markers s, u, v, w are used. The algorithm is

1. $s\alpha\beta \rightarrow \alpha u s\beta$
2. $sx \rightarrow xs$ $(x \in V)$
3. $\alpha u \rightarrow v\alpha$
4. $v\alpha\beta \rightarrow w$
5. $vw \rightarrow \Lambda$
6. $vx \rightarrow v$ $(x \in V \cup V')$
7. $w \rightarrow \Lambda$
8. $s \rightarrow .\Lambda$
9. $\Lambda \rightarrow s$

Consider, for example, the removal of $\alpha\beta = abca$ from *ababcaca*. We are left with a new *abca*, which we do not wish to delete. Marker s prevents deletions of this type. Production 1 marks *all* substrings $\alpha\beta$; Production 3 makes a marker substitution and shifts each marker to the start of its substring. Production 4 deletes nonoverlapped substrings, and, after their deletion, markers v and w enclose parts of overlapped substrings that remain to be deleted. This deletion is effected by Production 6.

4.46 Strings (i) and (iv) are sentences. String (ii) is not because *The* $\notin V$ (only *the* $\in V$), and string (iii) is not because *an* $\notin V$.

4.48 (ii) $G = \langle \{a, b\}, \{S\}, P, S \rangle$, where P is $\langle S \rangle ::= b \,|\, a \langle S \rangle a$. G is Type 2.

(v) The grammar derives from D.2.8. It is Type 2. A possible set of production rules is

$$\langle \text{var} \rangle ::= x_1 \,|\, x_2 \,|\, \cdots \,|\, x_n$$
$$\langle \text{cons} \rangle ::= 0 \,|\, 1$$
$$\langle \text{unop} \rangle ::= \,'$$
$$\langle \text{binop} \rangle ::= \oplus \,|\, *$$
$$\langle \text{prim} \rangle ::= \langle \text{var} \rangle \,|\, \langle \text{cons} \rangle$$
$$\langle \text{form} \rangle ::= \langle \text{prim} \rangle \,|\, (\langle \text{form} \rangle) \,|\, \langle \text{form} \rangle \langle \text{unop} \rangle \,|\, \langle \text{form} \rangle \langle \text{binop} \rangle \langle \text{form} \rangle$$

4.49 (ii) $\{a^n b c^n \,|\, n \geq 0\}$.

(iv) $\{\alpha a c a \beta \,|\, \alpha \in \{a, a d b^n d\}^*, n \geq 1;$ if $\alpha = s_1 s_2 \cdots s_k$, then $\beta = s_k \cdots s_2 s_1\}$.

4.52 Denote the symbols by $a_1, a_2, \ldots, a_i$. Assume that $\frac{1}{2} n(n+1) + 1$ rules are sufficient to produce all permutations of n symbols. There is an initiating rule $S \to A_1 A_2 \cdots A_n$, n rules of the form $A_t \to a_t$, and the remaining $\frac{1}{2} n(n-1)$ rules, which have the form $A_s A_t \to A_t A_s$, transpose the metalinguistic variables. To get a particular permutation, say $a_3 a_2 a_1 a_4$ when $i = 4$, one first produces string $A_3 A_2 A_1 A_4$ by means of transpositions, and then replaces the variables with terminal symbols. When a_{n+1} is added, the initiating rule becomes $S \to A_1 \cdots A_{n+1}$, and, to generate a particular permutation, one permutes symbols $A_1, \ldots, A_n$ and then sends A_{n+1} to its required position in the string (see the discussion preceding A.1.5). This requires n additional transposition rules

$$A_t A_{n+1} \to A_{n+1} A_t \ (t = 1, \ldots, n),$$

and we need the further rule $A_{n+1} \to a_{n+1}$; i.e., the total number of rules becomes $\frac{1}{2} n(n+1) + 1 + (n+1) = \frac{1}{2}(n+1)(n+2) + 1$, as required. To establish the base of the induction proof consider $P_2 = \{S \to A_1 A_2, A_1 A_2 \to A_2 A_1, A_1 \to a_1, A_2 \to a_2\}$. These rules produce the two permutations $a_1 a_2$ and $a_2 a_1$, and $|P_2| = 4 = \frac{1}{2} i(i+1) + 1$ when $i = 2$.

Chapter 5

5.1 There are two phases. (i) The check on indegrees is made by computing the sum of elements for each column of the adjacency matrix. This should come to 0 for one column (store its number in NROOT), and be 1 for every other column. (ii) The digraph can be shown to be acyclic, or to be connected and without slings. It is easier to establish acyclicity: Find the path matrix and test its diagonal elements; they should all be 0. Digraph D is a directed tree if both tests are passed, and then it has a root, which is identified by NROOT.

5.3 The string *abab* can be produced in two different ways:

$$
\begin{array}{lcl}
S \Rightarrow abSb & \quad \text{or} \quad & S \Rightarrow aAb \\
 \Rightarrow abab & & \Rightarrow abSb \\
& & \Rightarrow abab
\end{array}
$$

$L(G) = \{(ab)^n ab^n \,|\, n \geq 0\}$. An unambiguous grammar is $G_1 = \langle \{a, b\}, \{S\}, P, S \rangle$, where P is

$$\langle S \rangle ::= ab \langle S \rangle b \,|\, a.$$

5.5 One Type 3 grammar that generates the language has the productions

$$\langle S \rangle ::= \langle A \rangle \,|\, \langle B \rangle b \,|\, b$$
$$\langle A \rangle ::= ab \,|\, \langle A \rangle ab$$
$$\langle B \rangle ::= bc \,|\, \langle B \rangle bc \,|\, a \,|\, \langle B \rangle a$$

A simple algorithm for converting a syntactic chart to a state graph does not appear to exist. One might get some guidance in the design of the automaton from the syntactic chart, but this would be a purely subjective matter.

5.6   The contents of the stack are

$$1 \quad 2 \quad 3 \quad 4 \quad 5 \quad 6 \quad 10 \quad 9 \quad 8 \quad 7 \quad 6$$

(6 is the topmost datum).

5.7   Use common sense: Treat the stack storage area as a normal Fortran array.

5.8   Let N be the array used for the FIFO store, and let its size be 100. Two pointers are needed. Let us call them IH and IL. Pointer IH indicates the element that was last stored; IL points to the element that is next to be extracted. In IPOP one should first evaluate (IL.GT.IH). If this expression is true, then there is underflow; otherwise N(IL) is extracted, and IL incremented by 1. In PUSH one should first test IH. If (IH.EQ.100) is true, then a further test has to be made. If (IL.EQ.1) is also true, then there is overflow; otherwise all elements in the FIFO store are shifted down, and IL and IH adjusted, perhaps as follows:

```
      IH = 101 - IL
      DO 20  I = 1, IH
      N(I) = N(IL)
  20  IL = IL + 1
      IL = 1
```

Then IH is incremented by 1, and the datum placed in N(IH).

5.13   Append the specified substring to the given string, separating the two with a symbol that does not appear anywhere in the string. Then apply A.5.1 with d equal to the length of the specified substring.

5.15   For B-tree T of Figure 5.9 the nodes are processed in the following order under the three modes of traversal:

Preorder:

$$1 \quad 2 \quad 4 \quad 5 \quad 7 \quad 8 \quad 3 \quad 6 \quad 9 \quad 10 \quad 11 \quad 12 \quad 13 \quad 14 \quad 15 \quad 16;$$

Inorder:

$$4 \quad 2 \quad 7 \quad 5 \quad 8 \quad 1 \quad 3 \quad 9 \quad 11 \quad 10 \quad 13 \quad 12 \quad 15 \quad 14 \quad 16 \quad 6;$$

Postorder:

$$4 \quad 7 \quad 8 \quad 5 \quad 2 \quad 11 \quad 13 \quad 15 \quad 16 \quad 14 \quad 12 \quad 10 \quad 9 \quad 6 \quad 3 \quad 1.$$

5.26   There are three full trees of order 2. Their roots are defined by the sequences Λ, 01, 011. The algorithm given as Example 2 of A.5.4 is the more efficient.

5.29   The grammar might have the following productions:

$$\langle S \rangle \quad ::= (\langle var \rangle = \langle expr \rangle) \,|\, (\langle var \rangle = \langle var \rangle)$$
$$\langle expr \rangle ::= (\langle var \rangle \langle op \rangle \langle var \rangle) \,|\, (\langle expr \rangle \langle op \rangle \langle expr \rangle) \,|\, (\langle var \rangle \langle op \rangle \langle expr \rangle) \,|$$
$$(\langle expr \rangle \langle op \rangle \langle var \rangle)$$
$$\langle var \rangle \quad ::= a \,|\, b \,|\, c \,|\, \cdots \,|\, z$$
$$\langle op \rangle \quad ::= + \,|\, - \,|\, / \,|\, \times$$

Strictly speaking, the definitions of ⟨var⟩ and ⟨op⟩ are invalid in a parenthesis grammar. These productions could be corrected to

$$\langle var \rangle \ ::= (a)\,|\,(b)\,|\,(c)\,|\cdots|\,(z)$$
$$\langle op \rangle \ ::= (+)\,|\,(-)\,|\,(/)\,|\,(\times)$$

but since we prefer $(a = (b + c))$ to $((a)(=)((b)(+)(c)))$, say, we would be reluctant to write the productions this way. The alternative is to omit the last two definitions altogether. Then, in the definition of ⟨S⟩, we would have to replace $(\langle var \rangle = \langle expr \rangle)$ with the 26 alternatives $(a = \langle expr \rangle)\,|\,(b = \langle expr \rangle)\,|\cdots|\,(z = \langle expr \rangle)$, and make similar replacements elsewhere. However, our grammar is equivalent to this parenthesis grammar, and this is our justification for writing it the way we have written it. (A grammar that is not a parenthesis grammar, but is equivalent to one, is called a concealed parenthesis grammar.)

5.35 Each K-formula must be provided with an end-of-formula marker to avoid ambiguity; otherwise a string **abcd*, for example, could be interpreted as a single (invalid) formula **abcd* or as a pair of K-formulas {**abc, d}. Let \$ be the end-of-formula marker, and use & to indicate the end of the string. The set on which the algorithm is to be tested is then written

$$**a***a*bc**dcbef\,\$**bf**e**bad*ac\$\&$$

Let A be the set of arcs, and N the set of isolated nodes. A stack is used to process the string, which we write as $s_1 s_2 s_3 \cdots$, in the following manner:

1. Set $i = 1$.
2. If $s_i = *$, then go to 8.
3. Add s_i to N.
4. Set $i = i + 1$.
5. If $s_i \neq \$$, go to 17.
6. Set $i = i + 1$.
7. If $s_i = \&$, stop; else go to 2.
8. Push s_i.
9. Set $i = i + 1$.
10. If $s_i = \$$, go to 17.
11. If $s_i = *$, push s_i and go to 9.
12. Set $u = s_i$.
13. If stack empty, go to 4.
14. Pop up v.
15. If $v = *$, push u and go to 9.
16. Add $\langle v, u \rangle$ to A, set $u = v$, go to 13.
17. Error exit; the string is not a representative set of K-formulas.

Steps 1–8 process the first symbol in a K-formula and the markers. A special case is made here of a K-formula that consists of just one node symbol (the K-formula of an isolated node). To gain an understanding of the rest of the algorithm take a specific K-formula and look at how the algorithm processes it. In converting the algorithm to a program one must first choose a representation for the string that is to be processed. The string can be written into a linear array, one symbol to an element. The K-operator can be represented by 0, node symbols by positive integers, and markers by negative integers.

5.38 The average number of comparisons for the next word coming into the dictionary is (i) unbalanced—4.79, balanced—3.92; (ii) unbalanced—5.66, balanced—4.10.

5.39

		Array P	
the	1	2	4
only	2	5	3
problem	3	0	13
to	4	0	8
be	5	10	6
faced	6	22	7
in	7	9	11
using	8	14	0
foregoing	9	16	0
algorithm	10	12	17
obtain	11	19	21
a	12	0	0
solution	13	15	24
traveling	14	0	0
salesman	15	0	0
for	16	0	0
an	17	0	18
arbitrarily	18	0	0
large	19	23	20
number	20	0	0
of	21	0	0
cities	22	0	0
is	23	0	0
storage	24	0	0

5.40 Call the two trees A and B, respectively, and assume that B is to be merged into A. Their roots are *the* and *assuming*. All words that precede *the* and *assuming* in the two trees are reached by taking the left arc out of the root of the appropriate tree, and, since *assuming* precedes *the*, all such words in B (including *assuming*) can be sent into A through the left arc. Moreover, in going down the leftmost path in A, we reach in succession *only*, *be*, and *algorithm*. We find that *assuming* precedes the first two of these words, but that it does not precede *algorithm*. Therefore, all words in B that are reached by the left arc out of the root (i.e., *all*, *an*, *and*, and also *assuming* itself) can enter tree A at node *algorithm*. This discussion should be enough of a hint as to how an efficient merging algorithm can be designed.

5.45 Extended-entry decision tables:

Input 1	1	1	1	1	0	0	0	0
2	1	1	0	0	1	1	0	0
3	1	0	1	0	1	0	1	0
Action (Part ii)	A	A	A	B	A	B	B	B
(Part iv)	B	A	A	A	A	A	A	B

Limited-entry decision tables:

Input 1	1	1	1	0	0	0
2	1	0	0	1	1	0
3	–	1	0	1	0	–
Action (Part ii)	A	A	B	A	B	B

Input 1	1	1	1	0	0	0
2	1	1	0	1	0	0
3	1	0	–	–	1	0
Action (Part iv)	B	A	A	A	A	B

Note, however, that if we rearrange the second limited-entry table as follows

Input 1	1	0	1	0	1	0
2	1	0	1	0	0	1
3	1	0	0	1	–	–
Action (Part iv)	B	B	A	A	A	A

then, in searching the table for a column that corresponds to a given data vector, only the first two columns have to be examined. If the data vector does not match either of these columns, then the action must be A.

5.47   The limited-entry tables are

	0.30	0.25	0.25	0.20		0.35	0.25	0.20	0.20
q_1	N	Y	Y	Y	q_1	–	Y	N	Y
q_2	–	–	Y	N	q_2	–	Y	–	N
q_3	–	Y	N	N	q_3	Y	N	N	N
	A1	A1	A3	A2		A1	A3	A1	A2

The average number of comparisons in the two cases is

$$0.30 + 2 \times 0.25 + 3 \times 0.25 + 4 \times 0.20 = 2.35,$$
$$0.35 + 2 \times 0.25 + 3 \times 0.20 + 4 \times 0.20 = 2.25.$$

This analysis shows that the second table is more efficient. Note again that a further simplification is possible (see solution to Exercise 5.45):

	0.25	0.20	0.55
q_1	Y	Y	–
q_2	Y	N	–
q_3	N	N	–
	A3	A2	A1

Under this scheme the average number of comparisons is

$$0.25 + 2 \times (0.20 + 0.55) = 1.75.$$

5.49   The sequence of evaluation of conditions in the two trees is q_1—q_3—q_2 or q_3—q_1—q_2 respectively, and the average costs are, respectively,

$$1.5 + 0.50 \times 2 \ + 0.25 \times 4 = 3.50,$$
$$2 \ + 0.50 \times 1.5 + 0.25 \times 4 = 3.75.$$

The first procedure is more efficient.

Chapter 6

6.8 The proof is in the doing. An algorithm for the task can be defined as follows: Draw the root (distinguished by a zero entry in vector t—if $t(k) = 0$, then k is the root). Pick an unmarked node k in the tree under construction, find all i such that $t(i) = k$, draw arcs $\langle k, i \rangle$, and mark node k. Repeat until no unmarked nodes remain.

6.11 This is just the "backward" component of A.6.7.

6.13 The optimal pouring sequence is defined by a path over nodes labeled $\langle 16, 0, 0 \rangle$, $\langle 6, 10, 0 \rangle$, $\langle 6, 4, 6 \rangle$, $\langle 12, 4, 0 \rangle$, $\langle 12, 0, 4 \rangle$, $\langle 2, 10, 4 \rangle$, $\langle 2, 8, 6 \rangle$, $\langle 8, 8, 0 \rangle$.

6.19 The ith term in the sum over i gives the number of cycles of length i. When $n = 5$ the terms have values 10, 20, 30, and 24, respectively, and their sum is 84. Denote the formula by $N(n)$. The problem is to make the formula separable for an induction proof. Some rather involved rearrangements finally result in

$$N(n) = \sum_{i=2}^{n} \left(\sum_{j=2}^{i} \left(\prod_{k=1}^{j-1} (i - k) \right) \right),$$

and then

$$N(n) = N(n-1) + \sum_{j=2}^{n} \prod_{k=1}^{j-1} (n - k),$$

to which an induction proof can be applied.

6.22 (i) $\{a, b, c, d, e\}$.

    (iii) $\{1, 2, 3, 4\}, \{5\}, \{6, 7, 8\}, \{9\}$.

6.29 In the adjacency matrix of the network show that the elements of exactly one column and of exactly one row are all zero.

6.31 Of the five critical paths in the network of Figure 6.16 there are just two left: (1, 3, 5, 7, 8, 9) and (1, 4, 3, 5, 7, 8, 9).

6.33 Smith can be away for 11 days.

6.38 Let D be the matrix of path lengths and let $P = (1, \ldots, n)$ be the longest path found by the program of Exercise 6.16. There is more than one longest path from 1 to n if there exists some $k (k = 2, \ldots, n - 1)$ such that $d_{1k} + d_{kn} = d_{1n}$ and k does not lie on P. Moreover, the existence of such a k is a necessary condition for the existence of more than one longest path. This requires some explanation. Referring to the network of Exercise 6.31, what if the program had found (1, 4, 3, 5, 7, 8, 9) for the longest path? In general, if subpath $(i, \ldots, j)$ of $P = (1, \ldots, i, \ldots, j, \ldots, n)$ is equal in length to arc $\langle i, j \rangle$, then the existence of longest path $(1, \ldots, i, j, \ldots, n)$ is not detected. However, if the program of Exercise 6.16 is written sensibly, then this situation does not arise; i.e., a properly written program selects $(1, \ldots, i, j, \ldots, n)$ in preference to $(1, \ldots, i, \ldots, j, \ldots, n)$ for the longest path.

6.40 A.6.12 merely tells whether the network contains cycles. A.3.4 identifies all arcs that belong to cycles; i.e., it enables the designer of the network to locate the cause of error with much greater efficiency.

Chapter 7

7.3 Presume that A.3.1 is used to find the path matrix in the program of Exercise 7.2 and take a hint from Exercise 3.16. A further note: Elements in the lowest $k + 1$ rows of the adjacency matrix are all zero; hence iteration on i in Steps 2 and 3 may be limited to $i = 1, 2, \ldots, n - k - 1$ alone.

7.5   Consider the digraph $\langle \{a, b, c, d, e, f, g\}, \{\langle a, b \rangle, \langle a, d \rangle, \langle b, c \rangle, \langle c, d \rangle, \langle c, f \rangle, \langle d, e \rangle, \langle e, b \rangle, \langle e, g \rangle, \langle f, g \rangle \} \rangle$, in which (a, d, e, b, c, f, g) is a forward path by our new definition. Therefore, according to the new definition $\{\langle e, b \rangle\}$ is not a return path. Now take $P = (a, b, c, d, e, g)$ and $Q = (a, b, c, d, e, b, c, d, e, g)$. We have that P is a simple path, $P \subset Q$, and Q does not contain a path that is parallel to a subpath of P. Hence $(Q - P) = \{\langle e, b \rangle\}$ is a return path in terms of the definition of Section 7c.

7.6   No to both questions. Add arc $\langle b, d \rangle$ to the digraph of the solution to Exercise 7.5. The number of cycles increases from 1 to 2, but the number of return paths and final arcs remains 1.

7.8   Consider a digraph $D = \langle A, R \rangle$. For every arc $\langle a_i, a_j \rangle \in R$ generate sets

$$B_i = \{b_i \mid a_i \text{ is reachable from } b_i\},$$
$$B_j = \{b_j \mid b_j \text{ is reachable from } a_j\}.$$

Arc $\langle a_i, a_j \rangle$ is a separator if and only if (1) $\{B_i, B_j\}$ is a partition of A, and (2) $\langle a_i, a_j \rangle$ is the only arc in R such that $a_i \in B_i$, $a_j \in B_j$. Sets B_i and B_j can be generated very rapidly from column i and row j of the path matrix of D; note that every node a_i is reachable from itself, even though p_{ii} in the path matrix may be zero. Condition (2) is tested in the adjacency matrix. As an added exercise you should prove that the procedure works.

Chapter 8

8.1   9.7 and 1.0, respectively.

8.3   Arcs $\langle 1, 2 \rangle$ and $\langle 3, 6 \rangle$ (c_{12} increased to 2, or c_{36} increased to 5).

8.8   For every capacitated node a add a dummy node a'. Also add dummy arc $\langle a, a' \rangle$, and assign the capacity of node a to this arc. Arcs that terminated at a still terminate there, but arcs that originated from a now originate from a'.

8.10   The union of the five sets {CS1, CS13, CS248}, {CS1, CS31}, {CS1, CS248, CS31}, {CS1, CS13}, and {CS1, CS13, CS31} has only four elements. Therefore, by Th.8.3, it is impossible to set up a one-to-one correspondence between faculty members and courses.

Chapter 9

9.1 $loc(5, 6, 7) = loc(1, 1, 1) + 456,$
$loc(10, 9, 8) = loc(1, 1, 1) + 987,$
$loc(1, 5, 9) = loc(1, 1, 1) + 48.$

9.5   Assume that bit positions are numbered $0, 1, 2, \ldots, 35$. Then we write

```
      SUBROUTINE PLACE (LOGIC,LDIM,I,J,K,LWD,LBIT)
      DIMENSION LOGIC(LDIM)
      LOC = LOGIC(2)*LOGIC(3)*(I-1) + LOGIC(3)*(J-1)
     1      + (K-1)
      LWD = LOC/36 + 1
      LBIT = MOD(LOC,36)
      RETURN
      END
```

If *MN* is stored instead of *M* in `LOGIC(2)`, then we can write

$$\texttt{LOC = LOGIC(2)*(I-1) + LOGIC(3)*(J-1) + (K-1)}$$

Note, however, that an identical improvement in efficiency (reduction of the number of multiplications by one) can be achieved under the existing scheme by nesting:

$$\texttt{LOC = LOGIC(3)*(LOGIC(2)*(I-1) + (J-1)) + (K-1)}$$

The routine does not require dimension *L*. Therefore `LOGIC(1)` can be made to contain $(LMN - 1)$, and this quantity may then be used in a check as to whether the specified a_{ijk} is within array bounds:

$$\texttt{IF (LOC.GT.LOGIC(1)) GO TO 999}$$

where the transfer is to an error exit.

9.8   The representation of X^3 is

$$QQ = \begin{bmatrix} 1 & 1 & 1 & 2 & 2 & 2 & 2 & 3 & 3 & 3 & 5 & 6 & 6 & 6 & 6 & 9 \\ 2 & 3 & 5 & 1 & 2 & 6 & 7 & 2 & 3 & 5 & 6 & 2 & 3 & 5 & 6 & 9 \\ 1 & 1 & 1 & 1 & 1 & 1 & 1 & 1 & 1 & 1 & 1 & 2 & 1 & 1 & 1 & 1 \\ 5 & 9 & 10 & 0 & 8 & 11 & 0 & 12 & 13 & 14 & 15 & 0 & 0 & 0 & 0 & 0 \end{bmatrix}$$

$$NC = [4 \quad 1 \quad 2 \quad 0 \quad 3 \quad 6 \quad 7 \quad 0 \quad 16]$$

$$NR = [1 \quad 4 \quad 8 \quad 11 \quad 11 \quad 12 \quad 16 \quad 16 \quad 16 \quad 17]$$

Chapter 10

10.1

```
       SUBROUTINE INITIO
       COMMON LIST (500,2)
       DO 5 K = 11,499
   5   LIST(  K,2) = K + 1
       LIST(500,2) = 0
       DO 6 K = 1,10
       DO 6 J = 1,2
   6   LIST(K,J) = 0
       LIST(1,1) = 11
       RETURN
       END
```

10.35   To get our representations straight take it that the parenthesized strings corresponding to Figures 10.34 and 10.35 are $a(b(d)c(efg))$ and $a(def)bc$, respectively. First consider the representation in which the tree has all nodes labeled. Then both the threaded list (as in Figure 10.29) and the symmetric list (as in Figure 10.34) have $2n - 1$ elements, where n is the number of alphabetic symbols in the string. Next consider the representation in which only terminal nodes of the tree are labeled. Then the symmetric list (as in Figure 10.35) contains $n + m$ elements, where n is the number of alphabetic symbols and m is the number of opening parentheses in the string.

Chapter 11

11.1   The structure is a file containing 50 records. The properties are V, Y, $Z(1,1)$ $Z(1,2)$, $Z(2,1)$, $Z(2,2)$, and X. A record contains seven measures. Note, however, that there are no hard and fast rules. For example, an interpretation under which Z is a single property having a 2×2 matrix for its measure is just as consistent with D.11.1.

11.6   Descending order would do as well. The reason for order is that it takes less time to find the set union or set intersection of reference vectors when their elements are ordered. (For example, if we were searching for documents described by index terms, "data structures" *and* "operating systems," then we would require the documents defined by the intersection of the reference vectors associated with these two terms.)

11.8   What follows is merely an analysis rather than a full solution. The procedure for deleting a document is determined by the design of the file. The index terms associated with documents were either retained in the document register, or the entries in the register were stripped of index terms when the index was being constructed. In the former case one searches for the appropriate index terms in the sort tree and deletes the document number in the reference vector of each such index term; in the latter case *all* reference vectors must be examined. If the number of the document that is being deleted is the only document number in a reference vector, then we are left with an empty vector, and the entire node should be removed from the sort tree. However, there is no great harm in leaving the index entry in the tree; a zero in the field that would point to the reference vector tells that no document has this particular index term associated with it. We can go even further and confine the deletion procedure to the document register alone. Provide each entry in the register with a marker. Normally the marker shows that the document is *active*. Deletion is merely the process of changing the marker to the *inactive* setting. The retrieval system responds to a retrieval request by generating a set of document numbers, and printing document register entries corresponding to these numbers, but output of inactive entries is suppressed.

11.13   A worst case can arise in which all 1500 keys generate the same hash address. Hence the overflow area must be capable of holding 1499 records, leaving just 301 record locations for the primary storage area. This is a strong argument against the use of the basic method F.

11.22   Have a scatter table HASH and a separate record table FILE. Make FILE a list store of the form described in the final paragraph of Section 10g. Initially it is a single block of available space. As records are entered, blocks of the size required for their storage are chopped off the block of available space and become multiword list elements. The first word in each of these list elements indicates the size of the block and contains a pointer field; the record occupies the rest of the block. All records associated with hash address N are linked in a list, and HASH(N) is the name of the list. A record is processed as follows: (a) Store the record in FILE; since there is no erasing, records are stored sequentially in order of input. (b) Compute the hash address. Let it be N. (c) If HASH(N) $= 0$, create a list by inserting in HASH(N) a pointer to the block that holds the record. If HASH(N) $\neq 0$, then a list already exists. Look for the last block in this list and insert the pointer in its pointer field; i.e., add the block that is being processed to the list.

11.31   The procedure consists of tracing through the two lists, deleting elements that are common to both. Assume that neither list is empty, and that locations AA and BB contain addresses of first elements of lists A and B. Denote the forward pointer in element N of list X by $X_N(F)$, and the datum stored in this element by $X_N(D)$; e.g., $A_{AA}(F)$ denotes the forward pointer in the first element of list A.

   1. Set $J = AA$ and $K = BB$.

   2. If $A_J(D) < B_K(D)$, go to 5; if $A_J(D) > B_K(D)$, go to 6.

   3. Set $JTEMP = A_J(F)$ and $KTEMP = B_K(F)$; delete elements A_J and B_K; set $J = JTEMP$ and $K = KTEMP$.

   4. If $J = AA$, stop; else go to 7.

   5. Set $J = A_J(F)$. If $J = AA$, stop; else go to 2.

   6. Set $K = B_K(F)$.

   7. If $K = BB$, stop; else go to 2.

(Your solution should contain an explicit procedure for deletion of an element in a symmetric list.)

11.42   The approximate expected number of runs is $\frac{1}{2}n$.

Bibliography

Parentheses at the end of an entry enclose the following items of information: (a) the number of references cited in the work (usually omitted in the case of a book), (b) the number of its review in *Computing Reviews*, and (c) the chapter or chapters to which it is relevant. The fact that some very important and not too recent papers do not carry a review number is a warning that a thorough literature search should not be confined to a search through *Computing Reviews*.

The following abbreviations, some of which may be non-standard, are used in titles of periodicals:

AFIPS   American Federation of Information Processing Societies
BIT   Nordisk Tidskrift for Informationsbehandling
CACM   Communications of the Association for Computing Machinery
FJCC   Fall Joint Computer Conference
ICC   International Computation Centre
IEEE   Institute of Electrical and Electronics Engineers
JACM   Journal of the Association for Computing Machinery
JCC   Joint Computer Conference
SIAM   Society for Industrial and Applied Mathematics
SJCC   Spring Joint Computer Conference
RIRO   Revue Française d'Informatique et de Recherche Opérationelle

Ab64   Abramowitz, M., and Stegun, I. A., eds., *Handbook of Mathematical Functions with Formulas, Graphs, and Mathematical Tables*. U.S. Govt. Printing Office, Washington, D.C., 1964. xiv + 1046 pp. (CR 10100—errata are published in *Math. Comp.*; Chapters 1, 2.)

Ab68   Abrahams, P. W., Symbol manipulation languages. *Advances in Comput.* 9, 51–111 (1968). (41 refs.; CR 17684; Chapter 10.)

Ab69   Abbott, J. C., *Sets, Lattices, and Boolean Algebras*. Allyn and Bacon, Boston, Massachusetts, 1969. xvi + 282 pp. (Chapter 2.)

Ah72   Aho, A. V., Denning, P. J., and Ullman, J. D., Weak and mixed strategy precedence parsing. *JACM* 19, 225–243 (1972). (23 refs.; CR 23838; Chapter 12.)

Al69   Allen, F. E., Program optimization. *Ann. Rev. Automatic Programming* 5, 239–307 (1969). (15 refs.; Chapter 7.)

Au70   Augustson, J. G., and Minker, J., An analysis of some graph theoretical cluster techniques. *JACM* 17, 571–588 (1970). (43 refs.; Chapter 8.)

Ax67   Axsom, L. E., An expression recognition routine in LISP 1.5. See Ro67a, pp. 481–489. (4 refs.; CR 16236; Chapter 10.)

Ba59a   Backus, J. W., The syntax and semantics of the proposed international algebraic language of the Zurich ACM-GAMM conference. *Proc. Internat. Conf. Inf. Proc., Paris, 1959*, pp. 125–132. (No refs.; CR 3158; Chapter 4.)

Ba59b   Samelson, K., and Bauer, F. L., Sequential formula translation. *CACM* 3, 76–83 (1960) (reprinted in Ro67a, pp. 206–220). Earlier publ. in German: Bauer, F. L., and Samelson, K., *Elektron. Rechenanlagen* 1, 176–182 (1959). (14 refs.; CR 219; Chapter 5.)

Ba60   Barrett, J. A., and Grems, M., Abbreviating words systematically. *CACM* 3, 323–324 (1960). (1 ref.; CR 221; Chapter 11.)

Ba62   Banerji, R. B., The description list of concepts. *CACM* 5, 426–432 (1962). (6 refs.; CR 3595; Chapter 11.)

Ba64   Bach, E., *An Introduction to Transformational Grammars*. Holt, New York, 1964. xii + 205 pp. (Selected bibliography of 86 items; Chapter 4.)

Ba67   Battersby, A., *Network Analysis for Planning and Scheduling*, 2nd ed. Macmillan, London, 1967. x + 414 pp. (Chapter 6.)

Ba68   Barron, D. W., *Recursive Techniques in Programming*. Macdonald, London, 1968, viii + 64 pp. (CR 17273; Chapter 5.)

Ba69   Baer, S. L., Matrice de connexion minimale d'une matrice de précédence donnée. *RIRO* 3, No. 16, 65–73 (1969). (6 refs.; Chapter 3.)

Ba72a   Baer, J-L., and Caughey, R., Segmentation and optimization of programs from cyclic structure analysis. *Proc. AFIPS* 40 (*SJCC*, 1972), 23–35. (15 refs.; CR 23943; Chapter 7.)

Ba72b   Baker, F. T., Chief programmer team management of production programming. *IBM Systems J.* 11, 56–73 (1972). (3 refs.; CR 23113; Chapter 10.)

Ba72c   Barnes, B. H., A programmer's view of automata. *Comput. Surveys* 4, 221–239 (1972). (10 refs.; CR 25228; Chapter 4.)

Ba72d   Barton, D., and Fitch, J. P., A review of algebraic manipulative programs and their application. *Comput J.* 15, 362–381 (1972). (110 refs.; CR 25375; Chapter 12.)

Be58   Berge, C., *Théorie des Graphes et ses Applications*, Dunod, Paris, 1958 (English transl.: *The Theory of Graphs and its Applications*, Methuen, London, 1962. x + 247 pp.). (Chapter 3).

Be64a   Beckenbach, E. F., Network flow problems. In *Applied Combinatorial Mathematics* (E. F. Beckenbach, ed.), Chapter 12, pp. 348–365. Wiley, New York, 1964. (9 refs.; Chapter 8.)

Be64b   Berkeley, E. C., and Bobrow, D. G., eds., *The Programming Language LISP: Its Operation and Applications.* MIT Press, Cambridge, Massachusetts, 1966 (originally published in 1964 by Information Internat.). x + 382 pp. (CR 10865; Chapter 10.)

Be65   Berztiss, A. T., A note on storage of strings. *CACM* **8**, 512–513 (1965). (3 refs.; CR 9713; Chapter 10.)

Be69a   Berztiss, A. T., and Watkins, R. P., Directed graphs and automatic flowcharting. *Proc. 4th Austral. Comput. Conf., Adelaide, 1969,* pp. 495–499. (20 refs.; CR 22860; Chapter 3.)

Be69b   Bell, J. R., A new method for determining linear precedence functions for precedence grammars. *CACM* **12**, 567–569 (1969). (7 refs.; CR 18261; Chapter 12.)

Be70   Bellman, R., Cooke, K. L., and Lockett, J. A., *Algorithms, Graphs, and Computers.* Academic Press, New York, 1970. xvi + 246 pp. (CR 20885; Chapter 6.)

Be72   Berman, G., and Fryer, K. D., *Introduction to Combinatorics.* Academic Press, New York, 1972. xiv + 300 pp. (Chapter 1.)

Be73   Berztiss, A. T., A backtrack procedure for isomorphism of directed graphs. *JACM* **20**, 365–377 (1973). (13 refs.; Chapter 3.)

Bi41   Birkhoff, G., and MacLane, S., *A Survey of Modern Algebra.* Macmillan, New York, 1941 (3rd ed., 1965, x + 437 pp.). (Chapter 4.)

Bi70   Birkhoff, G., and Bartee, T. C., *Modern Applied Algebra.* McGraw-Hill, New York, 1970. xii + 431 pp. (Chapter 4.)

Bl66   Blair, C. R., Certification of Algorithm 271. *CACM* **9**, 354 (1966). (No refs.; Chapter 11.)

Bo60   Booth, A. D., and Colin, A. J. T., On the efficiency of a new method of dictionary construction. *Information and Control* **3**, 327–334 (1960). (2 refs.; Chapter 5.)

Bo63   Bourne, C. P., *Methods of Information Handling.* Wiley, New York, 1963. xiv + 241 pp. (Good sets of references throughout; Chapter 11.)

Bo64   Bobrow, D. G., and Weizenbaum, J., List processing and extension of language facility by embedding. *IEEE Trans. Electronic Computers* **EC-13**, 395–400 (1964). (6 refs.; Chapter 9.)

Bo67   Boothroyd, J., Algorithm 22: Shortest path between start node and end node of a network. *Comput. J.* **10**, 306–307 (1967–1968). (2 refs.; Chapter 6.)

Bo70   Bowman, R. M., and McVey, E. S., A method for the fast approximate solution of large prime implicant charts. *IEEE Trans. Computers* **C-19**, 169–173 (1970). (5 refs.; CR 19120; Chapter 2.)

Bo72   Bobrow, D. G., Requirements for advanced programming systems for list processing. *CACM* **15**, 618–627 (1972). (40 refs.; CR 24102; Chapter 10.)

Br72   Brillinger, P. C., and Cohen, D. J., *Introduction to Data Structures and Nonnumeric Computation.* Prentice-Hall, Englewood Cliffs, New Jersey, 1972. xxii + 629 pp. (Chapter 10.)

Br73   Bron, C., and Kerbosch, J., Algorithm 457: Finding all cliques of an undirected graph. *CACM* **16**, 575–577 (1973). (6 refs.; Chapter 8.)

Bu65   Busacker, R. G., and Saaty, T. L., *Finite Graphs and Networks: An Introduction with Applications.* McGraw-Hill, New York, 1965. xiv + 294 pp. (Chapters 3, 6, 8.)

Ca63   Carlson, C. B., The mechanization of a push-down stack. *Proc. AFIPS* **24** (*FJCC, 1963*), 243–250. (5 refs.; Chapter 5.)

Ca73   Cardenas, A. F., Evaluation and selection of file organization—a model and system. *CACM* **16**, 540–548 (1973). (28 refs.; CR 26117; Chapter 11.)

Ch63   Chomsky, N., Formal properties of grammars. In *Handbook of Mathematical Psychology* (R. D. Luce, R. R. Bush, and E. Galanter, eds.), Vol. 2, pp. 323–418. Wiley, New York, 1963. (78 refs.; Chapter 4.)

Ch68   Childs, D. L., Feasibility of a set-theoretical data structure: a general structure based on a reconstituted definition of relation. *Proc. IFIP Congr., Edinburgh, 1968*, pp. 420–430. (2 refs.; Chapter 11.)

Ch69a   Chapin, N., A comparison of file organization techniques. *Proc. 24th ACM Nat. Conf., 1969*, pp. 273–283. (25 refs.; CR 18276; Chapter 11.)

Ch69b   Chapin, N., Common file organization techniques compared. *Proc. AFIPS* **35** (*FJCC, 1969*), 413–422. (14 refs.; CR 18580; Chapter 11.)

Ch70a   Chapin, N., Flowcharting with the ANSI standard: A tutorial. *Comput. Surveys* **2**, 119–146 (1970). (21 refs.; CR 20001; Chapter 7.)

Ch70b   Chandler, J. P., and Harrison, W. C., Remark on Algorithm 201: Shellsort. *CACM* **13**, 373–374 (1970). (1 ref.; Chapter 11.)

Ch71a   Chang, S-K., Fuzzy programs—Theory and applications. In *Computers and Automata* (J. Fox, ed.), pp. 147–164. Polytech. Inst. of Brooklyn, Brooklyn, New York, 1971. (26 refs.; Chapter 1.)

Ch71b   Chen, W-K., *Applied Graph Theory*. North-Holland Publ., Amsterdam, 1971. xiv + 484 pp. (Chapter 3.)

Cl62   Clippinger, R. F., Information algebra. *Comput. J.* **5**, 180–183 (1962–1963). (No refs.; CR 4164; Chapter 2.)

Cl74   Claybrook, B. G., LPL—A generalized list processing language. *Proc. AFIPS* **43** (*Natl. Comp. Conf., 1974*), 659–663. (8 refs.; CR 27600 Chapter 10.)

Co60   Collins, G. E., A method for overlapping and erasure of lists. *CACM* **3**, 655–657 (1960). (5 refs.; Chapter 10.)

Co64   Comfort, W. T., Multiword list items. *CACM* **7**, 357–362 (1964). (11 refs.; CR 6686; Chapter 10.)

Co66   Collins, G. E., PM, a system for polynomial manipulation. *CACM* **9**, 578–589 (1966). (14 refs.; CR 10884; Chapters 9, 10.)

Co67   Cohen, J., and Trilling, L., Remarks on "garbage collection" using a two-level storage. *BIT* **7**, 22–30 (1967). (8 refs.; CR 12758; Chapter 10.)

Co70a   Codd, E. F., A relational model of data for large shared data banks. *CACM* **13**, 377–387 (1970). (10 refs.; CR 20780; Chapter 11.)

Co70b   Corneil, D. G., and Gotlieb, C. C., An efficient algorithm for graph isomorphism. *JACM* **17**, 51–64 (1970). (10 refs.; Chapter 3.)

Co72a   Codd, E. F., Further normalization of the data base relational model. In *Data Base Systems* (R. Rustin, ed.), pp. 33–64. Prentice-Hall, Englewood Cliffs, New Jersey, 1972. (5 refs.; CR 25954; Chapter 11.)

Co72b   Codd, E. F., Relational completeness of data base sublanguages. In *Data Base Systems* (R. Rustin, ed.) pp. 65–98. Prentice-Hall, Englewood Cliffs, New Jersey, 1972. (9 refs.; CR 25496; Chapter 11.)

Co73   Corneil, D. G., Gotlieb, C. C., and Lee, Y. M., Minimal event-node network of project precedence relations. *CACM* **16**, 296–298 (1973). (5 refs.; CR 25578; Chapter 12.)

Cr70   Crespi-Reghizzi, S., and Morpurgo, R., A language for treating graphs. *CACM* **13**, 319–323 (1970). (7 refs.; Chapter 10.)

Cu63   Curry, H. B., *Foundations of Mathematical Logic*. McGraw-Hill, New York, 1963. xii + 408 pp. (Chapter 4.)

De64   Demoucron, G., Malgrange, Y., and Pertuiset, R., Graphes planaires: Reconnaissance et construction de représentations planaires topologiques. *Rev. Française de Rech. Opérationelle* **8**, No. 30, 33–47 (1964). (2 refs.; Chapter 3.)

De67   Desaulets, E. J., and Smith, D. K., An introduction to the string processing language Snobol. See Ro67a, pp. 419–454. (9 refs.; CR 16235; Chapter 10.)

De73   Delobel, C., and Casey, R. G., Decomposition of a data base and the theory of Boolean switching functions. *IBM J. Res. Develop.* **17**, 374–386 (1973). (14 refs.; CR 26625; Chapter 11.)

De74a   Dewar, R. B. K., A stable minimum storage sorting algorithm. *Inf. Proc. Letters* **2**, 162–164 (1973–74). (2 refs.; Chapter 11.)

De74b   Deo, N., *Graph Theory with Applications to Engineering and Computer Science*. Prentice-Hall, Englewood Cliffs, New Jersey, 1974. xviii + 478 pp. (Chapters 3, 8.)

Di60   Dijkstra, E. W., Recursive programming. *Numer. Math.* **2**, 312–318 (1960) (reprinted in Ro67a, pp. 221–227). (4 refs.; CR 17275; Chapter 5.)

Dr69   Dreyfus, S. E., An appraisal of some shortest-path algorithms. *Operations Res.* **17**, 395–412 (1969). (35 refs.; Chapter 6.)

Dr72   Dreyfus, H. L., *What Computers Can't Do*. Harper and Row, New York, 1972. xxxvi + 259 pp. (CR 23463, 24357; Chapter 4.)

Ea72   Earnest, C. P., Balke, K. G., and Anderson, J., Analysis of graphs by ordering of nodes. *JACM* **19**, 23–42 (1972). (4 refs.; CR 23985; Chapter 7.)

Ea74   Earnest, C., Some topics in code optimization. *JACM* **21**, 76–102 (1974). (5 refs.; Chapter 7.)

Ed72   Edmonds, J., and Karp, R. M., Theoretical improvements in algorithmic efficiency for network flow problems. *JACM* **19**, 248–264 (1972). (7 refs.; CR 23548; Chapter 8.)

Ed73   Edwards, F. H., *The Principles of Switching Circuits*. MIT Press, Cambridge, Massachusetts, 1973. xiv + 329 pp. (CR 26695; Chapter 2.)

Eh73   Ehrlich, G., Loopless algorithms for generating permutations, combinations, and other combinatorial configurations. *JACM* **20**, 500–513 (1973). (9 refs.; CR 26429; Chapter 1.)

El74   Elshoff, J. L., Some programming techniques for processing multi-dimensional matrices in a paging environment. *Proc. AFIPS* **43** (*Natl. Comp. Conf., 1974*), 185–193. (11 refs.; Chapter 9.)

En72   Engles, R. W., A tutorial on data-base organization. *Ann. Rev. Automatic Programming* **7**, 1–64 (1972/74). (21 refs.; Chapter 11.)

Ev73   Even, S., *Algorithmic Combinatorics*. Macmillan, New York, 1973. xii + 260 pp. (CR 25710; Chapter 1.)

Fa63   Fang, J., *Abstract Algebra*. Schaum, New York, 1963. xii + 339 pp. (Chapter 4.)

Fe50   Feller, W., *An Introduction to Probability Theory and Its Applications*, Vol. 1. Wiley, New York, 1950 (3rd ed., 1968, xviii + 509 pp.). (Chapter 11.)

Fe60   Ferguson, D. E., Fibonaccian searching. *CACM* **3**, 648 (1960). (No refs.; Chapter 11.)

Fe70   Ferber, K., and Jürgensen, H., A programme for the drawing of lattices. In *Computational Problems in Abstract Algebra* (J. Leech, ed.), pp. 83–87. Pergamon, Oxford, 1970. (2 refs.; CR 20881; Chapter 2.)

Fi68   Fisher, A. C., Liebman, J. S., and Nemhauser, G. L., Computer construction of project networks. *CACM* **11**, 493–497 (1968). (7 refs.; CR 18221; Chapter 12.)

Fi73   Fitch, J. P., On algebraic simplification. *Comput. J.* **16**, 23–27 (1973). (29 refs.; Chapter 12.)

Fl62   Floyd, R. W., Algorithm 97: Shortest path. *CACM* **5**, 345 (1962). (1 ref.; Chapter 6.)

Fl64   Floyd, R. W., Algorithm 245: Treesort 3. *CACM* **7**, 701 (1964). (2 refs.; Chapter 5.)

Fl67   Floyd, R. W., Nondeterministic algorithms. *JACM* **14**, 636–644 (1967). (4 refs.; CR 14587; Chapters 3, 6.)

Fl70   Flores, I., *Data Structure and Management*. Prentice-Hall, Englewood Cliffs, New Jersey, 1970. x + 390 pp. (CR 20916; Chapter 11.)

Fl71   Flores, I., *Job Control Language and File Definition*. Prentice-Hall, Englewood Cliffs, New Jersey, 1971. xiv + 268 pp. (CR 22224; Chapter 11.)

Fo62   Ford, L. R., and Fulkerson, D. R., *Flow in networks*. Princeton Univ. Press, Princeton, New Jersey, 1962. xiv + 194 pp. (CR 4845; Chapter 8.)

Fo67   Foster, J. M., *List Processing*. Macdonald, London, 1967. vi + 54 pp. (33 refs.; CR 13446; Chapter 10.)

Fo73a   Foster, C. C., A generalization of AVL trees. *CACM* **16**, 513–517 (1973). (9 refs.; CR 26159; Chapter 5.)

Fo73b   Fox, B. L., Calculating kth shortest paths. *INFOR* **11**, 66–70 (1973). (10 refs.; Chapter 6.)

Fr66   Fraenkel, A. A., *Abstract Set Theory*, 3rd ed. North-Holland Publ., Amsterdam, 1966. viii + 295 pp. (Chapter 1.)

Fr72   Frazer, W. D., and Wong, C. K., Sorting by natural selection. *CACM* **15**, 910–913 (1972). (5 refs.; CR 24586; Chapter 11.)

Ga73a   Ganapathy, S., and Rajaraman, V., Information theory applied to the conversion of decision tables to computer programs. *CACM* **16**, 532–539 (1973). (14 refs.; CR 26188; Chapter 5.)

Ga73b   Gates, G. W., and Poplawski, D. A., A simple technique for structured variable lookup. *CACM* **16**, 561–565 (1973). (4 refs.; CR 26094; Chapter 10.)

Gi69   Gibbs, N. E., A cycle generating algorithm for finite undirected linear graphs. *JACM* **16**, 564–568 (1969). (6 refs.; CR 19833; Chapter 3.)

Gi71   Gildersleeve, T. R., *Design of Sequential File Systems*. Wiley, New York, 1971. xiv + 49 pp. (CR 22953; Chapter 11.)

Gl64   Glushkov, V. M., *Introduction to Cybernetics*. Academic Press, New York, 1966. x + 322 pp. (Original Russian edition: *Vvedeniye v Kibernetiku*. Acad. Sc. Ukr. S.S.R., Kiev, 1964.) (CR 11012; Chapter 4.)

Go63   Gorn, S., Processors for infinite codes of the Shannon-Fano type. In *Mathematical Theory of Automata* (J. Fox, ed.), pp. 223–240. Polytech. Inst. of Brooklyn, Brooklyn, New York, 1963. (7 refs.; Chapter 3.)

Go65   Golomb, S. W., and Baumert, L. D., Backtrack programming. *JACM* **12**, 516–524 (1965). (13 refs.; CR 9442; Chapter 3.)

Go67   Goldstein, A. J., Recursive techniques in problem solving. *Proc. AFIPS* **30** (*SJCC, 1967*), 325–329. (3 refs.; CR 17027; Chapter 5.)

Gr68   Griswold, R. E., Poage, J. F., and Polonsky, I. P., *The Snobol 4 Programming Language*. Prentice-Hall, Englewood Cliffs, New Jersey, 1968 (2nd ed., 1971, xii + 256 pp.). (CR 17858; Chapter 10.)

Gr71   Gries, D., *Compiler Construction for Digital Computers*. Wiley, New York, 1971. xvi + 493 pp. (Chapters 5, 12.)

Ha50   Hamming, R. W., Error detecting and error correcting codes. *Bell System Tech. J.* **29**, 147–160 (1950). Reprinted in *Algebraic Coding Theory: History and Development* (I. F. Blake, ed.), pp. 10–23. Dowden, Hutchinson, and Ross, Stroudsburg, Pennsylvania, 1973. (3 refs.; Chapter 4.)

Ha60   Halmos, P. R., *Naïve Set Theory*. Van Nostrand, Princeton, New Jersey, 1960. viii + 104 pp. (Chapter 1.)

Ha62a   Hardgrave, W. W., and Nemhauser, G. L., On the relation between the traveling-salesman and the longest-path problems. *Operations Res.* **10**, 647–657 (1962). (10 refs.; Chapter 6.)

Ha62b   Haley, A. C. D., The KDF9 computer system. *Proc. AFIPS* **22** (*FJCC*, *1962*), 108–120 [or *Proc. 2nd Austral. Comput. Conf.*, *Melbourne*, *1963*, Paper C.1 (22 pages)]. (11 refs.; CR 5466; Chapter 5.)

Ha65a   Harrison, M. A., *Introduction to Switching and Automata Theory*. McGraw-Hill, New York, 1965. xviii + 499 pp. (Extensive bibliography; CR 9109; Chapter 2.)

Ha65b   Harary, F., Norman, R. Z., and Cartwright, D., *Structural Models: An Introduction to the Theory of Directed Graphs*. Wiley, New York, 1965. x + 415 pp. (CR 8421; Chapters 3, 8.)

Ha66   Hamburger, P., On an automated method of symbolically analyzing times of computer programs. *Proc. 21st ACM Nat. Conf.*, *1966*, pp. 321–330. (5 refs.; CR 11052; Chapter 7.)

Ha67a   Hall, M., *Combinatorial Theory*. Ginn (Blaisdell), Boston, Massachusetts, 1967. x + 310 pp. (Chapter 1.)

Ha67b   Hays, D. G., *Introduction to Computational Linguistics*. Amer. Elsevier, New York, 1967. xvi + 231 pp. (CR 15139; Chapter 5.)

Ha67c   Haddon, B. K., and Waite, W. M., A compaction procedure for variable length storage elements. *Comput. J.* **10**, 162–165 (1967–1968). (8 refs.; CR 13547; Chapter 10.)

Ha68a   Hauck, E. A., and Dent, B. A., Burroughs' B6500/B7500 stack mechanism. *Proc. AFIPS* **32** (*SJCC*, *1968*), 245–251. (3 refs.; Chapter 5.)

Ha68b   Hayden, S., and Kennison, J. F., *Zermelo–Fraenkel Set Theory*. Merrill, Columbus, Ohio, 1968. xii + 164 pp. (Chapter 1.)

Ha69   Harary, F., *Graph Theory*. Addison-Wesley, Reading, Massachusetts, 1969. x + 274 pp. (CR 19472; Chapter 3.)

Ha73   Harary, F., and Palmer, E. M., *Graphical Enumeration*. Academic Press, New York, 1973. xiv + 271 pp. (CR 25843; Chapter 3.)

He62   Hellerman, H., Addressing multidimensional arrays. *CACM* **5**, 205–207 (1962). (3 refs.; CR 2619; Chapter 9.)

He72   Henderson, P., and Snowdon, R., An experiment in structured programming. *BIT* **12**, 38–53 (1972). (5 refs.; Chapter 10.)

Hi62   Hill, U., Langmaack, H., Schwarz, H. R., and Seegmüller, G., Efficient handling of subscripted variables in Algol 60. *Symbolic Languages in Data Processing*, pp. 331–340. Gordon and Breach, New York, 1962. (1 ref.; Chapter 9.)

Ho63a   Hopley, J., Algorithm 152: Nexcom. *CACM* **6**, 385 (1963). (No refs.; Chapter 1.)

Ho63b   Hoffmann, T. R., Assembly line balancing with a precedence matrix. *Management Sci.* **9**, 551–562 (1962–1963). (16 refs.; Chapter 6.)

Ho66   Hohn, F. E., *Applied Boolean Algebra*, 2nd ed. Macmillan, New York, 1966. xiv + 273 pp. (CR 12078; Chapter 2.)

Ho67   Howden, W. E., A program for the construction of PERT flowcharts. *Comput. J.* **10**, 278–281 (1967–1968). (2 refs.; CR 13792; Chapter 12.)

Ho69   Hopcroft, J. E., and Ullman, J. D., *Formal Languages and their Relation to Automata*. Addison-Wesley, Reading, Massachusetts, 1969. x + 242 pp. (CR 20188, 20525; Chapter 4.)

Ho71   Hope, A. K., A planar graph drawing program. *Software—Practice and Experience* **1**, 83–91 (1971). (3 refs.; CR 21650; Chapter 12.)

Ho72a   Hoare, C. A. R., and Allison, D. C. S., Incomputability. *Comput. Surveys* **4**, 169–178 (1972). (8 refs.; CR 25241; Chapter 4.)

Ho72b   Hoffman, A. J., and Winograd, S., Finding all shortest distances in a directed network. *IBM J. Res. Develop.* **16**, 412–414 (1972). (4 refs.; CR 25536; Chapter 6.)

Ho73   Hoaglin, D. C., An analysis of the loop optimization scores in Knuth's 'Empirical study of Fortran programs.' *Software—Practice and Experience* **3**, 161–169 (1973). (3 refs.; Chapter 7.)

Hu68   Hu, T. C., A decomposition algorithm for shortest paths in a network. *Operations Res.* **16**, 91–102 (1968). (9 refs.; Chapter 6.)

Hu69   Hu, T. C., and Torres, W. T., Shortcut in the decomposition algorithm for shortest paths in a network. *IBM J. Res. Develop.* **13**, 387–390 (1969). (7 refs.; Chapter 6.)

In66   Ingerman, P. Z., *A Syntax-Oriented Translator*. Academic Press, New York, 1966. x + 131 pp. (95 refs.; CR 11509; Chapter 5.)

In71   Ingels, F. M., *Information and Coding Theory*. Intext, Scranton, Pennsylvania, 1971. x + 229 pp. (Chapter 4.)

Is71   Idoda, S., Goto, E., and Kimura, I., An efficient bit table technique for dynamic storage allocation of 2^n-word blocks. *CACM* **14**, 589–592 (1971). (3 refs.; CR 22301; Chapter 10.)

Jo70   Jones, B., A variation on sorting by address calculation. *CACM* **13**, 105–107 (1970). (2 refs.; Chapter 11.)

Jo73   Jones, N. D., *Computability Theory: An Introduction*. Academic Press, New York, 1973. xiv + 154 pp. (CR 25842; Chapter 4.)

Ka60   Karp, R. M., A note on the application of graph theory to digital computer programming. *Information and Control* **3**, 179–190 (1960). (16 refs.; CR 3563; Chapter 7.)

Ka62   Kahn, A. B., Topological sorting of large networks. *CACM* **5**, 558–562 (1962). (2 refs.; CR 4359; Chapter 6.)

Ka66   Karp, R. M., and Miller, R. E., Properties of a model of parallel computations: Determinacy, termination, queueing. *SIAM J. Appl. Math.* **14**, 1390–1411 (1966). (7 refs.; Chapter 7.)

Ka72a   Kain, R. Y., *Automata Theory: Machines and Languages*. McGraw-Hill, New York, 1972. xviii + 301 pp. (CR 23833; Chapter 4.)

Ka72b   Karp, R. M., Miller, R. E., and Rosenberg, A. L., Rapid identification of repeated patterns in strings, trees and arrays. *Proc. 4th Annual ACM Symp. Theory of Computing, 1972*, pp. 125–136. (1 ref.; Chapter 5.)

Ke71   Kernighan, B. W., Optimal sequential partitions of graphs. *JACM* **18**, 34–40 (1971). (9 refs.; CR 21429; Chapter 7.)

Ke72   Kershenbaum, A., and Van Slyke, R., Computing minimum spanning trees efficiently. *Proc. ACM Annual Conf., 1972*, pp. 518–527. (27 refs.; CR 24587; Chapter 6.)

Ki72   King, C. A., A graph-theoretic programming language. In *Graph Theory and Computing* (R. C. Read, ed.), pp. 63–75. Academic Press, New York, 1972. (13 refs.; CR 25095; Chapter 10.)

Ki73   King, P. J. H., and Johnson, R. G., Some comments on the use of ambiguous decision tables and their conversion to computer programs. *CACM* **16**, 287–290 (1973). (8 refs.; CR 26028; Chapter 5.)

Kl67   Klein, M. M., Scheduling project networks. *CACM* **10**, 225–231 (1967). (7 refs.; CR 12275; Chapter 6.)

Kn65   Knowlton, K. C., A fast storage allocator. *CACM* **8**, 623–625 (1965). (2 refs.; Chapter 10.)

Kn66   Knowlton, K. C., A programmer's description of L^6. *CACM* **9**, 616–625 (1966). (9 refs.; CR 11513; Chapter 10.)

Kn67   Knuth, D., A characterization of parenthesis languages. *Information and Control* **11**, 269–289 (1967). (3 refs.; CR 14350; Chapter 5.)

Kn68   Knuth, D. E., *The Art of Computer Programming*, Vol. 1, *Fundamental Algorithms*. Addison-Wesley, Reading, Massachusetts, 1968 (2nd ed., 1973, xxii + 634 pp.). (CR 14505; Chapters 1, 5, 7, 10.)

Kn69   Knowlton, P., An algebraic extension to LISP. *Proc. AFIPS* **35** (*FJCC, 1969*), 169–178. (1 ref.; CR 18881; Chapter 10.)

Kn71   Knuth, D. E., An empirical study of Fortran programs. *Software—Practice and Experience* **1**, 105–133 (1971). (19 refs.; CR 22300; Chapter 7.)

Kn73a   Knuth, D. E., *The Art of Computer Programming*, Vol. 3, *Sorting and Searching*. Addison-Wesley, Reading, Massachusetts, 1973. xii + 722 pp. (CR 25533; Chapters 3, 5, 11.)

Kn73b   Knuth, D. E., and Stevenson, F. R., Optimal measurement points for program frequency counts. *BIT* **13**, 313–322 (1973). (7 refs.; CR 26627; Chapter 7.)

Kn74   Knott, G. D., A numbering system for combinations. *CACM* **17**, 45–46 (1974). (5 refs.; CR 26659; Chapter 1.)

Ko66   Korfhage, R. R., *Logic and Algorithms*. Wiley, New York, 1966, xii + 194 pp. (CR 11339; Chapter 4.)

Ko70   Kohavi, Z., *Switching and Finite Automata Theory*. McGraw-Hill, New York, 1970. xvi + 592 pp. (CR 20050; Chapter 2.)

Ko74   Korfhage, R. R., *Discrete Computational Structures*. Academic Press, New York, 1974. xiv + 381 pp. (Chapter 1.)

Kr64   Krider, L., A flow analysis algorithm. *JACM* **11**, 429–436 (1964). (No refs.; CR 6954; Chapter 3.)

Kr68   Kral, J., One way of estimating frequencies of jumps in a program. *CACM* **11**, 475–480 (1968). (6 refs.; CR 16713; Chapter 7.)

Kr71   Krolak, P., Felts, W., and Marble, G., A man–machine approach toward solving the traveling salesman problem. *CACM* **14**, 327–334 (1971). (8 refs.; CR 21696; Chapter 6.)

Kr72   Krolak, P. D., and Nelson, J. H., A man–machine approach to creative solutions to urban problems. *Machine Intelligence* **7**, 241–266 (1972). (48 refs.; CR 26356; Chapter 6.)

Ku62   Kurtzberg, J., Algorithm 94: Combination. *CACM* **5**, 344 (1962). (No refs.; Chapter 1.)

Ku67   Kurtukov, A., On optimal arrangement of graphs. *ICC Bull.* **6**, 143–159 (1967). (2 refs.; Chapter 7.)

La61   Lasser, D. J., Topological ordering of a list of randomly numbered elements of a network. *CACM* **4**, 167–168 (1961). (1 ref.; CR 1192; Chapter 6.)

La65a   Lass, S. E., PERT Time calculation without topological ordering. *CACM* **8**, 172–174 (1965). (No refs.; Chapter 6.)

La65b   Lapidus, A., and Goldstein, M., Some experiments in algebraic manipulation by computer. *CACM* **8**, 501–508 (1965). (13 refs.; Chapter 10.)

La67   Langdon, G. G., An algorithm for generating permutations. *CACM* **10**, 298–299 (1967). (No refs.; Chapter 1.)

Le49   Lederman, W., *Introduction to the Theory of Finite Groups*. Oliver & Boyd, Edinburgh, 1949 (3rd ed., 1957). x + 170 pp. (Chapter 4.)

Le70   Learner, A., and Lim, A. L., A note on transforming context-free grammars to Wirth-Weber precedence form. *Comput. J.* **13**, 142–144 (1970). (4 refs.; CR 20713; Chapter 12.)

Le71   Lewis, P. M., and Rosenkrantz, D. J., An Algol compiler designed using automata theory. In *Computers and Automata* (J. Fox, ed.), pp. 75–87. Polytech. Inst. of Brooklyn, Brooklyn, New York, 1971. (6 refs.; CR 25048; Chapter 4.)

Le74a   Ledgard, H. F., The case for structured programming. *BIT* **14**, 45–57 (1974). (6 refs.; CR 27180; Chapter 10.)

Le74b   Levi, G., Graph isomorphism: A heuristic edge-partitioning-oriented algorithm. *Computing* **12**, 291–313 (1974). (13 refs.; Chapter 3.)

Li64   Lipschutz, S., *Theory and Problems of Set Theory and Related Topics*. Schaum, New York, 1964. vi + 233 pp. (Chapter 1.)

Li68   Liu, C. L., *Introduction to Combinatorial Mathematics*. McGraw-Hill, New York, 1968. x + 393 pp. (CR 16455; Chapter 1.)

Li73   Lindstrom, G., Scanning list structures without stacks or tag bits. *Inf. Proc. Letters* **2**, 47–51 (1973–74). (4 refs.; Chapters 10, 12.)

Li74   Lindstrom, G., Copying list structures using bounded workspace. *CACM* **17**, 198–202 (1974). (5 refs.; Chapter 10.)

Lo64   Lockyer, K. G., *An Introduction to Critical Path Analysis*. Pitman, London, 1964. viii + 111 pp. (CR 16373; Chapter 6.)

Lo66   Lockyer, K. G., *Critical Path Analysis; Problems and Solutions*. Pitman, London, 1966. 118 pp. (CR 16318; Chapter 6.)

Lo69   Lowe, T. C., Analysis of Boolean program models for time-shared, paged environments. *CACM* **12**, 199–205 (1969). (15 refs.; CR 17862; Chapter 7.)

Lo70a   Lowe, T. C., Automatic segmentation of cyclic program structures based on connectivity and processor timing. *CACM* **13**, 3–6, 9 (1970). (8 refs.; CR 18876; Chapter 7.)

Lo70b   London, R. L., Certification of Algorithm 245 Treesort 3: Proof of algorithms—a new kind of certification. *CACM* **13**, 371–373 (1970). (7 refs.; Chapter 5.)

Lo71   Lorin, H., A guided bibliography to sorting. *IBM Systems J.* **10**, 244–254 (1971). (49 annotated refs.; CR 23246; Chapter 11.)

Lo73   London, K. R., *Techniques for Direct Access*. Auerbach, Philadelphia, Pennsylvania, 1973. x + 326 pp. (CR 26074; Chapter 11.)

Lo74   Loeser, R., Some performance tests of "quicksort" and descendants. *CACM* **17**, 143–152 (1974). (17 refs.; Chapter 11.)

Lu71   Lum, V. Y., Yuen, P. S. T., and Dodd, M., Key-to-address transform techniques: A fundamental performance study on large existing formatted files. *CACM* **14**, 228–239 (1971). (18 refs.; CR 21728; Chapter 11.)

Lu72   Lum, V. Y. and Yuen, P. S. T., Additional results on key-to-address transform techniques: A fundamental performance study on large existing formatted files. *CACM* **15**, 996–997 (1972). (2 refs.; CR 24906; Chapter 11.)

Lu73a   Lum, V. Y., General performance analysis of key-to-address transformation methods using an abstract file concept. *CACM* **16**, 603–612 (1973). (4 refs.; Chapter 11.)

Lu73b   Lurié, D., and Vandoni, C., Statistics for Fortran identifiers and scatter storage techniques. *Software—Practice and Experience* **3**, 171–177 (1973). (8 refs.; Chapter 11.)

Lu74   Lukes, J. A., Efficient algorithm for the partitioning of trees. *IBM.J. Res. Develop.* **18**, 217–224 (1974). (10 refs.; CR 27215; Chapter 7.)

Ly71   Lynch, M. F., Harrison, J. M., Town, W. G., and Ash, J. E., *Computer Handling of Chemical Structure Information*. Macdonald, London, 1971. xii + 148 pp. (CR 23745; Chapter 8.)

Ly73   Lynch, M. F., Compression of bibliographic files using an adaption of run-length coding. *Inf. Storage Retrieval* **9**, 207–214 (1973). (14 refs.; Chapter 11.)

Ma60   Marimont, R. B., Applications of graphs and Boolean matrices to computer programming. *SIAM Rev.* **2**, 259–268 (1960). (9 refs.; Chapter 7.)

Ma67   Martin, D., and Estrin, G., Models of computations and systems—evaluation of vertex probabilities in graph models of computations. *JACM* **14**, 281–299 (1967). (7 refs.; CR 12864; Chapter 7.)

Ma68   Martin, D. F., Boolean matrix methods for the detection of simple precedence grammars. *CACM* **11**, 685–687 (1968). (5 refs.; CR 16231; Chapter 12.)

Ma71a   Marshall, C. W., *Applied Graph Theory*. Wiley, New York, 1971. xiv + 322 pp. (CR 24286; Chapter 3.)

Ma71b   Martin, W. A., Sorting. *Comput. Surveys* **3**, 147–174 (1971). (100 conventional refs. and 37 refs. to sorting algorithms; Chapter 11.)

Ma71c   Martin, W. A., Determining the equivalence of algebraic expressions by hash coding. *JACM* **18**, 549–558 (1971). (6 refs.; CR 22731; Chapter 12.)

Ma72a   Martin, D. F., Formal languages and their related automata. In *Computer Science* (A. F. Cardenas, L. Presser, M. A. Marin, eds.), pp. 409–460. Wiley, New York, 1972. (56 refs.; CR 23541; Chapter 4.)

Ma72b   Martin, W. A., and Ness, D. N., Optimizing binary trees grown with a sorting algorithm. *CACM* **15**, 88–93 (1972). (7 refs.; CR 23365; Chapter 5.)

Ma72c   Massey, J. L., and Garcia, O. N., Error-correcting codes in computer arithmetic. In *Advances in Information Systems Science*, Vol. 4 (J. T. Tou, ed.), pp. 273–326. Plenum Press, New York, 1972. (47 refs.; CR 25813; Chapter 4.)

Ma72d   Maurer, W. D., *The Programmer's Introduction to LISP*. Macdonald, London, 1972. viii + 112 pp. (CR 24967; Chapter 10.)

Ma73   Manna, Z., Program schemas. In *Currents in the Theory of Computing* (A. V. Aho, ed.), pp. 90–142. Prentice-Hall, Englewood Cliffs, New Jersey, 1973. (CR 26580; Chapter 7.)

Mc60   McCarthy, J., Recursive functions of symbolic expressions and their computation by machine, Pt. I. *CACM* **3**, 184–195 (1960) (reprinted in Ro67a, pp. 455–480). (5 refs.; CR 479; Chapter 10.)

Mc62   McCarthy, J., Abrahams, P. W., Edwards, D. J., Hart, T. P., and Levin, M. I., *LISP 1.5 Programmer's Manual*. MIT Press, Cambridge, Massachusetts, 1962. vi + 99 pp. (CR 5689; Chapter 10.)

Mc63a   McGee, W. C., The formulation of data processing problems for computers. *Advances in Comput.* **4**, 1–52 (1963). (82 refs.; Chapter 2.)

Mc63b   McBeth, J. H., On the reference counter method. *CACM* **6**, 575 (1963). (3 refs.; Chapter 10.)

Mc67   McNaughton, R., Parenthesis grammars. *JACM* **1 4**, 490–500 (1967). (3 refs.; CR 13260; Chapter 5.)

Mc68   McDaniel, H., *An Introduction to Decision Logic Tables*. Wiley, New York, 1968. ix + 96 pp. (CR 15397; Chapter 5.)

Mc69a   McIlroy, M. D., Algorithm 354: Generator of spanning trees. *CACM* **12**, 511 (1969). (4 refs.; Chapter 3.)

Mc69b   McKellar, A. C., and Coffman, E. G., Organizing matrices and matrix operations for paged memory systems. *CACM* **12**, 153–165 (1969). (11 refs.; CR 18675; Chapter 9.)

Mc71   McNamee, J. M., Algorithm 408: A sparse matrix package (Part 1). *CACM* **14**, 265–273 (1971). (No refs.; Chapter 9.)

Mc72   McAfee, J., and Presser, L., An algorithm for the design of simple precedence grammars. *JACM* **19**, 385–395 (1972). (9 refs.; CR 24433; Chapter 12.)

Me67   Mealy, G. H., Another look at data. *Proc. AFIPS* **31** (*FJCC*, 1967), 525–534. 6 refs.; CR 14726; Chapter 2.)

Me70   Mei, P-S., and Gibbs, N. E., A planarity algorithm based on the Kuratowski theorem. *Proc. AFIPS* **36** (*SJCC*, 1970), 91–93. (9 refs.; CR 20587; Chapter 3.)

Mi67   Minsky, M. L., *Computation: Finite and Infinite Machines*. Prentice-Hall, Englewood Cliffs, New Jersey, 1967. xviii + 317 pp. (Chapter 4.)

Mi74   Minieka, E., On computing sets of shortest paths in a graph. *CACM* **17**, 351–353 (1974). (13 refs.; Chapter 6.)

Mo63   Moshman, J., Johnson, J., and Larsen, M., RAMPS—a technique for Recursive Allocation and Multi-Project Scheduling. *Proc. AFIPS* **23** (*SJCC*, 1963), 17–27. (12 refs.; CR 5599; Chapter 6.)

Mo67   Montalbano, M., High-speed calculation of the critical paths of large networks. *IBM Systems. J* **6**, 163–191 (1967). (6 refs.; Chapter 6.)

Mo68   Mooers, C. N., How some fundamental problems are treated in the design of the TRAC language. In *Symbol Manipulation Languages and Techniques* (D. G. Bobrow, ed.), pp. 178–190. North-Holland Publ., Amsterdam, 1968. (7 refs.; CR 15199; Chapter 10.)

Mo69   Moyles, D. M., and Thompson, G. L., An algorithm for finding a minimal equivalent graph of a digraph. *JACM* **16**, 455–460 (1969). (4 refs.; CR 19127; Chapter 3.)

Mo70   Mossige, S., Generation of permutations in lexicographical order. *BIT* **10**, 74–75 (1970). (5 refs.; CR 19834; Chapter 1.)

Mo71   Moses, J., Algebraic simplification: A guide for the perplexed. *CACM* **14**, 527–537 (1971). (33 refs.; Chapter 12.)

Mo72   Moler, C. B., Matrix computations with Fortran and paging. *CACM* **15**, 268–270 (1972). (6 refs.; CR 23651; Chapter 9.)

Mu70   Muthukrishnan, C. R., and Rajaraman, V., On the conversion of decision tables to computer programs. *CACM* **13**, 347–351 (1970). (6 refs.; CR 20110; Chapter 5.)

Mu71   Munro, I., Efficient determination of the transitive closure of a directed graph. *Inf. Proc. Letters* **1**, 56–58 (1971–72). (5 refs.; Chapter 6.)

Mu72   Mullin, J. K., An improved index sequential access method using hashed overflow. *CACM* **15**, 301–307 (1972). (6 refs.; Chapter 11.)

Na63   Naur, P., ed., Revised report on the algorithmic language Algol 60. *CACM* **6**, 1–17 (1963) (reprinted in Ro67a, pp. 79–117, and in various other publications). (No refs.; CR 4540; Chapter 4.)

Na72   Naur, P., An experiment on program development. *BIT* **12**, 347–365 (1972). (6 refs.; CR 25213; Chapter 10.)

Ne57   Newell, A., and Shaw, J. C., Programming the logic theory machine. *Proc. Western JCC, 1957*, pp. 230–240. (2 refs.; Chapter 10.)

Ni66   Nicholson, T. A. J., Finding the shortest route between two points in a network. *Comput. J.* **9**, 275–280 (1966–1967). (3 refs.; CR 12877; Chapter 6.)

Ni71   Nilsson, N. J., *Problem-solving Methods in Artificial Intelligence*. McGraw-Hill, New York, 1971. xvi + 255 pp. (CR 22015; Chapter 5.)

Ni72   Nievergelt, J., and Farrar, J. C., What machines can and cannot do. *Comput. Surveys* **4**, 81–96 (1972). Reprinted as Chapter 6 in [Ni74]. (19 annotated refs.; CR 27289; Chapter 4.)

Ni73   Nievergelt, J., and Reingold, E. M., Binary search trees of bounded balance. *SIAM J. Comp.* **2**, 33–43 (1973). (13 refs.; Chapter 5.)

Ni74   Nievergelt, J., Farrar, J. C., and Reingold, E. M., *Computer Approaches to Mathematical Problems*. Prentice-Hall, Englewood Cliffs, New Jersey, 1974. xiv + 257 pp. (CR 26696; Chapter 3.)

Ob69   O'Brien, J. J. (ed.), *Scheduling Handbook*. McGraw-Hill, New York, 1969. xii + 605 pp. (Chapter 6.)

Or71   Ord-Smith, R. J., Generation of permutation sequences. *Comput. J.* **13**, 152–155 (1970); **14**, 136–139 (1971). (52 refs.; CR 22064; Chapter 1.)

Ov73   Overholt, K. J., Efficiency of the Fibonacci search method. *BIT* 13, 92–96 (1973). (4 refs.; CR 26007; Chapter 11.)

Pa64   Pandit, S. N. N., Some observations on the longest path problem. *Operations Res.* 12, 361–364 (1964). (12 refs.; Chapter 6.)

Pa69   Paton, K., An algorithm for finding a fundamental set of cycles of a graph. *CACM* 12, 514–518 (1969). (4 refs.; CR 18332; Chapter 3.)

Pa70   Pager, D., A number system for the permutations. *CACM* 13, 193 (1970). (1 ref.; CR 18998; Chapter 1.)

Pa74   Pape, U., Netzwerk-Veränderungen und Korrektur kürzester Weglängen von einer Wurzelmenge zur allen anderen Knoten. *Computing* 12, 357–362 (1974). (2 refs.; Chapter 6.)

Pe60   Perlis, A. J., and Thornton, C., Symbol manipulation by threaded lists. *CACM* 3, 195–204 (1960). (4 refs.; CR 214; Chapter 10.)

Pe61   Peterson, W. W., and Weldon, E. J., *Error-Correcting Codes*. MIT Press, Cambridge, Massachusetts, 1961 (2nd ed., 1972, xii + 560 pp.). (Chapter 4.)

Pe66   Penny, S. J., and Burkhard, J. H., Multidimensional correlation lattices as an aid to three-dimensional pattern reconstruction. *Proc. AFIPS* 28 (*SJCC, 1966*), 449–455. (3 refs.; CR 10394; Chapter 3.)

Po66   Ponstein, J., Self-avoiding paths and the adjacency matrix of a graph. *SIAM J. Appl. Math.* 14, 600–609 (1966). (3 refs.; Chapter 6.)

Po71a   Pollack, S. L., Hicks, H. T., and Harrison, W. J., *Decision Tables: Theory and Practice*. Wiley, New York, 1971. xii + 179 pp. (CR 21882, 22955, 23938; Chapter 5.)

Po71b   Pollack, S. L., Comment on the conversion of decision tables to computer programs (with reply by C. R. Muthukrishnan). *CACM* 14, 52 (1971). (3 refs.; Chapter 5.)

Po71c   Pohl, I., Bi-directional search. *Machine Intelligence* 6, 127–140 (1971). (19 refs.; CR 21862; Chapter 6.)

Po73   Pooch, U. W., and Nieder, A., A survey of indexing techniques for sparse matrices. *Comput. Surveys* 5, 109–133 (1973). (46 refs.; CR 27190; Chapter 9.)

Po74   Pooch, U. W., Translation of decision tables. *Comput. Surveys* 6, 125–151 (1974). (108 refs.; Chapter 5.)

Pr67   Prather, R. E., *Introduction to Switching Theory: A Mathematical Approach*. Allyn and Bacon, Boston, Massachusetts, 1967. xvi + 474 pp. (Chapter 2.)

Pr71a   Pratt, T. W., and Friedman, D. P., A language extension for graph processing and its formal semantics. *CACM* 14, 460–467 (1971). (13 refs.; CR 22308; Chapter 10.)

Pr71b   Pratt, T. W., Pair grammars, graph languages and string-to-graph translation. *J. Comp. Syst. Sciences* 5, 560–595 (1971). (17 refs.; CR 25836; Chapter 7.)

Pu70a   Purdom, P., A transitive closure algorithm. *BIT* 10, 76–94 (1970). (8 refs.; CR 20884; Chapter 6.)

Pu70b   Purdom, P. W., and Stigler, S. M., Statistical properties of the buddy system. *JACM* 17, 683–697 (1970). (4 refs.; CR 21038; Chapter 10.)

Qu59   Quine, M. V., On cores and prime implicants of truth functions. *Amer. Math. Monthly* 66, 755–760 (1959). (6 refs.; Chapter 2.)

Qu67   Quillian, M. R., Word concepts: A theory and simulation of some basic semantic capabilities. *Behavioral Sci.* 12, 410–430 (1967). (37 refs.; CR 14875; Chapter 8.)

Ra64   Raphael, B., A computer program which "understands". *Proc. AFIPS* 26 (*FJCC, 1964*), 577–589. (21 refs.; CR 7207; Chapter 10.)

Ra66a   Ramamoorthy, C. V., Analysis of graphs by connectivity considerations. *JACM* 13, 211–222 (1966). (14 refs.; Chapter 7.)

Ra66b   Ramamoorthy, C. V., The analytic design of a dynamic look ahead and program
         segmenting system for multiprogrammed computers. *Proc. 21st ACM Nat.
         Conf., 1966,* pp. 229–239. (7 refs.; CR 11502; Chapter 7.)
Ra67   Ramamoorthy, C. V., A structural theory of machine diagnosis. *Proc. AFIPS*
         30 (*SJCC, 1967*), 743–756. (13 refs.; CR 12903; Chapter 7.)
Ra68a   Raphael, B., Bobrow, D. G., Fein, L., and Young, J. W., A brief survey of com-
         puter languages for symbolic and algebraic manipulation. In *Symbol Manipulation
         Languages and Techniques* (D. G. Bobrow, ed.), pp. 1–54. North–Holland Publ.,
         Amsterdam, 1968. (36 refs.; CR 15196; Chapter 10.)
Ra68b   Ramani, S., SLIP operations on trees and their relevance to problems of linguistic
         interest. In *Symbol Manipulation Languages and Techniques* (D. G. Bobrow, ed.),
         pp. 312–339. North-Holland Publ., Amsterdam, 1968. (10 refs.; CR 15341;
         Chapter 10.)
Ra71   Ramamoorthy, C. V., Computer program models. In *Computers and Automata*
         (J. Fox, ed.), pp. 137–146. Polytech. Inst. of Brooklyn, Brooklyn, New York,
         1971. (8 refs.; CR 24434; Chapter 7.)
Re68   Reiter, R., Scheduling parallel computations. *JACM* **15,** 590–599 (1968). (8 refs.;
         CR 17864; Chapter 7.)
Re71   Redish, K. A., Comment on London's certification of Algorithm 245 (with reply
         by R. L. London). *CACM* **14,** 50–51 (1971). (13 refs.; Chapter 5.)
Re72   Reingold, E. M., On the optimality of some set algorithms. *JACM* **19,** 649–659
         (1972). (6 refs.; CR 24440; Chapter 11.)
Rh72   Rheinboldt, W. C., Basili, V. R., and Mesztenyi, C. K., On a programming
         language for graph algorithms. *BIT* **12,** 220–241 (1972). (19 refs.; Chapter 10.)
Ri67   Richards, R. K., *Electronic Digital Components and Circuits.* Van Nostrand,
         Princeton, New Jersey, 1967. xii + 526 pp. (About 1000 refs.; CR 14809; Chapter
         9.)
Ri72a   Rich, R. P., *Internal Sorting Methods Illustrated with PL/I Programs.* Prentice-
         Hall, Englewood Cliffs, New Jersey, 1972. xiv + 154 pp. (CR 24135; Chapter
         11.)
Ri72b   Rivest, R. L., and Knuth, D. E., Bibliography 26: Computer Sorting. *Comput.
         Rev.* **13,** 283–289 (1972). (Chapter 11.)
Ri73   Rickman, J., and Walden, W. E., Structures for interactive on-line thesaurus.
         International J. Comp. Inf. Sciences **2,** 115–127 (1973). (15 refs.; Chapter 11.)
Ro55   Robbins, A., A remark on Stirling's formula. *Amer. Math. Monthly* **62,** 26–29
         (1955). (2 refs.; Chapter 1.)
Ro59   Roy, B., Transitivité et connexité. *C. R. Acad. Sci.* **249,** 216–218 (1959). (Chapter
         3.)
Ro67a   Rosen, S., ed., *Programming Systems and Languages.* McGraw-Hill, New York,
         1967. xvi + 734 pp. (Contains reprints of Ba59b, Di60, Mc60, Na63, and original
         papers Ax67, De67, Sm67; CR 15975.)
Ro67b   Ross, D. T., The AED free storage package. *CACM* **10,** 481–492 (1967). (6 refs.;
         CR 13437; Chapter 10.)
Ro68   Robert, P., and Ferland, J., Généralisation de l'algorithme de Warshall. *RIRO* **2,**
         No. 7, 71–85 (1968). (6 refs.; CR 18698; Chapter 6.)
Ro72   Roberts, D. C., File organization techniques. *Advances in Comput.* **12,** 115–174
         (1972). (203 refs.; CR 25778; Chapter 11.)
Ro73   Roy, M. K., Reflection-free permutations, rosary permutations, and adjacent
         transposition algorithms. *CACM* **16,** 312–313 (1973). (6 refs.; CR 25711; Chapter
         1.)

Ru65   Rutherford, D. E., *Introduction to Lattice Theory*. Oliver & Boyd, Edinburgh, 1965. x + 117 pp. (CR 8591; Chapter 2.)

Ru72   Ruth, S. S., and Kreutzer, P. J., Data compression for large business files. *Datamation* **18**, No. 9, 62–66 (1972). (15 refs.; CR 24512; Chapter 11.)

Sa62   Samelson, K., Programming languages and their processing. *Proc. IFIP Congr., Munich, 1962*, pp. 487–492. (18 refs.; CR 7262; Chapter 5.)

Sa64   Salton, G., and Sussenguth, E. H., Some flexible information retrieval systems using structure matching procedures. *Proc. AFIPS 25 (SJCC, 1964)*, 587–597. (17 refs.; CR 6916; Chapters 3, 8.)

Sa66   Sammet, J. E., An annotated descriptor based bibliography on the use of computers for non-numerical mathematics. *Comput. Rev.* **7**, No. 4, B.1–B.29 (1966); later, expanded version in *Symbol Manipulation Languages and Techniques* (D. G. Bobrow, ed.), pp. 358–484. North-Holland Publ., Amsterdam, 1968. (About 300 and 380 references, respectively; CR 15211; Chapter 10.)

Sa67   Sager, N., Syntactic analysis of natural language. *Advances in Comput.* **8**, 153–188 (1967). (54 refs.; CR 14435; Chapter 5.)

Sa68a   Salton, G., *Automatic Information Organization and Retrieval*. McGraw-Hill, New York, 1968. xiv + 514 pp. (CR 16841; Chapter 8.)

Sa68b   Sakoda, J. M., DYSTAL: *d*ynamic *st*orage *al*location *l*anguage in Fortran. In *Symbol Manipulation Languages and Techniques* (D. G. Bobrow, ed.), pp. 302–311. North-Holland Publ., Amsterdam, 1968. (5 refs.; CR 15202; Chapter 9.)

Sa68c   Sammet, J. E., *Programming Languages: History and Fundamentals*. Prentice-Hall, Englewood Cliffs, New Jersey, 1968. xxx + 785 pp. (CR 17682 and 17854; Chapter 10.)

Sa70   Sattley, K., and Millstein, P., Comments on a paper by Lowe (with reply by T. C. Lowe). *CACM* **13**, 450–451 (1970). (1 ref.; Chapter 7.)

Sa71   Salton, G. ed., *The Smart Retrieval System; Experiments in Automatic Document Processing*. Prentice-Hall, Englewood Cliffs, New Jersey, 1971. xx + 556 pp. (CR 23170; Chapter 8.)

Sa73   Salton, G., Recent studies in automatic text analysis and document retrieval. *JACM* **20**, 258–278 (1973). (34 refs.; CR 27300; Chapter 8.)

Sc64   Schurmann, A., The application of graphs to the analysis of distribution of loops in a program. *Information and Control* **7**, 275–282 (1964). (5 refs.; CR 8016; Chapter 7.)

Sc67   Schorr, H., and Waite, W. M., An efficient machine-independent procedure for garbage collection in various list structures. *CACM* **10**, 501–506 (1967). (13 refs.; CR 13179; Chapter 10.)

Sc68   Schurmann, A., GAN, a system for generating and analyzing activity networks. *CACM* **11**, 675–679 (1968). (3 refs.; Chapter 12.)

Sc70   Schwarcz, R. M., Burger, J. F., and Simmons, R. F., A deductive question-answerer for natural language inference. *CACM* **13**, 167–183 (1970). (27 refs.; CR 19390; Chapter 8.)

Sc73   Schaefer, M., *A Mathematical Theory of Global Program Optimization*. Prentice-Hall, Englewood Cliffs, New Jersey, 1973. xx + 198 pp. (Chapter 7.)

Sh72   Sheng, C. L., *Introduction to Switching Logic*. Intext, Scranton, Pennsylvania, 1972. xvi + 365 pp. (Chapter 2.)

Sh73a   Shneiderman, B., Polynomial search. *Software—Practice and Experience* **3**, 5–8 (1973). (22 refs.; Chapter 11.)

Sh73b   Shneiderman, B., Optimum data base reorganization points. *CACM* **16**, 362–365 (1973). (5 refs.; CR 26112; Chapter 11.)

Sh74   Shneiderman, B., A model for optimizing indexed file structures. *International J. Comp. Inf. Sciences* **3**, 93–103 (1974). (14 refs.; Chapter 11.)

Si64   Sikorski, R., *Boolean Algebras*, 2nd ed. Springer, New York, 1964. x + 237 pp. (Chapter 1.)

Si65   Simões Pereira, J. M. S., On Boolean matrix equation $M' = \bigvee_{i=1}^{q} M^i$. *JACM* **12**, 376–382 (1965). (3 refs.; CR 9805; Chapter 3.)

Si70   Simmons, R. F., Natural language question-answering systems: 1969. *CACM* **13**, 15–30 (1970). (79 refs.; CR 19053; Chapter 8.)

Sl70   Slagle, J. R., Chang, C-L., and Lee, R. C. T., A new algorithm for generating prime implicants. *IEEE Trans. Computers* **C–19**, 304–310 (1970). (20 refs.; CR 21588; Chapter 2.)

Sm67   Smith, D. K., An introduction to the list-processing language SLIP. See Ro67a, pp. 393–418. (7 refs.; CR 16427; Chapter 10.)

Sp73   Spira, P. M., A new algorithm for finding all shortest paths in a graph of positive arcs in average time $O(n^2 \log^2 n)$. *SIAM J. Comp.* **2**, 28–32 (1973). (4 refs.; Chapter 6.)

St61   Stoll, R. R., *Sets, Logic, and Axiomatic Theories*. Freeman, San Francisco, California, 1961. x + 206 pp. (Chapter 1.)

St63   Stoll, R. R., *Set Theory and Logic*. Freeman, San Francisco, California, 1963. xiv + 474 pp. (CR 5428; Chapter 1.)

St65   Stockham, T. G., Some methods of graphical debugging. *Proc. IBM Sci. Comput. Symp. Man-Machine Communication, White Plains, May 1965*, pp. 57–71. IBM Data Proc. Div., White Plains, New York, no date. (11 refs.; Chapter 7.)

St73   Stone, H. S., *Discrete Mathematical Structures and their Applications*. Sci. Res. Assoc., Chicago, 1973. xiv + 402 pp. (Chapter 4.)

Su65   Sussenguth, E. H., A graph-theoretical algorithm for matching chemical structures. *J. Chem. Doc.* **5**, 36–43 (1965). (3 refs.; CR 7812; Chapter 8.)

Sz63   Szasz, G., *Introduction to Lattice Theory*, 3rd ed. Academic Press, New York, 1963. 229 pp. (Chapter 2.)

Ta67   Tate, F. A., Handling chemical compounds in information systems. *Ann. Rev. Inf. Sci. Tech.* **2**, 285–309 (1967). (179 refs.; Chapter 8.)

Ta72   Tarjan, R., Depth-first search and linear graph algorithms. *SIAM J. Comp.* **1**, 146–160 (1972). (15 refs.; Chapter 6.)

Ta73   Tarjan, R., Enumeration of the elementary circuits of a directed graph. *SIAM J. Comp.* **2**, 211–216 (1973). (4 refs.; CR 27217; Chapters 6, 12.)

Th72   Thorelli, L-E., Marking algorithms. *BIT* **12**, 555–568 (1972). (8 refs.; Chapter 10.)

Th74   Thurber, K. J., Interconnection networks—A survey and assessment. *Proc. AFIPS* **43** (*Natl. Comp. Conf.*, 1974), 909–919. (48 refs.; Chapter 11.)

To71   Tobey, R. G., Symbolic mathematical computation—Introduction and overview. *Proc. 2nd Symp. Symbolic and Algebraic Manipulation*, 1971, pp. 1–16. (49 refs.; Chapter 12.)

Tr62   Trotter, H. F., Algorithm 115: Perm. *CACM* **5**, 434–435 (1962). (1 ref.; Chapter 1.)

Tu68   Turner, J., Generalized matrix functions and the graph isomorphism problem. *SIAM J. Appl. Math.* **16**, 520–526 (1968). (8 refs.; Chapter 3.)

Un64   Unger, S. H., GIT—a heuristic program for testing pairs of directed line graphs for isomorphism. *CACM* **7**, 26–34 (1964). (8 refs.; CR 5749; Chapter 3.)

Va72   Van der Pool, J. A., Optimum storage allocation for initial loading of a file. *IBM J. Res. Develop.* **16**, 579–586 (1972). (9 refs.; Chapter 11.)

Va73a   Van der Pool, J. A., Optimum storage allocation for a file in steady state. *IBM J. Res. Develop.* **17**, 27–38 (1973). (7 refs.; CR 26624; Chapter 11.)

Va73b   Van der Pool, J. A., Optimum storage allocation for a file with open addressing. *IBM. J. Res. Develop.* **17**, 106–114 (1973). (12 refs.; CR 25955; Chapter 11.)

Ve66   Veinott, C. G., Programming decision tables in Fortran, Cobol or Algol. *CACM* **9**, 31–35 (1966). (2 refs.; CR 9724; Chapter 5.)

Ve71   Ver Hoef, E. W., Automatic program segmentation based on boolean connectivity. *Proc. AFIPS* **38** (*SJCC, 1971*), 491–495. (9 refs.; CR 22034; Chapter 7.)

Wa62   Warshall, S., A theorem on Boolean matrices. *JACM* **9**, 11–12 (1962). (2 refs.; Chapter 3.)

Wa73a   Waite, W. M., *Implementing Software for Non-numeric Applications*. Prentice-Hall, Englewood Cliffs, New Jersey, 1973. xvi + 510 pp. (CR 26038; Chapter 10.)

Wa73b   Watkins, R. P., A survey of automatic flowchart generators. *Austral. Comput. J.* **5**, 132–140 (1973). (27 refs.; Chapter 7.)

Wa74   Wagner, R. A., and Fischer, M. J., The string-to-string correction problem. *JACM* **21**, 168–173 (1974). (1 ref.; Chapter 5.)

We63   Weizenbaum, J., Symmetric list processor. *CACM* **6**, 524–544 (1963). (4 refs.; CR 5023; Chapter 10.)

We64   Wengert, E. R., A simple automatic derivative evaluation program. *CACM* **7**, 463–464 (1964). (No refs.; CR 6698; Chapter 9.)

We66a   Welch, J. T., A mechanical analysis of the cycle structure of undirected linear graphs. *JACM* **13**, 205–210 (1966). (6 refs.; CR 10573; Chapter 3.)

We66b   Weizenbaum, J., ELIZA—a computer program for the study of natural language communication between man and machine. *CACM* **9**, 36–45 (1966). (6 refs.; CR 9655; Chapter 10.)

We67   Weizenbaum. J., Contextual understanding by computers. *CACM* **10**, 474–480 (1967). (6 refs.; CR 13062; Chapter 10.)

We69   Weizenbaum, J., Recovery of reentrant list structures in SLIP. *CACM* **12**, 370–372 (1969). (3 refs.; CR 18051; Chapter 10.)

We71   Wells, M. B., *Elements of Combinatorial Computing*. Pergamon, Oxford, 1971. xiv + 258 pp. (CR 23549; Chapter 1.)

Wh72   Whitney, V. K. M., Algorithm 422: Minimal spanning tree. *CACM* **15**, 273–274 (1972). (6 refs.; Chapter 6.)

Wi64   Wiseman, N. E., Application of list-processing methods to the design of interconnections for a fast logic system. *Comput. J.*, **6**, 321–327 (1963–1964). (11 refs.; CR 6256; Chapter 10.)

Wi65   Wikes, M. V., Lists and why they are useful. *Comput. J.* **7**, 278–281 (1964–1965) [or *Proc. 19th ACM Nat. Conf.*, *1964*, Paper F1 (5 pp.)]. (4 refs.; CR 6945; Chapter 10.)

Wi66   Wirth, N., and Weber, H., Euler: A generalization of Algol, and its formal definition. *CACM* **9**, 13–23, 25; 89–99 (1966). (17 refs.; CR 16240; Chapter 12.)

Wi69   Wiest, J. D., and Levy, F. K., *A Management Guide to PERT/CPM*. Prentice-Hall, Englewood Cliffs, New Jersey, 1969. vi + 170 pp. (CR 19210; Chapter 6.)

Wi71a   Williams, R., A survey of data structures for computer graphics systems. *Comput. Surveys* **3**, 1–21 (1971). (113 refs.; CR 21621; Chapter 10.)

Wi71b   Wirth, N., Program development by stepwise refinement. *CACM* **14**, 221–227 (1971). (4 refs.; CR 21630; Chapter 10.)

Wi73   Williams, T. A., and White, G. P., A note on Yen's algorithm for finding the length of all shortest paths in N-node nonnegative-distance networks (with reply by J. Y. Yen). *JACM* **20**, 389–390 (1973). (1 ref.; CR 27214; Chapter 6.)

Wo65   Wolman, E., A fixed optimum cell-size for records of various lengths. *JACM* **12,** 53–70 (1965). (No refs.; CR 8218; Chapter 10.)

Wo70   Woods, W. A., Transition network grammars for natural language analysis. *CACM* **13,** 591–606 (1970). (33 refs.; CR 20611; Chapter 5.)

Wo74   Wolverton, R. W., The cost of developing large-scale software. *IEEE Trans. Computers* **E-23,** 615–636 (1974). (22 refs.; Chapter 10.)

Ye71   Yen, J. Y., On Hu's decomposition algorithm for shortest paths in a network. *Operations Res.* **19,** 983–985 (1971). (9 refs.; Chapter 6.)

Ye72   Yen, J. Y., Finding the lengths of all shortest paths in N-node nonnegative-distance complete networks using $\frac{1}{2}N^3$ additions and N^3 comparisons. *JACM* **19,** 423–424 (1972). (1 ref.; CR 24138; Chapter 6.)

Yn72   Yngve, V. H., *Computer Programming with Comit II.* MIT Press, Cambridge, Massachusetts, 1972. xvi + 203 pp. (Chapter 10.)

Za65   Zadeh, L. A., Fuzzy sets. *Information and Control* **8,** 338–353 (1965). (3 refs.; Chapter 1.)

Zi73   Zissos, D., and Duncan, F. G., Boolean minimization. *Comput. J.* **16,** 174–179 (1973). (1 ref.; Chapter 2.)

Zz62   An information algebra—phase 1 report, language structure group of the CODASYL development committee. *CACM* **5,** 190–204 (1962). (No refs.; CR 2621; Chapter 2.)

Zz71   CODASYL Systems Committee, Introduction to " Feature analysis of generalized data management systems." *CACM* **14,** 308–318 (1971). (4 refs.; CR 22137; Chapter 11.)

Index

Computer Science and Applied Mathematics

A SERIES OF MONOGRAPHS AND TEXTBOOKS

Editor
Werner Rheinboldt
University of Maryland

HANS P. KÜNZI, H. G. TZSCHACH, and C. A. ZEHNDER. Numerical Methods of Mathematical Optimization: With ALGOL and FORTRAN Programs, Corrected and Augmented Edition

AZRIEL ROSENFELD. Picture Processing by Computer

JAMES ORTEGA AND WERNER RHEINBOLDT. Iterative Solution of Nonlinear Equations in Several Variables

AZARIA PAZ. Introduction to Probabilistic Automata

DAVID YOUNG. Iterative Solution of Large Linear Systems

ANN YASUHARA. Recursive Function Theory and Logic

JAMES M. ORTEGA. Numerical Analysis: A Second Course

G. W. STEWART. Introduction to Matrix Computations

CHIN-LIANG CHANG AND RICHARD CHAR-TUNG LEE. Symbolic Logic and Mechanical Theorem Proving

C. C. GOTLIEB AND A. BORODIN. Social Issues in Computing

ERWIN ENGELER. Introduction to the Theory of Computation

F. W. J. OLVER. Asymptotics and Special Functions

DIONYSIOS C. TSICHRITZIS AND PHILIP A. BERNSTEIN. Operating Systems

ROBERT R. KORFHAGE. Discrete Computational Structures

PHILIP J. DAVIS AND PHILIP RABINOWITZ. Methods of Numerical Integration

A. T. BERZTISS. Data Structures: Theory and Practice, Second Edition

N. CHRISTOPHIDES. Graph Theory: An Algorithmic Approach

ALBERT NIJENHUIS AND HERBERT S. WILF. Combinatorial Algorithms

AZRIEL ROSENFELD AND AVINASH C. KAK. Digital Picture Processing

SAKTI P. GHOSH. Data Base Organization for Data Management

DIONYSIOS C. TSICHRITZIS AND FREDERICK H. LOCHOVSKY. Data Base Management Systems

WILLIAM F. AMES. Numerical Methods for Partial Differential Equations, Second Edition

```
   7
C  8
D  9
E  0
F  1
G  2
H  3
I  4
J  5
```